Persuasive Communication Campaigns

Michael Pfau
Augustana College

Roxanne Parrott
University of Georgia

Allyn and Bacon
Boston • London • Toronto • Sydney • Tokyo • Singapore

TO OUR CHILDREN, WITH OUR LOVE

The Children of Michael and Ginger Pfau
Michael William Pfau
Julie Ann Pfau

The Children of Roxanne and John Parrott
Benjamin Allan Parrott
Joy Laryn Parrott

Series Editor: Stephen Hull
Series Editorial Assistant: Brenda Conaway
Editorial-Production Service: Spectrum Publisher Services
Manufacturing Buyer: Louise Richardson
Cover Administrator: Suzanne Harbison

Copyright © 1993 by Allyn and Bacon
A Pearson Education Company
160 Gould Street
Needham Heights, Massachusetts 02194

Library of Congress Cataloging-in-Publication Data

Pfau, Michael.
    Persuasive communication campaigns/Michael Pfau, Roxanne Parrott.
        p.   cm.
    Includes bibliographical references and index
        1. Advocacy advertising.   2. Advertising campaigns.
    3. Electioneering.   4. Campaign speeches.   Communication.
    6. Persuasion (Psychology) I. Parrott, Roxanne.   II. Title.
    HD59.3.P43 1992
    302.2–dc20   92-24093
    ISBN 0-205-13977-9   CIP

Printed in the United States of America

10 9 8 7 6 5 4 3   01 00 99 98

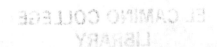

Contents

Preface

I am prepared to argue that at least in the social sciences a great deal of the empirical research that goes on today is in fact directed toward the image of the image. This research is scattered over many different fields, and for this reason the results are not often communicated among the researchers, and hence a good deal of effort is wasted through this lack of communication.
—SOCIAL SCIENTIST KENNETH E. BOULDING (BOULDING, 1977, P. 156)

We believe . . . [that] heightened interest in applied problems will help researchers uncover some of the cross-situational universals of communication that critics have contended do not exist in principle, or at least are not discoverable. [We maintain]. . . that general principles of influence apply in situations ranging from physician-patient interactions to expensive mass media campaigns.
—COMMUNICATION PROFESSORS MICHAEL BURGOON AND GERALD R. MILLER (BURGOON AND MILLER, 1990, P. 154).

Persuasive communication campaigns, as we will explain in Chapter 1, are conscious, sustained, incremental communication efforts, which involve multiple messages over time that seek to achieve clearly defined persuasive goals. All campaigns involve the process of persuasion at their very core, persuasion aimed at commercial, political, or social action ends, depending upon the particular type of campaign.

Although persuasive communication is probably as old as oral language, persuasive campaigns are a more recent phenomena, owing their growth to the rise of mass media outlets over the past 100 years. Today, persuasive communication campaigns are a pervasive feature of American life. We are bombarded with campaign appeals daily, which seek to influence our attitudes and behaviors about commercial products, political candidates, and social issues. As Leo Bogart (1990) describes, the sheer volume of just commercial campaign messages boggles the mind.

Each day, 12 billion display and 184 billion classified advertising messages pour forth from 1,710 daily newspapers, billions of others from 7,600 weekly newspapers, and 6 billion more each day from 430 general magazines and 10,500 other periodicals. There are 4,658 AM and 3,367 FM radio sations broadcasting an average of 2,600,000 commercial messages a day; 844 television stations broadcast 330,000 commercials a day, redisseminated by 5,000 cable systems. Every day, millions of people are confronted with over 500,000 outdooor billboards and painted bulletins, with 1.5 million car cards and posters on buses, subways, and commuter trains, with 40 million direct mail pieces and leaflets, and with billions of display and promotion items (pp. 1–2).

Furthermore, Bogart (1990) notes that the total number of daily commercial messages, which has increased significantly over the past 15 years, will double again during the next 15 years. The proliferation of political and social action campaign messages have paralleled the growth of commercial campaign messages, such that, when coupled with communication via other modalities than simply mass media, the average American is exposed to over 5,000 persuasive messages per day (Larson, 1989).

Are we influenced by campaigns? Most of us *prefer* to think that we are autonomous decision makers, responsible for our own conclusions concerning what brands to purchase, what candidates to support, and what social behaviors to exhibit. However, the truth is that all of us are influenced by campaign communication. This becomes evident to most people when they attempt to isolate the basis for their preferences, among brands of toilet tissues, soft drinks, or long-distance telephone providers; between two or more candidates for particular local, state, or national offices; and concerning smoking in public places, wearing automobile lap and shoulder belts, drinking and driving, and other social action issues. Typically, most people's first reaction is to justify such preferences with specific reasons, but when they are asked the origins of the specific information used to underpin these reasons, they more often than not will cite claims that closely parallel those featured in long-standing persuasive communication campaigns.

Given the pervasiveness of persuasive campaign communication in contemporary society, and its central role in the marketing of products and services, the election of political candidates, and the cultivation of desirable social behaviors, we believe that a book that draws together extant theory and knowledge dealing with persuasive campaign communication is long overdo. In this book, we examine the theories and strategies of persuasion in applied campaign settings: commercial, political, and social action.

This book is written for students, academics, practitioners, and others with an abiding interest in the workings of persuasive communication campaigns. This book integrates extant theories of influence with research findings in persuasion generally and with applied research findings about commercial, political, and social action campaigns.

As a result, this book is unique. While there are textbooks that focus on persuasion, on commercial advertising, on political campaign communication, and on social action campaigns, there is no book that attempts to integrate these areas. This omission is an unfortunate one, because what Boulding (1977) observed in very general terms leading off this preface, applies perfectly to the status of theorizing and research in influence: much is presently known, but because scholars and practitioners focus their efforts in very specific fields, and because of inadequate communication across fields, there is duplication and wasted effort. We agree with Burgoon and Miller (1990) that macro principles of influence apply across situational boundaries, and therefore that it makes more sense to approach persuasive communication campaigns as one genre of persuasion, applying the extant theory and knowledge in commercial, political, and social action contexts, rather than to treat each as a unique, distinct field.

This book is ideally suited as a primary text in an advanced course in persuasion or persuasive campaigns. In both instances, students would have had prior exposure to theories and strategies of influence, and thus would be in a position to explore them in greater depth in an applied context. The book can also be used to supplement a primary text in a number of courses, including: persuasion, political communication, health communication, and advertising. In these cases, this book provides an integrated view of the theories and strategies of influence in commercial, political, and social action campaign contexts, complementing a primary text.

The book consists of 14 chapters, organized in five parts. Part I focuses on the nature and history of campaigns. Part II examines theoretical approaches to influence, stressing active and passive approaches to receivers. Part III introduces the essential tools of contemporary campaigns, including planning, assessment, and research design. Part IV concerns the uses of communication in persuasive campaigns. It includes an opening chapter on the nature of communication, a detailed discussion of the uses of free and paid communication modalities in campaigns, and concludes with a chapter on the use of mass media. Part V consists of three case studies: a commercial, political, and a social action campaign. Although all chapters provide examples drawn from actual campaigns to illustrate concepts, this section of the book provides an opportunity to further apply the theories and strategies of persuasive campaigns in applied contexts.

We approached the task of writing this book as scholars, who are deeply interested in social influence, and in its application in various contexts. We want to acknowledge the contributions of a number of people who have helped make this book possible. We thank Stephen Hull, communication editor with Allyn & Bacon, for his unwavering support for this project.

We appreciate the help we received from Bridget Lindquist, an Augustana College graduate and law student at the University of Minnesota, who conducted interviews with key individuals in the Wellstone Senate campaign, which is the focus of Chapter 13. We thank the people who were involved in the Wellstone campaign for taking the time to provide personal insights concerning the campaign, including: Bill Hillsman, North Woods Advertising, who created and produced all media advertising for the Wellstone campaign; Patrick Forceia, who works with the Minnesota North Stars, who served as director of that campaign; David Lillehaug, former Augustana graduate, now an attorney with Leonard, Street, and Deinard, who prepared Wellstone for televised debates; and Dennis McGrath, a reporter with the *Minneapolis Star Tribune*, who covered the Wellstone/Boschwitz campaign for Minnesota's largest newspaper.

We are grateful for the contribution of Steven R. Thomsen, a doctoral student in the School of Journalism at the University of Georgia, and a former Publications Editor for Toyota USA, who authored Chapter 12, focusing on Toyota's inoculation campaign against protectionism.

We also appreciate the help of three doctoral students in Speech Communication at the University of Georgia. Kim Powell collected the original Meatout campaign materials, many of which are depicted in Chapter 14, and Kathryn Greene and Rhonda Parker conducted numerous literature searches. In addition, we thank Tracy Diedrich, an Augustana College graduate, just beginning advanced study in communication, who worked tirelessly to secure permissions from various sources for most of the pictures which appear in this book. Finally, we acknowledge the many special students that we have had the opportunity to work with in our respective persuasive campaigns classes, who, because of their enthusiasm for the content area, and their tough questions, have made our teaching tasks such a delight.

Our thanks also to the reviewers of the manuscript which include Dr. Douglas Jennings of Illinois State University, Dr. John Lucaites of Indiana University (Bloomington), Dr. Anne Gabbard-Alley of James Madison University, Dr. James P. Dillard of the University of Wisconsin, Dr. Anne Johnston of the University of North Carolina–Chapel Hill, Dr. Susan Hellweg of San Diego State University, and Dr. Henry Kenski of the University of Arizona.

Last but not least, we acknowledge the influence of Michael Burgoon, an International Communication Association Fellow, who is a professor of Communication and Family and Community Medicine at the University of Arizona. Professor Burgoon is one of the most widely recognized scholars of social influence. He served as our mentor and trained us as scholars.

About the Authors

MICHAEL PFAU is Professor and Chair of Communication at Augustana College, Sioux Falls, SD. He has published more than 40 articles, most dealing with social influence, appearing in such journals as *Communication Education, Communication Monographs, Communication Quarterly, Communication Reports, Communication Research, Communication Studies, Human Communication Research, Journal of Broadcasting & Electronic Media*, and others. He has co-authored three previous books: *Debate and Argument: A Systems Approach to Advocacy* (1987), with David Thomas and Walter Ulrich; *Attack Advertising: Strategy and Defense* (1990), with Henry C. Kenski; and most recently, *Televised Presidential Debates: Advocacy in Contemporary America* (1992), with Susan A. Hellweg and Steven R. Brydon. He is a past recipient of the Speech Communication Association's Golden Anniversary Monograph Award.

ROXANNE PARROTT is a faculty member in the Department of Speech Communication and Fellow in the Institute of Behavioral Research at the University of Georgia, Athens, GA. She is also a member of the Center for Risk and Health Communication at Emory University, and a consultant with the Centers for Disease Control in Atlanta regarding AIDS campaigns. Her research interests involve interpersonal, organizational, and societal messages concerning health. She has received four national, and one international, top research paper awards on health topics during the past five years. She has published in *Communication Monographs, Social Science & Medicine, Health Communication, The Journal of Language & Social Psychology*, and *Family Relations*.

P a r t *I*

Nature and History of Campaigns

Nature of Persuasive Communication Campaigns

"Two generalizations strike me as appropriate. . . . First, with the possible exception of language, more undoubtedly has been written and said about persuasion than any other single process, problem, or issue relating to human communication. . . . Second. . . . students of communication find it impossible to shake the uneasy feeling that we have precious little reliable, socially relevant knowledge about it [persuasion]."
GERALD R. MILLER, COMMUNICATION PROFESSOR
(MILLER, 1987, PP. 446–447).

". . . there has been more progress in designing and conducting campaigns in the past 20 years than in the [previous] 125 years. . . . "
WILLIAM PAISLEY, ELECTRONIC PUBLISHER (PAISLEY, 1989, P. 38).

More than three decades have passed since the publication of Vance Packard's (1957), *The Hidden Persuaders*, which opens in the following fashion:

> *This book is an attempt to explore a strange and rather exotic new area of American life. It is about the large-scale efforts being made, often with impressive success, to channel our unthinking habits, our purchasing decisions, and our thought processes by the use of insights gleaned from psychiatry and the social sciences. Typically these efforts take place beneath our level of awareness; so that the appeals which move us are often, in a sense, "hidden." The result is that many of us are being influenced and manipulated, far more than we realize, in the patterns of our everyday lives (p. 1).*

Persuasive communication campaigns are a pervasive feature of contemporary American life. Persuasive campaigns deal with systematic attempts to inform, change, and reinforce people's attitudes and/or behaviors concerning commercial, political, or social action issues. Such attempts may employ a highly active cognitive approach or a more passive strategy. Both approaches are examined in this book. Regardless of the general strategy employed, however, there is nothing "strange" or "exotic" about the process of influence. Social science theory and research guide these efforts. People are not victims of "hidden influence," and old assumptions about communication and mass media influence have been discarded since Packard's book. Commercial campaigners no longer operate on the assumption that advertising controls and manipulates the masses (Berman, 1981; Schudson, 1984). Similarly, political (Barnes and Kasse, 1979) and social action (Elmore, 1983) campaigners have abandoned a mass model, which assumed that human communication is a linear process and that mass media are all powerful.

In part, this revolution in approach to persuasive campaigns is a direct result of societal changes that began following World War II (Gibson and Haritos-Fatouros, 1986). "After the war . . . a conscious effort was made to stamp out the kind of upbringing that made people receptive to Nazism" (Pines, 1981, p. 65). Whereas parents used to encourage obedience to authority as an end in itself in their children, parents now prefer that their children develop self-reliance and tolerance for others (Remley, 1988). Children raised to be more self-reliant and to question authority also are likely, as children and later as adults, to be more critical of commercial, political, and social messages.

Moreover, numerous individual variables have been found to affect campaign outcomes, including perceived self-efficacy (Bandura, 1982; Phillips and Lord, 1980) and self-evaluation (Bandura and Cervone, 1986). Both contribute to individuals' motivation to think, to feel, and to behave, all of which are of interest to the persuasive campaigner.

This book applies the theory and research from the social sciences to commercial, political, and social action campaigns. Although there are a few successful campaigners who continue to operate on an intuitive level, that does not help the rest of us achieve success in persuasive communication campaigns. It is our belief that successful persuasive communication campaigns rarely just happen. Instead, we can promote success by specifying in advance what is to be achieved and how to achieve it, employing theories drawn from several disciplines, including psychology, communication, and sociology, to inform campaign practices.

This first chapter overviews what we mean by persuasive communication campaigns, thus answering the questions that appear in Table 1-1. The questions establish the boundaries for the book's perspective.

TABLE 1-1 Central Questions about the Nature of Persuasive Campaigns

1. What is a persuasive communication campaign?
2. What is the difference between a persuasive message and a persuasive campaign?
3. What are the goals of persuasive communication campaigns?
4. Do campaigners use communication theory?
5. What are the essential components of a persuasive communication campaign?

Definitions and Characteristics

A campaign involves more than just getting someone elected to office or convincing consumers to purchase new products, although both of these may be within the realm of campaigns. Campaigns are inherently persuasive communication activities. However, communication involves more than designing and sending messages (Berlo, 1960), and persuasion is not always concerned with attitude and behavior change (see Delia, 1987). Definitions of these three terms integrate the book's focus.

Communication

. . . If a tree falls down in the forest and no one is there to witness the event, does the tree make a sound? . . .

In this book, we will emphasize communication as a process that employs verbal and nonverbal codes to symbolically transact understanding between two or more people. We stress the role of receivers in campaigns. Traditional definitions of communication concentrated almost exclusively on the uses of communication by sources and reactions by receivers. However, over the past three decades, communication has been "acquiring the trappings of a discipline" (Berger and Chaffee, 1987, p. 15). Along with it, the focus of human communication has evolved to concerns about how individuals mutually define themselves, their relationships, and society (Shimanoff, 1980). The close examination of most past and some recent campaigns reveals the failure to carefully consider these issues. This often leads to failed persuasive campaigns, as is illustrated in the following example.

In November, 1981, Arizona lawmakers adopted the Arizona Health Care Cost Containment System (AHCCCS), a three-year Medicaid-demonstration program touted as the "Arizona Experiment" (Christianson, Hillman, and Smith, 1984). Like many states in the nation facing rapidly rising indigent health care expenses (Wing, 1984), Arizona wanted to provide adequate health care to the poor, but needed to do so affordably (Murphy and Kauffman, 1984). In the case of Arizona lawmakers, the decision was made to use Health Maintenance Organizations (HMOs) to provide health care services to indigents (Christianson, 1984). The success and affordability of using HMOs to provide health care depends upon members' use of preventive services, which reduces the use of more expensive acute and long term care (Christianson, 1984; Christianson et al., 1984).

In the example, policymakers seemingly failed to consider whether individuals for whom the program was designed viewed themselves as wanting, needing, and using preventive health care services. Four traditional assumptions concerning campaign communication are illustrated by this oversight (see Dervin, Harlock, Atwood, and Garzona, 1980). First, the reformers assumed that information is absolute, and thus can be transferred from the information source to the receiver like a physical object. Second, communication revolved around the policymakers' world views, which suggests reliance on an observer construction of reality assumption. The reformers simply assumed that because they would use such a program, indigents would use the program. No consideration was given to how health care may be socially constructed by the perceivers. Third, individual differences were not addressed, suggesting the assumption that all people react similarly to message stimuli. And fourth, policymakers assumed that health care providers were the appropriate agents to instill in indigents an understanding of the preventive health care actions that were expected of them. This assumption rests on the premise that persuasion is about what a source does to a receiver.

The greatest challenge to cost containment for indigent health care reform is to direct these patients away from a crisis orientation to medical care (Hale, Immel, and Moher, 1984). If this group does not use health care except when sick or injured, a program whose cost savings is based on prevention is doomed to fail. Indeed, at the end of the three-year experiment, the program had not achieved its purpose (Nichols, 1984). This is just one modern example of a traditional and linear approach to campaign communication.

Persuasion

This book will focus on the systematic use of communication to attain persuasion, which we define as the shaping, changing, or reinforcing of receivers' responses (Miller, 1980), including attitudes, emotions, intentions, and behaviors. In the example of Arizona's system for indigent health care, minimally some effort was needed to understand how targeted receivers view preventive health care. Quite likely, based on such an understanding, the primary purpose for communicating about preventive health care with this receiver group would ultimately become a persuasive one.

Persuasion is one function of communication and in this book will be used interchangeably with the phrase, social influence. The paradigm case of persuasion is intentional, as is the case in most campaigns. In addition, persuasion can be an unintentional, but no less real, outcome of communication. For example, President Ronald Reagan broadcast this message to the nation at the time of the space shuttle *Challenger* disaster:

> *We will never forget them nor the last time we saw them this morning as they prepared for their journey and waved goodbye and "slipped the surly bonds of earth to touch the face of God" (cited in Magnuson, 1986, p. 25).*

Although President Reagan's purpose for this message was probably not persuasion, one unintended outcome of the broadcast may have been that several citizens' responses to Reagan were positively affected, leading to potential support for such a compassionate individual. In this instance, the instrumental goal of the communicator may have been to console the nation, but one of the outcomes attained may have included persuasion. The fact that a message may be designed with one purpose in mind, achieve or not achieve that function, and result in additional outcomes, is in itself valuable information for the campaigner, as is discussed later in this chapter, and in more detail elsewhere in this book.

A functional approach to communication considers the motives or purposes for a communicator's message, as well as the outcomes associated with communication

FIGURE 1–1   Front Panel of a Box of Raisin Bran Breakfast Cereal

Source: Courtesy of *Kellogg* Company. *Kellogg's*® is a registered trademark of Kellogg Company.

(Burgoon, Buller, and Woodall, 1989; Miller, 1973). Examine Figure 1–1, which depicts the front of a cereal box. The message says that this cereal "Provides 13 essential vitamins and minerals," and is "fiber-rich."

If this is an intentional attempt to influence consumers' purchasing habits (which is likely), the motive for communicating is persuasive; this is what the verbal message was designed to achieve. In such a case, the communicator's goal is instrumental in nature, based on the conscious intent of the message designer.

Not all persuasion is instrumental, of course. Individuals may be influenced in their purchasing and other habits without a specific intent on the part of a source or in ways that the source did not intend. Social psychologist Robert Cialdini, for example, recounts the tale of a friend who wanted to move some merchandise and gave instructions that the product's price be cut in half (1984a, 1984b). Instead, the price of the merchandise was accidentally doubled, and yet all of the merchandise sold! Cialdini attributes this result to humans' mechanical patterns of action; in this case, shoppers associated the higher price with a more valuable good. Such fixed-action patterns may be used as weapons or "triggers of influence" (Cialdini, 1984a, 1984b).

Cialdini (1984a) brings to the forefront of this discussion of persuasion the debate concerning human behavior and action. He acknowledges (1984a, p. 20) that ". . . automatic, stereotyped behavior is prevalent in much of human action because in many cases it is the most efficient form of behaving, and in other cases it is simply necessary." Nevertheless, to view all human behavior as automatic is, again, to invite failure. Campaigners should consider their audiences as proactive choicemakers, as well as reactive agents.

Examine Figure 1–1 again. A message designer might believe that consumers have learned an automatic, habituated, or mindless response to the phrase, "fiber-rich." Given the information that the cereal is rich in fiber, a consumer may choose to buy it as opposed to another brand. The outcome associated with providing information, therefore, is expected to be an automatic response that leads to influence on purchasing behavior. However, just because a message is designed to influence does not mean that the goal will be attained, even when the designer intentionally employs a "trigger of influence." A person who prefers sugar-coated cereals might be influenced by the message, but probably not in the intended fashion. Another person who simply likes raisins may purchase the cereal, oblivious to the persuader's claim about its fiber content. Campaigners have learned that to ignore individual factors often dooms campaigns to failure.

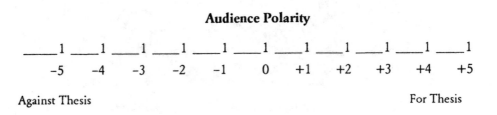

Audience Polarity

___ 1	___ 1	___ 1	___ 1	___ 1	___ 1	___ 1	___ 1	___ 1	___ 1	___ 1
−5	−4	−3	−2	−1	0	+1	+2	+3	+4	+5

Against Thesis   For Thesis

FIGURE 1–2 A Transactional Model of Persuasion

A traditional definition of persuasion forms a model like the one pictured in Figure 1–2, whereas our definition forms a model like the one depicted in Figure 1–3. The message on the front of the cereal box, for example, might inform ambivalent purchasers and influence them to form positive feelings about the product. The messages also could motivate already informed consumers and change their purchasing behavior, causing them to buy one of these cereals rather than other cereals because of the messages' content. Or, the messages may reinforce positive attitudes and commitment to the product on the part of consumers who have purchased them in the past.

Purchasing habits are certainly not the only area where influence occurs. Indeed, too much importance and significance may be attached to commercial messages in discussing the origins of communication theory (Delia, 1987). Certainly social issues

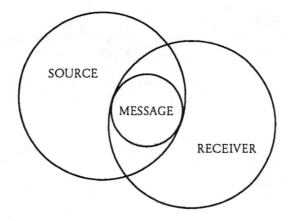

Affective Objectives:
1. Form/shape feelings about the influence topic.
2. Change feelings about the influence topic.
3. Reinforce feelings about the influence topic.

Cognitive Objectives:
4. Form/shape cognitions about the influence topic.
5. Change cognitions about the influence topic.
6. Reinforce cognitions about the influence topic.

Behavioral Objectives:
7. Form/shape behavior regarding the influence topic.
8. Change behavior regarding the influence topic.
9. Reinforce behavior regarding the influence topic.

FIGURE 1–3 A Transactional Model of Persuasion Campaigns

are the focus of considerable efforts by persuaders. During the past three decades, Americans have witnessed appeals designed to influence on issues as general as concern for the environment and as specific as individual rights based on ethnicity, gender, and sexual preference. Examine Figure 1–4, for example.

In the cover letter to "The Report of the Commission on Population Growth and the American Future," John D. Rockefeller (1972) overviews the commission's recommendations as follows:

> *The recommendations offered . . . are directed toward increasing public knowledge of the causes and consequences of population change, facilitating and guiding the processes of population movement, maximizing information about human reproduction and its consequences for the family, and enabling individuals to avoid unwanted fertility.*

Compare the Rockefeller message with the following communication concerning AIDS.

> *I encourage you to practice responsible behavior based on understanding and strong personal values. This is what you can do to stop AIDS (Koop, 1988).*

Koop, the Surgeon General at the time of the publication of the brochure pictured in Figure 1-4, addressed the nation about AIDS and made explicit statements about his desire to influence readers' behavior. The instrumental motive for Koop's message is behavioral change, a traditional persuasive objective, whereas Rockefeller's message focuses more on shaping responses. Both are one-shot messages, the kind that historically have failed, and neither alone constitutes a campaign. However, when taken together, the two might be seen as part of the government's sustained effort to affect society's sexual behavior, bringing them potentially within the realm of a campaign.

Campaign

Campaigns are sustained communication efforts involving more than a single message for the purpose of social influence. Note the following excerpt from Leon Jaworski's discussion of stories about former President Nixon's personal finances.

> *As far back as July, 1973, stories about Richard Nixon's personal finances had begun appearing in the newspapers. The Washington Post led the way with a story about the president's donation of his vice-presidential papers to the National Archives during his first term in office. The President had taken a $482,018 income tax deduction on his gift (Jaworski, 1976, p. 57).*

This represents a situation where a public figure might claim that the media was campaigning to remove him from office. Undoubtedly, all of us can recall some time when an untrue or exaggerated rumor was spread about a relative, friend, or public figure. One of the statements often made by individuals in these situations is that, "It's a

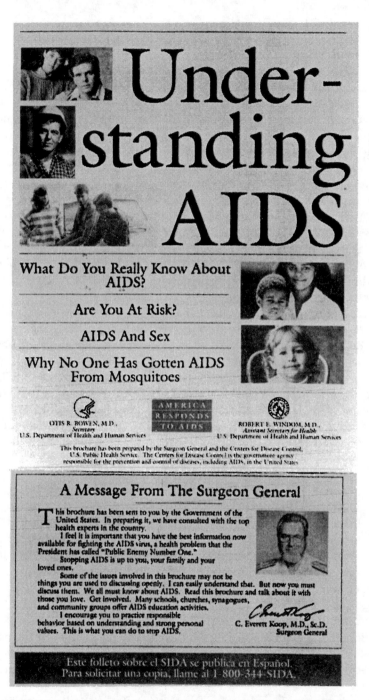

FIGURE 1–4 Pamphlet from the Department of Health and Human Services

Source: Courtesy of National AIDS Clearinghouse, Rockville, MD.

smear campaign designed to get me." Use of the term campaign in this way is usually a misnomer. Typically, these events involve a single message, which is not a campaign. These events are often communication, and they might even be persuasion, if the source sought to influence receivers' thoughts, feelings, or behavior. However, these events are not campaigns, unless they involve a sustained effort aimed at some predetermined objective.

Persuasive campaigns, in short, are integrated, sustained communication efforts, involving multiple messages that seek clearly defined persuasive goals (Simons, 1986). In campaigns, persuasive messages occur over a period of time, with one message necessarily related to another. Single messages can result in the failure of entire campaigns. For example, George Romney's, "I was brainwashed" response to a press inquiry concerning his reversal of positions about U.S. involvement in Vietnam ended his 1968 presidential campaign. Edmund Muskie's attack against the *Manchester Union Leader*, when he broke down and cried during an attempt to defend his wife against the newspaper's charges, put the brakes on Muskie's frontrunning campaign for the Democratic presidential nomination in 1972. More recently, Senator Joseph Biden's plagiarized speech brought an abrupt halt to his bid for the 1988 Democratic presidential nomination. Thus, campaigns carry a history.

Successful campaigners are aware of and utilize past events to shape current efforts. When we process campaign information, "new evidence is rarely regarded strictly on its merits. Rather, what we already know and believe significantly influences how we interpret any new information" (Moyer, 1985, p. 33). This is particularly important since receiver perceptions about products, candidates, or social issues initially are formed quite easily, but then change only grudgingly. Research indicates that voters form impressions of political candidates during the primary phase of campaigns, and that subsequently it is very difficult to alter them (Patterson, 1980; Kennamer and Chaffee, 1982). Moreover, it is usually easier to gain market entry for a new product than to reposition an old one when it involves making a fundamental alteration in product image.

A persuasive campaign seeks multiple, but clearly defined, persuasive objectives and goals. A movement is broader still, involving many campaigns over time. Movements pursue broader and less clearly specified objectives and goals, but the three communication levels are interrelated. The content communicated, the image generated, and the success of each message affects the broader campaign, much as the content, image, and success of a campaign affects a movement. Single campaigns can sometimes, due to success or failure, break broader movements. The success of the campaign for women's suffrage secured ratification of the Nineteenth Amendment to the Constitution, but in doing so, it sapped the strength of the women's movement, which embodied more than simply the right to vote, placing it on the back burner for nearly 40 years (Hole and Levine, 1971). In addition, the failure of Barry Goldwater's 1964 presidential campaign probably set the conservative movement back more than a decade.

There are several broad types of campaigns, and we will make comparisons and contrasts involving commercial, political, and social action campaigns. Many marketing books discuss commercial campaigns, and some provide considerable detail to describe how to influence consumers' purchasing practices.

Marketing originated out of economics and initially focused on services such as retailing, with little or no regard for the social outcomes attributed to activities (Choudhury, 1974). During the decade of the seventies, marketers were criticized for failing to be socially responsible. In turn, various individuals within the marketing area argued that marketing techniques could be used to successfully achieve social change (Kotler and Zaltman, 1971). The latter gave rise to the phrase, social marketing, and attention to marketers' potential social responsibilities. In fact, many campaigns analyzed in the social marketing literature (Kotler and Zaltman, 1971) are the same ones analyzed as public communication campaigns (Rice and Atkin, 1989) and will be discussed in this text.

The difference between marketing, social marketing, and a persuasive communication campaign is often one of emphasis and degree. Persuasion is interested more in social outcomes, but marketing is interested more in profit. This book focuses on persuasion as a guide to explaining the past and predicting the future with regard to sustained influence attempts. Persuasive communication campaigns fundamentally concern influence.

Persuasive Communication Campaign: A conscious, sustained, and incremental process designed to be implemented over a specified period of time for the purpose of influencing a specified audience.

FEEDBACK

When considering how we have narrowed the scope of discussion for this text with our definition of persuasive communication campaign, imagine the following scenario and answer the questions.

Scenario: The National Institute of Health has approved a five-year project that will study individuals who are at high-risk for colon cancer. The participants will receive regular health care check-ups, some will be put on special diets, and all will be compensated for their time. They will be given a great deal of printed material and asked to read it. Some of the information has already been prepared. Other information will be developed as the study progresses. Participants will also attend small group and mass meetings that range from lectures to movies about colon cancer. The participants will keep a record of a number of specific behaviors during the course of the study.

1. Does this meet the criterion specified for defining a persuasive communication campaign? Consider the source, the message, and the receiver of the message. Does this represent a sustained effort? Is it incremental in nature?

2. What are the desired outcomes or end products of this effort?

Essential Components

In order to explain the implications of our definition of persuasive communication campaigns, we need to carefully examine the essential components of a campaign.

Campaigns have several elements and are of several types. This book develops campaign strategy, and we assert that each component of a campaign must be consciously and intentionally executed by campaigners. When a persuader makes a conscious decision to conduct a persuasive communication campaign, the efforts should be vested with as much insight from previous successes and failures as possible. The essential components of persuasive communication campaigns include planning, implementation, and evaluation.

Planning

The first component of a persuasive communication campaign is planning. Planning requires answers to three questions: what is the influence topic, who is being influenced, and what is the campaign goal associated with who is being influenced? Within the planning phase, the most critical and often overlooked step is selecting a goal or goals for the campaign. Refer again to Figure 1-3. Campaigners are generally interested in three broad objectives: hostility reduction, attitude formation and change, and intensification (Miller, 1980). Within each of these broad objectives, there are a number of primary campaign goals which are appropriate.

Attitude formation and change involve campaigners' efforts to shape an attitude or actually swing an unfavorable view to a favorable one with regard to the influence topic. The objective of reinforcement addresses a campaign's supporters. Some people who are already committed to a campaign will be asked to do more, and agreement is likely to intensify favorable attitudes and behavior. A recent experience comes to mind with regard to this; a local elementary school PTA membership chairperson reported to the PTA that 100 percent membership had been achieved. However, the membership chair was not satisfied; she wanted more than 100 percent. She urged: "Get the children's grandparents to join, as well as friends who do not have any children of their own." She asked, "Where else can they get so much for so little?" referring to the modest membership dues.

Within each general campaign objective, persuaders specify multiple goals. As the campaign progresses, these goals change, in part as a response to the campaign's success in accomplishing initial goals. Some specific goals under the broad objective of reinforcement are: reinforcing favorable attitudes, activating favorable attitudes, increasing behavioral commitments, and maintaining high levels of attitudinal and behavioral commitments (see Burgoon and Miller, 1986). It should be evident that even people who are extremely committed to the persuader's position must not be overlooked in planning the campaign.

To illustrate the intensification objective, examine Figure 1-5. The Children's Wish Foundation attempted to accomplish this by enclosing one of these certificates in every invoice mailed to individuals who had pledged monetary support over the phone.

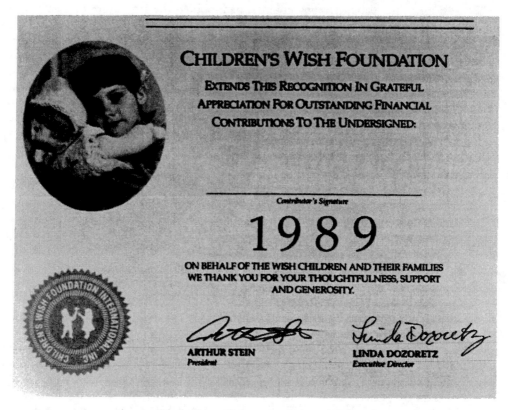

FIGURE 1–5 Certificate from the Children's Wish Foundation

Source: Courtesy Children's Wish Foundation, Atlanta, GA.

To be able to monitor the success or failure of a persuasive communication campaign demands care in specifying the desired outcomes. Campaign designers should forecast by use of survey or other means, such as a pilot study or field interviews, what the audience feels and thinks, and how the audience behaves with regard to the influence topic. Such formative research that is conducted before a campaign is undertaken helps both to eliminate unimportant but potentially confounding variables and to illumine variables that must be considered to enhance the likelihood of success (Rice and Atkin, 1989; Rice and Paisley, 1981). Formative research combines the disciplined application of social science theory and method with creative observations and recommendations of a particular situation (Palmer, 1981). Thus, formative research provides the means to approach a campaign guided by the lessons of the past as well as the specific needs of the present. The last three chapters of this book provide an in-depth analysis of specific campaigns, but for purposes of illustrating campaign components, we will use an example of the social action campaign that eventually led to health-care reform in Arizona.

In tracing the origins of AHCCCS, an appropriate starting point is societal conditions at the time. Arizona counties had lobbied the legislature to pass a state law that would establish a Medicaid program, and, in 1974, such a law was passed (Murphy and Kauffman, 1984). No funds were appropriated for the program, however, and so counties continued to have full responsibility for providing indigent health care, while county tax revenues paid the bill (Christianson, 1984). The existence of a state law to establish a Medicaid program and the absence of such a program comprise the topic of influence in this campaign. Reformers' basic planning strategies developed around the issue of setting statewide eligibility and health-care standards. Basing the state's health-care program on an HMO model was first suggested by Governor Bruce Babbitt in 1978. At that point, however, messages regarding the topic were piecemeal and often unrelated.

In 1981, city council supervisors, business owners, and health services people formed a coalition to mobilize community interest in a state Medicaid program (Resnick, 1984). At this time, health-care reform took on the dimensions of a campaign. Sustained efforts were designed and targeted to influence specific audiences. Two groups in particular were the targets of campaigners' efforts. One was the legislators who would have to pass laws to implement health-care reform. The second group was the general public who would have to pay for the reforms with their tax dollars. Some legislators were openly hostile and opposed to health-care reform, as illustrated by such statements as Phoenix Republican Wayne Stump's, "It's socialism, it's redistribute-the-wealth, it's enslave-the-taxpayer" (Lopez, 1985). Some taxpayers were also opposed because of the cost (Easterbrook, 1987), although survey data indicate that most Americans believe that health care should be available to everyone, regardless of ability to pay (Freeman, Blendon, Aiken, Sudman, Mullinix, and Corey, 1987). Thus, taxpayers might be viewed as an audience which held attitudes that needed to be reinforced and specifically linked to support for AHCCCS.

In sum, during the campaign's planning stage, campaigners seek to establish an accurate starting point for the campaign. Then, based on this information, campaigners select a goal or goals.

Planning: The campaign component that formally specifies an influence topic, identifies and attempts to understand the group or groups to be influenced, and outlines the persuasive objective associated with each group and the influence topic.

Implementation

The implementation component of persuasive communication campaigns is when the learning and application of theory most significantly come into practice. Having identified the influence topic, group(s), objective(s), and goals, the next component of a campaign is implementation. Many campaigns undoubtedly self-destruct during the planning phase. Lack of money is certainly not the only reason to explain a campaign's failure at this stage. Another reason is the inability to go forth with a sustained and incremental strategy.

FEEDBACK

Consider the following scenario and answer the questions.

Scenario: Arizona has an extremely high rate of skin cancer, and in recent years has begun to consider what might be done to promote skin cancer prevention (Parrott, Glassman, and Burgoon, 1989). Several groups and organizations have become involved in skin cancer-related persuasive communication campaigns. These groups' efforts have been multi-faceted and involve diverse audiences, such as elementary school children, college students, and Hispanics.

   1. Consider elementary school children as an audience. As a campaigner, you speak with them and learn that they know very little about the dangers of overexposure to the sun. What is your objective as a campaigner with this audience?
   2. College students, on the other hand, may or may not be aware of the sun's potential harmfulness. They are very aware, however, of a societal norm that associates a tan with beauty and health.
      One only need consider such expressions as "sickly pale" to realize that college students are unlikely to change their sun-worshipping behaviors if all they are given is information about the sun's potential harmfulness. What is your objective as a campaigner with this audience?
   3. Hispanics as a group to be influenced by a skin cancer prevention campaign represent yet another challenge to planners. Many believe the myth that darker skin pigment protects skin from the harmful rays of the sun. What is your objective as a campaigner with this audience?
   4. If the objective was reinforcement, what group or groups would you expect campaigners to target?

A large portion of this text is devoted to discussion of theories to be employed during the implementation component of campaigns. However, the planning component should serve as a guide for campaigners' decision making during implementation with regard to which theory or theories will most usefully guide the campaign toward achieving desired end products. Theory guides campaigners' decisions with regard to four elements of campaign implementation: message, source, receiver, and channel.

Messages

The implementation component involves the vital construction of campaign messages. Sometimes, a campaign source is as direct as Koop was in the AIDS brochure in stating the intent of the message. Other times, messages are designed that are less direct about their intent. Theory and research should guide a campaigner's decision making about when to adopt each style in order to facilitate the desired outcomes.

   Memorable campaign slogans, particularly if designed to be integrated into the overall sustained and incremental strategy, may facilitate the achievement of desired outcomes. During the implementation of health care reform in Arizona, AHCCCS took on the label of "ACCESS" in the press, one way to establish the notion that the program's purpose was to provide access to health care for groups that could not otherwise afford such care.

Campaign messages are designed within specific parameters, considering such issues as the number of arguments to be used (Insko, Lind, and LaTour, 1976), and how often to communicate the message (Belch, 1982; Calder and Sternthal, 1980; Gorn and Goldberg, 1980), issues which concern content and frequency.

Sources

The source of a message, as much as the message itself, must be consciously considered during the implementation phase of campaigns. Sometimes, a given source is ideal for the influence topic, and is preselected as a campaign spokesperson. When a source or spokesperson is chosen before a message is written, that sometimes guides the activities associated with message design, depending upon the theoretical approach guiding the campaign. Some sources are more effective when using more intense or opinionated language, for example, while other sources delivering an identical message would be ineffective (Bradac, Bowers, and Courtright, 1979). In addition, the source's physical attractiveness and likability are important considerations (Kahle and Homer, 1985).

Receivers

The implementation component formally addresses what receiver characteristics campaigners should consider when writing messages for the purpose of influence. The planning component identifies the campaign audience or audiences. The implementation phase considers variables such as receiver anxiety and involvement with the issue, which have been evaluated from several perspectives (Borgida and Howard-Pitney, 1983; Chaiken and Baldwin, 1981). Quite likely, formative research of the indigent group for whom health care reform in Arizona was designed would have found that these individuals were generally uninformed and/or apathetic regarding the topic. Providing them with more information may have been an appropriate strategy. However, the presentation would only have a chance for success if variables such as the group's poverty, ethnicity, and education were considered in an effort to make the information salient. Since ultimately, specific behaviors were sought from this group, campaigners should also have planned for incremental change and sustained efforts with this group, as well as legislators and taxpayers. Initially, the objective and related goals may have been to generate positive feelings and thoughts in receivers about use of preventative health care. Additionally, the goals should have included motivating the informed indigents to use the services.

Channels

Finally, during the implementation component of persuasive communication campaigns, decisions are made regarding the most appropriate channel (e.g., Chaiken and Eagly, 1976) to be used in delivering messages to specified audience. Campaigners have a wide range of possible options, from intimate face-to-face interpersonal communication to free or paid messages carried via print, radio, or television. Here, perhaps more than in previous areas of the implementation phase, an issue of funding for the campaign may drive many decisions. Nonetheless, past research and theory will also suggest the appropriate mix between mediated and interpersonal modes for message delivery. As previously noted, the press took on a significant role in campaigning about AHCCCS. Taxpayers became informed through newspaper stories about the rising cost of indigent health care in terms of taxes; legislators became aware of a significant issue in the minds of their constituents.

Implementation: The conscious and intentional theoretical decision-making processes associated with message design and source and channel selection to achieve a specified goal with an audience.

Evaluation

The final component of persuasive communication campaigns that is vital to our perspective is evaluation. In the same way that implementation will not occur simply because campaigners plan a campaign, evaluation is not automatic. Research during the evaluation phase of campaigns parallels formative research during the planning phase. Campaigners must sustain the efforts of the campaign through an evaluation process, which is too often overlooked. Evaluation involves the critical examination of the planning and implementation phases. Evaluation may occur simultaneously with implementation and send campaigners back to the planning phase.

One purpose of an evaluation component is to determine if the goals specified in the planning stage have been attained through the decisions made in the implementation phase. If not, why not? Campaigners need to address such questions as: Were there factors in the environment beyond campaigners' control that contributed to failure to achieve the goal? Were incorrect assumptions made about receivers? Did receivers get the message?

In addition to the primary campaign goals, several secondary outcomes of persuasive communication campaigns can be evaluated. One secondary goal is the reinforcement of values. For example, many proponents of school prayer may have reconciled themselves to the realization that achieving mandatory prayer in the public schools is unlikely. However, supporters may believe that just keeping the question in the public eye focuses discussion on key value questions that are significant. Another secondary goal of campaigns is winning on a subproposition of belief. It is not uncommon for some political candidates to campaign for office even though they don't expect to win an election. However, by campaigning for office, they bring a policy to the forefront of discussion, and get other candidates to support some part of the policy.

Additionally, a worthwhile campaign outcome may be the increased credibility of a political candidate, a company associated with a product, or an organization promoting some social issue. When women were first beginning to run for political office, for example, they may have had little hope of being elected. However, each woman who campaigned for an office represented not only her individual policies but women as a group as well. Those early candidates enhanced the credibility of women as a group, which allows the modern voter's attention to turn more to the merits of the individual rather than the individual's gender. Also, companies associated with products that have been the center of controversy, such as the Tylenol scare, carefully plan how to restore an image of credibility in consumers' minds. Attaining that goal is a worthwhile outcome. An appreciation of language and style is also noteworthy in a persuasive communication campaign, as is providing an ethical example for others to follow or bolstering an audience's esteem.

The determination that a goal has or has not been achieved is only the first step in evaluation. As Jacoby and Kyner (1973) argue regarding brand loyalty and purchasing behavior, findings have focused too often on the outcomes of rather than the reasons for behavior.

Evaluation is not easy or inexpensive, which may explain the tendency to overlook this component of campaigns. More than a checklist of questions must be answered, and success or failure must be viewed within a broader vision of the larger societal scene and events beyond the planning and implementation of the campaign. With regard to AHCCCS, for example, underestimation of the number of eligible Arizonans plagued the program from the beginning (Nichols, 1984). Clinic administrators reported negligible assistance with marketing, so enrollees did not use available services and reverted to use of the nearest emergency room at county expense (Hale et al., 1984). Moreover, the health-care providers who would be expected to provide care to the program enrollees should have been considered as a separate group whose support was vital to the successful implementation of reform. The evaluation component of campaigns will be fully developed in chapter 6 of this text.

FEEDBACK

One of the best (and, also, the most fun) ways to become familiar with the campaign process is to be involved in a campaign. Thus, we make the assignment to our classes that they form groups (from three to six members) and select a campaign topic. Topics in recent classes have included: blood donation, Greenpeace, food safety, organ donation, recycling, voting, obscenity in musical lyrics, drunk driving, and others. Groups should be formed early so that there is sufficient time to plan and implement a succession of messages during the campaign. The following is a list of activities associated with the campaign assignment:

1. Specify research questions or hypotheses which will be tested.
2. Determine receiver groups that will be targeted.
3. Draft a survey instrument designed to determine existing attitudes and behaviors of receivers. Administer the instrument. Compute the mean, median, and mode for items.
4. Determine campaign goals for each of the receiver groups.
5. Devise strategies to attain each goal. Select a theory for each strategy to explain why the strategy should be effective in achieving the goal.
6. Implement the campaign.
7. Administer the survey instrument and assess the results.

Evaluation: The conscious and intentional measurement of outcomes associated with message design and source and channel selection to achieve a specified goal with an audience.

Conclusion

This chapter introduced the perspective to be used in this text on persuasive communication campaigns. The focus utilizes a modern perspective of persuasion and communication. Persuasive communication campaigns will be discussed within the framework of planning, implementation, and evaluation. Future chapters will develop and elaborate the concepts and ideas introduced in this first chapter.

Suggestions for Further Reading

Cialdini, R. B. (1984). *Influence: The New Psychology of Modern Persuasion*. New York: Quill.

Delia, J. G. (1987). *Communication research: A history*. In C. R. Berger and S. H. Chaffee (Eds.), Handbook of Communication Science (pp. 20–98). Beverly Hills, CA: Sage Publications.

Dervin, B., Harlock, S., Atwood, R., and Garzona, C. (1980). The human side of information: An exploration in a health communication context. In D. Nimmo (Ed.), *Communication Yearbook* (Vol. 4, pp. 591–608). New Brunswick, NJ: Transaction Books.

Miller, G. R. (1987). Persuasion. In C. R. Berger and S. H. Chaffee (Eds.), *Handbook of Communication Science* (pp. 446–483). Beverly Hills, CA: Sage Publications.

Miller, G. R, and Burgoon, M. (1973). *New Techniques of Persuasion*. New York: Harper and Row.

Chapter 2

=====

History of Persuasive Campaigns

"As soon as several Americans have conceived a sentiment or an idea ... hey seek each other out, and when found, they unite. Associations substitute for the power of 'powerful private persons."
—ALEXIS DE TOCQUEVILLE, DEMOCRACY IN AMERICA
(CITED IN MAYER, ED., 1969, P. 516)

"The history of advertising is ... entwined with the development and availability of media forms ... The availability of new media and new media forms has undoubtedly facilitated the growth of advertising."
—WILLIAM M. WEILBACHER, ADVERTISING CONSULTANT
(WEILBACHER, 1984, P. 10)

"... these developments in [mass media] communication markedly changed the nature of propaganda, political and otherwise, and probably profoundly altered the nature of political power, by making it possible for national leaders to reach and influence mass opinion directly without heavy reliance on an intermediate network of party workers." —V. O. KEY, JR., POLITICAL SCIENTIST (KEY, 1953, P. 499).

Although persuasive communication is probably as old as oral language itself, persuasive campaigns, which we characterized in Chapter 1 as integrated and sustained communication efforts which target multiple persuasive goals, are a more recent phenomenon, owing their rise to the growth of mass communication outlets during the past 100 years. As Table 2–1 indicates, the content of this chapter seeks to provide a broad understanding of the history of campaigns. The chapter first briefly focuses on the origins of commercial, political, and social action campaigns, and then examines the most significant developments during the past 100 years that have shaped the nature of modern persuasive communication campaigns.

Origins of Persuasive Campaigns

The Beginnings

Persuasive communication has its origins in antiquity. The first advertising, for example, most likely took place "in the dawn of history" prior to the development of a written language (Ulanoff, 1977). At that time, people employed word-of-mouth tactics to promote interest in their goods. Criers or barkers were used later in Babylon, Egypt, and Greece as a primary vehicle to pronounce public edicts or announce goods for sale. Following the invention of *papyrus*, a primitive form of paper, written advertisements became possible.

It was the ancient Greeks, however, that laid the foundation for contemporary persuasion and persuasive campaigns. The Greeks recited epic poetry as a form of entertainment and political and social commentary. Homer's *Iliad* and *Odyssey* promoted cultural unity during the sixth century B.C. The prose of Isocrates and his students during the fourth century B.C. exploited historical myth in the pursuit of Pan-Hellenism.

However, the most important and precisely articulated Greek contribution to persuasion, and an early example of a receiver-centered view of persuasion, was made by Aristotle. Aristotle characterized rhetoric as the search for "the available means of persuasion," whether based on logic, emotion, or personal appeal (cited in Solmsen, 1954, pp. 24–25). He called for speakers to base their appeals on the nature of the audience.

TABLE 2–1 Basic Questions about the History of Campaigns

1. What are the origins of contemporary persuasion?
2. How did early social action campaigns contribute to the founding of the United States?
3. What circumstances led to the use of political campaigns which targeted a mass audience?
4. What circumstances led to the proliferation of commercial campaigns which targeted a mass audience?
5. What circumstances led to the increased use of social action campaigns which targeted a mass audience?
6. How did World War 1 serve as a catalyst for the growth of persuasive communication campaigns?
7. Who contributed to developments in campaign theory and research following World War II? How did they contribute?
8. What is the difference between the powerful and limited effects views of mass media communication? What implications do these perspectives carry for persuasive campaigns?
9. How has television changed the very nature of persuasive campaigns?

> *Aristotle's theory of ethos is causally conditioned by the speaker's generating or controlling expectations in his audience . . . to be accepted he [the speaker] needs to identify with the audience's views of the true, right, and good . . . the speaker must adjust to his audience in both temper and character (Yoos, 1979, p. 45).*

Aristotle's theory of rhetorical discourse has withstood the test of time, furnishing axioms that guide today's practitioners of persuasion and campaigns.

While the advent of political and social action campaigns would await the establishment of democratic institutions in the eighteenth century, advertising became prevalent following the invention of the printing press in the fifteenth century, and the subsequent appearance of books, journals, and newspapers by the seventeenth century. The first use of print advertising is attributed to Englishman William Caxton, who printed and then posted notices to market his books around 1480. However, the first journal advertising didn't appear until 1612, when want-ads were employed in the French publication, *The Journal of Public Notices*, to help defray publishing costs.

The American Experience

The first newspaper, the Oxford *Gazette*, which made its appearance in 1665, carried no advertising. Nor did the first American newspaper, *Publick Occurrences*, which debuted in 1690. However, by the early eighteenth century newspaper advertising was common practice (Pope, 1983). The first American newspaper to utilize advertising was the *Boston News-Letter* in 1704. Soon thereafter, Benjamin Franklin pioneered a number of advertising techniques, including headings, white spacing, illustrations, and others, in his *Pennsylvania Gazette*.

Early print advertising was primitive by contemporary standards, and could hardly be characterized as a communication campaign since it employed single messages designed to achieve narrow and specific persuasive objectives. The postings of individual items for sale were the most common advertisements.

The first persuasive campaigns took on more of a political and social action flavor. In 1721-1722, Cotton Mather launched one of the first social action campaigns in colonial America. He employed a combination of printed pamphlets and personal appeals in rather systematic fashion to convince citizens of Boston, Massachusetts Bay Colony, that they should inoculate against smallpox (Kotler and Roberto, 1989). Thomas Paine played a major role in one of the first significant and uniquely American political campaigns with the publication of *Common Sense* in 1776. *Common Sense* offered a strong rationale for independence from Great Britain. Because it was widely

---

FEEDBACK

Scenario: A seventeenth century aristocrat posts a notice at the general store and places an advertisement in the local newspaper for the sale of two horses.
Is this an example of an advertising campaign? Why or why not?

distributed throughout the colonies, selling an unprecedented 100,000 copies in less than three months, it played an important role in the mustering of public support for American independence.

The publication of 85 installments of *The Federalist Papers* in New York City newspapers commencing in 1787, and subsequent combined distribution throughout New York and Virginia, was one of the most extensive early political campaigns (Rossiter, 1961). *The Federalist Papers*, authored by Alexander Hamilton, James Madison, and John Jay under the pseudonym of Publius, offered a series of arguments to support the adoption of the United States' *Constitution*. This was no small persuasive task, since a clear majority of New Yorkers and other colonists opposed creation of a strong central government, despite the rather apparent failings of the government created under the *Articles of Confederation*.

FIGURE 2-1 Typical Temperance Movement Poster

The authors of *The Federalist Papers* systematically articulated a powerful case for a stronger union, anticipating the major objections by opponents, and then refuting them with well-reasoned arguments. Although most argue that *The Federalist Papers* exerted a modest overall influence on ratification, the collected works served as a "debaters handbook in Virginia and New York" (Rossiter, 1961, p. xi). In both states *The Federalist Papers* were thought to have "played an important part in getting the new government ratified" (cited in Lewis, 1967, p. 29).

Persuasive communication campaigns to support individual causes have helped to forge the American experience. These campaigns targeted issues in an attempt to shape public attitudes and motivate public support. Some of them are classics. They illustrate how social movements employ persuasive campaigns as a part of their effort to attain specific objectives.

In an effort to eradicate American slavery, the abolitionist movement employed books, newspapers, public speakers, political dialogue, demonstrations, and occasionally open confrontation aimed at various objectives during the three decades preceding

FIGURE 2–2 1912 Demonstration for Women's Suffrage in New York City

Source: Photograph by the Pictorial News Co. Courtesy of Sophia Smith Collection.

the Civil War. For example, helping slaves escape the South via the Underground Railroad was a specific objective within the broader abolitionist movement.

The Underground Railroad exemplifies many features of a successful persuasive communication campaign. The name stemmed from an incident in 1831 when one slave reached the Ohio River with slave catchers close behind. Once on the Ohio side, the slave seemed to disappear, prompting one of the slave catchers to remark, "He must have gone on an underground road" (Franklin, 1967). The phrase spread, adapting to the growth of railroads in the North. "Road" became "railroad." Individuals

"Jackson is to be President, and you will be HANGED."

FIGURE 2–3   Opponents Vilify Andrew Jackson during the 1828 Campaign

Source: An 1828 wood engraving, artist unknown.

helping slaves became "conductors," "stationmasters," "brakemen," and "firemen," while hiding places were termed "stations" or "depots," and the movement from one hiding place to another was called "catching the next train."

Individuals working with the Underground Railroad employed multiple strategies, including vigilance committees in Boston and Philadelphia. These groups formed to protect fugitives, raise money, and enlist public support for their efforts.

Two other classic historical movements employed persuasive campaigns in the pursuit of specific objectives. For example, the Evangelical Protestant movement of the nineteenth century spawned the temperance campaign, which sought an end to the manufacture and sale of alcohol (Cott, 1987). The temperance campaign achieved that objective with the adoption of the Eighteenth Amendment to the *Constitution* in 1919, which was subsequently repealed following more than a decade of prohibition with the enactment of the Twenty-first Amendment (Gusfield, 1976). Figure 2–1 illustrates a typical temperance campaign poster.

FIGURE 2–4 Harrison and Tyler's "Common Man" Appeal during the 1840 Campaign

Source: 1941 lithograph published by T. Sinclair, Philadelphia.

The women's movement sought equal rights as an overarching goal, but "operated on a number of fronts, including education, employment, legal and civic rights, social reform, personal behavior" (Cott, 1987, pp. 17–18). Nonetheless, the movement's most vivid late nineteenth and early twentieth century effort was embodied in the suffrage campaign. The suffrage campaign sought the franchise for women, and employed speakers, books, leaflets, newspapers, demonstrations, and other communication in the pursuit of this objective (Flexner, 1975). Figure 2–2 shows a rally for women's suffrage in New York City in 1912.

The campaign was successful in securing its objective with the adoption of the Nineteenth Amendment to the *Constitution* in 1920. Having achieved its objective, the suffrage campaign came to an end, although the women's movement remains active even today.

These early campaigns were the forerunners of contemporary political and social action campaigns. They flourished in an era that preceded the growth of governmental authority and the mass media. They were a unique response to particular circumstances.". . . [T]he limited authority of American governments. . . created an early reliance on communication campaigns as instruments of social change" (Paisley, 1989, p. 23). This was noticed by Frenchman Alexis de Tocqueville who marveled at the extensive use of voluntary associations designed to promote specific interests in nineteenth century America.

The first political campaign that bears any resemblance to contemporary variants was the 1828 presidential contest featuring John Quincy Adams and Andrew Jackson. Prior to 1828, politics was elitist, because a limited number of powerful men controlled the nomination and electoral processes. Jackson directed his appeal to the aspirations of the "ordinary common man," taking his case directly to the people. Jackson's appeal threatened opponents, prompting visceral negative responses, such as the one depicted in Figure 2–3. Kathleen Jamieson (1984) terms the 1828 election a "watershed year in presidential campaigns." She notes that it was accompanied by the rise of political parties and a tripling of the number of participating voters. For the first time, American citizens were able to play a direct role in the election of a president (Jamieson, 1984).

The first media campaign occurred during the election of 1840 (Melder, 1989). Incumbent Democrat Martin Van Buren was pitted against Whig William Henry Harrison. The 1840 campaign featured extensive use of image politics, communicated via a network of Whig newspapers, led by Horace Greeley's weekly, *The Log Cabin*. The Whig newspapers used the symbol of the log cabin, reinforced by campaign posters and badges, to foster an image of Harrison as "a man of the people" (see Figure 2–4), while harshly attacking Van Buren.

The 1896 presidential campaign, featuring Democrat William Jennings Bryan and Republican William McKinley, institutionalized the personal campaign approach. In previous campaigns, political candidates did very little campaigning, permitting their backers to assume the responsibility for promoting the candidate to the general public. However, in 1896, while McKinley stayed home, Bryan took his case directly to the people, traveling 18,000 miles and campaigning in 27 states. Bryan's campaign, though unsuccessful, institutionalized the expectation that political candidates should appeal directly to the public.

In sum, by the late nineteenth century, the potential of persuasive communication campaigns was evident. Social action campaigns in support of various causes became a common fixture, and political campaigns made their debut. In addition, the use of both mass media and interpersonal channels of influence were evident. Nonetheless, the political campaigns of the nineteenth century, and to an even greater degree, the commercial campaigns of this era, bore very little resemblance to their contemporary counterparts.

Growth of Persuasive Campaigns

A number of factors during the last three decades of the nineteenth century and the first three decades of the twentieth century contributed to the growth of persuasive campaigns. The rise of a mass market, and the resulting competition for the control of product distribution to that market, the growth of literacy, the development of mass media communication, and World War I all facilitated the expanded use and continued refinement of commercial, political, and social action campaigns.

Development and Control of the Mass Market

The industrial revolution intensified during the decades following the Civil War. The changes wrought were profound, producing what one historian called an "economic transformation" (Bailey, 1966). First, a rising volume of manufactured goods required the development of a mass market for their consumption. Manufacturing production increased 2 1/2 times during the brief 15-year period from 1877 to 1892, but market expansion failed to keep pace, resulting in "chronic" excess manufacturing capacity across the economy (Ginger, 1965).

The development of a true mass market required systematic techniques to stimulate and maintain consumer demand, requiring extensive use of marketing and advertising techniques. It also necessitated transportation systems for the quick distribution of goods from manufacturers to wholesalers and retailers and for the movement of people within and between communities. The response to the nation's transportation needs was dramatic. The total miles of completed railroad track grew from 35,000 in 1865 to 200,000 in 1900, "more than all Europe, including Russia" (Blum et al., 1968, p. 438). In America's cities, the construction of durable road surfaces and mass transit facilities paralleled the growth of the railroad system (Bailey, 1966).

Second, a growing industrial economy sped the transformation of America from a largely rural to an increasingly urban society, which provided a mass market for the consumption of manufacturing goods. The drift to the cities was nothing short of spectacular. During the decades from 1800 to 1890, urban population multiplied eighty-seven-fold. During the two decades from 1880 to 1900, the populations of Denver, Minneapolis, and St. Paul quadrupled, Chicago tripled, while New York City, Buffalo, Milwaukee, Detroit, and others nearly doubled (Blum et al., 1968). These changes exerted a powerful impact on marketing and advertising.

The effects of these changes on society in general, and on advertising in particular, were quite profound. "The Industrial Revolution not only made possible the quantity and forms of advertising we have today, it transformed every aspect of the economy and of life in general" (Norris, 1989, p. 103). With the growth of cities, and of transportation to facilitate movement of people, retail trade became more and more impersonal. In this climate, merchants had to attract customers, and they turned to more variety in goods, smaller and more visible packaging, *and* the use of promotional activities to lure increasingly anonymous customers into stores (Shudson, 1989). The initial appearance and subsequent success of the department store and the mail order catalog service epitomized this trend.

Such a climate was particularly conducive to the growth of commercial advertising. The creation of national markets for the standardized products of manufacturers during the late nineteenth and early twentieth centuries served as the main catalyst to the development of contemporary advertising practices (Pope, 1983). The ". . . advertisements themselves, no longer the afterthoughts of local merchants, were now elements in campaigns based on marketing strategies" (Pope, 1983, p. 6).

The growth of mass markets is only one of the reasons for the growth of commercial advertising during this period. Some maintain that manufacturers used advertising as a tool to wrest *control* over product distribution and pricing from wholesalers and retailers (Norris, 1989). Manufacturers had to distinguish their product from others, and to generate consumer demand for their product directly, enabling it to be pulled through the distribution system. They accomplished this by assuming full responsibility for packaging and promotion of their products. National advertising was the tool to achieve product promotion. "[T]he manufacturer who began to brand and advertise his goods could avoid the rigors of price competition. He could compel the distributor to buy *his* brand at *his* price" (Norris, 1989, p. 105).

The growth of advertising during the late nineteenth and early twentieth centuries was phenomenal. By 1920, advertising expenditures surpassed $1 billion a year, with Proctor and Gamble, Goodyear Tire, and Quaker Oats spending more than $1 million on magazine advertising alone (Pope, 1983, p. 6). During this time, the top companies in specific market sectors assumed dominance in their respective sectors in advertising expenditures, a tendency that continued as modern advertising campaigns came into their own. These developments prompted Pope to reflect that: "By 1920, American advertising had more in common with its counterpart today than with the advertising of a generation earlier."

Rise of Literacy and Changes in Mass Media

The growth of literacy, and the resulting changes in mass media communication, accompanied, and were no less significant than, the intensification of the industrial revolution during the late nineteenth and early twentieth centuries. During the last three decades of the nineteenth century, public schools replaced private academies as the primary vehicle for educating America's youth. By 1900, all but two states outside the South had adopted compulsory school attendance laws, and the length of each school day and of the school year increased. The number of high school graduates ballooned from 16,000 in 1870 to more than 311,000 by 1920, and illiteracy was nearly cut in half (Jeffres, 1986).

The growth of advertising, the rise in literacy, and the availability of more economical printing techniques facilitated the development of mass circulation newspapers and magazines. The growth of newspapers and magazines contributed directly to the potential for persuasive communication campaigns since they relied on the print media for mass communication. Total daily newspaper circulation rose from 2,602,000 in 1870 to 15,102,000 in 1900, at which time the United States published more than half of all the newspapers in the world (Blum et al., 1968). During the last decade of the nineteenth century, mass circulation magazines flourished as well. Spurred on by the cheap postal rates, magazines, including *McClure's, Saturday Evening Post, Cosmopolitan, Ladies Home Journal,* and others built a substantial readership, and moved to supplement direct reader revenue with advertising income.

Also, during the last decade of the nineteenth century, advertising revenues surpassed sales as the primary source of revenue for newspapers, triggering a set of circumstances that facilitated social action campaigns. Because "sensationalized news" promoted circulation, and circulation in turn dictated advertising rates, more and more newspapers turned to "yellow journalism," with a heavy emphasis on "sin, sex, and violence" (Jeffres, 1986, p. 36) and to "muckraking," or exposé journalism, which featured crusades against various social evils. The last decade of the nineteenth century was a period when "... newspaper men discovered that circulation could be greatly increased by making literature out of the news" (Park, 1975, p. 20). More and more, the nation's leading newspapers used exposés on political and social issues to promote readership. In this manner, the media's need for greater mass circulation to bolster revenues, contributed to the simultaneous growth of commercial, political, and social action campaigns.

The foci of journalists' reporting included many of the issues previously brought to the nation's attention, including women's suffrage and temperance. New issues, based on excesses of industrialization, such as working conditions and wages, child labor, price fixing, and the purity of food and drugs also were addressed (Paisley, 1989). During this period, "initiative for reforming many social problems shifted from associations to the mass media" (Paisley, 1989, p. 28). As both national and state governments passed laws to deal with these and other so-called social evils, government came to overshadow associations and the mass media as primary initiators of social action campaigns.

> *Inevitably, the federal government's communication programs overlapped both the associations and the media. Associations found that their programs ... could be overshadowed by federal programs with large budgets and urgent mandates from Congress. As federal agencies developed their own public information arms, their ability to scoop the media with "breakthroughs" discouraged the essential but slower process of investigative reporting (Paisley, 1989, p. 30).*

The invention of radio broadcasting was the next in what seemed like a series of lightening-fast changes in mass media during the late nineteenth and early twentieth centuries. The invention of the vacuum tube in 1906 made it possible for the commercial development of radio broadcasting that exploded on the national scene following World War I. The first regular station was KDKA, in Pittsburgh, whereas the first station to air a commercial was WEAF in New York. Radio was yet another medium that relied on commercial support and provided a forum for the expression of political and social ideas.

Two developments spurred the growth of radio communication. The National Broadcasting Corporation established its red and blue networks for national broadcasting in 1926. Then, Congress passed the Federal Radio Act in 1927, creating the Federal

FIGURE 2–5   Typical World War I Military Recruitment Poster

Radio Commission (forerunner of the Federal Communications Commission), which was charged with licensing radio frequencies and requiring stations to serve in the public interest.

Radio availability quickly multiplied. "In 1924 there were three million radios in America; by 1935 ten times that number existed" (Jamieson, 1984, p. 19). Radio, which transported an audio message into millions of homes simultaneously, carried tremendous potential for campaign communication. By the late 1920s, experimentation with various formats, commercial sponsorship of national and local radio programming became institutionalized.

FIGURE 2–6 CPI Depiction of the German "Hun" in Domestic Propaganda

Source: Committee on Public Information

The use of radio in political campaigns also became standard fare by the late 1920s. In 1928, both the Republican and Democratic candidates for president earmarked most of their publicity budgets for radio (Jamieson, 1984). It was Franklin Roosevelt, however, as president, and as candidate (the 1936 and 1940 campaigns), who was the first politician to truly "master" this medium (Nimmo, 1970). "In his 'Fireside Chats,' which at their peak reached upwards of 60-million listeners, Roosevelt capitalized on this preciously unappreciated strength of the new medium" (Jamieson, 1984, p. 21).

World War I

America's eventual entry into World War I in 1917, nearly three years after actual commencement of hostilities in Europe, presented two important challenges: to offset enemy propaganda efforts and to mobilize domestic support for the war effort. World War I unleashed the concept of "total war," based on requirements for the mass mobilization of national resources: including finance, industrial production, as well as manpower. "It became essential to mobilize sentiments and loyalties, to instill in citizens a hatred and fear of the enemy, to maintain their morale in the face of privation, and to capture their energies into an effective contribution to their nation" (De Fleur and Ball-Rokeach, 1982, p. 159). To accomplish these ends, within two weeks of the United States' declaration of war against Germany, President Wilson established the Committee on Public Information (CPI) under George Creel. Figure 2–5 depicts one of the most popular military recruitment posters of the era.

The CPI, which employed more than 150,000 workers, attempted to convince the public that America was fighting for freedom and democracy, and conversely that the Germans were bent on an evil mission of world conquest. Creel viewed his mission as a battle "for the minds of men" (Thum and Thum, 1974), and unashamedly stereotyped German behavior as barbaric, while suppressing dissent at home as unpatriotic (Sproule, 1987). Creel's CPI distributed more than 100 million posters and pamphlets, and recruited 75,000 four-minute men to speak between features at movie houses to promote the war effort and the sale of "liberty bonds." The CPI also produced a series of "Hang the Kaiser" movies, prepared "red, white, and blue" books, and wrote editorials for newspapers and magazines, whose editors were under pressure to run. Moreover, the organization used records, sermons, news stories, billboards, and other media to accomplish its ends (Jowett and O'Donnell, 1986). The portrayal of the German "Hun" in Figure 2–6 is typical of CPI efforts to vilify the enemy in domestic propaganda efforts.

Allied propaganda efforts were also intended to sap German military and civilian morale. The Propaganda Section of the American Expeditionary Forces used balloons, airplanes, and later "leaflet bombs and mortars" to distribute millions of leaflets behind enemy lines (Jowett and O'Donnell, 1986). These propaganda leaflets were "essentially antimilitaristic and prodemocratic . . . food was the most popular subject of appeal, for this had become an obsession with the starving German soldiers and civilian population" (Jowett and O'Donnell, 1986, p. 129). Although there is no quantitative research, there is some anecdotal evidence that the Allied propaganda efforts were successful. For example, after the Battle of Meuse-Argonne, one in three German soldiers taken prisoner had allied propaganda leaflets in their possession (Thum and Thum, 1974). Following the war, German Chief of Staff, General Erich von Ludendorff, commented that, "We were hypnotized by the enemy propaganda as a rabbit by a snake" (cited in Thum and Thum, 1974, p. 59).

It is clear that the prevailing sentiment at the time was that the propaganda efforts were stunningly successful. Harold Lasswell (1927, p. 220) characterized the coordinated propaganda of the Allies as "one of the most powerful instrumentalities propaganda efforts during the war." "America's most noteworthy contribution to the 'science' of warfare was in 'mobilizing the mind of the world' " (Bailey, 1966, p. 737).

The *apparent* effectiveness of the sustained propaganda campaigns during the war, coupled with the unique opportunities for "on-the-job training" on the part of practitioners, resulted in a number of specific peacetime applications after the war. The war had provided a tremendous laboratory for developing and testing the basic tenets of mass persuasion. Experts selected sources, crafted messages, chose an appropriate medium for their persuasive appeals, and then attempted to assess their impact on receivers. Contemporary influence scholars trace "the roots of the scientific study of persuasion" to the war (Miller, Burgoon, and Burgoon, 1984, p. 404).

After the war, those who were responsible for the planning, implementation, and assessment of wartime propaganda campaigns shifted their foci to peacetime advertising, public relations, and political campaigns. Ivy Lee, considered to be the first public relations counsel, adapted the lessons learned during the war to corporate public relations, pioneering a number of public relations techniques that continue to be used today. Edward Bernays, who served on the Creel Committee during World War I, also put the experience he gained during the war to work for corporate America. He advised corporations to tap basic human motivations, particularly the male sex drive, as a tool to market products. Charles Merriam, who ran the U.S. public information program in Italy during the war, pioneered behavioral research in politics, culminating with a series of studies of attitudes and voting behavior.

Psychologists applied the behavioral perspective to the practice of commercial advertising following the war. The early advocates of scientific advertising included Walter Dill Scott of Northwestern University and John Watson of Johns Hopkins University, later a vice-president at J. Walter Thompson, who authored the influential book, *Behaviorism.* Watson viewed the concept of attitude as instrumental in the process of persuasion. During the same period, market research arrived on the scene. Daniel Starch of Harvard University pioneered recognition methods for testing advertising copy, and George Gallup launched the first formal advertising agency research department for Young and Rubicam. Later, George Gallup would pioneer the use of political polling in his mother-in-law's campaign for the office of secretary of state in Iowa, and from there oversee the growth of one of the most successful contemporary political survey firms.

Developments Underlying Contemporary Campaigns

Two developments in the last half of the twentieth century provide the underpinnings for contemporary persuasive campaigns. The literal explosion of theoretical scholarship and empirical research in basic and applied persuasion in the years following World War II, in conjunction with the increasingly pervasive role of television communication, shaped the parameters that govern contemporary campaigns.

World War II

America's entry into World War II, following the Japanese attack on Pearl Harbor, once again was followed by the creation of an agency for propaganda. This time the agency was called the Office of War Information (OWI). It was directed by journalist Elmer Davis and contained a Psychological Warfare Division with the mission of undermining enemy military and civilian morale (Thum and Thum, 1974).

Overseas Allied propaganda made extensive use of radio to reach behind enemy lines. And, while misinformation campaigns were utilized, one of the most effective propaganda ploys was to simply broadcast the facts about wartime conditions to enemy civilian populations (Jowett and O'Donnell, 1986).

At home, the propaganda efforts, while extensive, were nonetheless much more factual and moderate in tone than during World War I. In particular, the use of enemy atrocity appeals were minimized, perhaps in anticipation of public skepticism, the direct result of postwar public revelations concerning the lack of probity of so many of the atrocity stories in the previous war (Jowett and O'Donnell, 1986). The *Why We Fight* films typified the propaganda effort. The films, which were shown to soldiers and civilians, were designed to provide a clear justification for America's role in World War II.

The Advertising Council, which today is the primary conduit for public service advertising, originated during World War II. In response to public criticism of commercial advertising during wartime, the advertising industry launched the War Advertising Council, which was renamed the Advertising Council following the war, to employ the techniques used to market commercial products and services to promote ideas in the public interest.

World War II served as a laboratory for the investigation of influence. Top researchers employed social science methods to assess the effectiveness of various propaganda efforts. Three such researchers, Carl Hovland, Authur Lumsdaine, and Fred Sheffield (1949), subsequently summarized the results of a number of studies sponsored by the military and completed during the war, including the famous *Why We Fight* films. They concluded that the films, while informative, did not significantly impact viewer attitudes (Hovland, Janis, and Sheffield, 1949).

Major Developments in Theory and Research

World War II served as a catalyst for further scholarship in persuasion. Research programs in basic and applied persuasion sprung up at major universities throughout the

---

FEEDBACK

The public found out after World War I that the Committee on Public Information (CPI), the propaganda arm of the government, had deliberately and systematically distorted the truth about German war atrocities.

Scenario: Assume that you were a literate American adult living during World War II.

　　1. If you were assigned to the OWI, what approach would you recommend for promoting the war effort among the American people? Justify your recommendation.
　　2. If you were a typical working person, how would you respond to initial reports of Nazi atrocities against the Jews filtering out of Eastern Europe?

---

nation, resulting in considerable progress. This section highlights significant developments in theory and research during the years immediately following the war, which provides a foundation for understanding persuasive communication campaigns. Later chapters of this book will discuss more recent developments in theory and research as they pertain to specific content areas.

Following the war, Hovland returned to Yale University and continued his research on persuasion. He attracted a number of top research psychologists to the Communication and Attitude Change Program, including some who had worked with him during the war. The Yale studies, as Hovland's program of research came to be known, focused on the manner in which communication variables interact with predispositional variables (e.g., receiver gender, intelligence, personality) in the process of attitude change. During the 1950s, the Yale scholars, operating from a learning theory perspective, completed a number of studies that exerted considerable impact on scholars and practitioners of social influence (McGuire, 1966). The Yale investigations were "... the most sophisticated, elaborate studies of attitude change in controlled environments conducted up to that time" (Miller et al., 1984, p. 405). As a result, Hovland is viewed as one of the "Founding Fathers" of modern communication study (Schramm, 1983, p. 8).

Another of the "Founding Fathers" of modern communication was the sociologist Paul Lazarsfeld of Columbia University. He brought a psychology of marketing orientation to the study of political influence, which shaped his expectations. Thus, Lazarsfeld anticipated that the mass media, in conjunction with population demographics, would explain "... how and why people decided to vote as they did" (Lazarsfeld, Berelson, and Gaudet, 1968, p. 1). Lazarsfeld and colleagues completed two major studies, the first examining the effects of the 1940 presidential campaign on Erie County, Ohio, and the second, using a more complex design, on the effects of the 1948 campaign in Elmira, New York.

Although the Erie County study did find that perception of socioeconomic status was "important" in determining how people voted, it revealed that the primary effect of the mass media was to reinforce partisans (Lazarsfeld, Berelson and Gaudet, 1968).

of the mass media was to reinforce partisans (Lazarsfeld, Berelson and Gaudet, 1968). Because the data failed to support their initial view, they conceived a sociological explanation of voting, consisting of two primary arguments. First, social influences determine political predispositions. As a result, most people commit to a presidential ticket early—usually prior to the formal start of an election campaign. Mass media communication exerts minimal influence on such voters, because both selective attention and selective perception operate full force.

Second, the authors conceived the "two-step flow" of mass communication. They had anticipated direct media influence. Although they found direct influence (more than half reported radio or newspapers as the "most important" influence on their voting decision), they detected a surprisingly strong personal influence on voting decisions (Lazarsfeld et al., 1968, pp. 127 and 154). Thus, they maintained that political influence occurs in two stages. Mass media political messages reach opinion leaders; and opinion leaders, in turn, carry the messages to others. The authors argued that secondary influence is especially powerful because people tend to discuss politics with others with their defenses down, thus making them more susceptible to influence. The second study dealing with mass media influence in the 1948 presidential campaign confirmed the original findings (Berelson, Lazarsfeld, and McPhee, 1954).

The Lazarsfeld research turned assumptions about mass media influence on their head. Although never formally articulated as a theory (Chaffee and Hochheimer, 1985; De Fleur and Ball-Rokeach, 1982), and underpinned by a largely illusory research base, the powerful effects view of mass communication captured the popular imagination, largely as a result of the *seeming* effectiveness of propaganda efforts in wartime (De Fleur and Ball-Rokeach, 1982). It accorded great power to mass media communication, which, as a result of its reach, carried tremendous potential to shape the commercial preferences, political disposition, and social issue views and behaviors of targeted receivers (Kornhauser, 1959; Lasswell, 1935; Packard, 1957). The powerful effects perspective constituted a classical linear view of communication, with the primary emphasis on source and message, and limited emphasis on receiver.

The first two Lazarsfeld studies, plus subsequent research that extended the scope of the limited effects position to the commercial realm (Katz and Lazarsfeld, 1955), produced no less than a complete paradigmatic transition. The studies ushered in the limited effects perspective, based on the persuasive impotence of mass media communication (Kraus and Davis, 1976, p. 119). This perspective, formally articulated as a theory by Klapper (1960), provided an axiomatic view of mass media communication, although it too constituted a linear perspective. Furthermore, it carried important implications for the practice of persuasive campaigns. If the power of mass communication is limited as this theory suggests, since the mass media is the primary conduit for most persuasive campaigns, then the potential of campaigns is limited.

Another important post war development was the creation of the Survey Research Center (SRC) at the University of Michigan in 1948. Angus Campbell and Rensis Likert envisioned the SRC as a vehicle to collect and analyze data involving consumer and voting behavior. They anticipated that an individual's perceptions, attitudes, motivations, and identifications determined their product and voting preferences. Their orientation was uniquely psychological (Chaffee and Hochheimer, 1985).

Campbell directed two national election studies during the 1950s which posited the psychological theory of voting. Campbell, Gurin, and Miller (1954) examined the 1952 presidential election, whereas Campbell, Converse, Miller, and Stokes (1960) analyzed the 1956 election. These studies dealt with the impact of party identification and campaign events on political cognitions. Campbell, Converse, Miller, and Stokes further refined the psychological theory of voting in *Elections and the Political Order* (1966), which examined congressional and national elections from 1948 through 1960.

Campbell and colleagues maintained that party identification exerted the most influence on political cognitions, but that short-term forces *can* exert psychological cross-pressures, occasionally overcoming the force of party identification. Such cross-pressures generate attitude conflict. This occurs when issue or candidate image considerations cause pressure opposite normal party disposition. However, absent psychological cross-pressures, party identification dictates voter decisions.

The psychological theory of voting, grounded in the gestalt of its era, relegated persuasion to a limited role in political campaigns. This resulted from two predispositions. First, the Michigan researchers assumed that specific issues exert minimal impact on political behaviors (Campbell, Converse, Miller, and Stokes, 1960). Therefore, Campbell maintained that mass media communication played a negligible role in voting decisions. If important cognitive factors that underlie party identification occur early, and if issues exert minimal influence on political decisions, then there is no significant role for the mass media in political influence. As a result of this view, the SRC questionnaires contained few items on mass media, and these were designed primarily to assess political participation as opposed to media influence (Chaffee and Hochheimer, 1985).

Other major developments in theory and research following the war included the development and refinement of the various cognitive consistency theories of attitude change, including balance (Heider, 1946; Newcomb, 1953), congruity (Osgood and Tannenbaum, 1955), and cognitive dissonance theories (Festinger, 1957). Moreover, the systematic examination of the role and impact of fear appeals in persuasion was undertaken (Janis and Feshbach, 1953). The notion of resistance to persuasion was examined, including the initial formulation of and subsequent research on inoculation theory (McGuire, 1961). Extensive field research on the diffusion of innovations (Rogers, 1962) and refinement of the techniques used for measuring communication effects [reported in Miller et al., (1984)] also took place.

Expanding Role of Television

The most significant change in the mass media environment during the twentieth century has been the increasing presence of television communication. It is important to realize that this medium is relatively new. Lazarsfeld's and Campbell's research was conducted prior to the penetration of television into most American homes, and prior to the full exploitation of the unique channel capabilities of this medium. V. O. Key (1953), writing five years after the second Lazarsfeld study and one year after the first Campbell study, commented on the use of television in the 1952 presidential campaign (the first campaign that it was used extensively). He speculated: "The impact of the new medium of communication on campaigning apparently will be quite important" (p. 504).

Television exploded onto the American scene in the postwar period. In 1948, there were 17 stations broadcasting to a mere 102,000 television sets in the United States, two-thirds of them in New York City (Hearold, 1986, p. 66). Twelve years later, in 1960, nearly 90 percent of American households had a television set, and by 1978, more than 98 percent of all households had at least one television set (nearly half had more than one), which was on an average of seven hours each day (De Fleur and Dennis, 1985). Today, the average American adult watches from two to three hours of television each day, and public opinion surveys indicate that 48 percent of American adults consider television viewing as their favorite leisure activity (Jeffres, 1986).

During television's first two decades, it was not much more than radio with pictures. Television news and commercials, for products, candidates and causes, simply featured someone talking at viewers. The overwhelming emphasis was on the verbal content of television messages (Ogilvy, 1963). However, this emphasis began to change in the 1970s as practitioners learned how to exploit the unique visual nature of television, thus tapping the medium's full potential (Clark, 1988; Jamieson, 1988).

Contemporary television communication places much greater emphasis on images, emotions, and experiences (Krugman, 1971; Jamieson, 1988; Meyrowitz, 1985; Pfau, 1990; Wright, 1974), and constitutes a fundamentally unique symbol system (Chesebro, 1984; Salomon, 1987). The change is a profound one. Edmund Carpenter (1986, p. 353) maintains that it has ushered in a "new language" in politics, and Huntley Baldwin (1989, p. 10) claims it has launched "a creative revolution" in commercial advertising.

Today, television is the medium of choice for persuasive campaigns. Contemporary attempts to persuade people to purchase particular brands, support certain candidates, or alter social behaviors all rely heavily on television to achieve their objectives. As a result, paraphrasing Richard Armstrong (1988, p. 29), who was referring specifically to television and politics, and extending his claim across commercial, political, and social action campaigns: Today, for all intents and purposes, campaigns *happen* on television.

Conclusion

This chapter provided a brief synopsis of the evolution of persuasive communication campaigns. While persuasion traces its origins to antiquity, persuasive campaigns, which involve more integrated, sustained communication efforts, are more recent in nature, owing their inception and development to the growth of mass communication during the past three centuries.

Social action and political campaigns trace their beginnings to the efforts of private citizens working together to achieve specific social or political ends in seventeenth and eighteenth century America. Later, newspapers and government overshadowed associations as primary sponsors of social action campaigns. In the meantime, as the base of American political participation broadened, candidates directed their appeals to a mass audience, relying more on mass media communication, and political campaigns began to take on the shape of contemporary variants.

Commercial campaigns took on modern form during the latter nineteenth and early twentieth centuries as a direct result of the development of a mass market, the rise of literacy, and the growth of mass media communication. America's involvement in each of the World Wars, and the evolution of electronic media communication during this century, further contributed to the growth and sophistication of persuasive campaigns.

Suggestions for Further Reading

Flexner, E. (1975). *Century of Struggle: The Women's Rights Movement in the United States* (rev. ed.). Cambridge, MA: Harvard University Press.

Jamieson, K. H. (1984). *Packaging the Presidency: A History and Criticism of Presidential Campaign Advertising*. New York: Oxford University Press.

Jowett, G. S., and O'Donnell, V. (1986). *Propaganda and Persuasion*. Newbury Park, CA: Sage Publications.

Paisley, W. (1990). Public communication campaigns: The American experience. In R. E. Rice and C. K. Atkin (Eds.), *Public Communication Campaigns* (2nd ed., pp. 15–38). Newbury Park, CA: Sage Publications.

Pope, D. (1983). *The Making of Modern Advertising*. New York: Basic Books, Inc.

Part II

Theoretical Approaches to Influence

$$Chapter \quad 3$$

Focus on Receivers

"Communication cannot be conceptualized as transmission. Rather it must be conceptualized in terms of both parties involved in creating meanings, by means of dialogue. The sense people make of the media messages is never limited to what sources intend and is always enriched by the realities people bring to bear."
—BRENDA DERVIN, COMMUNICATION PROFESSOR (DERVIN, 1989, P. 72)

". . . communication campaigns will seldom be effective if they are directed to a mass audience."
—JAMES E. GRUNIG, JOURNALISM PROFESSOR (GRUNIG, 1989, P. 222)

In Chapter 1, we characterized communication as a process that employs verbal and nonverbal codes to symbolically transact understanding between people. This definition highlights the importance of the receiver in persuasive campaigns. We further noted that the receiver is an active participant in persuasion, whether messages are processed in a consciously mindful or a habitual mindless mode.

This chapter, the first dealing with theoretical approaches, focuses on the central role of receivers in persuasive campaigns. The chapter contrasts traditional and contemporary perspectives on receivers, examines needs in receiver decision processes, and deals at some length with segmentation and targeting, the most popular strategy for tailoring persuasive communication to the specific needs of groups of similar receivers. The chapter will address the questions posed in Table 3–1.

Traditional and Contemporary Assumptions about Receivers

As we observed in Chapter 2, a linear view of communication, with the primary focus on source and message, and a more limited emphasis on receiver, dominated theory and research in persuasion throughout much of the twentieth century. As a result, experts acknowledge that almost all early communication campaigns as well as many contemporary ones operate from "an explicit linearity" (Rogers and Storey, 1987, p.

47

830). This traditional view stresses the role and the impact of sources, messages, and channels *on* receivers. There is no place for feedback in the traditional model. Instead, campaigns based on this model "closely resemble a monologue by the campaign organization" (Rogers and Storey, 1987, p. 830). This traditional model underpinned both the powerful effects view, as well as the limited effects perspective, of mass media influence.

Receiver Implications of a Linear View of Communication

All perspectives on communication are based on fundamental assumptions about receivers, or in more basic terms, are based on assumptions about the nature of human beings. The argument about whether people are largely rational beings, and thus subject to reasoned appeals, or basically irrational, and thus vulnerable to deceptive and emotional appeals, is an old one, with its origins in classical Greek thought (Allport, 1954). The argument becomes particularly important if persuaders direct campaigns toward mass audiences, which was the common practice well into the 1960s, and continues to persist among some practitioners even today.

The more rational view of people gained prominence during the Enlightenment, and was prevalent in the United States during the founding period. Indeed, *The Federalist Papers*, containing the prevailing thinking which underpins the *Constitution* of the United States, acknowledges the tension between the rational and irrational views.

TABLE 3–1 Basic Questions about the Role of Receivers in Campaigns

1. What basic assumptions about receivers underpinned the linear view of communication that was prevalent during the first half of the century?
2. Did these assumptions carry implications for the conduct of persuasive communication campaigns? What implications?
3. What assumptions about receivers stem from the transactional view of communication that has emerged in recent years?
4. What should be the starting point in persuasive campaigns?
5. List examples of successful commercial, political, and social action campaigns. What do these campaigns have in common?
6. What determines the need for information in most persuasive communication campaigns?
7. Identify the dominant consumer need at each stage of the disposition toward purchase model.
8. Identify the dominant receiver need at each stage of the disposition toward candidate choice model.
9. How does receiver need relate to the selection of campaign strategies in commercial and political campaigns?
10. What are segmentation and targeting? How are they used in persuasive communication campaigns?

The Federalist Papers argued forcefully for majority rule but also recognized the potential for excesses, reasoning that procedural safeguards, manifested by a rather elaborate system of checks and balances, would safeguard against "misguided majority sentiment" (Rossiter, 1961). The writings of Jefferson, Madison, Hamilton, and others offer "a well-balanced view of rational and irrational factors in the social nature of man" (Allport, 1954, p. 16).

During the late nineteenth and early twentieth centuries, the irrational view of receivers emerged as the more dominant perspective. Various factors contributed to this change. The disappearance of clearcut ideological choices between national political parties produced a decline in issue consciousness, and thus interest in electoral outcomes (Burnham, 1965). Ironically, the adoption of the Australian, or secret ballot, further reduced political participation (Rusk, 1970). Before the secret ballot, party bosses could observe votes being cast for one candidate as opposed to another. This enabled bosses to insure that turnout directly translated in to votes for their candidate. Adoption of the secret ballot made the benefits of turnout more problematic, reducing incentive to herd people to the polls. In addition, the *seeming* success of propaganda efforts during World War I, along with the rapid growth of behaviorism in commercial advertising, suggested an almost unlimited potential for receiver manipulation (Curti, 1967).

One thing is certain, during this period the very nature of persuasive messages began to change, as emotional appeals became increasingly dominant. This trend is evident in the commercial advertising appeals of the era. An examination of the trade journal, *Printers' Ink*, from its inception in 1888 through the 1950s, reveals that during the period from 1910 to 1930, and again during the 1950s, there was an upsurge in the characterization of human nature as "nonrational, emotional, and susceptible to manipulation" (Curti, 1967, p. 357). Even those scholars who question the methodology of this study, nonetheless concur with its conclusion. "There have been changes in American advertising in the past half or three-quarters of a century and they are consistent, in general, with a move toward viewing the consumer as driven by emotions, not cost-benefit calculation" (Schudson, 1984, p. 60).

Furthermore, the emerging picture of receivers, whether as consumers or voters, grew increasingly less flattering. On the whole, ". . . psychologists and practitioners in the early years of the century shared a low opinion of the intellectual and logical capabilities of consumers" (Pope, 1983, p. 246). It was during this period that promoter Phineas T. Barnum was alleged to have remarked that, "There's a sucker born every minute" (cited in Trenholm, 1989, p. 204).

Other writers characterized adult men and women as "grown-up children," encouraging marketing and advertising professionals to examine "the savage mind" in order to better understand receivers (cited in Pope, 1983, p. 247). One writer recommended the use of "heart-throb devices" to promote products (cited in Curti, 1967); another admonished advertising professionals against giving "the public credit for too much intelligence" (cited in Clark, 1988, p. 163). Also, "several writers in *Printers' Ink* subscribed to the idea that most men are unable to weigh the pros and cons of evidence with a judicial mind [because] emotional factors interfere" (Curti, 1967, p. 351).

The view of receivers as basically irrational and emotional culminated in the 1950s as advertisers, bolstered by the more popular psychological theories of the era, attempted to trigger hidden motivations in receivers (Martineau, 1957). This is the decade that Packard's popular book, *The Hidden Persuaders* (1957), was published. During the 1950s, advertising professionals speculated that: men perceive convertibles

FIGURE 3–1 General Motors' 1958 Campaign for its Chevrolet Convertible

Source: Courtesy of Chevrolet, a division of the General Motors Corporation.

as a substitute for a mistress; women manifest suppressed desires to "appear naked or scantily clad in a crowd;" men purchase fountain pens for their body image; women equate baking a cake with giving birth; men prefer large, smelly cigars because they express their masculinity; and so forth (Packard, 1957). Figure 3–1 depicts a common commercial advertising appeal of this era.

The irrational view of political receivers gained strength throughout the twentieth century, peaking during the 1940s and 1950s. The research on voting behavior conducted by Lazarsfeld at Columbia and Campbell at Michigan, discussed in Chapter 2, contributed to an increasingly pejorative depiction of the electorate. Subsequently, additional research supported the perspective that people do not care about, and do not know about, political content. For example, Woodward and Roper found most Americans to be politically inactive. All together, 73 percent of respondents scored no higher than 3 on their 12-point activity index; and, of those, 38 percent scored 0 or 1, indicating "extreme inactivity" (cited in Holloway and George, 1979, p. 55).

Other studies characterized voters as shockingly uninformed. A 1954 study called attention to widespread political ignorance among U.S. citizens. The results identified 20 percent of the electorate as "hard-core know-nothings" (Hyman, 1959). A study by Campbell and colleagues in 1948 reported that only one-third were aware, or had an opinion, about what government was doing in terms of major issues. For example, labor unrest was a major issue in 1948. Strikes and the threat of strikes were common, and well publicized in the media, and the Democrats made the newly enacted Taft-Hartley Act a major point of attack in the fall campaign. Nonetheless, as the authors conclude: "Almost seven out of every ten adult Americans saw the curtain fall on the presidential election of 1948 without knowing whether Taft-Hartley was the name of a hero or a villain" (Campbell et al., 1960, p. 172).

Other studies indicated that more than half of adults who were surveyed did not know such basic information as: the number of senators from each state, the length of a term in the House of Representatives, who their congressman or senators were. Also, more than two-thirds of adults could not name the three branches of the federal government, identify a single provision of the Bill of Rights, or relate what happened in America in the year 1776 (Barber, 1978, pp. 181–182).

The implications of this pejorative view of the American electorate for political campaign practices are clear. If most potential voters are uninterested and uninformed, then campaign appeals need to stress the candidate as opposed to issues, and communicate information to potential voters using simple themes, repeated over and over.

That was the approach that advertising specialist Rosser Reeves brought to the Eisenhower presidential campaign in 1952. Reeves, characterized as "the Dean of the hammer-it-home school of advertising" for his commercial campaigns for such package goods as Anacin, M & M's, and others, was considered to be the master of simplicity and repetition in television advertising (Moyers, 1984). In one of the most memorable television spots for the 1952 Eisenhower campaign, Reeves combined animation from

---

FEEDBACK

Scenario: Think of a political advertising campaign on behalf of one of the presidential candidates during the last election. Put yourself in the position of a critic and respond to the following questions:

1. What groups of receivers did the campaign target?
2. What implicit assumptions were made about each group of receivers?
3. What was the persuasive objective associated with each group? Do you think it was successful in achieving its objective? Why or why not?

---

the Disney Studios with the musical jingle: "You like Ike, I like Ike, Everybody likes Ike; Ike for President, Ike for President, Ike for President . . ." (Moyers, 1984). The Reeves approach to political advertising during the 1952 Eisenhower campaign was a by-product of the prevailing view of the American electorate.

A more optimistic view of the electorate emerged in data reported during the 1970s and 1980s. This view holds that, "where the electorate may have been wanting, it now meets the demands of democratic political systems and is more than able–if not always ready and willing–to participate rationally and effectively in the political process" (Pierce and Sullivan, 1980, pp. 16–17). Another study examined University of Michigan voting data of the 1960s and 1970s, revealing notable changes in the American electorate. The results showed that the electorate is more ideologically oriented, both willing and able to evaluate issue appeals, and less inclined to vote a straight party preference at the polls (Nie, Verba, and Petrocik, 1976). Another examination of the Michigan data, focusing on questions in the data which permit historical comparisons about the electorate, concluded that, ". . . the political climate of the country has not only changed over the past four elections, but that it has changed significantly–in the direction of greater reliance on ideological factors in making voting decisions" (Robinson and Holm, 1980, p. 53).

Other scholars employing various research procedures also supported the revisionist view. One study reported an increase in the tendency of voters to perceive issue differences between the political parties (Axelrod, 1972). Other studies indicated that the role of issue content in voting decisions had increased significantly. The reexamination of Michigan Survey Research Center data revealed that path coefficients altered from 1965 to 1972 with issue orientation rising from .10 to .35, suggesting that the role of issues in voting decisions had more than tripled (Pomper, 1975). Another study reported that the correlation between presidential voting and issue attitudes had steadily grown, from .16 in 1956 to .53 in 1972 (Nie and Anderson, 1976).

A synthesis of electoral studies over the past two decades indicated that the issue coherence of the average voter has risen dramatically. The researchers concluded that: "Greater issue constraint is now found in the general electorate than prevailed among presumably articulate activists [congressional candidates] of an earlier period" (Pomper and Lederman, 1980, p. 70).

Receiver Implications of a Transactional View of Communication

Of course, the debate over whether people are more rational or emotional misses the mark, at least insofar as it takes place within the confines of a linear view of communication. The most important change in communication scholarship over the past four decades has been the abandonment of a linear view, and with it, assumptions about mass audiences. Most contemporary scholars maintain that communication is minimally interactive, stressing the give-and-take between source and receiver, or transactional, involving the dynamic interplay of all of the elements in the communication's process. In addition, most mass media theorists accept one or another of the "moderate effects" explanations of mass media influence (Rogers and Chaffee, 1983).

The transactional view and the moderate effects perspective operate on the assumption that communication is a dynamic two-way process in which receivers play an active role. Hence, dwelling on what the mass media does *to* receivers is incomplete. Instead, one must examine receivers in order to determine what they are likely to do with the mass media, and how they might respond to specific appeals. "A transactional model recognizes that effects can probably be understood best by combining knowledge of message characteristics and the level of exposure given them with an understanding of *orientations* of the audience members to those messages" (McLeod and Becker, 1981, p. 72).

Individual receivers respond to persuasive messages based on specific circumstances. In response to persuasive communication, some receivers are motivated to attend the message, while others are not, and the motivational trigger varies across receivers and contexts. Some receivers can be reached by more rational appeals, while others require more emotional appeals, and responses vary depending on message content and context. An established program of research by Richard Petty and John Cacioppo, which is explored in some detail in Chapters 5 and 6, is based on the position that there are two routes to attitude change: the central route which requires conscious thought; and a peripheral route which involves minimal conscious effort (Petty and Cacioppo, 1984). In order to instrumentally attain the desired goals, persuasive communication must be adapted to the appropriate message processing strategy, which varies across receivers.

As a result, campaigners are advised to put receivers first, employing ways to determine how they will respond to messages.

Communication cannot be conceptualized as *transmission*.

> *Rather it must be conceptualized in terms of both parties involved in creating meanings, by means of dialogue. The sense people make of the media messages is never limited to what sources intend and is always enriched by the realities people bring to bear (Dervin, 1989, p. 72).*

The appropriate starting place for persuasive campaigns is the receiver; nothing else makes sense. Who are the targeted receivers? What do they think and feel? How do they act? Why do they think, feel, and act as they do? These are central questions, and they lead to a consideration of receiver needs.

Emphasis on Receiver Needs

Identification of targeted receivers' needs for information is an important starting point in persuasive campaigns. Receiver need for information is a product of uncertainty, either in terms of some attitude object or the attitude object as it relates to the individual's ability to cope with their environment (Atkin, 1973). Thus, need for information provides the motivation for receivers to attend communications, thus reducing uncertainties.

Because "... research has shown that people inform themselves primarily at moments of need" (Dervin, 1989, p. 80), needs are viewed as an integral component in commercial, political, and social action influence. Consumer need, for example, has been characterized as "the most important factor in marketing and advertising..." (Schultz, Martin, and Brown, 1984, p. 55). Needs may be: (1) active, where the consumer recognizes the need and actively attempts to satisfy it; or (2) latent, where a need is not recognized until called to the attention of the consumer (Schultz and Tannenbaum, 1989, pp. 40–41).

The methods persuaders use to gear their appeals to receiver needs, and identification of more common needs, are discussed further in Chapters 5 and 6. At this time, we simply want to emphasize that receiver need is an appropriate starting point for campaigners. The presence or absence of receiver needs determines whether, once information is provided, it will produce the desired effect. Receiver needs also determine what kind of information should be provided.

The persuasive campaign literature is replete with examples of failures. Advertising research reveals that most television viewers can not remember a commercial that they saw the day before, even after repeated prodding (Schudson, 1984). Empirical data indicates that, in spite of practitioners' personal convictions to the contrary, most political campaign communication exerts very little impact on voters (McGuire, 1986). Finally, experts claim that most health campaigns attain, at best, very "limited success" (Atkin and Freimuth, 1989). Strikingly, a consistent reason for failure is the undertaking of persuasive campaigns without consideration of receivers' needs.

Yet, there are also ample documented cases of commercial, political, and social action successes. In most cases, these campaigns were able to tap an unmet need; often, in the case for commercial advertising for packaged goods, a latent need, which the consumer is unaware of until the advertising calls attention to it.

For example, Marlboro's efforts to create a masculine image for its filtered cigarette was a huge success. Marlboro's print advertisements have changed very little over four decades. The advertisements feature the "Marlboro man," a rugged individual set in a western backdrop. They are solely designed to promote a masculine image of Marlboro smokers, thus appealing to a strong psychological need in male smokers. As a direct result of this campaign, "Marlboro changed from being a woman's cigarette and a minor brand to *the* macho brand and not just the world's biggest selling cigarette–but

FIGURE 3-2 Wendy's "Where's the Beef" Campaign Sharply Increased Sales

Source: Courtesy of Wendy's International, Dublin, OH.

the world's largest selling packaged good," with annual sales in excess of $6 billion (Clark, 1988, p. 244). In fact, the commercial campaign's success led to the use of the "Marlboro man" in television commercials which promoted smoking cessation. The social action advertisements depicted the "Marlboro man" on horseback, wearing a portable oxygen tank, and proclaiming: "If I'd known then what I know now." This smoking cessation message appealed to an obvious basic need: to live a long and healthy life.

Miller Lite's campaign, featuring a contrived controversy, "Tastes great, less filling," is another example of a successful commercial campaign. The Miller Lite advertisements focused on the two product attributes that the company sought to stress in its marketing. The attributes appealed to the needs of male consumers, who previously had been reluctant to switch to low-calorie brands, for a beer with taste that also contained less calories, thus allowing them to drink even more. The "Tastes great, less filling" campaign played an instrumental role in catapulting Miller Lite into third position among American beer brands (Vadehra, 1982).

Among fast food chains, Burger King's campaign, "Have it your way," sought to stress a unique characteristic of their burger outlets compared to competitors: their willingness to prepare hamburgers based on customers' preferences. The Burger King "Have it your way" campaign contributed to a 38 percent increase in sales.

Wendy's implied comparative, "Where's the beef?", depicted in Figure 3–2, focused on a unique feature of their outlets compared to competitors: namely the quantity of beef contained in their hamburgers. The Wendy's "Where's the beef?" campaign produced a 31 percent increase in revenues (Hume, 1988b). These and other successful commercial campaigns were directed at unmet consumer needs.

The need for information in political campaigns has grown during the past two decades as political party identification, once the dominant determinant of voting intention, has steadily eroded (Wattenberg, 1986). As party identification has weakened, the proportion of nonaffiliated voters has increased to over one-third of the electorate (Opinion Roundup, 1984), increasing the amount of cross-over voting (Mann and Wolfinger, 1984). In a more unstable political environment, absent traditional anchors for voting, the potential for campaign communication to significantly impact candidate preference grows. Receivers turn to campaign communication, principally advertising, as a source of information. Thus, receiver indecision "... prompts attention to campaign advertising," thus contributing to its persuasive potential (Atkin, 1973, p. 316). There is ample documentation for the persuasive effectiveness of commercials in recent state and national political campaigns (Pfau and Kenski, 1990).

The 1988 presidential campaign serves as a classic case in point. American voters had no clear image of Democratic nominee Michael Dukakis as the last campaign headed into its final two months (Broder et al., 1988). Voters sought more information, and they found it in the Bush advertisements, particularly the messages attacking Dukakis for being soft on crime and failing to back the Pledge of Allegiance in schools. These commercials are credited with turning Bush's 16-point June deficit in public opinion polls into a 19-point lead by September (Hershey, 1989). Again, the key is that the effective political commercials satisfy the receiver's need for specific information, whether active or latent.

There are a number of successes in social action campaigns that are based on the ability to satisfy needs and/or depict the issue/behavior in a new light. The United States Army's, "Be all you can be" campaign has been credited with turning around the Army's numbers and quality problems (Denton, 1983). In just two years, the proportion of high school graduates among recruits rose from 54 percent to 86 percent (Meyers, 1988b). The campaign made a direct appeal to young people's needs for more education and training before entering the workplace, and at the same time, changed perceptions about the Army.

One of the most successful public health campaigns, which has become the model for contemporary campaigns, is the Stanford Three Community Study and the follow-up Five City Project. This campaign appealed to people's concerns about their own health, providing specific information and reinforcement in an attempt to chang behaviors that contribute to coronary heart disease. In the Three Community Study, a

CRIME PREVENTION CAMPAIGN
MAGAZINE AD NO. CP-2913-91—4⅝" x 4⅞"
Volunteer Agency: Saatchi & Saatchi Inc.
Campaign Director: Robert A. Marchese, Aetna Life & Casualty

FIGURE 3–3 Spokesdog McGruff Urges Americans to "Take a Bite Out of Crime"

Source: Courtesy of Advertising Council with the permission of Saachti and Saatchi Advertising.

systematic mass media campaign was used in one community, mass media plus "face-to-face skills training, incentives, and support" in a second community, while the third community served as a control group. The extensive communication efforts have achieved significant reductions in coronary heart disease risk scores, with the results being the most striking in the media plus face-to-face condition (Flora, Maccoby, and Farquhar, 1989). The Five City Project provided for further refinements in methodology to enhance generalizability. The Stanford research continues today to provide important new insights about public health campaigns.

Finally, the "take a bite out of crime" campaign, depicted in Figure 3-3, appealed to Americans with a need for information about how to reduce their risk of becoming victims of crime. One follow-up study reported that 25 percent of adults have initiated preventative measures against crime after viewing the ads, while another investigation revealed that as many as 97 percent of young children follow the instructions provided by the cartoon character, McGruff (Wallach, 1988).

These and other successful commercial, political, and social action campaigns illustrate the maxim: when there is a need for information, or when communicators can create the perception of a need for information, receivers can be motivated to attend—and utilize—campaign communication.

Need for Information in Commercial Campaigns

In commercial campaigns, consumer need for information is determined on the basis of disposition toward purchase. "All product- or service-purchasing decisions made by consumers are based on satisfying a want or a need" (Schultz and Tannenbaum, 1989, p. 39). This is best depicted by examining disposition toward purchase in stages, employing a hierarchical model, much like the one originally advanced by Russell Colley (1961). In the years following the appearance of Colley's book, *Defining Advertising Goals for Measuring Advertising Results*, a plethora of similar hierarchical models appeared patterned after Colley's original model (Raymond, 1976).

We prefer a modification of the hierarchical model which starts at the most basic level, awareness, moving to the next stage, information-seeking, then to discrimination, choice, and finally to post decision. Our modified hierarchical model is shown in Figure 3-4.

Receivers' needs vary at each of the stages of the model, which in turn dictates appropriate communication goals. At the awareness stage, no needs are manifest, and thus the primary communication's objective is simply to generate awareness of a product or service and what it might do for the consumer. When operating at the awareness stage, communicators can choose from among a wide variety of strategies, although more image-oriented approaches which presume passive message processing are clearly more common. Communication strategies, which are the by-product of theories, are considered in some detail in Chapters 4 and 5. If successful, the communication will precipitate what Schultz and Tannenbaum refer to as a latent need, thus elevating the consumer to the next stage of the hierarchy.

At the information-seeking stage, the overriding receiver need is information, and the communication's objective is geared to providing relevant information concerning product attributes, price, and availability. At the discrimination stage, consumers are beginning to compare available brands. The most appropriate communication's objective is to provide information concerning the relative strengths of a particular brand. This suggests the appropriateness of comparative messages, in which one brand is "explicitly compared with one or more competing brands" (Barry and Tremblay, 1975). This stage, the last in which advertising is able to exert significant direct impact, is a crucial stepping stone in route to the purchase decision. This fact may explain the surge in comparative advertising during the past 20 years to the point where it accounts for approximately half of all ads (Levy, 1987).

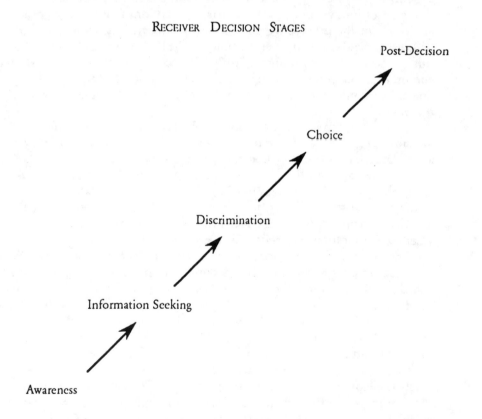

RECEIVER DECISION STAGES

Post-Decision

Choice

Discrimination

Information Seeking

Awareness

FIGURE 3–4   Modified Hierarchical Model of Receiver Decision Stages

> **FEEDBACK**
>
> **Scenario:** Think of a major purchase decision (e.g., automobile or stereo system) that you have made. Consider the various sources of influence, as you ponder the following questions:
>
> 1. How did you first learn of the brand you chose?
> 2. Where did you get information about various brands:
>
>   A) When you initially began to consider a purchase?
>   B) Just before you decided which brand to purchase?

At the choice stage, the interpersonal modality dominates. This is consistent with the two-step flow explanation of mass media influence (Lazarsfeld et al., 1968) and the diffusion of innovations model (Rogers, 1962). Consumers turn to other people for advice about the prospective purchase, including friends, family, and other persons with expertise (Jugenheimer and Chowins, 1981). It might be more accurate to label this process a "three-or-more step flow of communication," because mass media communication more often triggers a series of person-to-person exchanges, winding down the opinion hierarchy in stages from the most interested and knowledgeable to the least (Sheth, 1971).

One scholar involved in interpersonal communication as it relates to consumer decisions described word-of-mouth as "one of the most important, possibly *the* most important source of information for the consumer" (Arndt, 1967, p. 238). Although sales people can, and do, play a significant role at this stage (Reynolds and Wells, 1977), the role of advertising is limited, except for the cumulative impact generated at all the previous stages. Finally, at the post decision stage, the most prevalent need, only recently recognized, is for reinforcement of the purchase decision. Advertising and other communication can service this objective.

The process of identifying consumer needs is complicated by two factors. First, since consumers are at various points on the hierarchy, targeting is difficult. Second, available evidence indicates that it is difficult to pinpoint consumers at either the discrimination or choice stages because buying ntent is a volatile notion. For example, one Bureau of Advertising study (Bogart, 1967) reported the results of interviews done with 10,000 women in five cities. The results revealed that many who planned to make purchases, did not make them, whereas many who did not plan on purchases, did make them. This was true across a variety of general merchandise items. Another study, which was conducted by the Survey Research Center (SRC) at the University of Michigan, reported that two-thirds of new automobile purchases were made by people who did not plan on such a purchase just one year earlier (Kosobud and Morgan, 1964). These factors emphasize the necessity for commercial campaigns to design and maintain communications simultaneously targeting more than one stage of the disposition toward purchase hierarchy.

Need for Information in Political Campaigns

In political campaigns, a similar hierarchy exists, with need for information determined on the basis of disposition toward candidate choice. Receivers' needs vary depending on whether they are on the hierarchy. Needs, in turn, determine appropriate communication goals, which dictate strategies.

At the awareness stage, the primary communication objective is to generate awareness of a candidate and what she/he might do for the voter. This is attempted via political commercials that stress name identification, general qualifications, and reasons for seeking an office (Young, 1987). At the information-seeking stage, the overriding receiver need is information. This stage occurs in two main waves: for more politically active citizens, during the final days leading to their respective state primary or caucus, and for less active citizens, particularly in those campaigns that do not involve an incumbent, during the weeks that precede the general election. During the information-seeking phase, the communication's objective is oriented to providing relevant information concerning a candidate's attributes and positions.

There is a strong foundation of research indicating that political campaign communication exerts maximum possible impact on voter learning and attitudes about candidate character and issue positions during the formative period of a campaign when perceptions are as yet unformed or conflicted (Becker and McCombs, 1978; Chaffee, 1978; Gopoian, 1982; Kennamer and Chaffee, 1982; Mendelsohn and O'Keefe, 1976; Patterson, 1980; Pfau, 1987, 1988). The reason is that political campaigns proceed in phases, and need for information is most pronounced in the initial phase. "[T]he very early phase is characterized by [the] widespread lack of information among those who are not following the campaign closely, and uncertainty even among those who are" (Kennamer and Chaffee, 1982, p. 647). As a result, ". . . the primary season may be the formative period for many voters—a time when they mold their attitudes" (Becker and McCombs, 1978, p. 302).

Even later in a campaign, information can exert considerable impact if the conditions are ripe. Communication in political campaigns that features a large proportion of uninformed and/or conflicted voters, for whom information holds greater utility, will generate greater learning and attitude impacts (Chaffee and Choe, 1980; Geer, 1987; Hofstetter and Buss, 1980; Sears and Chaffee, 1979).

At the discrimination stage, voters are actively comparing candidates, and the appropriate communication's objective is to provide information focusing on the strengths of one candidate and/or the weaknesses of the competing candidate. At this stage, comparative messages, which examine the attributes, record, or positions of two candidates to the advantage of one of them (Salmore and Salmore, 1985), or attack messages, which focus on the negative attributes or positions of the opposing candidate (Pfau and Kenski, 1990), are the most suitable vehicles to deliver this information.

The importance of the discrimination stage as a precursor to candidate choice, and the documented effectiveness of negative political messages (Armstrong, 1988; Ehrenhalt, 1985; Guskind and Hagstrom, 1988; Pfau and Burgoon, 1989; Sabato, 1981, 1983; Surlin and Gordon, 1977; Taylor, 1989) explains their rising popularity. Negative

FEEDBACK

Scenario: Recall your candidate preference during the latest presidential campaign, and consider the following questions:

1. Was your preference based more on positive features of the chosen candidate, negative features of the unchosen candidate, or on a combination of the two?
2. How did you learn about those particular features of the candidates?

advertising is growing in proportion to all political advertising. "Experts estimate that today one of two political ads is negative; twenty years ago only about one in five was" (Young, 1987, p. 60). Political attack messages work best when they utilize basic assumptions already present in the minds of receivers. Some of the harshest attacks in presidential campaigns have attempted to exploit preexisting doubts about candidates. Advertising guru Tony Schwartz, who created the "daisy girl" spot used against Barry Goldwater in the 1964 presidential campaign, calls this influence approach "partipulation" because its success depends on the receivers' active participation in their own manipulation (Moyers, 1984).

Once again, at the choice stage, interpersonal communication takes over, as voters turn to other people for advice about the decision. As was discussed in Chapter 2, the two-step flow of mass communication was originally posited as a response to the unexpected strength of personal influence on voter political attitudes in the 1940 presidential campaign. What is amazing is that decades later very little is known about the workings of the two-step flow in political influence (Sheingold, 1973).

There is research that indicates that 20 percent of adults are asked their advice on which candidate to support, and as many as 20–40 percent of adults discuss campaign events and candidates with other people (cited in Chaffee, 1981, p. 192). In addition, there is every reason to believe that people attempt personal influence in these discussions. A study of personal influence during interpersonal interactions indicated that people attempted to influence another in 47 percent of conversations, with change of opinion resulting in 21 percent of these cases (Greenberg, 1975). Further study of interpersonal information flow would fill in important gaps in the extant knowledge about the way in which mass media communication affects receiver voting behavior (Sheingold, 1973).

Finally, at the post-decision stage, the primary need is for reinforcement. At this stage, voters who have made a choice from among competing candidates, manifest a need for confirmation of that choice and for protection against incongruous information. This can be achieved via a combination of bolstering messages, which further stress the positive attributes of a candidate, and inoculation messages, which in the process of articulating and then refuting a candidate's potential vulnerabilities, promote a blanket of resistance against the potential effectiveness of an opponent's impending attack messages (Pfau and Kenski, 1990). The inoculation approach has been confirmed as an effective deterrent against political attack messages in two large experimental field studies (Pfau and Burgoon, 1988; Pfau, Kenski, Nitz, and Sorenson, 1990).

Need for Information in Social Action Campaigns

Social action campaigns differ from commercial and political campaigns. The hierarchical model still applies, although it is much more difficult to identify and meet receivers' needs at each of the stages in the hierarchy. Nonetheless, emphasis on real or latent receivers' needs remains the paramount consideration. The specific examples of successful social action campaigns described previously all provided information directed to receiver needs. However, unlike most commercial and political campaigns, social action campaigns usually target a more restricted audience, often consisting of people at risk, whether from smoking, illegal drug use, sexual activity, excessive drinking, etc., who, as a result, resist efforts to change their attitudes and behaviors. In these instances, the tasks of assessing receiver motivation to acquire information or segmenting the information market are especially difficult (Ettema, Brown, and Luepker, 1983).

In addition, most social action campaigns have to rely on free as opposed to paid media, which further undermines their ability to reach targeted receivers (Lynn, 1974). As a result, many campaigns, though successful in generating awareness among the broader public, have not been very effective in influencing attitudes of targeted receivers. This is particularly true for contemporary campaigns involving drug use (Pomice, 1990) and AIDS (Baggaley, 1989). This limitation of free media will be examined in greater detail in Chapter 9.

Segmentation and Targeting

At the outset of this chapter, James Grunig (1989, p. 222) warned that, ". . . communication campaigns will seldom be effective if they are directed to a mass audience." This caveat is echoed by those who study commercial advertising campaigns:

> *It is not realistic to assume that advertising provides a method for selling to the masses. Instead, one must recognize that people of various ages, income levels, and occupations, and from all places and walks of life do not all want the same things, have the same tastes, consume products at the same rate, think the same way, or live by the same scale of values (Sandage, Fryburger, and Rotzoll, 1989, p. 124).*

In order to tailor persuasive communication to common needs of receivers, persuaders initially subdivide or segment the mass audience into smaller groups of similar receivers, and devise communication that targets one or more of the specific groups. This process is termed segmentation and targeting.

Marketing theorist Wendell Smith coined the phrase, "market segmentation," in 1956 (Pope, 1983). Since then, the notion of segmentation has found a place in such fields as public opinion, mass communication, political science, sociology, and in anthropology, and in particular, marketing, where it has become an overriding strategic consideration (Grunig, 1989). Segmentation has become "one of the most influential and fashionable concepts in marketing," dominating the thinking of those charged with the responsibility of promoting products and services (Lunn, 1986, p. 387). It is often characterized as "basic to modern marketing" (Kumar and Rust, 1989, p. 23).

Segmentation and targeting are fundamental strategies for persuasive communication campaigns, whether commercial, political or social action, precisely because they enable communicators to zero in on specific receiver needs. Obviously, thorough audience research is an indispensable tool in segmentation and targeting. Initially, the persuader employs survey research techniques in order to identify specific segments. Then, persuaders use a blend of quantitative and qualitative research methods to learn as much as is possible about each segment. Research methods will be explained in some detail in Chapter 7.

In political campaign communication, public opinion polling, focus groups, and direct mail are considered to be indispensable because they enable candidates to identify and target specific receiver groups (Armstrong, 1988). Similarly, in social action campaigns, experts credit segmentation as ". . . one of the most important concepts in making modern communication campaigns efficient" (Simmons, 1990, p. 19). Thus, social marketers are advised to ". . . achieve a thorough understanding of the target-adoptor group and its needs" (Kotler and Roberto, 1989, p. 40).

There are many different ways to segment audiences. This section will highlight a few of the more common methods, using examples drawn primarily from commercial campaigns to illustrate each of the methods. As we indicated previously, segmentation and targeting have been employed most extensively in commercial campaigns. This is true because commercial campaigns are more likely to involve well-funded, sustained communication efforts compared to either political (Mauser, 1983) or social action campaigns (Atkin and Freimuth, 1989). In addition, commercial campaigns must deal with far more diffuse receiver attitudes. Whereas social action campaigns can segment primarily on the basis of receiver need, thus targeting those at greatest risk, and political campaigns can segment on the basis of receiver attitude toward a candidate, commercial campaigns have had to develop far more elaborate approaches.

At the outset of this section, we caution against thinking of segmentation approaches as mutually exclusive. Indeed, it is increasingly common for contemporary persuaders to combine two or more approaches in the process of identifying a specific segment (e.g., well-educated, working women with young children). The three most common segmentation approaches are based on receiver geographic, demographic, and psychographic groupings, with the latter emerging as particularly fashionable today (Clark, 1988).

Geographic Factors

Geographic factors involve place of residence. Sometimes audiences are segmented by region of the country. This is done when products are not distributed nationally (e.g., for years, Coors beer was only marketed in the West), or when messages need to be tailored to specific regions. For example, candidates in national political campaigns usually tailor their messages to specific regions, adapting to unique regional issues. At other times, audiences are segmented according to place of residence, such as rural, small town or city, or metropolitan area. In commercial campaigns, product type and presentational style are often adapted to receivers on the basis of place of residence. In national political campaigns, a disproportionate share of time and resources are directed at potential voters in metropolitan areas of a small handful of large and competitive states (e.g., California, Texas, Illinois, Michigan, Ohio, New Jersey, and Pennsylvania together possess 184 electoral votes) which experts claim hold the key to victory in presidential elections (Quirk, 1989).

Demographic Factors

Demographics involve segmentation based on socioeconomic characteristics of receivers, including age, gender, ethnicity, family life cycle, education, income, social class, and others. This is one of the oldest segmentation approaches. The trick is to pinpoint existing socioeconomic segments while simultaneously keeping an eye on emerging trends.

Age is one of the most important segmentation approaches in commercial campaigns. "The stage of life people have reached determines not only what they want but what they can afford" (Clark, 1988, p. 178).

During the 1970s and 1980s, it seemed as if most commercial television campaigns targeted younger consumers, particularly the 12–18 and 19–25-year-old segments. There was good reason for the emphasis on younger consumers. The 12–18-year-old segment, for example, spent $56 billion in 1989 on a wide range of products and services (NBC TV News Network Report, 1990). The research also indicates that approximately half of all teenagers do some of the family grocery shopping, and that they exert a significant influence on major family purchases, including vacations, home entertainment systems, new automobiles, and others (NBC TV News Network Report, 1990).

However, the post-World War II "baby boom," which focused attention on youth in American culture, was followed by what some termed a "baby bust" (Sandage et al., 1989). As a result, the 12–18-year-old segment will show very little growth during the 1990s. In addition, the 19–25-year-old segment, which peaked during the early 1980s, is projected to decline by 3 million during the coming decade (Francese, 1988). These developments will result in much less emphasis on young people in commercial advertising.

In the meantime, those people born during the population upswing from 1946 to 1965 will reach middle age, peak earning and spending years, during the 1990s (Francese, 1988). "Boomers," as this particular demographic segment is called, "excite special interest from advertisers, because acquisitiveness is regarded as one of the group's most dominant characteristics" (Clark, 1988, p. 178). As "boomers" pass through the age cycle, they generate tremendous economic and social impact. As they enter middle age during the last decade of this century and the first decade of the next century, marketers expect a surge of spending on motor vehicles, food, housing, entertainment, and retirement programs, characteristic of middle-age consumers (Francese,

1988). Analyst Peter Kim of the J. Walter Thompson agency claims this movement will be the "... single most important phenomenon, in terms of the way marketers and advertisers will try to sell products in the 1990s" (cited in Carton, 1990, p. 9D). This claim makes sense given the fact that "boomers" enjoy an estimated combined annual income of $985 billion (Hall, 1990).

The commercial and political implications of this trend are already being felt. Kellogg, for example, has shifted emphasis from children's cereals to adult brands in order to capitalize on the health consciousness among this surging demographic segment (Sandage et al., 1989). In addition, the musical accompaniment to contemporary radio and television commercials is increasingly drawn from popular songs of the 1960s and 1970s, the "boomers" adolescent years (Zeifman, 1988).

Finally, Pat Caddell (1985) has commented on the important, but misunderstood, role of "boomers" in contemporary politics. He argues that "baby boomers" tend to be economic conservatives but cultural and social liberals, a fact which neither Democrats nor Republicans have yet to come to grips with. Absent an appeal tailored to the unique political attitudes of this demographic segment, Caddell maintains that "boomers" will continue to split their tickets, voting for Republican presidents and Democratic House and Senate candidates (Caddell, 1985).

Older Americans are one of the most challenging demographic groups. Persons who are over 55 now constitute 20 percent of the population but are projected to grow three times as fast as the overall population between now and 2000, and then even faster as the baby boom generation passes through middle age (Lazer and Shaw, 1987). Older Americans are important because they control more than half the nation's discretionary income and three-quarters of its financial assets (Beck, 1990).

Compared with other age segments, older Americans use mass media more often as a primary source of information, relying less on interpersonal sources (Festervand and Lumpkin, 1989). These tendencies should potentially increase the impact of advertising in purchase decisions. Yet, advertisers have largely ignored older Americans (Festervand and Lumpkin, 1989). In addition, available evidence indicates that present commercial advertising underrepresents and misrepresents this group, resulting in negative attitudes (Beck, 1990). The problem is complicated by the fact that most older people think and feel 10 years younger than they actually are (Clark, 1988).

Most of the recent political appeals that have targeted older Americans have played on insecurities surrounding Social Security cuts. This approach was used by Democratic challengers in 1982, 1984, and 1986 House and Senate races, at times with considerable success (Pfau and Kenski, 1990).

Gender is another important segmentation approach. Once it was thought that women purchased products designed for their own consumption as well as most household package goods, while men purchased products intended for their consumption in addition to most large, manufactured items. However, more recent research findings reveal considerable overlap in family purchasing decisions (Ulanoff, 1977). This resulted in the first serious rethinking of the role of gender in marketing.

The most significant recent development involving gender as a variable in segmentation has been the increase of women in the workplace, and the resulting impact on purchase decisions. It is estimated that more than 50 million women now work

(Steinberg, 1988), 200 percent more than at the end of World War II (Bloom, 1989), thus requiring marketers and advertisers to rethink the role and impact of gender in purchase decisions. For example, the proportion of new automobiles purchased by women has grown from 20 to 50 percent during the past 15 years (Erickson, 1988). Women are also buying a rising proportion of financial services, insurance policies, homes, and other products (Erickson, 1988). Conversely, men now account for more than 40 percent of grocery purchases, which constitutes a significant increase over the past two decades (Sandage et al., 1989).

As a result, some claim that gender should be downplayed as a demographic variable. Lisa Watson of Ogilvy and Mather Direct notes that, "There are other demographic factors [including age, income, lifestyle, and others] that are stronger. There's nothing inherent in being female that drives your financial needs" (cited in Cleaver, 1988, p. 58).

In politics, however, the importance of gender as a vehicle to segment voters has gained ground. From the 1940s to the 1970s, there was very little substantive difference in the way that women and men responded to political candidates or issues (Frankovic, 1982). However, during the 1980s, a gender gap emerged (Mandel, 1982). The growing gap is based on women's more negative responses to at first Ronald Reagan's, and then George Bush's, personalities and positions (Carlson, 1988; Farah and Klein, 1988; Goodman, 1986).

Political polling indicates that, compared to men, women are more opposed to high defense spending, more concerned about war, less willing to support intervention as a foreign policy tool, more opposed to the death penalty, more supportive of limiting firearms, and more resistant to intrusions on personal freedom (Opinion Roundup, 1982). In addition, women are perceived as more compassionate, defined in terms of support for government's role in providing jobs and otherwise assisting people who are in need (Opinion Roundup, 1982). There is empirical support for Carol Gilligan's (1982) position that women's political attitudes express a "morality of responsibility." As one study of women's political attitudes concludes: "It is evident that even economic worries for women are more suggestive of a compassionate concern for the welfare of people in general, rather than reflecting narrow self-interest considerations" (Miller, 1988, p. 280).

Ethnicity is a common segmentation approach in commercial and political campaigns. African Americans and Hispanic Americans make up the largest non-Caucasian racial groups, accounting for approximately 12 and 7 percent of the population, respectively. However, Hispanics are the fastest growing group, projected to comprise 14 percent of the overall population by the year 2010 (Sandage et al., 1989). Commercial advertisers are targeting more messages to African and Hispanic Americans.

The income of African American households, after adjusting for inflation, rose 40 percent during the past decade (Where Black Is Gold, 1991). Advertisers, in turn, are now spending $743 million annually on national advertising campaigns that target African American consumers (Where Black Is Gold, 1991). One firm, Burrell Advertising, a black-owned agency in Chicago, which boasts some large clients including Proctor and Gamble and McDonald's, tailors communication specifically to the nation's African American market, arguing that more homogeneous approaches are ineffective with this distinctive segment (Clark, 1988). During the past two years, Proctor and Gamble doubled its ethnic marketing budget to $29 million in response to the rapid growth of the African and Hispanic American populations (NBC TV News Network Report, 1990).

There are ample print and electronic media with particular ethnic orientations (Sandage et al., 1989) that can be employed to target minority consumers (e.g., *Ebony* and *Jet* are popular magazines among African Americans). However, Leo Bogart (1967) cautions that general media reach far more receivers in specific minority groups than specialized ethnic media that are targeted to those groups.

Political campaign communication often targets minority segments, particularly African American voters, who have been overwhelmingly supportive of Democratic candidates ever since the 1960s. For example, in presidential contests from 1964 and 1988, between 85–95 percent of African Americans have voted for the Democratic nominees (Quirk, 1989). In the 1988 campaign, Michael Dukakis targeted Hispanic American voters, first in Texas during that state's primary, and then in the general election campaign, making a direct appeal to them in Spanish (Cook, 1989).

Another approach to demographic segmentation is based on family life cycle. Family life style is based on predictable stages that most people pass through over the course of their adult lives. The stages include: the bachelor stage, consisting of single individuals living alone; newly married couples without children; young married couples with the youngest child under six; young married couples with the youngest child over six; older married couples with dependent children; older married couples who are still working, but with no children living at home; older married couples who are retired; solitary survivors who are still working; and solitary survivors who are retired (Lansing and Kish, 1957). Consumption patterns involving many products and services vary significantly according to stage of the family life cycle (see Reynolds and Wells, 1977).

Education, income, and social class, are three additional approaches to demographic segmentation. In fact, these factors significantly interrelate, making it difficult to segment based on just one in isolation. Education facilitates access to the professions, serving as a prerequisite to greater income level and more elevated social class. "A college degree has long been recognized as a prerequisite for entering the professions of medicine, law, and engineering. . .[and] is becoming an almost universal requirement for top management positions in business and government as well" (Sandage et al., 1989, p. 133).

Education, income, and social class correlate inversely to Democratic Party leanings (Conway, 1985). Despite successes of Republican presidential candidates in attracting lower income (Polsby and Wildavsky, 1984) as well as blue-collar voters (Lemann, 1985) in recent elections, both of these groups are targeted by Democratic candidates as essential segments of their electoral coalition in election campaigns at local, state, and national levels. Furthermore, polls show that most voters still believe that "The Democrats are best for the workingman," favoring the party on basic pocketbook issues (Polsby and Wildavsky, 1984, p. 175).

Psychographics

Persons attaining higher income and status tend toward a more expansive life style. Indeed, psychographics or lifestyle is viewed by some as a more useful way to categorize consumers than via traditional demographic groupings. Today's advertisers want to know more than simple demographic information. They want to know about people's values, emotions, and lifestyles in order to more effectively motivate them to buy. This is the essence of psychographics or lifestyle segmentation.

The focus of this approach is on the psychology of the user, a combination of the way people view themselves and those things that they surround themselves with (Schultz et al., 1984). Various motivational theories and approaches, including the evolution of psychographics, will be discussed in much more detail in Chapter 5. In this section, we only want to introduce it as a way to segment consumers.

Psychographic research examines the motivation of users and potential users, looking for clusters of people called "types." Campaign practitioners maintain that they can design specific communications which trigger predictable responses among common "types," making this approach especially useful (Simmons, 1990).

Advertising agencies have devised various schemes to depict psychographic segments. The lifestyle groups identified by the Chicago firm, Needham, Harper and Steers, include (the proportion is identified in parentheses): "Ben, the self-made businessman (17 percent); Scott, the successful professional (21 percent); Dale, the devoted family man (17 percent); Fred, the frustrated factory worker (19 percent); Herman, the retiring homebody (26 percent); Cathy, the contented housewife (18 percent); Candice, the chic suburbanite (20 percent); Eleanor, the elegant socialite (17 percent); Mildred, the militant mother (20 percent); and Thelma, the old-fashioned traditionalist (25 percent)" (Schultz et al., 1984, p. 70).

One of the newest forms of psychographic analysis is the VALS (Values and Lifestyle) typology, based on psychological profiles of lifestyles and values. VALS was the concoction of social scientists working at the Stanford Research Institute (Beltramini and Kelley, 1983). It grew out of work involving Abraham Maslow's psychological hierarchy of needs and David Riesman's sociological profile of inner- and outer-directed people (Rice, 1988).

Such considerations as education, income, social class, and others merge to affect consumer position on the VALS hierarchy. The hierarchy, however, is based on a combination of capability, largely a function of income, as well as disposition, which is based on personality (Clark, 1988). Joseph Plummer of Young and Rubicam, describes the approach this way: "VALS places a premium on understanding a consumer's attitude towards life in general; it gets marketers closer to the people they are trying to reach" (cited in Clark, 1988, p. 172).

The VALS typology, which emerged in the late 1970s, has at the bottom rung, people who are largely need-driven, wholly preoccupied with providing life's basics (comprising about one-tenth of Americans). Next come outer-directed people who buy in order to impress others, including belongers, emulators, and achievers (about two-thirds of Americans). At the next rung are inner-directed people who purchase things

---

FEEDBACK

Scenario: Examine the VALS 2 typology described below. Think of people you know, and attempt to place them in appropriate groups.

   1. What was it about them that caused you to place them in the groups that you did?
   2. What kinds of commercial advertising appeals would work best with the people you placed in each of the groups?

---

to please themselves, constituting the "I-Am-Me's," "experimentals," and "societally conscious" (comprising slightly less than one-third of all Americans). The final group consists of integrateds, a melding of the power of outer-directed and the sensitivity of inner-directed people (about two percent of Americans) (Beltramini and Kelley, 1983).

Timex was one of the first large American corporations to employ VALS in marketing, designing packaging and advertising messages to target the "societally conscious" and "achiever" groups (Clark, 1988). By the middle 1980s, "SRI had 130 VALS users, including the major TV networks, advertising agencies such as McCann-Erickson, Young and Rubicam and Doyle Dane Bernbach, publishers such as *Time*, and major consumer companies," such as AT&T, Coca-Cola, General Motors, Proctor and Gamble, and others (Clark, 1988, p. 171).

More recently, SRI developed VALS 2, a slight modification of the original VALS typology. The VALS 2 system employs two underlying dimensions, the consumer's psychological orientation and their psychological and material resources, in order to cluster consumers into eight basic groupings. The specific segments include: (1) strugglers, people who lack basic financial resources; (2) experiencers, younger people who seek variety and excitement in their lives; (3) makers, people who are bound by traditional values, and possess the practical skills to use in the pursuit of self-sufficiency; (4) strivers, people less sure of themselves who look to others for social approval; (5) achievers, successful career-oriented people who feel in control of their own lives; (6) believers, conservative and deeply moral people who follow established routines; (7) fulfilleds, who are more mature, satisfied, and comfortable people who value order, knowledge, and responsibility; and (8) actualizers, take-charge people with high self-esteem and abundant resources (Russell and Lane, 1990). The VALS 2 typology provides marketing and advertising professionals with the most recent refinement in psychographic segmentation.

Conclusion

This chapter dealt with the central role of receivers in persuasive campaigns. Whether we are concerned with commercial, political, or social action campaigns, the same basic maxim applies: the more the persuader knows about targeted receivers, the more likely they will be able to set appropriate objectives, choose optimal sources, craft effective messages, select proper media, and assess outcomes.

The chapter examined the implications for receivers of the traditional linear and contemporary transactional assumptions about communication, examined the central role of receiver needs in persuasive campaigns, and then introduced the techniques of segmenting audiences for the purpose of targeting communication to the specific needs of individual groupings. Segmentation and targeting are viewed as "crucial" starting points for effective persuasive campaigns. As one marketing specialist put it, "If you're not thinking segments, you're not thinking" (cited in Grunig, 1989, p. 201).

Suggestions for Further Reading

Beltramini, R. F., and Kelley, L. D. (1983). Lifestyle research applications in advertising intermedia comparisons. In D. W. Jugenheimer (Ed.), *Proceedings of the 1983 Convention of the American Academy of Advertising* (pp. 6–9). Lawrence, K.S.: Donald W. Jugenheimer, William Allen White School of Journalism and Mass Communication, University of Kansas.

Curti, M. (1967). The changing concept of "human nature" in the literature of American advertising. *Business History Review, 41*, 335–357.

Dervin, B. (1989). Audience as listener and learner, teacher, and confidant: The sense-making approach. In R. E. Rice and C. K. Atkin (Eds.), *Public Communication Campaigns* (2nd ed., pp. 67–86). Newbury Park, CA: Sage Publications.

Grunig, J. E. (1989). Publics, audiences, and market segments: Segmentation principles for campaigns. In C. T. Salmon (Ed.), *Information Campaigns: Balancing Social Values and Social Change* (pp. 199–228). Newbury Park, CA: Sage Publications.

McGuire, W. J. (1986). The myth of massive media impact: Savagings and salvagings. In G. Comstock (Ed.), *Public Communication and Behavior* (Vol. 1, pp. 173–257). Orlando, FL: Academic Press, Inc.

Active Approaches to Receivers

"The basic aim of scientific theory is to provide explanations for observed phenomena."
–CHARLES BERGER, COMMUNICATION PROFESSOR
(BERGER, 1977, P. 7)

"A cognitive orientation to communication must be a prime factor in theorizing."
–SALLY PLANALP AND DEAN E. HEWES, COMMUNICATION
PROFESSORS
(PLANALP AND HEWES, 1982, P. 70)

Campaign messages concerning health and welfare, politics, and commercial products and services are being disseminated at an increasing rate to wider and wider audiences (Haug and Lavin, 1983; Salmon, 1989). Also, the channels that are available to carry campaign messages have increased. Television is one of the most widely used media (Argenta, Stoneman, and Brody, 1986; Kulman and Akamatsu, 1988), providing campaigners with a vehicle which enables them to reach a large audience with diverse needs and motivations to attend messages. Print media also are used extensively (Bowen and Grunberg, 1987), with many special interest newsletters and other technical forms of communication available to provide specific messages to designated audiences. The computer has contributed significantly to proliferation of print messages, particularly via direct mail.

In addition to an increase in the number of messages, the distinction between informative and entertaining message content has become blurred. Popular television programs, in addition to newspaper, radio, and magazine stories, communicate content about politics, marketing, and social issues, including topics such as child abuse, rape, AIDS, and drug use, in addition to voting and purchasing behavior. Fictional characters wear and use some of the products that are advertised, work for and against candidates running for office, and become involved in real social issues of the times.

The Active Message Processing Paradigm

With so many messages available from so many communication channels, it is important for campaigners to know what kind of campaign messages and media people are likely to thoughtfully use and process, which involves an active approach to information processing, and what kind of messages and media they are likely to superficially use and process, which embodies a more passive approach. As noted in Chapter 3, campaigners design and target some messages at people's more rational side and other messages at their more emotional side. Active approaches depend more on logical arguments, which embody a systematic approach that describes objective characteristics (Pechmann and Stewart, 1989). Passive approaches focus on previously established or learned preferences, and/or other affective responses. This chapter addresses these issues, defining active receivers, discussing the predictors of cognitive activity, and identifying methods to enhance active message processing. The questions outlined in Table 4–1 will be answered.

Definition of Active Receivers

One of the first steps in campaign planning is for message designers to decide how actively they want the target audience to process their communications and whether the audience is willing and able to match this expectation. Sometimes, campaigners want to invoke more passive message processing. They can do this by either taking advantage of what receivers already know, thereby invoking a learned response, or by triggering a more emotional response in receivers. Other times, campaigners want to promote more active message processing, by making receivers aware of new information and/or by invoking a new response. A convenient way to conceptualize these

TABLE 4–1   Questions about Active Message Processing

1. What is an attitude?
2. What are the components of attitude?
3. How does the concept of attitude contribute to understanding active approaches to theorizing about campaigns?
4. Distinguish mindful and mindless message processing.
5. How does the concept of schema relate to attitude?
6. What receiver variables may facilitate the motivation to actively process message content?
7. What receiver variables facilitate the ability to actively process message content?
8. What message variables facilitate the motivation and/or ability to actively process message content?
9. What source variables facilitate the motivation and/or ability to actively process message content?
10. What channel variables facilitate the motivation and/or ability to actively process message content?

differences in message processing is via a continuum of awareness that ranges from mindless to mindful thought (Langer, 1978).

Mindful message processing assumes that receivers will be active in making distinctions, assigning meanings, and creating categories, while mindless processing relies on distinctions and meanings previously developed (Langer, 1978), or on triggering emotion. In other words, the mindless processing of campaign messages and information depends either upon existing mental habits (past knowledge or experience with similar messages) in order for receivers to assign meaning and to interpret messages or on emotion, and thus constitutes a more passive approach.

The amount of mental activity that individuals invest in processing messages also relates to a core assumption of Petty and Cacioppo's (1986) Elaboration Likelihood Model (ELM), which addresses people's ability and motivation to process persuasive communication. Elaboration, one of the ELM's derived terms, is defined as the degree of issue-relevant thinking that receivers engage in about a persuasive communication (Petty and Cacioppo, 1986). With this definition of active receivers as more mindful audience members who think about message content, thus making a greater number of elaborations of message content than passive receivers, the challenge for campaigners is to determine when such activity is more or less likely to happen.

Need for Information

With so much information available, how do people decide which messages to attend and which messages to ignore? Perhaps the most important predictor of whether receivers will actively attend and process information in campaign messages is their need for the information. Chapter 3 stressed that people's need for information is the most significant contributor to, and predictor of, how they will respond to campaign messages, both cognitively and affectively. Cognitive responses encompass all points on the continuum of mindfulness and elaboration previously described, whereas affective responses encompass a broad range of types and intensities of emotion. Where the need for information is high, campaigners should expect more mindful or elaborated message processing.

Receiver need for information is predicated upon awareness and understanding of some attitude object (e.g., a commercial product, political candidate, or social issue) as it relates to the receiver's immediate environment. When people perceive that the attitude object directly affects their immediate environment, the information encountered regarding the attitude object will be more actively processed. Conversely, if people perceive that the information does not affect their immediate environment, passive processing is likely. Thus, people's attitudes are an important starting place to assess how actively they will process campaign message content, since attitudes suggest how likely it is that a receiver perceives a need for information.

Role of Attitudes

Attitude research is linked to the development of cognitive persuasion theories. An underlying assumption of much theory and research in persuasion is that attitudes are directly related to behavior. In other words, if someone holds a positive attitude about a specific product, he or she will be inclined to purchase the product; if someone has a positive attitude toward a political candidate, he or she would be expected to vote for that candidate; and so on.

Experience has demonstrated, however, that attitudes do not always precede behavior. Sometimes, behavior precedes attitude formation; sometimes, attitude and behavior appear to manifest a reciprocal relationship to one another; and sometimes, attitudes appear to have no relationship to behavior. Nonetheless, in the planning and implementing of campaigns, an audience's attitudes are a pivotal starting point to make receivers integral in the process. Current attitudes may be the best indicator we have of future behavior, as present behavior is often situational and not linked to an individual's future behavior (McGuire, 1986).

Many definitions of attitudes have been advanced. We prefer McGuire's (1986) which defines attitude as "a mediating process grouping a set of objects of thought in a conceptual category that evokes a significant pattern of responses" (p. 239). This definition includes the following elements: (1) that attitudes intervene in responses even though attitudes are not directly observable; (2) that people tend to group common sets of stimuli, such as types of desserts or types of personalities, and order their importance accordingly; and (3) that cognition is causally related to responses (McGuire, 1986). As we will demonstrate in Chapter 7, a wide range of methods exists to identify receiver attitudes. In gathering attitude data, a campaigner narrows the focus for campaign messages, determining what information people already have and what information they may need.

Many ways of conceptualizing the structure of attitudes also have been suggested, but three common components are cognition, affect, and conation (McGuire, 1986). The cognitive component of attitudes highlights the relationship between thoughts or beliefs and attitudes, and is considered to be an integral feature. So, for example, students' attitudes about college tuition include their beliefs about the amount they pay in comparison to other students at other colleges. The affective component links the importance of feelings to attitudes. Students' expressions of anger or frustration regarding college tuition rates are also part of their attitudes. Finally, the conative component of attitudes is the most closely related to behavior, reflecting the intentions associated with the attitude object. Students' convictions that a further increase in the rate of tuition will prompt them to change colleges, for example, provides further information about their attitudes concerning tuition increases.

Active approaches to campaign theory emphasize the cognitive component of attitudes. What receivers presently think about an attitude object determines whether the campaign objective should be formation, change, or resistance. Persuasion theorists and researchers have long maintained that: "The key to understanding a given attitude is to learn the context in which the attitude is expressed and the standards of comparison that exist in the given situation" (Stouffer, 1949, p. 6). Students, for example, may have friends who attend other schools with equal academic repute but pay less tuition; parents may have friends or acquaintances who pay less tuition for their childrens' educations; thus, parents and students may believe that tuition costs are already higher than what others pay. In their efforts to identify the cognitions of receivers about an attitude object, campaigners are addressing the very basic issue of the audience's storehouse of knowledge and beliefs, or what is referred to as mental schemata or schema (Thomas, 1985).

Relevance of Schema

Schema are defined as the cognitive structures of organized knowledge that people acquire over time (Taylor and Crocker, 1981). Schema develop from a person's experiences, including exposure to media messages (Salomon, 1981), and function to direct their perception, interpretation, storage, and recall of information (McGuire, 1986). The concept of schema relates to the belief component of attitude (Smith, 1982).

Types of Schema

Three general categories of schema, or cognitive structures of organized knowledge, have been identified: self or person schemas, event schemas, and role schemas (Fiske and Taylor, 1984; Taylor and Crocker, 1981).

Self or Person Schemas Self or person schemas constitute stereotypes about others, such as those associated with student athletes ("jocks"), certain women ("blondes"), or intellectuals ("eggheads"), in addition to thoughts about oneself, such as attractiveness, intelligence, or honesty. Suppose a campaign message concerns college tuition, for example, and you are a college student. You probably would perceive the message as one that may affect your immediate environment, and therefore would perceive a need for the information in the message.

Campaigners focusing on college tuition increases could conduct their formative research in a number of ways, but one approach would be to start by defining the attitudes associated with the use of money collected through students' tuition. One relevant attitude object is professors, since their salaries, it would be assumed, are associated with the use of money collected through students' tuition. In this case, it becomes important to determine an audience's schema about professors. Are professors perceived as overpaid and underworked, underpaid and overworked, or are people relatively neutral on the topic? Campaigners also need to identify the audience's perceptions about themselves. Do they value education or see college as a hoop to jump through on the way to a high-paying job?

Campaigners focusing on immigration policy would want to identify the audience's schema about immigrants. If you are a U.S. citizen and a college student, you would probably perceive this message as less likely to affect your immediate environment than a message about college tuition. If this is the case, you would be expected to process messages about immigration policy less actively than you would messages about college tuition. If formative research indicates that most receivers are relatively uninformed and apathetic about immigration policy, and the goal is to increase receiver attention to, and processing of, messages about the issue, something will have to be done to involve this response, since receivers themselves do not currently perceive the need for such information.

To establish what might be done to invoke greater mental activity, campaigners might begin by identifying the audience's schema about immigrants. For example, are immigrants perceived as hard workers and poor, as trespassers and a tax burden, or is the audience relatively neutral about this topic? Campaigners also need to identify the audience's perceptions of themselves. Do they see themselves as altruistic, patriotic, freedom-loving, or are their views unformed? Obtaining information about the audience's schema regarding the campaign topic offers insights about receivers' needs for information, thus informing message design.

The importance of self-schema is demonstrated in research such as that conducted by Cacioppo, Petty, and Sidera (1982). Researchers presented proattitudinal messages that were either relevant or irrelevant to self-schema. In this investigation, some students were classified as "religious," while others were defined as "legalistic." The results indicated that legalistic messages were more persuasive for the legalistic rather than the religious subjects, while religious messages were more persuasive for religious rather than legalistic subjects. Thus, altruistic messages associating immigration policy with greater freedom, for example, should be more effective in promoting active thought and possible support of liberal immigration policies if the audience views itself as altruistic and freedom-loving, but less effective otherwise.

Event Schemas A second broad category of schema is called event schemas or scripts. Event schemas are based on situations, and consist of the knowledge that an individual holds regarding the appropriate sequence of actions or behaviors in any given context. One example of an event schema is a restaurant script, which identifies behaviors we expect to occur in a restaurant setting. A restaurant script acts as a guide to indicate how we should behave and how we can interpret others' behavior. Other examples of event schemas might include medical examinations, job interviews, weddings, and funerals. We are probably all able to generate a list of behaviors that we associate with each of these events.

Campaigners focusing on immigration policy are advised to understand the audience's schema about the event or process of immigrating in order to generate important insights about how receivers might respond to messages. The audience's lack of awareness about the laws governing immigration may demonstrate the need to start with messages which contain such information. Similarly, campaigners addressing a college tuition increase need to identify what the act of attending college means to receivers. Is it having access to current books and journals and to modern facilities? If so, messages may include information about the need to increase tuition to provide students with these. Or, is it having sufficient funding to support athletic programs? If it is, messages may be needed to reshape an audience's event schema before attempting to persuade them to support more tuition for the academic mission. Learning what knowledge an audience has about an event or events associated with a campaign issue aids campaigners' efforts to determine how actively an audience will process campaign messages, and ultimately helps focus campaign communication on the audience's need for information.

Role Schemas Another category of knowledge that organizes our perceptions is role schemas, which are independent of the person or event, but deal with an occupation, such as physician, professor, or lawyer. What an audience thinks that they know about the specific responsibilities of a role as it relates to a particular campaign topic may also facilitate or deter campaign communication. For example, campaigners might elect to use a lawyer as a spokesperson for or against immigration policy, but only if the audience's knowledge structure is such that lawyers would be seen as credible sources of these messages. Similarly, if an audience views the professor's role as a teacher, but fails to understand his/her role in research and service, then professors would be perceived as credible when speaking in favor of college tuition increases to support teaching, but not when speaking in favor of increases to support research.

Use of Schemas

During periods of formative research, campaigners seek to understand an audience's attitudes, particularly with regard to the content of the knowledge structures or schema relevant to a campaign topic. This is important because mental anticipatory schema serve as the medium through which information already present acts to determine what will be picked up next, and this information, in turn, modifies the original schemata (Neisser, 1976).

In particular, two ways that individuals' thoughts affect their attitudes have been identified (Millar and Tesser, 1986). First, cognitions may change the very content of schema, thereby making thoughts more or less consistent with an initial attitude. Second, cognitions may change the structure of the schema to be more or less complex. Whereas a change in the content of schema indicates that more information is added to an already formed knowledge structure, a change in the structure of schema means that the scope or dimensions of a thought category have changed, as when a unidimensional concept becomes multidimensional.

Consider again the topic of U.S. immigration policy. Using formative research, campaigners might learn that the audience's knowledge about the topic is structured into a two-dimensional schema for the topic, with the dimensions being laws and effects of immigration policy. This suggests that the audience may have some understanding and awareness of present immigration laws and some beliefs about the effects of current policies. Campaign messages may confirm or deny the audience's schema regarding both dimensions, a change in the content of the schema, and one means of affecting attitudes. The initial attitude about immigration policy, for example, might be that it is too liberal, because immigrants hold jobs that citizens might otherwise hold. If campaigners determine that the audience holds this belief, then providing the audience with discrepant information would change the content of the schema and afford an opportunity to change the audience's attitudes about immigration policy.

On the other hand, suppose that campaigners determine that the audience has no beliefs about causes which led to the laws, a possible third dimension of the knowledge structure associated with immigration policy. Such causes might include the numbers of untrained and unskilled individuals that immigrate into the country, or the treatment of people seeking to promote democracy in some countries. If campaigners

---

FEEDBACK

Consider the following questions within the framework of receivers' use of information in campaign messages:

   1. What time of the year are commercial campaigners most likely to advertise toys? Why? Similarly, what time of the day and week are commercial campaigners most likely to advertise sugar-coated cereals? Consider the parents of young children as one audience, and young children as a second audience of these messages. What relevant schema do the two audiences hold, and how are these likely to be in conflict? Consider the parent's role schema, including the nutritional value of food products that parents provide for their children.
   2. When are political campaigners most likely to advertise? Why? How does this relate to voters' need for information and the activity that is most likely to be associated with receivers' message processing?

---

determine that most audience members regard themselves as humane, then messages that provide a humanitarian rationale for immigration might generate considerable support. At the same time, such messages would change the structure of current schema, which would now include antecedent conditions of policy as one dimension of immigration laws.

   In short, the receivers' need for information determines whether they will actively process campaign messages. If they perceive a need for information, messages are much more likely to generate active thought. Campaigners need to determine what attitudes an audience holds, particularly with regard to salient person, event, and role schemas, in order to assess what message content people are likely to attend.

Factors Affecting Active Information Processing

The remainder of this chapter is devoted to the development and discussion of issues surrounding active message processing. This discussion is based on persuasion theory and research from several academic disciplines, including social psychology, psychology, and sociology, as well as communication. Some of what is unique about our approach to campaign communication is the inclusion of communication theories specifically concerned with persuasion, such as contingency rules theory (Smith, 1982) and expectancy theory (Burgoon and Miller, 1985), in addition to theories drawn from interpersonal communication. In part, this effort is made to integrate theory and research from the areas of mass communication and interpersonal communication as they relate to persuasive campaigns.

   The theoretical integrative pursuits advanced in this book are desirable and appropriate, as illustrated by such issues as receivers' formation of parasocial relationships.

Parasocial relationships describe how audience members often personalize their thoughts about media characters and personalities, as if they had actual interpersonal relationships with them. These personalizations affect outcomes associated with message content, reflecting a positive impact in situations in which the bond a character or media figure forms with the audience is a positive one and vice versa (Perse and Rubin, 1989; Pfau, 1990). Thus, this research has important implications for the success or failure of campaign messages in terms of source and channel selection, and the likelihood that individuals will actively process information. The discussion that follows is organized around those receiver, message, source, and channel variables that have been demonstrated to impact active message processing, in addition to the theoretical frameworks that explain why these outcomes occur. Several questions guide the development of these issues: (1) When will people seek information about an issue? (2) What type of information will they look for? (3) How do individuals go about the process of obtaining information? And, (4) Why do they select some information sources or messages more than others?

The ELM's second postulate predicts that issue-relevant elaboration varies with individual and situational factors, such that elaboration should be viewed along "a continuum going from no thought about the issue-relevant information presented, to complete elaboration of every argument, and complete integration of these elaborations into the person's attitude schema" (Petty and Cacioppo, 1986, p. 8). A person's need for information predicts how much mental activity they are likely to engage in when they encounter information. However, a number of receiver variables predict how likely it is that an individual will be motivated to actively process information, even at times deliberately seeking out message content. Additionally, a number of variables predict receivers' ability to actively process the information that they need, seek, and/or obtain. Both the receivers' motivation to actively process information and ability to process information should be considered by campaigners during the planning stage of the campaign.

TABLE 4–2 Receiver Variables that Affect Active Message Processing

That Affect Motivation	*That Affect Ability*
Uncertainty	Egocentrism and transductive reasoning
Involvement	Education and expertise
Issue involvement	Self-efficacy
Commitment	
Personal relevance	
Self-reference	
Egocentric bias	
Discrepant information and dissonance	
Personal responsibility	
Network density	

Receiver Variables Affecting Motivation to Process Information

The receivers' motivation to actively process information is determined by their uncertainty about the topic, involvement in the issue, the presence of discrepant information, and feelings of dissonance. In addition, a sense of personal responsibility and network density may also affect their motivation to actively process information. These factors carry important lessons for the construction of persuasive messages. Table 4–2 summarizes the receiver variables that affect the audience's motivation and ability to process messages.

Uncertainty

Recall from Chapter 3 that an individual's need for information is often predicated upon uncertainty. Individuals must often exercise a form of judgment that has been called quasirational thought, a melding of objective analysis and intuition (Hammond, 1975). Hammond explains that, "One of the important reasons why quasirational thought is applied to the cognitive tasks of everyday life is that uncertainty is embedded in such tasks" (Hammond, 1975, p. 72). In this manner uncertainty motivates people to actively process information and to intentionally seek information to reduce uncertainty.

This information search process has been conceptualized as consisting of six stages: (1) *initiation*, when a person becomes aware of a lack of knowledge or understanding, thus recognizing a need for information; (2) *selection*, when a person identifies and selects the approach to use in reviewing available information; (3) *exploration*, when an individual investigates information to extend personal understanding; (4) *formulation*, when feelings of uncertainty dissipate, and then are replaced by confidence; (5) *collection*, when thoughts center on selecting specific rather than general information; and (6) *presentation*, when a person prepares to use the information (Kuhlthau, 1991).

One way to conceptualize information-seeking activity that is designed to reduce uncertainty is with the explanatory rubric of uncertainty reduction theory (Berger and Calabrese, 1975). This theory was originally conceived in order to explain interpersonal communication between two strangers during initial interaction. While the theory is not concerned with persuasion or campaigns per se, broadening its theoretical scope provides for explanation and prediction of campaign persuasion. Perse and Rubin (1989) demonstrate the usefulness of the theory as a tool to explain the development of parasocial relationships, supporting the theory's appropriateness for both interpersonal and mediated contexts. They contend that, "when people approach communication, they use the same cognitive processes for both mediated and interpersonal contexts" (Perse and Rubin, 1989, p. 59). The third axiom of the theory asserts that high levels of uncertainty trigger greater information-seeking behavior; and conversely, as uncertainty levels decline, information-seeking behavior also decreases.

Berger and Calabrese (1975) argue that human beings are influence-seekers, who employ passive, active, and interactive strategies to satisfy their need for information. A passive strategy in persuasive campaigns might encompass intentionally reading or listening to messages regarding some attitude object about which receivers feel uncertain. Thus, someone about to become a new parent should be more motivated to read articles he/she encounters about parenthood. Passive strategies to reduce uncertainty should not be confused with passive approaches to information processing. The former simply implies that, while people do not seek out specific information about a topic, when they encounter such information, they will pay attention to it.

An active approach to seeking information in order to reduce uncertainty about some issue might involve seeking out a variety of sources, such as magazines, television, or books, to provide relevant information, or structuring situations to encourage other people to talk about the issue, stopping short of actually asking direct questions about the issue. An interactive approach uses self-disclosure to elicit a reciprocal response in others. The interactive approach is most appropriate at the choice stage of the decision-making model presented in Chapter 3, because the interpersonal communication modality dominates at this stage.

In sum, if campaigners are able to identify an audience's perceptions of uncertainty associated with an attitude object, messages may be designed to address that uncertainty. To do so allows the campaigners to predict more active message processing in these situations. In addition to global uncertainty about an attitude object as motivation to actively process information, people also are likely to be more mindful when messages address attitude objects that they find interesting or important.

Involvement
Consideration of an audience's involvement in an issue or topic provides another starting point for campaigners' assessment of the motivation to actively process

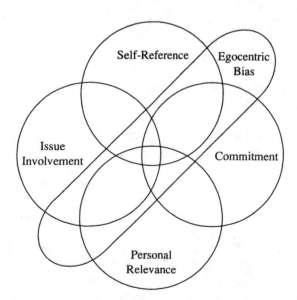

FIGURE 4–1 Model of Receivers' Involvement with Campaign Communication

information. Involvement is itself a multidimensional concept (O'Keefe, 1990) that has been examined with regard to the issue, the receiver's position on the issue, and his/her psychological reference to or identity with a subject. Many definitions of involvement exist. Petty and Cacioppo (1986), for example, define involved subjects as "those with extreme opinions or those who said the issue was important" (p. 139). We view involvement as multidimensional, minimally including the following elements: (1) *issue involvement*, the receiver's interest in, or judgment of the importance of, a campaign issue, (2) *commitment*, the receiver's formation of, and psychological identification with, a point of view on an issue, sometimes referred to as ego involvement, (3) *personal relevance*, the receiver's judgment that an issue relates to an ongoing or as yet uncompleted task, (4) *self-reference,* the receiver's judgment that an issue relates to an individual characteristic or trait; and (5) *egocentric bias*, a receiver's identification with an extreme point of view regarding a topic. All dimensions affect individuals' information processing. Figure 4–1 illustrates the construct of involvement using this multifaceted framework.

Issue Involvement Issue involvement, the perception that an issue is important or interesting, enhances active information processing. The belief that making an informed decision when we vote for political candidates is important, for example, suggests that we will pay attention to and may even seek information about the candidates. The belief that a purchase decision is important should motivate consumers to attend to and seek information about the price and quality of competing brands. The belief that good health is important should cause people to focus on information about how to behave in order to attain this goal. To promote active message processing, therefore, campaigners should design messages that stress receiver interest in, or the importance of, a campaign issue.

Commitment Commitment as a form of involvement indicates that an individual is not only interested in a topic, but also has formed a point of view and personally identifies with that position. For example, college students may be interested in the topic of college tuition because it relates to their immediate environment, but they may also be committed to the position that everyone has a right to a college education. Both situations provide considerable insight to campaign planners about how such audiences would react to messages about tuition increases, with the latter suggesting how to focus campaign messages to enhance persuasion. Information indicating that tuition increases are needed to update university facilities is unlikely to satisfy the student committed to the view that all students have a right to a college education, because such increases would not be viewed as expanding opportunity (they may be seen as restricting it). On the other hand, if tuition increases are justified on the grounds of providing more scholarship opportunities to students who might not otherwise be able to attend college, it should prove to be persuasive for this audience.

Commitment to a point of view may motivate receivers to seek particular kinds of information in lieu of others, as illustrated above. Commitment also suggests a greater likelihood of behavior being associated with an attitude. In assessing voting behavior, for example, researchers report that psychological involvement is a more accurate predictor of voting than interest in a political campaign (Traugott and Tucker, 1984).

Social judgment theory explicitly formalizes the notion of commitment, positing that attitudes can be visualized in terms of three zones or latitudes, reflecting receiver involvement in an issue (Sherif, Sherif, and Nebergall, 1965). The receiver's view is termed the anchor, and is placed on a continuum along with the position advocated in the message. Once the position of the anchor is established, receiver involvement dictates whether the anchor, compared to the position advocated, lies in the latitude or range of rejection, acceptance, or noncommitment. The range of rejection comprises all of the positions on an issue that an individual views as unacceptable in comparison to his/her own view. The latitude of acceptance includes all positions on an issue that an individual finds acceptable, including his/her own view. The latitude of noncommitment consists of positions that an individual perceives to be neither acceptable nor unacceptable when compared with his/her own view. When individuals judge few positions other than their own to be acceptable, then the range of acceptance is a narrow one, whereas the latitude of rejection is broad. People who manifest a narrow latitude of acceptance are defined as more ego involved, thus suggesting greater commitment and psychological identification.

In social judgment theory, ego involvement is the mechanism used to explain the impact of messages on receivers, and includes the processes of assimilation and contrast. Assimilation, or a polarized positive evaluation, is predicted to accompany messages which fall within the latitudes of acceptance or noncommitment, whereas contrast, or a polarized negative evaluation, occurs when messages fall in the latitude of rejection. Assimilation thus enhances persuasion, moving the anchor toward the position being advocated in the message. However, persuasion is also a function of the distance separating the anchor and the position advocated in the message. Thus, the potential for persuasion is limited if the anchor falls in the range of acceptance, in close proximity to the position of the message (Kiesler, Collins, and Miller, 1969). A contrast effect often produces distortion of the message, with receivers perceiving it as even more discrepant from their own position than it really is, and carries considerable potential for psychological reactance, or a boomerang effect.

To examine how ego involvement may affect audience responses to messages, DeCarlo and Parrott (1991) predicted effectiveness of alcohol warning labels using social judgment theory. People who consumed more alcohol were viewed as more ego involved with the topic and predicted to report less often reading alcohol warning labels, despite more frequent exposure to the warnings. Individuals who rated themselves as more health conscious were also regarded as ego involved with the topic, but predicted to report more often reading alcohol warning labels. These views were supported, although no differences were found between the two groups. Thus, although health conscious individuals report more often reading labels, the warning labels failed to produce a significant persuasive effect. It appears that for the health conscious, the warning labels evoked an assimilation effect, but absent much discrepancy between the position of the anchor and that of the message, limited movement of the anchor was possible.

In sum, when campaigners find that receivers are committed to a point of view positively associated with the campaign, then that commitment is likely to promote active message processing. If the campaign objective is to reinforce an already established point of view and/or behavior, then commitment and the provoked mental activity should facilitate campaign effectiveness. If, however, the campaign objective is to change behavior, positive commitment and mindful processing may actually inhibit campaign effectiveness. The determination that receivers are committed to a point of view that is negatively associated with the campaign is also very important information, since failure to address the commitment is likely to inhibit campaign success.

Personal Relevance   The concept of ego involvement has been defined not only within the framework of social judgment theory, but in a broader sense, as denoting personal relevance in terms of how information relates to an ongoing or persisting task as compared to a completed task (Greenwald, 1980). This provides for greater precision in segmenting a campaign audience.

"Personal relevance enhances motivation to process issue-relevant arguments" (Petty and Cacioppo, 1986, p. 149). Messages about health prevention, for example, should be most actively processed by individuals who either are experiencing, or have previously encountered, the condition that the campaign message is designed to prevent. Messages about heart ailments should be most salient for and sought after by those who have, have had, or have been exposed to heart conditions. Similarly, skin cancer prevention messages are more likely to be actively attended to by individuals who have, have had, or have been exposed to skin cancer.

Individuals who have had personal experience with a health issue have a schema for the issue, are involved with the topic, and should find content about it to be personally relevant. Studies of patients' health-seeking behavior have demonstrated that the persistence of a problem leads to exposure to medical institutions and medical doctors, but only after individuals first try home remedies and the local pharmacy (Low, 1981). Thus, personal relevance may not only lead to active processing of messages about the attitude object, but to information-seeking behaviors as well.

Messages that contain personally relevant information should be more actively attended by receivers, and receivers may become more committed to a point of view with regard to the issue. View Figure 4-1 again as we return to the example of college students and the topic of tuition. The topic of tuition increases should be personally relevant to college students. However, only some students will find the topic either interesting or important. Individuals whose parents pay the tuition bill are less likely to regard the topic as interesting or important, although it is still personally relevant. As noted above, some college students may be committed to a point of view regarding this issue, and also view it as interesting, important, and personally relevant. The more specific information that a campaigner is able to obtain about an audience's views regarding an issue, the more campaign messages may be tailored specifically to the audience.

Self-reference   The motivation to actively process message content is also affected by information that specifically refers to a receiver's personal characteristics and traits, such as age, ethnicity, gender, or income level. This information is better remembered, a concept termed the self-reference effect (Greenwald and Pratkanis, 1984). Audience segmentation partly relates to this issue too, as campaigners base messages on and call attention to particular variables associated with specific audience segments, thus expecting this to draw attention to the messages for those individuals who fit the description. Politicians call attention to the needs of the middle class, marketers call attention to problems such as the "frizzies," and social action campaigners alert women that harassment is illegal. In each instance, the reference to a specific characteristic remands attention to, and more active information processing of, message content.

Several theoretical perspectives can be used to explain why self-reference situations invoke more active message processing. When messages specifically refer either to an individual trait or characteristic, or to ongoing tasks, then the self may become an object of conscious awareness and evaluation (Wicklund and Duval, 1971). To refer to a task such as parenting, for example, may cause parents in the audience to consciously think about their own parenting behavior and to evaluate it within a framework of what the message content has to say about such behavior. To refer to individuals with fair complexions during messages that promote sun screen may make such receivers self-conscious about their own behavior.

When individuals are motivated to be in an objective state of self-awareness, Bem's self-perception theory (Bem, 1965, 1967, 1972) proposes that they may evaluate their own behavior as a way to determine their attitudes. This self-perception hypothesis has been found to primarily apply to individuals with poorly defined prior attitudes (Chaiken and Baldwin, 1981). Thus, the finding that an audience is neutral in their attitudes about a campaign topic that otherwise is personally relevant to them is strategically significant information for campaigners. It allows them to construct messages that identify particular behaviors as a means to invoke more active thought about a personally relevant issue. Once an audience is thinking about the behavior, thoughts about attitudes should occur as well. Campaigners also may want to indicate what attitudes specific behaviors suggest. Assuming that the attitudes and the behaviors are not the ones that either the campaigners or the audience want to display, the stage has been set for specific influence to occur.

As an example of how the self-perception hypothesis might guide the efforts of campaigners, suppose that a parents' group determines that many licensed day-care centers fail to supervise infants, choosing instead to leave them unattended, often crying, in cribs. The group decides to conduct a social action campaign to change the situation. As part of the campaign, they invoke reference to all parents who leave infants in licensed day-care centers. The campaigners also suggest that these parents assume that a license means that the center is regularly and rigorously inspected, and meets certain criteria, including supervision of infants. Such messages should elicit more active processing in the targeted audience. The suggested attitude, for those in the audience who behave in the described fashion and who have never really thought about their beliefs, does not appear to be one that would be rejected. It implies nothing offensive. Thus, the stage is set for campaigners to provide evidence contrary to what receivers believe, expect receivers to thoughtfully process the evidence, and to produce positive action by audience members.

For individuals who are committed to a position, attribution approaches may explain how we go about trying to understand and explain our own and others' behaviors when we are in a state of objective self-awareness. Such theories suggest that we act much like naive scientists, in order to determine what causes and consequences are associated with behavior (Harvey, Ickes, and Kidd, 1976). "It is a special feature of social interaction that each participant is both a causal agent and an attributer. His own behavior may be a cause of the behavior he is trying to understand and explain" (Kelley, 1972, p. 1).

We may explain our own behavior as parents, for example, in terms of how we have behaved in similar situations in the past, thus exemplifying the covariation principle (Kelley, 1973). This principle asserts that effects are attributed to causes with which they covary over time. It emphasizes the importance of prior beliefs on current information search and assessment. So, if a parent of three children has left two infants at a day-care center with no harm, the parent may be positively disposed to day-care centers and negatively disposed to messages that depict day-care centers in a disparaging way.

The covariation principle has been observed in a variety of settings. Consumers, for example, may hold beliefs that strike at the very heart of commercial campaigns designed to focus on low price as a positive feature of some products. In a study of 175 women shoppers at a suburban mall, for example, respondents were asked to provide answers to questions that measured beliefs about the relationship between price and quality for various products (John, Scott, and Bettman, 1986). Findings demonstrated that shoppers who believed that price is a true reflection of quality chose brands with higher average prices than shoppers who did not hold these beliefs. Campaign messages emphasizing lower prices probably would boomerang with such audiences.

In situations where we do not have multiple observations of ourselves and others to explain behaviors, attribution theory indicates that we employ a discounting principle (Kelley, 1973), whereby the potential of a particular cause is discounted in the presence of other plausible causes. Again, assuming that parents have formed attitudes about day-care centers, the revelation that their infants were unattended may be explained as an effect that was caused by the illness of staff members and employees on call, perhaps due to a flu outbreak or a holiday season. In short, one might construct a number of possible ways to explain the lack of supervision, particularly when one is committed to the point of view that the licensed day-care centers provide appropriate care for children. The possibility that audience members will invoke the discounting principle should be weighed by campaigners, who might deal with it by preempting the alternative explanations an audience might accept, besides the explanation that campaigners want the audience to adopt.

Egocentric Bias   The notion of egocentric bias is the final dimension of receivers' involvement. This condition relates to the practice of viewing the content of messages in relation to oneself, and focusing on one's personal needs and interests with very little or no regard for others. When this tendency relates to audience members' age and

---

FEEDBACK

Scenario: You are planning to launch a campaign concerning U.S. immigration policy. Your formative research reveals a sizable audience segment consisting of people seeking U.S. citizenship, but an even larger segment of people who agree with the statement that, "The United States has a responsibility to its own citizens first."

1. Based on just this information, assess each audience segment for the possibility that it contains a sizable proportion of individuals who are:
   a. involved in the issue;
   b. committed to a point of view;
   c. ego involved; or
   d. egocentrically biased?
2. Justify your assessment.

---

stage of cognitive development, the effect is referred to as egocentrism and affects the ability to actively process information (Bee, 1985). This will be discussed in more detail under the topic of receiver variables that affect the ability to actively process information. What is important at this time is the impact of this concept on message processing. When receivers' prior knowledge of an issue produces extreme or intense views regarding an attitude object, the motivation to actively process information is likely to be enhanced, but the net result is often biased elaboration (Petty and Cacioppo, 1986). Individuals who hold extreme views rapidly form strong judgments during information processing episodes (Schul, and Burnstein, 1990).

As with ego involvement, the finding that audience members are egocentrically biased about a campaign topic is important information. Whereas favorable biases suggest that audiences will be positively disposed toward message content, it does not necessarily mean that they will understand that message content applies to them. Unfavorable biases must also be addressed. If a negative consequence can be logically linked to the receiver's view, and personal responsibility invoked, campaigners may move toward a reduction in the egocentric bias.

Discrepant Information and Dissonance

We previously discussed two ways that information may affect schema: by changing the content of the schema or the structure of the schema. Often, receivers' interest in an issue leads them to actively process and seek information about a topic, sometimes resulting in exposure to inconsistent information.

How do receivers handle discrepant information? Bandura's (1977b) social learning theory indicates that when individuals encounter information that is inconsistent, they turn either to their past experience or observations of others' behaviors to help resolve the discrepancy. In this manner existing schemas play an important role in determining which information will be internalized and which will be discarded. Smokers, for example, may encounter not only the information that links smoking with lung cancer, but the positive correlation between lung cancer and heredity. A smoker faced with such discrepant information may be aware of a family member in their seventies, who has smoked two packs of cigarettes a day for more than five decades. This may suggest to the smoker that the more salient piece of information is the link between heredity and cancer.

One objective of conducting formative research is to isolate relevant discrepant information that an audience may hold. When an individual encounters two discrepant pieces of information, and one supports a point of view that the receiver is committed to, while the other does not, cognitive dissonance theory posits that the two inconsistent or incompatible thoughts will produce uncomfortable arousal, or dissonance (Festinger, 1957; 1964). Brehm and Cohen (1962) note that, "the concept of commitment helps to specify the point at which a dissonant relationship occurs" (p. 300). Dissonance is a form of arousal which may motivate the individual to seek information, although it also could invoke one or more selectivity mechanisms as a vehicle to cope with inconsistent cognitions (Cotton, 1985). These mechanisms include selective exposure, attention, perception, and retention, which respectively involve avoiding, ignoring, distorting, and forgetting discrepant information.

Most research supports the position that, when a person's cognitions and/or behaviors are inconsistent, they are likely to be in a highly active mental state. However, this may or may not result in attempts to reduce arousal. In some situations, people may actually prefer dissonant to consonant information (Cotton, 1985; Frey, 1986). For example, when individuals are capable of counterarguing dissonant information, they may prefer to receive it, as one means to elaborate on arguments that support their own point of view. Also, if people expect to encounter situations in the future that are similar to the one that produced dissonance, the dissonant information may be viewed as useful. In addition, when individuals are already familiar with consonant information, the dissonant information may be preferred because it is novel. Finally, if a norm of fairness is perceived to exist, people may prefer dissonant information, so that they have heard both sides. "Dissonance motivation only occurs when the individual labels his state of arousal negatively and attributes that arousal to his having freely produced an aversive consequence" (Cooper and Fazio, 1984, p. 256).

Thus, campaigners try to identify not only the pieces of inconsistent information held by an audience, but the level of commitment and consequences associated with the situation. For example, social action campaigners targeting a state's daycare system may determine that parents perceive their children to receive quality care at affordable prices, despite the fact that once in awhile, their children may not be closely supervised due to staffing problems. In this situation, an aversive consequence such as the kidnaping of an infant, and the responsibility that parents hold due to their awareness of problems of supervision, might promote more active thought about the campaigners' message. Indeed, personal responsibility is another receiver variable that is associated with more active message processing.

Personal Responsibility
Behavior is perceived to have objective consequences for people (Triandis, 1979). When a person believes that he/she is personally responsible for an unwanted

consequence, there is greater motivation to process issue-relevant arguments (Petty and Cacioppo, 1986). As a result, an important step in dissonance arousal is to get the receiver to accept responsibility for the adverse consequence (Cooper and Fazio, 1984). The individual must perceive personal responsibility for an unwanted consequence for dissonance to occur.

Campaigners should seek to enhance an audience's perception of personal responsibility for an adverse consequence, which in turn, triggers receiver dissonance, and thus more active message processing. Campaigns to solicit contributions to combat world hunger initially had to overcome the perception that the problem was overwhelming, and therefore that Americans were helpless to affect it. In response, most

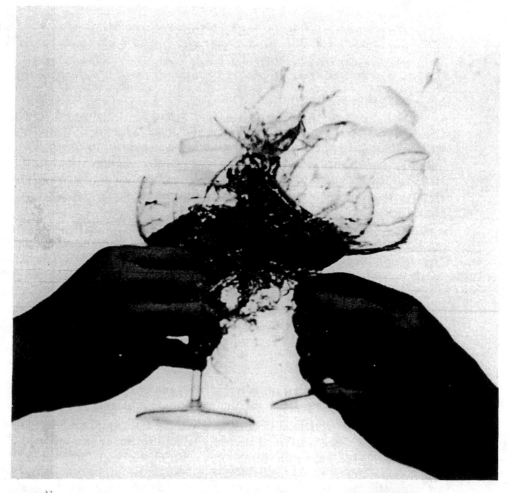

FIGURE 4–2 "Crashing Glasses" Television PSA to Combat Drinking and Driving

Source: Courtesy of The Advertising Council, Inc.

hunger campaigns shifted tactics, appealing to receivers for small contributions to save a single child. This approach placed the responsibility for the plight of a single child on the receiver, giving them the choice to act or not. Research indicates that the perception of responsibility is enhanced if receivers believe that they possess choices (Converse and Cooper, 1979; White and Gerard, 1981).

Other social action campaigns have responded to the need to make receivers take personal responsibility for the consequences of their actions. One of the first was U.S. Forest Service's, Smokey Bear campaign, featuring the familiar slogan, "Only *you* can prevent forest fires." DDB Needham's Mike Rogers (cited in "As Creatives Rate Them," 1991, p. A–10) explains the success of the Smokey Bear campaign in terms of personal responsibility.

This campaign is the first and maybe the best ever in stressing individual responsibility—only you—delivered by a likable character who makes us want to help. But its real brilliance is that while it targets everyone, it gives kids a special sense of duty and makes them believe they can make a difference. They can. And this campaign has. (Rogers, 1991, pp. A–10)

The shift in tactics in the campaign to reduce drinking and driving provides another example. For years, campaign messages targeted drinking drivers, who, invoking the selectivity tactics described previously, refused to accept personal responsibility that *their* drinking and driving might cause a serious accident. Indeed, some research found that these messages resulted in a boomerang effect, such that targeted receivers developed more positive attitudes about drinking and driving (Kohn, Goodstadt, Cook, Sheppard, and Chan, 1982).

As a result, the campaign changed tactics, targeting the friends of people who drink and drive, on the grounds that they would be less susceptible to selectivity. The approach of the current campaign is to motivate individuals to take personal responsibility for their friends' behaviors. The message shown in Figure 4–2, "crashing glasses," concludes with the slogan, "Drinking and driving can kill a friendship." In commenting on the success of the campaign, one analyst observed that, "It's a beautifully simple and deadly concept, and makes a hero of anyone who is willing to keep a friend from driving drunk" ("Expert Ratings," 1991, p. A–12).

Network Density
The density of audience members' social networks is another variable that determines message processing. For example, human service programs for low income groups sometimes have resulted in minimal use and high dropout rates. Research has shown that a dense social network is inversely related to use of many services (Birkel and Reppucci, 1983). Individuals with more people in their social networks use those interpersonal resources to meet their needs for support and information, rather than seeking or using other services. If campaigners learn that an audience's network contains many members, they should attempt to include network members in campaign messages and strategies. Conversely, the finding that an audience's network contains few members

should lead to careful evaluation of media messages that may compete with the campaign's messages.

Receiver Variables Affecting the Ability to Process Information

Receivers' motivation to actively process information may sometimes be inhibited and at other times facilitated by receivers' ability to actively process information. Receivers' egocentrism and transductive reasoning processes, their education and level of expertise, in addition to their perceptions of self-efficacy are important variables to consider when campaigners are making decisions about how actively they want an audience to process messages. No matter how much the campaigners would like the audience to attend to and elaborate the arguments contained in specific messages, if receivers lack the cognitive abilities, they probably will not get the intended meaning from the message content. Moreover, if the content of a message is beyond the receivers' level of education or expertise (e.g., an important reason that some patients do not understand conversations with their physicians), then receivers may be motivated to actively process message content but, again, lack the ability to do so. Finally, there are many situations in which receivers have been found to be motivated to actively process information, and may even attempt to actively process message content, but fail to do so because they do not perceive themselves to have the abilities or resources to complete the process. Perceptions of inefficacy also affect the amount of mental effort individuals put into such pursuits.

Egocentrism and Transductive Reasoning

When we examined receiver variables that may motivate active processing of information, we identified egocentric bias as one variable that may facilitate receivers' motivation to mindfully attend to message content. In addition to this, the receivers' stage of cognitive development may inhibit or facilitate their ability to process specific messages. The preoperational level of Piaget's cognitive development theory, a stage theory that represents the levels of individuals' ability to use information, addresses the limited intellectual ability of many young children (Bee, 1985; Shaffer, 1988).

Children's egocentrism, or self-centered view of reality, contributes to interaction that is focused on single, salient aspects or features of situations; egocentric individuals are unable to conceive how something may look any different from the way it appears at the moment (Gross, 1985; Shaffer, 1988). In addition, children in the preoperational stage of development, which is characterized by egocentrism, possess limited ability to think logically. As a result, thought is highly transductive or intuitive in nature, thereby failing to recognize cause-effect relationships (Shaffer, 1988). Children, and others in this stage of cognitive development, reason from the specific, or particular, to the specific or particular. Individuals in this stage move toward development of proficiency at using images and symbols to represent objects and events (Gross, 1985).

The concept of egocentrism provides a useful framework for evaluating advertising effects on children who display obesity, anorexia, bulimia, and iron deficiency due to poor nutritional habits, including snacking (Story, 1990). The latter was found to be related to the amount of time spent watching television, leading to the recommendation that critical viewing skills be taught to children so they can interpret information received from commercials and programs (Story, 1990).

In conclusion, some audiences, particularly young children who are receiving increasing attention, not only from commercial campaigners, but also from social action campaigners who seek to instill a sense of personal responsibility for their own health, may be unable to process message content in an active, elaborated fashion. Such audiences may only make literal interpretations of campaign information. If this is anticipated, perhaps messages should be designed that are explicit and direct in their intent.

Education and Level of Expertise
Some research has shown that education is directly related to active use of information, evaluation of alternatives, and longer decision time in purchasing situations (Gronhaug, 1974). In addition, the receiver's level of expertise in terms of the subject matter being presented affects his/her ability to actively process information. Thus, an expert is more able to use information which is at odds with prior knowledge (Fiske, Kinder, and Larter, 1983). Therefore, campaigners should assess the education level and topic expertise of the target audience to insure the potential for active processing of message content.

Self-Efficacy
Self-efficacy also influences a person's ability to actively process campaign messages. In social learning theory, Bandura (1977b) conceptualized expectancy as the tendency to anticipate the outcomes stressed in learning. Two types of expectancy are described. Efficacy expectations concern a person's conviction that a behavior can be performed, whereas outcomes' expectations are probability estimates that a certain behavior will result in a particular outcome (Bandura, 1977). Efficacy expectations, in particular, are important to campaigners because they determine how vigorously a person will strive to attain an outcome, which affects how much effort they will put in to message processing. Unless receivers perceive that they are capable of performing a behavior, they are unlikely to attend to messages on the topic.

Contingency rules theory (Smith, 1982) is useful for those who seek to increase audience perceptions of self-efficacy. The theory posits that given a goal, a context, and a set of possible actions to achieve the goal, individuals will perceive certain choices to be more acceptable or effective than others. Smith develops the notion of self-evaluative rules as a way to explain what choices will be more acceptable. These rules relate to an individual's personal standards, including his/her self-identity and the image he/she wants to project. Therefore, recommendations to enhance receiver perceptions of self-efficacy must operate within his/her self-evaluative rule structure. People who view themselves as unaggressive, for example, are unlikely to accept messages that urge more aggressive behavior to achieve a personal goal, regardless of the potential efficacy of that behavior.

Smith (1982) posits that people also have beliefs concerning what actions will be advantageous in certain situations in order to achieve their goals, and campaigners should evaluate how to affect the audience's perceptions of these within a framework of existing self-evaluative rules for the purpose of increasing perceptions of self-efficacy and thus active message processing. Campaigners all too often assume that an audience knows how to behave, when, in fact, they lack specific advice about how to attain the goals campaigners have for them and they may have for themselves.

For example, patients in a drug and alcohol unit of a large public hospital in New York City received 90 minutes of education about AIDS. The most commonly asked questions after these presentations were: "Where can I get tested for AIDS?"; "Where do I get free condoms?" (Kramer, Cancellieri, Ottomanelli, Mosely, Fine, and Bihari, 1989). One might wonder why the answers to these questions were not contained in the messages communicated to the patients. One might also wonder how many other patients had the same questions but failed to ask for the information.

There are many considerations that shape the instrumental activity of campaign communication. Numerous receiver variables affect what is appropriate for a campaign's objectives, and what kind of messages are best to attain these objectives. Often, the receivers will be motivated to actively attend messages and have the ability to do so. In other situations, receivers do not have the motivation or the ability to actively process messages. Some specific variables concerning message construction may facilitate receivers' motivation and/or ability to actively process campaign messages.

Message Variables Affecting Information Processing

Mindful processing of information suggests that a receiver is voluntarily attending to a message in a way that stifles the first response and may lead to more differentiation. Campaigners often have this goal in mind as they design messages. However, designing effective campaign messages concerns more than simply determining the receiver's condition and then writing the message accordingly.

If campaigners want an audience to attend to messages, but the audience is not interested in the topic, for example, then messages should be designed with the clear purpose of attaining audience interest in the topic. If an audience lacks expertise required to process message content, then design of the message should be tailored to their level of understanding, and so on.

Several message variables have been examined in isolation, suggesting guidelines about the likelihood of active processing by audiences. Among the message variables that have been found to affect active message processing are the quality of message arguments, information utility, questions, and repetition.

Perceived Expectations

The theoretical framework of Burgoon's expectancy theory (Burgoon and Miller, 1985) provides useful guidelines for message design. Expectancy theory posits that people have expectations about how others will use language based on societal norms for use. Violations of those expectations are likely to be noticed, and should provoke active message processing. However, such violations may produce either positive or negative impact on persuasion. When a message conforms more closely to societal norms than is expected, the theory proposes that a positive violation occurs, facilitating persuasive outcomes (Burgoon and Miller, 1985). However, when a message deviates from expected conformity with societal norms, a negative violation occurs, inhibiting persuasive outcomes.

If receivers anticipate that a message will be more intense and emotional than societal norms dictate, for example, they may establish a readiness not to listen based on their expectation. If instead, receivers experience the message and find it to be presented in a rational and logical fashion, thus conforming more closely to societal norms for rational behavior and speech, then it should facilitate active processing and persuasive effects. Such propositions are important guidelines for campaigners to consider in reviewing strategic designs for messages aimed at specific audiences.

FIGURE 4–3   Finesse Hair Spray Advertisement

Source: Courtesy of FINESSE and Helene Curtis, Inc.

Quality of Message Arguments

The quality of the arguments used in a message is always a requisite factor in persuasion, at least in most situations with active message processing. Petty and Cacioppo (1984) make this point, maintaining that argument quality is more important when individuals are highly involved. This makes sense, of course, since such receivers are more likely to be motivated to actively attend and process the information in the first place, and thus more likely to notice if message content is inadequate. Research supports the position that more involved receivers will attend to the quality of a message (Borgida and Howard-Pitney, 1983; Petty, Cacioppo, and Goldman, 1981). These receivers are more likely to actively process any information about the topic, and therefore to notice and assess the adequacy of the arguments contained in the message. In this context, quality message content further enhances attention to the message. The application and practice of designing quality arguments for campaign messages will be discussed further in Chapter 8.

Message Stimulus

Learning theories, which have been identified as one group of persuasion theories most often associated with systematic message processing (Pechmann and Stewart, 1989), suggest that the quality of a message stimulus affects both message processing and persuasive outcome. This is particularly true under conditions in which receivers lack sufficient information.

A classical conditioning model of learning theories pairs some neutral stimulus (e.g., word, phrase, or campaign slogan) with a stimulus that elicits a reflexive response, the purpose being to form a connection in the receiver's mind (Thornburg, 1984). Examine Figure 4–3 to consider how advertisers might utilize such an approach.

The hair spray advertisement presumes that the audience has already learned two pieces of information. First, hair spray (stimulus) holds (response) hair in place. Second, hair that has been sprayed (stimulus) with hair spray is stiff and unpleasant to touch (response). The new connection to learn is that FINESSE Hair Spray (stimulus) is both pleasing (response) and soft to the touch (response).

An operant or instrumental conditioning model of learning theories introduces the consequence of behavior into the learning equation. This predicts a behavioral response to be contingent upon the learned connection to a desired reward or the avoidance of an undesirable punishment. This approach has been used in seat belt campaign messages, for example, where the stimulus is safety and the desired response is to wear seat belts, which is reinforced by indicating that the failure to wear seat belts may result in negative consequences. Such approaches to constructing quality message arguments are quite common.

Learning theories also provide useful explanations for the effectiveness of passive approaches to influence. They will be discussed in this context in greater detail in Chapter 5.

Information Utility

Swanson (1976) views the concept of information utility as a two-dimensional construct consisting of decisional utility and interpersonal utility. Decisional utility

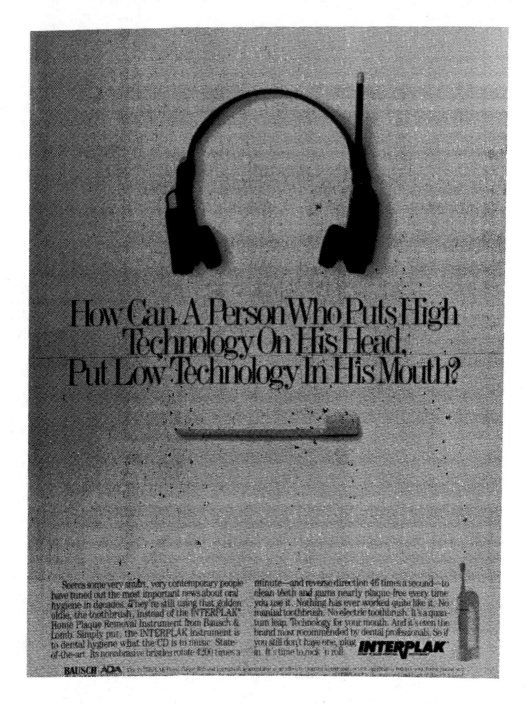

FIGURE 4–4 Bausch and Lomb's Print Advertisement for Interplak

Source: Courtesy of Bausch and Lomb Oral Care Division, Inc.

concerns the ability to use information in making a decision, whereas interpersonal utility deals with whether or not information is useful to the individual as something to communicate about with others. In more important commercial decisions, decisional utility takes precedence. In this context, consumers who require additional information are likely to more actively attend to messages that provide answers to their specific questions (Simonson, Huber, and Payne, 1988). Campaigners interested in invoking active message processing will emphasize the informational utility of message content.

Questions

Mindfulness may also be promoted by introducing a counter-attitudinal message with a question, which leads to more intensive processing of content than a simple opening statement, a finding that is supported even in low involvement situations (Burnkrant and Howard, 1984). Examine Figure 4–4.

The advertisement in Figure 4–4 poses the question, "How can a person who puts high technology on his head, put low technology in his mouth?" The question is designed to facilitate active message processing, and will do so for low involved receivers, probably the clear majority of toothbrush users. However, this strategy carries a risk for high involved receivers, people who take dental hygiene seriously and are committed to the use of a particular brand of toothbrush. Research indicates that use of opening questions can produce distraction in highly involved people (Petty, Cacioppo, and Heesacker, 1981). Thus, opening questions can be an effective tool to facilitate active message processing, except in those circumstances where the audience includes large numbers of highly involved receivers.

Message Repetition: Frequency and Recency

Research about message repetition indicates that moderate amounts of repetition facilitate message elaboration, perhaps by increasing the ability to engage in issue-relevant thought during additional exposure (Petty and Cacioppo, 1979). Also, learning theory posits that a stimulus must be presented frequently and recently enough in the presence of the response for the pairing to be learned. The presentation of message content frequently enough to attain adequate levels of comprehension and retention is associated with more active message processing. Frequency of exposure to a message is a prerequisite for full elaboration of the arguments contained in a message stimulus. The questions of reach and frequency are considered in more detail in Chapter 5.

Source and Channel Variables Affecting Information Processing

In addition to making decisions about the message content, campaigners must decide who shall be the source of the message, and how the message will be delivered to various audiences. The importance of the source to the success of a message, therefore, must be considered from the perspective of whether the source is expected to: (1) blend in with the message content and cause little effect in the audience's consideration or active thought about the message, (2) prompt greater attention and active thought about the message content; or (3) direct more attention to the source and increase the active thought about the source, while reducing active thought about the message. Three source variables in particular should be considered with regard to the issue of active message processing: credibility, source incentive value, and number of message sources.

Source Credibility

Source credibility is an important contributor to persuasive effects. In fact, source credibility is one variable that may increase a subject's message-relevant thought (Heesacker, Petty, and Cacioppo, 1983). When selecting spokespersons for campaigns, campaigners may desire to emphasize source credibility, which should focus greater attention to the message and content and more mindful processing, particularly if combined with message variables that promote active processing.

Deciding who shall be the source of a message is a very important decision for campaigners. Refer again to Figure 4–3. The individuals in this message are not recognized celebrities. However, selection of these sources suggests that an audience of a certain age and ethnicity, and perhaps even outlook on life (the sources could be in an office setting, for example) may be more likely to actively attend to the message content. Those receivers who do not like the source are less likely to attend to the message, a principle claimed by Heider (1946) in balance theory. Balance theory posits that receivers' attitudes toward persons and issues affect each other. An attitude toward an issue may change an attitude toward the person associated with the issue, or an attitude toward a person may change an attitude toward an issue.

One research application of balance theory in a political campaign had subjects assess whether new roommates would like or dislike each other based on each of their attitudes toward 1964 presidential candidates Goldwater and Johnson (Burnstein, 1967). After several weeks, researchers identified a clear case of positivity in that negative changed to positive more than the reverse. As predicted by balance theory, subjects in the study made the least number of changes necessary in order to achieve positivity or balance.

The importance of the source of a message to the success of the campaign, therefore, must be considered from the perspective of whether the source will: (1) blend in with the message content and produce little effect on the audience's consideration of active thought about the message, (2) prompt greater attention and active thought about the message content; or (3) direct more attention to the source, while reducing active thought about the message.

Source's Incentive Value

Another source variable that promotes more active thought about a campaign's information content is the source's incentive value. "Incentive value is defined as the belief that other persons can satisfy certain needs that one has or serve as potential sources of support" (Kellermann and Reynolds, 1990, p. 15). Again, this is a concept from the theoretical framework of uncertainty reduction theory (Berger and Calabrese, 1975). The source's incentive value appears to be one additional means of facilitating active message processing. When a receiver believes that a source may satisfy some need, the motivation to attend to what the source says should be greater.

Number of Message Sources

A final source factor that can promote more active message processing is the number of message sources. Some research has demonstrated that increasing the number of sources of a message enhances thinking about message content (Harkins and Petty, 1981). The outcomes associated with this increased mindfulness, however, depend foremost on the quality of message arguments. Thus, more sources can enhance the mindful processing, and if the quality of the content is good, facilitate persuasiveness.

Channel Use

The research and theorizing concerned with channel variables and message processing has received less attention. Many of the modes of influence are quite recent and have not been thoroughly examined. Primarily, a comparison between print and television media provides most of the knowledge base in this area. Mediated and interpersonal modes have also been compared, but most experts consider both as necessary to successfully disseminate campaign information, and both may promote more active message processing.

Various findings support the notion that written messages, particularly if composed of difficult material, are processed more mindfully than the same message via audio- or videotaped modalities (Chaiken and Eagly, 1976). Targeted receivers, however, also must possess the ability to process the message actively. Thus, the campaigner should consider audience expertise when a message is likely to contain difficult material. It has also been shown that campaigners can employ certain techniques in message construction to increase the chances that viewers will process television more mindfully (Salomon and Leigh, 1984).

Conclusion

In conclusion, if the goal is to invoke mindful processing of campaign messages, previous theory and research suggests a number of variables that may facilitate or inhibit this process. However, mindful processing may not always be the most effective way to promote a campaign's goals. There are times when mindless processing of messages may be more desirable.

Various biological, psychological, and social factors affect the cognitions associated with language use. Sometimes, mental activity leads to new elaborations, but often, it builds on already existing cognitive structures. What must be reckoned with, then, is that people will sometimes, depending on some variables that have been isolated and others that have not, flex their mental capacity, even pushing it to new limits. To be better equipped to effectively plan campaign activities, those situations in which more mindful or mindless processing is more likely should be identified with regard to each audience to be targeted in any particular campaign.

Suggestions for Further Reading

Atkin C. K., and Arkin, E. B. (1990). Issues and initiatives in communicating health information. In C. K. Atkin and L. Wallack (Eds.), *Mass Communication and Public Health* (pp. 13–40). Newbury Park, CA: Sage Publications.

Cooper, J., and Fazio J. (1984). A new look at dissonance theory. *Advances in Experimental Social Psychology, 17,* 229–266.

Dervin, B. (1989). Audience as listener and learner, teacher and confidante: The sense–making approach. In R. E. Rice and C. K. Atkin (Eds.), *Public Communication Campaigns* (2nd ed., pp. 67–86). Newbury Park, CA: Sage Publications.

Moore, D.W. (1987). Political campaigns and the knowledge-gap hypothesis. *Public Opinion Quarterly, 51,* 186–200.

Petty R. E., and Cacioppo, J. T. (1986). The elaboration likelihood model of persuasion. *Advances in Experimental Social Psychology, 19,* 123–205.

Passive Approaches to Receivers

"In nearly all cases. . . . feeling is not free of thought, nor is thought free of feelings . . . thoughts enter feelings at various stages of the affective sequence, and the converse is true for cognitions."
—*R. B. ZAJONC, PSYCHOLOGY PROFESSOR*
(ZAJONC, 1980, P. 154)

". . . [M]any broadcast ads persuade by evoking heuristic and/or affective processing rather than by stimulating purely systematic processing."
—*CONNIE PECHMANN AND DAVID STEWART,*
MARKETING PROFESSORS
(PECHMANN AND STEWART, 1989, P. 54)

We observed in Chapter 3 that receivers respond uniquely to persuasive appeals. What it is that motivates them to attend a message, and what causes them to respond, varies depending upon the receiver, message approach, and communication context. In Chapter 4 we examined the role of mindful message processing in campaigns, describing various theories that explain the role of cognition in influence. This chapter will focus on more mindless processing, describing the assumptions, theories, and strategies that explain the nature and impact of awareness and affect in campaign influence.

Chapter 4 employed Langer's continuum of awareness (Langer, 1978) and Petty and Cacioppo's ELM model (Petty and Cacioppo, 1986) to distinguish mindful and mindless message processing. Others have drawn the same distinction between message processing that is more- or less-involving, although specific terminology varies across the information-processing literature. Whereas Petty and Cacioppo (1986) use the terms central and peripheral processing, for example, Chaiken (1980) employs systematic and heuristic processing.

Whatever the chosen terminology, the two message processing approaches operate on very different assumptions about influence. The active, or high elaborative model assumes that receivers are motivated to attend communication, and that they will consciously process messages. As Fink, Monahan, and Kaplowitz (1989, p. 747) observe,

"Cognitive theorists believe that an individual must be able to identify a stimulus, classify it, and/or recognize it, for a mere exposure effect to occur." Further, the active model assumes that influence follows a hierarchical path in which each step is a necessary, if not sufficient, precondition to the next, working through the following stages: awareness ———➤ learning ———➤ attitude formation and/or change ———➤ action.

This chapter will examine passive or low elaborative message processing. Specific strategies and theories of influence will be discussed, with examples provided to illustrate them. Due to reasons that will be explained below, most of the examples used will be drawn from nationally televised commercial advertising campaigns. The chapter will answer the questions posed in Table 5–1.

The Low Elaborative Model

The passive, heuristic, or low elaborative model operates on very different assumptions about the process of influence. This model assumes that receivers are often unmotivated, and thus less involved in message processing. Under these circumstances, they are unlikely to actively process messages, and if messages exert a persuasive impact, they do so mindlessly (Chaiken, 1987).

The process of influence thus bypasses active cognition. As Chaiken (1987, p. 3) describes the heuristic processing model, ". . . opinion change in response to persuasive communications is often the outcome of only a minimal amount of information processing." Further, the notion of mindless processing has received considerable

TABLE 5–1   Questions about Passive Message Processing

1. What circumstances contributed to the initial formulation of the passive, low-elaborative model of influence?
2. Why is the passive model used more often in commercial as opposed to political or social action campaigns?
3. What changes in marketing and media contributed to greater use of the passive model in commercial campaigns?
4. What strategies do campaigners use to plant, and to prime, messages in receivers?
5. Distinguish classical and instrumental conditioning.
6. Explain how messages influence receivers using the classical conditioning and instrumental conditioning explanations for the role of awareness in persuasion.
7. Which stimulus factors make the greatest contribution to influence?
8. Explain how messages influence receivers using the learning and motivational explanations of affect in persuasion?
9. What are peripheral cues? Under what circumstances are they relevant in persuasion?
10. Why are source factors particularly relevant in commercial messages using television as opposed to other media?
11. How do commercial campaigners use source factors in modern television advertising?
12. What is the relationship between cognition and affect?

support in research. In reviewing this literature, Pechmann and Stewart (1989, p. 40) conclude that, "relatively permanent attitude changes can occur without systematic processing–without awareness, comprehension, and evaluation of arguments that support the advocated position or brand."

Evolution of the Concept

The low involvement perspective was originally conceived by Krugman almost three decades ago. In a seminal address, Krugman (1965) theorized that most successful influence occurs in low involvement circumstances, where our minds are virtually at rest. Krugman argued that this was particularly true of most commercial advertising, transmitted via television, which exerts an impact on viewers, but in a different way than was previously thought. Krugman (1965, p. 355) claimed artificial distinctions had, in effect, ". . . blinded us to the existence of two entirely different ways of experiencing and being influenced by [the] mass media." The two ways that Krugman referred to are distinguished by low and high personal involvement.

Krugman (1977) and Wright (1974) subsequently proved that much television communication generated very few cognitive responses, but did affect viewer behaviors. This process is an incremental one, however, as Salmon (1986, p. 248) describes: "Through the process of low involvement learning, an individual gradually becomes aware of an advertised product, purchases the product, and develops a favorable attitude toward the product." Salmon adds that, "Behavior is a step–not an outcome–in the overall change process."

While Krugman's thesis constituted an important first step toward an alternative, passive, conceptualization of persuasion, his own formulization of involvement was subsequently questioned, in part because it generalized about media forms irrespective of differences in content (Salmon, 1986). Nonetheless, more recent research suggests that television does manifest a unique symbol system (Chesebro, 1984; Meyrowitz, 1985; Salomon, 1987), which alters the process of influence (Pfau, 1990). We will return to this thesis later in this chapter. However, most scholars now accept Krugman's underlying assumption. As Batra and Ray (1985, p. 15) put it, "There do seem to be two different 'routes' to attitude change."

Primary Application to Commercial Campaigns

The remainder of this chapter will examine the theories and strategies of this low involvement, passive model, focussing on the role of awareness and affect as linchpins in the process of influence. The specific strategies and examples will be drawn from commercial campaigns that rely primarily on the television medium to carry their messages to receivers, precisely because they illustrate the passive alternative most clearly.

Political and social action campaigns tend to employ more active, cognitive approaches to influence. With some exceptions, in the political campaign context most messages, whether carried via news, speeches, debates, and even advertising, presuppose higher receiver involvement, and thus are more likely to contain specific content. Calder (1979, p. 27) slightly overstates the case, arguing that, "The individual is motivated to think about candidates over a period of time. He is set to make a rational evaluation, to weigh the positives and the negatives."

As a result, even the 30-second televised political spot, which has been subjected to an increasing barrage of criticism for polluting the democratic process with negativism (Jamieson, 1988), contains considerable candidate image and issue content (Patterson and McClure, 1976; Hofstetter and Zukin, 1979; Joslyn, 1980; Just, Crigler, and Wallach, 1990).

This is not to suggest that political advertisements are exclusively content vessels. The visual component of televised political spots plays a key role (Kaid and Davidson, 1986), and many of the spots are designed to elicit an emotive response (Kern, 1989). Indeed, Abelson, Kinder, Peters, and Fiske (1982) report that feelings contribute significantly to attitudes about candidates.

Nonetheless, most political spot advertisements assume more active receiver processing, and contain substantive content. As Berkman and Kitch (1986, p. 163) maintain, "In contrast to the viewer of product ads, the viewer of political ads seeks, and expects to find, information contained in the advertisement and attempts to evaluate its truth."

Social action campaigns also are inclined to rely on more active receiver processing. Health campaigns, in particular, have been largely information-oriented. Wallack (1989, p. 366), summarizing past approaches to health promotion, concludes that, ". . . we tend to define fundamental problems as a basic lack of information and then to rely on the mass media to provide the right information in the right way to the right people at the right time." Freimuth, Hammond, Edgar, and Monahan (1990), in synthesizing public service messages about AIDS, reported that "straightforward presentations of fact," in tandem with fear appeals, constituted 77 percent of all the messages. Indeed, many of the examples employed to illustrate active processing in Chapter 4 were drawn from social action campaigns.

Even commercial campaigns that utilized television as the primary medium once relied on active receiver processing. Most early television commercials featured "product-oriented, reason why" messages, in which a spokesperson appeared in front of the camera, usually with the product, and argued its merits (Clark, 1988). Early on, television simply was thought of as radio with pictures, and thus the same approaches that dominated radio news, programming, and advertising were adapted to the new medium.

Thus, early television commercials operated from an active model, with influence thought to follow a hierarchical sequence from awareness to learning to attitude formation/change and to action. It functioned as a verbal medium, presenting receivers with logical reasons for brand choices (Martineau, 1971).

Contemporary television is more effective at exploiting the full potential of the medium, particularly in communicating visual messages in a more intimate context. As a result, the maturation of television is one reason for the shift away from more informational advertising. "By its very nature, television is better able to convey images than facts" (Clark, 1988, p. 69). Not surprisingly, research reveals that low involvement is the most accurate characterization of contemporary television advertising, and consequently "the ordered learning hierarchy does *not* occur in a majority of advertising situations" (Batra and Ray, 1983).

That is not to say that all television commercial messages operate from a low elaborative model. The nature of the product also dictates the nature of the advertising campaign (Schudson, 1984). One advertising agency positions products on a grid in terms of whether they are thinking or feeling and low involvement or high involvement (Schudson, 1884). Of interest here is that advertising for products that are low or high involving require very different messages and media choices (Schudson, 1984).

The other reason why contemporary television advertising employs a preponderance of messages that are based on passive or heuristic processing concerns the nature of products. Package goods, characterized by low price and high consumption (e.g., detergents, toothpastes, cosmetics, soft drinks, beer, foods, etc.), and services dominate television network advertising. However, more often than not, in most of these product classes, there is little tangible difference among the competing brands. Schudson (1984, p. 50) observes that, ". . . with a number of widely advertised products, there is no significant difference from one brand to the next." Levin (1988, p. 10) adds that, "Most established consumer products and services are more alike than ever before, and new products aren't very new—or without competition—for very long."

This absence of clear differences among competing brands in a product class elevates the role of advertising in marketing and dictates potential advertising strategies. This is a dilemma for campaigners, because whereas a brand's ". . . success hinges more than ever on advertising" (Liesse, 1991), the lack of differences makes it impossible to make substantive claims in an effort to position a brand in a market. Levin (1988, p. 10) comments that, ". . . achieving that lasting element of exclusivity in an ad claim is becoming much more difficult in today's marketplace." Indeed, the campaigner who makes substantive claims about a brand runs a decided risk. Informational claims may trigger either a design or advertising response from competitors. As one practitioner notes (cited in Clark, 1988, p. 24): "With rapid technological advances in manufacturing methods, a product doesn't hold its advantage for very long. Any product advantages can be ripped off very quickly. If you sell purely on rational needs, the next manufacturer can not only duplicate those factors, but can make a feature of one upsmanship."

Increasingly, contemporary television advertising messages contain very little brand information, operating instead on the basis of passive, heuristic assumptions about receiver message processing. Pope (1983, p. 293) notes this trend, concluding: "Recent studies. . . . indicate that, even using a very broad definition of information, advertisements contain few facts." Employing the lax standard that an advertisement had to meet just one of 14 information criteria, one study of television advertising found that less than half of the 378 commercial messages contained *any objective product information* (Resnik and Stern, 1977).

The next two sections of this chapter will examine passive or low elaborative message processing, focusing on two distinct paths of influence, one involving message awareness, the other affect.

Role of Awareness in Influence

One path of influence that is grounded in low elaborative message processing places awareness at center stage. Using this model, campaigners attempt to achieve receiver awareness through various stimulus techniques and frequent repetition. Over time, and after significant repetition, the message may evoke action, and subsequently attitude formation and/or change in a receiver (Schultz, 1990).

The basic objective for campaigners is to trigger receiver awareness. Awareness, in turn, *may* result in action. Receiver attitude, which played such a central role in active message processing, is bypassed in the low elaborative model. Instead, campaigners rely on product use to shape attitude. As Batra and Ray (1983, p. 137) explain, with the low elaborative alternative, "messages leave attitudes unchanged, but do create awareness and mere exposure affect, which then influences action." Pechmann and Stewart (1989, p. 41) add: "Ads that solely evoke heuristic processing by brand identification cues do not influence brand beliefs or attitudes." Instead, awareness triggers behavior; "[t]hey stimulate purchase behavior simply because consumers are more likely to remember the advertised brands or to recognize them on store shelves." In short, advertising works because it generates brand awareness, and people are inclined to buy those brands that appear familiar to them (Sawyer, 1977).

Much commercial advertising aimed at brand identification operates from this perspective. Advertising seeks to make the consumer aware of the brand, and to encourage them to try it (Levin, 1988).

The Evoked Set

Evoked set, sometimes called evoked recall, is one useful perspective to explain how messages generate awareness, and how this in turn, elicits behavior. This perspective was devised by advertising guru Tony Schwartz, who created the infamous "daisy girl" commercial for Lyndon Johnson for his 1964 presidential campaign against Barry Goldwater (Moyers, 1984).

The evoked set involves mental schemata. One of the purposes of advertising is to plant the name and/or image of a brand in a receiver's mental schema. The campaigner accomplishes this via the repetition of messages, which make the consumer aware of the brand within the context of a purchasing scenario. Planting the name and/or image of a brand is accomplished via lengthy messages (often 60 seconds).

Pechmann and Stewart (1989, p. 41) explain how messages are planted, thus generating brand awareness: "Processing of the heuristic brand-identification cue restructures the contents of long-term memory." This may be accomplished via either verbal or nonverbal cues, as the authors acknowledge. "If awareness is conscious, a verbal representation of the brand is stored in memory, facilitating its recall. If awareness is subconscious, nonverbal material. . . is stored." Some claim that advertising generates its most important impact during the planting process, as campaigners attempt to maneuver brands into the evoked set of receivers (Schultz, 1990).

Once the brand is planted, it can be retrieved, or called up, during priming via subsequent repetitive advertising appeals, and eventually at the time of purchase.

Campaigners are able to accomplish this, using more abbreviated messages (usually 15 to 30 seconds) that trigger the planted schema. As Schwartz explains (cited in Pope, 1983, p. 292), all effective radio and television commercial messages contain ". . . package of stimuli that resonates with the information already stored within an individual . . . Resonance takes place when the stimuli put into our communication *evoke meaning* in a listener or viewer."

When Chevrolet first introduced its "heartbeat of America" campaign, it employed a series of 60-second commercials. These messages employed a pictorial montage of fast-moving, colorful images, in conjunction with a catchy, repetitive musical score, extolling Chevrolet products with the words, "The heartbeat of America. That's today's Chevrolet." Later, Chevrolet shifted to shorter 15- and 30-second commercials, each focusing on just one of their vehicle lines. Although the message content varied, it utilized the same musical pattern, adapted to the image of the particular product (e.g., a rock adaptation for Camero; a much softer version for Cavalier), and it stressed the same slogan.

Larson (1982, p. 539) explains that, ". . . the evoked recall process is instantaneous," adding that "there is no conscious and time-consuming sifting and weighing of evidence in preparation for a decision." Once primed, the receiver rather automatically inclines toward selection of the advertised brand. As Schultz (1990, p. 104) describes, "By moving a brand into a consumer's evoked set, the advertiser can assure that the brand will at least be considered for purchase rather than be totally ignored in a particular purchasing situation."

This perspective *resembles* the way schemata function in the active processing mode. This is because the passive and active applications share an important point in common: that influence involves the process of moving information into a receiver's short- or long-term memory, and subsequently retrieving it. The differences between the two applications, however, are rather pronounced. The active perspective assumes that intentional thought is required to accomplish this; is based on more lengthy and intricate content bundles; and presumes that it is possible to significantly alter receiver schemata. By contrast, evoked set may or may not involve intentional thought; is based on simple content (e.g., the name and/or image of a brand); and instead of presuming that messages can change receiver schemata, attempts no more than to exploit existing ones.

The Conditioning Model

The classical and instrumental conditioning models provide another useful explanation for how messages elicit awareness in receivers. This section will describe these models, and apply them to commercial campaigns.

The Models The classical conditioning model is based on the pairing of an unconditioned stimulus, capable of eliciting a particular response, in the presence of a conditioned stimulus, normally not capable of eliciting that response. In time, as a result of frequent repetition of the pairing of the unconditioned and conditioned stimuli, the conditioned stimulus alone becomes capable of eliciting the response. The classic example of this model is Pavlov's dog. The presence of meat (the unconditioned stimulus) was capable of causing the dog to salivate (response). Then meat was used in conjunction with the ringing of a bell (the conditioned stimulus). The pairing of the unconditioned and the conditioned stimuli were repeated over time, and eventually the ringing of the bell alone caused the dog to salivate.

Classical conditioning was the brainchild of John B. Watson, a professor at Johns Hopkins University who went on to serve as a vice-president at J. Walter Thompson. In the book, *Behaviorism*, Watson, sometimes called the "father of behaviorism" (Burgoon, Burgoon, Miller, and Sunnafrank, 1981), delineated his theory. He posited the principles of stimulus generalization (once a pair has been conditioned, a similar stimulus may call forth the same response), stimulus discrimination (once a general pair has been conditioned, increasingly specific stimuli can be employed to elicit the response), recency (the more recently a pair has been conditioned, the more likely the unconditioned stimulus will be able to elicit the response), frequency (the more often the pair has been conditioned, the more likely the unconditioned stimulus will be able to elicit the response), and extinction (the less often a pair is reinforced, the less likely the unconditioned stimulus will be able to elicit the response) (Burgoon et al., 1981).

Instrumental or operant conditioning is based on the work of B. F. Skinner, and focuses on the use of reinforcement, which is the consequence or expected consequence of a behavior. Types of reinforcement include: positive (rewarding a behavior increases the likelihood of its reoccurrence), negative, (not rewarding a behavior reduces the likelihood of its reoccurrence), as well as punishment (punishing a behavior reduces the likelihood of its reoccurrence) (Burgoon et al., 1981).

Both perspectives provide useful explanations for the way that messages influence receivers. Based on the applications of the theories in commercial advertising, message content functions as a stimulus that elicits a persuasive impact; also, message approach and use serves as a stimulus that triggers awareness. The first application is direct; the second indirect.

Direct Influence   As indicated above, the two conditioning theories explain how message content can be viewed as a stimulus that elicits a persuasive impact. Classical conditioning offers one explanation.

Classical conditioning suggests that advertising that can get receivers to associate something positive with a brand will generate awareness and possibly purchase. The association may involve a product attribute (e.g., low price or quality), or a social attribute (e.g., prestige, security, esteem, etc.). The former is cognitive; the latter, affective. Pechmann and Stewart (1989, p. 42) explain the process in these terms:

> *Ads that contain attractive and gratifying verbal and/or nonverbal stimuli (or unconditional stimuli, the UCS) and evoke pleasant affective responses...eventually create associations between the UCS and the advertised brands (the conditioned stimuli, or CS). Initially, only the ads themselves will elicit affective reactions. However, if consumers are repeatedly exposed to these ads, eventually the advertised brands themselves will evoke the same pleasant feelings . . .*

FIGURE 5–1 Buick Regal Print Advertisement

Source: Reprinted with permission from Buick Motor Division.

We will focus on the capacity of advertisements to evoke a social attribute in more detail later in this chapter, when we turn our attention to the role of affect in influence. Figure 5–1 depicts a Buick print message that is designed to associate Buick and a product attribute, namely quality.

Instrumental conditioning implies that advertising appeals, which are successful in causing consumers to perceive that a brand will reward them, will generate awareness and contribute to increased likelihood of purchase. In fact, some maintain that consumption itself is a learned response (Kassarjian and Robertson, 1973). A consumer's positive experience with a brand enhances the probability of a subsequent purchase of that brand, whereas negative experience reduces the chance. In this way, consumers develop routine patterns of brand choices over a period of time, eventually reaching the point of habitually choosing a certain brand (Bennett and Kassarjian, 1972, p. 37). Thus, two important tasks of advertising are to generate awareness sufficient to elicit a trial purchase, and to suggest rewards for continued use.

Stimulus Factors Message approach and use functions as a stimulus that triggers receiver awareness, which as we indicated previously, can enhance purchase. In this instance, message approach and use is the stimulus; awareness is the response. We will examine message size and distinctiveness, repetitions, the approach, and visuals as stimulus factors.

Commercial campaigners strive to attain as much reach and frequency as possible to attain their objectives. Reach deals with the number of people who are exposed to a message, while frequency concerns the number of exposures. Campaigners usually determine how much reach and frequency is desired, only to have to scale back their ideal levels in the face of limited budgets. In commercial campaigns the nature of the product, market, stage of the product cycle, size of the advertising budget, and the competition's efforts are some of the factors that affect decisions about reach and frequency.

Message approach and use affects both reach and frequency. Message size (length when applied to radio and television) and distinctiveness are stimulus factors. The research indicates that greater size is positively associated with more awareness, but that the relationship is not linear, suggesting diminishing returns (Russell, Lane, Nicholson, and Nelson, 1990; Sissors and Surmanek, 1982). Furthermore, because advertising budgets are limited, there are inherent tradeoffs between size, reach, and frequency (Bogart, 1967). As a result, a number of studies on the relative effectiveness of 15, 30, and 60-second television commercials indicate that the shorter messages (15- versus 30-second; 30- versus 60-second) constitute the superior advertising buy, generating as much as two-thirds or more of the recall of the longer versions, but at less cost (Krugman, 1986). Initially distinctive messages can produce a desired response, then similar messages elicit evoked recall.

The data on distinctiveness are somewhat mixed. Creative novelty, bright colors, loud sounds can help a message stand out from others (Taylor and Fiske, 1978; Taylor and Thompson, 1982), but they do not contribute to attitude formation or change (Taylor and Thompson, 1982). Nonetheless, just getting receivers to notice a message is an increasing challenge due to commercial clutter, the presence of more and more advertisements. "The average American is bombarded by 1,000 television commercials a week" (NBC News, 1990). And that's just television commercials!

As a result, contemporary campaigners place greater stress on message distinctiveness. However, message distinctiveness is not a panacea to clutter. First, distinctiveness may initially attract attention, but wears out in time (Bogart, 1967), thus requiring even more distinctiveness for continued effectiveness. This places an almost impossible burden on campaigners, who must generate increasingly unique messages.

In addition, distinctiveness can backfire. Use of humor in messages, for example, can distract receivers, thus undermining effectiveness. The classic Alka Seltzer campaign of the late 1960's and early 1970's is a perfect illustration of this caveat (see Figure 5–2). The commercials earned rave reviews from creative people and the public for their humor. Yet, they failed "to move the product" (Koten, 1984). The bottom line is that for humor to be fully effective, "[it] must grow out of the product and must contribute to the communication, not simply to the memorability of the commercial. The humor must be relevant" (Baldwin, 1989, p. 90).

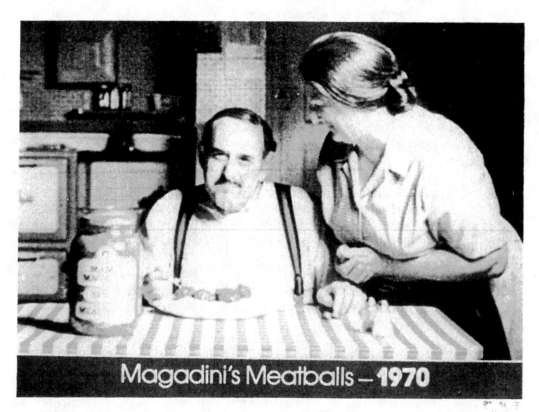

FIGURE 5–2 This Alka-Seltzer Campaign Was Heralded for Its Use of Humor

Source: Courtesy of Alka-Seltzer, a division of Miles, Inc.

Humor should not poke fun at the product or the consumer. The Wendy's "Where's the beef?" campaign, discussed in Chapter 3 (see Figure 3-6), created by Joe Sedelmaier, who also concocted the "fast talker" Federal Express campaign, won rave reviews, and significantly enhanced sales. During the first year of this campaign, the company's gross revenues rose 31 percent, and its net income jumped 24 percent (Hume, 1988b). Unfortunately, the campaign was perceived as offensive to senior citizens, and thus discontinued (Koten, 1984). A final caveat is that, "Humorous commercials . . . generally have a shorter life span than other ads," thus requiring frequent updating (Koten, 1984). Miller Lite's humorous, "everything you always wanted in a beer, and less," campaign was successful but only because they were willing to bear the costs associated with producing and airing a variety of different message vignettes (Vadehra, 1982).

The use of bright colors may secure attention but undermine mood. And boisterous messages can irritate consumers, a lesson seemingly lost on most local car dealers who continue to bombard local television airwaves with the most outrageous commercials. Still, given the limitations noted above, distinctive messages are more likely to enhance receiver awareness of a brand.

Repetition is the strategy advertisers use to attain a level of frequency. It also serves as a stimulus factor, contributing to awareness. Advertisers believe that repetition is essential to campaign effectiveness. "There has been a feeling in the industry for years that high frequency (or repetition) represents a strong form of persuasion in selling a product . . . At least, that is a widely held assumption" (Sissors and Surmanek, 1982, p. 155).

This assumption requires qualification. Research indicates that repetition does increase message effectiveness, but only to a point, especially assuming active receiver processing. Miller (1976), Cacioppo and Petty (1979, 1980), and others indicate that "persuasion first increases [and] then wears out as the number of repetitions increases" (Cacioppo and Petty, 1985, pp. 96–97). The research involving repetition and persuasiveness under conditions of active message processing suggests that three repetitions may be optimal, with psychological reactance setting in after about five repetitions (Schultz, 1990). This confirms the axiom that moderate repetitions insure optimal effectiveness (Cacioppo and Petty, 1985). However, McCullough and Ostrom (1974) and Calder and Sternthal (1980) provide evidence indicating that campaigners that vary message content and/or style, may be able to forestall receiver tedium, thus extending the effectiveness of messages following repeated exposure (cited in Cacioppo and Petty, 1985). Thus, message repetition offers limited utility, at least in high elaborative circumstances.

Other research indicates that message repetition contributes to awareness of the brand, but exerts minimal impact on attitudes (Batra and Ray, 1983). This is especially true under conditions of low involvement (Krugman, 1965; Ray and Webb, 1976). Batra and Ray (1983, p. 142) explain that in this circumstance ". . . repetition can be effective because it serves to maintain high awareness . . . " Tyebjee (1979) also argues that repetition is a crucial feature of advertising effectiveness under low-involvement conditions, contributing to receiver awareness of brand name, bypassing the intermediary step of attitude, thus affecting purchase decisions directly. He warns, however, that this effect is diluted when multiple competing brands simultaneously pursue the same high-frequency strategy.

Also, campaigners who vary their messages some can further enhance their effectiveness following as many as eight to ten repeated exposures (Leavitt, 1966; Weiss, 1966), an advantage of the passive over the active model. Indeed, repetition appears to be ideally suited to passive processing. That is the opinion of Batra and Ray, who conclude: "It would thus seem that message repetition, or high levels of frequency, are appropriate only in situations characterized by low consumer involvement in the product and/or media" (1983, pp. 142–143).

Message approach can also serve as a stimulus factor, thus contributing to awareness. Although message approach is a broad notion, we are interested in positive and negative approaches as stimulus factors.

There is evidence that extreme commercials, both positive and negative, increase brand awareness (Batra and Ray, 1983; Ray, 1982; Silk and Vavra, 1974). This may appear counterintuitive, especially in the case of negative messages (e.g., the attack message, which communicates negative information concerning a competing brand or opposing candidate; the irritating message, which employs a hard-sell approach to a product or candidate), which people *would like to believe* are ineffective.

Nonetheless, extreme messages can work. Their very nature insures penetration. They capture receiver attention because of their unusually positive or negative nature. And, as has been noted previously, with passive message processing, awareness is sufficient to trigger behavior, absent the intermediating role of attitude formation and/or change.

This makes perfect sense for positive messages, but not for negative ones. At first glance, we assume that, if the receiver noticed, but didn't like, the message, then they would be less likely to buy the product or vote for the candidate supported in the message. That's where the concepts of disassociation and differential decay enter the picture. These constructs provide two competing explanations as to why receivers often fail to respond predictably to a negative message.

Disassociation, which receives considerable attention in the work of Hovland (Hovland, Janis, and Kelley, 1953), sometimes known as the sleeper effect, postulates separation of new information from its origin over a period of time. Differential decay, a slightly different formulation of the sleeper effect, posits that a discounting cue, such as source, will deteriorate more rapidly than a message cue. Whereas research often failed to confirm disassociation, it has supported differential decay (Pratkanis and Greenwald, 1985).

Thus, negative messages generate awareness, and because of differential decay, the message content, and not its source, is the most enduring effect, thus leaving awareness to exert its usual impact on behavior. This thesis has been supported in research by Moore and Hutchinson (1985).

Visual images also serve as a stimulus factor. Receivers remember pictures better than words (Alesandrini, 1982; Horton and Mills, 1984; Krugman, 1986; Pavio, 1971). They respond more to the visual than the verbal component of television commercials, remembering such information as brand name after just one or two exposures to the message (Rossiter and Percy, 1983). The visual channel is more low involving, and in comparison with the audio channel in television commercials, generates more impact on awareness (Hollander and Jacoby, 1973).

Role of Affect in Influence

Another path of influence that is based on low elaborative message processing involves affect. In this model, campaigners attempt to generate positive affect in receivers, and that in turn evokes action. The principle objective for campaigners is affect. Affect, in turn, may contribute to attitude formation and/or change and then action, or may bypass attitude en route to action. In the latter case, action may in time impact receiver attitude.

Affect may act independent of cognitive thought; indeed, it can occur even in the absence of stimulus recognition (Moreland and Zajonc, 1977; Zajonc, 1980; Zajonc and Markus, 1982). Or, affect and cognition may occur conjointly. Zajonc (1980, p. 154) posits that, "In nearly all cases . . . , feeling is not free of thought, nor is thought free of feelings." Pechmann and Stewart (1989), referring specifically to commercial advertising, concur. They recommend classification based on two dimensions: "a systematic-heuristic dimension and an emotional (or experiential) benefits dimension" (p. 51). In this section, we are concerned with messages that are processed more mind-lessly, and that employ more affective appeals.

Affect is a powerful appeal in its own right. For example, even when affect and cognition occur together, there is evidence suggesting that affect precedes, and may even dominate, cognition (Edell and Burke, 1987; Holbrook and Batra, 1987; Ittelson, 1973). For instance, Zajonc (1980, p. 156) cites research indicating that, in assessing facial cues, half the variance is explained by the pleasant/unpleasant dimension, while in semantic differential studies, half of the variance is attributed to the evaluative component of attitude.

Given the importance of affect in the process of influence campaigners are advised to elicit receiver feelings, confident that feelings will trigger action. The remainder of this chapter examines the uses of affect in persuasive campaigns, beginning with classical conditioning, then focusing in some detail on motivational theories and approaches, and finally examining the significance of peripheral cues.

The Learning Model

We have already examined the classical conditioning model, which operates on the principle of association. This model is useful in explaining how pleasant feelings toward a commercial eventually transfer to the object (brand, candidate, cause). As Pechmann and Stewart (1989, p. 43) explain:

> . . . *the classical conditioning of attitudes remains a viable and useful theory for understanding . . . advertising. One of the reasons classical conditioning has such potential is because it and low involvement theory are the only theories that explain how commercials use emotion*

to influence purchase behavior without necessarily implying that the products themselves will provide emotional, experiential, or psychological benefits.

This, in part, explains the current preoccupation among many commercial campaigners with the construct of attitude toward the ad (Aad). According to Lutz (1985, p. 56), ". . . Add serves as a useful summary construct for a peripheral processing route to changes in brand attitudes and purchase intentions." Lutz argues that, for most television advertising, ". . . the consumer is seen as devoting little cognitive capacity to the ad; instead, prior attitudes toward the advertiser, advertising in general, or the situation (i.e., mood) transfer over to Aad, which in time transfers over to brand attitude" (p. 59). Calder and Gruner (1989) add that, "[Emotional appeals] create a favorable mood or image that surrounds the product. And it is this mood or image that is expected to sell the product, not the product's feature's per se" (p. 277). Sid Hecker of New York's Young and Rubicam ad agency acknowledges (cited in "Finding out What Makes Us Tick," 1987, p. 16) that, ". . . the advertising is the product. Consumers are buying the advertising more than the product." Indeed, Aaker and Bruzzone's (1981) research on the effectiveness of prime-time television advertising confirms that the receiver's liking of an advertisement enhances its effectiveness.

The Motivational Model

Motivational theories provide useful explanations for how messages generate receiver affect. As we observed in Chapter 3, grounded in a pejorative view of receivers, emotional appeals became increasingly dominant in the political and commercial advertising messages of the late nineteenth and early twentieth centuries.

Although this view peaked in the 1950s it has continued in the commercial advertising realm. Martineau (1957) captures this position well, arguing that consumers are not rational, driven by brand features and price in their purchase decisions. Instead, their emotional side usually drives these decisions.

Today, commercial television advertising continues to rely heavily on motivational appeals in order to reach consumers. As one practitioner puts it, "Informing people about a brand with which they are already familiar doesn't sell products any more. You

---

FEEDBACK

Think about the learning (conditioning) model as employed in the awareness and affect sections of this chapter and answer the following questions.

1. How does learning enhance awareness?
2. How does learning facilitate affect?
3. Based on the commercials that you've seen on television (other than the ones used as examples in this chapter), note and justify examples of those that are best explained as persuasive communication in terms of learning theory.

have to make them feel an emotional response" (cited in NBC News, 1990). Paine Webber ad industry analyst, Alan Gottesman (cited in Levin, 1988, p. 10), argues that increasing similarity in brands "created a demand for advertising to deal with more and more intangible aspects . . . ; [t]he emotional quotient of a brand as opposed to the functional aspect." Noel Baumwoll, who heads New York agency Baumwoll and Tannen Associates (cited in "Finding Out What Makes Us Tick," 1987, p. 16) concurs: "There are more and more categories [of products] where the difference between brands are minimal. You have to get involved with the product you *like* best. Your feelings take over." Saatchi and Saatchi research director, Penelope Queen, adds that advertisers must direct their appeals to the underlying feelings that drive consumer behavior (cited in NBC, 1990).

This brings us to motivational theories, which function as affective or emotional triggers for human behavior. Before we examine theories of motivation, we need to pinpoint more clearly what motives are. Drives are defined as bodily states, based on physiological needs, that produce anxiety in a person. They are universal across the species and are innate. Motives are defined as learned, directive states that incite people to act. Motives are more psychological in nature than drives; they are learned, whereas drives are innate; but like drives, they are powerful. Actually, drives and motives are best thought of as flip sides of the same coin, with drives characterized as deficiencies, and motives as abundancies (Kretch and Crutchfield, 1948). Thus, it's not sex, it's sex appeal; it's not hunger, it's taste; it's not the basic need for shelter, it's the desire for comfort and prestige, etc. (Kretch and Crutchfield, 1948).

Motivational Theories   In Chapter 3, we examined some of the first applications of psychological theories in commercial advertising. These were primitive attempts, at best. Subsequent applications provided more reasonable explanations for people's consumer behaviors.

Maslow (1943) offered what turned out to be one of the most popular and useful explanations that integrates drives and motives. He maintains that a person's motivational trigger depends on how successful he/she has been in satisfying more basic needs. Maslow used a hierarchy, reaching from "the belly to the brain," encompassing in order of importance the following needs: physiological, including oxygen, sleep, water, food, excretion, shelter, and avoidance of pain; *safety*, dealing with the desire to be safe and secure; *belongingness* and *love*, comprising love, belonging, and approval; *esteem*, encompassing recognition and respect; and *self-actualization*, involving personal fulfillment (Maslow, 1970).

Based on Maslow's hierarchy, the motivational trigger for people will vary, depending on where they are on the hierarchy. Moreover, people sometimes jump steps, or may move both up and down the hierarchy. For example, people may climb rungs of the ladder, perhaps reaching esteem, only to slide backwards as circumstances warrant. Such personal tragedies as death of a loved one, divorce, job loss, and others can result in a change in priorities, as the person becomes preoccupied with more basic needs.

Most Americans, as a result of our relative affluence, are free to concentrate on their personal needs located on the upper three rungs of the ladder: belongingness and love, then esteem, and finally self-actualization (Maslow, 1970). Thus, one of the most common advertising approaches is to get the receiver to perceive the brand as a vehicle to address a motivational need, or as Howard and Sheth (1969, p. 116) put it, causing them to perceive a brand "instrumentally."

In Chapter 3 we discussed receiver needs, employing rather traditional models. An important point to remember is that needs can be rational or emotional. The latter is particularly common in commercial television advertising where the products are most often common, low risk, and undifferentiated, where risk is not an important consideration. In such instances, the information imparted is much less important than the feelings and emotions that are associated with the brand.

Thus, Chapter 3 focused at some length on psychographic segmentation and targeting, which is based primarily on people's motivations, including their values, emotions, and lifestyles. Psychographic approaches are a direct descendent of motivational research, which used techniques such as depth interviews, word associations, and others in order to determine why people buy things. Psychographic approaches are based on the assumption that the essence of a particular brand is not in what it does but what consumers perceive it as. Clark (1988, p. 76) writes, that these approaches are based ". . . on the assumption that many of a person's decisions are governed by motivations over which he or she not only has no control but of which that person is probably unaware." Hence, an advertisement is not a series of statements about a brand, but a package of stimuli that trigger responses in specific types of receivers.

What kind of responses? Responses based on feelings about the brand and about the kind of person that uses it. Hence, the purpose of today's television advertising is to employ images to appeal to consumer needs, directed by motives. "[Campaigners] hone in on consumers whose life-styles and personalities have been carefully profiled" (Pope, 1983, pp. 189–290). With the results of formative research in hand, contemporary advertisers "concentrate on using the product's attributes in a metaphorical way to symbolize the brand personality, which embodies the brand values" (Houghton, 1987). As Richard Vaughn of Foote, Cone and Belding Communication (cited in "Finding Out What Makes Us Tick," 1987, p. 16) argues, "You focus on establishing a personality, building an emotional aura that will appeal to a certain person."

Commercial campaigns focus on images of the brand and what it can do for the consumer. The messages embody motivational appeals, using imagery to play on such consumer needs as to be in control, esteemed, loved, and self-actualized. Political campaigns also project images of candidates, stressing what they might do for the voter. Social action campaigns often emphasize images of the audience as altruistic and caring.

Approaches　There are numerous approaches that stem from a motivational underpinning. This section will highlight a few of the more common approaches. One advertising strategy is to create an image of a brand. "For products that are best in their class [the reality of what a product is and the values it embodies] are usually one in

E. & J. GALLO WINERY
"MOST RESPECTED"
:60 Commercial

Chardonnay . . .

Zinfandel . . .

Gewurztraminer . . .

Sauvignon Blanc . . .

Cabernet Sauvignon . . .

The varietal wines of Ernest
and Julio Gallo . . .

Among the most respected in
the world . . .

Today's Gallo . . .

All the best that a wine
can be . . .

FIGURE 5–3   E. & J. Gallo Winery "All the Best a Wine Can Be" Commercial

Source: E. & J. Gallo Winery 1986. Printed with permission.

the same" (Houghton, 1987). This is a common advertising approach. Campaigners coordinate the images, music, and message to elicit an image of a brand, more often grounded in emotion (Cohen, 1990).

E. & J. Gallo Winery commercials illustrate this particular approach well. Gallo is a moderately priced, American wine, a product that people buy to impress others, and which European brands have been perceived as the best. In addition, Gallo's marketing problem is compounded by the fact that, while people seek quality wines, most consumers can not judge quality directly, and thus rely on indirect signs, such as price, brand image, as established via advertising, and packaging.

Gallo commercials are among the best in creating imagery that exudes quality. The campaign, shown in the storyboard for one of the television spots in Figure 5–3, included both generic and brand-specific commercials. All the commercials in this campaign feature distinctive music, crisp and breathy enunciation of words, rich visual imagery, and the use of opinion leaders to foster a perception of quality, all in conjunction with the slogan, "Today's Gallo. All the best a wine can be."

Another strategy employs a "feel good" approach, focusing on the product as an effective vehicle to enhance togetherness among family and/or friends (Aaker and Bruzzone, 1981). The "feel good" approach attempts to project warmth, and has been identified as one of the most frequent strategies in contemporary television advertising (NBC News, 1990). Aaker and Stayman (1989, p. 297) describe how this approach works. "One or more characters in a commercial may be experiencing warmth, and the viewer may experience the same emotion vicariously."

Aaker and Stayman (1989) cite the example of a recent campaign for Lowenbrau. The commercials employ a vignette involving two or more family members or good friends. In the example cited, the commercial depicts a dinner scene involving a proud father and his son, who just passed his bar exam. The commercial exudes warmth, causing the viewer "to share vicariously the emotional experience with one or perhaps both characters" (Aaker and Stayman, 1989, p. 297). Research by Aaker, Stayman, and Hagerty (1986) indicates that commercials employing warmth generate considerable impact on purchase intentions, and do so within the first few seconds of the message. Also, Aaker and Stayman (1989) report that this approach enhances the longevity of messages, allowing more repetitions prior to "wear-out."

Many other commercial campaigns utilize the "feel good" approach. Some of the Gallo messages, described above, employ warmth. Their commercial, "the wedding," elicits warmth "with various shots of weddings drenched in sunshine and sentiment. Music by Vangelis added to the mood" (Baldwin, 1989, p. 84).

Maxwell House's "bringing people together" campaign employed a "feel good" approach to sell coffee. Its commercials depicted Maxwell House coffee as the one for those special moments when, in the presence of family and/or friends, you feel good. The ads project Maxwell House coffee as a vehicle for socialization. Maxwell House was the first coffee to use this strategy, though others have followed suit in recent years (NBC News, 1990).

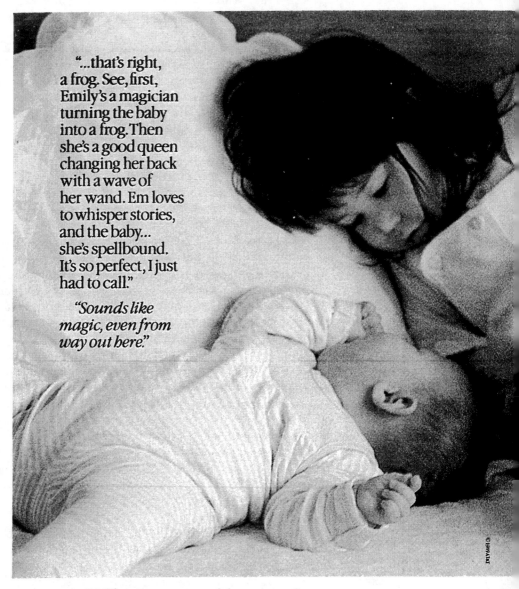

"...that's right, a frog. See, first, Emily's a magician turning the baby into a frog. Then she's a good queen changing her back with a wave of her wand. Em loves to whisper stories, and the baby... she's spellbound. It's so perfect, I just had to call."

"Sounds like magic, even from way out here."

AT&T's uncompromising sound clarity takes you right there and keeps you this close. So go ahead, call. Reach out and touch someone.

FIGURE 5–4 AT&T's "Reach Out and Touch Someone" Campaign Generates Warmth

Source: Courtesy of NW Ayer Incorporated, as agent for AT&T.

AT&T's "reach out" campaign, depicted in Figure 5-4, uses a very similar approach. Long-distance telephone calls through AT&T are depicted as the vehicle to turn the sadness of being separated from loved ones almost instantly in to the happiness of making a connection with them. One study that compared the emotive impact of a number of prime-time television commercials reported that AT&T's "reach out" messages scored the highest in eliciting pleasure (Holbrook and Batra, 1987).

The cola campaigns also make use of this approach, sometimes also using celebrities to assist. For example, the Coca-Cola classic "hilltop" commercial, similar to the advertisement shown in Figure 5-5, caused people to feel good about Coca-Cola. The television spot depicted a large group of people, representing diverse nationalities, religions, and ethnic backgrounds, drawn together in song to celebrate their universal love of Coca-Cola. Coca-Cola's "hilltop" commercial is one of the most popular ever produced.

FIGURE 5-5 Coca-Cola's "General Assembly" Television Commercial

Source: Coca-Cola is a registered trademark of the Coca-Cola Company. Permission for use granted by the company.

Another approach is to employ motives more directly, using products as vehicles to meet receiver needs. Thus, the brand is projected as enhancing sex appeal, eliciting esteem, or as a mark achievement. Consumers are susceptible because these needs are never fully met. As psychologist Carol Moog (cited in NBC News, 1990, p. 3) observes, "Advertising taps into the insecurity of never having enough, never measuring up well enough."

Numerous campaigns employ this approach. One consultant describes the strategy employed in most contemporary commercial television appeals as ". . . finding a consumer's need and filling it, whether it be sexual aspirations, social needs, or self-esteem . . . " (cited in Liesse, 1991).

Commercials that project a brand as enhancing esteem, or as a mark of achievement, abound. Most liquor, jewelry, and luxury automobile campaigns target these psychological needs. Citizen depicts their watches as part of a stylish appearance. Their commercials' visual images, language, and music are designed to suggest that others notice people who wear Citizen. The Citizen campaign's slogan reinforces this message: "Time is what you make of it. We prefer it beautiful." Also, campaigns for Cadillac, Lincoln, Mercedes Benz, and other fine automobiles for years have employed appeals based on the notion of ownership as a mark of individual achievement. Ownership of these cars is projected both as a personal reward and as a sign for others. Cadillac's recent campaign, "The only way to travel is Cadillac style," stresses the distinctiveness of Cadillac ownership, thus directly enhancing people's image of the car (Serafin and Horton, 1988).

Other campaigns suggest that the brand enhances sex appeal. We should distinguish between two strategies. One strategy uses sex as an attention device. This is a common strategy. "Sex has been a favorite weapon in the advertiser's armory at least since the beginning of the century" (Clark, 1988, p. 113). Its primary function is to grab receiver attention. In fact, Packard (1957) characterizes the use of scantily-clad women in advertisements that are directed to males as "eye stoppers." However, there is a downside to this approach. First, in much the same manner as other attention devices previously discussed (e.g., humorous or extreme approaches), sex may call attention to the ad, but not necessarily to the brand. Some research supports this prospect (Clark, 1988; Steadman, 1969). Second, some people find such messages offensive, thus making this a risky approach (National Organization for Women, 1972).

A second strategy is grounded directly in receiver needs. Here campaigners project the brand as enhancing the user's sex appeal, making them more attractive to those of the opposite sex. Many campaigns for cosmetics, deodorants, breath fresheners, clothing, and perfumes and after shave employ this approach. Some of them are explicitly suggestive. For example, Chanel's campaign, "share the fantasy," utilized visual images, graphics, and music to present female viewers with a sensual fantasy. Many viewers responded to the commercials, and thus to the brand, in "sexual and provocative" terms (Vadehra, 1982, p. M-43). Others are mildly suggestive, such as Dentyne's, "just the two of us," campaign.

Significance of Peripheral Cues

As we have indicated, the high- and low-elaborative models operate on very different assumptions about influence. In the passive processing model, receivers are less involved in message processing, and when messages exert a persuasive impact, they do so absent conscious thought about content. As a result, in this model, peripheral cues play a more prominent role in influence (Petty and Cacioppo, 1986). The most important category of these peripheral cues deals with the source of the message. Source factors as a peripheral cue in the process of influence will be explained and applied in this section.

Theoretical Basis

Two factors in tandem elevate the role of source factors in influence. First, the processing model determines the relative weight of content versus source factors. The presence of high-involving, active processing elevates content factors, whereas low-involving, passive processing enhances source factors. The explanation offered by Cacioppo and Petty (1987, p. 43) is that, ". . . [W]hen people are generally unmotivated or unable to think about an issue, such as when personal relevance is very low, credibility serves as a simple acceptance or rejection cue affecting agreement with little or no argument processing."

This is a repeated finding in the information-processing research. Petty and Cacioppo's research program stresses that, ". . . under high relevance, attitudes were influenced primarily by the quality of the arguments in the message, whereas under low relevance, . . . by the expertise of the source" (Petty et al., 1981, p. 847). Similarly, Chaiken (1987, p. 3) posits that in low-involvement processing circumstances, ". . . people exert little cognitive effort in judging the validity of the persuasive message and, instead, may base their agreement with a message on a rather superficial assessment of a variety of extrinsic persuasion cues," such as communicator characteristics. The evidence indicates that passive, low-elaborative message processing elevates source factors in the process of influence.

The second factor that contributes to the primacy of source factors in influence is the communication modality. Television contributes in two ways. First, because people consume it more passively than other media, while often simultaneously involved in other endeavors, television itself facilitates low-elaborative message processing. Some communication modalities, like print, require active receiver processing, while others, particularly television, do not (Krugman, 1965; Salomon, 1981; Wright, 1974). Television, thus contributes to low-elaborative processing, and to the importance of source factors in influence. As Chaiken's (1987, p. 81) research indicates, "The peripheral cue was used more with video . . . In these cases, attention would be drawn to communicator likability cues because of their salience and vividness."

Television also contributes to source factors in a second, and independent, way. It does so through its unique emphasis on visual images in communication. Television's visual component elevates person variables in influence. The reason is that we *watch* television. Obviously television contains both a verbal and visual component, but it is the visual element that tends to dominate. Paletz and Guthrie (1987, p. 20) refer to "the primacy of the visual over the audio channel," a point that draws support from many other scholars (Burgoon, 1980; Chesebro, 1984; Krugman, 1971; Meyrowitz, 1985; Salomon, 1979, 1981; Wright, 1974).

What do we see on television? Many things for sure, but predominantly we watch human faces. Television affords viewers immediate access to a communicator's face. Through its use of close-up shots, in conjunction with its relatively small viewing screen, television places considerable emphasis on communicator expressions (Brummett, 1988; Meyrowitz, 1985). Altheide and Snow (1979, p. 39) note that, "With television, the viewer is allowed the anonymity to read faces intensely." As a result, Meyrowitz (1985, p. 103) argues that, "On television, expressions usually dominate words."

In addition, some research indicates that visual messages can distract receivers, interfering with verbal processing, and thus inhibiting the learning of nonvisual content (Gunter, 1980; Paletz and Guthrie, 1987; Warshaw, 1978). Over time, as industry professionals grew more accustomed to television, they recognized its intrinsic communication features, and thus stopped trying to communicate more intricate verbal messages via the medium. We previously discussed the marked shift away from message content in contemporary television advertising.

Thus, television, because of the way that people consume it, and because of what people consume, with particular emphasis on human expression, downplays the role of specific information and elevates the impact of source factors in influence. This carries important implications for all campaigners, but especially in the commercial context.

Application

Commercial campaigners have enlisted celebrities to assist their efforts since the 1930s. From these early radio messages to the television spots of the 1950s and 1960s, celebrities were employed as spokespersons in commercials, verbally endorsing the brand. Today, nearly one in five television commercials feature celebrities (Cain, 1986), "hawking everything from credit cards to underwear" (NBC News, 1990).

However, campaigners today use celebrities much differently than in the past. Celebrities are much less likely to verbally endorse brands, instead appearing in vignettes, stories, or narratives in which the brand and brand name are displayed. Phil Dusenberry of the BBDO advertising agency provides the rationale for the change in approaches. He explains (cited in NBC News, 1990, p. 5): "To just put a celebrity up there and have him hawk his product won't work. Putting him there in a way that is engaging, is charming, has a bit of story going for it, we have found, is really a most successful formula."

One of the purposes of using celebrities is to grab viewer attention; to provide "instant recognition. Advertisers want to take advantage of the popularity of the presenter to make their product stand out" (Baldwin, 1989, p. 105). Cain (1986, p. 1E) argues that, "Research suggests that the presence of a celebrity on a commercial spot draws viewer attention . . . " In addition, other studies have compared the use of celebrities with other approaches, confirming that ". . . celebrity ads are more effective than others at grabbing viewers' attention" ("The Big New Celebrity Boom," 1978). John Vanderzee, advertising manager of the Lincoln Mercury Division of the Ford Motor Company (cited in "The Big New Celebrity Boom," 1978, p. 78), adds that, "When you're competing for a TV viewer at $100,000 per minute, you want to get every ounce of consumer attention out of it that you can."

But, that's not all. Campaigners also employ celebrities to establish an emotional bond with viewers, an objective that ties directly to the passive, heuristic, low elaborative perspective. The underlying rationale is that, viewers transfer their feelings about the celebrity to the brand. "One of the reasons celebrity ads work is that a viewer knows the celebrity and already has an emotional response to him and research has

FIGURE 5–6 Michael J. Fox Vignette for Pepsi-Cola

Source: Courtesy of Pepsi-Cola Company. Pepsi and Diet Pepsi are registered trademarks of PepsiCo Inc.

shown emotion to be a very effective way to grab a consumer's attention" (NBC News, 1990, p. 8).

Figure 5-6, which features Michael J. Fox who appeared in a series of recent commercials for Pepsi-Cola, illustrates the use of celebrities as a vehicle to elicit receiver feelings about the brand. Fox acted in a number of vignettes, each focusing on the lengths he'd go to get a Pepsi. As Fox comments on why he did these commercials, aside from the money (estimated in excess of $1 million an ad), he stresses his role as an actor (cited in NBC News, 1990, p. 6): "It didn't seem strange to me. It didn't seem like, like out and out saying, Hi, I'm me, I'm using this, to sell you this. It seemed like they wanted an actor to be able to execute these vignettes and to catch people's attention . . . "

FIGURE 5-7 James Garner Endorsement of Mazda Automobiles

Source: Courtesy of Fotte, Cone & Belding.

Alan Potash, who directs Pepsi's advertising, explains the role of attention and affect in these commercials. He observes (cited in NBC News, 1990, p. 7): "You'd better get their interest early. And that's why a Michael J. Fox, whose face you like, or we know that a large number of people are crazy about him, as soon as you see him, you say, Oh, I wonder what this is gonna be about." Potash ads that, ". . . it's gonna sell Pepsi, because it's gonna make people feel good about Pepsi. It's that one last foot in the supermarket . . . between your hand reaching this direction or that direction [which] is an emotional one and that's the bonding you want to get. I want you to feel good about Pepsi-Cola." The research indicates that this strategy has worked for Pepsi-Cola, eliciting pleasure in viewers (Holbrook and Batra, 1987).

The underlying assumption is that viewers will be attracted to the celebrity. "Agencies use a variety of criteria to measure the effectiveness of celebrities, their attractiveness, honesty, and age-group association" (Cain, 1986, p. 1E). More often than not, they rely on research, such as "Q" ratings which measure the recognizability and likability of hundreds of celebrities (Cain, 1986).

Since campaigners seek to transfer viewer feelings from the celebrity to the brand, the trick is in the casting, providing an optimal match involving the image of the celebrity and the image that the campaigner seeks to establish for the brand. Baldwin (1989, p. 105) advises that, if celebrities are to be effective, "they must fit the products they represent." Casey Wojciechowski of Grey Advertising (cited in Cain, 1986, p. 1E) stresses that, "The key lies in matching the celebrity to the product."

Sometimes campaigners may desire to establish an image of warmth, as in the case of the Michael J. Fox Pepsi-Cola spots or the James Garner commercials for Polaroid cameras or Mazda cars (see Figure 5–7).

Other times, the campaigner may seek to project an image of trust, as was the case for the Firestone commercials featuring Jimmy Stewart, which followed a number of negative news stories about Firestone 500 tires blowing out at high speeds; or an image of toughness, as was the case for the Everready commercials using Robert Conrad; or competence, as in the AC Delco commercials with Chuck Yaeger.

Other commercial campaign approaches stress source factors, but do not employ celebrities. One approach is to use ordinary people in vignette or narrative formats, drawing the viewer into an unfolding story, using the characters, visuals, and music to

---

FEEDBACK

Examine the advertisements in Figures 5–1 and 5–7 and answer the following questions.

1. Compare the persuasive approaches used in these two commercials. What strategies are the campaigners using to influence receivers?
2. What information-processing approaches do these messages assume?
3. Assuming the messages are successful, what outcomes will they produce?

elicit a response. This approach is particularly well-suited to television because its emphasis on visuals is able to focus attention on human expression.

Two successful examples involve AT&T's "reach out and touch someone" campaign, discussed previously in this chapter, which projects warmth resulting from families and friends maintaining contact with one another (see Figure 5–4), and McDonald's "it's a good time for the great taste of McDonald's" commercials, which stress the warmth that comes when people enjoy each other's company, naturally at McDonald's restaurants. In both instances, ordinary people serve as the vehicle to elicit affect in viewers.

Another approach is to employ what Baldwin (1989) refers to as "continuing characters, a character or personality created for the product (as opposed to being borrowed, as celebrities are)." The characters are often very ordinary, except that they usually are expressive. Examples include Folger's Mrs. Olson, Charmin's Mr. Whipple, Maytag's lonely repairman, Bartles and Jaymes's Frank and Ed, Bountie's Rosie, Palmolive's Madge, and others. In some ways this approach is safer than using celebrities, whose images may change suddenly, either because of controversy involving their professional life (e.g., Pepsi-Cola decided against airing of a number of expensive spots featuring Madonna after she released a provocative musical video), or their private life (e.g., Florida Orange Juice discontinued their association with Anita Bryant after she became increasingly vocal in opposition to homosexuality and then went through a well-publicized divorce)

Conclusion

This chapter dealt with passive, heuristic, low elaborative approach to influence. This approach assumes that receivers are often unmotivated, and thus less involved in message processing. Under these circumstances, they are unlikely to actively process messages, and if messages exert a persuasive impact, they do so mindlessly.

FEEDBACK

Think about the commercials you've seen on television and answer the following questions.

1. What commercials were the most effective with you?
2. Justify your choices. What did these commercials accomplish? Did they cause you to be aware of, learn about, form a positive attitude toward, or buy the brand?
3. Why were these commercials effective with you? What was it about the commercials that made them effective?

The chapter examined the theoretical underpinnings of the low-elaborative model, beginning with its first articulation by Krugman (1965), and then focused on how the passive alternative is used in persuasive commercial campaigns on behalf of package goods, which are inherently low-involving. The passive model relies on two explanations, positing that messages which elicit awareness or affect can directly influence behavior, bypassing receiver attitudes. Theories and examples drawn from commercial campaigns were presented to explain and illustrate the role of awareness and affect in influence.

At the outset of the chapter, we warned against thinking of active and passive approaches as mutually exclusive alternatives. At a macro level, campaigners usually need to use a combination of approaches, since the content of most political and social action campaigns, and even some commercial campaigns, will prove high-involving to some receivers and low-involving to others. At a micro level, campaigners will employ individual messages that contain a mix of content and affect, defying pure categorization. Zajonc (1980) reminds us that feeling and thought occur together. Nonetheless, it is useful for campaigners to think of active and passive processing in general terms, since the approaches suggest important nuances for influence. As Tybout (1989, p. 1) writes, ". . . persuasive communications . . . may include both cognitive and affective components and . . . these components engender distinct but interrelated responses . . . "

Suggestions for Further Reading

Baldwin, H. (1989). *How to Create Effective TV Commercials*. Lincolnwood, IL: National Textbook Company.

Burgoon, J. K., Burgoon, M. and Miller, G. R. (1981). Learning theory approaches to persuasion. *Human Communication Research, 7*, 161-179.

Cafferata P. and Tybout, A. (1989). *Cognitive and Affective Responses to Advertising*. Lexington, MA: Lexington Books.

Holbrook M. B., and Batra, R. (1987). Assessing the role of emotions as mediators of consumer responses to advertising. *Journal of Consumer Research, 14*, 404–420.

Krugman, H. E. (1965). The impact of television advertising: Learning without involvement. *Public Opinion Quarterly, 5*, 349–356.

Zajonck, R. B. (1980). Feeling and thinking: Preferences need no inferences. *American Psychologist, 35*, 151–175.

Part III

Essential Tools of Campaigns

C h a p t e r **6**

Managing Campaigns

> *"Social marketers. . . . [should] plan a campaign and establish its objectives systematically, comprehensively, and deliberately, in writing and with a purpose. A marketing plan establishes [the] standards for implementing a campaign and evaluating its outcomes."*
> —PHILIP KOTLER AND EDUARDO ROBERTO, MARKETING PROFESSORS
> (KOTLER AND ROBERTO, 1989, P. 275)

> *"Management by objectives provides a viable structure to control the design of messages, but it also serves in a later stage to make clear the criteria for evaluation."*
> ROBERT SIMMONS, COMMUNICATION PROFESSOR
> (SIMMONS, 1990, P. 202)

On a recent shopping trip, one of the authors ran across a T-shirt that depicts a professor standing at a chalk board while reading a student's notes and calculations. In the middle of the scribblings, formulas, and numbers is the statement: "And then a miracle occurs." The professor comments to the student: "You might want to be a little more explicit in step two . . . "

Such is the business of managing campaigns. The temptation might be (and far too often appears to be) to simply conclude that "the campaign succeeded" or "the campaign failed." When it succeeds, it is almost as if "a miracle occurred." And, when it fails, it is as if some sort of "a natural disaster" must have happened. In either case, of course, the reality is far more complex.

As first introduced in Chapter 1, the campaign process is comprised of three primary components: planning, implementation, and evaluation. The management of persuasive campaigns consists of the campaigner's efforts to systematically decide what will be done with regard to all three components. If campaigners do not clearly specify a plan and implement it in a prescribed fashion, evaluators may find themselves standing at the chalk board, so to speak, and concluding something similar to, "And then a miracle occurs." This happens all too often because campaigners are not systematic in

---

TABLE 6–1   Questions about Managing Campaigns

---

1. What is the difference between taking a societal needs versus an individual needs perspective in selecting the campaign's influence topic?
2. What is a causal and an intervention hypothesis?
3. What must be attained during the planning stage of the campaign?
4. What is the importance of operationalizing campaign goals?
5. What are the primary tasks associated with the implementation component of campaigns?
6. When does the implementation component deviate from the activation of the planning component?
7. What types of evaluation should be conducted in campaigns?
8. What is the purpose of campaign evaluation?

---

integrating objectives, strategies, and assessment (Simmons, 1990). In order to make sure that does not happen, a thoughtful and sequential process should be followed.

This chapter describes a series of interrelated steps that are involved in effective campaign management. The questions posed in Table 6-1 will be answered in this chapter.

The chapter will refer to theories and principles discussed in Chapters 3, 4 and 5 at appropriate junctures in explaining the process of campaign management. Table 6-2 suggests how campaigns may be initially visualized in terms of time.

TABLE 6–2   Managing the Campaign Process: A Sample Timeline

Goals and Objectives	Year				
	One	Two	Three	Four	Five
Conduct Focus Groups	- - O X - - - - - - - - -				
Fundraising for Year 4		- - - - - - OOOOO X - - - - - - - - - - - - -			
Design Messages	- - - - - OOOOO	X - - - - - - - - - - - - - - - -			
Pilot Test Instruments	- - - - - OOOOO	X - - - - - - - - - - - - - - - -			
Recruit Volunteers	- - OX - - - - - - - - OX - - - - - - - - - - - -				

X: indicates date by which objective is to be attained.
- - - - -: indicates planning associated with objective.
OOOOO: indicates work-in-progress/implementation of plan.
— — — —: evaluation of effects and effectiveness associated with campaign objective.

TABLE 6–3   Managing the Campaign Process: An Overview

Decision to Conduct ⟶ a Campaign	Societal Condition ⟶ Impending Election New/Competing Product	Overall Campaign Goal⟶

Stage One: Planning

Needs Assessment and Specification of Influence Topic ⟶

a. Individual Needs	**VS.**	**b. Societal Needs**
Why should anyone be concerned about this issue?		How does this issue affect societal good?
Why should anyone care about this candidate's platform?		How will this candidate affect societal good?
Why should anyone purchase this product?		How will this product affect societal good

Specification of Audience(s) and Objective(s), Prioritization, Causal and Intervention Hypotheses, Campaign Procedures ⟶

a. *Specify Criteria for Audience Selection*
Why should this audience be included within the campaign to attain the goal associated with the influence topic (formulate a causal hypothesis)?

  1. Is this a group responsible for the present societal condition?
  2. Is this a group within the candidate's district?
  3. Is this a group likely to purchase the product?

b. *Specify the Objective(s) Associated with Audience(s)*
Has the audience formed a point of view regarding the influence topic (formulate an intervention hypothesis)?

  1. If yes, is the point of view favorable to the campaign goals?
     a) If yes, the objective is reinforcement.
     b) If no, the objective is conversion.
  2. If no, the objective is formation.

c. *Specify Criteria for Entrance of Audience Member(s) into Campaign*
What data is to be collected; what measurement instruments will be used?

  1. Is this a representative audience?
  2. Have funds been raised to implement the campaign?

What order and priority will be given to entry of audiences into the campaign?

d. *Specify Activities and Procedures to Attain Audience Objectives*
What will be done to raise funds to support the campaign?

  1. Who might be solicited as major donors (e.g., business for a social action campaign; political parties for a political campaign; marketing department for a commercial campaign)?
  2. What special events might be orchestrated: celebrity auctions; dinners; galas; sports events (runs, walks . . .)?

Continued

TABLE 6–3   *Continued*

   3. If "planned giving" (via wills, . . .) is appropriate, how will it be promoted?

What major themes will be advocated and promoted in association with campaign content?

e. Specify Criteria for Exit of Audience Member(s) from Campaign
What data are to be collected; what measurement instruments will be used?

   1. Is the objective attained; did the audience indicate intention to vote, purchase product, make donation . . . ?

   2. Is the campaign over; have funds been exhausted?

Stage Two: Implementation

I. What messages ⟶
   Consider the audience and objective:

      a. Audience members' level of education, age . . .
      b. One-sided versus two-sided message, novel evidence, clear and precise language . . .

   Delivered by whom⟶
   Consider the budget:

      a. community leaders;
      b. persons of authority;
      c. effectors;

   Via what channel
   Consider the budget:

      a. radio: direct and immediate;
      b. TV: visual;
      c. daily newspaper: more detail and background;
      d. weekly magazines: richer context;
      e. monthly magazines: perceptions over time;
      f. books: documentation and perspective.

II. Recruiting, Training, and Retaining Campaign Personnel
   Examine Personnel's Motivation:

      a. personal goals;
      b. personality traits;
      c. past experience;
      d. community rootedness.

Stage Three: Evaluation

Consider Evaluation Audience ———➤
Policy makers, Campaigners, Planners, Targets:

   a. Effects   b. Effectiveness

   What happened that was   Did that campaign attain
   unexpected: objectives?

                             Was the overall campaign
                             goal attained?

Meta Evaluation ———➤
What have others said about the campaign?

Interpret effects, effectiveness, and meta-evaluation ———➤

Make recommendations for future campaigns ———➤

Planning the Campaign

The decision to conduct a campaign stems from any number of broadly conceived objectives. Political campaigns are most often initiated because an election is impending. Commercial campaigns are undertaken to launch a new brand, maintain or enhance market share of an existing brand, or in response to marketing efforts of a competing brand. Social action campaigns are initiated as a response to a public need, at times emerging at the grass roots level, and at other times launched by powerful public or private entities.

    Regardless of what the impetus for a campaign is, the first step to be undertaken once the decision to conduct a campaign has been made is planning. Recall from Chapter 1 that it is during the planning phase of a campaign when the influence topic is formally specified, the group or groups to be influenced are identified, and the persuasive objective and goals for each group are outlined. Several specific issues need to be addressed, as summarized in Table 6–3.

Why: Needs Assessment and Specification of Influence Topic

In specifying an influence topic, campaigners must consider why an audience may desire specific information. One reason is uncertainty reduction. An audience may need information about a candidate in order to reduce uncertainty about the candidate's positions on key issues, thus facilitating a decision regarding for whom to vote. Consumers may need to select from among three similarly priced products and require additional information in order to do so. Citizens may need information regarding a social issue's relevance to them.

    In specifying an influence topic, the campaigner is likely to make a decision during the planning stage to focus in one of two directions. Sometimes campaigners focus

TABLE 6–4   Example of Campaign Planning Process Based on an Individual Need

Planning Stage: Specification of Influence Topic, Audience(s), Objectives

INDIVIDUAL NEED: Save Money

	Overall Goal	*Influence Topic*
Social Action Campaign	Establish free prenatal care clinics	Tax cut: reduce the cost of indigent health care through creation of free prenatal care clinics (poor mothers fail to seek prenatal care); reduce the incidence of low birth weight babies; reduce the cost of care.

Audience	*Criteria*	*Objective*
INDIGENT MOTHERS	Selection: pregnant women Entrance: residents Exit: delivery	Form positive attitudes about prenatal care.
TAXPAYERS	Selection: taxpayers Entrance: randomly selected Exit: campaign ends, or attain objective	Change negative attitude about using taxes to build prenatal care clinics.
LEGISLATORS	Selection: office holder Entrance: campaign begins Exit: campaign ends, or attain objective	Reinforce positive attitudes about supporting state prenatal care clinics.

Order and Priority

1. Legislators and taxpayers are the first priority; the goal of reinforcement should be easier to attain, but is likely to follow only on the heels of constituents' support; thus, taxpayers must be addressed at the same time, and with the recognition that conversion will be far more difficult than reinforcement to attain.

2. Once support for the clinics is obtained, in order to attain the positive outcomes projected to be associated with them, indigent mothers must specifically be targeted to form positive attitudes and behavior about use of the clinics and prenatal care.

INDIVIDUAL NEED: Save Money

	Overall Goal	*Influence Topic*
Political Campaign	Gain support for candidate	Tax cut: Candidate supports an increase in emphasis on preventative care and less spending on catastrophic care; reduce the incidence of low birth weight babies; reduce the cost of care.

Audience	*Criteria*	*Objective*
FAVORABLE VOTERS	Selection: potential voters Entrance: randomly selected Exit: campaign ends, or attain objective	Reinforce positive attitudes about the candidate.
INDIGENT MOTHERS	Selection: pregnant women Entrance: residents Exit: delivery	Form positive attitudes about prenatal care.
OPPOSED VOTERS	Selection: potential voters Entrance: randomly selected Exit: campaign ends, or attain objective	Change negative attitude about the candidate.

Order and Priority

1. Favorable voters are the first priority; reinforcement should be an easier objective to attain, and making sure that those who are favorably predisposed toward the candidate follow through on their views by voting, raising funds, . . . , should be the highest priority.

2. To attain the positive outcomes projected to be associated with prenatal care clinics, indigent mothers must specifically be targeted, with the intent of forming positive attitudes and behaviors about use of the clinics and prenatal care.

3. The most difficult objective to attain is likely to be converting individuals committed to another political candidate, or whom—for whatever reason—are unfavorably predisposed to the candidate. Have reinforced positive attitudes among favorable voters, an effort might be made to obtain their assistance in converting unfavorable voters. Also, the mothers who are being targeted to use the clinics should also be encouraged to contact their representatives regarding support for prenatal care and clinics.

Continued

TABLE 6-4 *Continued*

	Overall Goal	*Influence Topic*
Commercial Campaign	Increase sales of milk	Tax cut: Candidate supports an increase in emphasis on preventative care and less spending on catastrophic care. Poor mothers do not eat well (they do not consume emough milk or healthy foods). The company will distribute coupons to be used for the purchase of milk.

Audience	*Criteria*	*Objective*
MILK-BUYING CONSUMERS	Selection: milk consumers Entrance: shoppers Exit: campaign ends, or attain objective	Reinforce positive attitudes about the milk producer.
INDIGENT MOTHERS	Selection: pregnant women Entrance: residents Exit: delivery	Reinforce positive attitudes about milk consumption during pregnancy.
OPPOSING DAIRY COMMISSION	Selection: Commission members Entrance: membership Exit: campaign ends, or attain objective	Change negative attitudes about a coupon campaign.

Order and Priority

1. The mothers are the first audience of concern, and promotion of use of coupons, as well as actual use, shall be encouraged and demonstrated.

2. In order to attain the company's objective, and increase sales of the company's milk, positive attitudes about the coupon campaign should be encouraged.

3. The state's Dairy Commission is found to regard this company's tactics as manipulative, and may have to be shown that actual benefits are accrued from the campaign before attitudes will change, making this the final objective to be focused on in the campaign

more specifically on the receivers' desire for information to satisfy individual needs and at other times on receivers' desire for information to satisfy societal needs.

Individual Needs Influence topics often specifically focus on individual needs. One reason campaigners may decide to target individual needs instead of societal needs is because the latter has been deemed as unlikely to promote active message processing. Given the number of times people are exposed to messages about societal issues, there is a tendency for them to simply ignore these messages. Therefore, when campaign messages concentrate on societal needs, people may respond passively—exhibiting an indifference to the topic.

To determine whether or not to focus on societal as opposed to individual needs, campaigners should ask the question, "What individual need could be satisfied by addressing the topic of the nation's infant mortality rate?" One answer may be the need to save money and pay lower taxes.

Examine Table 6–4 to see how campaigners might plan a social action, political, or commercial campaign on an individual need on the influence topic of infant mortality in the United States. A social action campaign may stress the need for more federal tax revenues to fund the costs required to provide expensive acute care to infants born prematurely and/or at low birth weights. A political campaign could support the election of candidates who are more sympathetic to the passage of legislation that leads to more tax revenues for health programs that reduce the incidence of low birth weight babies. Finally, a commercial campaign might endorse one or more products that promote maternal health during pregnancy, thus reducing the incidence of infants born with low birth weights, thereby ameliorating infant mortality.

At this early point in the planning stage, statements may mix outcomes, interventions, and causes (Berk and Rossi, 1990). The next matter to be considered in managing the planning stage is the identification of the audience or audiences to be influenced.

Societal Needs Campaigners often conduct campaigns aimed at audiences with no perceived personal need for the information that is at the core of the campaign. In these situations, they approach the influence topic from the perspective of societal needs. A societal needs' approach is not restricted to social action campaigns, although this arena may be the most salient. An emphasis on societal needs and other benefit in social action campaigns is quite natural. However, this focus also might be appropriate for commercial and political campaigns.

FEEDBACK

Consider the following societal needs that might be used as influence topics in current campaigns.

   1. How might the issue of homelessness, which represents a societal need, be an influence topic for a social action campaign, a political campaign, or a commercial campaign?

   2. What about the topic of hunger in the United States? How might social action, political, and commercial campaigners use this societal need in shaping the planning of the campaign?

Examine the following purpose statements and indicate a societal need that might become the influence topic for a campaign:

   1. Purpose: To determine the need for drug awareness in elementary schools.

   2. Purpose: To determine whether or not a black woman would be a viable candidate for president.

TABLE 6–5 Example of Campaign Planning Process Based on a Societal Need

Planning Stage: Specification of Influence Topic, Audience(s), Objectives

SOCIETAL NEED: Reduce Infant Mortality Rate

	Overall Goal	*Influence Topic*
Social Action Campaign	Establish free prenatal care clinics	Infant mortality and the need for prenatal care for indigent mothers (poor mothers fail to seek prenatal care); reduce the incidence of low birth weight babies; reduce the cost of health care.

Audience	*Criteria*	*Objective*
INDIGENT MOTHERS	Selection: pregnant women Entrance: residents Exit: delivery	Form positive attitudes about prenatal care.
TAXPAYERS	Selection: taxpayers Entrance: randomly selected Exit: campaign ends, or attain objective	Form positive attitudes about reducing infant mortality rate.
LEGISLATORS	Selection: office holder Entrance: campaign begins Exit: campaign ends, or attain objective	Form positive attitudes about reducing infant mortality rate.

Order and Priority

This campaign illustrates the difference between taking an individual versus a societal need approach in a social action campaign where the overall goal is to establish free prenatal care clinics. In this case, legislators and taxpayers are depicted as uninformed with regard to the U.S. infant mortality rate. Thus, not only will the audience of indigent mothers have to be informed and motivated to use prenatal care clinics, but, simultaneously, legislators and taxpayers have to be informed that a problem even exists before the campaigners can solicit support for specific programs to deal with the problem. Focus on societal needs may require more time in order to attain the objective of establishing free prenatal care clinics than focus on an individual need to save money.

	Overall Goal	Influence Topic
Political Campaign	Gain support for candidate	Candidate is concerned about infants' health and supports an examination of the causes of high infant mortality rates.

Audience	Criteria	Objective
FAVORABLE VOTERS	Selection: potential voters Entrance: randomly selected Exit: campaign ends, or attain objective	Reinforce positive attitudes about the candidate.
OPPOSED VOTERS	Selection: potential voters Entrance: randomly selected Exit: campaign ends, or attain objective	Change negative attitudes about the candidate.

Order and Priority

1. Favorable voters are the first priority; reinforcement should be an easier objective to attain, and making sure that those who are favorably predisposed toward the candidate follow through on their views by voting, raising funds, . . . , should be the highest priority. This is no different than if the focus were on an individual need, such as "to save money," as previously developed.

2. The most difficult objective to attain is still likely to be associated with converting individuals who are committed to another political candidate, or whom—for whatever reason—are unfavorably predisposed to the candidate. Having reinforced the positive attitudes among favorable voters, an effort might be made to obtain their help in converting unfavorable voters. This particular societal issue may be found to strike a chord with some unfavorable voters, both pro and con.

Note: The indigent mother group is no longer a target audience in this campaign, because the candidate is not being projected as promoting anything specific; the candidate expresses concern about a societal issue.

	Overall Goal	Influence Topic
Commercial Campaign	Increase sales of milk	For every carton of milk sold, a donation to the World Health Organization (WHO) is promised

Continued

TABLE 6–5   *Continued*

Audience	Criteria	Objective
CONSUMERS	Selection: milk consumers Entrance: shoppers Exit: campaign ends, or attain objective	Form positive attitudes about milk producer; inform consumers about problem of infant mortality and WHO's role in solving it.

Order and Priority

1. The milk-buying consumers are the only relevant audience, and they require information about WHO and the infant mortality rate in order to understand why the donation is important. This could be a more expedient approach to increasing sales, depending upon audience response to the information about WHO and infant mortality rates.

Take the infant mortality example employed above. Table 6–5 proposes how this topic might become the focus of a campaign that is based on societal needs. An audience may already have formed a response to the societal issue that complements the desire to undertake the campaign: most people want healthy babies born to survive and lead long productive lives. This desire links to the societal need to reduce infant mortality, thus comprising the influence topic in a specific social action campaign that seeks to establish free prenatal care clinics as its goal. The need for clinics may become the specific influence topic.

Savvy political campaigners may also recognize an important societal need that can be addressed during a political campaign (Meadow, 1989). The infant mortality example applies here as well. Political campaigners may base a campaign on the position that the election of certain individuals to political office is more likely to reduce the infant mortality rate. Thus, whereas the influence topic is still broadly conceived and grounded in societal needs, the specific type of campaign and the goals of the campaign differ from one expressly aimed at the reduction of infant mortality rates through a social action campaign.

Commercial campaigners should also consider how societal needs may fit into their definition of the campaign's influence topic (Solomon, 1989). Some phone companies, for example, have offered to make a contribution to a fund designed to save the rain forests with each minute of long distance calls that a customer pays for. This is a way to promote use of the specific phone company, within the framework of an influence topic that is linked to societal needs. Other commercial organizations could promise a donation to a relevant organization, whose mission is to reduce infant mortality, as a promise associated with the sale of each unit of milk, baby food, disposable diapers, and so on. The identification of the purpose of the campaign as stemming from the societal need to reduce infant mortality gives a very different emphasis to all the steps of the campaign to follow than would emphasis on individual needs.

Who: Identify the Audience(s)

The identification of the audiences that will be addressed in a campaign requires the specification of criteria to be used to: identify the audience(s), establish their entrance into the campaign, and determine when they will exit from the campaign. Refer to Table 6–2 to visualize the ordering of these events.

Criteria for Selection Some of the criteria for audience selection and involvement in a campaign will be obvious. For example, in a commercial campaign to sell baby food, individuals who have babies, care for babies, or are in some way are related to someone who presently has a baby are appropriate audiences for the campaigners' planning. Thus, the criteria for selection may involve some present, but transient, experience. Other criteria include individual characteristics like age, or, in the case of skin cancer campaigns, hair and skin color. Recall from Chapter 4 that involvement may be predicted by these variables based on their personal relevance or self-reference effect.

Socioeconomic status is another very common criteria for selecting individuals into or out of a campaign. In addition to identifying the criteria to be used for selection of individuals into a campaign, campaigners should identify the aggregate to be used during the campaign's evaluation. For example, the audience may comprise a specific neighborhood, state, region, or district. This may be particularly true in the case of political campaigns.

Criteria for Entrance into the Campaign Once the criteria to be used in selecting the audience(s) for a campaign are set, campaigners should specify what criteria will be used to include specific individuals in the campaign. This generally focuses on the selection of a research design for the campaign in order to provide reliable and valid data for assessment of the campaign's outcomes during the evaluation component. Campaigners must decide, for example, whether random samples will be selected, and what number of individuals will be specifically included for measurement of the intervention's effects, and whether or not a control group will be included for comparison.

In addition to selection of the research design, the sample size, and the type of sample to be selected, criteria for entrance into a campaign may stipulate oversampling of specific groups, such as minorities, to insure an adequate group size for comparison. This topic is developed further in Chapter 7, which deals with research design.

Criteria for Exit from the Campaign Just as campaigners should specify the criteria for entrance into the campaign, they should also elaborate on the specific criteria for exit from the campaign. If a consumer purchases the promoted brand once, does this qualify as trial or product switching? How about the second purchase? The third? If an individual indicates an intention to vote for a candidate, is that the criterion for measurement of a political campaign's success, or should the same individual be expected to do more: encourage others to support the candidate, contribute time or money to the campaign, or vote for other candidates of the same party? Perhaps the fact that someone votes for a straight party ticket because they support the party's choice for president is a better measure than simply the vote for the candidate. Once someone makes a \$10 donation to support a social issue, does that constitute behavior in support of the social action campaign, or does volunteering time, or some other additional form of commitment need to be included in the assessment?

These issues may seem simple or even unnecessary on first pass, but campaigners who fail to specify a very clear definition of the criteria for exit from a campaign run the risk of either (a) overgeneralizing, or (b) underreporting, the actual campaign results associated with the individuals who participate in the campaign. Advertisers in particular have moved from relying on day-after recall scores to more sophisticated and individualized measures of persuasion with audience media consumption by group becoming highly specific (Honomichl, 1988). Having specified the influence topic and the campaign audience(s), campaigners next identify the appropriate goals to be associated with each audience.

What: Establish Campaign Objectives

Many typologies for the establishment of a campaign's goals and objectives have been developed through years of conducting campaigns. Some are specific to the marketing setting (Pollay, 1989), others are applicable to political campaigns (O'Keefe, 1989), and still others have emerged as the result of general persuasion research (Patton, 1982). We briefly overviewed a typology of persuasive objectives in Chapter 1, which now will be discussed in much greater detail. Refer to Tables 6–4 and 6–5 as you read this section.

Selection of campaign objectives should be determined on the basis of formative research, defined as the attempt to collect background information regarding an audience's present attitudes and behaviors to compare with the campaigners' desired ideal for the audience's attitudes and behaviors (Atkin and Freimuth, 1989). Commercial campaigners, in particular, allocate ever-increasing amounts of money up front when developing television commercials in order to enhance the likelihood that the optimal appeal for the targeted audience is being employed (Honomichl, 1988).

Through the selection of campaign objectives, campaigners attempt to make explicit the purposes, questions, and concerns to be addressed in campaign messages for specific audiences. Each campaign objective should contain only one outcome, and clearly indicate what is to be attained by the campaign in relation to the audience, the campaign objective, and the outcome (Patton, 1982).

Attitude Formation Objective   Formative campaign research is likely to identify various audiences that are neutral about the topic of the campaign due to lack of information. Because these audiences are uninformed, they often are unable to provide responses to questions that they are asked, thus making formative research more difficult, as will be discussed further in Chapter 7.

However, the uninformed are relatively easy for campaigners to influence, as long as they are not also apathetic (a common occurrence in political campaigns). Campaigners can focus the campaign on providing specific information about the particular brand, candidate, or issue in a straightforward manner, possibly taking advantage of already learned responses that are positive and may be linked to the campaign topic.

If only thoughts flowed as smoothly as a Parker Duofold Roller Ball.

FIGURE 6–1 Parker Pen Magazine Advertisement

Source: Courtesy of Parker Pen, USA, Ltd.

The construction of informative messages should be novel and distinctive, as discussed in Chapter 5. Through the process of informing, the campaigner hopes to attain awareness of a product, candidate, or social issue. Information may also establish a preparedness to try a product, to vote in an election, or to be involved with an issue. At the very least, information announces the availability of a product or candidate, and may build an image for the product, person, or issue. The advertisement in Figure 6–1 is a unique way of emphasizing the smooth quality of the writing instrument's performance. The audience who needs to purchase an ink pen may remember this brand name because of the novel presentation.

An audience may display awareness of, even support for, some brand, candidate, or issue and still not indicate willingness to act: to purchase the brand, vote for the candidate, or support the issue. In this case, the audience is defined as apathetic, or lacking motivation concerning the campaign topic. They may passively receive information associated with the topic, so campaigners are faced with the task of designing messages that will prompt more active thought.

The audience must understand why the topic is one in which they should be involved. Messages should be designed to link already learned passive but positive responses to a related topic to the present topic in order to generate the desired response. Messages may also be designed to involve the audience with the topic, motivating them to attend to content. Information alone is unlikely to be the important ingredient. Rather, a way of producing a sense of personal involvement regarding the topic is necessary in this case.

The print message in Figure 6–2 illustrates this strategy. Public opinion polls consistently indicate that most Americans favor tighter controls on the manufacture and sale of handguns in the United States (Conference of Mayors, 1980). Nonetheless, Americans who support stricter controls also are more apathetic on this issue than those who oppose controls. As a result, the gun lobby has been effective in thwarting legislation designed to restrict handgun availability (Gergen and Gest, 1989). The print message in Figure 6–2 uses an oxymoron to capture the reader's attention and force him/her to think about the message, enhancing involvement.

The Conversion Objective   Persuasive campaigns are most commonly associated with change or conversion as the objective (Geller, 1989; Greenberg and Gantz, 1989; O'Keefe and Reid, 1989). In this situation, the audience has information on the issue, but that information has left their attitude either conflicted or opposed to the campaigner's position. Such individuals may not be ready to change. In those circumstances, the messages attempting conversion will be ineffective.

Formative research may reveal that people are conflicted in that they possess information on the topic but are undecided in their position. They may be aware of disparate claims based on contradictory information about the issue. Ironically, receivers who are conflicted often possess too much information, and as a result, they see merit in arguments on both sides of the issue in question.

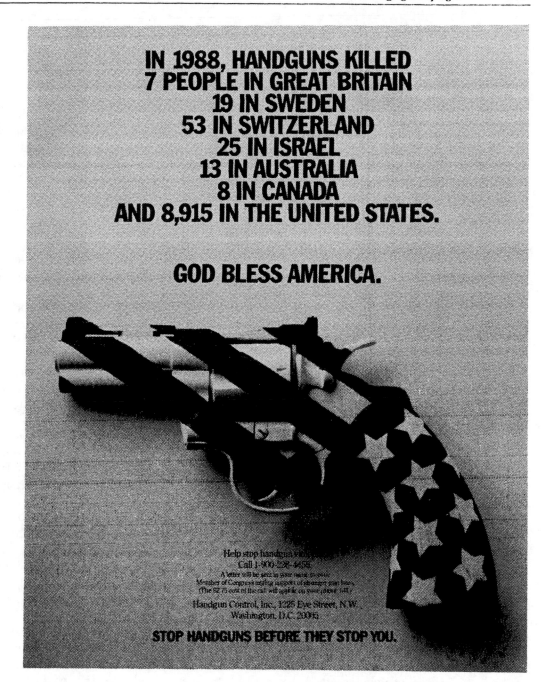

FIGURE 6–2 Attention-Grabbing Magazine Advertisement Opposing Handguns

Source: Courtesy of Handgun Control, Inc.

In these situations, campaigners should design messages to settle the seeming dispute. The conflicted audience needs help in making a decision and campaign messages can provide resolution in the dispute. Such messages should be substantive, since the conflicted audience is usually informed on the issue. Messages should be designed for active processing.

Formative research may indicate that people are opposed to the position advocated. Converting the opposed is a difficult undertaking at best. Indeed, experts maintain that advertising, one of the most important communication modalities in campaigns, has limited capacity to actually change people's attitudes about brand preference, candidate preference, or some issue position (Keim and Zeithaml, 1981).

In many cases, campaigners may decide to ignore an audience opposed to their position, reasoning that such efforts would not be cost-effective, and could unwittingly activate opponents. At the most, campaigners may attempt to establish the readiness to listen, reduce overt opposition, or generate indecision in those hostile to their position.

In many instances, campaigners are faced with audiences who already have strong loyalties to a product, a candidate, or a side of a social issue opposed to the campaign objective. Often in these situations, campaigners must establish the readiness to listen to influence appeals. When individuals possess a strong, specific position, their likelihood of attending to messages that take another point of view is minimal. As we observed in Chapter 4, an active response is more likely when an individual is highly ego-involved, committed, and views the information as personally relevant. In those circumstances where an audience has already formed attitudes and behaviors regarding the influence topic, it is more likely to actively attend to information which supports current attitudes and behaviors, while passively and negatively responding to information which opposes them.

Consider a political campaign, in which the candidate is a male who working women view as detrimental to the promotion of their interests, specifically with regard to day-care allowances and tax credits for child care. Furthermore, the candidate is on record as opposing such measures. In the planning process, campaigners may decide that it is vital to address working women as one audience that may overtly oppose the candidate's election. Campaigners may determine that the likelihood of this audience actually being persuaded to vote for the candidate as minimal. Nonetheless, this audience also may be viewed as one that is instrumental to the task of persuading other audiences that the campaigners believe could become supporters of the candidate.

In this situation, campaigners must attempt to reduce the overt opposition of working women. The candidate might make a public apology for a past position and present a reformed view. On the other hand, some supporters of the candidate may approve of the previous behavior and disapprove of any retraction of that point of view. In these instances, the campaigner's task will be compounded by the desire to not forsake the achievement of a goal associated with another audience while simultaneously striving to attain the goal with the present audience. In such a case, the campaign may focus on something substantive and deemed valuable to the group who is displeased, such as the candidate's support for job site day-care centers. At any rate, campaigners can not afford to simply neglect this audience in the planning stage of the campaign.

Campaigners in social action and commercial campaigns should consider which audiences are likely to object to their positions and evaluate how best to deal with this opposition. Again, one important reason for doing so is that these audiences are likely to affect the campaign's success by negatively impacting members of other audiences who either already support the campaign or who can be influenced to support it.

In addition to audiences who possess intense views opposing the influence topic, formative research may reveal audiences who are not as strongly entrenched in their responses to a product, candidate, or social issue. In a large campaign with multiple audiences, campaigners may determine that a negatively disposed group, which is generally quiet in its opposition, simply is not worth the campaigners' time, attention, and money.

It may be the case, however, that one of the most important audiences in the campaign is one that is mildly opposed but open to change. For example, if the goal is to get mothers to bring children in for preventative health care check-ups, but mothers reflect some negative responses, perhaps due to the cost of such care, addressing this specific need is likely to lead to success. If voters reflect some opposition to the election of a female for a major office, these doubts can be directly addressed. And, if consumers report that they do not see a need to use prespotters on their laundry, this can be dealt with, and the change may lead them to try the product. Formative research at the outset of the campaign will inevitably indicate the presence of opposition. Campaigners must decide the most appropriate way to respond to it.

The Intensification Objective   Broadly speaking, the goal of intensification focuses on individuals who already believe or behave in ways that the campaigners desire. Given the constant likelihood of exposure to messages that run counter to these attitudes and behaviors, even with the possibility of passive processing of such messages or negative responses to these messages, campaigners should not assume that the supportive audiences will be unaffected by competing messages.

When formative research reveals people who are favorably predisposed to the campaign topic, those attitudes should be reinforced. Reinforcement messages should offer reassurance, refute other's claims, and support the audience's taste for a product or candidate, as well as the importance of a specific social act. A majority of television commercial advertising for established brands is designed to reinforce favorable attitudes, thereby maintaining market share of the brand.

That is not to suggest that reinforcement is the only goal of commercial campaigns. Campaign messages often are designed to address two or more audiences. Campbell, for example, learned that viewers of the program, "All My Children," buy 46 percent more V-8 juice than the average television viewer, while viewers of "Search for Tomorrow" purchase 27 percent more spaghetti sauce than is usual.

Campbell has pitched the virtues of Prego spaghetti sauce on "Search" and those of V-8 on "Children" and will probably do so again, a low-risk, high-gain strategy aimed at maximizing sales among the likeliest customers (Kessler, 1986, p. 59).

FEEDBACK

Consider the advertisement in Figure 6–3, and the objective of conversion, when answering the following questions. Jim Brady has become an important spokesperson in the campaign to control handguns.

1. Why would Brady be more persuasive than other sources in the effort to convert individuals who are conflicted about, or opposed to, efforts to restrict handgun availability?

2. This message makes a reasoned appeal. Why is this an appropriate strategy for these audiences?

Campbell thus targeted the audience that is positively disposed to their product in the overall campaign plan at the same time that they attempt to convert additional viewers.

Planning for activation of campaign audiences who are ready to behave in the desired fashion assures that planners consider whether or not the audience has the necessary information and skills to behave as they are predisposed. McGuire (1989), for example, emphasizes skill acquisition as one important outcome in persuasion campaigns.

The American Cancer Society is one organization that has recognized the need to specifically address audiences who are ready to behave in a desired fashion but may lack the skills and information to do so. For example, in promoting the practice by women of regular breast self-examinations as one method of early detection of potentially cancerous lumps, a video was developed specifically to assist women in understanding and learning how to perform a self-examination. Similarly, parents of infants have been found to lack some of the basic skills and understanding associated with parenting although they were predisposed to behave in a health-promoting fashion. This became the focus of a video entitled, "Your Baby's First Six Months" (Williams, Hall, Lapointe, Parrott, Siegert, and Shapiro, 1990).

Commercial campaigners also commonly consider the audiences that are likely to be predisposed to purchase, seeking to inform them where the specific product may be obtained, as well as how to finance the more expensive purchases. Political campaigners have learned that providing assistance for voters to get to the polls to vote is an important aspect of activating the predisposition to vote.

Buy more of a brand, vote for more candidates of the same political party, and support the social action goal through the donation of more money and time. These are also messages common to campaigners who plan to address the reinforcement objective. Political and social action campaigners particularly focus time and energy on increasing the involvement of their volunteers (Brudney and Brown, 1990).

According to a 1985 Gallup poll commissioned by Independent Sector, 89 million Americans fourteen years old and older (48% of the population) reported volunteering an average

-- James S. Brady --
President Reagan's Press Secretary
Shot on March 30, 1981 by John Hinckley

Please Help Me Save Lives

"Add your voice to mine. Help me beat the gun lobby.

I know firsthand the daily pain of a gunshot wound. But I'm one of the lucky ones. I survived. Since I was shot ten years ago, more than 200,000 men, women and children have been killed here in handgun fire. That's more Americans than we lost in the Korean, Vietnam, Panama and Persian Gulf conflicts, combined. And America's random gun violence rages on.

I'm calling on Congress to pass a common sense law -- the Brady Bill -- requiring a seven-day "cooling-off" period before the purchase of a handgun so police can run a thorough background check on the buyer. Seven days to cool-off a hot temper. Every major police group supports this public safety measure.

So why hasn't Congress passed the Brady Bill? Because too many Members of Congress are afraid of the hardcore gun lobby and too many take the gun lobby's PAC money. The gun lobbyists say a seven day wait is "inconvenient." I'd like to see one of them try spending a day in my wheelchair.

Can we beat the gun lobby? Yes! Thanks to citizens like you, we passed the Brady Bill in the House of Representatives -- despite the gun lobby spending millions of dollars against us. How did we do it? People across America contacted their legislators in Washington and demanded action.

Let your Senators know you want an end to gun violence -- before someone you love becomes a statistic."

Now the Brady Bill is before the U.S. Senate. We can pass it if you help me now. It's real easy. Here's how.

Just call 1-900-226-1990

and for only $3.75, charged to your phone bill, we'll send letters in your name to your Senators in Washington urging a vote for the Brady Bill (S.257). We'll also send you copies.
Call anytime -- our lines are open 24 hours a day!
Help me "cool-off" gun violence and make America safer.

This public safety message brought to you by Handgun Control, Inc. 1225 Eve St., NW, Washington, DC 20005

FIGURE 6–3 Newspaper Advertisement Supporting the Brady Bill

Source: Courtesy of Handgun Control, Inc.

of 3.5 hours per week up from 2.6 hours in 1980. It is no longer considered women's work either, according to the same poll, 51% of women volunteer, and 45% of men do also. In 1985 this total of 16.1 billion hours of volunteer time was estimated at $84 billion which is the equivalent of 5 million paid workers (Raynolds and Raynolds, 1988, p. 16).

Volunteers often report that it is their assessment of an organization's significance to society that is likely to affect their decision to volunteer (Lynch-Schneider, 1991). In view of this finding, campaigners would be well-advised to construct messages to increase volunteers' behavioral commitment based on the organization's significance to society, which is grounding the influence topic on a societal need. Others have found that volunteers participate to attain skills (Lynch-Schneider, 1991). Thus, to increase behavioral commitment, campaigners may also want to emphasize the possibility of acquiring specific skills and experience, which comprises a focus on individual needs.

Finally, campaigners will have audiences who are committed in every possible way to helping to attain the objectives that are associated with the campaign. These audiences hold positive attitudes, which result in appropriate behaviors. An emphasis on personal and social responsibility in the political and social action realms of campaigns may help to maintain high levels of involvement (Hamilton and Fenzel, 1988). The physiological and psychological effects associated with doing good works have been associated with feelings of warmth and energy (Luks, 1988), which may also contribute to maintenance of high levels of involvement.

Order and Priority

In most campaigns, multiple audiences and objectives will be identified. In fact, it is not unusual for more than a single objective to be associated with a specific audience. Before completing the planning component of the campaign, campaigners must determine what order and priority to assign to the goals. Again, review Tables 6–4 and 6–5 to see how campaigners might prioritize the audiences and objectives in these campaigns.

Consider a campaign designed around the influence topic of skin cancer prevention. Suppose that the groups to be targeted in this campaign include individuals who already use sun block whenever they are outdoors, individuals who seldom use sun block and are often outdoors, and individuals who seldom use sun block but are seldom outdoors. A priority might be attached to the group who spends a lot of time outdoors without using sun block. This group seems to be most at risk. Based on formative research about this group, the campaigners may determine that the group opposes the notion of using sun block and believes that a tan protects them from the sun. These findings determine the order of the steps to be taken in the campaign. First, attitudes about the relationship between a tan and protection must be changed. Then, behavior related to sun block use can be targeted. The ultimate goal may be to activate favorable attitudes regarding sun block. Assigning a priority to campaigners' objectives is also likely to be associated with the overall budget that the campaigners are working with.

Operationalizing the Objectives

The planning stage also includes the identification of the causal and intervention hypotheses to be associated with the audience(s) and the campaign topic. The causal hypothesis formally posits a relationship between a present situation and a particular variable believed to contribute to the situation. The intervention hypothesis specifies the expected relationship between the campaign's intervention and the situation. Examples of causal hypotheses include: (1) availability of free clinics leads (causes) poor mothers to seek early prenatal care, (2) lack of awareness of brand X leads to (causes) the purchase of brand Y, (3) belief that candidate A supports abortion leads to (causes) overt opposition to the candidate; and so on. Examples of intervention hypotheses include: (1) more free clinics will lead to more poor mothers seeking early prenatal care, (2) more awareness of brand X will lead to the purchase of brand X rather than brand Y; and (3) information about candidate A's reason for supporting abortion will lead to a reduction in overt opposition to the candidate.

In addition to the hypotheses associated with a campaign, for each objective during the planning stage, campaigners should stipulate: (1) what data will be collected, (2) what instruments will be used, (3) what activities the audience will participate in; and (4) what procedures will be followed by individuals involved in the campaign. Failure to plan these activities may lead to an incomplete treatment or intervention. It may also lead to the wrong intervention. Finally such failure may contribute to an unstandardized intervention in the campaign.

Eolithism: Strategies for Situational Responsiveness

The discussion to this point has stressed the systematic specification of an objective for each audience with regard to the influence topic. Some campaigns, however, benefit from the flexibility of establishing objectives based on responding to the situation that campaign personnel specifically find themselves in. This strategy has been discussed by campaigners within the principle of eolithism (Patton, 1982).

In consulting with campaigners in the state of Georgia who attempted to assist elderly people in understanding how to more economically consume energy in their homes, for example, it was deemed likely to be most effective to meet with each elderly person or couple in their home to promote the campaign's energy conservation objective. The plan to be flexible in the energy conservation campaign allowed the campaign personnel to observe how the individual lived, and to converse with each individual in order to assess the individual's vocabulary and likely level of education and literacy. The personnel were trained to be flexible during interaction with the elderly audiences. If the campaign succeeded in meeting its objective, however, there would be no single method to recommend as a successful intervention. However, failure to adapt to each situation was viewed as more likely to lead to overall failure in the campaign. Therefore in some situations campaigners deem specification as secondary in importance to attaining the broader objective, which is viewed as requiring the flexibility to respond to the individual.

When and Where: Timeline for Activating Objectives and Sites

During the planning stage, campaigners should also formulate a schedule for data collection associated with the campaign's goals and audience(s), as was illustrated in Table 6–3. Modifications may occur along the way, but an initial discussion regarding how long each stage is expected to take refines the overall plan. Planners will need to include periods designated for recruiting and training personnel, constructing messages, selecting sources of the campaign's messages, and selecting channels to deliver the messages, the activities that broadly describe tasks associated with the implementation phase of campaigns.

Implementing the Campaign

The implementation component of campaigns is associated with the conscious theoretical decision-making processes, concerning message design as well as source and channel selection, designed to achieve a specified goal with a given audience. At the end of the planning stage, campaigners have compiled an intervention model that identifies audiences, goals, priority and order of goals, and a timeline for entrance of an audience into the campaign. What has not been established is what will be said to

---

FEEDBACK

The efforts associated with trying to reduce drug use have expanded to include many campaigns in public elementary schools. Consider the following audiences that should be addressed.

1. The community's parents have been informed about the introduction of a program into their children's school by a letter sent home. What assumptions regarding the parents' attitudes have been made? What is the objective of the campaign with regard to the parents as an audience?

2. The school's teachers have been given buttons to wear with the message, "We care about our children and teach them to say 'No!'." What assumptions regarding the teachers' attitudes have been made? What is the objective of the campaign with regard to the teachers as an audience?

3. The public has been informed about the introduction of the program through the media, including newspapers and television news reports. What assumptions regarding the public's attitudes have been made? What is the objective of the campaign with regard to the general public as an audience?

4. The students have been informed about the introduction of the program through announcements in school regarding when each class will participate in discussion about drug use and abuse. What assumptions regarding the students' attitudes have been made? What is the objective of the campaign with regard to the students as an audience?

the audience, who will say it, and via what modality. These decisions will be determined in part by the budget that is associated with the campaign. Nonetheless, even within the most modest of budgets (and sometimes more so for modestly budgeted campaigns), the range of choices available to campaigners necessitates careful, systematic, and creative implementation strategies.

Recruiting, Training, and Retaining Campaign Personnel

Who should be the personnel involved in a campaign? In a commercial campaign, is it important whether the source of the advertising or other personnel involved in the campaign use the product or service? During a political campaign, must the speech writer be an individual who supports the candidate? In a social action campaign, does it matter if the campaigners themselves are activists regarding the issue? These decisions are ultimately made during the implementation phase of the campaign, as the personnel associated with the campaign are hired or volunteer to work for the campaign.

It has been argued that, "Communities form individuals' behavior both symbolically and tangibly" (Finnegan, Bracht, and Viswanath, 1989, p. 56). Thus, individuals who hold positions of formal authority in a community as leaders in government, business, and the nonprofit sector may legitimize the campaign, not only by acting as its spokespersons but by working for the campaign. Others in the community may not hold positions of formal authority but still may be active influence agents in the community. These effectors, as Nix, Dressel, and Bates (1977) refer to them, are also important individuals to consider in recruiting the campaign's personnel. Some campaigns have been criticized for placing too much emphasis on individuals while failing to recognize the influences that community, nation, and the larger global community have on an individual's behavior (Hubley, 1986).

The training of campaign personnel, as will be discussed in greater detail in Chapter 7, will depend for the most part upon the nature of the research design selected for the campaign. In those situations where interviews are to be conducted, interview schedules need to be developed, pilot-tested, and refined. Campaign personnel should be trained to conduct the interviews, in-person and by phone, in a consistent and systematic fashion. Additionally, campaigners should form training sessions around the questions that individuals might be expected to ask about the campaign. The focus once more should be on providing consistent responses across all those individuals who are likely to be asked the questions.

Finally, to retain campaign personnel, consideration should be given to their motivations for working with the campaign in the first place. Even in commercial campaigns, the personnel often have a choice among various products to work on at any given time during their careers. They may select the one that they actually work on based on their own goals (Gillespie and King, 1985) or personality traits (Lafer, 1989). In political campaigns, past experience may lead individuals to associate themselves with the campaign (Vinokur-Kaplan and Bergman, 1986). In social action campaigns, community rootedness (Wandersman, Florin, Friedman, and Meier, 1987), social gratification (Daniels, 1985), and serving the community (Hamilton and Fenzel, 1988) seem likely to contribute to individuals' motivation to work for a campaign.

Constructing the Message(s)

The design of campaign messages should draw on theory and research to form the guiding principles. Thus, reference to the principles developed in Chapters 4 and 5 will enhance the campaigner's goals during the process of constructing messages. Based on some of the variable analytic research associated with language use and persuasion, several rules of thumb cut across the active and passive boundaries of this advice. More specific statements regarding the role of symbols and the nature of messages in campaigns is reserved for discussion in Chapter 8. Generally speaking, however, the broad objectives that have been advanced to represent campaigns' consistent themes afford message designers with several important insights to be considered during the implementation stage of campaigns.

First, for campaigners who are concerned with the objective of conversion, success appears more likely when the content of the message is two-sided. After all, the audience opposes the campaigner's position and holds steadfast to another view, which may set up expectations for the campaigner to pitch a hard-sell one-sided version of the campaigner's story. Recognizing and expressing the opposition's point of view before even suggesting a single claim associated with the campaigner's position should create a greater readiness to listen among the hostile groups.

When the broad campaign objective is formation, different strategies are suggested by the various goals. For example, when information is truly the desired ingredient, campaigners have learned that the use of unambiguous language is vital (Siegel, 1988). To motivate the apathetic audience, the focus shifts to personalizing the message (Terris, 1968). For disbelievers, the use of novel evidence may be the most important component of the message (Hample, 1977). When the objective is reinforcement, it might be more effective to forecast the arguments that might be raised against a point-of-view and provide messages that contain preemptive refutation of those arguments than to employ messages that attempt to bolster initial attitudes.

Selecting the Source(s)

The implementation phase of the campaign also requires campaigners to confront the selection of specific individuals to act as the sources of the campaign messages. These decisions, too, should draw foremost on the principles that have already been advanced during previous discussion of passive and active approaches to message processing.

Campaigners should consider, for example, whether or not the audience will respond to the message in an already learned and habitual fashion or if the audience is more likely to consciously assess the message. The campaigners must consider whether or not active or passive message processing is more desirable.

The selection of the source of the message will influence the subsequent process-ing approach. In a political campaign, the individuals who speak in favor of a candi-date may be beloved and trusted societal figures who are likely to evoke a favorable response. If a campaign source is to provide important content to an audience, however, the use of a source that evokes passive message processing may not be the most desirable choice. Rather, the campaigner may choose to select someone who is unknown to the audience but seemingly similar, or in some other way acceptable so that the audience's attention is focused on the message rather than the source.

Often, the selection of sources for messages in a campaign is deemed worthy of a pilot-test:

> *For example, as part of the planning and design of "Sesame Street," staff were concerned about which particular TV characters should be chosen to be the agents of the messages to be communicated to the children. Relatively simple experiments were undertaken in which the same learning messages were transmitted by different characters and in different sequences. Groups of children viewed the presentations on a television screen, and variations in their attention to the screen were measured. These measures of attention became one of the important bases for successful decisions about the format of the program (Rossi and Freeman, 1989, p. 141).*

Many of the issues associated with the selection of a campaign source or sources, as with the specific language variables that are associated with message construction, have been the focus of study in communication for many years. The source's credibil-ity, attractiveness, expert power, legitimate power, referent power, and celebrity status may contribute to the success or failure of a message. The possible interaction between specific source and message variables, and the importance of each to campaigners, comprises the discussion in Chapter 8.

Selecting the Mode(s) of Delivery

The decisions concerned with how to achieve exposure of an audience to a message are also multifaceted in a campaign. The mix of forms of media and interpersonal sources used to convey the campaigners' messages should be implemented in a thoughtful and systematic fashion.

We have an expectation that most advertising campaigns are conducted with attention to every detail. The lighting, the environment, the clothing that the actors wear, and so on. We also have come to expect political candidates to be polished and similarly attentive to details when appearing in a televised debate or a public forum. However, savvy campaigners also consider how the product appears in the grocery stores where the consumers shop. Is it at eye level, or above or below eye level? What other products are near the one that the commercial campaigner is interested in promoting? How does the candidate appear when in public but not scheduled for a public appearance? What does the candidate look like at home in the backyard? Who are the people that represent the social action campaign by getting framed in the media's eye? Do they attend church? What religion are they?

The issues associated with the use of media in a campaign are thoroughly developed in Chapters 9, 10, and 11. For now, however, consider Atkin and Arkin's (1990) discussion of the six tiers of media coverage. Atkin and Arkin assert that radio is primarily useful because it is direct and immediate. Television adds the cinematic revelation that is beyond the scope of radio. Daily newspapers can function to provide more detail and background to stories. Weekly magazines add the rich context that dailies, due to space restriction, seldom achieve. Monthly magazines provide the advantage of perceptions over time due to more widely spaced deadlines. Finally, books provide a more formal mode of documentation and perspective. Campaigners often avail themselves of all of these means to deliver appropriate content to their audiences.

Progress Reports

One final ingredient of the implementation component of campaigns is the scheduled progress reports. These provide minievaluations along the campaign trail. Progress reports are important for the campaigners who may use the information to modify the campaign plan, which might make a difference in the overall outcomes. Also, progress reports may answer questions that could not be answered during the planning stage, providing information for the further development and refinement of the campaign.

Several decisions must be made by campaigners about progress reports, including what instruments should be employed to most effectively assess progress. This issue focuses, as do all the questions associated with operationalization and instrumentation in campaigns, on the instruments' relevance, validity, and reliability. Once these issues have been addressed, the campaigners are better able to draw conclusions regarding what progress has been made, what features of the campaign appear to be promoting success, what ones are hindering progress, and what recommendations emerge for action. In sum, the progress reports will figure prominently in the final phase of the campaigns, the evaluation component.

Evaluating the Campaign

The evaluation component of campaigns addresses the conscious and intentional measurement of outcomes associated with message design and source and channel selection to achieve a specified goal with an audience. Evaluations may be framed in different ways depending upon the audience for whom they are intended. For example, one audience is likely to be the people who can use the information that the campaign uncovers regarding various audiences and the effects of the planned intervention on these audiences. If one audience in a health prevention campaign is a group of women who entrust their care to a curandero, or a modern medicine man, rather than the local organized health-care system, even when the latter provides free services, this information should be distributed among those responsible for making policy regarding free clinics for this group. Another audience that evaluators may address are those to whom the information makes a difference because it can answer important questions. Continuing with the same example, physicians may want to know why more women are not using free clinics. The most common failure associated with the evaluation process is the unsuccessful dissemination of evaluation research into future decision making (Hubley, 1986).

A campaign evaluation provides an overall description of what the campaign looked like. Questions that are addressed focus on several issues. (1) How was the program implemented? (2) Was the implementation consistent with the plan? (3) What groups were targeted during implementation? (4) Which audiences and members within the audiences were pretested? And, (5) what campaign components were dropped, modified, or added? Through the process of answering these questions, the evaluator moves toward making an assessment of the campaign's costs and benefits. Ultimately, campaign evaluations should be comprised of a meta-evaluation, effectiveness evaluation, effects evaluation, interpretations, and recommendations. Each of these contributes something important but significantly different to the understanding of a campaign and the workings of a campaign.

Conducting a Metaevaluation

A meta evaluation is the campaigners' examination of others' evaluations of the campaign. It is not unusual for individuals outside of the campaign structure to undertake an examination of specific campaigns (McAlister, Ramirez, Galavotti, and Gallion, 1989; Reardon, 1989). Campaigners may save themselves time and money associated with duplicating others' efforts by examining these reports. Additionally, in those instances where a campaign has been in progress for a period of years, previous campaign evaluations, which may consist of a compilation of periodic progress reports, should provide useful information to campaign evaluators.

When a metaevaluation is conducted, campaigners look for others' assessments of the over- or underinclusion of target populations and other problems that have been identified for comparison with the present status of the campaign (Rossi and Freeman, 1989).

> *Inefficient target estimation and identification often has serious consequences for the overall program effort. It is questionable in terms of costs, for example, to expose entire communities to educational, housing, medical, and cultural programs when only a small percentage of the community population is at risk (Rossi and Freeman, 1989, p. 136).*

A meta evaluation may contribute to the development of an evaluation plan. The evaluation plan may be to examine the campaign's effectiveness in attaining the goals of the campaigns, as well as the effects that were unplanned. Too often, campaigns focus on whether or not the intended outcomes were attained without examining what other effects may be associated with the campaign (Atkin and Freimuth, 1989).

Examine Effectiveness: Objective-Based

An assessment of a campaign's effectiveness usually takes one of three different forms (Berk and Rossi, 1990). Broadly speaking, an examination of a campaign's effectiveness is an attempt by campaigners to seek an answer to the question, Did the campaign achieve its objectives? First, in answering this question, the campaigner might want to evaluate the marginal effectiveness of the campaign. Such an approach considers whether or not more or less of the campaign intervention would have led to the same outcomes. For example, could the commercial campaigners have advertised in half as many markets and obtained the same market share overall? Could the political campaigner have purchased half as many television spots and obtained the same number of voters? Could the social action campaigners have mailed half as many direct mailings and ended up with an equal number of contributors? If these types of evaluation questions were planned for initially, then the campaign's implementation will have included the collection of data necessary to attain answers to these questions through the appropriate application of statistical analyses.

A second focus that evaluation addressing a campaign's effectiveness may take is to examine the relative effectiveness of the campaign in attaining its goals. Here the issue is whether or not the outcome associated with the audience would have been achieved in the absence of the campaign intervention. Or, the campaigners may consider two or three approaches to addressing the same goals with the same audiences and make comparisons among the outcomes attained via these approaches to answer the questions about relative effectiveness. Obviously, the care with which the campaign is designed and data collected throughout the campaign will contribute to the validity of the assessment of the campaign's relative effectiveness.

Third, campaigners assessing effectiveness are likely to consider cost effectiveness. In this case, the focus is on the units of outcome attained per dollar of cost. For example, if the campaign is designed to promote HIV testing in order to reduce the spread of the HIV infection, then an effort to get *everyone* who practices particularly risky behaviors to be tested would be more effective than a campaign aimed only at a specific group within the at-risk population.

Kim, McLeod, and Palmgren (1989) provide one example of an evaluation of the effectiveness of a social action campaign. The researchers focused on the "I'm Special" program targeted at fourth-graders for the purpose of reducing the use of illegal drugs. The researchers describe the program, which consists of nine sessions conducted once per week for a period of nine weeks.

The theoretical framework for the campaign is depicted as combining elements of social learning theory and Maslow's hierarchy of needs (1970). The student's use of 17 drugs, including alcohol, cigarettes, marijuana, snuff, chewing tobacco, amphetamines, clove cigarettes, stimulants, amyl or butyl nitrite, cocaine, tranquilizers, and hallucinogens was examined. Also, the students' absenteeism, school suspension, and arrest record were evaluated. A longitudinal design covering eight years was used.

The findings demonstrated that current substance users and the incidence of other problem behavior was significantly lower among the students who had completed the "I'm Special" program, particularly for fifth through seventh grades. The effectiveness appears to dissipate around ninth grade, and during eleventh and twelfth grades may even go in the reverse direction. The researchers attribute the latter to a "catch-up" mentality on the part of the students. The recommendations made are to inoculate the students again in junior high and high school rather than relying on the exposure obtained in fourth grade to carry with the students throughout their public school experience.

Examine Effects: Goal-Free

When campaigners conduct an evaluation, they are most likely to focus on the campaign's effectiveness. However, not only should the goal-based effects of a campaign be examined, but also the goal-free effects of campaigns should be evaluated. "Goal-free evaluation essentially means gathering data on a broad array of actual effects and evaluating the importance of these effects in meeting demonstrated needs" (Patton, 1978, p. 109).

For example, Patton (1978) describes one state's campaign designed to teach welfare recipients some basic information regarding parenting and household management. The state welfare department was responsible for conducting workshops, distributing printed materials, and training case workers about ways for low income families to manage their meager resources and become better parents. One major city was picked as a pilot-test location. An independent research institute was contracted to conduct the evaluation of this social action effort. The state legislature and the welfare department proclaimed their support for the campaign and their intent to use the evaluation's findings in future decision making. The evaluators conducted extensive interviews and surveyed the eligible participants. No measurable change was found after 18 months in the parenting skills nor in the household management abilities of the pilot group. The effectiveness of the campaign was deemed null and void; the campaign was canceled; no further funding was to be provided.

This evaluation taken one step further beyond the intended outcomes, however, revealed that when the funds were initially allocated by state government to municipalities, welfare rights' organizations asked what right the government had to tell poor people how to spend their money or how to raise their children. Thus, the actual campaign was delayed; no parenting brochures were ever even printed. In short, the campaign was never implemented in the planned fashion. It generated effects that the planners had not predicted, which inevitably led to the campaign's failure to attain the prescribed goals.

Two campaign maxims may be associated with this example. First, the final acceptance of a plan is never certain during the planning phase of the campaign. Second, campaign implementation is a process that seldom looks like the ideal when the campaign becomes operational:

> *The reality is that actual programs look different from ideal program plans. The evaluation challenge is to assist identified decision makers in determining how far from the ideal plan the program can deviate, and in what ways it can deviate, while still meeting fundamental criteria (Patton, 1978, p. 162).*

In evaluating the effects of a campaign, campaigners should consider the quantity and quality of effort and activity that was put into the campaign. This presses the questions of, "what did the campaigners do," and "how well did they do it." Also, in examining the effects, campaigners must look at the process. What worked and what didn't work? Kim, McLeod, and Shantzis (1989) examined the "Just Say No" campaign and found that, in terms of effectiveness, the campaign failed. More students felt it was more difficult to say, "No," after they had participated in the campaign than before. In terms of effects, the process of making students attentive to issues that surround saying, "No," such as peer pressure, made the students more sensitive to saying, "No," and less able to do so in the posttest period of the campaign.

In sum, the evaluation component of the campaign serves a vital function not only in answering the question, how effective was the campaign in attaining the goals, but in addressing the likely reasons why a goal was or was not attained. Campaigners should share the results of these findings with a number of audiences, including the internal groups who may receive the information in the form of technical reports, colleagues at conferences through the presentation of professional papers, articles, public meetings, media appearances, and news releases to promote the use of interpretations and recommendations in future decision making.

Conclusion

This chapter examined the complex issues and ideals that face those responsible for the management of a campaign. The planning process is intended to afford campaigners with a road map for conducting the campaign. The planning component of persuasive campaigns is particularly concerned with identifying the audiences and the goals of the campaign. Moreover, some priority and ordering of the goals must be assigned. Campaign planning should result in a model of what the campaigners' intentions are for the duration of the campaign and include the causal and intervention hypotheses that emerge from the grand scheme.

The implementation of the actual campaign may, however, be a very different process from the ideal plan. Budget constraints, or other issues that could not be foreseen in advance, may result in modifications of the original plan. Messages, sources, and modes of delivery within the prescribed theoretical framework may be piloted and fail to attain the predicted response. In these instances, the implementation is likely to take a different turn from the original prescribed plan. The evaluation component of the campaign should reflect all of these nuances, both planned and unplanned. Then an assessment of the effectiveness and the effects associated with the campaign is likely to enhance the understanding of the entire campaign process.

Suggestions for Further Reading

Alcalay R., and Taplin, S. (1989). Community health campaigns: From theory to action. In R. E. Rice and C. K. Atkin (Eds.), *Public Communication Campaigns* (2nd ed., pp. 105–130). Newbury Park, CA: Sage Publications.

Augustin M. S., Stevens, E., and Hicks, D. (1973). An evaluation of the effectiveness of a children and youth project. *Health Services Report, 88,* 942–946.

Chen, H., and Rossi, P. H. (1980). The multigoal, theory driven approach to evaluation: A model linking basic and applied social science. *Social Forces, 59,* 106–122.

King, J. A., Morris, L. L., and Fitz-Gibbon, C. T. (1987). *How to Assess Program Implementation.* Beverly Hills, CA: Sage Publications.

Chapter **7**

═══════════════════════════════

Measurement and Research Design in Persuasive Campaigns

Practical but creative data collection consists of using whatever resources are available to do the best job possible. There are many constraints. Our ability to think of alternatives is limited. Resources are always limited. This means that data collection will be imperfect, so dissenters from evaluation findings, who want to attack a study's methods, can always find some grounds for doing so. A major reason for actively involving decision makers and information users in making methods decisions is to deal with weaknesses in the design, and consider tradeoff threats to data quality, before data are generated.
—*MICHAEL QUINN, SOCIOLOGY PROFESSOR*
(CITED IN PATTON, 1982, P. 211)

For many of us, hardly a week goes by that we do not receive either (1) a phone call in which the caller wants to ask our opinion regarding a political candidate, a social issue, or a product on the market; or (2) a piece of direct mail that seeks our input regarding the same issues. One mass mailing from a national animal rights group (People for the Ethical Treatment of Animals—PETA, 1990), received by one of the authors, employed a series of questions, as shown in Table 7-1.

The respondent is asked to reply by checking either "yes" or "no," in response to each question and to, "PLEASE RESPOND WITHIN 10 DAYS!" Presumably, the questions have been designed with some purpose in mind that is associated with measuring attitudes and behaviors related to the objectives of the organization's social action campaign. Indeed, an important part of the process of managing campaigns is planning for testable results. Planning for testable results requires the selection of measurement tools and appropriate research designs, which are the topics of this chapter.

This chapter examines the purposes of research design in persuasive campaigns. Research plays an indispensable role in campaigns. Without it, many bad decisions are

TABLE 7–1 Questions Posed by People for the Ethical Treatment of Animals

1. Before reading this mailing, were you aware of the vast numbers of animals who suffer and perish every year in American research laboratories?
2. Did you realize that the vast majority of painful animal experimentation has no relation at all to human survival or the elimination of disease?
3. Do you approve of lethal animal experimentation to test new cosmetics and household products?
4. Do you approve of military testing of new weapons, poison gases and radiation on live animals?
5. Would you support Congressional legislation such as the Consumer Products Safe Testing Act extending protection to all experimental subjects? (Nearly 90 percent are currently excluded from any protection.)
6. Would you like to see your tax dollars directed toward research that emphasizes alternatives to animal experimentation?
7. Do you see any need for a major public education effort to expand awareness about animal rights?

made, thereby dooming campaigns. The relationship between formative studies, impact studies, and efficiency analyses in persuasive campaigns is developed in this chapter. The goals and types of research designs common to persuasive campaigns will be overviewed. In addition, possible approaches to collecting and assessing data in persuasive campaigns are evaluated, and the questions posed in Table 7–2 will be addressed.

Purposes of Research Design

It becomes somewhat obvious when one considers the planning, implementation, and evaluation of persuasive campaigns that some sort of framework is needed to weave

TABLE 7–2 Questions about Measurement and Research Design

1. What are the purposes of research design in persuasive campaigns?
2. Compare and contrast incidence and prevalence.
3. What are three strategies that campaign research design should include?
4. When constructing interview or survey questions, what outcomes are campaigners interested in assessing and forecasting?
5. Discuss four types of surveys.
6. Discuss indirect methods of gathering quantitative information.
7. What are some advantages and disadvantages associated with qualitative research designs?
8. What are some advantages and disadvantages associated with quantitative research designs?

these efforts together. The theoretical perspective that campaigners adopt should guide many if not most activities. However, most theoretical propositions are broad enough in scope to allow several interpretations, so it requires more than just theory to execute a campaign plan. Once again, consider the questions that appear on the survey regarding animal rights.

An important objective for the animal rights' campaigners may have been conversion or change. The campaigners who adopted this survey may have conceptualized the questions after a period of formative research in which they interviewed members of an audience with already formed negative responses to the animal rights' issue. If this is the campaigners' basis for developing the survey questions, the purpose of asking questions associated with animal experimentation and its resulting pain and suffering may be to provoke an already learned response that emerged during those interviews. Perhaps few of the interviewees associated animal experimentation with pain and suffering. The campaigners may also have learned from the interviews, however, that few of the interviewees would want to perceive themselves as responsible for inflicting pain and suffering on animals. The point is that the questions on the survey may reflect the results of formative research, an early strategy in the design of campaign research.

If the animal rights' questionnaire was designed with no specific input from the audience, then the questionnaire items may be based on the campaigners' *assumption* that people do not want to perceive themselves as causing pain and suffering to animals, and that very few members of the audience presently perceive animal experimentation to be associated with animals' pain and suffering. The campaigners may reason that to inform the audience of the connection will lead to cognitive dissonance and a motivation to change. In reality, however, the audience may already perceive that animal experimentation causes pain and suffering to animals, but this realization is outweighed by their belief that animal experimentation promotes the health and welfare of human beings. In this case, the questionnaire items may further polarize the audience in a negative direction due to the manner in which the questions are framed, a fact that could have been learned during a period of formative research. The use of formative research can avoid such mistakes.

The primary purposes of campaign research are to assess and forecast an audience's needs. In order to enhance the likelihood of a campaign's success, in terms of effectiveness as well as the generation of testable results, it is wise to include information users at the earliest stages of the campaign during the period of formative research, which takes place during the planning phase of the campaign. Campaigners most often assess and forecast the audience's needs, however, during impact studies conducted as part of the implementation component of campaigns. Recall that implementation of a campaign requires development of messages, the content of which should reflect audience needs. Campaign research designs should also include an assessment and forecast of needs during an efficiency analysis at the campaign's end, during the evaluation component of campaigns. Thus, campaign research design attempts to assess and forecast audience needs.

Needs Assessment

When the purpose of campaign research design is to assess an audience's needs, campaigners are attempting to answer one or more of the following questions: (1) What individual needs are most salient with regard to the campaign topic and audience? (2) What societal needs are most salient with regard to the campaign topic and audience? (3) Should the campaign focus on individual or societal needs, or both?

On the animal rights' issue, campaigners might have focused on an individual need, such as people's love for their pets, as a way to involve the audience with the issue and promote active message processing. Or, they might have focused on the desire to discover cures for illness and disease, an important societal need that should also promote issue involvement, and therefore active message processing. If formative research indicated that the latter was determined to be the most salient need, then the campaigners could have considered the option of using messages counterarguing the use of animal experimentation for medical purposes.

The American Cancer Society (ACS) provides another example of the use of formative research to assess audience needs. The ACS has undertaken an image campaign for the 1990s (Hanily, 1991). Previous slogans associated with the ACS, such as "Fight cancer with a check-up and a check," "You do make a difference," and "Together we're better," combine individual and societal needs simultaneously. However, no qualitative or quantitative data were collected to assess the effectiveness of these slogans.

The current campaign, by contrast, has been undertaken in a much more systematic manner, involving several steps. A research company initially conducted focus group interviews with about 40 ACS staff and regional volunteers. The focus group interviews revealed information that was used to design questions in the next phase of the research, a national survey of approximately 1,000 men and women. The interviews attempted to assess awareness of progress in the fight against cancer and awareness of the ACS. The national survey indicated that the public is deeply concerned about cancer and is willing to support cancer research. However, the results also revealed an image problem for the ACS, finding that the public is generally unaware of ACS activities, and does not perceive the ACS as any better or worse than other organizations. Thus, an important function of needs assessment is to establish the incidence and prevalence of those attitudes and behaviors related to the individual and/or societal needs associated with the campaign topic.

Incidence

In establishing the incidence of an attitude or behavior, campaigners attempt to determine the degree or the range of occurrence of an effect with regard to the number of new cases identified in a specified area during a specified period of time (Rossi and Freeman, 1989). For example, during formative research, PETA campaigners may determine that 10 percent of adults surveyed acquired a pet during the previous year, or that 25 percent know someone who has benefited from medical treatments which may be associated with animal experimentation. ACS campaigners may learn that 53 percent of adults surveyed have had a friend or relative who has had cancer during the past five years. Perhaps 35 percent of them are aware of the ACS having done something to benefit the friend or relative.

Based on such formative research, messages, sources, and channels will be chosen to implement the campaign. At the end of the implementation period, ACS campaigners will probably want to know the incidence of awareness of the organization's activities. If research indicates that the campaign is having the predicted impact, it would probably be continued until another assessment is conducted or the campaign ends. If the predicted impact is not achieved, adjustments may be mandated before the campaign progresses further.

Prevalence

Prevalence of an attitude or behavior concerns the number of existing cases of an attitude or behavior in a particular area at a specified time (Rossi and Freeman, 1989). In order to determine the prevalence of an attitude or behavior, campaigners focus on how prominent or widespread the attitude or behavior is. PETA campaigners may determine, for example, that 50 percent of adults surveyed have a pet that they consider to be like a member of the family. The prevalence of the condition tells nothing about the period of time during which such bonds were created. Campaigners may find that 75 percent of adults interviewed in New York City know someone who has benefited from medical treatments that may be associated with animal experimentation. Again, it is unclear whether this is over the course of their lifetimes or during the previous six months. ACS campaigners may learn that 95 percent of Americans have a friend or relative who has had cancer.

In another example, during formative research campaigners may learn that five out of 1,000 students at a large southwestern university tested HIV positive, thus indicating the prevalence of the AIDS virus in the sample. Campaigners might retest the same 1,000 students one year later and find seven to be HIV positive. Campaigners then may conclude that the rate of incidence in that sample for the year tested was two per 1,000 students.

Yet another example of campaigners using formative research to assess audience needs in terms of incidence and prevalence involves the finding that 20 percent of elementary-age children who reside in a large southeastern city have experimented with some form of illegal drugs, a statement about the prevalence of the condition. The finding that five percent of third graders in a sample school experimented with drugs during the past twelve months addresses the incidence of use. Both findings would be important during the planning phase of a campaign to determine the campaign's audiences and objectives, and the order and the priority for both. These findings could also be important if obtained during the implementation component of the campaign to pilot test the success of the intervention, or during the evaluation component of a campaign to assess the campaign's effects and effectiveness.

Needs Forecast

Once campaigners assess the current needs of an audience based on the incidence and prevalence of specific attitudes and behaviors displayed by the audience, the information is used by campaigners to *forecast* an audience's future needs, which also is done in terms of incidence and prevalence. Again, needs forecast occurs not only during formative research, but also during impact studies and efficiency analyses. Since the campaigners' goal is to project from a current situation to the future, the problems

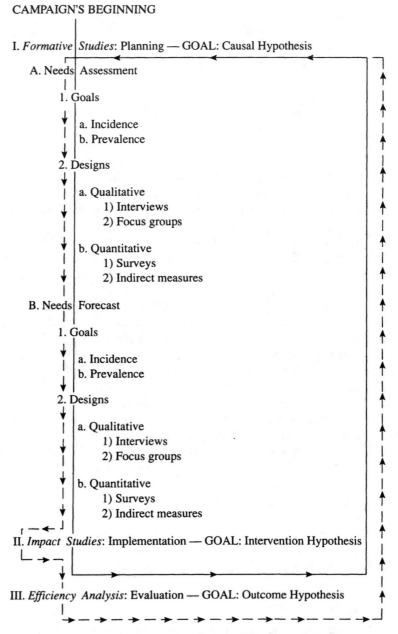

CAMPAIGN'S BEGINNING

I. *Formative Studies*: Planning — GOAL: Causal Hypothesis

   A. Needs Assessment

      1. Goals

         a. Incidence
         b. Prevalence

      2. Designs

         a. Qualitative
            1) Interviews
            2) Focus groups

         b. Quantitative
            1) Surveys
            2) Indirect measures

   B. Needs Forecast

      1. Goals

         a. Incidence
         b. Prevalence

      2. Designs

         a. Qualitative
            1) Interviews
            2) Focus groups

         b. Quantitative
            1) Surveys
            2) Indirect measures

II. *Impact Studies*: Implementation — GOAL: Intervention Hypothesis

III. *Efficiency Analysis*: Evaluation — GOAL: Outcome Hypothesis

FIGURE 7–1 Measurement and Research Design in Persuasive Campaigns

associated with this projection include the assumption that the future will be like the past. Thus, variables that are likely to be related to future incidence must also be forecast, rather than assuming that conditions today automatically reflect conditions in the future.

For example, if the incidence of testing HIV positive among college students is increasing, campaigners may forecast that the incidence will continue to increase if no specific efforts to arrest the condition are made. If during formative research the campaigners determine that 33 out of every 100 American college students surveyed believe that AIDS is a disease that occurs only among certain groups, the prevalence of this belief may lead campaigners to forecast that students need more information regarding the incidence of AIDS. A problem with this conclusion is that college students may change their thinking as evidence of AIDS victims contradicts their present belief. Magic Johnson's revelations, for example, contributed to such change. However, they will not know what behaviors to adopt unless campaigners specifically focus on messages about the prevention of AIDS. Thus, in forecasting the audience's future needs, it appears reasonable to project that the audience needs information about the incidence of HIV positive cases among college students, plus information about how to prevent or arrest this trend.

Several factors affect the incidence of AIDS among college students, including the practice of unprotected sex with multiple partners. If campaigners find through their surveys that 88 out of every 100 American college students engage in unprotected sex with multiple partners, prevalence of this behavior should guide campaigners' attempts to forecast the target audience's need for information. Specifically, they may decide that students need information regarding the prevention of AIDS, as much or more than they need information about the incidence of AIDS, among college students as a means to decrease the incidence of AIDS in this group.

Campaigners forecast an audience's needs during the planning component of campaigns to further guide the selection of campaign objectives. Campaigners forecast an audience's needs to tailor or refine the campaign during the implementation component of campaigns. Campaigners forecast an audience's needs at the end of a campaign to project future directions for efforts in the area. Thus, the forecasting of audience needs is a vital part of campaigns at every stage. Campaigners select from two basic research design strategies and numerous research tools to assess and forecast audience needs.

Research Design Strategies in Persuasive Campaigns

Campaigners' research designs are a blueprint for attaining testable results. Figure 7–1 provides a visual summary of the strategies, purposes, and decisions that are involved in campaign measurement and research design, which will be discussed in this chapter. This model will be systematically applied, drawing upon a campaign designed to enhance cultural diversity in American law schools (Harris, 1992a, 1992b). This campaign sought to change internal and external policies of American law schools and justify legal organizations. The steps undertaken to achieve multiculturalism will be examined within the model's framework in the chapter's feedback sections.

Formative Studies: Planning

As depicted in Figure 7-1, campaign research begins with formative studies. Formative studies, conducted to shape and guide campaign decision making during the planning stage, may be based on a causal hypothesis, such as unemployment increases the incidence of crime. Formative studies should always result in causal hypotheses, however tenuous, as a means to suggest the appropriate intervention or interventions.

Formative research during a political campaign may indicate that the candidate has a poor image among working middle-class adults, and that many working women perceive the candidate as insensitive to their needs. An assessment of the audience's needs may show that working women need more sites of affordable day-care. The prevalence of this attitude may be found among 75 of 100 working women surveyed. Further efforts to accurately assess this audience's needs may determine that 15 percent of women who had obtained jobs in the state's capital city during the previous six months failed to find affordable child care and had placed their children in temporary care situations. Based on this data, political campaigners: can forecast the incidence of need for such care; or, can lobby to draw attention to the need. Campaigners may also construct the following causal hypothesis suggested by these findings: "the candidate's lack of support for day-care leads to lack of support for this candidate by working middle class voters, particularly working women." If these audiences are important to the candidate's election, the goals of the campaign will have to focus on reducing hostility among these voters.

As another example, consider a commercial campaign in which formative research determines that the target audience is not able to discern a difference between several brands of the same product, for example, frozen orange juice. The prevalence of this attitude might involve 20 percent of adults surveyed who use the product. The incidence may stem from the finding that 20 percent of those adults interviewed who had tried three different brands of the same product during a month's time perceived virtually no differences. Campaigners may learn that whichever brand is on sale or available is the one that the consumer purchases. The causal hypothesis in this instance might be that, "absence of perceived brand differences leads to the purchase of the

---

FEEDBACK

According to Harris (1992b), the campaign to enhance cultural diversity in American law schools employed a causal hypothesis that lack of awareness is responsible for underrepresentation of minorities in law schools.

1. How might campaigners use an individual need to promote increased awareness?
2. How might campaigners use a societal need to promote increased awareness?

cheapest or the most available brand." This suggests that, assuming some difference in orange juice brands exists, campaigners will need to make that difference known to consumers.

Many unsuccessful campaigns have been criticized for failing to include formative studies in their research design (Salmon, 1989). This failure may have resulted from a presumed causal hypothesis that formative research may have shown to be false. Thus, successful campaigns include careful formative research (Flora et al., 1989).

For example, American dairy producers were concerned at one point that American consumers needed to be convinced not to worry about cholesterol in milk. However, formative research revealed that most consumers were not concerned about this. Thus, dairy producers saved the costs of a large campaign, and perhaps more important, avoided the risks associated with messages concerning cholesterol in milk, which might have caused consumers to begin to worry.

In the animal rights' survey (Table 7–1), the first question asks about the reader's level of awareness with regard to the use of animals in American research laboratories. This may have been designed to satisfy a formative research function to assess the audience's need for information about the topic. If most people who responded to the survey indicated a lack of awareness of the use of animals in research laboratories, campaigners may conclude that, in the future, they will need to focus their efforts on the audience's need to be so informed. If most who responded to the survey indicated that they were aware of the use of animals in research laboratories, however, campaigners may correctly or incorrectly conclude that the campaign does not need to focus on providing such information. It also may be true that those people who are most likely to respond to the survey are precisely the ones who are already informed and support the campaign. That does not, however, preclude the need for information among the audience that campaigners would like to convert, or among the audience that campaigners hope to reinforce.

Other research design issues which are discussed in this chapter contribute to campaigners' ability to draw conclusions from needs assessment and forecast. Such issues include: (1) the selection of the type of research design; (2) the choice of the method to collect information; and (3) the choice of a means to assess the information. Before discussing these, however, we consider the unique contributions that continued needs assessment and forecast during the implementation and evaluation components of campaigns make to the campaign process.

Impact Studies: Implementation

Impact studies also deal with the implementation component of campaigns. Refer again to Figure 7–1. A similar process of needs assessment and forecast occurs during the implementation phase but for different reasons. The results of formative studies lead quite naturally to the development of a campaign plan and the design of an appropriate intervention. Commercial campaigners may determine during a period of formative research, for example, that consumers prefer "fresh" ingredients in their foods and beverages. As a result, they may forecast that many consumers need information regarding a product's freshness. The intervention hypothesis might be:

"perceptions that a product contains fresh ingredients will lead to the product's purchase." The intervention to follow then may focus on promoting the product's freshness, and impact studies can determine, while the campaign is ongoing, the effects that the campaign intervention is having on the target audience. Just such a situation has, in fact, occurred with enough regularity in commercial campaigns that the Food and Drug Administration (FDA) has stepped in to prevent what it perceives as misuse of the term, "fresh".

The advertising campaign associated with the sale of Citrus Hill Fresh Choice orange juice provides an illustration of the FDA's policy. The FDA seized 12,000 gallons of the juice, which is made from water and concentrate, from a suburban Minneapolis supermarket warehouse, charging that the juice was mislabeled and confused customers (*Atlanta Journal*, 1991, April 25). The FDA charged that, "Using the term 'fresh' for any food that has been heated or chemically processed is false and misleading" (*Atlanta Journal*, p. A-1). Thus, a campaigner's intervention occasionally is constrained by federal, state, and local laws. In such cases, the government's assessment and forecast of the audience's needs subsumes campaigners' activities. Formative research should be able to identify such constraints, thereby saving the expense of a misdirected campaign. In this case, impact studies revealed the need to change the campaign's direction and focus.

As another example, consider a situation in which political campaigners determine, through strategic formative research, that voters have more interest in how the government is going to care for an increasingly older population than voters have interest in how the government is going to pay for an increasing number of AIDS cases in the population. A political candidate may focus attention on addressing the need regarding provision of care for the elderly, or the candidate may address the issue of making care for AIDS victims a more salient issue in voters' minds. The intervention hypothesis in the former situation might be that, "addressing care for the elderly will generate support for the candidate." The intervention hypothesis in the latter situation might be that, "increased awareness regarding the cost of care for AIDS patients will generate greater interest in the issue and in those candidates addressing the issue." The two hypotheses suggest quite different objectives for political campaigners and different levels of initial issue involvement for the audience. The latter forecasts variance in the amount of mental effort likely to be expended to process messages associated with the two topics.

Questions three and four in the animal rights' survey may have been designed to assess the impact of the mailing's message on readers' attitudes regarding the use of animal experimentation to test cosmetics or military weapons, including poison gases and radiation. If respondents indicate that they approve of animal experimentation to serve these purposes, campaigners may conclude that the message intervention has failed and must be adjusted in some way. In response to this finding, campaigners may change the content of their messages, or they may decide to increase the frequency of their messages. Such actions would be designed to enhance intended campaign outcomes. However, these actions may be inappropriate responses, particularly if respondents favor spending tax dollars on research to find alternatives to animal experimentation, suggesting that they prefer some other means to attain the same ends.

FEEDBACK

According to Harris (1992b), the campaign to increase cultural diversity in American law schools used an intervention hypothesis that, "Increased awareness will lead to increased representation of minorities in American law schools." Provide a justification for your answer to each of the following questions.

   1. What audiences should campaigners target?
   2. What objectives are appropriate for each audience?
   3. What sources would be the most effective in delivering campaign messages to each audience?

The animal rights' survey is an example of an instrument that is too broad in scope to specifically assess any particular audience's responses. The survey seems to focus on formative issues that should inform campaigners' decisions regarding specific interventions to be used during the implementation component of the campaign. The survey also seeks to measure comprehension and response to an already formulated message, which is an appropriate part of an impact study. A campaign is an incremental process, and, to be most effective, campaign research must be sensitive to and reflect this fact through the selection and use of the three design strategies. In addition to formative and impact studies, an efficiency analysis should be included in the research plan.

Efficiency Analysis: Evaluation

When conducted with precision, the results of impact studies contribute to campaigners' ability to conduct thorough efficiency analysis, which is an important part of the evaluation component of campaigns. Refer again to Figure 7-1. Note that the choices and decisions to be made parallel the choices and decisions which go in to the formation of impact studies. An efficiency analysis helps to generate outcome hypotheses, statements regarding the actual relationship between the campaign's intervention and the campaign's outcomes once the campaign ends. For example, more information increased college students' level of knowledge about AIDS; however, more information did not reduce the incidence of unprotected sex among college students.

The first step in an efficiency analysis is to specify the costs and benefits of a campaign (Sandefur, Freeman, and Rossi, 1986). Then, to assess the benefits, campaigners may compare the incidence and prevalence of an audience's needs at the end of a campaign compared to at the beginning. Campaigners for animal rights, for example, may have some initial figures regarding the audience's willingness to use tax dollars to support research designed to find alternatives to animal experimentation. In this instance, the responses to the sixth question on the animal rights' campaign survey

(Table 7–1) may lead to a conclusion regarding the overall success of the campaign in generating this support. Starting figures are essential if such a comparison is to be made. Without them, it would be difficult to draw these conclusions, demonstrating once more the importance of formative study. Campaigners working to enhance the cultural diversity in American law schools, for example, possess data on the admission of minorities to American law schools each year, which will provide an important source of information that can be used to evaluate the campaign at its end.

In summary, three basic strategies are used to attain the primary purposes associated with research design in persuasive campaigns. The strategies include the use of formative studies during the planning phase of the campaign, the use of impact studies during the implementation component of the campaign, and the use of efficiency analysis during the evaluation component of the campaign. The purposes associated with these strategies are to assess and forecast the incidence and prevalence of specific attitudes and behaviors associated with the campaign topic in the campaign audience, and to plot changes in these over the course of a campaign. To accomplish these purposes, campaigners must specify the type of research design to be used in conjunction with each design strategy.

Types of Research Designs

Campaigners may employ two general types of research designs when planning for testable results. Campaigners may elect either a qualitative approach or a quantitative approach, or combine the two designs in some meaningful fashion. Qualitative research favors reliance on critical analysis and synthesis of information that is primarily verbal (Maddala, 1983; Miles and Huberman, 1984). For example, political campaigners may gather information during a period of formative study from the records of public speeches made by various community organizations to determine what voters perceive to be the most important issues facing them. A qualitative political campaign research design based on this information may generate the conclusion that the public is concerned about the values of today's young people. This conclusion could be reached after critically synthesizing the main topics of the speeches.

Quantitative research, on the other hand, favors reliance on techniques for counting and measuring relevant information (Kish, 1987). Political campaigners using organizational speeches during a period of formative quantitative research may conclude that 45 percent of public concerns about young people involves their use of illegal drugs, 20 percent deals with their lack of goals for the future, 15 percent focuses on young people's indiscriminate sexual behavior, and the remaining 20 percent deals with various issues relating to their lack of involvement in the community. Campaigners should remember that "design and data-collection decisions are a far cry from being neutral, objective, or rational; such decisions are political, subjective, and satisficing" (Patton, 1978, p. 202). The discussion which follows illustrates this, noting the advantages and disadvantages associated with the choices.

Qualitative Research: Approaches to Collecting Information

Qualitative research designs are often less expensive than quantitative approaches and may be sufficient during periods of formative research to pinpoint the nature of an audience's needs. The general disadvantage associated with qualitative research is an inability to generalize beyond self-selected participants (Rossi and Freeman, 1989).

Refer again to Figure 7–1. Remember that campaigners have to decide whether to use qualitative or quantitative research at three points in time.

Several options are available to campaigners who elect to collect information using a qualitative research design during periods of formative, impact, and/or efficiency study. The most common qualitative methods for collecting campaign information are (1) open-ended interviewing and (2) focus groups. An example of each is included in the discussion to follow. In both cases, interviewers or moderators may use projective questions and/or may pretest campaign messages on the interviewees or the focus group members. Projective questions ask respondents to predict what someone else, such as a spouse or a neighbor, thinks or does in a particular situation. This technique may provide insights in to individuals' feelings that otherwise would not be available through self-report measures.

Open-Ended Interviewing

The most important task involved in open-ended interviewing is the construction of questions to provide useful information. Several principles guide the campaigners' efforts. See Table 7–3 for an example. First, the interviewer should strive to insure that the questions are really open-ended. For example, political campaigners attempting to assess audience needs during a period of formative research before actually designing a presidential candidate's campaign might ask, "What problems do you have with the present administration?" This implies, of course, that respondents have some problems. A better way to do this is to first ask a filter question, "Do you have any problems with the present administration?" Then, for those who answer in the

---

TABLE 7–3 Standardized Open-Ended Interview about Smoking in Public Places

1. Should people smoke in public?
   PROBE: Why or why not?
2. Should airports ban smoking in waiting areas?
FOLLOW-UP: Is segregation of smokers in waiting areas sufficient?
   PROBE: Why or why not?
3. Should grocery stores ban smoking in their facilities?
FOLLOW-UP: Is smoking in grocery stores harmful to public health?
FOLLOW-UP: Does smoking in grocery stores present a fire hazard?
4. Should restaurants ban smoking in dining areas?
   PROBE: Why or why not?
5. Should employers ban smoking in employee offices?
   PROBE: Why or why not?

---

affirmative, pose the follow–up question, "What problems do you have with the present administration?"

A second consideration during the construction of interview questions is whether or not the questions are clear and neutral in tone. The same political campaigner might ask, "Are you aware that the increased property tax millage rate in your county is a direct result of the incumbent's decision to elevate national education requirements?" This question may prove confusing to someone who is unclear about the meaning of the terms "millage," "incumbent," or "elevate" in the context of the question. The tone of the question also suggests that the increased millage rate is a negative outcome, when the connection to education may, in fact, make the rate a positive outcome in relation to the present administration. A different approach to the same question might be, "How do you feel about property taxes going up in your county?"

Care also should be taken in the construction of interview questions to frame them in a sensitive manner. The question, "Don't you realize that it's your duty and responsibility as an American citizen to make an informed decision when voting for the individual who will lead this country?", fails to be sensitive to the many reasons why an individual would not be informed and may not vote. A more sensitive approach would be, "What would you like to know about the candidates to help you decide whom to vote for in the election?" Another question might be, "What help do you need in order to get to the polls on election day to vote?"

Campaigners should also prepare potential followup questions and probes as potential responses to interviewees' answers. For example, if an individual indicates that they work full time and are in need of a sitter in order to get to the polling place, the campaigner should be prepared to ask, "What time do you get off work?"; "Would that be a good time for us to schedule someone to come by and watch your children while you vote?". If an elderly individual indicates that they have no means of transportation to get to the polling place, the interviewer should be prepared to inquire, "What would be a good time for us to arrange to give you a ride to where you can vote?" Such information has been useful in past campaigns in order to "get out the vote." It requires that campaigners strategically anticipate responses to questions in order to plan follow–up questions.

Other times, interviewees may provide information that is too broad or general in nature to provide sufficient insight to campaigners. In these instances, campaigners may want to probe the general response to seek more specific information. For example, in response to the question, "Do you have any problems with the present administration?", an interviewee might answer, "Other than the fact that they're Republican, you mean?" The interviewer may nod, and the interviewee may respond, "Isn't that enough?" Interviewers should be prepared to respond to these situations with persistence and patience in an effort to provide more substantive information. It is also helpful to remind the interviewee that there are no right or wrong answers; that their opinions on the matter are what is being sought.

An interviewer may further increase the cooperativeness of the interviewee by communicating the reason that a particular question is being asked. This shows respect for the interviewee and contributes to the two-way nature of the communication that is taking place. For example, the interviewer might say, "We are trying to understand the effects of the recent property tax increase on voters. Will you be able to afford the increase?" If the interviewee answers, "No," then the interviewer may probe by asking, "Will you have to sell your property?"

Words of support or gratitude from time to time during the course of the interview will also contribute to the willingness of interviewees to more fully and accurately disclose their attitudes and behaviors. For example, the interviewer may say early on during the interview, "I really appreciate your taking the time to talk to me like this." After the interview has been completed, the campaigner might again acknowledge the time given, "Thank you for taking your time to talk to me. It's the best way for us to find out what the voters are really thinking."

Three basic approaches to qualitative interviewing are used to collect information to be employed in formative, impact, and efficiency studies during persuasive campaigns (Patton, 1982). One approach to qualitative open-ended interviewing is informal, with the interviewer's generation of questions occurring as a natural part of the conversation. This may be most common when an interviewer participates in, or observes, some activity in the field that directly relates to the campaign's topic area. For example, social action campaigners may participate in sit-ins, marches, or other activities at the grass roots level in order to assess what participants are thinking and why they are behaving in particular ways. The advantage of this approach is that the interviewer is able to be responsive to individual differences, as well as situational changes. On the other hand, it requires a great deal of time to get the information necessary to move ahead with the campaign, the primary disadvantage of this approach.

A second approach to qualitative interviewing involves the formulation of a list of questions or issues to be used during the interview. Refer again to Table 7–3. The broad issues of this interview are the boundaries for the regulation of smoking in public places and the underlying reasons for those boundaries. An interview guide for this research might consist of: (1) Should smoking in public be banned? (2) Does smoking in grocery stores present any risks other than the health consequences of passive smoke? (3) Is smoking in an employee's own office a private or public matter? The formulation of this interview guide acts as a way to enhance the likelihood of obtaining the same information from those who are interviewed. What varies in this approach is the way that a particular issue may be framed when speaking with different interviewees, or the order in which the questions are asked.

For example, campaigners may interview individuals from a variety of age or educational groups and frame their questions accordingly. The advantage of this approach is the provision of a more systematic and comprehensive set of issues to frame the informational context. The disadvantage is that some important topics are likely to be omitted, since the questions do not grow out of the situation, and campaigners may overlook important issues in constructing the original questions.

A third approach to qualitative interviewing involves the formulation of a standardized, open-ended interview, such as the one in Table 7–3. This consists of a set of specific questions, which have been carefully worded and specifically arranged in a logical sequence, that will be asked of each interviewee in precisely the same fashion. Thus, the information gathered is more systematic and may be more thorough in its revelations. Differences among interviewers will also be less likely. The disadvantage of this approach involves loss of flexibility and spontaneity, which interviewers find desirable, particularly based upon some respondents' answers.

When conducting an interview, the issue of how to collect the data becomes vital. Interviews should be tape-recorded to increase the accuracy of the data collection and to grant the interviewer the ability to pay more attention to the interviewee. The interviewer is likely to still want to take notes during the interview to provide a quick reference for specific highlights of a given interview, and to transcribe the interviews when possible to provide a useful form for information analysis. In summary, open-ended interviews provide an important method for assessing the nature of an audience's needs but are unable to specify the extent of the need.

Focus Groups

Focus groups usually consist of 8 to 12 individuals brought together to interact in a comfortable manner, with a moderator encouraging free expression of opinions. The primary purpose of a focus group is to obtain information that people are likely to pass to one another during their own free daily discussions. One of the goals of the focus group leader is to encourage free and open discussion. To do this, the leader must stress that there are no right or wrong answers; that all input is valued. Table 7–4 offers an example of a focus group agenda.

One of the authors received a phone call from an area radio station that desired to increase its listening share. In order to gather information about how to be successful in this effort, the station had identified several screening questions to be used in obtaining individuals to comprise several focus groups. The questions focused on how often the individual who answered the telephone listened to the radio, which stations the individual preferred, the listener's age, and his/her music preference(s). Based on responses to these questions, some of the respondents were asked to meet at an area conference center to share their ideas for improving the station's format, an attempt to increase the audience share, for which participants often receive modest compensation.

TABLE 7–4 Focus Group Agenda: Public Awareness of American Cancer Society

1. What diseases are you most concerned might affect your own or your family's health?
FOLLOW-UP: Why are you concerned about this?
2. What health organizations are you aware of?
FOLLOW-UP: How are you aware of these?
3. What do health organizations do?
4. How are health organizations funded?
5. What does the American Cancer Society do?
6. Who benefits from research conducted and sponsored by the American Cancer Society?
7. What are the warning signs of lung, breast, and colon cancer?
8. What are early detection programs?
FOLLOW-UP: Where are such programs available?
9. What is the Great American Smokeout campaign?

Through the use of focus groups, the moderator is able to obtain information similar to what might be obtained from open-ended interviews. Because a small group of people are involved in answering the moderator's questions, a variety of questions are likely to be raised in response to participants' answers. Not only does the moderator respond to participants' responses with additional questions, other members of the group may ask questions, as well. This provides the flexibility associated with informal open-ended interviews, while facilitating the systematic collection of information.

The use of focus groups has become increasingly popular in all types of campaigns. This technique played an instrumental role in George Bush's 1988 presidential election campaign (Ross, 1989). Prospective themes for Bush's television spots were pretested using focus groups, enabling the campaign to learn in advance how "Reagan Democrats," the key target audience for the Bush campaign, would respond to the spots (see Chapter 10). Despite their value in providing insights concerning people's reactions to brands, candidates, or causes, however, campaigners need to remember that focus groups are not a substitute for good quantitative research.

> *As with any qualitative research approach, however, care must be taken not to interpret focus group interview results quantitatively. If for example, 5 out of 10 respondents in a focus group do not understand portions of the messages, it does not necessarily mean that 50% of the total target population will be confused. Such lack of understanding among the pretest respondents suggests, however, that the message may need revisions to increase comprehension. In sum, focus group testing is indicative, not definitive (Atkin and Freimuth, 1989, p. 145).*

In sum, campaigners often use qualitative research designs to gather information during a campaign, often because the cost associated with qualitative data collection is comparatively less than the cost associated with gathering information through the use of a systematic quantitative design. However, qualitative research carries inherent limitations, such as the inability to generalize beyond the particular participants and,

---

FEEDBACK

If you were given the task of assessing (a) undergraduate pre-law students, (b) law school faculty, and (c) the legal community of their awareness of and support for greater cultural diversity in American law schools:

1. What would you be interested in learning during periods of formative research?
2. Design a focus group agenda for use with undergraduate pre-law students.
3. Design an open-ended interview for use with law school faculty.
4. How would you assess the legal community's awareness? Justify your approach.

quite often, its time-consuming nature, which may direct campaigners to the selection of quantitative research designs in many settings.

Quantitative Research: Approaches to Collecting Information

David Ogilvy, the founder and director of Ogilvy and Mather, credits much of his own professional success to a reverence for numbers (Wilson, 1988). He asserts that in product advertising, the emphasis is more commonly placed on creativity rather than on research. The time, money, and skills necessary to produce valid and reliable quantitative information may explain why campaigners are less likely to emphasize research. The individuals who are assigned the task of planning for a campaign's testable results may not have the background and training to conduct the research themselves. Finding individuals who are trained to take on the task requires the investment of more time and money, which are usually in short supply for campaigns. Although a thorough discussion of any of these issues is beyond the scope of this text, the two basic types of quantitative research designs, and the goals associated with the use of these approaches, will be overviewed before discussing the ways to collect and assess quantitative information during persuasive campaigns.

The use of quantitative research methods in campaigns is often reserved for assessing the impact of campaign intervention, specifically with regard to messages, during the implementation phase. Refer again to Figure 7-1. The two types of quantitative designs available for impact assessment include experimental and quasi-experimental (Ross, 1989). In either design, researchers may use projective techniques, as discussed within qualitative design, and are also likely to copy or pilot test their message based on theory, to promote a product, social action cause, or political candidate.

The use of a randomized or true experimental design requires the researcher to randomly assign participants to experimental and control groups. The purpose of this assignment is to be able to explain the impact of specified input variables on selected outcome variables. The input variables usually consist of some combination of: (1) manipulations constructed by the campaigners; and (2) naturally occurring differences among target audiences.

The outcome variables include what the campaigners predict to be affected by the input variables. The minimum information that must be collected in order to use a randomized approach includes measures that are collected after a planned intervention. More commonly, information is collected before, during, and after the campaign intervention.

Randomization is the best method to obtain comparability between experimental and control groups, but is costly and time-consuming. Some have argued that it is unlikely to attain high generalizability or external validity, because a treatment that is delivered in an actual campaign will differ considerably in comparison to the controlled experimental setting (Sandefur et al., 1986).

In the nonrandomized (quasiexperimental) approach, the assignment of participants to groups is nonrandom. Typically, intact groups are used, and selected targets may be compared to unselected targets through use of before and after intervention outcome measures. An intervention group also may be matched with controls selected by the researcher, or exposed targets may be compared to information available about the general population. This approach has been argued to be more valid than many true experiments for collecting campaign information (Sandefur et al., 1986). It allows campaigners to use more naturalistic settings. For example, a follow-up phone survey of a target audience might place those individuals who chose to view a particular television program, and so were exposed to a particular message, in one group for comparison with those who did not watch the program, and so on.

Various methods are available to quantitative researchers to collect information from the campaign audience, as summarized in Figure 7–1. However, the two most common approaches are: (1) surveys; and (2) various indirect methods, such as physiological or mechanical measures. Simulation may also prove to be a useful method of collecting quantitative information, as campaigners design formal computer-based modeling to predict the outcomes of specific interventions.

Surveys

Probably the most common method of collecting quantitative information in campaigns is the use of a survey. The strengths of the survey approach involve its low cost and speed, whereas the weaknesses concern its artificial nature and overreliance on first impressions. Surveys may be administered by mail or over the telephone. Of course, the introductions would differ. For example, a telephone survey might be introduced:

> *Hello, my name is [insert caller's name] with [insert the organization's name]. We are conducting an opinion poll in your community concerning health practices. Your telephone number has been selected at random. The survey will only take about ten minutes of your time, and your participation would be greatly appreciated.*

By comparison, a mail survey may be introduced as follows:

> *The [insert organization's name] is sponsoring a survey of people's opinions about health care. We would very much appreciate your participation in this survey. Your answers will be treated in strictest confidence, and will only be seen by the researchers. The survey requires only about ten minutes to complete, and a preaddressed, stamped envelope is enclosed for you to return your survey. We thank you in advance for your participation in this important project.*

Researchers should be careful in wording questions for use in a survey. One common error in survey construction is failure to consider whether a statement includes the use of singular or plural items, rendering questions double-barreled. For example, the following statement, "Communism is evil and dangerous," contains two items. Campaigners would be unable to identify whether or not participants' agreement or disagreement was in response to the concept that, "communism is evil," or that, "communism is dangerous." The use of conjunctions, such as "and," "or," and "either" generally indicate that a survey item has a plural idea in it. Other common errors include jargon-laden questions, too much verbiage, poor grammar, and complex syntax.

Several scaling techniques may be used to design survey instruments for campaigns. These include: (1) Thurstone's method of equal-appearing intervals; (2) Likert's method of summated ratings; (3) Osgood's semantic differential; and (4) Guttman's scalogram. One final approach discussed is the Q-sort method.

Thurstone's Method of Equal-Appearing Intervals The first major method of measuring attitudes was formulated by Thurstone in 1929 (Zimbardo and Ebbesen, 1969). This approach is based on several assumptions. First, an individual is assumed to be able to provide statements of opinion about an issue. Second, it is assumed that the survey statements can be ordered in terms of their expressed favorableness versus unfavorableness toward the issue. Third, the ordering of the statement is assumed to be equal distance between adjacent statements. Fourth, statements are uncorrelated, so each statement has a position such that is independent of the others. This indicates that acceptance of one does not imply acceptance of others. The primary disadvantage associated with this method of surveying a target audience is that construction is extremely laborious and time-consuming to attain a useful instrument.

Construction of a Thurstone scale begins with compilation of large numbers of opinion statements about a particular issue. A group of judges sorts the statements in 11 categories, reflecting the degree of favorableness toward the issue. Statements about which judges do not agree, or that fail to reflect roughly equal intervals, are then culled out. The final scale consists of about 20 statements that obtain high inter-judge agreement and fall at fairly equal intervals along the continuum. "A subject is then asked to check those statements with which he agrees. His score on the attitude test is either the median or the mean of the scale valuers with which he agrees" (Cronkhite, 1969, p. 117). Thurstone (1928) initially developed the scale to assess attitudes toward religion.

Examples of statements that might comprise such a measure about the involvement of the state in religion include (from the least to most favorable toward government involvement): the state should take no actions that affect the practice of religion; the state should intervene to protect citizens only in extreme cases of religious discrimination; the state should provide rhetorical support for religion; the state should remove legal impediments to encourage prayer in the public schools; the state should pass legislation requiring prayer in the public schools.

Likert's Method of Summated Ratings The Likert scale is a summative model that includes a series of statements about an issue (Lemon, 1973). A participant is asked to indicate the extent to which he or she agrees or disagrees with each item. The items are constructed using a five- or seven-point scale, ranging from strong agreement with the statement to strong disagreement. The individual's score is calculated by finding the sum of individual ratings.

Each statement is designed as a linear function of the same attitude dimension, so that scale items are highly correlated. Technically, this method assumes equal intervals between scale values, which is achieved by pretesting scale items. More often, however, this assumption is ignored, thus resulting in what is called a Likert-type scale. The Likert Scale assumes that each participant's frame of reference will influence his or her responses. For example, consider that the animal rights' campaigners might decide to measure respondents' opinions about animal experimentation through the use of a survey that contains Likert scales. The statements might include the following:

	Strongly Disagree				Strongly Agree
Animal Experimentation is good	1	2	3	4	5
Animals suffer during animal experimental	1	2	3	4	5
Animal experimentation informs modern medicine	1	2	3	4	5

Those respondents who believe that animal experimentation informs modern medicine would be expected to agree that animal experimentation is good and that animals do not suffer during animal experimentation. If this is confirmed, campaigners may decide to build a campaign around the statement, "Animals suffer during animal

FIGURE 7–2   A Portion of a Sun Awareness Survey Using Likert Scales

SUN AWARENESS SURVEY

This set of questions asks you about sun awareness. Please read each statement carefully. Then circle the number that indicates your level of disagreement or agreement with the statement. For example, if the statement reads, "It is important to take care of my appearance," and you disagree, circle number 2; if you agree circle 4; if you strongly agree, circle number 5.

1. Long-term exposure to sunshine increases the likelihood of getting skin cancer.
    Disagree   1   2   3   4   5   Agree
2. A suntan improves people's appearance.
    Disagree   1   2   3   4   5   Agree
3. Clouds filter out most of the harmful effects of the sun.
    Disagree   1   2   3   4   5   Agree
4. If you have a suntan, being in the sun is not dangerous.
    Disagree   1   2   3   4   5   Agree
5. Sunscreen lotions prevent people's skin from being damaged when exposed to the sun.
    Disagree   1   2   3   4   5   Agree
6. Sunscreens lotions are a great deal of trouble to use.
    Disagree   1   2   3   4   5   Agree
7. Sunscreens lotions are too greasy.
    Disagree   1   2   3   4   5   Agree
8. A higher SPF (sun protection factor) number means more protection from the sun.
    Disagree   1   2   3   4   5   Agree

experimentation." If respondents are found to perceive that animals suffer during animal experimentation, this should produce conflict for those who also believe that animal experimentation is good, even if it does inform modern medicine.

One problem with this method, not inherent in the approach, but in the way researchers use it, is that the scales are loaded cognitively, virtually ignoring affect. Since attitude consists of both cognition and affect, scales that tap the cognitive and not the affective are really measuring beliefs and not attitudes. This problem can be avoided if researchers employ items that are assessed in terms of "bad-good" in addition to those assessed in terms of "false-true." The example above contained both type of items, as does the example in Figure 7–2, a portion of a survey of attitudes about sun awareness.

Osgood's Semantic Differential   The semantic differential taps both the cognitive and affective dimensions of attitudes. It is based on the assumption that people assign meaning to a concept on the basis of three independent dimensions of judgment that may be represented by scales of bipolar adjectives (Osgood, Suci, and Tannenbaum, 1957; Osgood, 1965). The semantic dimensions that Osgood's research revealed to be important in such judgments include an evaluative dimension, involving how good versus bad a concept is perceived to be. For example, consider the following concept in terms of an evaluative factor:

The concept of animal experimentation might be assessed in these terms to evaluate respondents' negative or positive perceptions of the practice.

ANIMAL EXPERIMENTATION

unattractive	1	2	3	4	5	attractive
unsafe	1	2	3	4	5	safe
common	1	2	3	4	5	uncommon

Osgood viewed potency as a second important dimension used to judge concepts. These dimensions also provide a way for us to make comparisons among our repertoire of concepts. Again, consider the same concept, but in terms of a potency factor:

ANIMAL EXPERIMENTATION

small	1	2	3	4	5	big
weak	1	2	3	4	5	strong
insignificant	1	2	3	4	5	significant

Animal experimentation might be judged in these terms to assess the strength or intensity with which participants hold particular views.

The third dimension that Osgood found to be important in assessing individuals' judgments of a concept is activity. To examine this dimension, assess the same concept for activity:

ANIMAL EXPERIMENTATION

fast	1	2	3	4	5	slow
exciting	1	2	3	4	5	dull
lethargic	1	2	3	4	5	energetic

Semantic differential measures are relatively easy to construct and particularly useful in providing campaigners with a means of making comparisons among an audience's attitudes on different concepts that may be important in a campaign. One disadvantage associated with this survey method is respondents' failure to understand how to mark the scales. Another problem involves respondents' failure to carefully read each pair of adjectives, making the assumption that all negative terms are on one end and all positive terms are on the opposite end. To reduce the occurrence of these problems, introductions and instructions to the survey should be carefully constructed. Figure 7–3 includes an example of a portion of a survey designed to assess people's attitudes about a commercial brand, using the semantic differential method. Notice the instructions to respondents.

Guttman's Scalogram Another scaling technique is based on the assumption that a single unidimensional trait can be measured by a set of statements ordered along a continuum of difficulty of acceptance (Guttman, 1944). In this situation, the scale items are cumulative. Statements range from those which are easy for people to accept

FIGURE 7–3 Portion of A Commercial Survey Using Semantic Differential Scales

KELLEY'S HOUSE OF FLOWERS SURVEY

The following questionnaire items are designed to assess your attitudes about the business, Kelley's House of Flowers. Please respond to each of the pairs of adjective opposites. Between each pair of adjective opposites there are five numbers. Circle the number which best captures your attitude about Kelley's House of Flowers. In the example below, if you feel that Kelley's is fairly gloomy, you would circle 2; if you feel that Kelley's is fairly cheerful, you might circle 4; if you feel that Kelley's is very cheerful, you would circle 5.

KELLEY'S HOUSE OF FLOWERS IS:

Gloomy	1	2	3	4	5	Cheerful

THE QUESTIONNAIRE ITEMS OCCASIONALLY REVERSE POLARITY (e.g., the more positive adjectives are sometimes on the left and carry a low value; at other times they are on the right and carry a high value). PLEASE READ EACH CAREFULLY BEFORE CIRCLING A NUMBER.

KELLEY'S HOUSE OF FLOWERS IS:

Negative	1	2	3	4	5	Positive
Valuable	1	2	3	4	5	Worthless
Good	1	2	3	4	5	Bad
Foolish	1	2	3	4	5	Wise
Pleasant	1	2	3	4	5	Unpleasant
Favorable	1	2	3	4	5	Unfavorable

to those which few persons would endorse, which form a continuum of "difficulty of acceptance." Acceptance of one item implies acceptance of all statements of lesser magnitude or less difficult to accept. A Guttman scale is also extremely time-consuming to develop (Lemon, 1973).

The initial step in constructing a Guttman Scale resembles the Thurstone Scale. Researchers have people rate statements in terms of their degree of favorableness toward an issue. These items are then pretested to determine whether they constitute a unidimensional scale, such that if a respondent agrees with one of the middle items on the scale, then they will accept all of the lower items and none of the higher items. If the test meets this standard, it is said to be "perfectly unidimensional. . . . " (Cronkhite, 1969, p. 119). However, most things do not conform to a unidimensional pattern, limiting the use of the Guttman Scale.

Q-Sort Methodology   Another method for measuring peoples' attitudes about issues is to have them rank order, or Q-sort, a series of statements, issues, brands, or even persons from most favorable to least favorable, or from most important to least important (Lemon, 1973). Campaigners must limit the number of items to a relatively low figure, so that participants are more likely to be able to make distinctions among their feelings regarding the issues. The advantage associated with this form of measurement is its low cost and speed in being obtained. However, ranking hides respondents' quality determination, so participants may view all their choices as good, for example, or all their choices as bad.

In sum, campaigners often use surveys to assess and forecast an audience's needs, particularly during impact studies. The more meaningful information to be obtained from this method may require more than a single administration to refine the survey instrument, and to enhance the reliability and validity of the measurement tool.

Physiological (or Mechanical) Measures

In addition to the self-report pencil and paper measures of participants' attitudes and behaviors, campaigners may also employ the use of more indirect methods to determine a target audience's responses. These are restricted for use, however, primarily in a laboratory setting. Included among such measures are the use of a polygraph, electromyographic recordings (EMG), galvanic skin response (GSR), and pupillary size to assess levels of arousal, which may be used to indicate a participant's attitude more or less accurately. Researchers have also used such devices as split-cable test panels (Mayer, 1970).

GSR measures the electrical resistance of the skin, or how well the skin conducts an electric current that is passed between two electrodes, usually placed on the surface of the hand. This measure is based on the assumption that a sweaty hand conducts electricity better, and people are predicted to perspire more when emotionally aroused. EMG recordings measure contractions of the major facial muscles. Pupillary expansion is said to occur when an individual is presented with stimuli they like; constriction occurs when the stimuli is disliked. The advantages of assessing attitudes toward a

---

FEEDBACK

The campaign to enhance cultural diversity in law schools used students at the University of California at Berkeley as sources for messages that targeted undergraduate pre-law students.

Design a quantitative measure to assess the target audience's perception of the credibility of the source in communicating the campaign messages.

---

message or issue through the use of a physiological measure include the fact that individuals are unable to lie and have less control over these physiological responses. The disadvantages associated with these measures include the fact that they may cause an increase in arousal and so, therefore, not be accurate measures of an individual's reaction (see Le Poire, 1991).

In some instances, particularly with regard to assessing commercial campaign messages, cable sends test commercials to some homes with point-of-purchase scanners. The purpose is to determine whether particular commercials exert an impact on sales. Microcomputers record whether or not the television set is on and which channel it is tuned to, but cannot identify, of course, whether or not anyone is actually watching. A consumer uses identification card for purchase, the data are coordinated and analyzed, and the researchers then correlate viewing and buying habits. In addition to the failure of such an approach to determine whether specific ads are actually observed, this method also assumes that advertising must directly affect purchase to be successful, totally ignoring the incremental nature of campaign influence.

Reliability and Validity

When choosing a quantitative research design to use during periods of formative study, impact research, and efficiency analysis, campaigners are concerned with selecting designs and methods of measurement that will be most likely to achieve high reliability and validity, two key goals of quantitative research design. Reliability is a measurement issue, indicating whether an instrument is consistent or stable. Researchers are concerned with two forms of reliability when assessing the information that has been collected from quantitative research. Whereas *external reliability*, or consistency, determines whether a measurement instrument has been applied and reapplied with the same results, *internal reliability* demonstrates that the subparts of a measure contribute equally to the results.

The ultimate goal of a quantitative research design is to achieve high validity. Validity is a set of criteria by which to judge the research both in terms of the measurement tools used and the sampling plan selected. Measurement is the systematic means of assigning numbers to objects, and validity gauges how well measurement does this. Validity of a measure is assessed by three criteria. One criterion, *construct or measurement validity*, assesses the systematic and random measurement error to determine whether an instrument is actually assessing the concept in question. Systematic error destroys the construct validity by overestimating or underestimating the nature of the "true" attribute being measured.

Predictive and criterion or concurrent validity concerns the degree to which an investigator is able to predict the value of some criterion by using the measurement tool. *Content and face validity* indicates whether or not a measure represents the actual behavior, or is at least an adequate sample of the behavior, able to discriminate it from other behaviors.

Validity of the design's sampling methods is assessed by two criteria. *Causality and internal validity* involves a comparison between the outcome had the intervention been introduced compared to outcome had intervention not occurred. Consideration of the alternative explanations must be addressed. *Generalizability and external validity* refers to how broadly one can generalize the findings. An unbiased sample justifies greater generalization back to the population. Replication of an effect may be used to assess the boundaries of the generalization.

Approaches to Assessing Information

Once the information has been collected, campaigners face the task of making sense of what has been learned. Collection of information goes hand-in-hand with the assessment of information. For example, if open-ended interviews are the method selected to collect information, campaigners should consider how the answers to questions will be assessed during the process of constructing the questions. Several usual methods of assessing information include an evaluation of the audience's awareness/recognition, recall, comprehension/understanding, attitude change, behavioral intention/behavioral change.

Awareness and Recognition

When campaigners are planning the questions to be used in open-ended interviews or focus group discussions, or designing survey statements, they may be most interested in assessing the audience's need for information regarding the campaign topic. In this instance, they may want to select questions or statements that will: (1) reflect the specific knowledge about which an audience is expected to demonstrate awareness; (2) examine awareness of the specific knowledge items that an intervention has implemented; or (3) evaluate awareness of the specific knowledge items that were included in a campaign.

For example, campaigners involved in designing questions to assess the need for information on AIDS among college students might ask: (1) what causes AIDS; (2) how can individuals protect themselves from AIDS; (3) what is the HIV virus; (4) how is the HIV virus transmitted; (5) what is AZT; (6) when was the AIDS virus first discovered; and (7) where was the virus discovered? The accuracy or inaccuracy of responses would be indicative of how knowledgeable the audience is regarding these issues.

The construction of survey statements to assess awareness and recognition could be based on possible responses to these same questions. In statement form, participants would have the opportunity to demonstrate their understanding of these same issues.

Recall

Campaigners often utilize day-after recall to examine the impact of televised commercials. Again, specific questions for interviewers or moderators, or survey statements, or stimuli to use in assessing more indirect responses, may be designed to address respondents' ability to remember. Political campaigners may be interested in an audience's memory of a candidate's image during a previous campaign as a precursor to planning a present campaign. Or, political campaigners may want to identify whether or not specific slogans are being associated with the campaign. After a political campaign is concluded, campaigners may want to assess what specific information about the campaign overall individual voters are able to recall. A comparison of the campaign's actual content and the respondents' memory of campaign content is once more indicative of future campaign direction and strategy.

The questions or statements that a campaigner formulates to evaluate recall should be designed to specifically assess content that an audience should have encountered. The same questions or statements designed to assess awareness and recognition may be used to assess recall if campaigners know that an audience has been exposed to the information.

Comprehension and Understanding

As with the discussion of the multiple goals of campaigns, the discussion of ways to assess information gathered during the research conducted for the campaign highlights the multifaceted nature of this information. The target audience may be aware of the issues that campaigners ask about, and may recall particular slogans or highlights of speeches and informative presentations such as print ads, but still not comprehend the message content or understand its personal relevance.

Moderators' and interviewers' questions or survey statements may also be constructed, therefore, to specifically assess an audience's comprehension and understanding. In this case, the campaigners may provide the participants with specific messages, request that the participants read the messages, and then make inquiries regarding the content. The same questions that were identified as being useful to measure awareness and recognition might also be used in this situation, assuming that the messages given to the audience were designed to address these issues. Such questions would give some indication of the audience's comprehension.

Understanding might be assessed by having the interviewer or moderator ask receivers: (1) what changes in your behavior does the message suggest that you make to avoid getting AIDS, (2) what assistance does the message indicate is available to help you in making these changes; (3) what does the message say is likely to happen to you if you make these changes in your behavior; and (4) what does the message say is likely to happen to you if you do not make these changes in your behavior?

Attitude Change

Campaigners are often looking for evidence of attitude or behavioral changes. If the purpose of the study is to examine attitude change, the questions constructed for use during the interviews and focus group sessions, and survey statements, should reflect this goal. During the initial formative research, responses to particular questions regarding attitudes must be collected to provide information for comparison later. It should be obvious that asking a target audience if they are aware of a piece of information, can recall a particular message, or even comprehend and understand the message is quite different from making inquiries regarding changes in their beliefs, feelings, and future intentions.

In this instance, interviewers and moderators would attempt to construct questions, for example, to address: (1) how do you feel about money that is being spent to conduct research on AIDS; (2) what do you think is the cause of AIDS; (3) do you intend to behave differently now than in the past because of AIDS; and (4) if so, how will you behave differently now than in the past?

Behavioral Change

When campaigners decide to seek information which reflects behavioral change, questions and statements are constructed to focus on the audience's behavior. Once more, it is vital that information be collected during the early formative stages of the campaign regarding an audience's behavior in order to facilitate comparisons during later stages of the campaign.

Obviously, the problems associated with the self-report of behavior are numerous, including the audience's desire to give socially desirable responses. These problems may be exacerbated in a setting where interaction is taking place face-to-face, so that the interviewee or the focus group members are publicly known to the interviewer, the moderator, and other focus group members. To encourage more open and honest self-disclosure, questions or statements regarding behavior require the campaigner to be particularly sensitive to the audience and the need for privacy.

Conclusion

This chapter examined both research design and measurement strategies to be used in persuasive campaigns. The purposes of research design were discussed in terms of the assessment and forecast of audience needs. Differences between incidence and prevalence of needs were illustrated. Both qualitative and quantitative methods of collecting campaign information were considered, together with a discussion of usual approaches for doing both. The methods of assessing the information collected during campaign research was examined in terms of the multiple objectives that are associated with campaigns.

Suggestions for Further Reading

Allen, R. L., and Taylor, B. F. (1985). Media public affairs exposure: Issues and alternative strategies. *Communication Monographs, 52*, 186–201.

Bradburn, N. M., and Sudman, S. S. (1988). *Polls and Surveys: Understanding What They Tell Us.* San Francisco: Jossey-Bass.

Fowler F. J., Jr. (1984). *Survey Research Methods.* Newbury Park: Sage Publications.

Freimuth, V. S., and Van Nevel, J. P. (1981). Reaching the public: The asbestos awareness campaign. *Journal of Communication, 31*, 155–167.

McAlister, A., Perry, C., Killen J., Slinkard, L. A., and Maccoby, N. 1980. Pilot study of smoking, alcohol, and drug abuse prevention. *American Journal of Public Health, 70*, 719–721.

Miles, M., and Huberman, A. M. (1984). *Qualitative Data Analysis.* Beverly Hills, CA: Sage Publications.

Part *IV*

Campaign Communication

The Symbolic Nature of Communication

"When I use a word," Humpty Dumpty said, in a rather scornful tone, "it means just what I choose it to mean—neither more nor less." "The question is," said Alice, "whether you can make words mean so many different things." "The question is," said Humpty Dumpty, "which is to be master— that's all."

(CARROLL, 1960, P. 186)

The country of Japan has been characterized as an empire of signs (Barthes, 1982). This is literally and figuratively the case when one observes the signs, which are so carefully lettered and posted everywhere in Japan. Moreover, the Japanese signs are also symbols, which are signs deliberately created to stand for and represent something else. Whereas smoke may be a sign of fire, for example, human beings did not deliberately create the smoke to represent fire. In the English language, however, human beings have created letters of an alphabet, purposively strung together to create the word, "smoke," and the word, "fire," which have meaning only because and when one understands and is able to interpret the symbols. In the Japanese language, signs have been deliberately created by human beings to symbolically represent "smoke" and "fire." Again, the symbolic signs only have meaning when one understands and is able to interpret them.

Persuasive campaigns' effects and effectiveness depend upon the symbolic nature of communication, specifically with regard to the messages designed for use in the campaign, but also in terms of the choice of, for example, a trademark to be associated with the campaign. Commercial companies, such as Pillsbury, carefully select and maintain the use of a symbol, such as Pillsbury's doughboy, to represent their products. In fact, the Pillsbury company has sued Sunshine Biscuits for use of the Drox character, which Pillsbury maintains infringes on the doughboy trademark ("Atlanta Journal", 1991). Similarly, Proctor and Gamble has long battled against use of the company's trademark by Satanic cults. In political campaigns, systematic efforts are put into associating a particular candidate with a specific platform and sometimes with a particular symbol as well. In social action campaigns, a particular symbol or slogan provides unity among supporters and organizations identified with the campaign. The American Cancer Society, for example, employs the sword to represent it, characterizing the image of waging and winning the battle against cancer.

The symbolic nature of the images associated with campaigns is no small matter in the minds of campaigners. Moreover, the theorizing and research associated with impression formation and management comprises an extensive and extant body of work within the communication discipline (e.g., Tetlock and Manstead, 1985). This pursuit, in combination with the study of language use and message design in communication, provide persuasive campaigners with substantive support for the expenditure of time, energy, and money on the careful testing and development of messages, and selection of message advocates. These are the tools to be used by campaigners in order to meet audience needs.

Persuasive campaign messages should be constructed with purposive intent based upon the belief that in the minds of the audience members, the words will become a reality, affirming once more that all campaigns are situational. This is a complex task and one that may well lead campaigners, at times, to throw up their hands and ask, as did Alice, "Can we make words mean so many different things?" Persuasive campaigners, however, hope to be the master of the situation, based on their selection of messages rooted in theory and research. In fact, message design is often the event most under the control of campaign planners. Thus, many of the issues discussed in Chapter 7, relating to quantitative analysis during the planning, implementation, and evaluation of campaign effects and effectiveness, are relevant to discussion of the process of message design in persuasive campaigns.

The *choice* of spokespersons to represent the campaign is also within the realm of the campaigners' control and is a very important consideration during the message design process. It must be remembered, however, that a campaigner has less control

---

TABLE 8–1   Questions about the Symbolic Nature of Communication

1. What are the major philosophical contributions to the study of language in communication?
2. What are the major linguistic contributions to the study of language in communication?
3. What do we know about invention that informs the choice of arguments in persuasive communication campaigns?
4. What issues should be considered in arranging the arguments to be used in campaign messages?
5. What considerations should govern the campaigners selection of stylistic appeals or word choices?
6. What might campaigners do to facilitate audience retention of campaign messages?
7. What images should campaigners strive to promote during the planning of campaign messages and the selection of campaign advocates?

over the behavior of spokespersons than the words selected for use in campaign messages. Consider Anita Bryant as the source for the Florida Orange Juice campaign as but one example. Her private behaviors called into question her effectiveness as a continuing spokesperson for Florida Orange Juice. Campaigners for organizations concerned with social issues, such as the Christian Children's Fund, select spokespersons such as Sally Struthers, hoping that past positive associations of that person in the audiences' minds will be a difficult bond to break.

A brief overview of the philosophical and linguistic origins and traditions of functional and formal approaches to language study in communication follows. This introduces discussion of Cicero's five rhetorical canons as they relate to the symbolic nature of communication and the status of social scientific approaches to persuasive campaign message design. The questions posed in Table 8–1 will be addressed in this chapter.

Origins and Tradition of Language Study in Communication

Language use is an important consideration in all areas of communication. Different functions of communication, such as persuasion versus relational development and maintenance, for example, suggest various uses of language. Societal norms often govern language use in both one-to-many and one-to-one settings, focusing on the rule-governed nature of language use (Burgoon and Miller, 1985). Even discussion of the nonverbal communication may be clarified by comparison and contrast with characteristics of language (Burgoon, Buller, and Woodall, 1989).

Despite the somewhat banal conclusion that language is a vital and integral component of communication, the study of language use and message design, which is of vital interest to persuasive communication campaigners, has been fragmented and disjointed. In general, such research has taken two disparate paths of inquiry. A functional perspective, treats language as a "socially shared means for expressing ideas," while a formal or structuralist view, emphasizes "all conceivable sentences that could be generated according to the rules of the grammar" (Miller, 1973, p. 7). Historically, language study, and thus message design, have been influenced by several disciplines, including philosophy and linguistics.

Philosophical Contributions

Aristotle believed that verbal definitions expressed an object's immanent essence, suggesting that language and reality existed in a one-to-one state of correspondence (McKeon, 1947). Consider one example from the Japanese culture, which so often depends upon behavior that is governed by extensive interaction ritual (Sherry and Camargo, 1987), to illustrate Aristotle's belief. One of the authors has a spouse whose business dealings have led to participation in the Japanese practice of exchanging business cards, "meishi." In the extreme, the Japanese practice of meishi suggests an Aristotelian perspective. The underlying purpose of this practice is to establish ground rules for the interpersonal communication behavior to follow. The symbols exchanged are used to assign a hierarchical classification to the human being who carries the symbol, as if the card is somehow immanently the essence of the person. That appears to be rather arbitrary to many Westerners, who prefer to believe that their accomplishments and identity cannot be relegated to the space of a two-by-three-and-one-half-inch piece of parchment typically peppered with little more than a dozen or so words. The fact of the matter is, however, that the Japanese, in their business dealings, view this ritual as a valid and important one.

Persuasive campaigners must consider group, subcultural, and intercultural customs during the design of messages. After all, the messages used in a campaign constitute an important symbolic representation of what the campaign is all about, in spite of the fact that they are not the campaign. The U. S. Army's efforts to increase the number and quality of recruits provides one example of how important verbal and visual persuasive messages associated with the campaign are in representing the campaign. The Army's advertising campaigns of the 1970s focused on "blood and guts," stressing the message that "the Army wasn't for sissies" (Meyers, 1988b). One ad showed troops "slogging through a swamp," where one soldier was "sucked under the slime" (Meyers, 1988b). Retired Colonel William Graf, the Army's head of advertising and sales promotions from 1980 to 1984, told how, "One recruiter said that every time he showed it [the swamp ad], five people would walk out," concluding: "Being shot and killed in some foreign country never appealed to new recruits" (cited in Meyers, 1988b, p. 94). The Army's manpower levels hit "rock bottom" in quantity and quality by 1980, the year the Army launched the "Be All You Can Be" campaign (see Figure 8–1), which succeeded in turning things around (Meyers, 1988b). This slogan stressed an individual need, namely young peoples' needs for experience, education, and maturity to lay a foundation for their future, as a means to attain an important societal goal.

In the seventeenth century, John Locke argued that words do not express the real essence of a thing but only the nominal sense (Oldroyd, 1986). Attempts to label or name things often involve the use of symbols, frequently verbal symbols, but the very same thing might just as well have been given a different name. To understand the real essence as opposed to the nominal essence of something requires, according to Locke, observation or scientific experiment. Certainly, within the American culture, we are more likely to accept our own or someone else's label based on actual observation. Even in this instance, however, the tendency may be to stereotype based on a nonrepresentative sample. Many Americans, for example, may belittle the Japanese practice associated with business cards, but turn right around and assert that the Japanese spend too much time focusing on their jobs and not enough time enjoying life. This may be based on their expectations, stemming from the selective exposure to information confirming that Japanese workers spend more time working than do American workers. Persuasion campaigners must take the time to determine the nominal sense, how things and events are labeled by members of the campaign audience. For example, "hood" will be understood to represent "neighborhood," or "barrio," for some audiences. Others would interpret the word to mean an adornment for one's head. Still others would envision a criminal.

FIGURE 8-1   U.S. Army's, "Be All You Can Be," Campaign Message

Source: Army Photographs courtesy U.S. Government as represented by the Secretary of the Army.

FIGURE 8–2 Chrysler Print Advertisement Promotes Commitment to Safety

Source: Courtesy of Chrysler Corporation, Detroit, MI.

More than a century after Locke began the debate regarding words and the essence of meaning, Emmanuel Kant extended Locke's notion, asserting that the human mind is the active agent that imposes meaning on objects (Aiken, 1956). Kant argued that the mind, as an active agent of perception, shaped the understanding and interpretation of objects. Schema researchers still uphold such views, as explained in Chapter 4. Thus, as businesspersons attempt to understand the importance of interacting with one or another representative of an organization, the symbols contained on business cards are interpreted by the human mind. For some, the symbols are used to assign an individual to a role schema that supports the preference for some behaviors over others. For others, the business card represents little more than a name tag. For still others, it is a source of legitimacy, indicating that the carrier is a representative of a specific organization.

At the beginning of this century, Wittgenstein advanced his picture theory of language, stating that the logical structure of language reflected the logical structure of the world, with the limits of the former imposing limits on the latter (Oldroyd, 1986). Our ability to understand the world, in other words, was limited by our ability to impose, through arbitrarily constructed symbolic speech, meaning on events or objects in the environment. According to the theory, a picture of an apple, for example, had some association to the apple, as did the language that was used to represent the apple. From this comes the appropriateness of assigning the label, "picture," to the theory. Campaigners need to select their slogans, much like their spokespersons, in order to facilitate campaign objectives. An examination of a picture establishes some understanding of those things in the picture. Typically, that meaning will translate to the language we have to express what we observe in the picture. In English, the picture of an apple may be said to portray an object that is red with a shape that is generally round. A great deal of information regarding the apple, however, is missing from either of these conceptualizations. A more scientific undertaking to understand the actual object, the apple, could reveal that the interior texture of the apple differs from the exterior skin. Even more information could be attained by tasting the apple. Yet, even these observations are limited by our own ability, or lack of, to verbalize the experience. The

---

FEEDBACK

A slogan that appears on a major U. S. automobile manufacturer's ads is, "Chrysler understands family matters." The picture in the ad, features a young child, secured in a carseat, holding a teddy bear. The picture is a close-up, so no image of the car itself, except for a small portion of the interior where the child sits, is visible. Thus, the picture does not provide information on the car's appearance.

Carefully examine the ad in Figure 8–2 and ponder the following questions.

1. What need does this slogan address?
2. Is the use of the slogan and the picture more likely to invoke an active or passive approach to message processing on the part of readers?
3. What are campaigners attempting to achieve with this ad?

parameters associated with our own ability to understand the apple, according to this theory, bear a direct relationship to the limits and the logical structure of our language.

In later years, Wittgenstein became dissatisfied with his earlier conceptualization of language (Taylor, 1981). How, for example, was such a theory to deal with hopes, beliefs, or values? The logical form of language did not function to afford such meaning. Moreover, how does a portrait become a portrait of some particular person? Both, Wittgenstein reasoned, depend upon intention, one in the mind of the speakers, and the other in the mind of the painter. This suggests what is termed in philosophy as the problem on intentionally, defined as, "a sense of purpose or motivation in thought or action" (Lanigan, 1979, p. 33). If a campaigner intends to construct a persuasive message, then the statement's form or the logical structure of the language used may be dictated by social praxis, but the statement's function depends upon the campaigner's intention. Indeed, this—in a nutshell—presents the challenge that faces the campaigner during the process of message design. The campaigner may well understand how to use the language within the rules of sentence construction, but the campaigner's intention is to discover, among all the available means, the construction that will serve the intended purpose.

The final philosopher to be considered in this discussion is John Searle, whose speech act theory hypothesizes that "speaking a language is engaging in a (highly complex) rule-governed form of behavior" (1969, p. 12). Searle maintains that, although individuals may not be able to verbally speak exactly what they mean, *in principle* the possibility to do so exists. To achieve that end, individuals may have to increase their knowledge of the language, or even add new terms to the language. "[W]here there are thoughts that cannot be expressed in a given language or in any language," asserts Searle, "it is a contingent fact and not a necessary truth" (1969, p. 20). Searle also observes that just because it is possible to express one's meaning does not indicate that the effects produced in hearers will always be the intended ones. This represents the problem associated with the challenge to select among the available forms to construct campaign messages.

From the ancients to the moderns, philosophers have stressed a distinction between function and form, an important distinction to the campaigner interested in constructing effective messages. The influence of Aristotle's search for immanent forms is still apparent in efforts to design messages. Also, Locke's injunction to observe and experiment to clearly discern an act or activity's distinctive features guides social scientific endeavors. These searches are undertaken by campaigners in an effort to determine how campaign planners' intentions may be communicated in order to increase the likelihood of a one-to-one correspondence between intention and understanding.

Linguistic Influence

"Throughout the history of modern linguistics, the ideas of philosophers have been plundered for the purposes of the related concerns of linguists" (Taylor, 1981, p. 263). The philosopher's notion of a universal, for example, is applied by linguists who define a universal as a necessary category to describe the total set of human languages (Smith and Wilson, 1979). Formal universals in linguistics address the form of rules in a grammar, while functional universals concern ways in which such rules may be applied to conversation (Bailey, 1981). Linguists proceed from the assumption that individuals of a speech community who speak the same language use the same forms to do so, including words and sentences. Another's speech can be understood, therefore, because it is recognized as a "token" of a particular type of language (Taylor, 1981). Chomsky exemplifies a linguist who has focused substantial effort on the issues related to form rather than on questions associated with communicating meaning.

Rules are central to the study of linguistics, with primary emphasis being placed on the ways in which words are put together to produce phrases, clauses, or sentences—the sentence structure (Postal, 1973). Human language, as we have previously observed, is arbitrary, relying on an almost universal use of an arbitrary code called an alphabet, which again attests to the symbolic nature of human communication (Pribram, 1976). Functional linguistic rules relate to understanding when and how to use formal linguistic rules. Individuals engaged in speaking the English language, for example, may understand the rule of how to form the passive in English, but that says little about whether they understand how or where to apply the rule (Smith and Wilson, 1979). Later discussion in this chapter dealing with verbal immediacy will demonstrate the relevance of this very issue to modern campaigners and message design.

Chomsky's generativist school of linguistics led to much interest in and focus on formal properties, or systems of rules, that generate the endless combination of words in a language (McGregor, 1984). Chomskians define the syntactic component of language as consisting of two parts, a deep structure and a surface structure. The deep structure may be "produced by inserting words from the lexicon into trees created by the phrase-structure rules" (Smith and Wilson, 1979, p. 199). Each individual selects from an available repertoire of words or vocabulary, and applies known rules about how to construct comprehensible sentences to produce the deep structure component of language. Chomsky's approach to linguistics has been credited with motivating others to develop approaches to language that could account for human communication and actual language use (Koerner, 1983).

Use of language in campaign message design depends on understanding syntactical and lexical information, as well as conceptual knowledge of the world and a system of beliefs within which to evaluate what is heard (Miller, 1973). Whatever the linguistic skills individuals possess owing to the language-learning process, to communicate requires effort to make words suit needs, which is the persuasive campaign message designer's task.

Persuasive Campaign Message Design

Perhaps the only useful "universal" to campaigners is the notion of words themselves. Consider the following example:

> One day Helen was playing with the water coming from the pump when her nurse vibrated out the word "water." Immediately, in a flash of revelation, Helen saw the idea of words. "Everything has a name!" she cried. She made a remarkable inference, developing the new

concept, or universal, of "words," a thing no animal can do. From that moment on, Helen became human and her mental life became organized. She could communicate and become a social being (Cherry, 1973, p. 78).

Language is thought to have evolved as a part of social living. Within groups, each individual's behavior affects others, and language may serve as a method of social control (Hogan, Jones, and Cheek, 1985). Rousseau observed that when humans are brought together and forced to live together, they develop a common idiom much sooner than humans who wander freely in the forests (Kendall, 1954). Thus, language acquisition occurs in the social context of discourse, which takes place in settings where communicative intentions may be converted into communicative conventions (Bruner, 1981).

All logical thought is said to be socialized because it implies the possibility of communication between individuals (Piaget, 1962). The listener's sharing of a context with the speaker suggests language for communicating. Language is a tool of exchange which is used to represent and classify experience, but different individuals use language resources for different purposes (Brinker, 1982; Prideaux, 1985; Sterelny, 1983).

Delia (1977) observes that an analogy between rule-analytic approaches in communication and linguistics tends to be implicit rather than explicit. Ellis (1982) argues that language studies in communication must go beyond the linguistic level of sentence structure. Indeed, much research regarding the symbolic nature of communication has been conducted, and, as Golden observes:

We have had students in each communication age and system who have preserved and advanced out knowledge of language. . . . Although Cicero's challenge to have someone create "a science of conversation" was not adequately met for 2,000 years, today the gauntlet has been accepted by many current scholars (1987. pp. 266-267).

To organize the theory and research that has utility for message designers in persuasive campaigns, Cicero's five rhetorical canons provide a useful framework. Cicero, of course, was the great Roman orator who authored, "De Inventions" (Hubbell, 1949). His writing foreshadowed a great many of the pursuits of modern social scientists, particularly with regard to the topics of message design.

Invention

Invention, according to Cicero, concerns ". . . the discovery of valid or seemingly valid arguments to render one's cause plausible . . . " (cited in Hubbell, 1949).

The topic of a campaign is usually stated easily enough, but making decisions regarding the arguments that campaigners view as likely to promote the goals associated with the topic is a far more difficult undertaking. The first question associated with this issue is, "What is the campaign's objective?" Answers to this question suggest guidelines about how the campaigner should proceed. Audiences who know nothing about the issue, for example, require information. Audiences who know nothing about the issue and are uninvolved with the topic need motivation to attend to the information. Audiences who know about the issue, but behave in ways that are inconsistent with the information they possess need information concerning this discrepancy. Audiences who know about the issue and behave in ways that are consistent with the information may require some form of reinforcement.

Argumentation is the "ongoing transaction of advancing claims, supporting them with reasons, and the advancing of competing claims with appropriate support, the mutual criticism of them, and the granting of adherence to one" (Reike and Sillars, 1975, p. 6–7). Jensen (1981) contends that argumentation is "a human communication process which emphasizes the rational (logos) while at the same time recognizing the importance of the appeal to the credibility of the arguer (ethos), and the appeal to the emotions of the audience (pathos)" (p. 6). Jensen also asserts that persuasion differs from argumentation, in that the role of emotion is proportionately greater in persuasion compared to the importance attached to reason. Toulmin's (1959) structural model of argument provides a convenient method to use in outlining the construction of campaign messages.

Claims, Warrants, and Data

Toulmin (1959) includes three core components in his model of arguments: claims, warrants, and data. In composing the campaign's claims, planners are identifying the assertions that they hope the audience will accept by the end of the campaign. Claims may be worded in a positive or a negative fashion. "You should join the Army," is a legitimate claim, as is, "You should not join the Army." As with attitudes, claims may be linked to a network of other claims; on the other hand, a single claim may stand alone. The claim, "you should join the Army," for example, may be linked to statements such as, "the United States needs volunteers to enlist in the Army," "joining the military is a patriotic act," and/or "patriotism is good." As campaigners go about the process of identifying or "inventing" the central arguments of the campaign, consideration should be given to whether or not important claims are associated with other claims for a particular audience. If a campaigner seeks to persuade highly educated people to volunteer for military service, then the promise of additional training or education should not be used. However, this appeal would be intrinsically appealing to people who have no training and no way of attaining an education without support. Thus, claims must also be carefully considered in terms of specific campaign goals.

Toulmin (1959) suggests that three types of claims are sufficient to cover the domain of the topic. Fact claims assert the existence or nonexistence of a particular state of affairs, such as, "the United States needs volunteers to enlist in the Army." The situation can be verified by objective data, such as sensory perception. Some fact claims assert that a cause and effect relationship exists to explain why some state of affairs exists; at times, these claims become very difficult to prove.

The core messages of a campaign often evolve around facts, as in Wodarski and Lenhart's (1982) curriculum for teaching adolescents about alcohol. The messages center around the biological, psychological, and sociocultural determinants of alcoholism, together with some basic knowledge about alcohol consumption and usage. The audience is taught information about topics such as how much alcohol a body can absorb in a given period of time and the amount of alcohol contained in various products.

The following example in the campaign against AIDS illustrates a message based on a fact claim:

> *People infected with HIV can develop many health problems. These can include extreme weight loss, severe pneumonia, a form of cancer, and damage to the nervous system. These illnesses signal the onset of AIDS. In some people, these illnesses may develop within a year or two. Others may stay healthy for as long as 10 or more years before symptoms appear (Department of Health and Human Services, p. X).*

Value claims make judgments or give opinions regarding issues, people, and events. "Military service to your country is good," is a value claim, as is, "failure to serve your country when. it needs you is unpatriotic." People hold inherently fewer values than they do beliefs or opinions, and values tend to govern more than a single behavior. Messages designed around values, if successful, may be linked to long term behavioral or attitudinal change, as values tend to be more resistant to change.

Policy claims are statements that propose that something should, or should not, be done by someone, such as, "All high school graduates should enlist in the military for a tour of duty to serve their country." When people are adequately informed and motivated to behave, a policy claim may provide a road map of explicit instruction regarding action, as in this example: "Any woman who is considering having a baby and who thinks she might have placed herself at risk for HIV infection—even if this occurred years ago—*should* seek counseling and testing before she gets pregnant" (Department of Health and Human Services).

Warrants, within Toulmin's (1959) model are defined as bridging statements that link a claim with the data. Warrants may be implicitly or explicitly stated. In asserting that, "individuals should wear sun screen"—a policy claim, a campaign message may also include the statement that, "more people, as the result of overexposure to the sun, are being diagnosed with skin cancer," which may provide an explicit warrant associated with the policy claim. If the audience does not accept the warrant, it becomes another claim—in this instance, a fact claim—in need of substantiation, detracting from the success of the message.

Data is what is specifically offered to support the claim (Toulmin, 1959). McCroskey (1968) elaborates on the concept of data by suggesting three types. First order data is support for a claim that is shared by the audience and the message advocate. These beliefs may be implicitly or explicitly stated. During times of war, the policy claim, "You should enlist in the military," may be supported by the belief that recruits are needed to serve in the war. The success of the policy claim depends, in part, upon whether or not the audience shares the belief. Second order data, according to McCroskey, are beliefs held by the message advocate but not known or shared by the audience. The success of this type of data, therefore, depends upon the credibility and referent power of the advocate in the situation. Commercial campaigners often depend upon connections with the audience. Pepsi-Cola's use of the slogan, "You got the right one baby, uh huh," in their ads featuring Ray Charles has been a tremendous success. Third order data are what is more commonly called evidence, support for a claim that comes from a third party besides the communicator or the audience (McCroskey, 1968).

A great deal of research has focused on the use of evidence in persuasive messages. Reinard's (1988) review of the status of persuasive effects associated with evidence after 50 years draws several conclusions that have specific relevance for campaign message designers. First, the use of evidence has more impact on persuasive effectiveness for active message processors than for passive message processors. Also, evidence has a positive impact as compared to lack of evidence on persuasive effectiveness when a message is personally relevant. Testimonial evidence, the judgments and opinions of others, is particularly effective. In terms of the use of evidence, the persuasive success is linked to specifically citing the source of the evidence. Both high and low credible sources are more persuasive when they use evidence.

Too little research is available regarding the persuasive effects of statistics to draw specific conclusions, although the study that has been done shows no significant difference between use of statistics and testimonial evidence in terms of impacting persuasive outcomes. It has been suggested that, since effective arguments create vivid mental images, "cold statistics may not come alive" (Reinard, 1988, p. 24) for the audience. Evidence that supports the desirability of a particular attribute or activity has been found to be more persuasive than evidence that attempts to establish simply that something is true, so called truth evidence. Providing an audience with evidence has proven to be extremely important in helping to inoculate individuals to later attacks on a position they have accepted, suggesting that it is a vital component of messages when the objective is resistance. To be effective, however, evidence should be new to the audience.

Audiences appear to expect messages to contain support for their claims. Johnson (1985) found that individuals were biased against commercial ads for which evidence about some important point was absent. In addition to the outline of messages within the skeletal framework of an argument, the invention of campaign messages should consider the audience's drives, motives, needs, and motivations.

Drives, Motives, Motivations, and Needs

Hull's (1943) drive theory proposes that several variables are likely to intervene between the independent and dependent variables in a learning or persuasion process. Primary among these variables is an individual's drive, a temporarily activated state of an organism that includes sex, hunger, and thirst.

Indeed, in creating messages for campaigns, these drives are often the focus of content, although some experts have recently questioned the effectiveness of using sex to sell goods. Scott (1989) asks the questions, "Does selling with sex, which used to be such a snap, still work?" (p. G-1). Recent industry trends show some movement away from emphasizing sex in the invention of messages as companies, such as Gitano, have started to emphasize family.

FEEDBACK

Read the following excerpt concerning the issue of gender as it relates to smoking.

Women have a bigger emotional investment than men [in the smoking issue]. Cigarettes represent one of the ways of uncorking those feelings that society teaches them to suppress. Mrs. X, who is 64 and smokes 20 cigarettes a day, puts it another way: "Cigarette smoking not so much calms the nerves as dulls the sensibilities so that I, at least, do not care so much that I am frustrated." Men do not, of course, escape similar frustrations, but there are more channels through which they can express these pent-up emotions. Society may not like a drunken man, but it approves even less of a drunken woman. Aggressive behavior—whether desirable or not—is always an easier avenue for release of tension for men. This does not necessarily mean that women are innately less aggressive than men, but rather that women are expected to be so. Despite living in an age of "sexual liberation," sexual freedom does not apply equally for men and women. Even exercise—a seemingly innocuous outlet—is still a more acceptable activity for men than for women (Jacobson, 1982, pp. 33-34).

This excerpt contains several claims and forms of data that could be employed in a campaign to reduce smoking by women. Examine it again as you answer the following questions.

1. How is personal testimonial used, and what segment of readership does the testimonial explicitly refer to?

2. What types of data are used to support the claim that aggressive behavior is an easier avenue of tension release for men than for women?

The AIDS crisis effectively brought an end to the sexual revolution and promiscuity as we knew it. More people are settling down with the same partners. But more important, the gulf between younger consumers and baby boomers has finally grown so much that Madison Avenue is having to send separate signals to address both (Scott, 1989, p. G-1).

The invention of messages based on sex drive is believed to be less appealing for people 35 to 60 years of age. Thus, a focus on other motives or motivations and needs may well become more crucial in message invention. Some examples of commercial campaigners' shift to other forms of human drive and motivation in campaigns include: Nike's selection of a solitary athlete running through city streets at night, with some heroic moments interspersed; and PacTel Cellular Car Telephone's use of the slogan, "We'll help you reach your calling" (Scott, 1992, p. D-2).

Motives or motivations are learned drive states that will differ from one culture to the next, and often, even within subgroups of a single culture. Americans may be motivated to attain success, power, and status, while another country's citizens may be motivated to achieve personal fulfillment and inner peace.

One researcher (Winter, 1988) has examined motivations to be president in the United States and found that by analyzing candidates' speeches, one could ascertain their motives for seeking the highest political office in this country. Winter (1988, p. 22) concludes that:

People who score high in power motivation seek prestige and influence over others. They can make good leaders, but unless they also have a high sense of responsibility, they are prone to impulsive aggression and risk-taking.

If an audience perceives that a candidate is motivated by power and prestige, and the audience positively identifies with such motives, support for the candidate should be enhanced. On the other hand, audiences who perceive the candidate to have such motives but devalue these motives will be inhibited in their support of the candidate.

A longitudinal and cross-cultural examination (Tse, Belk, and Zhou, 1989) of print ads from Hong Kong, the People's Republic of China, and Taiwan reveals that the Hong Kong commercials stress hedonistic values, promising easier and American lifestyles. Taiwan ads converge toward Hong Kong ads, while the People's Republic of China's ads emphasize utilitarian appeals, promising a better life, and focusing on states of being (Tse et al., 1989). In each country, the motives of the citizens guide the invention of messages and will contribute to the success or failure of campaign messages.

Sources of Inconsistency

Cognitive consistency approaches to persuasion have a long tradition within the study of persuasion and social influence (see Miller et al., 1984 for review). Campaigners may deem, primarily when the objective is change, that inventing messages around the inconsistency between attitudes and behaviors of an audience will reap the desired effectiveness. The focus of this invention may be on the logical inconsistencies of thoughts and/or behaviors, conflicting social roles held by the audience members, or historical and environmental changes.

Arrangement

Arrangement is defined by Cicero as, ". . . the distribution of arguments thus discovered in the proper order . . . " (cited in Hubbell, 1949).

During the invention process of message design in campaigns, campaigners are striving to "get it all down on paper," so to speak, providing an outline of what the content of the campaign is to focus on. Once that has been done, however, key decisions must be made regarding issues such as: How many arguments are to be used?

FEEDBACK

Collect a number of print ads associated with the promotion of a specific product, candidate, or social issue.

1. Identify the arguments used in the ad.
2. What types of claims are made?
3. What are the implicit or explicit warrants associated with each claim?
4. Identify the types of data used to support each claim.

Which arguments should be primary, and which secondary, in importance? And, how should the data be ordered to support the desired outcomes?

Deduction, Induction, and Abduction

Three general methods of arranging message arguments are available to planners. If a pattern of deduction is chosen, a generalization will lead to the statement of a specific rule. "By deduction, the rule and a given case entail a result" (Mick, 1986, p. 199). For example, a campaign's objective may be to increase the practice of attending preventive child health care appointments. The argument that the campaigners may wish to focus on is that part of being a good parent is taking children to well child exams. The form that this argument would take, deductively speaking, is:

> *Rule*: All women who regularly make and keep appointments for well child care for their children are good mothers.
> *Case*: You are a good mother.

So, by a process of deduction, one may reach the conclusion that:

> *Result*: You take your children to receive well child care.

Deductively arranged arguments move from general content to more specific application, which facilitates the conclusion.

When an argument takes an inductive form, a specific example leads to a general conclusion. "By induction, given a case and a result, the rule is inferred probabilistically" (Mick, 1986, p. 199).

> *Case*:   You are a good mother.
> *Result*: You take your children to receive well child care.

So, by a process of induction, one may reach the generalization that:

> *Rule*:   Good mothers take their children to receive well child care.

Inductively arranged arguments move from a particular case to the general rule, so that a conclusion always involves making a leap based on probability.

Within a process of abduction, "a result and the rule infer the given case probabilistically:"

> *Result*: You take your children to receive well child care.
> *Rule*:   Good mothers take their children to receive well child care.

So, by a process of abduction, one may make the inference that,

> *Case*:   You are a good mother.

For message designers:

> *The potency of abduction is particularly obvious if we consider Jane a new neighbor or a fictional character in an advertisement about whom little else is known. For the person who*

wonders why Jane acts as she does, abductively the person need only invent, or more likely, instantiate a rule that has been socioculturally learned and rehearsed, and the explanation for Jane's actions is derived (Mick, 1986, p. 199).

Particular emphasis should be placed on the selection of one of these general patterns of arrangement based on the competence of an audience in making deductions. Hypothetical reasoning becomes more accurate with age (Kamhi, Nelson, Lee, and Gholson, 1985; Li, Zhang, and Jin, 1985; Moshman and Franks, 1986; Tunmer and Nesdale, 1983). In fact, research indicates that the capability for using logical reasoning is not generally present yet in sixth graders (Overton, Ward, Noveck, and Black, 1987).

Numerous researchers have reviewed the existing research concerning organized versus unorganized messages, finding that organization enhances the credibility of the source, may result in greater comprehension and retention, but does not necessarily facilitate persuasiveness (Burgoon, 1988). Particular patterns of organization (for example, problem-solution versus solution-problem) have not been examined sufficiently to provide specific support for the superiority of one pattern over another. Based on the particular objectives of the campaign, the appropriate organizational pattern may emerge. For example, if an audience is unaware of a problem, the logical construction pattern would be to first inform them of the problem, thereby arousing need, before offering a specific solution. If the audience is aware of the problem, they may be most interested in the solutions that campaigners have to offer, and the discussion of the problem that follows the solution may afford greater resistance to future arguments that contradict the audience's support of the campaign. Other organizational plans may similarly fit the specific needs of the campaign.

Other Issues Regarding the Arrangement of Arguments in Messages

Sometimes, campaigners may decide to place the most central support for a claim at the beginning of an argument, believing that it will be remembered best if so positioned, supporting a primacy effect. Other times, campaigners may place important information at the end of an argument, believing that it will be remembered best, supporting a recency effect. Campaigners ought to ask themselves whether an audience is likely to be attentive enough early in the presentation of a message to comprehend important information, or if an audience is more likely to be receptive after the presentation of some attention-getting materials. If the former is the case, campaigners may choose to arrange a message to take advantage of a primacy effect, while in the latter situation, campaigners should arrange the message to promote a recency effect.

Researchers have also debated about the value of providing audience with implicit conslucions versus explicit conclusions regarding message content. Again, there may be occasions when the former is a superior approach, although research to date tends to support the superority of explicitly drawn conclusions (Tubbs, 1968). If a camapigner's primary objective is to reduce overt or covert hostility, drawing explicit conclusions with regard to the campaigner's position may not be warranted.

FEEDBACK

Once more, examine the ads or messages collected for the earlier FEEDBACK exercise in this chapter.

   1. Identify the organizational pattern used in each message.

   2. Does the message utilize a primacy or recency effect? If so, explain whether it appears to be appropriate in the context.

   3. Is the message inductively, deductively, or abductively presented?

Expression

Cicero defines expression as, ". . . the fitting of the proper language to the invented matter . . . " (cited in Hubbell, 1949).

   Watson asserts that, "Since man is a verbal animal the world is reacted to many times more often than the object itself. The word organization becomes dominant over all other organization" (Watson, 1924, p. 340). Indeed, as we observed in the opening pages of this chapter, words are the one universal notion that campaigners are likely to be interested in. Once the campaign arguments have been invented, and the patterns of arrangement have been selected, the campaigners face making decisions regarding what specific types of appeals and word choices will be used to construct the campaign messages.

   Ellis (1982), in reviewing research concerning language in communication, notes the tendency to treat language as a variable that influences outcomes; source, receiver, channel, and message are assumed to be variable and manipulated so that effects may be observed. Such variable-analytic studies have examined the use of intense or immediate language, as well as lexically diverse language (Bowers, Courtright, and Bradac review, 1979). These studies have often taken a micromessage approach and looked at language at the level of the words, while other investigations consider macromessage appeals such as the use of humor, fear, warmth, or emotion. Some researchers have argued that much of what we know regarding message design and effectiveness may be unique to a specific message or messages (Jackson and Jacobs, 1983). Morley (1988) asserts that advertisements in particular can be randomly sampled to promote the increased internal and external validity of the research results. Some of the research to be reported in this section has dealt with a specific message, while other studies have drawn from a population of messages. The results provide some wisdom for campaign planners during periods of message design.

Types of Appeals

Broadly speaking, campaigners may choose message appeals based on humor, fear, warmth, or other emotions. Humor and fear appeals have perhaps been examined most extensively, providing more information at present for campaign planners.

Humorous Appeals In terms of humor, Reeves (1988, p. 18) observes:

It took me a while to figure out that it takes the same number of Belgians or Poles or Norwe-gians or Swedes to change a lightbulb. You know: one to hold the bulb and two to turn the ladder.

There are only so many themes to be used in jokes, as comedy and what makes us laugh provide a defense against injustice and absurdity in life. The problem with using a humorous appeal is often, "who's left out." Investigations of humor consistently find that, "Often the widest division between who's in on the joke and who's left out is that between men and women. Both sexes don't necessarily find the same things funny" (Stechert, 1986, p. 37).

Researchers generally conclude that the appreciation of humorous appeals depends upon perceived incongruity (Holland, 1982; Paulos, 1977). In other words, the necessary component of humorous appeals is that two incongruous ways of considering someone or something are juxtaposed, which may provide an avenue of relief or feelings of superiority. Research indicates that individuals who perceive themselves to have control over their environment have been found to rate humor more positively than those who perceive themselves to be powerless or helpless (Trice, 1982; Trice and Price-Greathouse, 1986). Those individuals who display a sense of humor are perceived to be cheerful, relaxed and also are less disappointed by failure (Rossel, 1981; Rothwell, 1982). They also rate higher on sociability and character (Gruner, 1970). Humor's main utility to persuasion, however, is increasing attention.

Funny people are among the most highly regarded in our society. Not only are they able to lift our spirits, but their talents have socially redeeming value. For one thing, they are great equalizers. H. Allen Smith once wrote that a humorist is "a fellow who realizes, first, that he is no better than anybody else, and second, that nobody else is either" (Witty, 1983, p. 22).

Fear Appeals The necessary ingredients to construct a fear appeal are that the audience is made to feel vulnerable to a threat, told to take action to reduce threat, and, therefore, should accept recommendations contained in the message (Boster and Mongeau, 1984). Varied outcomes have been attained using fear appeals. Boster and Mongeau (1984) suggest several reasons why such differences have occurred. A drive explanation indicates that higher levels of fear produce an unpleasant drive, and so to avoid the unpleasantness, individuals will change, which explains why strong fear appeals may be effective. On the other hand, a resistance explanation asserts that as the perceived fear in a message decreases, individuals are more likely to attend to the message and so more likely to change in response to the message, which suggests why strong fear appeals would be ineffective. Another explanation suggests that if receivers are either very fearful or very unafraid, no change is likely to occur. This explanation, therefore, argues for moderate fear appeals. All fear appeals, to be effective, need to be delivered by a credible source, and should relate to receivers' self esteem, as well as being focused on an important topic (Robberson and Rogers, 1988).

Campaign messages sometimes select similar straight-forward factual information for the verbal component of a fear appeal, and vary the choice of the visual component to reduce or elevate levels of fear. For example, research indicates that the use of fear-oriented, compared to nonfear-oriented, posters to advocate use of condoms are more effective for all receivers regardless of their age, gender, or ethnicity (Rhodes and Wolitski, 1990).

Emotional Appeals   When campaigners construct other forms of emotional appeals they may be interested in responses such as anger or sadness and happiness or joy. A Canadian social action campaign employing television advertisements to influence basic childrearing skills reported positive impacts on basic parenting beliefs and behaviors, as well as positive emotions associated with parenthood (Ratcliffe and Wittman, 1983). As with the use of organizational patterns in designing messages, further theorizing and systematic and longitudinal research is required to develop principles to guide the use of emotional appeals.

However, many of the generalizations regarding the use of humor seem likely to be appropriate with regard to emotional appeals. Different groups may respond uniquely to such appeals. Animal rights' activists have learned this, for example, when their attempts to evoke sympathy instead elicited anger in some targeted audiences. Research examining the effects of emotional appeals before their actual use in a campaign can identify such problems in advance. Some research on commercial campaign themes indicates that the use or nonuse of brands is equated with basic dilemmas of being human, such as good versus evil and life versus death (Leymore, 1982). These themes are often represented, and evoke appeals to primary emotions. Sometimes, however, appeals are not intended to evoke primary emotions, but instead to arouse feelings of warmth.

Warmth Appeals   In addition to constructing their messages to elicit fear and other primary emotions, campaigners often try to design messages to arouse feelings of pleasantness and warmth. This is particularly true in commercial campaigns, as we observed in Chapter 5, and will again stress in Chapter 10. These appeals often utilize people's feelings (real or idealized) for family, friends, patriotism, or special occasions (e.g., ceremonies or holidays) to evoke the desired response. A culture's traditions and values provide themes for the content of such appeals. For example, McDonalds has consistently employed appeals to family in its campaign advertising, evoking warmth, and thereby increasing sales. Campaigns to increase blood donations have also used such appeals, employing posters depicting children and slogans such as, "Thanks to you, someone will live to have another birthday." Political candidates also use appeals designed to evoke warmth, especially in their spot advertising. The 1984 Reagan campaign spot, "Morning Again," employed music and visuals, and sought to tap feelings of patriotism. "The ad was subtle and reflected a golden glow . . . ," using a commentator to remind people how well things were going for America once again (Pfau and Kenski, 1990, pp. 22–23).

Word Choice

At the outset of a campaign, audience research is employed to determine "the level of familiarity with and comprehension of topic-related vocabulary and terminology" (Atkin and Freimuth, 1989, p. 137). For example, Atkin and Freimuth found that only 25 percent of the audience surveyed was aware of the legal blood alcohol level, and that there were many diverse interpretations for the meaning of "social drinker" and "moderation." Cook, Petersen, and Moore (1990) found that when counseling women about childbearing and childbearing risks, campaigners are advised to keep their messages "clear, simple, and realistic," adding that "neither sensationalism nor humor are effective approaches in dealing with this serious subject" (p. 47).

Two language constructs have received a great deal of attention with regard to the selection of the specific words to be used in composing persuasive messages: verbal intensity and verbal immediacy.

Verbal Intensity Bradac, Bowers, and Courtright (1979) review the use of verbal intensity in communication studies. Verbal intensity may be defined as the distance from neutral that a message presents itself to be. The use of adverbs, adjectives, and death and sex metaphors all contribute to the ability to move speech from a more neutral tone to a more intense tone. Examine the following newspaper headlines:

"Defenseless Disciples of Sanctuary" (Arnold, 1985);

"MASH Star Declares War on 'Rambo Thinking'" (Fimbres, 1985);

"Retarded in Arizona Have 'License to Kill'"(Medlyn, 1985).

The first headline is in reference to a story regarding the "Sanctuary Movement" of El Salvadoran refugees into this nation. The individuals who organized the movement were arrested and tried for their involvement in the situation. Many people, as summarized in this headline, viewed those who were assisting the refugees as nothing less than heroes. This headline is not neutral. It clearly expresses the author's opinion, forewarning the reader regarding the position to be taken in the accompanying story.

The second headline also appeared in a newspaper during the period of heightened activity surrounding the sanctuary movement. In this instance, Mike Farrell, the advocate for the message associated with the movement, is pictured as strongly taking a stand in the situation. There is nothing neutral regarding the phrase, "declares war." Moreover, the selection of Farrell as spokesperson, an actor and star of the hit television series, "MASH," further enhances the likelihood of success.

The final headline introduced an article about the issue of competence as a criterion for standing trial. As a result of this standard, the author of the article observes that many mentally retarded citizens of the state commit crimes for which they are never tried. Again, the phrase, "license to kill," leaves little doubt regarding the viewpoint to be developed.

Bradac et al. (1979) summarize the research concerning the verbal intensity construct, reaching conclusions that may be of specific interest to campaigners during the planning of messages. First, for highly aroused receivers, intense language often leads to less attitude change. Moreover, obscenity, which is generally considered to be a form of intense language, is inversely related to ratings of source competence and amount of attitude change.

Verbal Immediacy   Verbal immediacy has been defined as the degree of directness between a speaker and an object, as assessed by the message itself (Wiener and Mehrabian, 1968). In terms of forms of speech that are more or less immediate, Wiener and Mehrabian (1968) propose several. These speech forms provide very explicit information about construction of messages at the level of word choices.

The temporal component of verbal immediacy addresses the use of verbs and modifiers in a message in order to evaluate whether or not a present event or condition has been displaced to the past or future, which would make the speech more nonimmediate. Words such as, "before," "after," "at first," and "later," are examples of particular word forms indicative of temporally nonimmediate speech, as well as past or future tense verbs. The latter bears some relationship to understanding when to use the passive form in English.

Another dimension of verbal immediacy is denotative specificity. This, too, relates to our earlier discussion in this chapter regarding one's understanding of how to form the English passive, but failure to understand when to use the passive form. Specifically, Wiener and Mehrabian (1968) propose that when the subject or object of a message is not explicitly stated or is referred to only with reference to membership in a group, the speech is more nonimmediate. Thus, use of the word, "politicians," when a speaker is referring to a specific candidate is denotatively nonspecific and less immediate than a direct reference to the particular individual would be. Failure to name a subject or reference to "it" also characterize the speech as less immediate.

Spatial forms of nonimmediate speech address the use of demonstratives within the constructed message content. Use of "this," "these," and "here" are more immediate than the use of "that," "those," and "there." Again, the former indicate a close relationship between the message source and the message, while the latter distances the source from the message.

Qualifiers, too, are considered to be forms of nonimmediate language use. An advocate of a message who adds words or phrases such as, "perhaps" and "it could be" is sending a subtle message to the audience regarding his or her own support for the content of the message, according to proponents of verbal immediacy's ability to predict and explain language choices.

Researchers examining the concept of verbal immediacy have analyzed newspaper editorials to determine the effectiveness of more or less immediate speech. A study of President's Nixon's 1969 speech on the "Vietnamization" of the Vietnam War reported that favorable editorials were more verbally immediate (Hess and Gossett, 1974). Another study indicated that verbal immediacy relates to assessments by self and others of open communication content and style (Montgomery, 1981). In addition, Parrott (1992) used more immediate speech as a way to increase the audience's involvement with printed brochures designed to inform audiences about the risks associated with overexposure to the sun, and Saisslin and Parrott (1992) used immediate speech as a method of personalizing AIDS messages, indicating that the receivers who received the more immediate form of the message were more likely to alter risky sexual behavior. Though message designers may not often consider the design of messages at this level, such specifics afford more guidance and understanding.

Two theories, in particular, have been advanced in the field of communication that have specific relevance to the selection of words and appeals to be used in expressing the chosen arguments in campaign messages. In 1985, Burgoon and Miller published "An Expectancy Interpretation Language and Persuasion." The basic assumption of their article is that, "since language is a rule-governed system, people develop norms and expectations concerning appropriate usage in given situations" (p. 199). Burgoon, Jones, and Stewart (1975) advanced an earlier skeletal form of the theory.

Burgoon and Miller (1985) advance the rationale for a set of theoretical propositions, the first of which is: "use of language that negatively violates normative expectations about appropriate communication behavior inhibits persuasive effectiveness; use of language that positively violates expectations by conforming more closely than anticipated to normative expectations of appropriate communication behavior facilitates persuasive effectiveness" (Burgoon and Miller, 1985, p. 201). The theory's functional focus, then, is persuasion; formally, expectancy theory asserts that campaigners must determine normative rules of language use in order to employ the most appropriate stylistic appeals and word choices for their messages.

Speech accommodation theory advances the proposition that people attempt to converge linguistically toward others' speech patterns when desiring social approval and perceived costs for doing so are proportionally lower than anticipated rewards; and/or they desire a high level of communicational efficiency, and social norms are not perceived to dictate alternative speech strategies (Street and Giles, 1982). Investigations have shown that: (1) speakers were rated more positively when converging on content and speech rate than when converging on content, rate, and pronunciation (Giles and Smith, 1979); (2) normative expectations pressured in individuals t converge with high status individuals (Ball, Giles, Byrne, and Berechee, 1984); and (3) ratings of attractiveness of counselors and clients were higher when they used powerful speech (1984). These findings also provide some support for expending the time and effort necessary to determine what specific speech patterns an audience uses in order to enhance the likelihood of forming positive impressions through the specific design of message content.

Memory

Cicero defines mamory as, ". . . the firm mental grasp of matter and words . . . " (cited in Hubbell, 1949). A number of factors can be manipulated to facilitate comprehension and retention.

Repetition

Gorn and Goldberg (1980) found that multiple exposures to a message was superior in increasing the audience's retention to a single exposure to a message. Few would disagree with the statement that repeating a message enhances the ability of the listener to retrieve the information in the message (e.g., Sawyer and Ward, 1979). What has been observed regarding the repetition of a message, however, is that two ideas that are similar become linked in association through mere repetition, and one may elicit the other spontaneously (Alba and Hutchinson, 1987). "As two of several determinants of recall,

---

FEEDBACK

Again, examine the ads or messages collected for use in this chapter.

  1. What types of appeals have the message designers employed?
  2. Examine the use of language. Evaluate the intensity of speech forms, as well as the immediacy of speech forms. If you were the designer, based on discussion in this chapter, would you have done anything differently?

---

repetition, and recency are likely to be very influential in the decision process, particularly for novices" (p. 434). Burke and Srull (1988), however, found that repetition had a positive effect on receiver's ability to recall information only when there was little or no advertising for very similar products. Others have found that when content employs a "straightforward" approach rather than a "mood" appeal, multiple exposures increase the recall of the message's content (Donius, 1983).

Level of Knowledge

The understanding that an individual has about the subject, the number of known facts contributing to awareness or the level of expertise, also contributes to the ability to remember new information that may be presented (Brewer and Dupree, 1983). In other words, if an audience already has a preexisting schema regarding a candidate, a product, or a social issue, then their response to a message and memory of the message content differs from those individuals without such familiarity. Recognizing this, many magazines, particularly trade publications, employ controlled circulation distribution to target people with more precision. IBM, for example, launched two computing magazines in 1992, one aimed at customers, called *Profit*, and the other at potential customers, called *Beyond Computing. Profit* attempts to target small business owners, whereas *Beyond Computing* is aimed at executives in medium and large companies. The two audiences' differing expertise in computers will undoubtedly determine the development of the content of stories, although the topics may be quite similar. By tailoring their content accordingly, IBM may be able to enhance retention levels.

Coherence

"Coherence aids comprehension by allowing the consumer to understand how one assertion is related to another. It aids recall because the associations that are formed provide retrieval cues. If two assertions are linked, one may cue the other" (Alba and Hutchinson, 1987). Coherence relations also accounts for significant differences among people in reading time, such that increased coherence is positively related to decreased time to process information (Thorson and Snyder, 1984). Consider, for example, the following message on AIDS:

> *You won't get AIDS from a mosquito bite. The AIDS virus does not live in a mosquito, and is not transmitted through a mosquito's salivary glands like other diseases such as malaria or yellow fever. You won't get AIDS from bed bugs, lice, flies, or other insects, either (Department of Health and Human Services).*

The coherence of this message in making associations between a mosquito bite, AIDS, other diseases that mosquitoes do carry, and other insects that do not carry AIDS, should promote the reader's ability to remember the message.

Competing Messages

The greater the number of items that an individual learns, the greater the proportion of items that will not be recalled (Alba and Chattopadhyay, 1985). The number of competing brands advertising within a product category inhibits consumers' ability to retrieve specific information regarding a specific brand (Keller, 1987).

Audience Goals

When an audience is processing a message to make a decision, they are better able to recall specific information than when they are simply exposed to a message (Biehal and Chakravarti, 1986; Keller, 1987). This provides one more reason to establish the audience's readiness for responding before providing them with campaign content.

Visual and/or Verbal Messages

Pictures have been found to be more easily recalled than words (Lutz and Lutz, 1978). The most common explanation given for this finding is the superior ability of pictures to evoke use of mental imagery. Childers and Houston (1984) have demonstrated that picture superiority occurs in immediate and delayed recall tasks when processing is directed at appearance features, while verbal messages are recalled as well as pictures in immediate recall conditions but decay in delayed recall when processing is directed at semantic content. Additional discussion of message dissemination occurs in Chapters 9, 10, and 11.

In sum, the research that addresses an audience's ability to remember message content has provided some consistent findings over the years, particularly in terms of message repetition. Other variables also have been found to hold promise in this area, and with more and more researchers focusing programs of study on the cognitive area of communication, campaigners' understanding of memory should be further enhanced.

Delivery

Cicero defines delivery as, ". . . the control of voice and body in a manner suitable to the dignity of the subject matter and the style . . . " (cited in Hubbell, 1949).

Communication researchers have focused a great deal of effort on the examination of the available means to deliver a speech. Norton's (1978) inventory of communicator

---

FEEDBACK

Review the ads and messages collected for this chapter one more time.

1. Based on our understanding of message recall, evaluate the expected immediate and delayed recall of the messages' content.

styles provides one typology of approaches to communicating that a speaker may adopt. The verbal and nonverbal behavioral indices associated with these styles has been examined, as well as the impressions likely to be left by each style of communicator. Importantly, the nonverbal behaviors of speakers contribute significantly to the effects associated with messages. In fact, as we are all well aware, the very same verbal content may be interpreted quite differently from one person to the next, depending upon how that content has been delivered. Issues associated with specific style and delivery of a message are beyond the scope of discussion for this text. However, Chapter 9 will examine the research associated with the conveyance of specific relational messages (Burgoon and Hale, 1984) as related to the use of particular modes of communication.

The important issue for campaigners to consider in selecting advocates to be associated with a campaign is the maintenance or congruence of the delivery with the image of the campaign. Impression formation and management is typically examined with regard to impression formers and managers. Tedeschi and Norman (1985), for example, have identified a taxonomy of assertive and defensive impression management strategies used by individuals during conversation. Tedeschi and Norman identify credibility as the most important component of a positive public image. Others researchers provide further support for this conclusion (Bond, Welkowitz, Goldschmidt, and Wattenberg, 1987; Godfrey, Jones, and Lord, 1986). Although such research is specifically relevant to the individuals' maintenance of impressions and images, campaigns too will be associated with an image, and in all likelihood, the perceptions of credibility will be vital to their success.

Likability, next to credibility, is the image most commonly identified as important for impression managers to attempt to claim (Bird, 1987; O'Connor and Gifford, 1988). Thus, message advocates should be individuals that an audience is expected to find likable. Additionally, attractiveness (Albright, Kenny, and Malloy, 1988; Alicke, Smith, and Klotz, 1987) and power (sometimes called assertiveness) (De Meuse, 1987) are images that contribute vitally to the formation of impressions.

In sum, in selecting the spokespersons for a campaign and the advocates of campaign messages, the images to be promoted are credibility, likability, attractiveness, and assertiveness. Consider, for example, the General Mills symbol, Betty Crocker. Her image has evolved since her debut in 1936. In fact, she underwent five image changes through 1980, growing younger and more modern each time. In the sixth edition of General Mills' classic cookbook, Betty is a distinctly young urban professional:

Spiffed up in a business suit, Betty appears to be a woman who would feel as much at home in the boardroom as in the kitchen. According to General Mills, up to 30% of men do at least some of their own cooking, and the new Betty is intended to be "similar to someone businessmen work with. We wanted someone they would trust with their baking questions" (Time, 1986, p. 63).

FEEDBACK

Many cities have stepped up their campaign activities to promote themselves to three audiences: tourists, convention planners, and their own residents. The goal is to attract more people, thereby enhancing their economy. Place yourself in a position as advisor to campaigners in the city nearest you.

1. What arguments might be advanced to promote the city to each of the three audiences?

2. Within each argument for each group, develop both a fact and policy claim.

3. For each policy and fact claim, select an appeal based on humor, emotion, and warmth to advance the claim's content.

Conclusion

This chapter began with a brief historical overview of the origins and traditions of language study in communication that contribute to persuasive campaigners' message design. Following the introduction, Cicero's five rhetorical canons were employed to provide a framework for reviewing extant research and framing suggestions for campaign planners in the message design process.

The invention of messages was considered within the classic Toulmin model as a way of getting a skeletal outline of where message designers are headed. The arrangement of messages was examined in terms of inductive, deductive, or abductive patterns that are selected along with specific organizational patterns that promote a primacy or recency effect based on the campaign's goals. The expression of campaign messages was discussed within the framework of the various types of appeals and word choices that are available to campaigners. Ways of contributing to the audience's memory of campaign messages were considered, including repetition and the use of verbal versus visual content. Finally, the images that a campaign should strive to promote were viewed as part of the topic of delivery.

Suggestions for Further Reading

Bingham, S. G. (1991). Communication strategies for managing sexual harassment in organizations: Understanding message options and their effects. *Applied Communication Research, 19*, 88–115.

Edelman, M. (1967). *The Symbolic Uses of Politics.* Urbana, IL: University of Illinois Press.

Hunter, J. E., Hamilton, M. A., and Allen, M. (1989). The design and analysis of language experiments in communication. *Communication Monographs, 56*, 341–363.

Larson M. S. (1991). Health-related messages embedded in prime-time television entertainment. *Health Communication, 3*, 175–184.

Free Communication Modalities

In the world of television, public leaders and reporters are only seen and heard selectively. When the visual and the verbal dance in step, the power of each is magnified. But while the visual message is a flamenco dancer, its verbal partner is a wallflower.
KATHLEEN HALL JAMIESON, COMMUNICATIONS PROFESSOR
(JAMIESON, 1988, P. 60)

All [political] campaign messages . . . have come to look and sound suspiciously like political advertisements. Staging, scripting, and directing have become the order of the day. The real and momentous political consequences of the electoral process are masked and subverted by the staged drama of the campaign.
DIANA OWEN, POLITICAL SCIENTIST
(OWEN, 1991, P. 174)

This chapter concerns various free communication modalities that are available to campaigners, including traditional public speaking (including debates or joint appearances), interpersonal communication, news, and public service announcements. The task for campaigners is to manage these free communication modalities so as to simultaneously insure maximum exposure for, and maintain control over, their messages.

This chapter will examine each of these free communication modalities, drawing examples from the realm of campaigns which most frequently utilize them. While these free modalities are potentially available to all commercial, political, and social action campaigners, in practice the most desirable options are often limited. Political campaigns for acknowledged contenders for major office enjoy an advantage in using the most desirable modalities. Such campaigns carry an aura of legitimacy, which stems from a perception of importance, which in turn serves as a precondition for drawing crowds to speeches, insuring a hearing from potential supporters, or attracting mass media news coverage of speeches, debates, or other campaign activities. By contrast, most social action campaigns often must settle for a combination of interpersonal efforts, press releases for local media news, and public service announcements to influence receivers, whereas commercial campaigns rely exclusively on paid communication (in the form of advertising).

It is important to note as an overview to this chapter that campaign communication, whether passed along to receivers in the form of public speeches and debates, news, or paid advertisements, is highly managed, designed to convey basic themes, principally to television viewers through a combination of capsulized verbal messages and illustrative visual material (Owen, 1991). In the contemporary campaign environment, television clearly has become the medium of choice. Americans rely increasingly on television for news, and thus campaign speeches, debates, and other events are geared to television coverage. As a result, this chapter will place particular emphasis on the unique characteristics of the television medium, and will answer the questions that appear in Table 9-1.

Speechmaking (Speeches and Debates)

Traditional speechmaking was once a primary communication vehicle for political and social action campaigns. American history is replete with examples of spokespersons who advanced political appeals that exerted a profound impact on this nation's development. The speeches of Samuel Adams in Massachusetts and Patrick Henry in Virginia, along with Thomas Paine's book *Common Sense*, helped move colonists to support independence from Great Britain (Paisley, 1989). The rhetoric of Abraham Lincoln guided the nation safely through the perils of the Civil War, while the appeals of men like Charles Sumner of Massachusetts and Thaddeus Stevens of Pennsylvania steered the nation toward a more radical reconstruction policy than Lincoln desired (Bailey, 1966). The early speeches of Tom Watson in Georgia and of William Jennings Bryan in Nebraska turned undisciplined agrarian protest into a potent political force

TABLE 9-1   Questions about Free Communication Modalities

1. Why are the most desirable free communication modalities more available to political campaigners?
2. What is a sound bite? How can speakers exploit the desire of audiences and reporters for sound bites?
3. What is a set speech? What does it contain? How is it used?
4. Describe the nature of the "new eloquence."
5. What are relational messages? What dimensions of relational communication exert the greatest impact in speaker influence?
6. Describe the role and impact of interpersonal communication in influence.
7. What functions do personalized direct mail and telephone contacts serve in political and social action campaigns?
8. How does the nature of the medium affect what is reported in television news?
9. Is agenda-setting a useful theory to explain the impact of news in political campaigns? Why or why not?
10. Which communication objectives can be effectively met using public service announcements? What is their primary weakness?

(Hicks, 1961). And, the public speeches and radio broadcasts of Franklin Roosevelt guided America through the Great Depression and World War II (Blum et al., 1968).

Speech-making was once a most demanding endeavor. Speakers addressed specific audiences, some of whom traveled considerable distances in order to hear them, spoke at some length, and often shared the platform with someone representing an opposing view. Consequently, speech-making demanded more breadth and depth than it does today (Graber, 1981). For each claim advanced, a speaker was expected to provide sufficient warrants (reasons) and backing (support). This produced both lengthy and substantive discourse (Jamieson, 1988). On those occasions when two or more speakers shared the same platform, speakers were additionally expected to clash with their opponent(s), providing direct refutation of their claims.

Ironically, what has changed, some say "debased" (Graber, 1981), modern speech-making is the evolution of television. At first glance, the new medium seemed to possess the potential to enhance oratory by electronically multiplying a speaker's reach many times. Indeed, early television consisted largely of live events, including speeches, shot with one or two cameras and in black and white. A more careful examination, however, reveals that television, because of its unique channel characteristics, has changed speech-making dramatically, producing a "new language" (Carpenter, 1986, p. 353). As a result, "traditional . . . oratory has become rare" in campaign communication (Graber, 1981, p. 212).

Contemporary television consists of ". . . what is said (the verbal message), what is shown (the visual message), and how it is presented (production techniques)" (Nesbit, 1988, p. 20). It is the latter characteristics, the visual message, enhanced by sophisticated production techniques, that renders television communication unique, even when compared to live presentations. Contemporary speech- making is geared to the creation of sound bites, and consists of a limited number of basic themes, which are captured in a set speech.

The Sound Bite

Contemporary campaigners, especially in politics, continue to "take to the stump." However, their speeches are not directed primarily to those in the immediate audience; rather, as a result of the tremendous reach of contemporary television news, they are aimed at a national audience. What the television viewer sees is a 14-second snippet of a speech, called a "sound bite." A sound bite consists of a "memorable phrase," a one-liner, little more than an unsubstantiated claim often reinforced with a "memorable picture" (Jamieson, 1988). Sound bites constitute abbreviated communication, which reduce oral discourse to assertions, often backed by nothing more than a colorful anecdote or a visual. "In this electronic age, they [labels] are our politics" (1988, p. 248).

The increasing trend toward abbreviated communication has even affected the oral discourse found in televised political debates, which at first glance might appear immune as a result of more lengthy formats. Jamieson and Birdsell (1988, pp. 118–119) refer to contemporary televised debates as "a gladitorial contest in miniature," adding:

> *. . . the format [of televised debates] invites sloganeering. Brief answers on a shower of topics creates an informational blur. The press panel asks questions designed to elicit news headlines, not information of use to voters. The superficial is rewarded; the substantive spurned.*

Jamieson (1988, pp. 10–11) criticizes the format used in the 1984 Reagan and Mondale debates because it produced candidate answers that ranged from 1 to 2 1/2 minutes per topic, quite a change from the Lincoln and Douglas debates of 1858 where each man spoke for close to 90 minutes per topic.

This is not to suggest that speakers are less able to exert influence than in the past. Indeed, the success of the 1988 Bush presidential campaign, which employed a coordinated attack based on speech-making, designed to elicit sound bites, and advertising, attests to the potential persuasiveness of this more abbreviated communication. Nonetheless, while effective, using speech-making as a platform to generate sound bites undermines the substance of discourse, and results in a "dangerous oversimplification of what are, in reality, very complex matters" (Kymlicka and Matthews, 1988, p. 23).

Effective speakers adapt to the demands of the new oratory. They are aware that, because today's receivers prefer "quick, instant gratification," "long speeches are no longer tolerated" (Graber, 1981, p. 212). Jamieson and Birdsell (1988, p. 96) document that, "Since the advent of the broadcast media, the length of political messages has decreased steadily."

Further, effective speakers understand how to exploit the mutual desire of audiences and the news media for brief, catchy one-liners. Atkinson's research (1986) convincingly illustrates that speakers who are able to package message segments employing optimal combinations of verbal rhythm, intonation, volume, and timing/pacing increase the probability of audience applause, which in turn, enhances the likelihood that the message segment will be selected as a media sound bite. Atkinson (1986, p. 46) explains:

> *The selection of excerpts from speeches which receive applause has a number of advantages for the producers of news programs and other media reporters. The amount of approval . . . shown by an audience provides observers with a firm basis for assessing the impact of a particular speech. By showing sequences where audiences produce displays of affiliation . . . , television news producers are thus able to supply viewers with a snapshot both of what the speaker had to say and of how the audience responded.*

Atkinson offers three specific message strategies that are designed to accomplish this end. The use of "three-part lists" (audiences are likely to respond after a speaker communicates the third item in a series), "two-part contrasts" (audiences are more likely to respond after a speaker delivers a way out in the form of a solution following the presentation of a contrast), and the use of "combined formats" significantly increase the probability of audience applause. A large, follow-up study of 476 political speeches (Heritage and Greatbatch, 1986) both supports and extends Atkinson's thesis.

FEEDBACK

Select a speech that was crafted for, and delivered to, a live audience, the text of which was reported in local or national print media. Gather as much information as you can about the speech, paying particular attention to the source, the content matter, and the primary audience.

Then write a condensed version of the speech designed to enhance its likelihood of being reported by television news. Make sure that the rewritten version:

    1. adapts the content to the larger secondary audience that might receive it via television news;

    2. packages the main ideas in message segments that can be easily adapted to a "sound bite";

    3. includes at least one example of each of the following message strategies:

        a. three-part lists;

        b. two-part contrasts.

The study identified seven message strategies (including lists and contrasts) that accounted for more nearly two-thirds of the instances of applause (Heritage and Greatbatch, 1986, p. 137).

Whereas research has begun to study speeches to determine what stylistic devices promote audience applause, which in turn contributes to media sound bites, there has been scant interest in comparing the effectiveness of speech-making and alternative communication forms. One study (Mortensen, 1968) reported that televised political speeches contained fewer policy claims, more assertions, and less content development than network interview telecasts. This finding is consistent with the thesis that good speakers are able to adapt their discourse to the demands of the television medium.

The absence of manifest content in televised speech-making is much more pronounced in those instances when entire speeches are reduced to 14-second sound bites. Jamieson (1988) cautions that sound bites can seriously mislead viewers, especially when verbal content is supplemented with visual footage. She (1988) argues that people lack the ability to judge the sound bite, having not experienced the speech from which it was taken. "This means that the reporter not the speaker or the viewer now determines which moments in the speech will come to stand for the speech" (p. 112). It also means that people lack the ability to judge the veracity of speaker's claims, "because we lack a grammar to test whether a visual assertion can function as argument" (p. 116).

The abbreviated communication of the television era results in a bias toward problems, which can be depicted visually, and a bias against proposed solutions, which are more abstract, thereby requiring words and reasons (Hellweg, Pfau, and Byrdon, 1992). BBC executive David Webster observes that, "Television . . . happens to be better as a medium of experience . . . it is not . . . very good at explaining things" (cited in Linsky, 1983, p. 18). Thus, modern political campaigns stress problems (the contemporary vernacular is "values"), whose symptoms can be depicted in powerful, visual images (e.g., crime, inflation, and the environment), and avoid solutions.

The Set Speech

The focus on the televised audience in most speech-making has produced additional changes. First, since select sound bites of any speech may reach a broader audience, speakers must develop and maintain a limited number of consistent positions. This consistency is accomplished via the "set speech," a series of modules that contain the core ideas that are designed to appear and reappear throughout a campaign. In the case of political campaigns, "Each of these modules is used so often that the candidate can remember it and convincingly deliver it" (C. Smith, 1990, p. 122).

The set speech insures consistency and adaptability. The speaker can select from among various modules, depending on the audience. The repetition of the basic themes of the set speech insures consistency. In addition, the set speech facilitates adaptability. Speakers adapt the individual modules of the set speech to specific circumstances by simply adding, changing, or removing specific supporting material (e.g., examples, anecdotes, statistics, illustrations, quotations, etc.).

For example, candidates often utilize specific modules from the set speech in answering the questions posed by a moderator or journalists in political debates. In fact, this may be the most common criticism of contemporary televised debates, that debate formats encourage superficial answers, termed "worn commonplaces" (Hellweg et al., 1992). Candidates often ignore specific questions asked, instead resorting to "minicampaign speeches" (Johnstone, 1985). This may explain the tendency for televised debates to typically underperform both viewers' and journalists' expectations for specific content (O'Keefe and Mendelsohn, 1979).

The set speech contains the speaker's core philosophy. Each module is worked and reworked to update the content, particularly the examples and anecdotes, which Jamieson (1988) argues is one more integral feature of effective contemporary eloquence. In a television age, a speaker's ability to support claims with more illustrative backing insures success. Jamieson (1988) considers Ronald Reagan as "an effective communicator" because he possessed the rare ability to use ". . . verbal and nonverbal vignettes that capture his central claims" (p. 119).

Jimmy Carter delivered the same set speech throughout the 1976 presidential campaign. The basic theme, repeated over and over again, was that America's greatness is in her people; that we must elevate government so that it becomes worthy of people's support. This theme remained constant in Carter's speeches, but was adapted to specific content claims that Carter made during the campaign. Ronald Reagan's set speech, which he first used in 1964, contained two overarching themes: that "big government" is responsible for many of this nation's problems, and that America must remain strong and vigilant in the face of international communism. These themes permeated his 1976, 1980, and 1984 presidential campaigns, although the specific content varied.

FEEDBACK

Examine the campaign rhetoric of the Democratic and Republican nominees during the last presidential election. Identify the core modules that comprised the basic themes of the set speech employed by each candidate in the campaign.

The set speech, in short, must be consistent in its themes, but simultaneously fresh in its supporting content. This, in turn, places a tremendous premium on fresh material, which in part explains the expanding role and influence of speech writers in national campaigns.

The "New Eloquence"

While television features both visual and verbal channels, the former dominate the latter. Political consultant Ken Swope (cited in Kern, 1989, p. 35) says that, "In order of importance on television come pictures, music, then words." Most scholars concur, emphasizing "the primacy of the visual over the audio channel" (Chesebro, 1984; Graber, 1987; Paletz and Guthrie, 1987, p. 20; Salomon, 1987).

As a result of visual preeminence, television communicates a unique message, possessing quite "different possibilities and limitations" (Meyrowitz, 1985, p. 97). Television's limitations revolve around its lack of substance, as we explained previously. "Television is an information-poor medium: facts, statistics, charges, and counter-charges fly past the viewer, often too rapidly to be digested" (Diamond and Friery, 1987, p. 49).

Television's possibilities involve images. "It [television] directs us to respond to images, which are holistic, concrete, and simplistic. That is why it rarely matters what anyone says on television" (Postman, 1988, p. 18). "But because television is at the same time an emotion-rich medium, qualities of appearance such as 'competence' and 'trustworthiness' are easier to pick out" (Diamond and Friery, 1987, p. 49). The implications for speech making of television's limitations and possibilities are best understood in terms of the active and passive models of influence, explained in Chapters 4 and 5, respectively. Whereas traditional speech making once embodied active influence, with an emphasis on message content, contemporary speech making, which is targeted toward a television audience, conforms much more closely to the passive or heuristic model of influence, with an emphasis on source factors.

What matters in televised speech making is the communicator, and particularly the way in which he/she delivers the message. Television places a premium on the presentational dimension of communication, demanding that speakers employ a more personal, casual style, more similar to the way they would communicate in an interpersonal context. Atkinson (1984, p. 171) explains that, an effective television presentation requires that communicators deliver messages "...in such a way that viewers can feel they are *eavesdropping* on a scene, rather than being spoken to directly from the scene." This requires a warm, conversational delivery, what Ranney (1983, p. 103) calls ". . . a pleasant and friendly presence, a moderate tone of voice, small and natural gestures, and a general conversational manner."

Jamieson (1988) refers to this communication style as "a new eloquence," and points to Ronald Reagan as the epitome of this new discourse (see Figure 9–1). Political correspondents Peter Goldman and Tony Fuller (1985, p. 29) characterize Reagan's

FIGURE 9–1 Ronald Reagan Exemplifies the "New Eloquence"

Source: Courtesy of Teresa Labala, photographer, and the League of Women Voters.

"elegance" as follows: "he had a gift of intimacy, of plain speech, simple vision, and open feelings," perfectly suited to the demands of the television medium. Reagan communicated conversationally, illustrating his claims with vivid anecdotes. Schram (1987) credits Reagan's more conversational, intimate delivery with his success in exploiting television. "He skillfully mastered the ability to step through the television tubes and join Americans in their living rooms" (p. 26). Political consultant Thomas Edmonds (cited in Colford, 1988, p. 32) agrees, adding that, "Ronald Reagan . . . communicated one-on-one, even if he was talking to millions."

Reagan's communication style was also expressive. Reagan "doesn't just speak with words. He speaks with a frown, a smile, or [with] an expression of 'aw shucks.'" As a result, Meyrowitz (1985, p. 304) argues that the label, "great communicator," is misleading. In its place, he prefers "great expressor," a label that captures the former President's *true* communicative strength.

Interpersonal Routes

Interpersonal communication concerns the interaction of two or three people which usually occurs in face-to-face situations where each person can respond to the other(s). In this section we will examine interpersonal as a specific communication context in contemporary campaigns. The focus of this section will be on the role of person-to-person contact as an essential supplement to mediated influence in all persuasive campaigns. Personalized direct mail and telephone appeals to exert influence and raise monies will also be examined.

The Role of People in Influence

Person-to-person contact is an important source of influence in persuasive communication campaigns. Greenberg (1975) terms its role "crucial". There are two ways to view the influence of person-to-person influence in persuasive campaigns. On the one hand, person-to-person influence can be treated as an indirect, intermediating variable in mass media influence; on the other hand, it can be treated as a direct source of influence.

Lazarsfeld and colleagues posited a "two-step flow" of mass communication in reporting the results of their seminal study of the 1940 presidential election campaign in Erie County, Ohio (Lazarsfeld et al., 1968), and then reaffirmed it in an investigation of the 1948 presidential campaign in Elmira, New York (Berelson et al., 1954). As we indicated in Chapter 2, the studies found that mass media campaigns convert relatively few, instead serving mainly to reinforce partisans. However, the results also revealed, that in the instances when influence does occur, personal influence played a surprisingly strong role. Thus, Lazarsfeld reasoned that influence occurs in two waves: initially the mass media influence opinion leaders, ordinary people who, because of more interest in a content area (in this case, politics), are also greater users of mass media; then opinion leaders influence others. Subsequently, Katz and Lazarsfeld (1955) extended the "two-step flow" model to other influence contexts, including marketing.

We stress that opinion leaders are ordinary people; they are not elites. As Katz and Lazarsfeld (1955, p. 32) indicate, they are found among "all occupational groups, and on every social and economic level." It is their heavier mass media use that clearly distinguishes them. Katz and Lazarsfeld (1955, p. 312) continue: "In sum it can safely be stated that the opinion leaders in every realm tend to be more highly exposed to the mass media than are the nonleaders."

Lazarsfeld's research was the first to confirm the presence of face-to-face influence in mass media communication. However, two caveats should be noted. First, although the research was subsequently interpreted by some as evidence of the impotence of mass media influence, it indicated that the mass media exerted more than twice the influence of personal contacts, suggesting just the opposite. Chaffee (1972, p. 107) describes the irony in these terms: "Even in the famous Decatur study that was designed to demonstrate personal influence, a majority (58 percent) of the reported opinion changes 'were apparently made without involving any remembered personal contact, and were, very often, dependent upon the mass media'" (Katz and Lazarsfeld, 1955).

Second, and more important from the standpoint of trying to understand the nature of person-to-person contact in campaigns, Lazarsfeld's research posits that the process of influence goes from the media to opinion leaders, and then from opinion leaders to other people. What the Lazarsfeld research could not address is the manner that information diffuses. Sheingold (1973) says that a sociological methodology, grounded in the examination of social networks, constitutes the most promising approach. As he explains (1973, p. 714):

> *Social networks constitute social structures which exist independent of the perceptions of discrete individuals. The information an individual receives may emanate from others with whom he is not in direct contact and of whom he may be unaware. Thus, network structures cannot be directly studied within the confines of self-report data.*

Parrott and Ross (1991) examined people's use of mediated and interpersonal sources of influence in commercial and social action contexts. The researchers found that people rely more on television as a source of information about issues and opinions, but not about relationships or products. They added that people who had previously formed opinions about products increased their use of interpersonal interaction for the goal of social control, using it to bolster their own views.

In a political context, Kaid (1977) reminds us that, despite the mass media attention showered upon national presidential and senate campaigns, interpersonal communication continues to be the most important source of influence in the myriad of less visible state and local political campaigns. Such interpersonal tactics as door-to-door canvassing and small social gatherings constitute staples in state and local political campaigns. In these cases, "Interpersonal campaigning . . . is often the major thrust of the campaign, an essential means for compensating for the lack of media exposure" (Trent and Friedenberg, 1991, p. 249).

In national, state, and local political campaigns, the use of interpersonal communication remains a very important source of influence. One study (cited in Chaffee, 1981, p. 192) found that 20 percent of adults are asked their advice on which candidate to support, and that 20 to 40 percent of adults discuss campaign events and candidates with other people. Another study reported that an attempt to persuade occurs in 47 percent of conversations (an actual change of opinion resulted in 21 percent of cases), and that, "The data reveal that persuasion is attempted more often in political conversations than in nonpolitical ones" (Greenberg, 1975, p. 130). Previously, Katz and Lazarsfeld (1955) acknowledged that some people exert significant influence on the political attitudes of others.

In addition, Kotler and Roberto (1989) maintain that most social action campaigns depend heavily on interpersonal contact, particularly as a follow-up to mass media appeals. "Of the three main promotional communication tools [mass communication, what they term "selective communication," which includes direct mail, and personal communication] personal communication exercises the most powerful influence..." (Kotler and Roberto, 1989, pp. 222–223). The impact of personal influence is the most pronounced at the decision or adoption stage.

Kotler and Roberto (1989, pp. 223–224) explain three common strategies in which personal influence plays an important role in social action campaigns. These include: outreach, in which the communicator deals directly with potential adoptors; education, in which the communicator deals with relevant groups; and what they term, "word-of-mouth," in which the communicator uses some adoptors to relay the message to other potential adoptors.

The success of the Stanford Three Community Study and the Stanford Five City Project most vividly support the fundamental axiom that mass media and interpersonal influence are essential in health campaigns, serving complimentary functions: the former to generate awareness and impart knowledge, and the latter to provide training and reinforcement (Flora et al. 1989). This principle has been repeatedly demonstrated across social action campaigns (Rogers and Storey, 1987). Consequently, as a campaign progresses, emphasis must shift from mass media to interpersonal communication. That was the case in the Stanford community studies, where, "Over time, the number of broadcast media messages decreased and the number of face-to-face messages increased" (Flora et al., 1989, p. 250).

Personalized Direct Mail and Telephone Appeals

Targeted or direct mail and telephone appeals have come of age with the growth of computer technology. The computer made it possible to target specific individuals, thus "facilitating a volume of communication virtually impossible using traditional methods" (Frantzich, 1989, pp. 216–217). Personalized direct mail and telephone appeals are person-to-person, although they are obviously not face-to-face.

Nonetheless, we have included direct mail and telephone appeals as a subset of interpersonal communication because, when they are done right, they resemble one-on-one communication. As Robert Denton and Gary Woodward (1985, p. 64) posit, referring just to direct mail, it is targeted to very specific receivers. "The letter is conversational and personal using a lot of *I*'s and *you*'s." This language is more verbally immediate.

Kotler and Roberto (1989) characterize direct mail as a form of "personalized communication" (p. 213) and telephone appeals as "two-way interaction" (p. 217). Armstrong (1988, p. 144) agrees. In noting the more intimate, interactive nature of personalized telephone appeals, he refers to them as ". . . just like direct mail . . . only more so." Thus, although direct mail and telephone appeals require the use of mediated channels of communication, in their approach they resemble interpersonal communication because they provide an opportunity for two-way communication, complete with feedback, to occur.

As a result of its personalized nature, research indicates that people open and read direct mail appeals. Armstrong (1988, p. 89) estimates that, "When it comes to fund-raising mail, . . . over four of five survey respondents (81 percent) say they open and at least glance at the contents." Armstrong (1988, p. 90) goes as far as to claim that, ". . . despite what people themselves often say, the evidence suggests that most people actually *like* direct mail. Further, in terms of persuasion mail, one study found that direct mail inoculated supporters of political candidates against their opponents' attacks, in direct comparison with the control subjects, thus inferring that subjects opened and read the direct mail appeals.

> *Since inoculated and control subjects were alike in almost every respect, including exposure to campaign events . . . , differing only in that the inoculated subjects had received a direct mail inoculation message and the control subjects had not, the greater resistance shown by the inoculated subjects to the persuasive attack messages suggests that many of them read and internalized the inoculative material (Pfau et al., 1990, p. 38).*

Personalized direct mail and telephone appeals, whether in political or social action campaigns, seek one of two functions: influence or fund-raising. When used as a vehicle for influence, more common in political campaigns, direct mail, in particular, is a potent weapon. It can contain lengthy appeals, marshaling arguments and evidence on behalf of a specific candidate or cause (Godwin, 1988). Further, direct mail can employ such approaches as threat, fear, and/or attack more effectively than other media (Martinez and DeLegal, 1988). Armstrong (1988, p. 60) calls direct mail "the most insidious advertising medium in the world," with this explanation: "Attack your opponent's record on television, and he will respond in kind. Attack your opponent in the mail, and he will never know what hit him" (p. 60). This feature led Sabato to characterize direct mail as "a silent killer" (cited in Armstrong, 1988, p. 60). In addition, as we indicated above, there is evidence that direct mail can be employed to inoculate the supporters of a candidate against an opponent's attacks, thus making it a strategic linchpin in today's attack politics (Pfau et al., 1990). Both the attack and inoculation strategies will be explored in more detail in Chapter 10.

Direct mail and telephone attempts at influence in social action campaigns are thought to be the most effective in aiding adoption of a desired behavior or in reinforcing adoption (Kotler and Roberto, 1989). As with political campaign uses, the success of these approaches depends on the ability of the campaigner to carefully target receivers with highly personalized messages.

Direct mail and telephone appeals play an important role in fundraising in political and social action campaigns. Richard Viguerie started his direct mail business in 1965 with $400 and the membership list of the conservative group, Young Americans for Freedom (Sabato, 1981). With the example set by Viguerie, who has enjoyed tremendous success in championing conservative causes, the Republican Party has led the way in exploiting the direct mail vehicle for political fund-raising, raising four to five times more than Democrats (Denton and Woodward, 1985).

In political and social action fund-raising, the "prospecting phase" involves efforts to snare first-time contributors, and is much less cost effective than the "renewal phase," which deals with past contributors. Sabato (1981) claims that it is common to secure 50 to 75 percent renewal, "at a tidy profit for each renewal" (p. 253).

Direct telephone appeals can be used to supplement direct mail fund-raising efforts. While conceding greater cost, still Armstrong maintains that telephone appeals generate as much as ten times the response rate of direct mail (1988, p. 145). In addition, telephone appeals can facilitate renewal, thus serving as "an effective tool to recapture lapsed donors" (Armstrong, 1988, p. 158). Public Interest Communication estimates that 20 percent can be retrieved, "even after a group of lapsed donors has ignored [as many as] seven direct-mail notices" (cited in Armstrong, 1988, p. 158).

Campaigners should consider a few simple guidelines in using either direct mail or telephone appeals. The key is to capture and hold the receiver's attention and interest. In using direct mail, campaigners should design the envelope, employing slogans or teasers to motivate the recipient to open it. In both direct mail and telephone appeals, the opening lines are very important, determining whether the receiver will continue the communication. The first lines should be carefully designed. They should be crafted to insure that they generate a favorable impression, and so that they provide a sufficiently compelling reason for people to continue.

Because the specific arguments and supporting materials are contained in the body of the appeal, it should be long enough to develop this content adequately, yet not so long so that receivers lose interest. In part, the appropriate length is determined by: (1) the communication modality (e.g., telephone appeals should be brief; direct mail appeals may be longer); (2) the content of the message (e.g., because the issue is inherently more intricate, it requires more specificity to advance an effective case for energy conservation than for many other causes); and (3) the targeted audience's sophistication and attitude disposition on the issue in question. Finally, the communication should conclude with a direct appeal that is compelling and specific.

In addition, the caller plays a critical role in telephone appeals. The caller requires a pleasant voice and a strong, but friendly, tone. And most important, although operating from a script, the caller must be able to communicate so as to create the impression of a conversational style.

FEEDBACK

Gather a number of examples of direct mail appeals on behalf of candidates or causes. Compare the appeals.

1. Assess the overall appearance and the opening lines of the appeals. Do you think they are optimally effective? For what audience(s)? How could they be improved?
2. Examine the body of the appeals. Are they appropriate given the content area? For what audience(s)? How could they be improved?

Mass Media News

Mass media news coverage of campaigns provides credibility, and is thus an invaluable asset. One analyst (Steinberg, 1979, p. 228) placed the value of news coverage of a candidate in a political campaign at $1^1/2$ times an equal volume of paid advertising time.

Eliciting News Coverage

Unfortunately, not all campaigns are in a position to take full advantage of mass media news because of the perception that they lack sufficient importance. Although businesses engage in campaigns aimed at enhancing their image (public relations), it requires considerable effort on their part to attract media news coverage of these activities. Commercial campaigns promoting a brand rely almost exclusively on paid communication, which will be developed in some detail in Chapter 10.

Social action campaigns also require considerable effort to generate mass media news coverage. Because their actions may not be deemed sufficiently important by gatekeepers, campaigners will usually need to pursue media news outlets, instead of the other way around. The news release is the tool that public relations and social action campaigners use to elicit the assistance of mass media news in carrying their message to the general public. News releases, if they are prepared properly, and if they are judged to be newsworthy by media gatekeepers, can be an important source of influence.

The problem with this approach is that it puts campaigners at the mercy of mass media gatekeepers, who determine if, and how, these materials may be used (Freimuth and Van Nevel, 1981). News releases often are not used and, when they are, may contain a different perspective than the campaign intended. Nonetheless, if the social action issue has newsworthy potential, campaigners are advised to work with media gatekeepers, "enlisting their support and cooperation" (Freimuth and Van Nevel, 1981, p. 166).

Generally speaking, news releases should focus on a single potentially newsworthy item, should be written economically, and should be tailored to specific media outlets. The release should contain an appealing headline, should be dated, and written in an inverted pyramid style common in journalism, in which the lead paragraph provides

---

FEEDBACK

Select a campus or local social issue of interest to you. Gather as much information as you can about the cause, and then prepare a press release on the issue for newspaper publication. Examine your release as you consider the following questions:

1. Is the headline appealing?
2. Is the writing economical?
3. Is the story compelling?
4. What could you do to increase the likelihood that the campus or local newspaper will actually use your release?

---

the synopsis of the story while the remaining paragraphs fill in the specific details. A number of examples of news releases are provided in Chapter 14, which examines the 1991 "Meatout" campaign in considerable detail.

A more ambitious tactic is the use of media kits, containing a number of news releases and other promotional materials, which are adapted to the specific communication modality (e.g., video tapes for television, audiotapes for radio, and news releases and photographs for newspapers and magazines). The same caveat applies, however, in that mass media gatekeepers determine if, and how, the materials are used. For example, during the 1991 "Meatout" social action campaign, a prepared spot was mailed to all the radio stations in Atlanta, Georgia. One popular morning show played the spot, which urged listeners to abstain from the eating of meat for the day, after which the announcer exclaimed, "Not eat meat? That's downright un-American!" More than likely, the hoped-for persuasive effect was lost.

Most public relations and social action campaigns, as well as less visible political campaigns, are not perceived by mass media gatekeepers as important enough to automatically warrant coverage, especially by national media. These campaigners must pursue media news outlets in the hope of obtaining coverage.

Controlling News Coverage

More active mass media news coverage is largely limited to more visible political campaigns, primarily those at the national and state levels. Such campaigns are perceived as important by the public, at least in a ritualistic sense (Edelman, 1964), and therefore are viewed as worthy of regular coverage by the media. As Owen (1991, p. 74) explains:

> . . . *the mass public desires campaign news, or at least they feel that election information should be reported daily. Election coverage provides Americans with a sense of security in knowing that democracy is alive and kicking. People believe that they can fulfill their duty as citizens by turning in to election news, if only occasionally.*

From the beginning of the American experience, political matters were viewed as essential content, appropriate for news coverage. At first the focus was on political causes, such as the campaign for the adoption of the Constitution of the United States (Rossiter, 1961). Subsequently, the focus shifted to candidate contests. From the democratization of politics in the 1828 Adams and Jackson campaign to the present, politicians came to depend on mass media news coverage to help communicate their message to people, and the mass media came to rely on closely contested political races to sustain readers, and later viewers. Some of the early political campaigns are discussed in Chapter 3. As a result of the symbiotic relationship between media news and political campaigns, it is impossible to fully understand the one absent the other.

If news affords credibility, then television news affords the most credibility. The difficulty for political campaigners is to control television news coverage so that it promotes, and does not undermine, the campaign effort. This is no small task because of the very nature of television news.

Nature of Television News

If television is the primary medium for political campaign news, how does the modality affect what is reported? One way is by placing a premium on brevity. The network evening newscasts are limited to approximately 20 minutes of content. This is not enough time to provide depth of coverage on any one story. As a result, television news coverage consists of little more than "a headline service." The stories are short, ranging from 30 to 90 seconds in length, "which makes it difficult for them to convey much information. There is little time for providing either context or explanation" (Graber, 1990).

Television news, because of the serious time constraints, devalues political content, and, due to its quick-moving format, biases receivers toward even increasing brevity (Graber, 1990; Jamieson, 1988). "Politics now comes to us . . . in tiny bites . . . We no longer get visions or complete thoughts. We are lucky to get complete sentences . . . [The consequence is that] substance becomes obliterated" (Halberstam, 1981, p. 4). It is little wonder that researchers (Gunter, 1987; Robinson and Davis, 1990) report minimal viewer retention of television news content.

Another way that the modality affects what is reported is by placing a premium on visual as opposed to verbal content. Owen (1991, p. 65) maintains that, "Visuals are a key component, often filling in details that the accompanying audio does not project." Indeed, it is the visual dimension of television news that most directly contributes to its believability, since people are more inclined to believe what they see than what they hear. As one analyst describes (cited in Altheide and Snow, 1979, p. 98), " 'Viewability' is easily construed as reliability because any intervention by broadcasters is largely invisible, and because the dramatic intensity of film and video. . . carries conviction and guarantees authenticity in ways which words cannot." Altheide and Snow (1979, p. 99) argue that this is a false reliability, since visuals appear out of context, adding that: ". . . we are vulnerable . . . if we are not aware of the workings of media logic."

Television news' bias for stories that can be captured via the live camera or on film tends to distort its coverage. The reason is that some stories offer greater visual potential than others. Simply put, some events lend themselves very nicely to pictures. This works to the detriment of issue content, which lacks the requisite action features.

As Patterson and McClure (1976, p. 27) observed in their seminal study of the role and impact of television during the 1972 presidential campaign:

> *In its coverage of a presidential campaign, network news frequently places exciting pictures ahead of informative reporting. The nightly newscasts...often ignore the substance of election politics to concentrate on the trivial, but colorful, campaign shenanigans that provide good film.*

Furthermore, to maximize visual coverage, television news relies most heavily on planned or staged events. In response, candidates have learned to organize their campaigns around the media's needs. "Candidates have discovered the advantages of presenting the press with planned newsmaking opportunities" (Owen, 1991, p. 63), consisting of nonspontaneous events that are created for the purpose of being reported. Social action campaigns have learned the same lesson. Environmental, civil rights, and abortion activists, for example, often plan their activities in order to obtain maximum attention and coverage on television news.

This development means that campaigners need to plan their candidates' schedules to facilitate media news coverage; schedule major campaign events prior to journalist deadlines; provide advanced texts of speeches; and so forth. In addition, it means that campaigners can schedule candidate appearances in such a way as to dramatize an issue that is being featured in a candidate's communication (e.g., speeches and paid advertising). The 1988 Bush presidential campaign capitalized on such events. Bush's appearance with the Boston police was designed to emphasize his attack on Dukakis' record on crime, while his speech at Boston Harbor was intended to underscore his attacks against Dukakis' environmental record. These events, which were created by the Bush campaign, and which featured the requisite visuals which television news demands, were an essential component in a well coordinated communication effort.

Television's "Melodramatic Imperative" The television modality's emphasis on brevity and visuals explains television news' overriding concern with the dramatic. Owen (1991, p. 63) argues that, "Television news . . . thrives on stories that feature high drama." Combs (1980, p. 110) explains that: "The news is dramatized for entertainment purposes. News organizations . . . are well aware that news is part of the entertainment fare of mass audiences, and must cater to those expectations or risk losing their audience . . . " This is particularly true regarding political campaigns.

The reason for the dramatic imperative is that television news, to inform, must also entertain in order to command viewer attention (Berkman and Kitch, 1986). As a result, television news seeks to improve upon reality, making it more interesting (cited in Taylor, 1990, p. 24). Halberstam (1981, p. 4) captures the implications of television's need to entertain for the practice of political campaigns in these words: "Politics is television, television is entertainment, and entertainment is politics." The dramatic imperative of television news is well illustrated by a memorandum written by former NBC News executive producer Reuven Frank to his staff. He instructed: "Every news story should . . . display the attributes of fiction, of drama. It should have structure and conflict, problem and denouncement, rising action and falling action, a beginning, a middle and an end" (cited in Gregg, 1977, p. 224).

The Emphasis on "Horse Race"   This preoccupation with drama leads to another bias: toward the competitive aspect of campaigns that deals with who is winning and losing, or what is termed in political campaigns as "the horse race" (Graber, 1980; Patterson and McClure, 1976; Patterson, 1980). The reason for this emphasis is that the competitive aspect of campaigns tends to be much more dramatic, thus conforming more closely to the narrative format which is common in network entertainment (Gregg, 1977; Weaver, 1976). Patterson and McClure (1976, pp. 40-41) explain that certain features of a presidential contest fit the narrative mold.

> *For a presidential election is surely a super contest with all the elements that are associated with spectacular sports events: huge crowds, rabid followers, dramatic do-or-die battles, winners and losers. It is this part of the election that the networks emphasize.*

Weaver adds that ". . . television's politician acts out a clear and gripping melodrama . . . Television presents the candidates not as people who are running for elective office, but as figures [who are] deeply and totally embroiled in an all-out-struggle" (cited in Swanson, 1977, p. 242). As a result, television news slights issue coverage, and when it does touch on issues, it treats them "as tactical moves in the ongoing dramatic conflict" (Swanson, 1977, p. 242).

Research has consistently confirmed the "horse race" bias of television news coverage of political campaigns. Patterson and McClure's (1976, p. 41) study of the 1972 presidential campaign indicated that network coverage of campaign activities dominated its coverage of candidates' positions on the issues four to one, and its coverage of candidates' qualifications about nine to one. Patterson (1980) reported that nearly 60 percent of television network news coverage of the 1976 presidential election focused on "the game," winning and losing, strategy, logistics, hoopla, and appearances. Berkman and Kitch (1986, p. 125) explain that, "Within the context of the strategic game and the melodramatic imperative, campaign coverage takes shape," and that, "The most popular game story is the 'horse race' story." They report that television news coverage of the 1980 presidential election also stressed horse race over substance.

In sum, the real drama of campaigns concerns who is winning and losing (Patterson, 1980). This applies to social action as well as to political campaigns. In reporting on abortion, for example, television news gets caught up in whether momentum has swung to the pro-life or pro-choice side, losing sight of the specific arguments advanced by their spokespersons.

FEEDBACK

Reexamine the press release on a campus or local issue that you prepared for newspaper use. Devise a strategy to gain coverage of this issue by campus or local television news.

The television news networks seem aware of their substantive shortcomings. As a result, since 1980 network news coverage has featured candidate position segments, and in 1988 focused on the claims that the candidates made in their paid advertising, which, as we will explain in Chapter 10, contains a surprising emphasis on issue content. Perhaps as a result of these changes, but more likely due to the double-digit leads that Reagan maintained over Mondale and that Bush built over Dukakis during the fall of their respective campaigns, Owen's (1991) research reports a decline in television network news horse race coverage in the 1984 and 1988 presidential elections.

Undermines Political Discourse We previously explained that television has contributed to the demise of verbal content in contemporary discourse. Television news, in particular, has further undermined political discourse in two ways.

First, television's emphasis on visual content has resulted in an increase in "the image orientation of campaign news" (Owen, 1991, p. 67), a tendency previously documented by Graber (1987). As Graber (1987, p. 77) explains, "when candidates for political office are shown on the television screen, audiences tend to use the pictures to judge the candidates' personality traits such as competence, integrity, leadership, and empathy."

In this way, television's emphasis on visuals, elevates the impact of source factors, and undermines the role of discourse, in the process of influence. Research dealing with the factors responsible for influence in commercial, political, and social action campaigns supports this position. Comparing television and other communication modalities, Pfau (1990) indicated that source factors are responsible for more influence than content in television communication, whereas the content overpowers the impact of source factors in print, radio, and public address communication.

A second way that television news has undermined political discourse is caused by the way that it frames issues. Instead of employing thematic framing, which views political issues within some broader framework, television news relies more heavily on episodic framing, which focuses on individual events and causes. Iyengar (1987) argues that episodic framing obscures connections between problems and political action, thus undermining electoral accountability. In severing the connection between discourse and policy choices, television news further erodes the role of issue content in campaigns. Iyengar (1987, p. 143) thus characterizes television news as "the opiate of American society."

Impact of Mass Media News

Not surprisingly, research indicates that voters learn very little from television news about the candidate's qualifications for office or their positions on the issues (Graber, 1976; Kline, 1976; Patterson and McClure, 1976; Swanson, 1977). Robinson and Davis (1990) report that despite people's perception that they gain most of their information about the nation and the world from television news, the fact is that it is responsible for limited learning about the stories covered, especially over time. The authors conclude that, ". . . whatever TV's impact, it may be mainly short-lived. As news events unfold and additional contextual information becomes available, TV news influence pales in comparison to that of other news media." Furthermore, content that is remembered tends to be visual, not verbal (Graber, 1990), which would be expected based on the television modality's visual orientation.

The print media are better suited to communicating specific information, and therefore newspaper news exerts more impact on learning. As we explained in Chapters 4 and 5, print messages necessitate active involvement in message processing, thereby increasing the role and impact of content in the process of influence (Chaiken and Eagly, 1976, 1983; Keating and Latane, 1976; Krugman, 1971; Salomon, 1979, 1981).

As a result, newspapers enhance learning. In the political context, for example, Patterson (1980) indicates that newspaper reading is associated with greater knowledge of the candidates' qualification for office, knowledge of candidates' positions on the issues, and involvement in political activities. Clark and Fredin (1978) indicate that people learn more about candidates and their positions from newspaper reading, and that as a result, they are more likely to be able to provide reasons as to why they support one candidate over another.

Newspapers provide more substantive content and newspaper readers are more knowledgeable about political matters. This is not to suggest direct causality. What happens is that people who are more active and knowledgeable about politics are inclined to greater mass media use, including newspapers. In her study of the 1984 and 1988 presidential elections, Owen (1991) reported that people's interest in politics determined their exposure to newspapers, which in turn, was associated with their knowledge about the political campaigns.

Mass media news also generates impact by setting the agenda for the campaign. Walter Lippmann (1922) provided the rationale for agenda setting in reasoning that, unlike personal, family, and perhaps economic concerns, which people can verify on the basis of their own observations, the political world consists largely of "pseudoevents," determined on the basis of mass media reports. Politics involves the "unseen environment," in which people are at the mercy of mediated information.

The power of mass media news thus stems from its capacity to call peoples' attention to some things and not to others. As Cohen (1963, p. 13) put it: "The press may not be successful much of the time in telling people what to think but it is stunningly successful in telling its readers what to think *about*." This obviously applies to political campaigns, which is the context for research concerning agenda setting to date. However, it also applies to social action campaigns, as detailed in Chapter 14, and sometimes even to commercial campaigns, as illustrated in Chapter 12.

As we noted above, research on agenda setting has focused exclusively on the political context. Interest in agenda setting paralleled the decline of party identification, and the rise of candidate character and issues, in determining voting decisions. As candidate character and issues exerted increasing influence on voting, there was a resurgence in interest in mass media news as a potential contributor to people's perceptions about both.

Agenda setting suggests that mass media news might affect people's political cognitions in several ways. Initial research on agenda setting suggested that mass media news, particularly newspapers, influenced people's prioritization of issues during political campaigns (McCombs and Shaw, 1972; McLeod, 1965; Shaw and McCombs, 1977). This is a combined function of the importance and valancing of issues, and was reported to be particularly strong at the outset of a political campaign (Weaver, Grabber, McCombs, and Eyal, 1981). The media's capacity to set the issue agenda was found to be the most powerful among people who are less informed to begin with (Iyengar, Peters, and Kinder, 1982).

Subsequent research indicated that mass media news also can shape people's perceptions of candidate image (Brady and Johnston, 1987; Shaw and McCombs, 1977; Weaver, Grabber, McCombs, and Eyal, 1981) and of the campaign (Adams, 1987; Mayer, 1987). Mass media news determines the relative importance of criteria used in candidate evaluation (e.g., leadership, experience, integrity, etc.), and indicates what traits are ascribed to individual candidates.

Also, mass media news coverage determines which candidates, social issues, and to a lesser degree, which commercial products that the public perceives as viable. We observed at the outset of this section that news coverage affords credibility. In this sense, news coverage is a prerequisite to candidate legitimacy. The main reason that the early political contests in Iowa and New Hampshire are important, beyond the convention delegates earned, is that they dictate media news coverage: both its quantity and tone. Mayer (1987, p. 13) explains:

> *The most basic reason why New Hampshire is so important is because of its immense publicity value. The New Hampshire campaign itself is the focus of a large number of stories, and its results then play a major role in shaping newspaper and television coverage decisions during the rest of the primary season.*

Mayer (pp. 23–25) concludes that, "For the majority of recent candidates, New Hampshire and Iowa were no longer the first inning; they were the entire ballgame."

Agenda setting research has been subject to some criticism. First, the direction of causality remains unclear. Do mass media prioritizations determine people's agenda, or the reverse? This question has not been satisfactorily resolved (Severin and Tankard, 1979). Even proponents of the model have their doubts. Weaver, Graber, McCombs, and Eyal (1981, p. 84), while confirming a clear agenda setting impact for "unobtrusive issues," nonetheless caution that:

> . . . it is not possible to speculate further on whether the candidates were important agenda-setters of issues for the media or vice-versa, whether the process was reciprocal or whether some other sources . . . were setting the agenda for both candidates and the news media.

Second variability undermines existing findings. While some variability is inherent since the political context differs from study to study (Becker, 1982), much of it stems from imprecise operationalization of crucial terms across studies. Third, more recent research suggests that the media agenda interacts with a number of additional variables (e.g., interpersonal communication about politics, group pressures, need for information, stage of the campaign, etc.) to influence receiver political cognitions (Kaid and Sanders, 1985; O'Keefe and Atwood, 1981; Parrott and Ross, 1991).

Public Service Announcements (PSAs)

Public service announcements (PSAs) are messages that are intended to promote awareness, disseminate information, and/or influence attitudes/behaviors concerning public issues. The messages are prepared for delivery by radio or television at no cost to the sponsor. PSAs are a primary communication vehicle for social action campaigns, which lack the perceived importance to command regular access to mass audiences through media news coverage and the resources to purchase media space/time.

Although PSAs are produced by various sources, the most active source is the Advertising Council, which is a nonprofit organization that operates in cooperation with large advertising agencies, the mass media, and private firms. The Advertising Council alone was responsible for more than $1 billion worth of equivalent space/time placements in 1989, a 25 percent increase from 1983, accounting for nearly a third of all national public service advertising (Pomice, 1990).

Social action PSA media campaigns are designed primarily to generate awareness of an issue, and to a lesser extent, to affect attitudes. And, many of the campaigns that have been sponsored by the Advertising Council are familiar to most Americans. The messages usually feature "hard-hitting" fear appeals, and assume active receiver processing (Wallach, 1988).

The Advertising Council's campaign for the prevention of forest fires, featuring Smokey Bear, initiated in 1942, is "one of the most famous of all campaigns" (McNamara, Kurth, and Hansen, 1989, p. 215). Most people are familiar with this campaign's slogan, "Remember, only you can prevent forest fires," which was created by the advertising agency Foote, Cone, and Belding in 1947 (McNamara et al., 1989, p. 216). Yet, despite more than $17 billion in space/time placements over the past 30 years, and a 98 percent awareness rate, there is no hard evidence indicating that the campaign actually altered people's behaviors (McNamara, 1989). Indeed, Alcalay and Taplin (1989, p. 120) argue that, "PSAs alone are not likely to cause behavior changes," especially involving ingrained life-style issues. This position is echoed by, Steve Rabin, an Ogilvy and Mather executive, involved in the Centers for Disease Control's paid advertising on AIDS, who argues that: "We can create awareness. We can draw attention to the problem, and we can begin to raise the issues. But, if I had all the spots on the Super Bowl, it wouldn't change people's behavior" (cited in Meyers, 1988, p. 148).

Partnership for A Drug-Free America, a New York City group, directs the largest current PSA campaign. The campaign features more than 200 messages, the most familiar of which is the, "This is your brain on drugs" advertisement, depicted in Figure 9–2, a message that has appeared repeatedly in magazines and on network television. The Partnership is relying on $745,000 in space/time placements per day to get the antidrug message across. Although it is too early to tell, preliminary evidence indicates that the campaign has generated awareness and changed attitudes. Social researcher Gordon Black (cited in "Users are Losers," 1988, p. 10) posits that, "People are more likely than ever to see drug users as losers," and "In areas with high exposure to the media campaign, attitude changes were the most pronounced." Black's assessment is not shared by all. Other research indicates that, while the campaign has

FIGURE 9–2 "This Is Your Brain on Drugs" Campaign Message

Source: Courtesy of the Keye/Donna/Pearlstein agency and The Media Partnership for a Drug-Free America.

enhanced awareness among teenagers of the dangers of drugs, the powerful fear appeals may overpower many, causing receivers to tune them out (cited in Pomice, 1990).

The fact that PSAs are free is also their chief weakness. The competition for public service time is vigorous. While it is possible to overcome this obstacle by having the campaign adopted by the Advertising Council, they work with a very limited number of causes, and the competition for their endorsement is extremely intense. Also, campaigners have no control over the placement of their messages. "Most PSAs air whenever TV stations have unsold time—often late at night" (Pomice, 1990). Two studies of PSA placement report that most messages air before 9 A.M. and after 11 P.M., and that only about one in ten appear in prime time (Freimuth and Van Nevel, 1981; Hanneman, McEwen, and Coyne, 1973).

Campaigners who must rely heavily on PSAs to communicate their message have no ability to target them, since they can not control when they will air. The best the campaigner can do is to try to convince media gatekeepers (e.g., television station community affairs directors) to air the messages during optimal times (Alcalay and Taplin, 1989).

Conclusion

This chapter focused on free communication modalities that are available to campaigners, such as traditional speech making (including joint appearances/debates), interpersonal, mass media news, and public service announcements. However, we also noted that the most desirable of these options, which provide maximum possible exposure, are limited to more visible campaigns.

We stressed at the outset of the chapter that the focus of most free campaign communication, except for the interpersonal modality, is the televised audience. The campaigner's task is to communicate basic themes to a televised audience using a mix of capsulized verbal messages and illustrative visuals. This is difficult because campaigners have limited control over most of the free communication modalities.

The chapter also examined each of the free communication modalities, describing their nature and impact in contemporary campaigns. Traditional speech-making plays an important, albeit changed role, in modern campaigns. Speakers still take to the stump (the set speech remains an integral feature of political campaigns), but the focus is on the televised audience. Indeed, television has changed speech-making dramatically, placing the emphasis on short excerpts, called sound bites, which are most useful to journalists, and producing a new eloquence, which is more casual and intimate, and stresses relational over content messages.

Interpersonal communication is an important modality for all campaigners. Person-to-person communication, whether in the form of direct contact or targeted direct mail and telephone appeals, is an integral component of effective influence and fund raising efforts.

Mass media news coverage is a prerequisite to credibility in campaigns. Media news is television news, perceived as the most believable by the public. However, the idiosyncrasies of the television medium have exerted a significant impact on the nature of television news. Time constraints, television's visual bias, and its tendency toward the melodramatic affect the nature of news reporting. Effective campaigners have learned to capitalize on the unique characteristics of contemporary television news.

Finally, public service announcements are an important tool for social campaigners. PSAs are useful to provide exposure and impart information, but are less effective in the effort to alter attitudes and behaviors.

Suggestions for Further Reading

Atkinson M. (1984). *Our Masters' Voices: The Language and Body Language of Politics.* London: Methuen.

Combs, J. E. (1980). *Dimensions of Political Drama.* Santa Monica, CA: Goodyear Publishing Company, Inc.

Gold, E. R. (1988). Ronald Reagan and the oral tradition. *Central States Speech Journal* 39, 159–176.

Hellweg S. A., Pfau, M., and Brydon, S. R. (1992). *Televised Presidential Debates: Advocacy in Contemporary America.* New York: Praeger.

Jamieson, K. H. (1988). *Eloquence in an Electronic Age: The Transformation of Political Speech Making.* New York: Oxford University Press.

Kaid, L. L. (1977). The neglected candidate: Interpersonal communication in political campaigns. *Western Journal of Speech Communication, 41,* 245–252.

Keating, J. P., and Latane, B. (1976). Politicians on TV: The image is the message. *Journal of Social Issues, 32,* 116–132.

Chapter 10

Paid Communication Modality

Advertising exists to inform—but even more so to persuade. It sells goods and services by turning them into images and dreams.
ERIC CLARK, JOURNALIST
(CLARK, 1988, P. 15)

[The year] 1986 was the year of triumph for commercial principles in political advertising. The lessons were those of the winning Reagan campaign: acceptance of affect- and entertainment-laden messages, a focus on myth, the dovetailing of character and issue messages, and the careful integration of news and advertising efforts. Most important, perhaps, was an understanding of the importance of early candidate imagery. . . . [The] early image-making efforts are important on all levels . . . (congressional, senatorial, and presidential. . . . The early battle is therefore on to define not only one's own but one's opponent's imagery.
MONTAGUE KERN, POLITICAL SCIENTIST
(KERN, 1989, PP. 113 AND 210)

The reason that nastiness [in political spots] is on the rise is that nastiness works.
MARY MCGRORY, JOURNALIST
(MCGRORY, 1990, P. 10A)

Whereas Chapter 9 dealt with free communication modalities, this chapter examines advertising, a paid communication modality. While advertising is a potential option for all campaigners, its cost may prove to be prohibitive for many. The price of a 30 second spot on network television exceeds $300,000 for the more popular shows (Patti and Frazer, 1988, p. 390), and this nation's leading commercial advertisers, like Philip Morris and Proctor and Gamble, spend more than $2 billion per year to reach consumers ("100 Leading National Advertisers," 1992).

As a result of the cost, most social action campaigns have no choice but to fall back on free public service announcements to reach a mass audience. With few exceptions, this limits the advertising option to the most visible commercial and political campaigns. Commercial campaigns have to rely almost exclusively on paid communication since they lack the requisite legitimacy to command mass media coverage of speeches, debates, or other activities.

Political campaigns for candidates seeking major office have access to all communication options, but increasingly in the more visible races, candidate advertising drives speeches, debates, and news. Kern (1989) posits that the emergence of advertising as the most central communication modality in political campaigns during the past decade is a watershed event. Kern (1989) notes that, compared to television news coverage, advertising dominates political airtime by a four to one margin in presidential races and six to one in Senate campaigns. Furthermore, televised political spots are the most effective communication tool for reaching uninterested receivers, thereby enhancing their importance (Devlin, 1984). Thus, Kern distinguishes "the mass media election," a title that Patterson (1980) coined to characterize the role of the mass media, especially television news, in presidential campaigns of the 1960s and 1970s, and "the *new* mass media election," in which candidate advertising plays the dominant role (Kern, 1991, p. 5).

This chapter will examine the use of advertising in modern commercial and political campaigns. The chapter will integrate passive message approaches, which are common in most televised commercial campaigns, and active approaches, which are prevalent in political campaigns, thus illustrating many of the theories that were discussed in Chapters 4 and 5. The chapter examines four broad macro advertising strategies, answering the questions posed in Table 10–1.

Name Identification

Name identification is an important initial objective for a commercial or political campaign. Here the objective comes down to simple awareness of the brand or candi-

TABLE 10–1 Questions about Paid Advertising

1. How does the name recognition strategy work in commercial or political campaigns?
2. Distinguish the bolstering, attack, and refutation political advertising approaches.
3. What is the impact of political spot advertising on receiver attitudes and voting intentions?
4. Why is the story format so effective in commercial television advertising?
5. Provide examples of commercial advertising campaigns based on single and multiple themes. What disadvantages are associated with a multiple theme approach?
6. What strategies are employed to communicate brand image using affect?
7. How does television facilitate the influence of celebrities in commercial campaigns designed to communicate affect?
8. Explain why negative political spots work when people seem to dislike them so much.
9. Identify the factors that determine the relative influence of comparatives in commercial advertising.
10. What limitations are associated with the refutation response to political attack spots?
11. How does inoculation promote resistance to the influence of commercial or political attack spots?

date. In the commercial realm, Norris (1990, p. 53) characterizes the name of the brand as "a handle," "something for you to take hold of." "In every case . . . [it] is a device put there to start a chain reaction in your mind."

Generating awareness of a brand or candidate can prove to be difficult, particularly on behalf of an unknown commercial brand. Bogart (1990, p. 44) stresses that:

> . . . *[A] new brand faces a real problem in making the consumer aware of its existence . . . A new product must, by advertising, fight its way into the public's awareness and into a sector of the established market. It must work quickly to get past the initial months of heavy investment and learn to stand on its own feet within the designated payout period.*

This requires considerable advertising outlays. James Peckman's research indicates that during the first two years following the introduction of new brands of food, household goods, toiletries, and proprietary drugs, the most successful new brands "spent at a rate that gave them an advertising share of 60 to 70 percent greater than the market share they achieved at the end of this period," and that this spending was "consistently maintained" over this period (cited in Bogart, 1990, p. 45). Moreover, these spending levels are essential for new brands.

The bottom line is that new brands "have no way to go but up or out," and most entry attempts fail (Bogart, 1990, pp. 43–44). This explains why such a high proportion of the most successful new brand entries into established markets are accomplished by already established companies, such as Proctor and Gamble in such areas as food and household products, Campbells' in soups, and Kelloggs' in breakfast foods. These firms have the advantage of name recognition, which provides automatic credibility for the newly introduced brand, and the financial resources to provide sufficient advertising support.

Generating awareness is also difficult for many political candidates. Challengers who take on incumbents without having first achieved comparable visibility levels face a significant disadvantage. Less known challengers require large financial resources, even more than their more known opponents, in order to support extensive advertising to establish name recognition. Unfortunately, candidate visibility is also a precondition for fund-raising, thus making it difficult for challengers to mount effective campaigns. House incumbents, for example, are able to discourage opponents and their potential contributors. As a result, ". . . uncompetitiveness feeds on itself" (Jacobson, 1989, p. 133).

This is evident in the proportion of incumbents returned to office. In elections to the House of Representatives, in which challengers usually have less visibility and resources than their incumbent opponents, challengers seldom win. Usually, more than 90 percent of incumbents win reelection (Shannon, 1991), and this tendency, if anything, has increased during the 1980s (Jacobson, 1989). As a result, in the 1990 election, 96 percent of House incumbents won (Shannon, 1991). On the other hand, Senate races are usually more competitive, precisely because challengers, who are drawn from the ranks of sitting governors or popular House incumbents, possess the requisite visibility. During the 1988 elections, 63 percent of Senate challengers had previously held statewide office (Jacobson, 1989). "Senate contests are more often competitive than House elections because Senate challengers are more often experienced, high-quality candidates who are able to raise adequate funds. . . . [Thus] the same dynamic that inhibits competition in House elections encourages it in Senate elections" (Jacobson, 1989, p. 136).

Over the course of a campaign, advertising plays a crucial role in enhancing awareness of candidates. Political consultants indicate that name identification is one of the most important functions of political commercials, especially for challengers (Berkowitz, 1985). One study concludes that, public recognition of more "serious and active" candidates increases steadily over the course of a campaign, particularly for challengers. In one campaign, name recognition of a challenger rose 55 percent over a six month period (Mann, 1984). It is no wonder that political campaigners spend an increasing proportion of their budgets for television advertising. At all levels, between 1976 to 1986 the total spending for political advertising on network and local television more than quadrupled (Broadcast Advertising Reports, 1985). In the 1988 Bush and Dukakis presidential contest, each of the candidates spent approximately two-thirds of their total budgets, nearly $35 million each, on television advertising (Devlin, 1989). It is clear that political practitioners are relying increasingly on television advertising to carry their message to voters.

As we indicated in Chapter 5, early television operated on the basis of an active model of influence, communicating simple messages designed to elicit awareness. Rosser Reeves, an early pioneer of television advertising, believed that the "hard sell" approach was the most effective to communicate awareness. In the years following World War II, Reeves directed a number of highly successful television campaigns for products, including Anacin ("What do doctors recommend for pain?") and M & M's, and first introduced television advertising to national politics during the 1952 Eisenhower presidential campaign (Moyers, 1984).

The Eisenhower 10–second "I like Ike" and 30-second "Man from Abilene" spots were designed to introduce the candidate to potential voters, whereas the "Eisenhower answers America" ads were intended to spell out the candidate's position on three central issues: political corruption, inflation, and the war in Korea. Reeves wrote multiple scripts, "making the same points over and over in different words" (Fox, 1984, p. 309). In all, Eisenhower spent about $3 million on his television advertising (Devlin, 1986). "It hadn't been done before. And the spots had tremendous impact" (Axelrod, 1988). Then, just as now, name identification, plus image projection, were the primary goals of television advertising (Berkowitz, 1985).

Reeves believed that television advertising needed to take simple points and repeat them over and over. "You have to be terribly simplistic," he admonished (Moyers, 1984). He offered three maxims: first, reduce the product or candidate to their bare essentials (their name and perhaps a single attribute); second, package those essentials in memorable fashion; and third, repeat the message again and again (Moyers, 1984). This approach produced such memorable lines as: "M & M's, melts in your mouth, not in your hand." And, "You like Ike; I like Ike; everybody likes Ike." Subsequently, learning theory was used to explain strategies designed to promote receiver awareness.

FIGURE 10–1   Oscar Meyer's "The Fisherman," Television Spot

Source: Courtesy of the Oscar Meyer Foods Corporation.

While name identification strategy is employed to generate awareness of new brands in commercial campaigns and challengers in political campaigns, it also is used to maintain awareness of established brands in commercial campaigns. As we indicated in Chapter 5, most television advertising on behalf of package goods uses message repetition to evoke awareness, which in many cases is sufficient to trigger purchase (Pechmann and Stewart, 1989). The underlying assumption is that people are inclined to purchase those brands that are familiar to them (Sawyer, 1977), and that product use in time shapes attitude. Thus, advertisers initially plant, and then attempt to maintain, brand awareness. Maintaining brand awareness is accomplished via the repetition of the message over time (Batra and Ray, 1983; Krugman, 1965; Ray and Webb, 1976;

Schultz, 1990; Sissors and Surmanek, 1982). The evoked set and classical and instrumental conditioning models were used to explain this passive process of influence.

To generate a base of awareness for new brands, campaigners employ a combination of catchy print messages, high-visibility outdoor or transit advertising, and extensive television spots (Bogart, 1990). However, to maintain awareness, they rely more heavily on television, using short 15- to 30-second spots which stress brand name, and are repeated to attain frequency. This approach grows out of research indicating that television is a superior communication modality in generating awareness, mainly because it employs audio in conjunction with the more powerful video component (Grass and Wallace, 1974: McKelvie and Demers, 1979; Pavio, 1971, 1978).

Some of these messages are simultaneously ingenious in their creativity and classic in their simplicity in communicating brand name. Oscar Meyer, for example, has employed various spots that feature children singing about Oscar Meyer bologna. The spots, like "The Fishermen" advertisement depicted in Figure 10-1, one of the most successful of this genre (Vadehra, 1982), are cute, and yet they focus attention on the brand name. "The kids and the jingle are integral parts of these commercials . . . Oscar Meyer kids are adorable, innocent, natural, and eye-catching. Singing about the product, they appear honest and convincing" (Vadehra, 1982, p. M-42).

Other commercials feature vignettes in which the name is misspelled, as is true of the long-standing Wausau Insurance campaign, or mispronounced, as in the Poulin Chain Saw campaign, to generate attention to their brand name. Still others involve the simple repetition of the brand name within the advertisement, as is the case with the Doublemint Gum campaign, which employs a number of messages, each containing humor and music, woven around as many as 20 to 25 repetitions of the word "double." The simple repetition of words in an advertisement makes it more unique and memorable.

One of the most successful campaigns in maintaining brand name awareness is Rolaids. These spots, like the one shown in Figure 10-2, all pose the rhetorical question, How do you spell relief? The answer, "R-O-L-A-I-D-S," is spelled out in the ad, almost methodically, sometimes by a teacher printing the word on a blackboard, or perhaps by a carpenter tracing it amidst sawdust on a workbench. The teacher, carpenter, or other person repeats each letter as they print it, providing both verbal and visual communication of the brand name. In addition, this process is done slowly, thus causing receivers to complete the spelling in their own minds, motivated by a desire for more rapid completion of the vignette. Active receiver participation in the message contributes to the internalization of the message content.

The Rolaids' campaign communicates a simple, but effective, message, linking the brand name and its claimed benefit. Thus, when people think relief, they think Rolaids, and when they see Rolaids on a store shelf, they think relief. A popular anecdote illustrates this linkage. A number of years ago, an elementary school teacher reported that, during the routine administration of a spelling test, some of the children actually spelled relief, R-O-L-A-I-D-S.

FIGURE 10–2   Rolaids' Campaign Made their Brand Name Synonymous with "Relief"

Source: Courtesy of Warner-Lambert Company 1991

Promoting an Image

Another general strategy in advertising is to promote an image of the brand or candidate. This can be done through the use of campaign themes, which communicate one or more specific attributes, through the use of affect, which establishes a mood or general feeling that embodies the brand, and/or through the use of spokespersons for the brand, candidate, or idea.

Use of Themes

A campaign theme embodies the image of a campaign. It is somewhat open-ended, thus enhancing flexibility. By contrast, a slogan, is much more specific. Quera (1977, p. 80) distinguishes theme and slogan, as follows: "Campaign themes may say the same thing in different ways; a slogan always says the same thing in exactly the same way." A campaign theme may be cognitive, thus stressing a specific product attribute, candidate quality or position, or social action goal. Or, a theme may be affective, particularly in commercial campaigns, involving the way that people feel about a brand.

Political campaigns rely on themes, and various slogans, to convey reasons why voters should support a particular candidate. Indeed, experts label most political advertisements as "slogan ads," because they contain a claim, often embodied in a slogan, without a subsequent rationale. Kern's 1984 sample of political spots contained an overwhelming proportion of slogan ads: about 83 percent of presidential and 77 percent of Senate campaign ads (Kern, 1989, p. 52).

Most political commercials are designed to convey relatively simple messages about the candidate endorsed in the spot or about the opponent. The former are called bolstering messages; and the latter attack messages (Pfau and Kenski, 1990). In addition, there are response or rebuttal messages, in which a candidate responds to an attack initiated by an opponent (Salmore and Salmore, 1985), and there are inoculation messages, which attempt to preempt the lines of potential attacks by an opponent (Pfau and Kenski, 1990). The positive bolstering message remains the most common political spot. Kaid and Davidson (1986) found that their sample of 1982 Senate campaign spots contained 73 percent "candidate-positive" messages and 27 percent "opponent-negative" ones. However, use of the negative attack commercial has increased sharply during the 1980s (Kern, 1989; Pfau and Kenski, 1990). This approach will be discussed in more detail later in this chapter.

The primary vehicle employed by candidates to promote image is positive bolstering messages, which contain claims about the candidate's character, qualifications for office, or positions on the issues. Bolstering messages are more often the primary focus of candidate advertising during the initial stages of a campaign, each spot containing a single kernel of information, or a slogan, which together, comprise the broader campaign theme. The theme resides principally in the audio track of the television message (Shyles, 1986).

Contemporary political television advertisements are usually packaged as 30-second messages, thus restricting the quantity of information they can contain. Nonetheless, an impressive array of studies suggest that political spots contribute to increased knowledge about the candidates and their positions. This means, of course, that they do contain valuable information. Patterson and McClure's extensive study of the 1972 presidential campaign found that 42 percent of all televised political advertisements were "primarily issue oriented"; another 28 percent "contained substantial issue information" (1976). Jamieson (1984, pp. 446–447) concluded that campaign advertising has served issue and image formation. She argued that political advertising has (1) contributed to an increase in the role and importance of issues in presidential campaigns, and (2) provided a sharper definition of the public's image of the presidency.

Furthermore, issue and image information carried via spots reaches the receiver. Patterson and McClure (1976, pp. 116–117) reported that, ". . . people who were heavily exposed to political spots became more informed about the candidates' positions . . . on a typical issue, individuals who happened to see many commercials were nearly half again as likely to become more knowledgeable as people who saw few, if any, televised spots." Another study of the 1970 gubernatorial campaigns in Colorado and Wisconsin found that 64 percent of the voters who viewed the advertisements felt they "learned something about each candidate's qualifications for governor, and 56 percent gained a greater understanding about their position on major issues" (Atkin, Bowen, Nayman, and Sheinkopf, 1972, p. 10). Still another study compared viewer learning from candidate advertising as opposed to debates, concluding that advertising is superior in informing viewers about candidate positions (Just et al., 1990).

Research also suggests that political spots contribute to candidate choice. Although Patterson and McClure (1976) found that televised advertising exercised only a modest influence on voter choice during the 1972 presidential election, Republican pollster Robert Teeter indicated that the 1980 institutional televised advertisements sponsored by the Republican National Committee and the National Republican Congressional Committee exerted tremendous influence on voter choice. These messages urged Americans to: "Vote Republican. For A Change." Teeter (reported in Cannon, 1981) found that when voters were asked to justify their intention of voting for Republican congressional candidates, 22 percent identified the theme of the advertising campaign, "We need a change" or "Time for a change." Further, the Bush commercials in the 1988 presidential campaign, which will be discussed in more detail later in this chapter, exerted enormous impact on voter choice (Devlin, 1989; Hershey, 1989).

Other research supports the position that political spots affect voter preferences. Joslyn (1981) reported a "positive relationship" involving television spots and voting defections (tendency to vote contrary to traditional party identification) in a study of congressional and senatorial contests during 1970, 1972, and 1974. This influence is even more pronounced at the state level. Atkin, Bowen, Nayman and Sheinkopf (1972, p. 16) found: "The evidence shows that TV spots may be a contributing factor in the decision-making process of those voters who make up their minds during the campaign period. More than half of the group said that political ads for both the chosen and the unchosen candidates were helpful in arriving at their decision."

Commercial campaigns also utilize themes to communicate one or more attributes about a brand. Usually a variety of specific messages are used, each focusing on the attribute. Charmin, for example, has employed a long-standing campaign that features the character Mr. Whipple, a fictitious grocery store employee whose self-proclaimed mission is to guard the Charmin from shoppers who can not resist squeezing it (see Figure 10–3). Over the years, the campaign has used a myriad of vignettes, each designed to communicate the softness of the toilet tissue. Although the Charmin spots do not register high marks in terms of AAd (e.g., most viewers claim they do not like the commercials), the Charmin campaign has been remarkable in its effectiveness in etching the brand name and this single attribute in the minds of receivers. In a series of informal surveys conducted over a number of years with college students, one of the authors confirmed the effectiveness of Charmin's ads. More than 80 percent of respondents typically identify Charmin, when asked to name the softest toilet tissue. In

FIGURE 10–3 Charmin's Campaign Stresses the Product Attribute of "Softness"

Source: Courtesy of D'Arcy, Masius, Benton & Bowles and Proctor & Gamble.

addition, if presented with a list of 25 common product brands, and told to comment on the brand, almost all use some form of the word "soft" in association with Charmin.

Miller Lite's commercials, which pioneered the use of sports celebrities as real people in humorous vignettes, stress reduced calories and taste. The various messages communicate a unified theme, that Miller Lite is "a regular beer but better because it's less filling" (Vadehra, 1982). The humor of these advertisements contributed to their success, making Miller Lite's commercials the most liked and best remembered of the early and middle 1980s (Abrams, 1982; Alsop, 1986), propelling Miller Lite into second place in total beer sales in the United States, behind only Budweiser (Teinowitz, 1988).

Both the Charmin and Miller advertisements utilize a story format to communicate their thematic message. The story offers the receiver a context to use in processing the information that is contained in the message, and research indicates that context facilitates memory (Jenkins, 1974). Not surprisingly then, the story format has been found to provide superior recall (cited in Alesandrini, 1983). Research also indicates that the story format is particularly well-suited to television because "a story can be developed very quickly via pictorial communication" (Alesandrini, 1983).

FIGURE 10–4 Pontiac Stresses "Excitement" in Their Commercial Advertising

Source: Courtesy of Pontiac Division, General Motors Corporation, Pontiac, MI.

Other campaigns that have employed themes that communicate single attributes include State Farm and Pontiac. State Farm has stressed dependability in their advertising campaigns dating back to the 1960s. This theme is embodied in commercial messages that feature the company's agents, background music, and conclude with the jingle, "Like a good neighbor, State Farm is there." Pontiac has emphasized the excitement of owning and driving their line of cars with the theme: "Pontiac. We build excitement." The Pontiac campaign, now more than a decade old, is thought to be effective because it communicates a clear, consistent image about this line of cars. "The advertising works not only because it has given a consistent image to consumers but because . . . it reflects a company that knows where it is headed" (Serafin and Horton, 1988, p. 66). The "We build excitement" campaign, illustrated in Figure 10–4, has helped move Pontiac into third place in automobile nameplate sales in the United States.

Other times, themes are multiple, perhaps best illustrated in McDonald's advertising. McDonald's advertising is designed to foster an image of McDonald's restaurants as enjoyable places to visit, and to promote specific products, specials, and events as

FIGURE 10–5 McDonald's "McLean Deluxe" Commercial Promotes a New Menu Item

Source: Courtesy of McDonald's Corporation.

part of the firm's aggressive marketing approach. To accomplish the first objective, the company uses general commercials which are targeted to specific age cohorts. The slogan, "You deserve a break today," and later, "It's a good time for the great taste at McDonald's," embody a "celebrate life" theme, uniting diverse messages, some directed toward children, others toward families, teenagers, and seniors. The messages are often poignant, as was the case with their spots targeting seniors, projecting an image of McDonald's as "caring" (Vadehra, 1982).

To achieve the second objective, McDonald's uses a variety of commercials to promote specific products, such as their "Mac Tonight" or "Big Mac attack" messages on behalf of their Big Mac sandwich, two of the most best remembered commercials of 1988 (Hume, 1988a), their McDLT spot, or their McLean advertisement, shown in Figure 10–5. McDonald's employs multiple themes to maintain the initiative in its marketing, thus keeping its competitors on the defensive. This approach, however, is not appropriate for most commercial campaigners. First, campaigns may not require multiple themes. Second, those that do may not be able to afford it. Comparisons of cost efficiency, measured in terms of cost-per-thousand impressions, consistently indicate that McDonald's pays a high price for its multiple campaigns. The 1985 data are typical. They indicate that McDonald's spent $84.86 per thousand impressions, compared to $9.72 for Pepsi-Cola, making McDonald's the least efficient among the 25 most liked television campaigns of the year (Alsop, 1986).

Use of Affect

In addition to the use of themes, campaigners rely on affect to communicate the image of a product or candidate. As indicated in Chapter 5, affect may contribute to attitude formation and/or change, or it may bypass attitude and exert a direct influence on action. Commercial campaigners, in particular, are increasingly disposed to use favorable mood or image as the primary strategy to market products, based on the assumption that emotion, and not brand features, drives most consumer decisions (Calder and Gruner, 1989). Learning theory and motivational theories were examined in Chapter 5 to explain the role of affect in campaign influence.

One of the approaches introduced in Chapter 5 involved the use of affect to create the image of a brand: coordinating the images, music, and message to elicit the image of a brand, and linking that image with the kind of person the viewer is (or, more commonly, wants to be). This strategy is sometimes called "resonance," in that it attempts to evoke audience feelings. The message does not attempt to convey specific brand information. "Rather, it tries to present patterns of experience that match those of the audience" (Patti and Frazer, 1988, p. 301), thereby eliciting an image of the brand, grounded in affect.

Approaches based on affect have gained popularity in recent years, in part because of the absence of clear differences among competing brands in most product classes, particularly involving package goods, which rely more heavily on television advertising (Levin, 1988), and because of the growing belief among today's advertising practitioners that feelings are more powerful than thinking in influence (Clark, 1988).

FIGURE 10–6 Michelob's "Weekend" Campaign Communicated Quality and Warmth

Source: Courtesy of Anheuser-Busch, Inc.

Campaigners can employ any number of approaches to create and maintain the image of a brand. The approaches are based on vignettes that embody experiences. Regardless of the approach, however, the campaigner communicates experiences, "and it is the experience which is purchased . . . " (Larson, 1982, p. 540).

Product commercials may seek to create an image based on the quality of the brand, as the campaign for E. & J. Gallo wines described in Chapter 5, or the "Weekend" or "Night" campaigns for Michelob beer. The "Weekend" campaign, depicted in Figure 10-6, was designed to project the special quality of Michelob, a beer for special moments involving family or friends. The music and the imagery add to the perception of quality, while the setting, involving people enjoying each other's company, suggests warmth. The "Night" campaign was conceived in much the same way, except that it targeted a more youthful audience. The imagery of this campaign was intended to elicit a sense of excitement, as opposed to the warmth of the "Weekend" campaign, a feeling reinforced by the music of such contemporary artists as Christopher Cross and Steve Winwood, thus enhancing "Night's" more youthful appeal.

Product spots also may seek to promote an image of a brand based on warmth, as with the Michelob "Weekend" campaign above, or the Lowenbrau and Maxwell House campaigns described in Chapter 5. This approach, which has been identified as one of the most common strategies in contemporary television advertising (NBC News, 1990), is based on the capability of the spot to transfer the feelings projected by the characters to viewers. Viewers vicariously share in the emotional experience of one or more of the characters in the commercial (Aaker and Stayman, 1989). Each of the examples above is based on the warmth inherent in shared experiences.

Another way for advertisers to elicit warmth is to exploit the nostalgic images of special occasions. Gallo's "the wedding" commercial, depicted in Figure 10-7, taps the idyllic imagery of weddings, using rich visuals and music by Vangelis to create the appropriate mood (Baldwin, 1989). For years, Budweiser has aired its "Holiday Greetings" spots during the Christmas season. The Budweiser commercials use a combination of nostalgic Christmas scenes and music to capture the idyllic imagery of the holiday season. Both ads elicit warmth, grounded not in the reality of these occasions, but in the way people *want* to feel about them. Studies suggest that commercials that employ warmth can be shown more frequently prior to "wear-out" (Aaker and Stayman, 1989), and that they exert significant impact on viewer purchase intentions (Aaker, Stayman, and Hagerty, 1986).

Commercials also promote the image of a brand, suggesting that the products are vehicles to enhance sex appeal or elicit esteem. These spots make the viewer feel that using the brand provides emotional benefits. "When consumers use products to fulfill emotional needs, products take on symbolic meanings, and the product usage experience itself takes on imaginary or fantasy dimensions" (Baldwin, 1989, p. 88). The commercial's imagery is designed to project the feeling that comes from brand use. This approach was discussed at some length in Chapter 5.

Political commercials also employ affect to elicit the image of a candidate. Kern's (1989) research indicates that "positive affect-laden appeals," grounded in emotions such as compassion, nostalgia, intimacy, hope, pride, and others, constituted 55.9

E. & J. GALLO WINERY "WEDDINGS"
:60 Commercial

Theme throughout.

ANNCR: To dreams, and hopes, and promises . . . And years of happy days.

Today's Gallo.

All the best a wine can be.

FIGURE 10–7   E. & J. Gallo Winery's "The Wedding" Spot Features Rich Visuals

Source: Courtesy of E. & J. Gallo Winery 1986. Printed with Permission.

percent, the largest single category, of political spots in her 1984 sample. She argues that the emotional school of political advertising, pioneered by Tony Schwartz, communicates "by means of sights and sounds," and is more effective than communication of "concepts, rationales, or indeed the presentation of 'real life' " (1991, p. 12). Schwartz, who devised the evoked set to explain advertising's influence, believed that spots influence by tapping into images already present in the receiver (cited in Pope, 1983). Larson (1984) maintains that political spots must trigger memory responses within viewers, producing an emotional response. Thus, political commercials exert influence, not by providing new information per se, but by evoking perceptions already in place. Those people who develop a preference for a particular candidate as a result of campaign advertising are responding to the images or experiences associated with that candidate (Larson, 1982).

Kern (1989) argues that one of the most important tasks for campaigners is to communicate a clear, consistent positive image of the candidate and negative image of the opponent, and to do it as early in the campaign as possible. She posits that, ". . . early image-making efforts [which involves defining the candidate and the opponent] are important on all levels" (1989, p. 210).

Television, as we have indicated, is ideally suited for the communication of emotion, and Kern (1991) maintains that by the mid-1980s political practitioners, having ". . . absorbed the view of the world of commercial advertising . . . ," came to adopt a more emotional approach to political advertising, using a combination of ". . . positive, relating to elegiac expression of emotional appeals associated with trust, hope, and the like, and negative, associated with . . . soft 'soft-sell' and 'hard-sell' . . . " messages (Kern, 1991, p. 13). These soft, emotional ads were particularly prevalent during the 1990 Senate and House campaigns. "What marks 1990 is a concoction of mostly warm and fuzzy positive images that stress politicians' experiences outside government and how they have fought the government monster. Candidates' families and neighbors star" (Raasch, 1990, p. 16A).

Testimonials

Another strategy employed to promote the image of a brand is based on testimonials on the part of spokespersons for the brand, candidate, or idea. The spokesperson might involve a fictional character, as in the case of Frank and Ed for Bartles and Jaymes, Mrs. Olson for Folgers, or Mr. Whipple for Charmin; a company president, as in the

---

FEEDBACK

Using a recent political campaign for President or U. S. Senate, carefully examine each candidate's television advertising and answer the following questions.

1. Can you see Rosser Reeves' approach to influence in any of the spots?
2. Can you see Tony Schwartz's approach to influence in any of the spots?
3. Which approach strikes you as more effective? Why?

case of Lee Iacocca for Chrysler (see Figure 10–8); another politician, as when one political officeholder (e.g., a popular president or senator) campaigns for another's election; or more commonly, a celebrity, as with Michael Jordan for Wheaties and Nike, Bill Cosby for Jell-O, and Michael J. Fox for Pepsi-Cola. The use of celebrities in advertising has become a very popular approach, accounting for approximately ten percent of all television advertising dollars. "In the mid-1980s, this amounted to well over $2 billion" (Patti and Frazer, 1988, p. 315).

One function of testimonial ads in commercial, political, and social action campaigns is to capture viewer attention. The advertiser seeks to utilize the recognition of

FIGURE 10–8   Lee Iacocca Makes a Reasoned Appeal for Chrysler Quality

Source: Courtesy of Chrysler Corporation, Detroit, MI.

the presenter to make the message stand out, and research indicates that use of celebrity spokespersons, in particular, is an effective tool for capturing receivers' attention in commercial and social action campaigns (Cain, 1986; Sherman, 1985). Kaid and Davidson (1986) report that incumbent Senate candidates are more likely to employ testimonials in their political commercials.

Another function, even more important in this era of image advertising, is to use spokespersons to establish an emotional bond with viewers. This is common in commercial campaigns, as was explained in some detail in Chapter 5. Campaigners seek to transfer viewer feelings about the celebrity to the brand. One of the reasons why celebrities generally are more effective than other spokespersons in more emotional image advertising is that ". . . a viewer knows the celebrity and already has an emotional response to him . . . " (NBC, 1990).

The ability to establish an emotional bond between receiver and celebrity is enhanced with the television modality because it is more intimate in its communication. In Chapter 9, we pointed out that television demands a warm, personal, casual style, more akin to interpersonal communication. This is because television stresses facial communication, the impact of which is magnified because the viewer can stare at the communicator's face at will (Altheide and Snow, 1979). In addition, people view television in the privacy of their own homes, which accents its more intimate nature (Beniger, 1987; Brummett, 1989; Keating and Latane, 1976). As a result, Horton and Wohl (1956) and Perse and Rubin (1989) maintain that television is responsible for the creation of a "parasocial relationship" between television personalities and viewers, a relationship grounded on an illusion of intimacy.

In this context, viewers *feel* that those celebrities they see on television are their friends, even though they have had no direct contact with them. Alperstein (1991, p. 44) refers to "an imaginary social relationship . . . [that connects] the viewer to a celebrity who appears in a television commercial." Since viewers feel that a relationship exists, celebrities are in a position to exercise considerable influence in television commercials, a position previously argued by Caughey (1984) and Schickel (1985).

The secret in using celebrities to establish an emotional bond with viewers lies in providing an optimal match involving the image of the celebrity and the image campaigners seek to establish for the brand. Grey Advertising executive, Casimir Wojciechowski (cited in Cain, 1986) affirms that, "The key lies in matching the celebrity to the product." Baldwin (1989, p. 105) adds that, "Celebrities can provide stopping power. But to be convincing they must fit the products they represent." More explanation of, and examples of, this approach were provided in Chapter 5.

Attack Approach

An increasingly important strategy in modern commercial and political campaigns is attack advertising. Attack advertising is a very aggressive approach in which the message focuses on some negative aspect of the competing brand or candidate. The attack strategy relies more heavily on active message processing, which emphasizes the verbal stream, although in television spots, the visual stream is designed to reinforce the verbal, thus employing both cognition as well as affect.

There are two types of attack messages. Negative messages focus entirely on the opposing candidate's weaknesses, reminding the receiver of the alternative at the very end (Pfau and Kenski, 1990). Comparative messages feature an explicit comparison of two or more brands or candidates, claiming superiority for the sponsored one (Barry and Tremblay, 1975; Salmore and Salmore, 1985). Both negative and comparative messages are employed in persuasive campaigns.

The use of attack messages in political campaigns dates to this nation's first campaigns. During the 1800 election, Thomas Jefferson was ridiculed as "an atheist, a free thinker, and an enemy of the Constitution," whereas John Adams was attacked as an "aristocrat" and "monarchist" (Jamieson, 1984, p. 5). Political attacks continued in every presidential campaign thereafter, but took on a new twist in the 1952 election, in which television was used for the first time to deliver attacks in a national election campaign (Axelrod, 1988). The early television political attack messages remained relatively mild (the exceptions being a strong Eisenhower spot in the 1952 election which placed responsibility for the Korean war on the doorstep of Democrats, and a powerful Kennedy ad in 1960 which used Eisenhower's response, "If you give me a week, I might think of one," to a reporter's question about what major decisions Vice-President Nixon had played an important role, to discredit Nixon's credibility) (Sabato, 1981) until the 1964 campaign.

The 1964 Johnson and Goldwater presidential campaign was the one that escalated the use of negative messages (Pfau and Kenski, 1990). The campaign perhaps is best remembered for the airing of Tony Schwartz's "Daisy Girl" spot, featuring a little girl in a field, picking daisies, as the countdown to a nuclear explosion unfolds. The spot ends with the explosion, captured in sound and in visual images as a reflection in the girl's eye, and with the voice of Lyndon Johnson talking about what is at stake in the 1964 election (Pfau and Kenski, 1990). The spot was so controversial it aired just once, but ushered in a new era of deeper, more potent negatives, designed not just to win over undecided or conflicted voters, but also those who are weakly committed to the opposing candidate. "The Johnson media campaign, more than any other, foreshadowed the development of contemporary political media" (Axelrod, 1988, p. 91).

Attack politics continued to play a role in the political campaigns that followed the 1964 election, and then exploded in number and intensity in the political advertising of candidates during the 1980s, turning conventional wisdom about the use of negatives on its head. Whereas once it was thought that the use of negatives was dangerous, and thus constrained by caveats (e.g., a viable option for challengers, but not incumbents; available only after establishing a solid, positive image, thus never for use at the outset of a campaign; to be delivered only by third parties, and not by the candidate), the thinking of successful contemporary practitioners is quite different.

[During the 1980s,] . . . [n]egative campaigning, compared to positive advertising, was used with greater frequency. It was used by incumbents as well as challengers. The old practice about building up your positives first before attacking was abandoned, and attacks occurred

at the start of a campaign . . . , and candidates themselves sometimes attacked or responded personally (Pfau and Kenski, 1990, p. 60).

The 1988 presidential campaign perhaps best demonstrated the efficacy of attack advertising in defining an opponent. Bush's campaign manager, Lee Atwater, and media advisor, Roger Ailes, both believed in attack politics. Furthermore, in May and June, following the contests for nomination but prior to the nominating conventions, Bush faced a difficult task. He trailed Dukakis by 16 to 17 points in the polls (Farah and Klein, 1989), and complicating matters, "although roughly an equal number of voters liked Bush as disliked him, a staggering five voters liked Dukakis for every one who didn't" (Taylor and Broder, 1988, p. 14).

The task of the campaign was apparent to Roger Ailes: "Every single thing I did from debates to rhetoric to media was designed to define the two of them and push them further apart" (cited in Devlin, 1989, p. 392). That meant defining Bush more positively, but even more critically, defining Dukakis negatively. The staff considered the latter task easier because public attitudes about Dukakis, while positive, were

FIGURE 10–9 1988 Bush "Revolving Door" Attack Commercial

Source: Courtesy of the Republican National Committee.

malleable. Dukakis was perceived by most people as a moderate, in large part because he had waged the last three months of the nomination campaign against the more liberal Jesse Jackson. The purpose of the Bush campaign "was to define Dukakis to the voters before he was able, or willing, to define himself. The definition would be that Dukakis was a liberal in the mold of Walter Mondale, Jimmy Carter, and George McGovern" (Hershey, 1989, p. 82).

During the late spring the Bush staff pretested a series of negative messages, including the "Revolving door" message (see Figure 10-9), which attacked Dukakis for furloughing prisoners, the "Pledge" spot, which criticized the Governor for not supporting mandatory Pledge of Allegiance legislation, the "Boston Harbor" ad, which cast doubt on Dukakis' commitment to a clean environment, and others. The focus group pretesting of these and other messages confirmed the persuasiveness of Bush's negative themes. After hearing the themes, the attitudes of the Dukakis supporters, all of whom fit the Reagan Democrat prototype (precisely the swing voter that Bush needed to win over in order to capture the presidency), began shifting away from Dukakis and toward Bush (Pfau and Kenski, 1990). All together, half of the 30 focus group members changed their vote preference from Dukakis to Bush after hearing the themes (Hershey, 1989). "The Bush staff felt they had struck gold" (Hershey, 1989, p. 81).

The attack spots exerted their anticipated effect during the campaign. Bush attacked early and often, allowing him "to define Dukakis to the voters before he was able, or willing, to define himself" (Hershey, 1989, p. 82). Further, Bush coordinated his campaign appearances, speeches, and the resulting news coverage, to the themes developed in his advertising, an approach that adds to the effectiveness of political commercials (Jamieson, 1989). As a result of his coordinated attack, Bush was able to drive Dukakis' negatives up sharply, turning a 17-point deficit after the Democratic nominating convention into a 14-point lead by late October. Public opinion polls that reported negative ratings of the candidates illustrated most clearly what was taking place. They confirmed that while Bush's negatives remained relatively constant during the period from July to early November, Dukakis' negatives more than doubled, increasing sharply from 21 to 44 percent (Devlin, 1989). Marjorie Hershey, focusing specifically on the Bush campaign's "Prison Furlough" attack (as well as the National Security Political Action Committee sponsored "Willie Horton" ad), concluded:

> *By late October, even Jesse Jackson's approval ratings were higher than Dukakis's. Even more significantly, the proportion of respondents saying George Bush was "tough enough" on crime and criminals rose from 23% in July to 61% in late October, while the proportion saying Dukakis was not tough enough rose from 36% to 49%. It would be hard to find more convincing proof of the efficacy of attack politics (1989, pp. 95–96).*

The growing sophistication in using television in political advertising led to the emergence of campaign consultants as an inherent fixture in campaigns for major office. In turn, both of these developments, coupled with a heavy dose of public cynicism about politicians (Axelrod, 1988), are responsible for the rapid growth of attack commercials (Johnson-Cartee and Copeland, 1991; Nyhan, 1988; Pfau and Kenski,

1990; Taylor, 1986). Attack messages now comprise about half of all televised political commercials (Johnson-Cartee and Copeland, 1991).

The attack approach is more popular because of the mounting evidence available to practitioners that it works (Sabato, 1981; Taylor, 1989; Welch, 1988). The explanation for the efficacy of attack commercials in both commercial and political advertising is found in the information processing literature, which suggests that negative information generally carries greater weight than positive information, in part because it stands out, thus making it more likely to be noticed and processed (Hamilton and Zanna, 1972; Hodges, 1974; Kanouse and Hanson, 1972), and in part because voters in political campaigns and consumers of major purchases in commercial campaigns are motivated by risk aversion, the desire to avoid making a mistake in selecting a candidate or a brand, and therefore are more susceptible to fear appeals (Martinez and DeLegal, 1988).

Applying this theoretical premise to political campaign advertising, Kernell (1977), Lau (1982, 1985), and Pfau et al. (1990) indicate that people process negative information more deeply, and consequently, it exerts a disproportionate impact in the formation of candidate impressions.

The bottom line is that attack messages exert much greater impact on memory. Democratic pollster Mark Mellman (cited in Guskind and Hagstrom, 1988, p. 2787) claims that, "People process negative information faster." Whereas positive information may require five to ten viewings of a commercial to make its impact, negative information can penetrate in only one or two viewings (Guskind and Hagstrom, 1988). Frank Luntz of the Richard Wirthlin Group explains that, "Negative advertising is remembered better because it stands out" (cited in Kern, 1989, p. 26).

This explains the irony in people's reactions to negative spots: people say they hate negatives ads, but negatives work. Democratic pollster Paul Melman posits that, "We know from years of research psychology that people process negative information more deeply than positive information. When we ask people about negative ads they'll say they don't like them. . . [however] the point is that they absorb the information" (cited in Kern, 1989, p. 26). Janet Mullins (cited in Devlin, 1989, p. 407) explains it this way: "Everybody hates negative ads; then they rate them most effective in terms of decision making. There isn't any long-term effect . . . It is kind of like birth pains. Two days later you forget how much it hurt." CBS exits polls found that, although 61 percent of voters viewed Bush as running a more negative campaign than Dukakis in 1988, Bush won a "resounding victory" (Cutbirth et al., 1989), and won on precisely those negative themes stressed in his advertising (Devlin, 1989).

Early research focused on the short-term reaction, finding that attack spots elicit a boomerang effect against sponsors (Garramone, 1984, 1985; Merritt, 1984; Stewart, 1975). However, these studies ignored the notion of differential decay, explained in Chapter 5, which causes receivers to retain specific content of an attack long after they forgot the origins of that content (Moore and Hutchinson, 1985; Pratkanis and Greenwald, 1985). As a result, most practitioners now acknowledge that attack messages are an influential strategy in political campaigns (Armstrong, 1988; Axelrod, 1988; Ehrenhart, 1985; Nugent, 1987; Sabato, 1981, 1983; Taylor, 1986, 1989).

FEEDBACK

Contrast the bolstering and attack strategies in political spot advertising and consider the following questions.

 1. Under what circumstances would you recommend each?
 2. What, if any, ethical issues stem from the use of the attack approach in political advertising?

In commercial campaigns, the common variant of this approach is called comparative advertising because the advertised brand is "explicitly compared with one or more competing brands" (Barry and Tremblay, 1975). The Federal Trade Commission (FTC) unleashed this practice during the 1970s when it encouraged advertisers to name the competing brands rather than refer to them as, "Brand X". The FTC maintained that comparative advertising would enhance consumer information about brands (Boddewyn and Marton, 1978; Dougherty, 1973). Since then, the comparative approach has grown increasingly popular, and now accounts for approximately half of all commercial advertisements (Levy, 1987).

The relative effectiveness of the comparative advertising approach has been examined repeatedly in a vast array of studies during the past 15 years. The research findings, however, are described as "equivocal" (Belch, 1981), and as "inconclusive and inconsistent" (Atkin, 1984), thus failing to explain the increase in the overall proportion of comparative messages during the same period. Research is just beginning to specify the circumstances in which comparative advertising works best.

What is known is that the influence of comparative messages is affected by two factors: receiver involvement in the product class, defined as the strength of belief about a product class (Tyebjee, 1979), and its resulting implications for message processing, and the format of the comparative.

Receiver involvement in the product class is considered to be an "important mediator of consumer behavior" (Mitchell, 1978, p. 195). More receiver involvement in the product class results in "greater perception of attribute differences, perceptions of greater product importance, and greater commitment to brand choice," which should trigger more involved message processing (Zaichkowsky, 1985, p. 341). Comparative ads employ a unique message format in that they extol one brand at the expense of another. For those receivers for whom there is a discrepancy between their brand preference and the position advocated in the message, comparatives should prove threatening, a position that has received support in past research (Sujan and Dekleva, 1987). As a result, comparatives for brands in less involving product classes should prove to be the most effective. This conclusion was tested and supported in one study (Pfau, 1991b), and can be inferred from past studies that reported differences based on product class (Jain and Hackelman, 1978; Lincoln and Samli, 1979; Ogilvy and Mather, 1976, 1977; Shimp and Dyer, 1978).

The format of the comparative also affects its efficacy. In a series of studies of comparative advertising, Lamb, Pletcher, and Pride operationalized comparatives in terms of intensity and directionality. Intensity involves the style of the comparative.

Whereas low-intense comparatives feature casual mention of the competing brand, high-intense employ a point-by-point comparison (Lamb, Pletcher, and Pride, 1979; Lamb, Pride and Pletcher, 1978; Pride, Lamb, and Pletcher, 1977; 1979). Directionality involves the nature of the comparative. An associative message stresses the similarities of brands, whereas a differentiative message focuses on differences in brands. The researchers report differentiative comparatives are more effective in generating receiver interest, associative comparatives and noncomparatives are more believable, and moderate-intense comparatives are more persuasive than high intense comparatives (Lamb et al., 1979).

One study that examined the effectiveness of comparatives, taking into account receiver involvement in the product class, format, and receiver gender, found that while comparatives for brands in less-involving product classes were generally more effective, there were interactions involving all three factors (Pfau, 1991b). The results indicated that for females, moderate-intense differentiative comparatives were generally superior, whereas for males, moderate-intense comparatives were best on behalf of brands in high-involving product classes, while high-intense comparatives were superior with brands in low-involving product classes. This finding is consistent with the selectivity hypothesis, advanced by Meyers-Levy (1989) as an explanation for differences in the manner that female and male receivers respond to commercial messages. If males are inclined to judge a brand quickly, based on the information presented at the beginning of an advertisement, as Meyers-Levy (1989) posit, then comparatives for specific brands in more high-involving product classes, as well as those that feature more intense formats, risk triggering a boomerang effect among male receivers.

Comparative campaigns have been conducted for a variety of products. Pepsi-Cola's "Pepsi challenge" comparative campaign of the 1970s was credited with producing significant gains in market share for the soft drink company, particularly among younger consumers (Giges, 1977). In response, Coca-Cola launched a series of refutation spots which stressed reasons why consumers prefer Coca-Cola to "the other cola" (Giges). Then in 1985 the company introduced "new Coke," a much sweeter cola, much like Pepsi, which performed better against Pepsi in taste tests, but sparked a consumer revolt demanding return of the original product (Giges, 1987). More recently, Diet Pepsi has initiated a comparative campaign targeting Diet Coke, which rose quickly after its introduction in 1982 to a position as the third largest selling soft drink (Montgomery, 1984). The campaign features celebrities, such as Ray Charles, who employ humor in making their claim that Diet Pepsi tastes better.

Comparatives have played a particularly prominent role in two recent television commercial campaign battles: one concerning long-distance telecommunication services, featuring AT&T, Sprint, and MCI, and the other dealing with pickup trucks, involving both Chevrolet and Ford. Both battles have been intense.

The $55 billion telecommunications industry is dominated by AT&T. AT&T is the market leader, and spends nearly $145 million per year on advertising, as compared with MCI's $30 million and Sprint's $25 million (Fitzgerald, 1990b). AT&T, like most market leaders, was accustomed to expending most of its advertising on positive messages, designed to maintain its visibility and image as the most reliable, quality provider of long-distance services.

MCI launched a comparative advertising campaign in May 1989, stressing lower prices than AT&T, and challenging AT&T's claims of superior quality (see Figure 10–10). Sprint then changed policy, moving the starting time of its evening discount rate to 5 P.M. two hours prior to MCI's and five hours before AT&T's, and then launched its own comparative advertising campaign stressing its new rates (Fitzgerald, 1989b). This campaign, coupled with the long-standing implied comparative, featuring a pin dropping on a table, near a phone, thus stressing the clarity of their service, and MCI's explicit comparatives, were the first salvos in what was to become an all-out war against AT&T.

AT&T was particularly sensitive to the attacks because it had experienced a steadily declining market share, falling throughout the decade from a high of 90 percent to about 77 percent (Foltz, 1990). AT&T reduced its long-distance rates and simultaneously initiated a barrage of refutation and comparative advertisements of its own (Fitzgerald, 1989a). AT&T employed testimonial spots featuring people who had switched to MCI and Sprint but failed to experience the anticipated cost savings. These spots concluded with the question, "Aren't you glad you never left." These ads led to an aggressive AT&T comparative, "Put it in writing," that accused competitors of misleading the public with false promises of reduced rates, encouraging them to get competitors' claims in writing before switching ("100 Leading," 1990). In addition, AT&T initiated comparatives featuring testimonials by MCI and Sprint customers who claimed that they could not get the needed service with the other carriers.

AT&T's aggressive campaign produced immediate retaliation by Sprint. Sprint launched refutation ads in response to the AT&T refutation messages, running print

FIGURE 10–10   An MCI Comparative Advertisement Targets AT&T

Source: Courtesy of MCI.

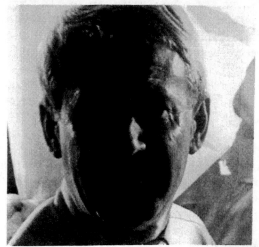

FIGURE 10–11   Chevy's "Ford County" Comparative Advertisement Targets Ford

Source: Courtesy of Chevrolet, a division of General Motors Corporation.

messages that posed the question, "Who is AT&T kidding when they say their rates are competitive?" (Fitzgerald, 1989c), and claiming they offered a 24-hour international directory (subsequent investigation by network television journalists revealed that Sprint operators were referring customers to number 10288, AT&T's long-distance directory service). Also, Sprint initiated two new comparative spots, one targeting the residential sector and offering one month of free telephone calls to people switching from AT&T (this actually amounted to a $25 credit on customer telephone bills) (Fitzgerald, 1989c), and the other targeting the business sector, which accounts for 60 percent of long-distance revenues, called "It's a new world" (Fitzgerald, 1989d). Then, after January 15, 1990, the day AT&T experienced a computer glitch that interrupted phone services for millions of customers, Sprint ran full-page print messages and a series of television spots both questioning AT&T's reliability (Fitzgerald, 1990a). MCI, in turn, produced a refutation ad claiming that they could provide instant credit for a misdialed long-distance call 24-hours per day.

Although the telecommunication's advertising battles have cooled down some, AT&T, MCI, and Sprint are still involved in very aggressive comparative and refutation advertising campaigns that require a steady stream of fresh commercials. It would be premature to speculate as to the impact of the three campaigns, although in the first year following MCI's opening comparative salvo, the overall market share of the three companies remained constant (Fitzgerald, 1990b).

Another recent advertising battle featured the nations two largest manufacturers of pickup trucks: Chevrolet and Ford. The feud began when Chevrolet launched its "Ford County" comparative campaign, claiming that Chevrolet outsold Ford in Ford County, a central Illinois farming community.

The six Chevrolet commercials, like the one shown in Figure 10–11, feature local residents, "countrified," and scripted to deliver out-of-character lines, which together contribute to the humor of the spots. The convenience store manager, who played a waitress in one ad, tells a homespun joke about a farmer who goes to heaven, proclaims that, "The cardiovascular benefits of eating a low-fat diet are well-documented in medical journals." Another woman observes that, "The understated simplicity even contributes to greater fuel efficiency" (Cox, 1990). All the spots conclude with the line, "People from Ford prefer Chevy trucks."

The campaign sparked considerable controversy following its debut in January 1990. Nationally, Ford sells more pickup trucks than Chevrolet (Cox, 1990). Even in Ford County, where Chevrolet outsold Ford by one truck through June 30, 1989, for the year as a whole, Ford claims that it outsold Chevy 113 to 106, something Chevrolet disputes (Cox, 1990). In any event, Ford responded at two levels. First, Ford launched refutation ads claiming that, "Ford outsells Chevy in Ford County, Ill., *and* Chadds Ford, Pa., Ford County, Kans., and Chevy Chase, Md. (It also called a news conference in Chicago to recognize its three Ford County dealers for outselling their Chevy competitors.). Second, Ford launched a positive, image-based campaign, "The best never rest," which focuses on the positioning of Ford trucks as the market leader, and stresses product features that contribute to Ford's success. Whereas Ford's refutation spots aired for a short time, The "Best never rest" campaign, illustrated in Figure 10–12, ran throughout 1990 and into 1991.

It's hard *not* to notice.

Because other trucks spend lots of time and money comparing themselves to Ford. America's truck leader.*

But if you're going to be the leader tomorrow, you can't afford to rest today.

That's why we're going to keep making the kinds of technical advances that have

Ford Trucks. The Best Never Rest.

helped make Ford Ranger America's most popular compact truck.

So even though we're proud of Ranger's exclusive pushbutton four-wheel drive system and advanced 4.0L engine, we're not going to rest. We're going to keep working to make Ranger better.

The same way we're going to keep working to make the best-built American trucks even better.** And continue to prove to you that there's really no comparison between our trucks. And theirs.

THE BEST-BUILT, BEST-SELLING AMERICAN TRUCKS ARE BUILT FORD TOUGH.

Did You Ever Notice Who The Other Trucks Compare Themselves To?

Optional light bar shown not for occupant safety.

FIGURE 10–12 Ford's "Best Never Rest" Campaign Answers Chevy

Source: Courtesy of Ford Motor Company.

283

Responses to Attack

When faced with the prospect or the reality of an attack or comparative commercial, companies or candidates have few viable options. First, they can ignore the attack, a more plausible option in past years, when conventional wisdom and the limited research on the efficacy of commercial comparatives indicated little, if any, differences (Etgar and Goodwin, 1978; Golden, 1974, 1979; Goodwin and Etgar, 1980; Jain and Hackelman, 1978; Mazis, 1976; Pride, Lamb and Pletcher, 1979; Sheluga and Jacobey, 1978; Shimp and Dyer, 1978; Wilson, 1976) and when research on the persuasiveness of both commercial (Levine, 1976; McDougall, 1977; Shimp and Dyer, 1978; Wilson, 1976; Wilson and Mudderisoglu, 1979) and political (Garramone, 1984, 1985; Merritt, 1984; Stewart, 1975) attack messages raised the spectre of a boomerang against the sponsor.

Ignoring the attack remains an option for a brand that is the dominant one in their market and for a candidate that enjoys a rather sizable lead in public opinion polls. In both cases, they may not want to provide further exposure to the attack, or worse, give it a degree of legitimacy by providing an answer. Bert Neufeld, a former creative director at Wells, Rich, Greene, Inc., cautions that, ". . . if the big guy answers back he loses points" (cited in "Should an Ad," 1979). Morner (1978, p. 104) adds: ". . . a product that is a market leader has little to gain from letting the world know that it has competition."

Thus, some criticized Coca-Cola's refutation spots against the Pepsi-Cola "Taste test" comparative campaign (Giges, 1977). Proctor and Gamble and General Foods, which manufacture a number of brands that are dominant in their respective markets, generally eschew advertising strategies that call attention to rival brands (Morner, 1978). Further, some incumbent politicians that enjoy substantial leads in their reelection bids have chosen to ignore opponents' attacks completely, or ignore the specific charges in the attack and initiate generic refutation spots against the use of "negative campaigning" (Cecil, 1990).

This strategy is risky, however. In politics, particularly, ignoring an opponent's attack leaves voters with the impression that the charges are true. Campaign advisor Richard Moe (cited in Taylor and Broder, 1988, p. 15) warns that, "Unless you are a prohibitive front-runner, an unanswered smear is believed."

We previously documented the stunning success of the Bush attacks on Dukakis in the 1988 presidential race. The success was due, in large part, to Dukakis' failure to respond. Farah and Klein argue that the Bush spots worked precisely because Dukakis failed to respond to them. They note: "Michael Dukakis did not find his voice to counter the charges made against him until very late in the campaign. The damage had already been done" (1989, p. 127). Hershey (1989, p. 87) adds that although he had been warned that, "unanswered smears are often believed, Dukakis refused to respond in kind." Robert Squier, democratic media consultant echoed the same conclusion. "With the Boston Harbor and furlough commercials, they [the Bush strategists] took the campaign straight at Dukakis, and the charges went unanswered for more than a month. It is a truism in politics: An attack unanswered eventually becomes an attack agreed to" (cited in Perry and Langley, 1988, p. A-24). Vice Chair of the Democratic

National Committee, Lynn Cutler, summarizes the crucial lesson that political practitioners learned from Dukakis' experience. When hit with an attack, "You can't ignore it. You simply can't ignore it" (cited in "A New Era," 1990).

A second option is to attempt refutation, which involves a rebuttal of the attack, perhaps employed in conjunction with an attack of their own. However, it is unclear whether refutation messages can militate the damage done by an attack, especially over the long haul, after the disassociation of the content of the attack and its origins (Hagstrom and Guskind, 1986; Pfau and Kenski, 1990). Indeed, the effectiveness of refutation messages in political campaigns is mixed. In an examination of attack politics in elections for House, Senate, and President since 1980, Pfau and Kenski concluded that, in response to attack campaigns, refutation messages only managed to reduce the final margins of defeat in the 1980 Senate reelection campaigns of Indiana's Bayh, Idaho's Church, and South Dakota's McGovern, and the 1986 reelection campaign of South Dakota's Abdnor, while they were able to salvage victories for incumbents Melcher in 1982 and Gramm and Humphrey in 1984 (1990, p. 70).

The bottom line is that refutation is post-hoc. Thus, in many cases, the attack advertising has already done its damage by the time the refutation message airs. In addition, refutation is useless as a response to an opponent's attack that comes late in a close political campaign, thus preempting the possibility of a response (Pfau and Kenski, 1990). This limitation is serious in the face of the increasing number of "last minute" attacks during 1988 presidential primary contests (Colford, 1988a).

An alternative and more promising option is the use of some form of refutational preemption, in which the brand or candidate attempts to undermine the potential for attacks before opponents initiate them. One form of preemption that is receiving more and more attention is the inoculation approach, which makes receivers resistant through the use of refutational pretreatments, which raise the spectre of content potentially damaging to a receiver's attitude while simultaneously offering direct refutation of that content (Papageorgis and McGuire, 1961). A number of early studies confirmed the relative superiority of inoculation as opposed to reinforcing bolstering messages in conferring resistance to attacks in laboratory conditions (Anderson and McGuire, 1965; McGuire, 1961, 1962; McGuire and Papageorgis, 1961; Papageorgis and McGuire, 1961).

More recent research has explored the application of the inoculation construct to confer resistance to attack messages in commercial and political campaigns. The early findings appear promising, indicating that refutational same (which involve the specific content of the impending attack) and different (which concern generic content) pretreatments provide resistance to commercial and political attacks.

Two large experimental field studies examined the viability of inoculation in political campaigns. The first study tested inoculation in a U. S. Senate campaign in South Dakota among 733 potential voters (Pfau and Burgoon, 1988), while the second study assessed inoculation via direct mail during the 1988 presidential campaign among 314 voters (Pfau, Kenski, Nitz, and Sorenson, 1990). The results of both studies indicated that inoculation of same and different pretreatments provide resistance to the influence of political attack messages, undermining the potential of attacks to influence attitudes or voting intention (Pfau and Kenski, 1990). A significant inoculation effect was observed among all receiver groups and on all the major dependent variables (Pfau and Kenski, 1990).

Political practitioners have only just begun to examine the potential of refutational preemption. Republican consultant Jim Innocenzi proclaims that, "Inoculation and preemption are what win campaigns" (cited in Ehrenhalt, 1985, p. 2563). Salmore and Salmore (1985, p. 80) suggest incumbents "anticipate negatives and preempt them," whereas consultant Charles Black advises that, "If you know what your negatives are, you can preempt" (cited in Ehrenhalt, 1985, p. 2563). Stephen Frantzich interviewed active political consultants, finding many willing to use "inoculation letters," explaining candidate's positions on sensitive issues (1989, pp. 220–221).

Research also has examined the viability of inoculation in commercial campaigns. Two of the earliest studies dealt with social marketing issues, nonetheless claiming application to commercial advertising. Bither, Dolich, and Nell (1971) took "a step toward marketing applications" in a study involving movie censorship. They found that inoculation pretreatments foster and strengthen initial beliefs, concluding that an advertiser should be able to inoculate users and nonusers. Szybillo and Heslin (1973) examined whether there should be air-bags in cars. Results supported the overall superiority of refutational as opposed to supportive pretreatments, suggesting that potential for inoculation in commercial advertising. Both studies prove inoculation's viability in social action campaigns, intimating its potential in commercial campaigns.

Subsequent research findings concerning message sidedness in commercial campaigns suggest that two-sided comparative messages are superior to one-sided messages in enhancing acceptance of an advertiser's claims (Hass and Linder, 1972; Kamins and Asseal, 1987; Swinyard, 1981). One study that used refutational preemption, a feature of two-sided messages, in conjunction with threat, thus operationalizing the inoculation construct, reported that both inoculation same and different approaches foster resistance to changes in receiver attitudes that would otherwise result from comparative advertising (Pfau, 1991a). In addition, this study indicated that inoculation pretreatments were more effective in conferring resistance against high- as opposed to moderate-intense comparatives for high-involving products (Pfau, 1991a). Thus, in commercial advertising, where most products are low-involving (Atkin, 1984; Krugman, 1965; Ray, 1976; Rothschild and Ray, 1974; Wright, 1974), inoculation is barely able to generate sufficient threat levels to trigger the receiver's internal motivational process, and the potential of inoculation is limited to specific circumstances, such as those discussed in Chapter 12.

One additional application of inoculation involves advocacy advertising, predominantly print messages in which corporations take positions on controversial public policy issues. While the practice is fairly widespread [Dardenne (1981) suggests that more than 20 percent of this nation's corporations employ some form of advocacy advertising], opinion is divided as to whether advocacy advertising exerts any appreciable impact on public opinion or on public policy (Dardenne, 1981).

One study examined Mobil's long-standing advocacy campaign on behalf of various issues, not as attempts to change receivers' attitudes, but as efforts to inoculate them. The corporation's "advertorials," like the one illustrated in Figure 10–13, appear regularly in such publications as *Time*, *The Economist*, and in a number of the nation's

The right time, the right idea

When does the time for an idea finally come?

For landmark civil rights legislation, it came in 1964, after the nation had witnessed the power and dignity of peaceful protest—and the brutality of rampant racism.

For the ascendancy of the free-market system, it came after ordinary citizens all over the world compared their living standards with those of the Western democracies—and found Marxism wanting.

And for the line-item veto, unsuccessfully sought by President Reagan, it may be coming soon, propelled by the need to cut wasteful spending and by the blatant politics played each year as Congress and the Administration attempt to write the national budget.

A prime example of the need for a line-item veto was offered up within recent weeks. An economic aid package of $420 million for Panama and $300 million for Nicaragua—fledgling democracies both—was contained in an omnibus supplemental spending bill. But instead of a cut-and-dried spending measure, Senate and House conferees had to wrestle with a rider involving a social issue. President Bush threatened to veto the entire bill as Nicaragua and Panama twisted in the wind.

If the President had the line-item veto authority enjoyed by the governors of 43 states, he could veto only appropriations he deems undesirable. Since he doesn't, he either has to take the bad with the good or throw out the good with the bad.

Currently, the line-item veto is gaining on two fronts. The Senate Judiciary Committee has voted out, albeit by a narrow 8-6 margin, two proposed constitutional amendments to give the President that power. One would let him reduce or veto individual spending items, subject to an override by a simple majority in both Houses of Congress. The other would let the President veto items but not cut spending. The veto could be overridden by a two-thirds majority in each chamber.

The other front in the line-item veto battle involves a bill that has been introduced in the Senate, and which its backers say won't require a constitutional amendment. Under this bill, the President would have 20 days after signing a spending bill to reduce or eliminate expenditures he considers wasteful. Congress would have 20 days to restore funding by a simple majority vote, but then the President could veto the so-called "resolution of disapproval." The President can already rescind spending, but his action is nullified unless both Houses approve within 45 days. The practical effect has been to sharply limit the use of rescission; of 164 attempted rescissions in the last four years, only eight won approval.

We have argued for the line-item veto on several occasions in the past. It works on the state level. It inhibits the blatant pork barreling and logrolling currently built into the budget process. And it gives our national leader—the President—the final say on what spending is in the best interest of all Americans, and not just a few from a select constituency.

The line-item veto, in short, is a good idea. We think its time is here.

Mobil®

FIGURE 10–13 **Mobil Advertorial Advocates a Line-Item Veto**

Source: Courtesy of 1990 Mobil Corporation. Reprinted with permission.

largest newspapers (Rubin, 1977). The study found that Mobil's "advertorials" generate considerable good will for the firm, and effectively inoculate most readers against efforts to sway them to positions that are contrary to Mobil's interests (Burgoon, Pfau, Birk, and Clark, 1985).

Conclusion

This chapter concerned the use of advertising in persuasive campaigns. Advertising is the principle vehicle that commercial campaigners employ to reach a mass audience, and also has become the most important communication modality available to political campaigners. However, advertising is costly, which means that it is unavailable to most social action campaigners.

The chapter examined four macro advertising strategies: name identification; the use of themes, affect, and testimonials both to establish and maintain the image of a brand or candidate; the attack message approach; and potential responses to attack. The chapter examined the nature and impact of each of the approaches in contemporary campaigns, providing examples to illustrate their use. Because each of the approaches are designed to accomplish specific objectives, campaigners may need to employ one or more of them depending on marketing or political circumstances.

Suggestions for Further Reading

Aleasandrini, K. L. (1983). Strategies that influence memory for advertising communication. In R. J. Harris (Ed.), *Information Processing Research in Advertising* (pp. 65-82). Hillsdale, NJ: Lawrence Erlbaum Associates.

Alperstein N. M. (1991). Imaginary social relationships with celebrities appearing in television commercials. *Journal of Broadcasting and Electronic Media, 35*, 43-58.

Bogart, L. (1990). *Strategy in Advertising: Matching Media and Messages to Markets and Motivations.* Lincolnwood, IL: National Textbook Company.

Keating, J. P. and Latane, B. (1976). Politicians on TV: The image is the message. *Journal of Social Issues, 32*, 116-132.

Kern, M. (1989). *30-second Politics: Political Advertising in the eighties.* New York: Praeger Publishers.

Pfau, M. and Kenski, H. C. (1990). *Attack Politics: Strategy and Defense.* New York: Praeger Publishers.

$$Chapter \quad 11$$

Using the Mass Media

Media create information and entertainment to attract an audience that will be of interest to advertisers.
—CHARLES H. PATTI AND CHARLES F. FRAZIER
(PATTI AND FRAZIER, 1988, P. 358).

[I]f the intervention goal is to orient a particular demographic group to act or interact in a certain way, then researchers should first identify the medium with which that group has the strongest orientation dependency relations. . . . The emphasis, therefore, is upon the quality of people's relationships with different media, rather than the quantity of their exposure.
SANDRA BALL-ROKEACH AND MILTON ROKEACH
COMMUNICATION PROFESSORS
(BALL-ROKEACH AND ROKEACH, 1989, P. 221)

In this last chapter of the book before we present the case studies used to illustrate persuasive communication campaigns, we consider the campaign audience's use of the mass media as one of the issues associated with campaigners' selection of media forms to deliver campaign messages. Individuals have many sources of media available to them, and their selection of one source or another, as well as the reasons behind the selection process provide important information for campaigners. We also review several other issues related to the campaigners' decision-making process in using the mass media.

As was discussed in Chapters 9 and 10, there are several free and paid communication modalities that campaigners may use to deliver the messages associated with a campaign. However, a problem associated with dependence upon free communication forms, such as PSAs, is that the intended audience may never be exposed to the campaign message. Sometimes, however, campaigners have few options other than to rely on free channels, whether or not an intended audience frequently uses the medium or not. In order to project the likelihood of audience exposure, and therefore the medium's potential reach for a message, a great deal of research has been conducted to increase our understanding of how and when people use various forms of media. At the very least, inadequate message exposure offers one explanation for evaluators who find that the desired effectiveness has not been attained. Sometimes, however, campaigners are too quick to blame lack of effectiveness on insufficient reach.

To preempt problems of reach, campaigners should project in advance the percentage of an intended audience who is expected to be exposed to the campaign message by each channel communicating the campaign message. Effectiveness regarding channel selection during a campaign relates not only to the audience's media use, but to the campaign budget and other constraints, which affect campaigners' decisions to use the mass media. The channel selection decision-making process, by both the audience and the campaigners, is the focus of this chapter. Specifically, the questions in Table 11–1 will be discussed.

Media Forms and Use: Campaigners' Perspectives

Reach versus Frequency: Impact on Recall

Planners must focus first on the practical problems of reaching the target audience as frequently as needed. That is where most programs flounder . . . The real questions are, What channels might be paid for with available resources? What channels can be sustained over the long run (Hornik, 1989, p. 313)?

When campaigners assess whether or not a message will reach the intended audience, the issue is not about content of messages or effects associated with the messages. Rather, the focus is on whether or not an audience has an opportunity to be exposed to the message content. Some have argued that the more valid and interesting question is whether specific information has been provided by a source to an audience rather than the simple volume or frequency of contact (Chaffee, 1982).

Hornik's (1989) evaluation of communication programs aimed at disseminating health information among people in developing nations, for example, illustrates the question of reach in a campaign.

TABLE 11–1   Questions about Using the Mass Media

1. Discuss the importance of reach in making decisions about the use of mass media.
2. How is frequency of exposure to a message related to recall of the message?
3. What motivates audiences to use mass media?
4. What is MTU?
5. How does age affect the use of mass media?
6. How do individuals use television, radio, newspapers, and magazines?
7. How is the audience's use of television, radio, newspapers, and magazines assessed?
8. What advantages and disadvantages are associated with use of television, radio, magazines, and newspapers?

In the African nation of Swaziland, the government implemented an intense public health communication campaign directed toward the treatment of diarrheal disease in children, beginning in September 1984 and continuing through March 1985 (p. 319).

Hornik reports that contact with a clinic nurse was related to about 18 percent greater likelihood of using the solution being promoted to reduce dehydration associated with diarrheal disease. Radio use was related to about 17 percent greater likelihood of using the solution, while contact with an outreach worker was associated with about a 20 percent greater likelihood. These figures are comparable. The dissimilarity between the three channels in affecting the audience's behavior occurs when one evaluates the reach of the messages. Radio messages reached 60 percent of the intended population, while only 16 percent of the target group was exposed to an outreach worker, and 22 percent were exposed to the message through a nurse. In sum, greater reach leads to greater numbers of successful converts, although the actual percentage of individuals who are converted in any single group may be quite similar. Thus, the medium that is able to reach 60 percent of the desired population with a campaign message will be viewed as more desirable to use, within the constraints of the campaign's budget.

With regard to the frequency of a message, the campaigners must make decisions regarding how often to expose an audience to the message. As Krugman (1972) phrases it, the first exposure to anything is primarily focused on answering the question, "What is it?" The second time that an audience is exposed to a message, the audience is likely to replace the, "What is it," response with a, "What of it" and/or "I have seen this before," so that the message is considered in terms of its salience for a particular individual. The third exposure, according to Krugman, will be associated with decisions regarding any consequences associated with earlier evaluations, as well as the start of disengagement. In sum, the number of exposures that Krugman deems necessary and generally sufficient to obtain the desired audience results is three. The problem is guaranteeing that an audience is actually exposed three times.

We spend a lot of money on repetition of advertising. Some explain this by noting that recall of the advertising will drop unless continually reinforced; others note that members of the audience are not always in the market for the advertised product, but that when they are, the advertising must be there. There's no choice but to advertise frequently (Krugman, 1972, p. 12).

The objective of repeating messages is to increase the likelihood that receivers will remember the message and behave according to the contents of the message. As was discussed in Chapter 8, campaigns can control several variables to increase the likelihood that a message will be more memorable. Both repetition and visualization, for example, are important in promoting message recall.

Krugman (1977) asserts that results supporting an audience's low recall of messages among television viewers ignores the high levels of message and pattern recognition; television is a visual medium and its impact relates to the presentation of continuous visual images.

Cost Effectiveness

"The basic task of media planning is to locate media that deliver the target audience efficiently and effectively" (Patti and Frazier, 1988, p. 360). Several questions must be considered in the process of assessing the media source's cost effectiveness. In general, campaigners seek to determine the cost per person (CPP), or the cost of placing an ad divided by the number of audience members expected to be exposed to the ad. Cost per thousand (CPM) is a more commonly used measure of effectiveness and is obtained by multiplying the CPP by 1,000. One decision regarding cost effectiveness is a question of comparing the CPM for one spot on one TV program versus a weekly newspaper, versus a monthly magazine, and so on, always within the context of the number of audience members who will be exposed to the message.

The use of CPM is the most common method of measurement, but should be used with caution. First, CPM measures efficiency in terms of reach and frequency rather than effectiveness: CPM will produce the same ratio whether 10 percent are reached 10 times; 100 percent are reached one time; or one percent are reached 100 times. CPM also is often used for comparison among nonequivalent forms of media. It is inappropriate, for example, to compare a one- and four-color print advertisement, but CPM treats them the same.

The validity of CPM as a measure of effectiveness has been challenged by researchers such as Clancy (1992), who asserts that, "CPMs are no longer relevant" (p. 26). Clancy prefers a measure for assessing television effectiveness that takes in to account program involvement, which influences the effectiveness of commercials shown during a program. He recommends a measure called cost per thousand people "involved" (CPMI), arguing that it is a more valid index than cost per thousand people "exposed" (Clancy, 1992, p. 26). His research demonstrates that involvement in a television program enhances involvement in, and the overall effectiveness of, the commercials shown during the program, as follows:

Advertising Response to Commercials by Program Involvement

	Program Involvement		
	Low	Moderate	High
Unaided recall	18.4%	21.0%	22.2%
Aided recall	34.0%	48.0%	54.0%
Purchace interest	13.2%	15.7%	17.9%
Behavioral change	6.4%	12.6%	14.4%

Cost of the media is an important consideration when Madison Avenue selects test markets (Scott, 1991). For example, Atlanta has been rated number seven in the nation for market testing of products for the period of January 1988 through June 1990, a period during which 43 new products were tried (Scott, 1991). Some of the products included, according to advertising staff research by Saatchi and Saatchi, are

Horizon cigarettes, Geritol Complete, U.S. Blues blue corn tortillas, and colonial oat bran buns (Scott, 1991).

> *. . . [E]ach test market represents a kind of microcosm of America. To make the Saatchi & Saatchi list, a city's demographics must fall within 20 percent of the national average, it should be somewhat isolated, local media should be relatively inexpensive, citizens shouldn't be extremely loyal to any particular brand and supermarkets should be impartial enough to give new products good display on their shelves (Scott, 1991, p. A-8).*

In sum, cost effectiveness is not just a matter of the cost of using a form of media per se. Rather, the reach associated with a message must be examined in relation to the cost of using the media. This, in combination with the attributes associated with each mass media form, the audience's motives for use, and their use patterns contribute to the campaigners' decisions.

Audience Perspective: Media Time Use

"Media time use (MTU) research is the quantitative analysis and description of the timing, frequency, and sometimes the sequential order of media consumption during a given period" (Hornik and Schlinger, 1981, p. 343). Thus, studies that focus on MTU seek to understand how people use the media and to identify how much time is spent using various forms of media.

> *. . . [M]ost media habits are formed and performed in social circumstances. With exceptions, of course, for certain individuals (single-person householders), situations (housewives on their own at home all day, motorists tuned to their car radios and cassettes), or forms of content (pornography), little media consumption is utterly private and unobserved"* (Blumler, 1985, p. 58).

FEEDBACK

You have been hired as the media director to plan a campaign to promote your community to tourists, convention planners, and its own residents.

1. Who are your audiences?
2. What media will you select to target each audience? Why?
3. Design a media plan that includes the following elements:
   a. targets gender, age, and education;
   b. reach objectives;
   c. frequency objectives.

Read and think about the following fictional scenario. It will be referred to from time to time in this chapter to illustrate various points about mass media use.

"Table Talk"

In the upper peninsula of northern Michigan, snow fell like curtains suspended from heaven. Children caressed the white flakes and tasted them; adults swept them aside. In the dusk that settled so early there, rows of house were reflected in the dim light of tall street lamps. Within one of these split-level constructions, a family had gathered about their rectangular chrome table for supper.

"This is the CBS evening news," a clear voice announced as the family began to once more recite in unison, "God is great and God is good. Let us thank Him for our food. By His hands we all are fed. Give us Lord our daily bread. Amen."

"Amen," the father echoed.

"Why do they have to put that on?" the mother asked, glancing at the television, which was centered in front of the living room window, plainly visible from the dining alcove. The screen showed battered bodies of young men peppering a distant foreign field.

"It's not real, television's not real," the youngest daughter repeated what she had many times been told.

"War is real, all right," the oldest daughter retorted. "Pass the butter, please, Mom."

"Mommy, my soup's too hot."

"Protesters on a Michigan university campus staged a peaceful–"

"Let it cool."

". . . anti-war demonstration today. Police on hand–"

"I hope the roads are clear tomorrow," the mother said. "I need to go to the commissary. We're out of milk."

"Today was the first in a series of planned protests in opposition to the conflict in Vietnam. Various meetings, church services, and marches took place across the country–"

"Mommy, do I have to eat this? It's got on-yuns in it."

"There's only a little bit of onion in it. Stop complaining, please, and eat."

"In Boston, nearly one hundred thousand people met on the Commons to hear speeches–"

"Salt–" the son gestured, and his oldest sister rolled her eyes.

"You might try saying please," she said.

"In Washington, forty-five thousand marchers descended on the White House–"

"If that were my son, I'd disown 'im!"

The mother's forehead furrowed and her eyes lifted to look long at her husband's face. The children all twisted in their seats to watch long-haired demonstrators, wearing faded bell-bottom pants, beads, beards, and headbands, parade across the TV screen, shouting at the camera, "Hell no, we won't go! Hell no, we won't go!" One protester even spat into the camera lens, and another lit a match to the document in his left hand.

"What's the matter with young people today!" the father asked.

"War is hell," the son shrugged, and his older sister again rolled her eyes.

"What's hell–" she retorted, "is expecting eighteen-year-olds to fight and die for this country when they're not even allowed to vote."

"But what does burning their draft cards prove?"

"Freedom of expression, Dad," she answered.

"And just who do you think fought and died for that freedom!"

"But what are we fighting for now!"

"I'm sorry you ever got on that debate team," the mother interrupted. "You like to argue too much." The daughter understood that her mother liked peace at the dinner table. If that meant quiet, too, so much the better.

"While anti-war demonstrators marched in the capital, another group also braved the frigid Washington temperatures."

"Equal rights for women!" "Equal pay for equal work!" "Equal opportunity!" Women marched with placards and chanted their refrain. The daughter sat a little straighter in her chair. She observed her father's clenched jaw and those little muscles were twitching in his cheeks again.

"I suppose you'd disown me if I joined the women's movement," she said. Her father's eyes narrowed. In his youth, children had spoken only when spoken to, and a woman's place had been in the home.

"Women will never be equal with men," he said.

"How can you say such a thing!"

"Women have never fought for those freedoms that you're so quick to take for granted."

"That's true, and if men are going to be drafted, women should be too," she said, thinking that on this point at least she and her father agreed.

"American men will never put up with having their women go into combat!"

"American men have got to stop treating American women like property or children!"

The father's jaw locked tight as his teeth ground together. The daughter bit the inside of her cheeks so hard, it brought tears to eyes shining with their truth. No one noticed the mother's strange expression.

"More soup, dear?"

It took several seconds before her husband responded, handing his wife an empty dish. The son also gave the mother a bowl, and she rose, looking down the table at her oldest daughter who interpreted the expression: No more, not tonight. Then the mother paced toward the kitchen, her lips moving in a silent prayer, as the oldest daughter got up from the table, too.

"More soup?" she asked her sister, and the little girl shook her head. "Well, I want some." The oldest daughter walked to the kitchen.

"In the White House today, the President—"

"What's Tricky Dicky done now?" the daughter laughed, passing her mother.

"Thanks, Mom," the son said as his mother placed a bowl of steaming soup in front of him.

As the wife placed the second filled dish in front of her husband, he took her hand and held it until she looked into his troubled eyes.

"A new batch of orders came down from headquarters."

"Can I get down?"

"May I," the mother automatically corrected her daughter.

"Yes, you may." Her eyes never wavered from her husband's expression. "Where?"

Continued

> "Where what?" the oldest daughter asked, returning to the table with her own refilled soup bowl.
> "Daddy, it's time for my show. Would you change the channel, please?"
> The father rose and crossed the room. "Thailand," he said, and the oldest daughter's smile faded.
> "How long," her mother asked.
> "A year."
> The filled bowl slipped from the daughter's fingers and fell to the tiled concrete floor, red rivulets cutting a pattern at the mother and daughter's feet.
> "Why don't you pay attention to what you're doing! Just look at this mess!" the mother said as the daughter knelt to sop up spilled soup with paper napkins from the table. Her mother knelt beside her to collect the pieces of cracked crockery.
> "I think I can mend that," the father said.
> The daughter followed her parents into the kitchen and watched as the mother washed and dried the broken bowl, then handed it to the father. The couple worked wordlessly, holding the earthenware vessel, waiting for the glue to set.

This short story illustrates important distinctions between the **motives for use** of the media and **how people use** the media, both of which are important topics when considering media time use from the audience's perspective to inform the campaigners' planning.

Motives for Media Use

Mike Koelker, executive vice president and creative director of Foote, Cone & Belding, one of the nation's largest advertising agencies, characterized as "the force behind some of the most influential campaigns of the past two decades" (Pendleton, 1988), was recently interviewed by *Advertising Age* about his influence on people's values and desires. In the interview, Koelker notes that, "advertising is like algebra," adding that, "Every ad or campaign starts as an answer to a problem that we believe can be solved through the media. . . whether it's a marketing problem, a sales problem, or an image problem" (Pendleton, 1988, p. 52).

Investigations operating from the uses and gratifications perspective of mass media relate to MTU, examining what motivates people to use the media (Rubin, Perse, and Barbato, 1988). Swanson (1987) concludes in his review of research conducted within the uses and gratifications perspective of mass media that support is generally obtained for the conclusion that gratifications predict exposure to media. The assumptions usually associated with uses and gratifications research include that (1) the audience is active, although, at times, habitually so, and, (2) much media use is goal-oriented (Palgreen, Wenner, and Rosengren, 1985).

One of the longest-lived controversies in the short history of communication research centers on the nature of the mass media audience. Is that audience an active or a passive participant in the communication process? How does this active or passive orientation arise? And what are its consequences for mass communication, especially most communication effects?" (Levy and Windahl, 1985, p. 109.)

One focus in examining individuals' purposeful use of media has been the debate about how actively individuals select and use media. In summarizing the research in this area, Rubin (1984) visualizes media-users' activity as existing along a continuum from more instrumental and goal-directed use to more ritualized and habituated patterns of use, as summarized in Table 11–2.

The specific motives associated with the more instrumental patterns of use include to learn, to seek behavioral guidance, and to become acquainted with topics for conversation. These are likely to include watching the news and/or documentary and interview shows. In the short story depicted above, the father appears to have an instrumental motive for having the television set turned on during the dinner hour. The motive he likely wants to serve is an informational one.

Political campaigners plan and implement messages based on instrumental use of media. People use the media to learn about candidates' character and positions, which are likely to become topics for conversation, and ultimately, to inform their voting

TABLE 11–2   Media Time Use Patterns: A Gratifications Map

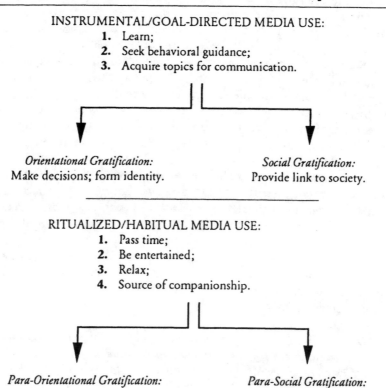

INSTRUMENTAL/GOAL-DIRECTED MEDIA USE:
1. Learn;
2. Seek behavioral guidance;
3. Acquire topics for communication.

Orientational Gratification:
Make decisions; form identity.

Social Gratification:
Provide link to society.

RITUALIZED/HABITUAL MEDIA USE:
1. Pass time;
2. Be entertained;
3. Relax;
4. Source of companionship.

Para-Orientational Gratification:
Reinforce existing attitudes.

Para-Social Gratification:
Gain a sense of identity.

behavior. Social action campaigners also design and use messages that seek to facilitate an audience's instrumental use of media. In designing messages to promote healthy lifestyles, for example, news reports of causes and cures of illness and disease appear on television news and documentaries and in newspapers. Audiences who learn new information about health behavior from the media are likely to discuss it with other people, and hopefully, such awareness will promote healthy behaviors.

On the other hand, commercial campaigners are less likely to depend on instrumental uses of media to promote their interests. Companies that advertise their products during news programs on television or in newspapers are likely to be targeting specific audiences that use these media. Commercial campaigns, as opposed to most social action and political campaigns, usually assume a more passive use of media, at least in terms of audience's use of television commercials.

At the other end of the activity continuum, Rubin (1984) considers motives such as to pass time, to be entertained, to relax, and to have companionship. He describes these motives as involving more ritualized media use, positing that more passive processing is likely. The most extreme form of ritualized use is the focus of the enculturation perspective (Gerbner, Gross, Signorielli, Morgan, and Jackson-Beeck, 1979), which treats users' media patterns as nonselective. Some uses and gratifications researchers claim that media exposure is habit, together with the content available at a given time, and within the current social situation (Weibull, 1985). In the short story, the youngest daughter appears to be oblivious to, or at least disinterested in, the content of the media news program. She wants the channel changed, however, when the time comes for her program, indicating that watching the program is a habit.

Political campaigners often attempt to place their messages in certain programs, which audiences view instrumentally instead of ritualistically, in order to take advantage of the more active message processing that such programs demand. Thus, campaigners find placement of spots during television news programs are very advantageous. Unfortunately, news program slots are also prized by certain commercial sponsors, who require more active message processing, and who make their media buys well in advance. In addition, some stations prohibit scheduling of political spots during newscasts, seeking a clear separation between their news coverage of campaigns and the partisan messages of campaigners. Political and social action campaigners sometimes decide to place their messages in such a way as to take advantage of the content of certain television programs, and conversely, to avoid the content of other shows.

Wenner (1985) utilizes much of the research done regarding motives for media use to propose a multi-dimensional framework to conceptualize audience activity. Within this model, which Wenner refers to as a gratifications map, the content of mass media is considered to satisfy orientational and social gratifications.

Orientational gratifications are message uses for information that provide for the reference and reassurance of self in relation to society. Social gratifications are message uses that link information about society derived from news to the individual's interpersonal network (p. 175).

At the end of the short story, it becomes apparent that the father is in the military and about to leave his family to serve an overseas tour of duty. Watching television news is likely, therefore, to satisfy an orientational need, as the content of the messages provides important information for making decisions, and may also contribute to his sense of personal identity.

The content of the media message also satisfies a social purpose in the short story, however, as it becomes the focus of conversation at the table, particularly between the father and son, and the father and his eldest daughter. The nature of the social relationships of the children with the father emerges during their conversations.

Wenner (1985) asserts that the content of the media is not always the focus of media use. Sometimes, simply the process of using media is gratifying, satisfying both parasocial and paraorientational needs, such as discussed in Chapter 10.

> . . . [P]arasocial interaction, are process uses that provide for personal identity and reference through ritualized social relationships with media actors who coexist with news content. . . . Paraorientational gratifications are process uses that ritualistically reorient news content through play activity that tends to reinforce predispositions by using expressive strategies that are often aimed at tension reduction or ego defense (p. 175).

Within Wenner's model, use of media content for information and decision making is considered to provide an orientational gratification, while the use of media content to imagine anticipated conversations with others serves a social need for people. Campaigners may too often focus on use of media to serve orientational as opposed to social needs. Moreover, they may fail to consider that media simultaneously serves both of these purposes.

The process of media use—indeed, the very act of having a television set turned on, or of glancing through a magazine or the local newspaper—may consume time, provide comedic entertainment, or just be a habit, all of which constitute paraorientational service of mass media use. Commercial campaigns depend on this process, based on the assumption that, as people read a magazine or watch a television show, they will notice and be influenced by an ad. This may happen because the content of the advertisement reinforced current attitudes about the brand, or perhaps because it generated awareness of the brand, provided useful information about the brand, or triggered an emotional response to the brand.

These uses are more likely to be positively associated with satisfaction of the orientational gratification served by media content, rather than social gratification, and to function as reinforcement. In a political context, for example, McLeod and Becker (1981) indicated support for the notion that individuals select media so as to reinforce attitudes concerning preferred candidates, selectively retaining information that reinforces their views. On the other hand, the process of media use for diversion and dramatic entertainment fits a paraorientational function, and is more likely to be positively related to satisfaction of social gratification, rather than orientational gratification. Mass media use for companionship, for example, is considered as a parasocial gratification satisfied by the process.

The motives that members of the campaign audience have for using the media provide one indication of the form that message content should take. For example, if members of an audience are expected to use the media more often to relax than to simply consume time, a message that might ordinarily seem to be one that could be delivered as information might be framed so that it has interpersonal utility. This is, according to Wenner's model, positively related to the likelihood that the audience will use the content obtained from the exposure, rather than simply being satisfied with the process of exposure. The audience's retention of the content of messages that have been included in dramatic entertainment shows, dealing with issues such as child abuse, condom use, and drug abuse, may be explained within this framework.

How People Use Media

Several variables affect people's use of the mass media in addition to the specific motives that are associated with use. There is a reciprocal relationship between MTU and the amount of time that individuals have to gratify certain needs in their lives. For example, when the motive for media use is leisure, the time spent using media to satisfy leisure needs will depend, in part, upon how much time an individual has for leisure activities. More leisure time is likely to result in more time spent using the media to serve this function. Research conducted by Robinson and Converse (1972), for example, indicated that Americans spent about 40 percent of their leisure time watching television. Individuals who only have a half hour each day for leisure may spend about 12 minutes watching TV to gratify this need; individuals who have 12 hours a day to devote to leisure activities may spend almost five hours daily watching TV.

FEEDBACK

There is a dispute among physical fitness experts as to whether performance- or activity-based standards are more appropriate in assessing the physical fitness of students. Critics argue that performance-based standards, supported by the President's Council for Fitness, can be counterproductive for less developed youth, who perceive the standards as too difficult (Godin and Shephard, 1990). Think of messages you have seen in the media that are designed to encourage exercise to promote physical fitness.

   1. With regard to commercial campaigns, do television ads for such products as athletic shoes promote a performance- or activity-based standard? Give examples.
   2. In terms of ritualized use of television, do situation comedies promote a performance- or activity-based standard? How about the show, "Roseanne?"
   3. Do magazine and newspaper articles that promote exercise depend on an audience's instrumental or ritualized use of media?
   4. Overall, as a campaigner, what uses of media would you recommend to promote exercise among adolescents?

The choices of media at individuals' disposal, of course, also affect how people use media. Some researchers conclude:

> . . . *[T]hat mass media do not serve as substitutes for one another—spending time with one medium does not necessarily reduce the time spent with another. This suggests that the media are not so much competing with each other for the consumer's time as they are competing with other activities. It also supports the previously noted findings that the introduction of new media (e.g., television) can lead people to extend their total MTU (Hornik and Schlinger, 1981, p. 348).*

An increase in choices, however, does not necessarily cause an increase in MTU. This issue involves collective use patterns. The principle of relative constancy, for example, suggests that the mass media compete for a limited quantity of consumer media time. If this principle is true, an increase in media choices does not necessarily increase MRU.

The issue is not just choices, however, it also involves the way that people use media. Heeter, D'Allessio, Greenberg, and McVoy (1983) found that cable subscribers change the channel a great deal, actively involving themselves in their choice of programs. Alfstad (1991) reports that young people, who cut their viewing teeth on "Sesame Street," and later on MTV music videos, ". . . have been programmed to switch their attention rapidly from topic to topic, image to image" (p. 20). Barwise et al., 1982 contend that often the first stage of viewing is passive, but what to watch is not passive. Thus, campaigners seek to understand *what* media choices individuals in the target audience typically have available to them, as well as *how* they choose to use those choices.

Age and education of audience members are also likely to have some impact on how the audience chooses to use the available sources. More educated audiences have greater ability to process information and greater interest in abstract topics, suggesting that media formats that use informational content are likely to be utilized more often by educated audiences (O'Keefe and Liu, 1980). Rubin (1984) found that more education relates to less overall television viewing, with the more ritualized forms of viewing, such as watching game shows, being greatly reduced in educated audiences.

With regard to age, people's viewing behaviors emphasize the importance of considering the motive for use rather than simply the number of hours of exposure to media. "Television use is important in the lives of children" (Rubin, 1985, p. 196). The available research demonstrates that children actively select media content to satisfy needs, which change almost year to year, with young children preferring action without complex motives, and adolescents interested in action and more complex motivations (Rubin, 1977). Adults increase the use of television to seek behavioral guidance, information, and affinity (Rubin, 1985).

The primary role of television in the lives of children may affect their disposition toward newspaper use when they grow to adults. A recent study conducted by the Times Mirror Center for the People & the Press reports that regular readership among younger people has fallen from 67 percent in 1965 to around 30 percent today. The authors of the study conclude that, "The under-30 generation knows less, cares less and reads newspapers less than any generation in the past five decades (cited in Zoglin, 1990, p. 64).

In addition to the simple exposure to a message as a primary determinant of the selection of the source, audience evaluations of the source's credibility contribute to the likelihood of use (Atkin and Freimuth, 1989). This is a fairly consistent finding in media research (McCombs and Washington, 1983). As has been previously emphasized, it is important to assess a particular audience's views regarding the images associated with campaign sources before making final decisions regarding their selection. Previously, this statement has been associated with particular individual spokespersons; the present recommendation concerns the specific audience impressions about media sources. Individuals may spend more time watching television, for example, but they consider newspapers as more credible when it comes to providing information to satisfy instrumental motives for use.

Use of Specific Media Forms

In considering how people use the media, several forms will be discussed, including television, radio, newspapers, and magazines. Use of all of these, however, will be affected by the amount of time individuals have to devote to media use, the sources of media available for use—including subscription to various channels on TV, the age and education levels of users, and credibility associated with the sources as previously discussed.

Television

At any time, each television network can expect a base of several million viewers to be tuned in by chance. Television is thus characterized as the most pervasive medium, through which a single message exerts maximum potential reach. Television is regarded as a highly credible form. Television has excellent mass penetration, but is viewed as ineffective on complicated issues, and is considered to be cost-prohibitive for nonprofit organizations (Alcalay and Taplin, 1989). Other strengths include impact, repetition, flexibility, and prestige.

The television viewing base level constitutes a "floor," to which programmers seek to add more viewers. . . . a basic difference between watching television versus watching programs" (Hirsch, 1980, p. 87–88). The floor includes individuals who are watching for the sake of the process and individuals who are watching for the sake of the content. To increase audience size, television decision makers are likely to focus on obtaining individuals who watch for the sake of the content, which is a more active process. Most campaigners also hope that their message content and style will motivate viewers to watch for the content, although often this is not the case.

One source provides information regarding media ratings, circulation, and exposure information concerning Americans' use of television. The source is the Nielson or Arbitron ratings. "Households using television (HUT) is the percent of all television households in the area surveyed with one or more sets in use. It is the sum of all program ratings for each time period" (Belville, 1988, p. 310). The rating is an estimated percentage of television households who view a specific program or station, while the audience share is the actual percentage of households tuned to specific programs for specific time.

Results of one Nielsen Media Research survey, for example, showed that Atlanta, Detroit, and Houston ranked in a three-way tie for first in television viewing during the period from April 25 through May 22 of 1991, viewing an average of 50 hours and 24 minutes of television per week (Dollar and Yandel, 1991). In an effort to explain the high viewership in Atlanta, it was observed that, "there was at least some rainfall 17 out of 28 of those days" (p. A-9) during the survey period. Thus, the motive being ascribed to viewers in this situation was quite likely more closely related to filling time, a process function, rather than genuine interest in media content. One Atlantan observed, "'Our TV stays on. It's a constant. The kids don't [always] sit in front of it; they come and go. But it stays on." (p. A-9). This, of course, illustrates a problem with both the validity and reliability of measurement in these surveys, as was discussed in Chapter 7.

This pattern of viewing may also be related to a finding published more than a decade ago:

> *Heavy television viewers tend to be unemployed and, like heavy radio listeners, live in households headed by someone in a relatively low prestige occupation. Heavy viewers complain that their families are in debt and they are unable to save money or get ahead financially (Hornik and Schlinger, 1981, p. 349).*

At the same time that the Nielsen data was gathered in Atlanta, Detroit, and Houston, the national economy was suffering, and these three cities displayed increased unemployment levels. In addition, there has been a decline in daytime television viewing as more women work outside the home. Limitations associated with the use of television include the fleeting nature of messages, its high cost, and lack of selectivity.

One important development concerning television use patterns that carries significant implications for campaigners involves a growing fragmentation of the television audience. Cable programs offer increasingly attractive alternatives to standard television network fare. With more than 50 percent of American homes now wired for cable reception, and with cable attracting as many as 25 to 33 percent of prime-time viewers, it offers campaigners "a cheaper and more efficient" vehicle to reach receivers (Walley, 1988). Advertising on cable is cheaper, and because of greater specialization in programming, provides an opportunity to target specific audiences with greater accuracy (Walley, 1988). Thus, since 1987, when Proctor & Gamble shifted significant advertising resources away from the networks and to cable, both commercial and political campaigners have been making greater use of cable television to reach viewers (Edel, 1988).

Cable established a $1 billion-a-year business by offering a less expensive option to advertisers. However, as cable shifts to higher rates, warranted on the basis of the growing audience, it risks losing its pricing advantage, thereby making it less attractive (Walley, 1988).

In addition, network television has encouraged the use of less expensive 15-second commercials as one response to cable's lower rates. The shift to the shorter spots began in 1986, and has accelerated since then. This option is not for everyone, however, since the 15-second spot limits how much information can be communicated. "You can only get across one specific point" (Bauer, 1986, p. 1), which renders the shorter spots of little value to advertisers who must communicate specific information, and who therefore rely on more active processing.

This may suggest that commercial campaigners, who rely more heavily on passive message processing, are in the best position to utilize 15-second spots. Political campaigners may view the content of their messages as inherently too information-laden to accommodate the shorter spots. Social action campaigners are also concerned about this issue. Some have questioned whether it is possible to educate about HIV transmission, safe sex, or proper condom use using even 30-second spots (Kroger, 1992). Thus, the very campaigns that are likely to be the most underfunded, those desiring to achieve social ends, are the least likely to be in a position to utilize these shortened television spots.

Another problem associated with the increase in the number of 15-second spots is clutter, caused by a sharp increase in the number of messages occurring in a fixed time frame. Research indicates that exposure to two competitive commercials reduces the effectiveness of both, decreasing "brand name recall by more than 25% and ad claim recall by roughly 40%" (Mandese, 1991, p. 6). However, the use of celebrities in television spots is one way to "stand out from the clutter" (Tsiantar and Miller, 1989).

Radio

Researchers have demonstrated that heavy media users are heavy radio listeners and television viewers (Hornik and Schlinger, 1981). Families, such as the one depicted in the fictional story earlier in the chapter, who are inclined to listen to television news reports during dinner, are also quite likely to have a radio station tuned in during times of the day when television is less accessible. The advantages of radio use include immediacy, low cost, flexibility, creativity, and mobility. Fragmentation and the transient nature of its messages are the medium's chief liabilities.

Arbitron ratings provide information concerning radio use. The content aired on radio is designed and purchased "on the basis of reach and frequency" (Alcalay and Taplin, 1989, p. 125):

> *In buying radio time or planning a PSA schedule, it is important to target audiences narrowly, combining dayparts 6:00 A.M. to 10:00 A.M., 10:00 A.M. to 3:00 P.M., 7:00 A.M. to midnight) and a sufficient number of stations to achieve, for example, an overall 60% reach goal and share of radio listeners in the particular target audience. Radio is often bought on a 12x, 24x, or 36x spot schedule on a weekly basis adding up to the GRP goal or the "reach" goal.*

The GRP goal is the *gross ratings points*, or the sum of all the rating points achieved or sought in a given market area for a particular time span. GRPs relate to the purchase of television and radio time, and may be calculated as the product of the reach or number of households expected to be exposed to a message times the average frequency or number of times each household is expected to be exposed to a message (Alcalay and Taplin, 1989).

TSA is the total survey area for radio, including metro area and counties in which at least two stations provide substantial strength to broadcast a signal. For television, the geographical area is defined in terms of the designated market area, or DMA. "Heavy radio listeners live in households where the head has a relatively low prestige occupation. In terms of lifestyle, they primarily are characterized by their interest in active recreational pursuits" (Hornik and Schlinger, 1981, p. 349).

Like television, the radio audience has grown increasingly fragmented in recent years. Whereas once AM radio dominated, in recent years the proportion of listeners tuned in to FM stations has steadily grown, now accounting for nearly 80 percent of all radio listeners (Harris, 1990). This nations 4,966 AM stations now compete for listeners and advertising revenues with 4,234 FM stations, which attract an average of $1.74 million in ad income per station (Harris, 1990).

Radio use patterns tend to complement television use, since listening peaks in the morning and again in the late afternoon as people make their way to and from work. These two peak listening periods are known as "drive-time." Radio use remains relatively high during the workday, but attention to radio drops, with its programming serving largely as background sound. Radio use falls precipitously during the evening, as people shift their focus to television.

In sum, radio has a broad frequency, reaches a "small but loyal audience, and allows for narrowly targeted campaigns" (Alcalay and Taplin, 1989).

Newspaper Reading

Newspapers are considered to be the best medium to penetrate specific geographic markets, especially with more high involving messages. Newspapers are also flexible, likely to carry prestige in the community, and can be used to achieve intense coverage of a specific area. However, the low grade of paper used in local newspapers limits the quality of reproduction. Also, newspapers possess a short life span, and are often hastily read.

The strength of newspapers stems from a combination of its potential to communicate in detail, in conjunction with a user's ability to consume information at their own pace. As a result, newspapers are regarded as an excellent medium for communicating complex and highly involving content. This makes newspapers the medium of choice for commercial campaigners to reach consumers at the choice stage of the decision hierarchy. Hence, local papers are effective vehicles to grocery stores, automobile dealers, and clothing stores to communicate specific information about sales.

In contrast to use of television and radio, newspaper use has been characterized as time-situational (Jeffres, 1975). Most people read the newspaper after dinner or while commuting, for example. In the fictional episode, "Table Talk," the father fit this characterization.

The Standard Rate and Data Service Reports (SRDS) are used to provide information about audience use of newspapers, consumer magazines, and outdoor billboards. In selecting newspapers as a form of media to convey a campaign message, campaign planners look at degrees of coverage and household penetration, as well as circulation.

While two-thirds of Americans still read newspapers daily, household penetration has dropped 10 percent in the last decade (Hulin-Salkin, 1987), and the future appears dim. Readership has dropped precipitously among the young, as we indicated earlier in this chapter. It has been demonstrated that people who spend a lot of time reading newspapers are often older than heavy users of other sources of media (Hornik and Schlinger, 1981).

Newspaper readership is highest among people who are heads of household, hold prestigious occupations, are well-educated and articulate, and are involved in politics. Consequently, the medium provides an excellent vehicle to elaborate and clarify political and social action content. At the same time, bargain hunters favor newspapers as a form of media to be used to gratify needs (Hornik and Schlinger, 1981).

Other research indicates that people's feelings regarding particular daily newspapers, together with their perceptions of accuracy, predict which newspaper an individual will use (Cobbey, 1980). In smaller geographic locations, there is much greater interest in local papers, and for such audiences, these become effective means of exposing an audience to a message. (Reimer, 1984)

In the same way that a reciprocal relationship is said to exist between amount of time available to pursue a particular motive and the use of a form of media to satisfy that motive, the size of a newspaper affects the time spent reading it. It has been observed, for example, that the volume of a morning paper, which was operationalized in terms of the amount of editorial content, influences reading time, with the metropolitan papers being read for longer a period of time than a provincial paper (Weibull, 1985).

National newspapers, such as *The Wall Street Journal, The Christian Science Monitor,* and others are secondary sources of information for most readers. However, political and social action campaigners find such newspapers to be among the most effective vehicles for reaching highly educated professional audiences.

Magazine Reading

Magazines have a wide latitude in selecting audiences, can reach more affluent consumers, are noted for the highest quality reproduction, provide prestige to advertisers, and facilitate pass-along readership (Alcalay and Taplin, 1989). In addition, magazines enjoy a long life, with approximately three-fourths of readers returning to reread something they previously had read. Finally, geographical and topical segmentation are most easily accomplished via the use of magazines.

People are likely to read magazines as a content-seeking activity (Hornik and Schlinger, 1981). A tremendous growth in the number and types of magazines occurred from 1975 to 1985, with more than 10,500 being published in the United

States alone. Golfers are likely to subscribe to golf magazines, while antique collectors choose to read magazines relating to this past time.

SRDS Reports provide information about people's patterns of reading consumer magazines, while the Simons Market Research Bureau informs with regard to other magazines' use. Given an audience's profile and the profile regarding who the readership of specific magazines will be, campaigners often elect to place the same ad in several different magazines to reach different audiences, and sometimes, the same audience. The "seven sisters" of women's service magazines, including *Better Homes & Gardens, Good Housekeeping, Ladies' Home Journal, McCalls, Women's Day, Family Circle,* and *Redbook,* are among the nation's most popular magazines (Levin, 1987). The same advertisements are often seen in these seven publications. Magazine readership is positively associated with education and occupational prestige (Hornik and Schlinger, 1981).

Magazine circulation and advertising revenues have declined somewhat in recent years. "The decline in spending by cigarette, liquor, and utility advertisers has generated intense competition among magazines for replacement pages" (Coen, 1987). *TV Guide* and *Reader's Digest,* the two biggest-selling magazines, topping 16 million subscribers each, have experienced flat circulations in recent years (Levin, 1987).

In summary, from an audience's perspective, the use of mass media is examined in terms of motives for use, which may include instrumental purposes and/or more ritualized functions. How individuals use the media, in addition to the reasons for which the media is used, provide important information for campaigners during the decision-making process regarding the appropriation of the campaign budget toward the selection of channels to deliver the campaign messages.

Other Media Forms

Billboards and transit cards are two additional media forms for campaigners to consider. Billboards are good when selecting geographical market, and have "high repetitive value, low cost, good color reproduction, reinforcement medium, large physical presence and attention" (Alcalay and Taplin, 1989, p. 112).

Transit cards are also a good reinforcement source for a captive audience, but require short messages (Alcalay and Taplin, 1989, p. 112).

In examining potential media forms, campaigners must examine the strengths and weaknesses of specific media, paying particular attention to issues associated with reach, frequency, and recall of messages, all within the framework of the campaign's budget. These judgments are vital in the decision making process regarding media forms and use.

Whether or not a specific audience is likely to elect to spend time using a particular communication modality, of course, affects campaigners' decisions regarding the use of various mass media forms. Although it is useful to identify the general media patterns of a campaign audience, more importantly, planners seek to ascertain the audience's exposure to specific media content regarding the campaign topic. This offers a means of assessing the likelihood of the audience receiving either competing or complementary messages during the campaign. Further, several other issues are important to guide the decision making process: the campaign's budget, information about cost-effectiveness of various media, and the relative strengths and weaknesses of the media forms, as they relate to the goals and strategies of the campaign.

Conclusion

Using mass media in persuasive communication campaigns is not simply a matter of what the budget might withstand. Rather, use depends upon campaigners' analysis of a campaign audience's motives for use of various media forms considered within a framework of the audience's age and education level, together with accessibility to and time available for media use. Once these have been determined, campaigners examine the reach and frequency necessary to attain the desired outcomes associated with media use. Then, within these findings, the cost analysis is a more valid assessment of ways to use the campaign's budget.

Suggestions for Further Reading

Cutler, N. E. and Danowski, J. A. (1980). Process gratification in aging cohorts. *Journalism Quarterly, 57,* 269–277.

Gunter, B., Furnham, A. and Jarrett, J. (1984). Personality, time of day and delayed memory for television news. *Human Learning, 2,* 261–267.

Horning, S. (1990). Television's NOVA and the construction of scientific truth. *Critical Studies in Mass Communication, 7,* 11–23.

P a r t V

Case Studies

Chapter 12

Commercial Campaigns

Toyota's Product Promotion and Antiprotectionism Campaigns

STEVEN R. THOMSEN*

*Like most great undertakings, the process of building an automobile begins
with an idea and plenty of questions. Who are we trying to reach?
What hole in the market are we trying to fill? What trends are we trying to set?*
—TOYOTA MOTOR SALES PRONOUNCEMENT
(TOYOTA TODAY, 1985C, P. 8)

*Perhaps the least noted of the postwar lessons is the need
to keep the world trading system fair —and expanding.*
EARL W. FOELL CHRISTIAN SCIENCE MONITOR EDITOR
(FOELL, 1985, P. A-1)

Speaking to the American Association of Port Authorities in the fall of 1985, Toyota
U.S.A. Vice President, James Perkins, warned his audience that the international trade
"waters" had become full of "alligators." He opened his speech with this statement:

*As some of you might know, I'm from Texas and we're known for doing things pretty big
down there. Let me give you a little example. Not too long ago I went to a barbecue at a
friend's ranch. In many ways it was your typical barbecue—big Texas drinks, a big country*

* Steven Thomsen, doctoral student in the School of Journalism at the University of Georgia, is the former
Publications Editor for Toyota USA.

western band, a big roast on the spit and a big old swimming pool filled with alligators—yes, alligators. (Perkins, 1985).

As he continued the speech, Perkins revealed how his friend had challenged anyone present at the barbecue to jump into the swimming pool and fight off the alligators for 20 minutes, with the promise of anything in the world he wants, if he survives. Perkins said that everyone was standing around thinking to themselves that no one would be that foolish when a splash was heard, and suddenly a guy was in the pool fighting off the alligators. After 20 minutes, the man climbed out of the pool, alive and just a little worse for wear with one chewed-up foot. Perkins' friend congratulated the man and asked him what he wanted. The man looked at Perkins' friend and said he wanted to know who pushed him in.

Those "alligators," Perkins explained, represent what his organization believes are obstacles to free trade and to the economic success of Japanese automobile distributors in the United States as well as support operations such as those found in Portland, Oregon. Fighting off "gators," Perkins continued, is serious business (Perkins, 1985). It has, in fact, been a serious part of Toyota U.S.A.'s public affairs strategy for more than a decade.

Sometimes in this business, my friends, we all feel like that man. There's protectionist alligators in those free trade waters. And it seems we're either fighting them off or looking for the guy who pushed us in. Today I want to talk to you about some of those "gators" and some of the ways we can keep them at bay (Perkins, 1985).

Trade issues, particularly involving the United States and Japan, have surfaced several times in the past decade and have become the focus of intense international disputes. In the early 1990s both the Japanese and Americans have pointed fingers at each other in an ongoing battle involving trade and international commerce.

TABLE 12–1 Basic Questions About Commercial Campaigns

1. What changes in approach turned Toyota's product promotion campaign into a success?
2. Explain the interrelationship between Toyota's commercial and public relation's campaigns:
    a. during the early 1980s ;
    b. during the early 1990s .
3. Why are lawmakers an important audience for many commercial campaigners to address?
4. When do free communication modalities become an important variable for commercial campaigners to consider?
5. How can inoculation messages be employed by commercial campaigners? Why is this a desirable campaign strategy?
6. What are the advantages and disadvantages associated with involving a company's employees in a commercial campaign?
7. How has Toyota altered its commercial advertising appeals during the early 1990s in the face of increasing attacks against Japanese imports? Has this approach worked?

This chapter examines Toyota's product promotion campaigns, in conjunction with its efforts to fend off protectionist attacks launched by U.S. automakers, directed at both Congress and the general public, and simultaneously to inoculate its dealers and employees against these attacks. Following a series of highly successful promotional campaigns during the 1970s and 1980s Toyota launched an extensive effort to undermine the specter of protectionist legislation in the mid-1980s, a time when trade issues took center stage on Capitol Hill. This chapter examines the evolution of Toyota's persuasive campaigns, concluding with a postscript, providing an update on where things stand as of the early 1990s. While U.S.-Japan trade relations remain an ongoing concern for Toyota and other Japanese companies selling cars in the United States, Toyota's antiprotectionist campaign of 1983 and 1984 provides some insights as to how a corporation can employ multifaceted communication efforts in order to promote its commercial interests.

More significant than a *single* commercial product promotion or advertising campaign, this campaign addresses much broader issues. The question of fairness in U.S.-Japan trade is debated before American lawmakers and via free communication modalities, as well as through paid advertisements. The "bottom line" is the bottom line in most commercial campaigns: profit. In the pursuit of profit, extensive and elaborate campaigns are undertaken. The consumer is an obvious target audience for such campaigns. But, increasingly campaigns also target supporters (e.g., employees, distributors, and supportive opinion leaders) for bolstering and inoculation, and target policy makers for influence. Some of the characteristics unique to commercial campaigns are examined in this chapter, and the questions posed in Table 12–1 are answered.

Toyota's Product Promotion Campaigns

Marketing-oriented product promotions are the most common of the persuasive campaigns undertaken by large corporations, and they are what we usually think of when we think of advertising. Indeed, product promotion is an important component of Toyota's efforts to market cars in the United States. An October, 1985 review of Toyota's advertising themes, for example (*Toyota Today*, 1985c), reveals that the major slogan, back in 1957, was: "We are quality oriented." In 1957, Toyota had just entered the United States automobile market with its first nameplate, the "Toyopet" (*Toyota Today*, 1985c). The car was a bomb! Critics claimed that it was "underpowered and built like a tank" (p. 8).

A decade later, Toyota was back, having carefully assessed the American market, armed with an understanding of differences between the tastes of the Japanese and U.S. consumers (*Toyota Today*, 1985). For example, nameplates like "Toyopet" or "Cutie" just will not make it in the United States.

Toyota had learned to ground its product promotion campaigns in receiver needs. As a Toyota sales pronouncement urged: "Like most great undertakings, the process of building an automobile begins with an idea and plenty of questions. Who are we trying to reach? What hole in the market are we trying to fill (*Toyota Today*, 1985c, p. 8)? This time, Toyota's slogans urged, "Get your hands on a Toyota, you'll never let go," and "See how much car your money can buy." During the mid-1970s the campaign adopted the slogan, "You asked for it, you got it." In the mid-1980s, the promotion campaign turned on the phrase, "Who could ask for anything more," with the word, "more," used as the major focal point in Toyota's print messages. Celebrities, such as Lee Travino, appeared in the advertisements.

Advertising research has demonstrated that consumer recall of Toyota's advertisements is markedly above the industry norm compared to all makes and models of cars and trucks (*Toyota Today*, 1985c). Charles Valentine, Toyota Motor Sales' national advertising manager for the United States in the mid-1980s, explained that the strategy behind the "Who could ask for anything more!" campaign was the establishment of "benefit-oriented" content, focusing on issues such as price, performance, quality, styling, and service (*Toyota Today*, 1985c), issues relevant to consumers in making highly involving purchase decisions.

> *There will be more competitive claims and comparisons, more aggressive copy, more emphasis on product attributes, especially performance characteristics, and a more rational, less emotional theme (Valentine, 1985, p. 13).*

Toyota kicked off the mid-1980s advertising campaign with gatefold ads in the October and November issues of such magazines as *Time, Newsweek*, and *Sports Illustrated*. Also, Toyota launched television spots with heavy saturation during the last week of October, expecting to reach millions of U.S. households, some more than once, over 90 percent of the television viewing population (*Toyota Today*, 1985b). All of this was taking place at about the same time that Toyota's relations with the community and government had become vitally important to the company's ability to conduct business at all in the United States.

Toyota's Antiprotectionism Campaign

Commercial campaigners' audiences include more than just consumers. Government relations, community relations, employee relations, and lobbying activities are an increasingly frequent component of commercial campaigns (Wilcox, Ault, and Agee, 1989). Moreover, corporations are discovering that employees can be motivated to undertake activities that serve the best interests of the organization. Employee publications are often used to build awareness of the problems and issues that confront an organization and to encourage employees to support the company's cause (Center and Walsh, 1985). In short, commercial campaigners are increasingly savvy when it comes to defending their interests from attack and inoculating supporters against potential change. For foreign companies that do business in the United States, the focus of such efforts is often protectionism, as shown in this case study.

Protectionism Defined

Most protectionist legislation is designed to impose quotas, which restrict the importation of foreign products to the United States, or tariffs, which are taxes on imports. In recent years, protectionist legislation has come in response to pressure from American firms and their employees, who have been directly hurt by imports.

> *For a brief period after 1945, the industrial nations tried trade protectionism. It was billed as a means for nations to shelter war-ruined industries while they rebuilt. But this lapse back to the approach that helped bring on the Great Depression was fortunately short (Foell, 1985, p. 2).*

The policy of protectionism has been a priority item on the agenda of Congress with increasing regularity during the past decade. During the early 1980s the United States experienced its worst recession since the Great Depression, followed soon by a strong recovery in which "the United States created—almost inadvertently and certainly unannounced—an informal new Marshall Plan for much of the world" (Foell, 1985, p. 2).

During the mid-1980s as Congress returned from a summer recess, protectionist legislation was at the top of the agenda, with several hundred bills having been introduced (Feldstein and Feldstein, 1985). In particular, protectionist legislation was being debated concerning trade and commerce between the United States and Japan.

> *No two economies affect each other so much as the American and the Japanese. If we cannot learn from each other—and apply the lessons quickly—we do a disservice to both nations and to the whole Pacific area depending on both engines of growth (Gibney, 1985).*

In the early and mid-1980s, Toyota and the other U.S. subsidiaries of the large Japanese automakers had to formulate campaign messages to directly address the following issues: (1) anti-Japanese sentiments in the United States; (2) possible protectionist legislation designed to force import automakers to use mostly American-made parts and labor; (3) pressure for import quotas; and (4) criticism over plans by Toyota and General Motors for a joint venture in California.

Toyota responded to the threat of U.S. protectionism in an increasingly systematic fashion, in part by stepping up its involvement in a Washington-based trade association representing import car dealers. Toyota also used a dealer magazine, *Toyota Today*, and a special publication, "Washington Report," to rally support on behalf of its dealers and employees in the campaign against protectionism. In short, Toyota addressed several audiences in addition to consumers in a broad effort to enhance its interests.

Pfau and Burgoon (1988) argue that contemporary political campaigns rely on four general message strategies. The same is true of commercial campaigns. The message strategies include: (1) bolstering, which highlights the positive attributes of a candidate or brand; (2) attack, which stresses the negative qualities of the opposing candidate or brand; (3) refutation, which responds to a competitor's attacks; and (4) resistance, which protects supporters against potential attacks. Use of these strategies is illustrated in this case study.

Product Promotion
Success Fuels
Protectionist Response

The "Big Three" U.S. automakers—General Motors, Chrysler, and Ford—reported a record $4 billion loss in 1980 (*Toyota,* 1977). They claimed that Japanese automakers had unfairly taken a sizable share of the U.S. car market. Ironically, it had been only 23 years since Toyota had struggled to sell its first cars in the United States. Indeed, more than 14 months after entering the U.S. market, Toyota U.S.A. had sold only 288 cars (*Toyota,* 1977). Through the mid-1960s, Toyota had sold only 12,953 vehicles, an average of less that 1,500 a year (*Toyota,* 1977). Its market area remained confined primarily to the West Coast, and it appeared as if Toyota might not be able to counter the popularity of American-made compacts that included the Falcon, Valiant, and Corvair.

In 1965, however, Toyota introduced the Corona, which became one of the most successful models in the company's early history. The next year, market expansion, aided by television advertising, moved Toyota into the Midwest. In the years following, Toyota dealerships reached from coast to coast. Rising gasoline prices and consumer demand for durable and economical cars made Toyota a household word by the mid-1970s when Toyota's vehicle sales averaged nearly 500,000 units a year (*Toyota,* 1977).

By the late 1970s the United States faced a recession, plagued by double-digit inflation, high interest rates, in conjunction with a high unemployment rate. With the recession, Detroit's "Big Three" pointed to the growing U.S. trade deficit with Japan as a cause of the nation's economic woes (Chira, 1985b).

> *In fact, it is precisely the economy's success in job creation that led to the trade deficit, as Americans enjoying new prosperity have bought more and more goods, many of them from abroad. The strength of the dollar against other currencies also has contributed to the deficit, by making exports more expensive and imports cheaper (Chapman, 1985).*

That deficit had jumped from $10.6 billion in 1979 to $12.1 billion in 1980, a year during which Japanese automakers sold a combined total of more than $9 billion worth of vehicles in the United States (Chira, 1985b).

In 1981, the United States' trade deficit with Japan climbed to $18.1 billion, as against the dollar value of all Japanese vehicles sold in this country of $10 billion (Chira, 1985b). Under pressure and fearing possible legislative retaliation, Japanese automakers in 1981 agreed to "voluntary" limits on the number of vehicles they would export to the United States. In what became known as the "Voluntary Restraint Agreement" (VRA), Japanese automakers agreed to a ceiling of 1.68 million units through 1983 (Brown, 1983). Under the VRA, each Japanese automaker received a quota that was proportionate to the number of automobiles it had sold previously in the United States' market. This was most beneficial to the larger Japanese car makers such as Toyota and Datsun (Nissan). These voluntary limits, however, did not stop the criticism of Japanese automakers.

Audience One: The U.S. Congress

On September 21, 1982, The House Ways and Means Committee's Subcommittee on Trade began hearing testimony on H.R. 5133, known as the "The Fair Practices in Automotive Products Act." The bill was intended to establish domestic content requirements for motor vehicles sold by foreign firms in the United States. The mood on the "Hill" was markedly protectionist. A press release issued by the Subcommittee on September 20 commented as to the nature of the pending legislation: "These requirements would have major implications not only for the U.S. automobile industry and its future competitiveness internationally, but for U.S. trading relations as well" (*Hearings*, H.R. 5133).

H.R. 5133 was designed to establish a ratio system requiring foreign automakers to gradually increase the percentage of American-made parts and labor in vehicles sold in this country during a three-year period. After 1985, any foreign automaker selling more than 900,000 vehicles, for example, would have been required to produce records proving that the cars contained 90 percent domestic content. For Japanese automakers, who earn a majority of their international profits in the U.S. market (Auerbach, 1983c), this posed a threat to profits.

During a nine-day period, the House subcommittee heard from more than 50 witnesses, allowing an additional 28 individuals or organizations to submit statements for the official record. Witnesses ranged from the United Auto Workers (UAW) President Douglas Fraser and General Motors' Chairman Roger B. Smith to representatives from American Honda and Nissan. These hearings established the precedent for future discussion of the bill, that would carry into the next legislative session and beyond.

U.S. Automakers Call for Protectionism

During the hearings, representatives from the major U.S. automakers took a cautious tone, even though sponsors of the bill had made it clear they intended to protect U.S. industry.

> *"The proposed legislation," Ford Motors Chairman Phillip Caldwell told the subcommittee, "should be viewed as an instrument of last resort to be considered when other measures to correct trade inequities and imbalances have been tried and have failed—in short, when Congress is convinced that there is no other way to solve these international competitive issues that disadvantage all U.S. industry" (Hearings, H.R. 5133).*

General Motors' Chairman, Roger Smith, was equally cautious in his remarks, stating:

> *I am sympathetic to the objective of the legislation, that is to strengthen the American auto industry and increase American jobs, but I do not agree that legislation is the best means of reaching that objective (Hearings, H.R. 5133).*

Despite General Motors' Chairman's statement in the Senate hearings for H.R. 5133, an analysis of the full content of his statement to the subcommittee illustrates how Smith bolstered the arguments in favor of protectionism. Smith reaffirmed the need to protect American jobs. Thus, supporters of domestic content legislation had found the thesis of their message—protection and creation of American jobs. Positioning the act as a "jobs bill," proponents of H.R. 5133 hoped opponents would be disarmed. Only one year earlier, the prime rate hovered at 20 percent and unemployment pressed double-digits. America needed jobs.

In his testimony, UAW President, Douglas Fraser, did his best to drive that point home:

> *If you use 1978 as a benchmark, the employment in the auto industry, in the motor vehicle industry, is down by 28 percent. The employment in the motor vehicle industry is now 720,000, and in 1978, it was 1,005,000. You can add to that the ripple effect of the unemployment in the auto industry. Some 670,000 jobs have been lost in industries that supply the auto industry. During that same period, 1978 to 1981, Japan has increased its production by 32.1 percent in cars and 32.7 percent in light trucks, and its share of the market has increased from 12 percent to 21.89 percent. In July and August,. . . the Japanese share will be around 27 percent of our market. As most of you know, the auto industry is crucial to the American industrial base. We consume 21 percent of all the steel in the country, 50 percent of the malleable iron, 34 percent of the zinc, 12 percent of the primary aluminum, 13 percent of the copper, and 60 percent of the synthetic rubber. H.R. 5133 is not a quota bill. It is not a tariff bill. We view it as an investment bill, and we say to the Japanese, let's put some capital where your market is. Let's create some jobs where your sales are (Hearings, H.R. 5133, pp. 145–46).*

This message illustrates how domestic automakers supported the view that American jobs are being lost to what they see as unfair foreign competition. The statistics bolster the claim that employment in the auto industry is down, as is employment in American industries that depend on automobile production.

The "Fair Practices in Automotive Products Act" never made it out of the 97th Congress. It was reintroduced with the same title, however, as H.R. 1234 in the next session of Congress. This time it was initially assigned to the House Committee on Energy and Commerce rather than the House Ways and Means Committee. That committee's Subcommittee on Commerce, Transportation, and Tourism held hearings in April and May of 1983. In September, the Ways and Means Subcommittee on Trade also resumed a day of hearings on the bill. Proponents of the bill had the momentum.

U.S. Automakers Attack the Japanese

In the case of Toyota cars, the United States' auto dealers began to display a unique form of attack message in the campaign to limit imports. They emphasized the "negative" qualities of Toyota and Japanese culture. "I believe that H.R. 1234 is a strong step in the proper direction," proclaimed John D. Dingle, Energy and Commerce Committee Member Representative, a Democrat from Michigan, in his opening statement at the hearings. "It serves a message on the Japanese and provides a mechanism for revitalizing the U.S. auto industry" (*Hearings*, H.R. 1234). In his statement, Dingle supported his position, pointing out that the United States' trade deficit had surpassed the $36 billion mark in 1982 and, that during the last half of 1982 and early 1983, unemployment remained above 10 percent–15.7 percent in his home state of Michigan. The U.S. trade deficit with Japan was at $18.9 billion in 1982. In 1983, it would climb to $21.7 billion, while the Japanese would sell about $10 billion worth of vehicles in the U.S. (Chira, 1985b). Dingle suggested it was time the United States did what other nations had already done:

> *Every nation in the world has some kind of constraints on imports of automobiles. The Brazilians and the Mexicans have domestic content legislation, and the Japanese accept these constraints with remarkable good grace. The British, the Germans, the Italians, and the French all have constraints on imports, many of which constitute local content requirements. I have never heard any complaint from the Japanese about the behavior of these countries (Hearings, H.R. 1234, p. 17).*

Dingle said that the United States was playing the role of "Uncle Sap," because it allowed virtually unrestricted import of foreign goods, even from those countries that discriminate against U.S. goods abroad.

> *The time for that to come to an end is now, or indeed is long past. While we work to establish a comprehensive trade and industrial policy that will put Americans back to work, legislation like this is an immediate and urgent necessity (Hearings, H.R. 1234, p. 17).*

During the hearings, the UAW's Douglas Fraser accused the Japanese of dealing unfairly with the United States. "I think the Japanese make fools of us," Fraser told the subcommittee.

> *They just make promise after promise, and never keep those promises. An editor of the Japan Economic Journal says that they have a technique, and these are his words, that they "make easy promises and postpone real action indefinitely" (Hearings, H.R. 1234, p. 171).*

With statements such as this one from Fraser, the content of messages about the production and sale of foreign automobiles in the United States had changed. The message content focused less on providing specific support for a policy of protectionism and instead attacked the Japanese, questioning both their business principles and practices. Specifically, the ethical and moral basis of the method used to negotiate business was cited as one way that the Japanese are able to make Americans appear foolish.

Representatives from both the UAW and Chrysler not only voiced support for the domestic content legislation, but they also brought up a new topic of discussion for the hearings–directly attacking Toyota's plans to build a car jointly with General Motors in Fremont, California. For pragmatic reasons, General Motors had formed an alliance with Japanese automakers on the quota issue. General Motors planned on importing 200,000 small cars from Isuzu (GM had a 34.2 percent interest in Isuzu), and 90,000 cars from Suzuki (GM had a 5.3 percent interest in Suzuki) for sale under GM nameplates. For GM, the problem with the proposal was that the 1.85-million vehicle limit would have left GM 120,000 vehicles *short* of its goal (Brown, 1983). Thus, GM objected, too, but for substantively different reasons.

Chrysler Vice Chairman, Gerald Greenwald, characterized the proposed joint venture as a "public relations coup" and a "Trojan horse for General Motors." Explaining that the plan was a "bad deal" because of the "antitrust questions," Greenwald testified (*Hearings*, H.R. 1234, pp. 243):

> *What were the U.S. antitrust laws intended for if not to prevent a linkage of two companies of this enormous magnitude. Together GM and Toyota would control 50 percent of the American auto market and 25 percent of all the cars sold on our planet. If that is not anticompetitive, and if that does not flunk the antitrust test, then I have to ask just what transaction would flunk that test.*

Again, the speech specifically attacks the Japanese, labeling their efforts as "anticompetitive."

Toyota Responds to the Attacks

On April 28, 1983, Toyota U.S.A. Senior Vice President, Norman D. Lean, appeared before the subcommittee. In addition to his testimony, Lean submitted a 25-page statement detailing Toyota's responses and rebuttals to the arguments supporting the bill. Recognizing that domestic content legislation had been tied to jobs, Lean pointed out that Toyota U.S.A. (at that time) employed 39,000 people in the United States and spent more than $1.6 billion on its annual payroll in this country. It was clear that his intention was to refute the opponents' attacks, directly addressing the "jobs" arguments.

Lean continued to point out problems with domestic content legislation, responding to the issues introduced by the bill's supporters.

> *In particular, domestic content requirements would be destructive and dangerous. They would be harmful to American workers and consumers. They would be harmful to the U.S. economy and to the domestic auto industry. The true effect of the proposed legislation would be a long-term system of quotas on imports that would emasculate the healthy competition that has been of increasing benefit to the United States and the world. The bill is sometimes represented as a jobs bill. It is not a jobs bill. Even if you could produce some small increase in jobs in the auto industry, they would come at the expense of more lost jobs in other industries (Hearings, H.R. 1234, p. 394).*

The statement that was submitted by Lean was signed by 58 organizations and major companies who sided with Toyota. This list of supporters including Boeing, Xerox, Caterpillar Tractor, Beatrice Foods, the Chamber of Commerce of the United States, the National Association of Wheat Growers, and American Electronics

Association. Calling H.R. 1234 "misleading, misdirected, and counterproductive," the statement signed by the 58 organizations and companies, submitted with Lean's testimony, warned that, if it was enacted, the bill's consequences would be "far-reaching." The statement predicted that American consumers would pay more for cars of all makes, American exports would be jeopardized as other nations retaliated against American-made products, and that by 1990, more than 104,000 jobs in the U.S. export sector would be lost against the creation of 38,000 auto jobs (*Hearings*, H.R. 1234, pp. 420–21).

Lean also focused attention on the advantages versus the disadvantages that the proposed legislation would accrue to the American public, introducing a new campaign strategy to the playing field.

Lean warned that, "Domestic content legislation would cost the country in higher unemployment, lower foreign investment, higher consumer prices, and reduced competition" (*Hearings*, H.R. 1234, p. 394). Lean's strategy was to stress that the domestic automakers had already begun a "revitalization" for their record losses nearly three years earlier. It appeared that the Toyota strategy was to make it clear that the problems plaguing the domestic auto industry were the result of changes in consumer preferences and the economic conditions of the past five years.

The second part of the strategy was to argue the position that the domestic industry was on the road to recovery. Lean emphasized that, "The U.S. auto industry is expected to be a major beneficiary of the economic recovery. Private forecasters, Wall Street analysts, investors, and Detroit top executives expect a strong and lasting recovery in auto sales starting this year" (*Hearings*, H.R. 1234, p. 410).

Nissan U.S.A. President and CEO, Marvin T. Runyon, had, in fact, already warned the lawmakers in earlier testimony that the bill would not force foreign investment in the U.S. and thereby create more jobs. "It would certainly not result in additional investment in the United States by Nissan. In fact, it would seriously jeopardize our project in Tennessee," where Nissan had been manufacturing light trucks for two years, Runyon told the subcommittee (*Hearings*, H.R. 1234, p. 374).

The strategy to persuade legislators and opinion leaders by presenting arguments concerning the potential loss of American jobs has been a consistent approach used by Toyota. In May 1984, Toyota U.S.A. Group Vice President, Harold Bracken, testified before Senate committee hearings held in Portland, Oregon. His message strategy was to bolster the company's existing approach by trying to drive home the point that Toyota plays a significant role in the U.S. economy, and that hurting Toyota with domestic content requirements would hurt the U.S. economy. Bracken also was quick to stress that Toyota U.S.A. employed more than 40,000 individuals and had an annual payroll in excess of $2 billion. He then defended the economic contributions of the import auto industry in general.

Today, the import auto industry in the United States employs more people than Mobil or Exxon. It pays more in wages than all iron and steel foundries in the country. It spends more on advertising in the United States than the travel, hotel and resort industries combined (Hearings, S. 707, p. 343).

Cognizant that he was speaking in a city whose very economic foundation depended on its port operations—156,000 Toyota cars entered the United States through the Port of Portland in 1983, contributing $112 million to the U.S. economy—Bracken forecasted that "overall auto imports would decrease by 19 million six years after enactment (of domestic content legislation)," and "the U.S. economy would be deprived of $1.4 billion in port-related auto revenue alone" (*Hearings*, S. 707, p. 344).

Bracken next attacked arguments that domestic content legislation was a "jobs bill"—an argument that supporters had been using, and that opponents had been refuting, for more than two years. His strategy this time, however, was to put his argument into human terms that would inoculate the Senators listening to his testimony and make them resistant to the "job bills" label in the future:

> *Let's be clear about something else: This is not a jobs bill, as its proponents claim. It is a job-transfer bill, and a net loss one at that, sacrificing far more jobs for dock workers, exporters, and those working in agriculture and the auto-import industry than it ever will create in the domestic auto sector. Mr. Chairman, at the opening day's hearing Senator Danforth said: "There's no free lunch in world trade." We agree, and this legislation is a perfect example. It would ask the dock worker in Portland, the import-car salesman in Missouri, the farmer in Nebraska, the machinist at Boeing in Seattle, and American consumers from Maine to California to sacrifice their pocketbooks—and, in many cases, their jobs—and to give protection to an industry whose products are in strong demand and whose profits have broken all previous records (Hearings, S. 707, pp. 344–345).*

That Detroit's "Big Three" were in the midst of a strong recovery certainly played into the hands of the opponents of domestic content. In 1983, the "Big Three"—General Motors, Ford, and Chrysler—had reported a record-breaking $6.3 billion in earnings. In the first quarter of 1984, their earnings were an impressive $3.2 billion—a pace that would push earnings beyond $10 billion by year's end ("Correcting Misperceptions . . . ", 1984). General Motors' Chairman Roger Smith's salary, bonuses and stock options exercised for 1984 totaled nearly $2.3 million, whereas Chrysler's Lee Iacocca reported his income, including bonuses, at just over $5.5 million for the year (Holuska, 1985). To argue that domestic content was necessary to help an "ailing" U.S. auto industry was no longer persuasive, and the Japanese automakers knew it.

In his written statement submitted to the committee, Bracken included one additional significant inoculation strategy. He portrayed import auto dealers as the same kind of entrepreneurs that built this country. Domestic content, in other words, would be a blow to the American pioneering spirit. Bracken explained:

> *In short, the import auto dealership is a small, entrepreneurial enterprise in the best American tradition. It employs local residents, purchases goods and services from other businesses in the area, and pays state and federal taxes. There is no question that the enactment of domestic content legislation would force many of these local businesses to close their doors (Hearings, S. 707, p. 347).*

One final hearing was held by the committee in July. In September, 1984, the Senate worked feverishly to put together a trade bill before the end of the 98th Congress. Before the Senate was H.R. 3398, a trade bill that encompassed a number of issues. Among other things, the bill included a "reciprocity" provision that would broaden presidential authority to respond to other countries' trade barriers. Supporters of S. 707 hoped to attach some form of domestic content requirements as an amendment to the bill. Those amendments, however, were fought off. When the Senate approved H.R. 3398 by a vote of 96 to 0, the bill *did not* include domestic content requirements. "Advocates of domestic content legislation . . . decided not to add their bill to the trade package" ("Senate Eludes Protectionists . . . ", 1984). Senator John Danforth, a member of Senate Committee on Commerce, Science, and Transportation, which had conducted hearings for S. 707, told the publication, "Frankly, I was surprised" (1985). Toyota, and the other import automakers, had succeeded in fending off domestic content legislation—at least this time.

Audience Two: The General Public

As developed in Chapter 9, a number of free communication modalities provide campaigns with coverage that also serves to afford legitimacy to a topic or issue. The commercial campaign regarding domestics or imports attained newsworthy status, as the debate appeared in the television news headlines. The print media, too, began regular coverage of the topic, providing, at times, more attention to the issue than the campaigners may have desired.

The Battle over Jobs

In early November, 1983, for example, as the House prepared to vote on the "Fair Practices in Automotive Products Act," Japan-U.S. trade relations were quite strained. On November 2, the *Washington Post* reported that the Japanese were planning to raise the ceiling on annual vehicle imports to the United States from 1.68 to 1.8 million when the VRA expired the following spring (Brown, 1983). Many legislators saw the continuation of the Voluntary Restraint Agreement and its modest increase of 170,000 units as an attempt to draw supporters away from domestic legislation. The news report of the Japanese plans, however, drew an angry backlash on Capitol Hill. Japan's agreement to continue export limits for cars, Representative Dingle told the *Washington Post*, "will in no way detract from the need for domestic content legislation" (Auerbach, 1983a). Chrysler's Lee Iacocca called the decision to raise the export ceiling "a major blow to U.S. auto producers . . . and laid off workers who are being hurt by the unfair advantages enjoyed by the Japanese industry" (Brown, 1983).

Popular magazine articles elaborated on newspaper headlines and TV sound bites regarding the issues associated with the debate, including laid off autoworkers.

> *"Autoworkers who have lost their jobs blame it on imports more than anything else," a Chrysler manager says. "One young woman who used to work in my division was so angry about being laid off that she went out and bought a Toyota, to spite Chrysler. She paid for it with benefits she gets under the Trade Adjustment Assistance Act, which aids workers who*

lose jobs because of foreign competition. Another guy piled his old junker into an Alfa Romeo parked on a suburban street. He rammed it and rammed it until it was almost unrecognizable" (O'Toole, 1981, p. 71).

Toyota and the major auto importers had also picked up another important ally. A devout free-trader, President Ronald Reagan had made it clear that he opposed the domestic content legislation (Auerbach, 1983a). The President appeared to agree with statements such as, "All customers in the free world want the freedom to choose the best products and the best prices," a statement made by Yuki Toga, then President of Toyota Motor Sales, U.S.A., Inc. (*Toyota Today*, 1985–1986, p. 15).

On the same day as the *Washington Post* report, the House debate raged into the evening hours. Concerns over the legislation's implications under the General Agreement on Tariffs and Trade (GATT)—which regulates most international trade—and fear of retaliation by other trading partners created the deadlock (Auerbach, 1983b). An amendment to the bill had been proposed that would have canceled the measure's effects if they were later found to be in violation of GATT (Auerbach, 1983c).

The following day, November 3, the House passed the bill by a narrow margin of 219 to 199 "after heavy overnight lobbying by the UAW to defeat (the amendment) that would have gutted the measure" (Auerbach, 1983c). President Reagan called the bill the "worst since the Smoot-Hawley Act raised tariffs in 1930;" the UAW's Owen Bieber hailed the vote as a "victory for American jobs," and Chrysler and Ford offered "lukewarm support" (Auerbach, 1983c). Attention then turned to the Senate version of the bill (S. 707) and the campaigners' need to sustain media interest to promote their own point-of-view regarding the issue.

Even though the Republican-controlled Senate had taken a free-trade stance, Toyota faced the very real possibility that domestic content legislation could in fact become public law. It faced a growing tide of anti Japanese sentiment in the United States and a number of Senators who were very intent on passing the Senate version of the "Fair Practices in Automotive Products Act." Because 1984 was a Presidential election year, it seemed likely that the bill would generate much attention in the media and on Capitol Hill. That at least was the hope of the UAW (Packwood, 1984).

Audience Three: Toyota's Dealers and Employees

Toyota prides itself on its relations with its U.S. work force. As Robert McCurry, the senior vice president of Toyota Motor Sales USA observes, "Any automaker who wants to survive, let alone prosper, better have more than just good products. He needs the people, the programs, the dedication, and whatever else it takes to keep the customer happy" (McCurry, 1985, p. 15). In their attempt to develop and foster these qualities, Toyota had implemented such programs as "Toyota Touch," which was designed to cultivate "people skills necessary to build better customer satisfaction," and in turn, "help ensure long-term profitability" (*Toyota Today*, 1985a, p. 7).

The main objectives of commercial product campaigns are to: maintain current users; win over those consumers who are thought to be good prospects but are not using; and persuade some users of competing brands to switch. To achieve these goals,

Toyota had to deal directly with protectionism, not only at a national level, with legislators and the general public, but perhaps more importantly, at the level of American dealerships. Thus, Toyota launched a strategy to inoculate its dealers and workers against the attacks of domestic automakers and their supporters.

In the spring of 1984, Toyota turned to its dealer body and employees, which exceeded 40,000, in an effort to inoculate them against the attacks of protectionists. Pfau and Burgoon (1988, p. 92) explain the inoculation approach in these terms: "The inoculation message strategy is designed to promote resistance against attitude change, deflecting persuasiveness of subsequent attack messages" Toyota used a strategy of resistance in communications directed to its dealers, employees, and select opinion leaders. The purpose was to deflect the persuasiveness of anticipated attacks.

Using publications such as its national dealer magazine, *Toyota Today*, and the special publication, "Washington Report," the automaker raised the specter of attacks so persuasive that the firm's U.S. market share was in jeopardy. At the same time, it provided dealers and employees with the ammunition with which to answer the attacks.

Toyota provided preemptive refutation to five major attacks. The first attack claim was that the Japanese yen and the American dollar are misaligned, giving the Japanese an unfair advantage in pricing. In response, the refutation claims indicated that there is no evidence the Japanese government manipulates its currency to keep prices low; that, if anything, the opposite is true: the government has repeatedly acted to strengthen the yen against the dollar (American International Automobile Dealers Association, 1984). The second attack claim was that Japanese cars exported to the United States carry low price tags because they pay no commodity tax when they leave Japan. The refutation claims in response to this attack argued that, like the U.S. sales tax, the Japanese commodity tax is levied on consumers, as recommended by the GATT agreement ("Washington Report," 1984), and that Japanese exported products are not assessed a commodity tax, nor are U.S. exported products assessed a sales tax, when sold overseas (American International Automobile Dealers Association, 1984).

A third attack claim was that imports cost the U.S. taxes. The rebuttal claims maintained that loss of taxes is a fact of life in international trade, but that the loss is offset by a gain in taxes from selling exports abroad, and that tax burdens on American and Japanese cars sold in the United States is approximately equal (American International Automobile Dealers Association, 1984). The fourth attack claim was that imports cost the United States jobs. In response, the rebuttal claim posited that this attack was misleading because it ignores the many thousands of jobs which are generated by the import automobile industry in the U.nited States ("Washington Report," 1984). The fifth attack claim involved the issue of quotas, that America favors free trade, but the rest of the world is not playing fair. In response, the rebuttal claim argued that the Japanese government imposes no quota or tariff on imported automobiles, making Japan the only major auto-producing country in the world that does not (American International Automobile Dealers Association, 1984).

Finally, Toyota drew attention to the potentially damaging bill, S. 707, encouraging participation in a postcard campaign aimed at members of the Senate. This postcard campaign effort was designed to activate supporters against protectionism, and simultaneously to raise doubts among legislators as to whether S. 707 had the support of their constituents.

Employing the campaign slogan, "This Is One Bill You Can't Afford," Toyota placed bright red and white posters, brochures and displays in dealerships around the country. These displays included preaddressed postcards ready for a sender's signature. The text of the postcard was simple and to the point.

> *Dear Senator:*
>
>   *As an American consumer, I think automobile "domestic content" legislation (S. 707) is a bad idea. Competition in the auto industry is essential to hold down prices, stimulate better quality and provide greater choice to consumers. I don't want to pay hundreds of dollars extra for my next car because Congress has restricted free competition.*
>
>   *I urge you to oppose domestic content legislation.*
>
> *Name:*
>
> *Address:*

This message is designed to persuade the reader, providing counterarguments to the claim that there should be a legislated restriction on new car imports. Some dealerships went one step further and sent handwritten, personalized letters to their state's Senators. The "Washington Report" noted that one New Jersey dealer had called his employees together for a meeting and then had each employee compose such a letter. The intent of the letters was to point out the effects the legislation would have on individuals and families whose livelihoods depended on Toyota dealerships. According to the "Washington Report," other import automakers conducted similar letter-writing campaigns, helping to flood the office of Senators from Oregon, Virginia, New York, Pennsylvania, Maryland, and Illinois. By the time the Senate Committee on Commerce, Science, and Transportation began hearings on S. 707 in May, 1984, more than 300,000 signed postcards had arrived at Senate offices on Capitol Hill ("Dealers and Consumers Unite . . . ", 1984). While supporters of S. 707 referred to it as a "jobs bill," Toyota chose to reposition it as an "anticonsumer bill" ("Dealers and Consumers Unite . . . ", 1984), as yet another attempt to promote protectionism.

In addition to the postcard and letter-writing strategies, more than 400 Toyota dealers went to Capitol Hill in mid-May to attend the seventh annual American International Automotive Congress, sponsored by the American International Automobile Dealers Association. The Washington-based trade association representing import auto dealers of all makes, had actively opposed both H.R. 1234 and S. 707. Its representatives had testified numerous times against domestic content legislation. The annual Congress gave the Toyota dealers the opportunity to meet face-to-face with lawmakers from their home states—nearly all 50 were represented—and express their opposition to domestic content legislation ("AIADA Congress . . . ", 1984). One of the keynote speeches at the three-day meeting was delivered by Senator Bob Packwood, whose committee had jurisdiction over S. 707.

Toyota continued to use its dealers, employees, and employee publications to generate support for its causes, motivating them to participate in the political process when trade issues are raised. The February, 1986 issue of *Toyota Today* warned the Toyota dealers of potential persuasiveness of the protectionist attacks, and told them explicitly how they could make an impact.

> *Become personally involved. Protectionists are dedicated and persistent. Their efforts must be matched by those with a direct, personal stake in free trade.*
> *Pay a call to the district offices of your senators and representatives when they are in the district. Don't settle for talking to an aide. You are an important businessman in the community who deals with the public daily; the member will welcome your views.*
> *Be well briefed on the issue, and armed with persuasion information.*
> *Write your senators and representatives as well. Enclose articles that express your viewpoint.*
> *Become active in political campaigns. Activity equals Access equals Influence (p. 17).*

Toyota also produced a report titled, "This Is Toyota U.S.A.," which emphasized the positive economic and social impact that Toyota Motor Sales has in this country (*Toyota Today*, 1985a). The "Washington Report," in fact, was changed from a special quarterly publication to a regular feature in the monthly dealer national dealer magazine, *Toyota Today*.

In March, 1985, President Reagan allowed Japanese automakers to raise the ceiling on import quotas 24.3 percent to 2.3 million vehicles a year (Chira, 1985a). The very same day, the Senate passed a resolution condemning Japan's "unfair" trade practices by a vote of 92 to 0 (Farnsworth, 1985). Two days earlier, Senator John Chafee, who had been a staunch opponent of S. 707, proposed legislation to bar the Japanese from selling telecommunications equipment in the United States until Japan fully opened its own market to similar American-made equipment. Other legislation had been introduced that called for a 20 percent surcharge on all Japanese imports (Farnsworth, 1985). In the months and years to follow, the voluntary restraints continued, the quota ceiling was raised, and more protectionist bills were introduced.

Illustrating the public opinion and public image challenge facing the Japanese import automobile industry is a Fall, 1985, *Los Angeles Times/Yomiuri Shimbun* (Japan's largest newspaper) poll, which indicated that most Americans believed that "trade with Japan is doing more harm than good" (Sing, 1985). The survey reveals a major irony involving the trade situation. Most Americans strongly support protectionism even though they do not believe it will work.

An Update on the Protectionist Debate and Toyota's Campaigns

While Toyota's efforts to influence Capitol Hill have been successful, it is clear that campaigners need to do a better job of influencing the American public. Events of the early 1990s seem to follow an interesting parallel to those of the early 1980s. In both cases, the United States was mired in recession, and domestic automakers were suffering from record losses. In the most recent discussion of U.S.-Japan trade, both sides have found ample photo opportunities and mass media forums to make their points. Scenes of individuals smashing Japanese cars have begun to reappear with frequency, and *Time* magazine made the U.S.-Japan standoff its cover story for February 10, 1992.

General Motors' Chairman Robert C. Stempel asserts that the U.S.-Japanese war of words should stop, allowing the marketplace to be the battlefield, but also adding:

> *U.S.-owned auto plants buy about 97 percent of their parts from U.S. suppliers, versus less than 50 percent for foreign-owned auto plants in the United States. The lower domestic content of the transplants resulted in the loss of nearly 125,000 U.S. supplier jobs ("U.S., Japan Should End Name-calling," 1992, p. C-3).*

Thus, the message remains the same: American jobs are being lost.

In response, Toyota changed its product promotion campaign. For example, some newspaper advertisements for the 1992 Camry include a picture of the car with the words, "Made in Kentucky," stamped across the side of the car. This is an obvious attempt to concisely counterargue the claims carried over free media concerning unfair trade practices on the part of Japanese firms, and their impact on American jobs. American automobile ads, on the other hand, are worded to remind consumers to make explicit comparisons between U.S.-made and foreign-made cars. Dodge and Plymouth, for example, launched comparative advertisements that argue that their low-price models have more room, more power, a superior warranty, and more safety features than Honda Civic.

Some other foreign automakers have increased the percentage of U.S.-made parts in their cars. Mazda, for example, plans to use 75 percent U.S.-made parts in their 1993 626 sedan and MX-6 coupe, making it the *first* Japanese car line to be classified as "domestic" (*Atlanta Journal & Constitution*, 1992, p. S-6). The free media provided a great deal of coverage of this event.

FEEDBACK

Read this excerpt from *The Atlanta Journal & Constitution* and respond to the following questions.

"Angry Georgia peanut farmers say they could lose up to $50 million this year because of President Bush's decision Friday to allow 100 million pounds of peanuts to be imported by July 31.

'There's absolutely no foundation or justification for doing that,' said Billy Griggs, 44, a Unadilla peanut farmer and vice chairman of the Georgia Peanut Commission.

'There's plenty of peanuts in the United States. I'm afraid that the direction they're taking is not based on sound logic and economics. It's based purely on politics.'

The action marks only the second time since 1953 that the import level has been raised for peanuts, which are governed by a strict quota system limiting production (Coady, 1991, p. A-1)."

1. How is this similar to the American automakers' campaign against Toyota?
2. What would you predict to be the bolstering, attack, and refutation messages used in this campaign?
3. What inoculation strategies could foreign peanut growers use in response?

Conclusion

In commercial campaigns, the interconnectedness of a firm's marketing and public relations' efforts is evident, with this campaign as striking evidence of the need to address important political leaders, the general public, and supporters. This case illustrates how commercial organizations use persuasive campaigns to protect their economic interests. The attacks on Japanese businesses and their success continue today. In response, Toyota and other Japanese companies continue to promote their products and articulate their point-of-view, attempting to militate the effectiveness of attacks leveled against them before the Congress and the American public, while simultaneously trying to inoculate supporters.

Suggestions for Further Reading

Gorn, G. J. (1982). The effects of music in advertising on choice behavior: A classical conditioning approach. *Journal of Marketing, 46,* 94–101.

Keller, K. L. (1987). Memory factors in advertising: The effect of advertising retrieval cues on brand evaluations. *Journal of Consumer Research, 14,* 316–333.

McCracken, G. (1986). Culture and consumption: A theoretical account of the structure and movement of the cultural meaning of consumer goods. *Journal of Consumer Research, 13,* 71–84.

Park, C. W., Easwar, S. I., and Smith, D. C. (1989). The effects of situational factors on in-store grocery shopping behavior: The role of store environment and time available for shopping. *Journal of Consumer Research, 15,* 422–433.

Rook, D. W. (1987). The buying impulse. *Journal of Consumer Research, 14,* 189–199.

Political Campaigns

On the eve of the 1990 elections an unpracticed observer might have supposed that the Washington landscape was about to be massively rearranged. Virtually every survey found voters "mad as hell." [Despite what was characterized as "record levels of dissatisfaction with congressional incumbents"] . . . the elections of 1990 changed the composition of Congress hardly at all. In the House 391 of 406 incumbents running for reelection were returned. . . In the Senate. . . , only one incumbent, Rudy Boschwitz (R,MN) met defeat [at the hands of challenger Paul Wellstone] . . .
—POLITICAL SCIENTIST W. WAYNE SHANNON
(SHANNON, 1991, P. 12)

Bill Hillsman and friends created the Wellstone TV ads which set a new standard for political advertising in Minnesota and perhaps in the nation.
—REPORTER DENNIS J. MCGRATH
(MCGRATH, 1990, P. 17A)

The hip, quirky, self-mocking style of Hillsman's ads [on behalf of Paul Wellstone] is clearly a product of the David Letterman generation. Most political ads, by contrast, seem stuck in the 1970s. And the Hillsman style is bound to become more popular, especially among long-shot challengers with little to lose. . . .
—POLITICAL ADVERTISING SPECIALIST M. ADAM GOODMAN
(MITCHELL, 1990, P. 62)

Chapters 12 through 14 are designed to provide an in-depth look at specific campaigns. Examples were selected which illustrate the concepts, theories, and strategies developed in previous chapters of the book. Whereas Chapters 12 and 14 focus on commercial and social action campaigns, respectively, this chapter examines the political campaign involving Republican incumbent Rudy Boschwitz and Democratic challenger Paul Wellstone for the U. S. Senate in Minnesota in 1990. This campaign is particularly interesting, in part because a little-known challenger upset a popular incumbent (no small feat in light of the overwhelming incumbent successes during the 1990 elections), and in part because of the Wellstone advertising, which constitutes a departure from existing genres, not so much in its strategy, but in its style.

This chapter will overview the dominant characteristics of contemporary political campaigns, and then provide an in-depth look at the 1990 Wellstone campaign. The chapter will address the questions posed in Table 13–1.

Characteristics of Contemporary Political Campaigns

Because all persuasive communication campaigns by their very nature seek to influence receivers, whether to shape, change, or in some way reinforce attitudes and behaviors, the three genres of campaigns, commercial, political, and social action, have much in common. However, there are differences as well, which affect potential strategies.

Unique Features of Political Campaigns

Three unique features distinguish political campaigns from commercial or social action campaigns. The first difference is that political campaigns are more person-oriented. This stems from the very nature of representative politics. While voters sometimes directly decide policy questions (e.g., they vote yes or no on a bond issue or referendum), it is far more common for voters to elect individuals who will decide such things. Thus, most political campaigns are designed to promote a selection of one person over one or more opponents. By contrast, commercial campaigns concern the selection of goods and services, and most social action campaigns involve social outcomes.

Not surprisingly, research about voter decision criteria in elections suggests the primacy of character over issue content (Miller, 1990; Miller, Wallenburg, Malanchuk, 1986; Wattenburg, 1991). This means that ". . . it is the personal characteristics of the nominee that have the greatest potentiality for affecting election outcomes" (Asher, 1980, p. 139). An election involves choices about people, and in this context, it would be expected that candidate personality affects that choice. Doris Graber's research

TABLE 13–1 Basic Questions about Political Campaigns

1. What are the unique features that distinguish political from commercial and social action campaigns?
2. How are contemporary political campaigns different from their counterparts of one to two decades ago?
3. What are the possible implications of these changes in the nature of political campaigns for American democracy?
4. How did the Wellstone campaign employ formative research in determining its goals and approach?
5. How did circumstances dictate the approach of the Wellstone campaign?
6. What are contrasts, and what role did they play in Wellstone advertising?
7. In what way was Wellstone's television advertising unique?
8. Do you think Wellstone's advertising will set a new standard for political campaigns of the 1990s?

confirms this thesis. She (1980, p. 184) finds that: "Overall, three out of four answers people give when asked . . . why they would vote or refrain from voting for a certain candidate concern personality traits."

The second unique characteristic of political campaigns is that their time frame is sharply defined, at least in terms of a definitive end point. Although all campaigns operate over some time frame, commercial and social action campaigns *can* take as long as they need to achieve their objectives. By contrast, political campaigns have until election day to accomplish their goals. Tony Schwartz called politics ". . . the most task-oriented area of advertising that ever existed" (cited in Moyers, 1984). Using the language of product commercials, Schwartz characterized elections as, "a one-day sale, in which every customer is allowed in the store for one or two minutes on that day, and where [the political campaigner] has to sell a majority or plurality on that day or [they] are out of business" (cited in Moyers, 1984).

The point is that all political campaigns culminate on some specified day, at least in terms of their primary objective which is to elect a candidate to some office. Once that objective is met, candidates are in a position to undertake further campaigns, utilizing many of the same techniques employed previously. For example, candidates might continue to employ campaign advisors, polling, and media consultants in an effort to mobilize public opinion in support of an upcoming legislative initiative or even to pave the way for the next electoral cycle. Sidney Blumenthal (1982) character-izes these efforts as constituting "the permanent campaign," precisely because candi-dates' efforts to shape public opinion are ongoing in contemporary politics. But, these are new campaigns, involving different objectives.

Because political campaigns are more limited in time, their communication activi-ties are more compressed than in commercial or social action campaigns. Indeed, as election day approaches, media are dominated by political campaign communication, in terms of advertising, news, and other public interest features.

The third way in which political campaigns differ from their commercial and social action counterparts is that they can turn to the entire range of communication modalities. As we indicated in Chapter 9, more visible national and state political campaigns possess the legitimacy to draw large crowds to speeches, secure an audience with a potential supporter, or attract mass media news coverage of such events as speeches, debates, and other campaign activities. By contrast, commercial campaigns almost always rely on paid communication and social action campaigns usually must settle for volunteer efforts in conjunction with public service announcements in order to influence receivers.

Changes in Political Campaigns

Technology has fundamentally altered the nature of political campaigns. First television, and then computers, have left their imprint on campaigns, fundamentally affecting the manner in which candidates communicate to voters, and therefore changing the very nature of political campaigning.

Television has come a long way from its primitive beginning. Today, political campaigns for major offices rely on television as the primary conduit of communication. Theodore White (1982, p. 165), reflecting on the evolution of presidential campaigning from 1952 to 1980, observes: "American politics and television are now so completely locked together that it is impossible to tell the story of one without the other." Michael J. Robinson (1981, pp. 177–178) notes the same development. "From the last dozen years, the media have become to campaign theory what sex has been to clinical psychiatry—the first and foremost factor analyzed."

These new technologies have altered the way that candidates communicate via available modalities, as we explained in detail in Chapters 9 and 10. Television has been responsible for most of the changes.

Television has affected traditional speech-making, producing more abbreviated oral discourse, designed to elicit sound bites, consisting of claims, supported by nothing more than an anecdote or visual (Jamieson, 1988). Campaigners craft catchy phrases in candidate speeches, anticipating that the one-liners will attract television news coverage, thus reaching a national audience. In addition, the constant focus on a broad national audience places a premium on consistency, which is achieved through repetition of a basic themes in all campaign communication (Patterson and Davis, 1985). Finally, television is responsible for a "new eloquence," featuring more casual and intimate communication, epitomized by the candidate's relational messages which stress nonverbal cues (Jamieson, 1988).

These changes epitomize all political speech-making, whether in the form of traditional stump speeches or candidate debates (Jamieson, 1988; Jamieson and Birdsell, 1988). The changes carry serious implications for political communication. They produce oversimplification of issue content (Kymlicka and Matthews, 1988), more emphasis in candidate communication on problems, which can be depicted visually, as opposed to solutions to problems, which cannot (Hellweg, Pfau, and Brydon, 1991), and greater potential for candidates to mislead receivers (Jamieson, 1988).

Television has also changed the nature of the news coverage of political campaigns. Television news coverage offers little more than "a headline service," featuring short segments which lack context or explanation (Graber, 1990; Halberstam, 1981). In addition, television news places a premium on stories that can be captured via pictures, which undervalues issue content because it requires verbal explanation and overvalues staged campaign events precisely because they contain more visual potential (Boorstein, 1975; Combs, 1980; Owen, 1991). Finally, television news has a demonstrated bias for the dramatic, which results in overemphasis on the "horse race," the contest between the candidates, much to the detriment of substantive content (Patterson, 1980).

However, the most significant change in political campaign communication involves television advertising. Television spots have emerged as the dominant communication modality in the more visible campaigns, driving candidate speeches, debates, and news (Kern, 1989). Candidate advertising is the primary vehicle that campaigners use to establish candidate name identification (Mann, 1984), communicate candidate image (Kern, 1989), posit candidate positions (Just et al., 1990), and compare/contrast candidates and their opponents (Pfau and Kenski, 1990). The role of the other communication modalities is reinforcement, insuring that all candidate communication is focused on the basic content contained in the television advertising. Such is the nature of "the new mass media election" (Kern, 1991).

In addition, the nature of political spots themselves has changed. Political practitioners have adopted the techniques employed in commercial advertising, where a premium is placed on affect (Kern, 1991). Although most political ads still contain substantive content, which is communicated via the audio track, they are also rich in affect, which is designed to trigger an emotional response to the candidate (Kern, 1989). In addition, attack spots are viewed as an integral strategic option for all candidates but prohibitive front runners (Pfau and Kenski, 1990).

In some ways the interpersonal communication modality has been relatively unaffected by the new technologies. Certainly the role of person-to-person contact remains an important source of influence in political campaigns, particularly at state and local levels (Kaid, 1977). Less visible, small budget campaigns must rely heavily on grassroots efforts, featuring door-to-door canvassing and small social gatherings to reach voters. Further, based on the potential availability of volunteers [MacWilliams, Burns, Greer and Associates, (1988a) estimate that, if asked, about 15 percent of voters would volunteer to work during a political campaign], and given the evidence by Kingdon (cited in Chaffee, 1981) and Greenberg (1975) of rather frequent, often successful, person-to-person influence attempts, all campaigners are advised to fully exploit all available opportunities for personal contact with voters (MacWilliams, Burns, Greer and Associates, 1988b).

However, in other ways, the computer has revolutionized the interpersonal modality. The computer enables modern campaigners to target specific individuals for personalized direct mail and telephone appeals (Armstrong, 1988; Frantzich, 1989). Thus, it is now possible to make what seem to be personalized appeals to specific receivers in order to exercise influence and/or solicit campaign funds.

Campaign Analysis: The 1990 Wellstone Senate Campaign

During his 12 years of service as a Republican Senator from Minnesota, Rudy Boschwitz had established himself as invulnerable to defeat. He won his second term in 1984 with 58 percent of the vote, had amassed $7.3 million in campaign contribu-

---

FEEDBACK

Consider two campaigns for political office in your area: one for the U. S. Senate seat from your state and the other for a seat on the City Council or Commission. How do these campaigns differ in terms of:

1. The role that formative research plays?
2. Use of available communication modalities?
3. Impact of candidate personality, as opposed to political party identification and issues?
4. The role and impact of candidate advertising?

tions to seal his reelection for a third term, and "entered the 1990 campaign as the state's most popular politician" in either political party ("Republican's Net Loss," 1990).

Moreover, Boschwitz faced an opponent, who was a political unknown, who was inexperienced in campaign politics, who lacked the financial resources to undertake a campaign for major office, and who defined himself as "a traditional liberal" (the "kiss of death" to recent Democratic candidates for Senate and President) (Johnson, 1990). Paul Wellstone, a political science professor at Carleton College, was given absolutely no chance to unseat the Republican incumbent. Political experts said he "was tilting at windmills" (Johnson, 1990, p. 14).

During an era in which incumbents' reelections are virtually assured, and where Boschwitz appeared so strongly positioned, how was Wellstone able to pull off one of the most surprising upsets in recent years? There is no question that part of the answer lies in unique circumstances surrounding Minnesota politics during the 1990 campaign, and that part of the answer lies in the ineptitude of the Boschwitz campaign. However, most observers maintain that the Wellstone campaign itself is the most important reason why he was able to unseat Boschwitz in 1990 (McGrath, 1990).

The rest of this chapter will scrutinize the 1990 Wellstone campaign. The Wellstone campaign was chosen as the focus of this chapter because it exemplifies so many of the concepts, theories and strategies that we have developed in this text, and because it broke new ground in political advertising. This analysis is based on published accounts and two days of personal interviews conducted with the Wellstone campaign "braintrust" during April 1991.

Formative Research Suggests Overall Approach

The Wellstone campaign began in his hometown of Northfield on April 24, 1989. "Over the next year and a half, he built a network of volunteers and supporters who helped him capture the DFL [Democratic Farmer-Labor Party] endorsement" (McGrath, 1990, p. 16A). After winning the primary, insuring the nomination as DFL candidate for the Senate, the Wellstone campaign took a hard look at available data and their circumstances in preparation for the general election campaign.

The data suggested the enormity of the task ahead. Wellstone started the general election campaign with a mere 17 percent name recognition, despite the attention generated during his campaign for the nomination. By contrast, Boschwitz enjoyed a 98 percent name recognition (Hillsman, 1991). Even more disturbing was the fact that Boschwitz's job approval ratings were well in excess of 70 percent, "which were the highest of any politician [regardless of political party] in the state" (Hillsman, 1991).

On the other hand, the data showed that most people did not really know what Boschwitz stood for. As Bill Hillsman (1991), the man in charge of creating Wellstone's advertising, explained:

When you investigate, you find out that people really think he's [Boschwitz's] a good guy. But as a legislator? It's like that thought never entered their minds. He was a good guy, he wore plaid shirts . . . and he had great constituency service. . . . But when it came down to votes, nobody knew what he had voted on for 12 years.

The data explained the difficult circumstances the Wellstone campaign faced on the eve of the campaign. The campaign was rich in terms of committed people, but poor as a church mouse in terms of financial resources.

The "senior staff" of the Wellstone campaign was comprised mainly of people in their twenties and thirties, "most of whom are barely out of college, few of whom have worked in a general election campaign" (McGrath, 1991, p. 17A). They were assisted at the grass roots by an army of volunteers, drawn from people who were disproportionately young, well-educated, female and/or racial minority, and who were deeply committed to the candidate and his ideals.

But, the Wellstone campaign lacked sufficient funds to run a traditional race. The campaign sought seed money from wealthy individuals and the Democratic Senatorial Campaign Committee. It took PAC monies, but only from those with a Minnesota connection (McGrath, 1990). Wellstone personally loathed appeals for funds, preferring to talk about issues as opposed to why individuals or groups should contribute to the campaign. The financial troubles were compounded by the early poll results, which suggested little possibility of unseating Boschwitz. As McGrath notes, ". . . what matters most are poll results and fund-raising ability. These people like to back winners. Convince them that you can win and they'll help make that happen with fat checks" (1990, p. 16A).

All together, the Wellstone campaign raised and spent about $1 million, with most of it coming in during the last two months of the campaign, in stark contrast with the Boschwitz campaign, which amassed close to $8 million (Johnson, 1990). As a result, the Wellstone campaign never had enough money. It scrimped on everything from needed equipment to campaign communication. As McGrath recounts:

> *The campaign gets most of the things it needs, but never enough of them. The St. Paul [campaign] headquarters has a fax machine, but the furniture is second- or third-hand, including a legless desk and a chair whose armrest drags on the floor. Blackshaw [John Blackshaw, the campaign manager] has a car phone, finally, but no business cards. (He explains that all his cards went into ads.] . . . To get phones installed, campaign workers reach into their own pockets to make deposits or borrow from friends . . . More than once, printers refuse to publish another piece of literature until overdue bills are paid.*

The available data and the circumstances suggested specific goals, target audiences, as well as the nature of the campaign. The data suggested three overriding, central objectives for the campaign. First, the campaign had to boost name identification. Hillsman (1991), pointing to the 17 versus 98 percent disparity in name recognition between the candidates, explained how easy, and yet tough, this would be.

> *I knew these numbers would jump as soon as the campaign started . . . Name awareness is solved by screen time; lots of screen time. The flip side is that you're never going to get*

Boschwitz's name recognition to drop; that's not something you have any control over and you also don't have enough money.

Second, the campaign had to establish a positive image for Wellstone, and third, the campaign had to simultaneously "chip away at Boschwitz's job approval rating." These objectives are treated as flip sides of the same coin because the campaign had to achieve both, and given limited resources, had to do it using an integrated communication's strategy.

These twin goals are difficult to achieve, especially with a limited campaign budget. Yet, this campaign, just like any other in which a relatively unknown candidate takes on a known and well-liked opponent, had to accomplish both objectives or lose. Under these circumstances, the campaign must drive up their candidate's positives and their opponent's negatives. As Hillsman (1991) put it, ".". . you know that with a 70 percent approval rating [for the opponent], you're not going to win . . . "

In order to achieve both objectives with limited resources, the campaign required a carefully conceived, tightly coordinated communication's effort in addition to the unwitting cooperation of their opponent. As it turned out, they got both.

The Wellstone campaign selected as its overriding theme that the candidate "represented the people that had been left out of the decision-making loop for the entire decade of the 1980s; people that were never given a seat at the decision-making table" (Forciea, 1991). The theme employed a "simple contrast," one of Hillsman's notions about political campaigns. By grounding their campaign theme in a contrast, the campaigners put themselves in the optimally efficient position to utilize dual-sided campaign messages, which are designed so that positive information about the candidate simultaneously carries negative information about their opponent, and vice-versa.

Conventional wisdom dictates that campaigners build up their candidate's positives before attacking in an effort to drive up the opponent's negatives (Pfau and Kenski, 1990). This approach, however, is costly, requiring two separate communication tracks. The Wellstone campaign, in employing contrasts, would design all communication to accomplish both objectives simultaneously, thus optimizing its scarce financial resources. The campaign designed a coordinated communication's effort, in which all of Wellstone's messages, whether in speeches, debates, or advertising, focused on this central theme.

As we indicated, the success of this strategy also requires the unwitting cooperation of the opponent. If the opponent goes on the attack, thus driving up your candidate's negatives, then the strategy will usually fall short. The Wellstone campaign was aware of this risk. In August, Boschwitz initiated a television blitz, running $300,000 of spots in a two-day period. Wellstone feared that this might be a preemptive strike, comparable to what Bush did to Dukakis in the 1988 presidential campaign. He mused: "He's going to try to end it in the next couple of weeks is what he's trying to do" (cited in McGrath, 1990, p. 16A).

Instead of an attack on Wellstone, the Boschwitz television blitz involved a series of "feel-good" spots designed to enhance his positives, already unusually high. The Wellstone campaign breathed a collective sigh of relief. Forciea, who understood that the campaign had just dodged a bullet, commented:

I cannot believe he's not snuffing this thing out right now. This megamillion-dollar outfit is choosing not to bang on us. I sense a high degree of overconfidence. If this race ever tightens up and we win, it will be because of this (cited in McGrath, 1990, p. 16A).

The Wellstone campaign targeted three key audiences, though it lacked the financial resources to conduct the polling and hire the specialized media to target more precisely. Journalist Dennis McGrath (1991) explained their limited targeting this way: "They had the brains to target audiences, but they simply didn't have the resources of the typical political campaign." Pat Forciea (1991) disputed this claim, arguing that the campaign "targeted carefully."

The Wellstone campaign targeted Twin City suburban voters, who Forciea described as "crucial to any Democrat's chance for winning a state-wide election" in Minnesota. He characterized suburban voters as "yuppies," but with concerns about children's issues and the environment, areas that tie nicely to Wellstone's strengths and Boschwitz's weakness, contribute to the campaign's overall theme, and thus appear perfect for framing as contrasts. The campaign also targeted the 8th congressional district in northeast Minnesota. Because the district contains "the largest block of Democrats" in the state, Forciea observed that, "If a Democrat is going to win, he or she must get 60 to 65 percent of the vote [Wellstone got 70 percent]" (Forciea, 1991). Finally, they targeted the inner cities of Minneapolis and St. Paul.

Campaign Strategies

The scarcity of resources dictated strategic options for the campaign. The Wellstone campaign capitalized on its strengths and compensated for its weaknesses. It enjoyed an abundance of dedicated volunteers, and it suffered a shortage of monies which is essential for today's media-driven campaigns, so it stressed person-to-person contact wherever possible, but especially for its targeted audiences.

Use of Volunteers

The campaign employed direct mail and personal appearances of the candidate and volunteers to reach suburban voters, and it relied heavily on its active pool of volunteers in northeastern Minnesota and the Minneapolis and St. Paul inner cities. Also, the candidate made weekly visits to the northeastern Iron Range throughout the campaign to appeal for votes and to "cement labor support" (McGrath, 1990).

FEEDBACK

The Wellstone campaign was poor as a church mouse in financial resources.

    1. Under these circumstances, what would you recommend that the campaign do in order to compensate?

    2. Would you employ attack advertising against Boschwitz? Why or why not?

Wellstone's volunteers played an important role in campaign communication. McGrath (1990, p. 20A) observed that the campaign employed dozens of phone banks, in all making more than 300,000 telephone calls to prospective voters during the final weeks of the campaign. In addition, volunteers constructed as well as distributed thousands of lawn signs.

Liz Borg, campaign field director, headed up the volunteer effort. She initially recruited, and then continued to motivate and direct the campaign's field organizers, each of whom in turn oversaw volunteers in their respective areas (McGrath, 1990, p. 19A). This was an ongoing effort. McGrath (1990, p. 19A) noted that, "Borg constantly frets about her rural staffers and tries to talk to them two or three times a day on the phone to make them feel included. But she also polices them, making sure they don't neglect their duties."

The Wellstone campaign utilized its volunteers in routine and novel ways. As an example of the latter, the campaign made extensive use of human billboards. Lacking funds to rent fixed billboard space, the campaign asked volunteers to hold banners and posters at the most traveled traffic spots throughout the Twin Cities during the morning and evening rush hours (McGrath, 1990).

Some of the banners were impressive in their size, like the four foot by eight foot banner held on overpasses in clear sight of commuters who traveled the city's interstates. Borg insisted that "the banners have more impact than billboards," explaining that: "The drivers are thinking, 'who would get up at 7 in the morning to do this? They must really like this guy.' We want people to think there are campaigners all over the place" (McGrath, 1990, p. 20A).

Turning the Tables

We previously explained how the Wellstone campaign employed contrasts to compensate for its lack of funds. As part of this approach, the campaign took Boschwitz's strength, his financial advantage, and turned it into a liability. The strategy was a by-product of the broader campaign theme, that Wellstone stands for the interests of those people who have been excluded from decision-making. Forciea (1991) explained the origins of this contrast:

I had felt that he [Boschwitz] represented much of what people disliked about the 1980's and was vulnerable. He spent a whole lot of time protecting the interests of the wealthy, whether it be on tax issues or budgetary issues. He spent tremendous time on fund-raising and rewarding contributors with access that common people just don't get.

The Wellstone campaign decided to make Boschwitz's strength, his ability to purchase much more television time, a major campaign issue. Bill Hillsman, in charge of advertising for Wellstone, explained this way (1991):

Early on you learn that you want to take someone's strength and use it against them. And we knew that Boschwitz was going to be on television way more than we could ever afford to be. The trick is to figure out a way that every time he's on TV it works against him.

The Wellstone campaign succeeded in turning the tables on Boschwitz's strength, making it a liability. They made money a fairness issue, charging that Boschwitz was trying to buy the election (Hillsman, 1991). The Wellstone campaign attempted to use information that was already planted in the minds of voters (the Boschwitz campaign's financial position had received ample mass media coverage prior to the general election campaign), and as the basis for their attack. This is a classic illustration of Schwartz's notion of partipulation, and it worked. As a result of the Wellstone attack, every time people saw Boschwitz in a television spot, it played right into an established mental set. Hillsman described the thinking of viewers: "This is the third time in the last half hour that I've seen one of his commercials. Dang right he's trying to buy the election" (1991).

Consistency of Message

Lacking sufficient finances, the Wellstone campaign had to emphasize a limited number of points, stressing each over and over again. Patrick Forciea (1991) admits: "I'm a big believer in repetition." The campaign tried to take a few simple messages and stress them in speeches, debates, television spots, and so forth (Forciea, 1991). As Forciea explained:

> *Consistency was key. People were only exposed to Paul over two months, September and October, so we made sure they were basically hearing the same things, over and over, regardless of the media context. We didn't have the luxury of doing it any other way.*

Thus, the insider-outsider theme was the focal point of the campaign's advertising, and was a major charge in the candidate's debate with Boschwitz. Debate advisor David Lillehaug, who also coached Walter Mondale in his 1984 presidential debates against Ronald Reagan, recommended this focus in the debate. "I want you to ring the anti-incumbency bell every time you can. If you ring the bell every 30 seconds, then the debate will be a success" (cited in McGrath, 1990, p. 18A). This also insured subsequent repetition of this basic theme on television news coverage, which followed up on the sound bites produced in the debate (Lillehaug, 1991).

Adaptation to Television

Another point that Lillehaug stressed in preparation for the televised debates, and that Hillsman wrestled with in producing the campaign's television advertising, was the speaking style of the candidate. Wellstone, like Dukakis in the 1988 presidential race, was an excellent orator, capable of rousing large audiences with an enthusiastic style. That style features a loud speaking voice and animated gestures and expressions.

We previously indicated that television requires a softer and more casual communication style, more akin to the interpersonal context. Lillehaug had observed Wellstone in his primary debate and was unimpressed. ". . . [I]t was the most horrible political television I've ever seen," he explained. "They started yelling and gesticulating frantically, and it just made them look like a couple of kids you'd want to throw out of the house" (Lillehaug, 1991).

Wellstone's oratorical style was far too hot, "completely counterproductive on television" (Lillehaug, 1991). "So, the first task was to tone Wellstone down, thus making him much more acceptable in people's living rooms, without robbing him of all emotion" (Lillehaug, 1991). At the same time, Lillehaug coached the candidate to pare down his speech, condensing each point to a few sentences, tailored to television news sound bites (McGrath, 1990). With coaching, Wellstone was able to both tone down his rhetoric, and simplify it, while still maintaining what Hillsman (1991) called, an "honest energy."

Television Advertising

We previously indicated that television advertising drives the communication of contemporary political campaigns. Despite inadequate finances, this was no less true of the 1990 Wellstone campaign. Indeed, because the campaign lacked sufficient funds, the advertising had to be innovative in order to compensate. It was!

Approach to Advertising

Bill Hillsman assembled an advertising team from the Twin Cities area, producing Wellstone's television advertising using his own "free-lance ad shop," North Woods Advertising (Mitchell, 1990). Wellstone, Forciea, and even Hillsman were nervous about their rather unorthodox approach to political spot advertising (Forciea, 1991). Nonetheless, they also recognized limitations of more traditional approaches.

Hillsman (1991) believed that the traditional approach was inappropriate. He termed that approach the "hammer the message home school," in the tradition of Rosser Reeves. It annoys the viewer, thus capturing their attention (Hillsman, 1991). And, because so many candidates employ the approach, their television spots all look alike, and distinctiveness is lost (Hillsman, 1991).

Hillsman prefers the British approach to advertising, which is more subtle. He argued that, "They aren't brazen like American ads; they don't come right out and say, 'buy me.' To the contrary, they employ humor and anecdote to make people feel good about the advertisement, thus making them feel good about using the product or supporting the candidate" (Hillsman, 1991). This "feel good" approach to advertising has become increasingly popular in the commercial sector, as we indicated in Chapters 5 and 10.

Hillsman (1991) justified the approach as appropriate for the cash-strapped Wellstone campaign, reasoning, ". . . if people want to watch your commercials, or at least don't want to tune them out, doesn't it stand to reason that you can spend less media dollars because you don't have to bang the stuff into an unreceptive subconscious?" His approach was grounded in subtle humor, and in what political advertising specialist, M. Adam Goodman (cited in Mitchell, 1990, p. 62) termed a "hip, quirky, self-mocking style," "clearly a product of the David Letterman generation." The spots employed humor. Hillsman said that, "We made people smile, and that's no small trick in politics these days" (cited in Johnson, 1990). Journalist Russell Mitchell (1990, p. 62) confirms that political spots rarely use humor, which consultants shy away from because it's too "undignified," "flippant," and "weird" (1990, p. 14).

Bolstering Spot

The first Hillsman spot was designed to introduce Wellstone to voters, but to do so in a distinctive way, thus insuring the maximum penetration for a limited run, and to simultaneously hit on the basic contrast involving campaign funds. The spot, called "Fast-Paced Paul," ran in September (see Figure 13–1), just before the DFL primary election, but was aimed at Boschwitz. "Fast-Paced Paul" stressed the "personal side of Wellstone–likable, caring, family man" (McGrath, 1990, p. 17A).

In "Fast-Paced Paul," the candidate explains that, unlike his opponent, he doesn't have $6-million to spend for television ads, so "I'm going to have to talk fast." McGrath describes the spot:

> *He races in front of the camera, moving from scene to scene showing his family, his modest home, the farm where his son and daughter-in-law live. His pace accelerates until he's literally running past the camera. Then he jumps onto the trademark campaign bus, which speeds away (1990, p. 17A).*

Wellstone also crams information about his personal background and positions on issues into the 30-second spot (Mitchell, 1990). During the filming of the spot,

FIGURE 13–1 "Fast-Paced Paul" Introduces the Candidate to Minnesota Voters

Source: Courtesy of North Woods Advertising.

Wellstone was not told how the ad eventually would be edited into a coherent spot (McGrath, 1990). "Hillsman was afraid he wouldn't approve," because the style of the spot is more than unconventional, it borders on being plain silly (McGrath, 1990, p. 17A). Even Forciea held the spot for 72-hours before running it, nervous about how people would react to it (Forciea, 1991).

Nonetheless, the spot worked, catapulting Wellstone to the victory in the primary, setting the tone for the general election campaign, and eventually winning national awards for creativity in political advertising (Forciea, 1991).

Attack Spots

Most of the other Wellstone television spots are accurately categorized as attack messages, but were structured as contrasts. Each spot simultaneously communicated negative information about Boschwitz, the flip side of which featured positive information about Wellstone. Like the introductory message described above, the attack spots were subtle. They employed humor, packaged in an unorthodox style. But, they were hard-hitting. As Hillsman (1991) admitted: ". . . we brutalized him on some things," but did it in such a way that people didn't realize the negative thrust of the ads. "We achieved the same purpose [as with a traditional negative ad], but without letting everyone know we were slashing someone to death" (Hillsman, 1991).

What the Wellstone ads did was to positively violate viewer expectations. Expectancy theory (Burgoon and Miller, 1985) offers a theoretical rubric to explain the influence of the Wellstone attack ads. Expectancy theory posits that people develop norms and expectations about language use, particularly its intensity. If source language intensity conforms to receiver expectations, it exerts very little impact on their attitudes. By contrast, if communicator language intensity violates receiver expectations, it triggers a significant impact on their attitudes, which can be positive or negative, thus either "facilitating" or "inhibiting" communicator influence (Burgoon and Miller, 1985).

As we indicated, the initial focus of expectancy theory is language intensity, with specific supporting research drawn from the public speaking context. However, Burgoon and Miller (1985) describe the theory as robust, suggesting broader applications. One such application involves the stylistic intensity of attack spots.

We have previously documented the increasing incidence of attack spots in contemporary political campaigns (Kern, 1989; Pfau and Kenski, 1990). In addition, these spots are remarkably similar in appearance. They include a "flip-flop" format, in which the opponent's past words or deeds are used to discredit them (e.g., the Bush "Boston Harbor" spot employed to undermine Dukakis' environmental record in the 1988 presidential race); a "humorous mocking" format, in which an opponent is made to appear foolish (e.g., the Bush "Tank" spot used against Dukakis in the 1988 campaign); an implied comparative, in which the opponent is attacked for an unpopular position on some issue (e.g., the Bush "Pledge of Allegiance" and "Revolving door" spots against Dukakis in the 1988 contest); or a "taking the high-low road" format, in which one candidate argues that they would never stoop as low as their opponent, perhaps in initiating attacks (Christ, Caywood, and Thorson, 1991).

These formats are stylistically similar in tone. They are grim, humorless, and mean. That's why most people are so quick to criticize negative ads, producing an initial backlash against sponsors (Garramone, 1984, 1985; Merritt, 1984). Despite their initial disgust, people are susceptible to attack spots. This irony was illustrated in 1988, when "61 percent of the voters viewed George Bush as conducting the 'most negative' campaign," and yet Bush won, and precisely on those themes stressed in his campaign advertising (Cutbirth, Monroe, Kirch, Case, and Mikesell, 1989).

People's expectations for political attack spots are based on their stylistic intensity. The 1990 Wellstone attack spots were more often subtle, humorous, and self-effacing. They made people chuckle, thus positively violating people's expectations, thereby facilitating attitude change (Mitchell, 1990). The ads literally "caught the imagination of voters" ("Profiles of," 1990), who were long accustomed to "viciously negative spots" as "the norm" (Mitchell, 1990).

The first attack spot was entitled "Faces." It's an upbeat, humorous ad, which alternates between Wellstone and Boschwitz's faces as Wellstone complains about how little money his campaign has, and thus how Minnesotans will not be seeing his face as often on television during the campaign. "'But, he says, 'he's better prepared to represent Minnesotans in the Senate—not to mention better looking'" (McGrath, 1990, p. 18A). Wellstone was nervous about the punchline, but went along with it.

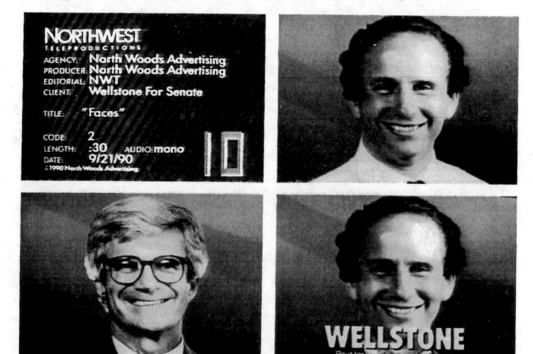

FIGURE 13-2 The "Faces" Spot Seeks to Offset Boschwitz's Financial Advantage

Source: Courtesy of North Woods Advertising.

The spot's creator justified the approach, arguing that the humor will work because it violates people's expectations about political ads. He explained: "The thing people don't expect in political advertising is a sense of humor. The thing about Rudy Boschwitz that my mother doesn't like is that he's one humorless s.o.b." (cited in McGrath, 1990, p. 18A). The contrast of styles will become even more apparent later.

The second attack spot was "Looking for Rudy." The spot was patterned after the movie, "Roger and Me," in which an unemployed automobile worker tries in vein to secure an interview with then General Motors President Roger Smith. The two-minute spot, long by advertising standards, "featured an exasperated Wellstone fruitlessly scouring the Twin Cities," including Boschwitz's own office, trying to track down his elusive opponent in an effort to arrange for candidate debates (Mitchell, 1990).

> *In one scene he is confronted by two tall Boschwitz campaign workers who tell Wellstone they don't want strangers wandering around the office. "Those guys were straight out of central casting," Hillsman says. "They were like bouncers at a Republican party. The only thing they didn't do is crack their knuckles" (McGrath, 1990, p. 17A).*

FIGURE 13–3 "Looking for Rudy" Became an "Instant Classic" Political Spot

Source: Courtesy of North Woods Advertising.

In the ad, Wellstone leaves his home telephone number at every stop. He asks a Boschwitz secretary if he can keep her pen because his campaign doesn't have much money. As he passes a BMW in a parking lot outside one of Boschwitz's offices, he says, "Nice car." As the spot ends, he's calling directory assistance seeking Boschwitz's home phone number in Plymouth (McGrath, 1990, p. 17A).

The spot was risky. In the first place, it was unique in its approach, possibly irreverent (Lillehaug, 1991). Forciea, for one, worried about how people would respond to it (Forciea, 1991). In the second place, it was long, thus violating norms. Some claim that, because of their brief attention spans, most voters will not stick with a two-minute spot. Also, because of its length, the spot cost more to air ($7,500 per showing on Twin Cities television), thus restricting its potential penetration.

This spot turned out to be a tremendous success. Although it formally aired only three times, because of its novelty, the spot received "dozens of free showings on local news reports" (Mitchell, 1990). The uniqueness of the ad captured viewers' attention, proved to be very influential, and became a major news event, thus insuring additional showings beyond those that the campaign had purchased. McGrath (1990, p. 17A) described the spot as "an instant classic, one of the most talked-about ads in Minnesota politics."

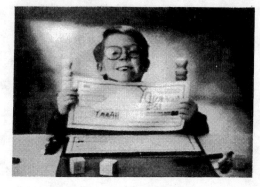 

FIGURE 13–4 "If Kids Had Money" Spot Assails Boschwitz on Children's Issues

Source: Courtesy of North Woods Advertising.

In what would prove to be a pattern involving inappropriate reactions to Wellstone campaign communication, a spokesperson for the Boschwitz campaign responded to the spot, calling Wellstone "an Abbie Hoffman-type character," "a leftist hustler," and "a self-promoting little fake." The Wellstone campaign had attacked Boschwitz with success, in large part because it had tempered its attack with humor. The Boschwitz campaign responded, not with a direct denial of the content of the Wellstone ad, but with mean-spirited name calling, thus providing a clear stylistic contrast that played into the Wellstone strategy. Forciea attributes this to the fact that "Boschwitz's people were unfamiliar with being reactive," the product of over-confidence (Forciea, 1991).

Two other Wellstone attacks are also unconventional in their approach. They focus on the two issues that formative research had indicated were key in winning Twin City suburban voters, one of the three "crucial" target audiences: children's concerns and the environment. One spot depicts young children, "scrawling on oversized checks made out to 'Rudy,'" concluding with Wellstone's comment that, "If kids had money, maybe he [Boschwitz] wouldn't have one of the worst records in the Senate on children's issues" ("Republican's Net Loss," 1990, pp. 3824–3825). The other "showed the candidate drawing a skull and crossbones while talking about his opponent's

FIGURE 13–5   "Skull and Crossbones" Spot Hits Boschwitz on the Environment

Source: Courtesy of North Woods Advertising.

environmental record" (Mitchell, 1990, p. 62). Both of these spots were "hard-hitting," according to producer Hillsman (1991), but they were stylistically subtle, even cute, which in effect "leavened Wellstone's otherwise harsh criticism of Boschwitz . . . " ("Republican's Net Loss," 1990, p. 3824).

Some observers of the 1990 Wellstone campaign argued that its creative approach to television advertising would set a new standard for future campaigns (McGrath, 1990; Mitchell, 1990). The Wellstone spots were, without any question, stylistically unique, because they were the product of an advertising man who, unfettered from the shackles of conventional wisdom concerning political spot advertising, and aware of the campaign's severe financial constraints, operated from the premise that, "We could make up a $3 to 4 million gap by having more creative advertising" (Hillsman, 1991). And, he did produce creative advertising. A column in the *New York Times* (Staples, 1990, p. 16) put it aptly: "Mr Wellstone's campaign ads were clean and funny, extraordinary political comedy."

Forciea (1991) cautions, however, that the campaign's use of humor in its television spots was effective in part because of a contrast in styles. Wellstone had a very comfortable style, and Boschwitz was a very easy person to be cynical about (Forciea, 1991).

> *Most people run campaigns while looking in the rear-view mirror (you know, whatever worked last year is what we'll do this year). . . . My guess is that even more people will try to copy the kinds of ads we did and look kind of foolish doing it. But for the right people and the right opponent, humor is a real effective tool (Forciea, 1991).*

Refutation

As opinion polls indicated that Boschwitz's once commanding lead was eroding, Boschwitz unleashed his own attack spots. He assailed Wellstone, using common Republican campaign themes, but extended to the extreme. Compared to the tone of the Wellstone spots, the Boschwitz attacks "struck many voters as strident or desperate" ("Republican's Net Loss," 1990, p. 3825). Nonetheless, the "million-dollar barrage of Boschwitz ads" (McGrath, 1990, p. 20A) seemed to be working, extending his lead in the polls from three to nine points over a two-week period (Smith, 1990b).

FEEDBACK

Given the success of Wellstone's advertising in contributing to the campaign's main objectives of promoting name identification, fostering a positive image for Wellstone, and chipping away at Boschwitz's image, the question is what comes next?

1. What could the Boschwitz campaign have done to reverse Wellstone's momentum?

2. What might the Wellstone campaign have done to prepare for the Boschwitz campaign's next moves?

Boschwitz attacked Wellstone as an "irresponsible liberal." A series of television spots claimed that Wellstone's plan for changes in health care was "socialistic," would result in the rationing of care, long delays for elderly patients, and "would double Federal income taxes paid by most households . . . " (Smith, 1990a, p. 12A). Other ads accused Wellstone of "wanting to put thousands of Iron Rangers out of work through his support of the Clean Air Act" [mining is important to the economy of the Iron Range, which is a part of the 8th congressional district in northeastern Minnesota] (Smith, 1990b, p. 4B), and "supporting abortion 'in all circumstances' including in the ninth month of pregnancies and when parents don't like the sex of the fetus" (Smith 1990c, p. 10A).

The Wellstone campaign, having failed to inoculate against what surely was anticipated, namely attacks portraying Wellstone as a "big-spending liberal," systematically refuted each of the attacks. Since they lacked the money to answer each charge with a refutation spot, the campaign had to rely heavily on speeches and press coverage as the communication modalities to rebut the attacks. McGrath (1991) commented that the attack ads "took a lot out of the campaign. They [the Wellstone campaign] had to respond to each one of these because if they didn't, the public would assume they were true."

At one point, Wellstone ridiculed the Boschwitz attacks as "a bunch of Boschwitz" (cited in Smith, 1990a, p. 1A). He also enlisted the help of former Vice President Walter Mondale, who termed the Boschwitz attacks as "a relentless, brutal, heavily financed, and in my judgment, untruthful television assault that is unprecedented in Minnesota's history" (cited in Smith, 1990b, p. 1B).

The Wellstone campaign, anticipating that Boschwitz would initiate attack ads against Wellstone, had prepared a generic refutation spot. The television message, called "Mudslinger," depicted Wellstone's face being pelted with mud. A newspaper version of the same message proclaims, "For God's Sake Senator, Enough is Enough" (McGrath, 1990, p. 20A). In response to the Boschwitz attacks, Forciea was ready to air the refutation spot, but Wellstone hesitated, maintaining that, "The campaign hasn't gotten dirty enough for us to put this ad on. We're running an upbeat campaign, and this ad might cover us with the same kind of mud that they're slinging" (cited in McGrath, 1991). Still, tracking polls showed that Boschwitz's attacks were undermining Wellstone support (McGrath, 1990). "They decide to stick to their original strategy . . . There will be no personal attacks on Boschwitz but, instead, a blitz of news conferences to battle each major assault" (McGrath, 1990, p. 21A).

Finally the Boschwitz campaign went too far and launched a personal attack on Wellstone that probably cost Boschwitz the election. The Boschwitz campaign released a direct mail letter to Jews, authored by a Boschwitz supporter and endorsed by the senator, suggesting that he is a better Jew than Wellstone is (McGrath, 1990). The direct mail letter charged that "Wellstone has no connection whatsoever with the Jewish community or our communal life. . . . His children were brought up as non-Jews" (cited in McGrath, 1990, p. 21A).

Wellstone's refutation of the letter was quick and decisive. In a press interview Wellstone responded, "I guess the senator is criticizing me for marrying a Christian." The response was just the right touch, an off-the-cuff remark "that Forciea and others recognize instantly as a turning point in the campaign" (McGrath, 1990, p. 21A). McGrath (1991) reflected later that Wellstone's response, "without any coaching or strategy session, . . . blew away the issue."

The previous attacks on Wellstone focused on his positions. Such attacks use issue content to assail character. They employ a rationale that looks something like this: "No candidate who would do "X" (restrict medical care for the elderly, increase taxes, etc.) is worthy of your support." This attack strategy, while distasteful to many voters, has proven to be effective.

However, the Boschwitz attack on Wellstone's religious life was decidedly personal. The attack, and Wellstone's refutation of it, may have proven pivotal in this election. In assessing the Wellstone victory, (*Time,* 1990) commented on the role played by the letter. "This crude tactic affronted voters of all faiths. It also drowned out Boschwitz's attacks on Wellstone's expensive proposals for a national health-care scheme and other ambitious programs" ("Boschwitz Botches It," 1990). *Star Tribune* reporter Dane Smith (1990d, p. 11A), citing tracking polls, concluded that:

> *The senator's fall from public grace appears to have occurred over the weekend and Monday, according to overnight tracking polls taken of 250 likely voters each day by the Star Tribune. That poll showed Boschwitz losing support at the same time Wellstone was gaining. Boschwitz slipped five points from Sunday to Monday. Wellstone gained slightly so the two were deadlocked at 45 percent each. . . . If there was any issue that closed the gap between incumbent and challenger, it was the letter to the Jewish community that was mailed late last week by the Boschwitz camp.*

Wellstone campaign manager John Blackshaw commented that, "(It) might have been the final straw that broke the camel's back." He added that, "There came a point in time when people just began to disbelieve what he had to say. He said so many bad things and so many things were out-and-out lies. I think people really saw through it toward the end" (cited in Hotakainen and Schmickle, 1990, p. 11A).

Wellstone won 51 to 49 percent, the only challenger able to unseat an incumbent senator in the 1990 elections.

Conclusion

Contemporary political campaigns differ from commercial and social action campaigns in that the former are much more person-centered, operate within a brief, fixed time frame, and are able to utilize the full range of communication modalities. They also differ from political campaigns of just a few years ago. Changes involving television and computers have fundamentally altered the way candidates communicate to voters. Television has produced a more abbreviated oral discourse, changed the nature of media news coverage, and catapulted the political spot to a role as the most dominant communication modality. In addition, computers make it possible for campaigns to target specific individuals for direct mail or telephone appeals.

This chapter provided a detailed examination of a campaign for the U. S. Senate in Minnesota in 1990. This campaign served to illustrate many of concepts, theories, and strategies that are featured in previous chapters of the book, and was particularly interesting because it broke new ground in political advertising that may carry over to other campaigns of the nineties (McGrath, 1990; Mitchell, 1990).

Suggestions for Further Reading

Armstrong, R. (1988). *The Next Hurrah: The Communications Revolution in American Politics*. New York: William Morrow.

Kaid, L. L., Nimmo, D., and Sanders, K. R. (Eds.) (1986). *New Perspectives on Political Advertising*. Carbondale, IL: Southern Illinois University Press.

McGrath, D. J. (1990, November 11). With more humor than cash, he won it his way. *Minneapolis Star Tribune*, pp. 1, 16A-21A.

Owen, D. (1991). *Media Messages in American Presidential Elections*. Westport, CT: Greenwood Press.

Trent, J. S., and Friedenberg, R. V. (1991). *Political Campaign Communication: Principles and Practices* (2nd ed.). New York: Praeger Publishers.

$$Chapter\ 14$$

Social Action Campaigns

... in order to survive we all must take responsibility...
—MOLLY PITCHER, REVOLUTIONARY WAR HEROINE

Researchers have concluded that these [health] education and persuasion campaigns achieved only limited success and have identified a key reason: Most are underdeveloped. . . . due to poor conceptualization and inadequate formative evaluation research inputs. This situation is in distinct contrast to commercial advertising campaigns, where strategies for influencing the audience are based on extensive precampaign research activities.
—CHARLES K. ATKIN AND VICKI FREIMUTH
COMMUNICATIONS PROFESSORS
(ATKIN AND FREIMUTH, 1989, P. 131).

This last chapter examines in some detail a social action campaign that was launched in the last half of the 1980s by a movement that had been in existence for some time prior to the campaign. Social action campaigns and social movements are often related to one another, as first discussed in Chapter 1. When a movement launches a campaign, the social action campaign has a ready base of funding resources, and particularly supporters, to call on. In fact, it is our observation, based on examination of social action campaigns in comparison to political and commercial campaigns, that the most distinctive difference regarding social action campaigns is their heavy emphasis on the intensification objective, as supporters are asked to make more extensive and/or intensive commitments to the campaign effort. Characteristics that distinguish social action campaigns are developed in this chapter, as highlighted by the questions in Table 14–1.

Characteristics of Social Action Campaigns

A social action campaign is a sustained, collective effort, either public or private, to influence attitudes and/or behaviors of people for the public good. As Salmon (1989) observes:

> *Any effort to engineer change in society is a value-laden activity, one in which not all persons agree upon the ends pursued and the means employed to achieve these ends. Instead, each phase of a campaign for social change involves an application and weighting of conflicting interests, some of which will be maximized at the expense of others. At the center of this conflict is the fundamental tension between social control and individual freedom (p. 20).*

Although the history of social action campaigns reveals a litany of failures (McGuire, 1968), there have also been a number of exemplary campaigns. For example, efforts to prevent forest fires have been highly successful. Originally, in 1940, a group of farmers from Oregon and Washington, many who had lost their homes and/or land to fire, banned together to form an association that would inform the public about the value of forested lands and the losses related to forest fires (U.S. Forest Service, 1973). Two years later, a forest fire prevention campaign was undertaken within the Forest Service by the U.S. Department of Agriculture in response to a Japanese submarine's shelling of the California coast (Daines, 1984).

The Wartime Advertising Council, a nonprofit organization, assisted the forest fire prevention campaign in designing two posters whose slogans were, "Careless Matches Aid the Axis" and "Our Carelessness, Their Secret Weapon" (U.S. Forest Service, 1960). These messages undoubtedly were intended to provoke feelings of psychological discomfort associated with being an American and behaving in any fashion that somehow might assist the enemy during the war.

Later posters used Walt Disney characters, such as Bambi, for whom the American audience had already learned a positive response, to take advantage of the classical learning principle of stimulus generalization. Smokey Bear was first painted by artist Albert Staehle in 1945 (U. S. Forest Service, 1960) and took full advantage of classical learning theory's stimulus discrimination principle. Individuals, perhaps partly due to the success of the Disney animal characters, were receptive to this animal character

Table 14–1   Basic Questions about Social Action Campaigns

1. What are the characteristics of a social action campaign?
2. What role, if any, do commercial organizations play in social action campaigns?
3. What is the role of the media in social action campaigns?
4. What is meant by the statement that, "successful social action campaigns are grounded in receiver needs?"
5. What contribution do interpersonal sources make to a social action campaign?
6. How important is the selection of a source for campaign messages?

representing the campaign. Subsequently, most Americans learned to associate Smokey with preventing forest fires, and discriminated this character from Bambi, who was also used by antihunting campaign proponents.

After the war, in 1946, the campaign became the Cooperative Forest Fire Prevention Campaign whose responsibility it was to sustain the effort to eliminate preventable fires (U.S. Forest Service, 1960). As a tribute to the campaign's success, U.S. Department of Agriculture (1986) data indicate that the number of acres lost to forest fires each year since the campaign began has been reduced by approximately 84 percent; the number of actual fires that occur has been reduced by approximately 47 percent.

In addition to increased public awareness of responsibility for the environment, the American middle class developed greater social awareness during the first two decades of the twentieth century. City and state governments took steps to deal with indigents in a more concerned manner. The federal government adopted a myriad of consumer protection laws and set up public regulatory commissions to police social evils. Middle class progressives also urged the passage of social insurance legislation to protect people who might not otherwise be able to protect themselves. Social insurance necessitates contributions through taxes and payroll deductions, using society's resources to solve lower class economic insecurities while maintaining the laborer's traditional self-reliance (Hirschfield, 1970). One area that warranted social insurance was health and medical care.

In 1906, the American Association for Labor Legislation (AALL), an educational pressure group concerned with health reforms in industry, sought compulsory health insurance as a solution to indigent medical care (Hirshfield, 1970). Initially, they concentrated on implementing workmen's compensation laws, which is viewed as the first successful social insurance program in the United States. Following the enactment of the workmen's compensation laws, the AALL's membership grew, and among the new members was Woodrow Wilson.

The effort involved in attaining the passage of workmen's compensation laws comprised a social action campaign. Future efforts of the AALL moved toward further health-care reform and used individuals such as Woodrow Wilson as credible sources of messages intentionally designed to influence specific audiences. Woodrow Wilson ran for political office and was elected governor of New Jersey in 1910 by a large majority. While governor, Wilson obtained passage of a number of reforms, including an insurance system to help injured workers. This success, in turn, contributed to Wilson's status as a national figure, and to his decision to run for the Democratic presidential nomination in 1912.

Although the United States was predominantly Republican at the time, Wilson was elected over Republican incumbent William Howard Taft and Bull Moose candidate Theodore Roosevelt. His previous accomplishments, in achieving successful outcomes in social action campaigns of that era, also contributed to the success of his political campaign.

Following his election, Wilson obtained passage of several social welfare measures, including the Child Labor Act, which prohibited children under the age of 14 years from working in factories, and the Adamson Act, which created an eight-hour work day for interstate railroad workers. This is just one example of how social action campaigns and political campaigns often become intertwined, as the promotion of the public welfare as an end in itself subsequently becomes part of promoting a candidate running for office or vice-versa.

Successful and unsuccessful past social action campaigns inform current practices, suggesting several generalizations, which will be illustrated in the case of "The Great American Meatout" campaign:

   1. Research is key.
   2. Messages must be personalized.
   3. The mass media can create awareness, provide knowledge or stimulate interpersonal discussion, but it is relatively ineffective in securing attitude and/or behavioral change.
   4. Message exposure is an obvious prerequisite to success..
   5. The credibility of the message source is crucial.
   6. Social and environmental support is important.
   7. Timing is critical.

Campaign Analysis: The Great American Meatout

Critical Event

In June of 1984, the U.S. Senate passed Resolution No. 396 that proclaimed the week of January 27 through February 2 of 1985 as "National Meat Week." This is the event that sparked the birth of "The Great American Meatout."

FARM ANIMAL REFORM MOVEMENT
Box 70123 Washington, DC 20088   301-530-1737

DIRECTORS

Alex Hershaft, President
Washington, DC
Melinda Marks, V Pres
Washington, DC
James Mason
Mount Vernon, MO
Thomas Hartmann
Plymouth, NH
Paul Obis
Chicago, IL

ADVISORS

Cleveland Amory
The Fund for Animals
Robert Brown
Food An. Concerns Trust
Cesar Chavez
United Farm Workers
Pegeen Fitzgerald
Millennium Guild
Brian Klug
Philosher
John Kullberg
ASPCA
Helen Nearing
Author and Philosopher
Gary Null
Author and Radio Host
Peter Roberts
Compass. in World
Robert Rodale
Rodale Press
Isaac Bashevis Singer
Nobel Laureate
Peter Singer
Author and Philosopher
Henry Spira
Animal Rights Activist
George Wald
Nobel Laureate
David Wallecninsky
Author
Gretchen Wyler
Broadway and TV Actress

COORDINATORS

Frances Arnetta
Selden, NY
Eric Baizer
Washington, DC
George Cave
State College, PA
Chas Chiodo
Miami, FL
Virginia Handley
San Francisco, CA
Ann Kory
Theo Kulessa
NJ
Marlene Lakin
Toronto, ON
Anne Morris
New York, NY
Susan Nielson
Denver, CO
Sheila Schwartz
New York, NY
Mary White
Rocky Mount, NC
Ted Zagar
East Chicago, IN

January 28, 1985

Dear Senator:

    We were shocked to learn that last June the U.S. Senate passed Senate Resolution #396 proclaiming the period between January 27th thru February 2nd, "National Meat Week."

    Production and consumption of meat pose a major threat to consumer health, world food supplies, conservation of resources, environmental quality, and animal welfare (see enclosed Fact Sheet). In fact, your own Select Committee on Nutrition and Human Needs recommended that Americans reduce their consumption of meat. The U.S. Senate must never again be associated with promotion of this violent and wasteful food.

    In the interest of fairness, we solicit your support for the Great American Meatout. This national campaign is asking all Americans to give up meat for one day on March 20th -- the first day of Spring and symbol of renewal and rebirth. May we count on you?

                              Very sincerely,

                              Alex Hershaft, Ph.D.
                              President

"To Alleviate and Eliminate Animal Abuse and Other Adverse Impacts of Animal Agriculture"

FIGURE 14–1 Letter to U.S. Senators Stresses Harm of Meat Consumption

Source: Courtesy of Farm Animal Reform Movement (FARM).

Every social action campaign has at its core at least one critical event, something that happens which propels people to action. This is one way in which timing is critical. Social action campaigners should recognize and use critical events to spark momentum, to enhance motivation, and to sustain their own enthusiasm. Other examples of critical events that have served as an impetus for action include an untimely death, which sparked Candy Lightener to form MADD, and has produced tougher laws for driving while intoxicated, and discrimination, which prompted a national reaction to the plight of Ryan White, the youngster who was denied the opportunity to attend public school after he was diagnosed with AIDS. In sum, this is one important distinction of social action campaigns. Whereas profit motivates commercial campaigners, and election motivates most political campaigners, altruism often motivates social action campaigners. However, as Salmon (1989, p. 21) concludes, "That some social condition is problematic means only that it has been defined as a problem or threat by someone or some group." In short, while commercial and political campaigners are often interested in the self-benefit to be gained by successful campaigning, social action campaigners are often motivated by other-benefit, with those "others" and the "benefits" to be accrued defined by social action campaigners. Examine Figure 14-1. This letter to Senators illustrates the notion of other-benefit, emphasizing the harm that arises from the consumption of meat. In similar fashion, smoking campaigns have designated individual and public health to be of paramount importance.

A critical event occurs against the backdrop of some larger societal situation. Thus, the Senate resolution was passed in an environment of declining beef consumption, attributed to greater public awareness of the health risks associated with eating beef, as well as the higher cost of eating beef. In all likelihood, the beef lobbyists who spearheaded the adoption of "National Meat Week" were campaigning for their very livelihoods. They sought to reverse the national trend toward reduced beef consumption.

Director and President of the Farm Animal Reform Movement (FARM), Alex Hershaft, recalls that the Senate action provoked the realization among FARM members that a response was necessary. However, Hershaft and others realized that the wrong response would be worse than no response at all by bringing more media attention to National Meat Week (Powell, 1990). Therefore, the group decided to respond in kind, initiating their own campaign. In this way, Meatout started as a counter-campaign, a response to an ongoing campaign that sought to enhance beef consumption. In fact, counter-campaigns are relatively common, particularly in the commercial and social action areas, where efforts on behalf of a competing brand or idea trigger a persuasive response from competitors. For example, campaigns have been conducted for and against abortion, sex education in schools, gun control, and a myriad of other social issues.

Intensification was a foremost object for FARM campaigners. They did not want to lose the momentum that had been achieved in moving the American public away from beef consumption, but more to the point for the movement, a less violent diet.

Initially, their primary campaign goal was to reinforce positive attitudes and behaviors of receivers. Planning focused on how to achieve this. Their meeting, an informal brainstorming session, produced the idea of launching a national campaign to be modeled after the American Cancer Society's highly successful "Great American Smokeout." A discussion follows of the yearly progression of "Great American Meatout" campaign events to illustrate the sustained and incremental process of this social action campaign.

Year 1

Planning

For a social action campaign, the focus during the planning stage is, as will be developed in more detail below, to determine (1) who is responsible for an unsatisfactory societal condition, (2) who is most harmed by the present state of affairs, and (3) who has the greatest likelihood of remedying the situation. FARM was most concerned with who is most harmed by messages designed to encourage beef consumption, with the "who" defined as cattle. However, the relatively extreme nature of this position prompted campaigners to focus on the harm to humans from beef consumption rather than the harm to animals. As in so many social action campaigns, health was the focal societal condition.

Once the decision was made to model a campaign after the "Great American Smokeout," the campaigners wrote to the American Cancer Society and obtained information and materials about that campaign. After studying the materials, the campaign planners drafted a preliminary prospectus that identified several campaign goals for the first year. The foremost goal was to get Americans to abstain from meat for at least one day, in the same way that the American Cancer Society strives to get smokers to quit for one day. Toward this end, campaigners sought to inform those uninformed Americans about harmful health effects associated with eating meat. Campaigners also worked to motivate the apathetic, as well as to convert the conflicted, by stressing the negative impact of meat consumption on the environment, national economy, animal welfare, and world hunger.

There was no formal formative analysis completed prior to implementing the campaign. However, campaigners targeted three diverse groups of individuals. One targeted group consisted of U.S. Senators, supporters of the "National Meat Week." Campaigners sought to inform this group. Another targeted group was the American public, most of whom are locked in a pattern of eating meat that dates from childhood. It was hoped that the campaign could convert many members of this group. The third targeted group was comprised of supporters of FARM who would be expected to endorse Meatout.

Implementation

Social action campaigns seek to involve individuals, groups, and organizations who will benefit from adopting a new social activity or policy. Campaigners also often seek to involve individuals, groups, and organizations who will adopt policy changes to facilitate new social activity. Messages, sources, and channels to attain campaign goals reflect these diverse audiences.

Broadly speaking, Meatout campaigners employed strategies based on principles drawn from a classical learning theory model. The campaign was designed to evoke an already learned response to Smokeout. Spokespersons and messages were selected for similar reasons. However, knowledge generated by other theories guided campaign implementation at various stages as well. Specifically, campaigners sought to move listeners from relative uninvolvement with the issue and messages, a more peripheral path of message processing, to feelings of increased issue involvement and more central routes of message processing. As a result, many of the generalizations drawn from the Elaboration Likelihood Model (ELM) apply, and several will be specifically noted.

Messages   The overarching message was "Meatout," a single easily remembered expression. A campaign logo was designed using a cut of meat with a universal sign for "no" or "banned" stamped across it (see upper left hand corner of Figures 14-2 and 14-3). The date for Meatout was carefully considered, and the first day of Spring, symbolic for new life, was selected. This, too, was an intentional act designed to evoke both cognitive and affective responses in the audience.

Additionally, the following slogans were adopted for the campaign in the first year: "Meat is a four-letter word," and "You deserve a break from meat today." Both of these took advantage of previously learned responses to messages. The second slogan, in particular, hoped to generalize to the very successful McDonald's campaign.

Another slogan was, "Choose life—kick the meat habit." It was designed to explicitly link the desired behavior with the concept of life—a term with double-meaning, the life of the individual who gives up meat, and the life of the animal who is not eaten. This was a generalization from the American Cancer Society and the antismoking efforts. Other slogans included: "If you like fat, cholesterol, and hormones, you'll love meat"; "Eat meat—subsidize world hunger"; and "Eat meat—subsidize cruelty." These last three messages aimed directly at generating feelings of inconsistency in audiences, who undoubtedly do not like fat, cholesterol, or hormones; and do not want to contribute to world hunger or cruelty (to animals). Additionally, fact sheets were put together as handouts to provide brief statements of the harmful effects associated with meat production and consumption, and tips for quitting meat.

Channel   Buttons, bumper stickers, posters, T-shirts, and tote bags were designed with the campaign logo on them. The efforts focused on repetition of the logo in enough forms and places to establish an automatic learned response. National media efforts included news releases, letters to editors, radio and television interviews with campaigners, and public service announcements—as many forms of free media as campaigners could attract. The fact sheets, buttons, bumper stickers, and posters were distributed at shopping malls and supermarkets. National and local information hotlines were established. Sport runs and other sport events were sponsored. Action guides and kits were assembled to be given to local organizers and support groups. Again, part of the advantage of having the Meatout campaign grow out of the FARM

THE GREAT AMERICAN MEATOUT

Box 70123-Washington, DC 20088-301-530-1737

March 7, 1986

National Chairman

Bob Barker—Host of
"The Price Is Right"

COORDINATORS
Alex Hershaft
Melinda Marks

ADVISORS
Cleveland Amory
The Fund for Animals
Pegeen Fitzgerald
Millennium Guild
John Kullberg
ASPCA
Helen Nearing
Author and Philosopher
Gary Null
Author and Radio Host
Peter Roberts
Compass. in World Farm.
Robert Rodale
Rodale Press
Isaac Bashevis Singer
Nobel Laureate
Peter Singer
Author and Philosopher
George Wald
Nobel Laureate
David Wallechinsky
Author
Gretchen Wyler
Broadway and TV Actress

**Sponsored by
FARM ANIMAL
REFORM
MOVEMENT**

The Honorable John F. Seiberling
House of Representatives
Washington, DC 20015

Dear Congressman Seiberling:

We would appreciate it if you would invite your colleagues
in the House and Senate to a reception on the occasion of the
Great American Meatout on March 19. The purpose and character
of this highly successful national campaign are explained in
the enclosed news release. Other Members of Congress asked to
co-sign the invitation are Representatives Lantos, Torricelli,
Scheuer, Jacobs, Fauntroy, Torres, and Solarz.

The program will include video, slide and photographic
displays of the hazards associated with excessive production
and consumption of meat, brief remarks by Members of Congress and
Meatout organizers, and, of course a delicious meatless luncheon
with compliments of the Meatout folks. Representatives of the
media will be attending as well.

Over 120 Members of Congress and their staffers attended last
year's reception. A copy of last year's invitation is enclosed. We
will be glad to furnish you sufficient copies of this year's invitation
to enclose with your letter.

Thank you in advance for your consideration and assistance.

Sincerely,

Alex Hershaft

Alex Hershaft, Ph.D.
National Coordinator

Choose Life—Kick the Meat Habit!

FIGURE 14–2   Letter Inviting Congressional Representatives to Join Meatout

Source: Courtesy of Farm Animal Reform Movement (FARM).

movement was the ability to utilize an already well-established network of information dissemination. Other social action campaigns must expend a great deal of effort to mobilize supporters.

Source   During the first year, campaigners mainly used the spokespersons identified in Figure 14-1. Alex Hershaft holds a Ph.D. in chemistry and, for most Americans, is not a household name. Similarly, other individual sources associated with the Meatout campaign were generally unknown. The campaign relied more on the organizational credibility of FARM as a source to enhance campaign goals and objectives during the first year, primarily among members of FARM, than they did on individual campaigners or campaign spokespersons. During that initial year, therefore, the process of organizing the campaign was the most time-consuming task, as further evidenced by the receivers.

Receivers   During the first year, the campaigners' audience consisted mostly of local FARM support groups, although the media carried the messages to a much larger audience. Local support groups, in turn, took the campaign directly to the public.

Evaluation

As with many social action campaigns, Meatout was privately funded, and there was no requirement to write formal reports of evaluation. This is unfortunate for reasons explained in the chapter about managing campaigns. Nonetheless, one can draw several conclusions about the organization's self-evaluation of the first year's campaign based on the changes made during the planning and implementation phases of the following year's campaign. Nonetheless, a plan to systematically evaluate the effects and effectiveness of "Meatout" would greatly enhance the validity and reliability of the conclusions.

It appears that campaigners probably concluded that the mass media did a good job of creating awareness, and many individuals were exposed to the messages, although qualitative rather than quantitative backing is all that is available to support this conclusion. Social and environmental support was there, primarily due to the association with FARM. In addition, it was recognized that individuals who were better known by the public would likely enhance outcomes should they be associated as spokespersons for the campaign. Perhaps most important, campaigners realized that timing could be improved, as can be observed by noting the date on the letter in Figure 14-1 (late January) and the date for Meatout (early March).

Year 2

Planning
During the second year of the "Great American Meatout," there was increased attention paid to actual behavior and behavioral intention. Planners decided to adopt the Meatout pledge. Campaigners focused on plans to get people to sign the pledge,

THE GREAT AMERICAN MEATOUT

Box 70123-Washington, DC 20088-301-530-1737

20 MARCH

News Release

CONTACT: Melinda Marks 301-530-1737

THE GREAT AMERICAN MEATOUT RETURNS ON MARCH 20th

National Chairman

Bob Barker—Host of "The Price Is Right"

COORDINATORS
Alex Hershaft
Melinda Marks

ADVISORS
Cleveland Amory
The Fund for Animals
Pegeen Fitzgerald
Millennium Guild
John Kullberg
ASPCA
Helen and Scott Nearing
Authors and Philosophers
Gary Null
Author and Radio Host
Peter Roberts
Compass. in World Farm.
Isaac Bashevis Singer
Nobel Laureate
Peter Singer
Author and Philosopher
George Wald
Nobel Laureate
David Wallechinsky
Author
Gretchen Wyler
Broadway and TV Actress

On March 20th, thousands of Americans in all major population centers will observe the second annual Great American Meatout by kicking the meat habit, according to the Farm Animal Reform Movement, principal sponsors of the national event. The date chosen is the first day of Spring, symbolic of renewal and rebirth. The concept is patterned after the highly successful Great American Smokeout campaign by the American Cancer Society which also advocates reduced intake of meat.

The Great American Meatout is designed to reduce the national consumption of meat and thereby to mitigate the destructive effects of intensive animal agriculture on consumer health, world agricultural resources, environmental quality, and animal welfare. Nearly 1.5 million Americans are crippled and killed each year by chronic diseases that have been linked conclusively with excessive consumption of animal products. Raising animals for food consumes up to 90 percent of our agricultural resources, depletes our topsoil and groundwater, pollutes our lakes and streams, destroys forests and other wildlife habitats, and causes intense suffering to six billion animals annually.

A number of special activities have been planned by local Meatout coordinators. Among these are "The Steakout" - an educational picket at restaurants and supermarkets, "The Meat Counter" - an information table in shopping malls, "The Meatout Teachin" - a presentation before a school or civic club, "The Meatout Cookin'" - a class in meatless cooking, "The Meatout Eatin" - a public meatless reception or dinner, and "The Healthline" - an information and support hotline.

Meatout supporters will be distributing thousands of "Meat Facts" - wallet-sized folders detailing the major problems with meat production and consumption and providing helpful "Quit Tips". Among these are putting away all meat in the house, cleaning the greasy stove, keeping around appropriate "munchies" for when the meat attack strikes, and visiting restaurants that offer salad bars and other meatless dishes. Most important, they will be asking passersby to sign "The Meatout Pledge" promising to kick the meat habit on March 20th.

Editors and producers are invited to contact us for advance feature stories or to schedule interviews with Bob Barker or one of our national coordinators. Additional updates will be released as new developments warrant it.

-- 30 --

Choose Life—Kick the Meat Habit!

FIGURE 14-3 News Release Announces the Great American Meatout

Source: Courtesy of Farm Animal Reform Movement (FARM).

ᵀᴴᴱ GREAT AMERICAN MEATOUT

Box 70123 - Washington, DC 20088-301-530-1737

January 6, 1987

Sample / sent to over 40 Celebrities

National Chairman

Bob Barker—Host of "The Price Is Right"

COORDINATORS
Alex Hershaft
Melinda Marks

ADVISORS
Cleveland Amory
The Fund for Animals
Pegeen Fitzgerald
Millennium Guild
John Kullberg
ASPCA
Helen and Scott Nearing
Authors and Philosophers
Gary Null
Author and Radio Host
Peter Roberts
Compass. in World Farm.
Robert Rodale
Rodale Press
Isaac Bashevis Singer
Nobel Laureate
Peter Singer
Author and Philosopher
George Wald
Nobel Laureate
David Wallechinsky
Author
Gretchen Wyler
Broadway and TV Actress

Sponsored by
FARM ANIMAL
REFORM
MOVEMENT

Ms. Susan Saint James
2645 Outpost Drive
Los Angeles, CA 90068

Dear Ms. Saint James:

The Great American Meatout is an annual national campaign designed to persuade the American people to "kick the meat habit" on March 20th (the first day of Spring), at least for the day, and to consider a less violent, more healthful diet. Additional details are provided in the enclosed news release and "Meat Facts" brochure.

The campaign is implemented through local promotional events and media interviews in nearly 100 locations throughout the U.S. These are handled by local animal rights and consumer groups that endorse the Meatout concept. The Farm Animal Reform Movement (FARM) provides national coordination and guidance, publishes promotional and educational materials, and handles national media interviews. FARM is a national, non-profit, public-interest organization working to moderate and eliminate the harmful impacts of intensive animal agriculture on animal welfare, consumer health, and resource conservation. (Please see enclosed "Veal" brochure.)

In light of your fortright position on diet and health and/or animal welfare, we would like to invite you to serve as the National Chairperson of the Great American Meatout for 1987. The position is strictly honorary, involving no financial or time commitment, although you may wish to do some national media interviews as the date draws closer. Bob Barker, who held this position for the past two years, has contributed considerably to the Meatout's current national renown.

We are well aware of the many intense demands on your time due to your national prominence and social consciousness. But please keep in mind that:

> America's excessive production and consumption of meat and other animal products causes more harm to animal welfare, consumer health, and resource conservation than all other human activities combined

Choose Life—Kick the Meat Habit!

FIGURE 14-4   Letter Inviting Ms. Susan Saint James to Serve as the National Chairperson of the 1987 Great American Meatout

Source: Courtesy of Farm Animal Reform Movement (FARM).

thereby making a public commitment to not eating meat for one day. Maintenance was not forgotten, however. For example, campaigners advised supporters that when dealing with more conservative groups, like government agencies, to identify activities as part of the observance of National Agriculture Day, also on March 20.

Because the second year's campaign followed on the heels of the evaluation of the first year, timing was used in a more thoughtful and careful fashion. For example, supporters were advised that one useful early activity would be to obtain a Meatout proclamation or resolution from local authorities. This would also provide further support and legitimization of the Meatout campaign.

Implementation

Campaigners continued the use of many successful approaches, and some were now given formal labels. The sporting events, for example, became the "Meat Romp", an opportunity to enhance public awareness of Meatout and get participants to sign the pledge. "Meatout Production" was a playlet to be performed on the street or a flatbed truck to dramatize the problems with eating meat. Suggestions for "Meatout Productions" included using vegetables to banish meat from the plate, or the grim reaper pointing to a scroll listing harmful ingredients contained in meat. The "Meat Outreach" was formed to facilitate contacts with mass media and sympathetic organizations that promoted local activities.

Messages   One slogan emerged as primary: "Choose life—kick the meat habit!" This was the most explicit generalization from the "Great American Smokeout." Moreover, efforts were made to lend significance and credibility to the social action associated with Meatout. The letter mailed to congressional representatives (see Figure 14–2), for example, includes the number of members of Congress who had attended the previous year's reception. Also, examine the news release in Figure 14–3. The significance of selecting the first day of Spring as the date for Meatout is explicitly stated, together with a number of additional claims important to the campaign.

Campaigners utilization of a "Meatout Pledge" may be viewed as a "foot-in-the door" compliance-gaining strategy. Having complied with the initial smaller request to sign the pledge, supporters believed that individuals were more likely to follow through with the behavior of not eating meat on March 20. The campaign also expanded its activities to include: "The Steakout"—use of informational pickets in front of supermarkets and restaurants to get passersbys to sign the meatout pledge; and "The Meat Counters"—information tables at shopping malls to get passersbys to sign the pledge.

Channel   The use of mass media, particularly the free modes, continued to be emphasized, but greater efforts were made in this second year of the campaign to reach individuals one-on-one, as can be seen by both "The Steakout" and "The Meat Counters." These further utilized local supporters, which functioned as an intensification strategy, reinforcing the beliefs and habits of nonmeateaters.

Sources Quite significantly, campaigners obtained Bob Barker as the National Chairman of "The Great American Meatout." Examine Figure 14–2 once more. Barker's name and picture appeared on most of the campaign literature and letters during the second year's campaign. This contributed to the campaign's ability to make connections between the familiar and trusted image of a celebrity and the less familiar claims and goals of the campaign.

Receivers The same three groups of receivers continued to be the focus of campaigners' efforts during the second year. The emphasis on individuals who already support "Meatout" is needed in order for the campaign to recruit others, an important goal, and one that contrasts to commercial campaigns where individuals who presently use a particular product are not persistently and specifically solicited to recommend the product to others. Social action campaigns must often depend on their supporters for continuance of the campaign.

Evaluation

Again, illustrating the sustained and incremental nature of campaigns, an evaluation of the second year of the "Great American Meatout" focuses attention on the following year's planning and implementation strategies. By these means, some conclusions may be drawn about what the campaigners thought was working, and what was not working, although it would have been better to have more explicit quantitative evidence. Examine Figures 14–4 and 14–5.

Judging by the letter in Figure 14–4, Meatout campaigners determined that their reach during the second year of the campaign included 100 locations throughout the United States. Headlines clipped from newspapers across the nation, as seen in Figure 14–5, attest to the campaign's reach. The campaign achieved further success in intensifying and reinforcing positive attitudes and behaviors, as well as in increasing and maintaining behavioral commitments. It is less certain whether the campaign was successful in securing much behavioral change or conversion.

Year 3

By the third year, the "Great American Meatout" had reached significant size, and campaign costs necessitated a direct and formal appeal to FARM supporters for financial support in the form of contributions designated to Meatout (see Figure 14–6).

Planning

During the third year, in addition to expanding efforts to raise campaign funds, Figure 14–4 reflects campaigners' expanded efforts to obtain national spokespersons to represent the "Great American Meatout Campaign." The letter seen in Figure 14–4 was sent to over 50 celebrities. The goal was to obtain a number of recognized celebrities to voluntarily chair the campaign, lending more visibility to the campaign. Previous research has demonstrated that increasing the number of sources of a message increases thought about the message (Harkins and Petty, 1981). Also, source credibility can increase subjects' message-relevant thinking (Heesacker et al., 1983).

FIGURE 14–5 Collage of Newspaper Stories about the Great American Meatout

Source: Courtesy of Farm Animal Reform Movement (FARM).

FARM ANIMAL REFORM MOVEMENT (FARM)
P.O. Box 70123, Washington, DC 20088   301-530-1737

23 February 1987

Dear Fellow FARM Member:

The Great American Meatout is our annual national campaign calling on the American people to "kick the meat habit" on March 20th, at least for the day, and to consider a less violent and more healthful diet. The purpose of the Meatout is to remind the American people of the destructive impact of intensive animal agriculture on consumer health, world food supplies, agricultural resources, environmental quality, wildlife habitats, and of course, on the abuse and destruction of six billion innocent feeling animals on American "factory farms." For every one percent reduction in the national meat consumption, we will be preventing the suffering of 60 million animals annually - a number equivalent to all the animals suffering in vivisection experiments.

Although FARM obtains national endorsements from prominent individuals and organizations, produces a large variety of educational and promotional materials, formulates guidelines for local activists, and procures national media coverage, the key protagonists of the Great American Meatout are the hundreds of FARM members and supporters like you, who arrange local promotional activities, disseminate the Meatout message, and get their friends and neighbors to sign the Meatout pledge (see over). Here are some of the key Meatout activities:

- MEATOUTREACH - Reaching out to other animal, health, consumer, environment, and peace groups in the community and to public officials to obtain their support

- STEAKOUTS - Small teams of activists armed with Meatout information, in front of a supermarket or a shopping mall, distributing "Meatfacts," getting people to sign the Meatout pledge, and rewarding them with a lapel sticker

- LIFESTIVAL - Fun-filled, life-affirming public festival featuring brief messages from local celebrities, musical entertainment, games and prizes, screening of videotapes, sampling of meatless foods, and signing of the Meatout pledge

The educational and promotional materials that we furnish are presented overleaf along with some clip art for use in pasting up and printing your own materials.

So, won't you complete and return the coupon below at your earliest convenience, so that we may ship you the needed materials? Thank you for your support.
Sincerely,

Alex
Alex Hershaft, Ph.D., President

Please send completed forms to: **FARM,**
P.O. Box 70123, Washington, D.C. 20088

Dear FARM Folks: yes, count me in on the Great American Meatout!

☐ I would like to organize something in my community. Send the following items:

_____

_____ Total cost: $ _____

☐ I can not organize anything this year, but I am enclosing a $ ____ contribution to help defray the promotional costs of Meatout.

☐ Here's my 1987 membership contribution of $ ____ and/or pledge of $ ____/month

Total amount enclosed $ ____. Please make sure that the address on the label overleaf is correct and add your home telephone number. If you have not done so before, please jot down any special skills and resources and interest in interning at FARM.

FIGURE 14-6 Mail Appeal for Financial Contributions for 1987 Meatout Campaign

Source: Courtesy of Farm Animal Reform Movement (FARM).

Implementation

Messages   "Choose life—kick the meat habit!" continued to be a central message used in the Meatout campaign. Additionally, "Our planet's loss is the meat industry's grain," "Mother was right! Eat your vegetables," and "A steak a day drives good health away" joined the ranks of the messages utilized in the campaign. Each plays on formerly learned messages, which should enhance the memorability of the messages.

Channel   The previous use of channel remained consistent, although the participation by recognized celebrities and physicians undoubtedly enhanced the campaign's efforts to obtain more media coverage than before.

Sources   Doris Day became the national chair; Casey Kasem and Ally Sheedy acted as national co-chairs. Alex Hershaft continued to be listed as the national coordinator, but his name moved to the last position in the list of sources associated with the campaign in the news releases generated for promotional efforts. This suggests that campaigners recognized the importance of name recognition and utilized the primacy effect with regard to celebrity sources.

Receivers   The audience remained a constant. As can be seen from Figure 14–6, the supporters were asked to do even more than before, further intensifying their support for the campaign. Commitments of time, money, and active involvement with campaign goals were solicited.

Evaluation

A formal annual report was written to evaluate the third annual Meatout campaign. It includes the finding that more than 150 members of Congress and their staff took part in a Meatout reception. Moreover, activists in Minneapolis, San Diego, and Seattle arranged "Meatout Feed-ins" for local homeless shelters. Thirty restaurants in the Dayton-Springfield area offered Meatout specials. Not one, but several national celebrities acted as spokespersons for the campaign. These figures were verifiable. Hershaft estimated that more than 20 million people were reached through 200 media interviews and news reports. The campaign's sponsors included FARM, the American Society for Prevention of Cruelty to Animals, the Fund for Animals, and the Animal Protection Institute are all recognized as playing vital roles in the Meatout campaign's success. Meatout was regarded as highly successful by this point in time in effectively achieving the necessary condition of audience exposure to the message.

Much actual desired behavior was also attained, as evidenced by the free media's record of the many Meatout events that took place and the absence of meat consumption for that date.

THE GREAT AMERICAN MEATOUT

Box 70123-Washington, DC 20088-301-530-1737

NATIONAL CHAIR

Doris Day

NATIONAL CO-CHAIRS

Casey Kasem

Hayley Mills

NATIONAL COUNCIL

Cleveland Amory
Columnist

Peter Burwash
Tennis star

Cesar Chavez
Labor leader

Andy Jacobs
US Congress

John McDougall, MD
Physician, author

Bob Mendelsohn, MD
Physician, author

Tom Scholz
Rock star

Isaac B. Singer
Nobel Laureate

George Wald
Nobel Laureate

Gretchen Wyler
Stage & TV star

NATIONAL COORDINATORS

Alex Hershaft, PhD
Don Lutz

January 1988

Dear Friend and Colleague:

For the past three years, the Farm Animal Reform Movement has undertaken an extremely successful national grass-roots campaign called the Great American Meatout. Its purpose is to reduce the national consumption of meat and thereby to mitigate the destructive effects of intensive animal agriculture on animal welfare, consumer health, world food supplies, and environmental quality. The concept was borrowed from the annual Great American Smokeout campaign of the American Cancer Society. The date selected was March 20, the first day of spring and symbol of renewal and rebirth. The renowned movie actress Doris Day has been kind enough to serve as our National Chairperson.

The types of activities suggested as part of the Great American Meatout campaign are outlined overleaf. The most common of these are the "Steakout" and the "Meat Counter." Over 100 animal rights and vegetarian groups across the U.S. have participated in one way or another. Dozens of newspapers, magazines, and radio and television stations have carried the Meatout message to millions of Americans. None of our other programs, including the Veal Ban Campaign and the World Farm Animals Day, has had such a remarkable activist and media appeal.

We invite you to share in our success by introducing a version of the Great American Meatout in your own country. You could use a similar name, e.g., the Great British Meatout, or another name, more suited to your own cultural and linguistic tradition. The campaign wouldn't even have to take place on March 20th, although a uniform date throughout the world would be more effective, as in the case of the World Farm Animals Day which is approximately six months later (October 2nd). The key message, however, should be to "kick the meat habit," at least for one day, to take a break from a meat-centered diet, and to consider a less violent, more healthful diet based on grains, vegetables, and fruit.

We are prepared to help by sending you a Coordinator Kit containing samples of the items marked by an * overleaf. Of course, you will probably need to translate and modify these items to suit your own needs.

We are looking forward to working with all of you to make this planet a better place to live for all its inhabitants, human and non-human alike. Don't hesitate to call or write if we can provide any assistance in reaching this goal.

Don Lutz
Education Director

Choose Life—Kick the Meat Habit!

FIGURE 14–7 Letter Promoting Meatout Campaigns in Other Countries

Source: Courtesy of Farm Animal Reform Movement (FARM).

Year 4

By the fourth year, the Meatout campaign was recognized as FARM's most publicity-generating event. Intensification efforts were sustained and even increased. The campaign was extended to begin on March 1 and culminate on March 20.

Planning

In the fourth year, individual supporters from previous campaigns received detailed plans for activities' dates and materials to be used during a three-week period. The name and telephone number of a national coordinator to be reached for assistance with individual local efforts was provided. A list of regional coordinators and phone numbers also was provided, contributing to the formalization of planning details. Moreover, the campaign moved beyond national boundaries. Examine Figure 14–7.

Implementation

As the campaign worked to extend the reach of its messages, it also sought to keep the campaign within the boundaries of a positive, upbeat approach to changing individuals' diets, generally avoiding the use of intense fear or threat appeals.

Messages   The previous messages were continued to be used. One new strategy was the use of a Meatout sticker to be put on the lapel of anyone who signed the Meatout Pledge or contributed to Meatout, much like those worn by voters on election days. This was intended as a reward that also would provoke questions from others and increase the use of the literature and word-of-mouth campaigning.

Channel, sources, and receivers   The continued use of all previous forms of getting the message out characterized this year of the campaign. Moreover, reliance on celebrities was extended, with Hayley Mills, for example, becoming a national co-chair. An additional audience was added, as the campaign extended beyond national borders.

Evaluation

An informed evaluation of the Meatout campaign's effects and effectiveness is possible by examining the letter that went out to supporters for the following year's campaign. Examine Figure 14–8.

By the fourth year, the reach of the Meatout campaign had increased to some 200 festivals, receptions, exhibits, and other events. This kind of success necessitated the request for even greater financial backing from supporters. Since social action campaigns are often privately funded, success costs supporters. In fact, the more costly the campaign to supporters, often the more successful the campaign is in attaining its goals.

20 MARCH

NATIONAL CHAIR

Doris Day

NATIONAL CO-CHAIRS

Casey Kasem

Ally Sheedy

NATIONAL COUNCIL

Cleveland Amory
Columnist

Peter Burwash
Tennis star

Cesar Chavez
Labor leader

Andy Jacobs
US Congress

John McDougall, MD
Physician, author

Tom Scholz
Rock star

Isaac B. Singer
Nobel Laureate

George Wald
Nobel Laureate

NATIONAL COORDINATOR

Alex Hershaft, PhD
Farm An. Ref. Mov't

℡ GREAT AMERICAN MEATOUT

Box 70123 - Washington, DC 20088 - 301-530-1737

15 January 1989

Next March 20th will mark the first day of spring. Once again, it will also be the day of the **Great American Meatout**, when thousands of consumer and animal rights advocates, manufacturers and distributors of wholesome foods, and other concerned Americans will be asking their friends and neighbors to kick the meat habit, at least for the day, and to explore a less violent, more wholesome diet. Selected materials illustrating recent **Meatout** observances are enclosed for your review.

In the brief four years of its existence, the **Great American Meatout** has already captured the imagination of the American public and the mass media beyond our wildest expectations. Our latest observance involved some 200 festivals, receptions, exhibits, and similar events throughout the U.S. We conducted over 200 media interviews resulting in 50 newspaper stories and countless radio and television reports.

Funding for the **Great American Meatout** is provided entirely by contributions from small manufacturers and distributors of meatless and other wholesome foods, personal foundations, and many compassionate individuals. Food manufacturers and distributors have been particularly supportive.

We invite you to become a Sponsor of the Great American Meatout by contributing $500 or more in cash, goods, or services to our 1989 Meatout campaign. As a token of our appreciation, your firm will be listed in our promotional literature and your handouts and samples will be distributed by our coordinators around the country. But, more importantly, you will be enhancing public awareness of the destructive impacts of animal agriculture on consumer health, environmental quality, and animal welfare. Finally, you will be encouraging American consumers to kick the meat habit and to explore a less violent, more wholesome diet and opening new markets for your products.

Whether you do become a Sponsor or not, we ask that you help our common cause by undertaking one or more of the exciting educational projects listed overleaf. We would be pleased to provide any supporting guidance and materials that you may require.

Thank you in advance for your compassionate concern. We look forward to hearing from you.

Sincerely yours,

Alex Hershaft, Ph.D., President

Choose Life—Kick the Meat Habit!

FIGURE 14-8 Mail Appeal for Financial Contributions for the 1989 Meatout Campaign

Source: Courtesy of Farm Animal Reform Movement (FARM).

^{HE} GREAT AMERICAN MEATOUT

Box 70123 - Washington, DC 20088 - 301-530-1737

A PROSPECTUS

NATIONAL CHAIR

Doris Day

NATIONAL CO-CHAIRS

Casey Kasem

Ali Sheedy

NATIONAL COUNCIL

Cleveland Amory
Columnist

Peter Burwash
Tennis star

Cesar Chavez
Labor leader

Andy Jacobs
US Congress

John McDougall, MD
Physician, author

Bob Mendelsohn, MD
Physician, author

Tom Scholz
Rock star

Isaac B. Singer
Nobel Laureate

George Wald
Nobel Laureate

Gretchen Wyler
Stage & TV star

NATIONAL COORDINATOR

Alex Hershaft, PhD
Farm An. Ref. Mov't

The Great American Meatout is a national educational campaign calling on Americans to "kick the meat habit" on March 20th, at least for the day, and to consider a less violent diet. March 20th was chosen because it's the first day of Spring, symbolizing renewal and rebirth. The purpose of the Great American Meatout is to alert the American people to the destructive impacts of intensive animal agriculture on consumer health, world food supplies, agricultural resources, the natural environment, wildlife habitats, and animal welfare and to caution them of their personal support for this destruction through their diet.

Since its inception in 1985, the Great American Meatout has been sponsored by the Farm Animal Reform Movement (FARM), a national public interest organization advocating greater moderation in the production and consumption of animal products. FARM obtains national endorsements from prominent individuals (see listing) and organizations, produces a large variety of educational and promotional materials, formulates guidelines for local promotional activities, and procures national media coverage (see enclosed report and clippings on Meatout '86).

However, the key players in the Great American Meatout are the thousands of animal and consumer activists who arrange local promotional activities, disseminate the non-violent Meatout message, and get the American people to sign the Meatout pledge to explore a less violent diet. The key Meatout activities are as follows:

- MEATOUTREACH - Reaching out to animal, consumer, health, environment, peace, and other kindred groups and individuals in the community who should be supporting the Meatout message to obtain their endorsement and cooperation; obtaining proclamations from public officials.

- STEAKOUTS - Placements of small teams of activists, preferably with a table and a Meatout banner or large posters, in front of supermarkets, in shopping malls, at fairs, in public parks, to attract passersby, hand them "Meatfacts" and other information, get them to sign the Meatout pledge and place a contribution in the collection can, and affix a Meatout sticker on their lapel.

- LIFESTIVAL - Large, fun-filled, life-affirming public festival, featuring brief messages from local officials, media representatives, and other celebrities, musical entertainment, games and prizes, screening of educational videotapes, sampling of meatless foods, and displays by supporting groups and merchants, as well as signing of the Meatout pledge.

- MEATFARCE - Short play or tableau, staged by costumed performers on the street or a flat-bed truck, on such themes as vegetables banishing meat from the plate and proclaiming their superior nutritional merits, or the "Grim Reaper" pointing out the hazards of meat; in conjunction with either "Steakouts" or "Lifestival."

Additional Meatout activities and a suggested schedule are shown overleaf.

Choose Life—Kick the Meat Habit!

FIGURE 14–9   Letter Highlights Schedule of Activities for Meatout Campaign

Source: Courtesy of Farm Animal Reform Movement (FARM).

Year 5

Planning

Campaign costs became a primary focus of campaigners' time and attention during the fifth year. More effort was also directed to details related to the timing of campaign events. Letters to supporters directly address the time issue and set deadlines for responding so that materials would be mailed to activists in "a timely fashion." A sample timeline for a schedule of activities was provided to participants (see Figure 14–9). Thus, the previous years of experience contributed to the ability to further formalize more details for local supporters.

Implementation

Messages Hershaft, the national coordinator, signed some invitations and requests to supporters with "Yours, for life," a personalized and facilitative approach to refer to the bond among supporters. Campaigners had also been highly successful in attaining the support of local mayors for Meatout. During the fifth year, therefore, the national campaign office provided local campaigners with examples of proclamations (see Figure 14–10). This further enhanced the ability of local groups to obtain proclamations in their own areas.

Channel As media coordinator for Meatout, Susan Smith began extensive efforts to formally assist the local activists with media messages. For example, sample public service announcements were mailed to public service directors around the nation. Ten, 20- and 30-second spots were included:

> *Do you know that one-and-one-half million Americans are crippled and killed each year by chronic diseases linked with a high-meat diet? That billions of animals are terribly abused in U.S. "Factory Farms?" That our environment is being destroyed by animal agriculture? It's time for a change! On March 20th, the first day of spring, join thousands of concerned folks in the Great American Meatout. "Kick the meat habit," at least for the day, and explore a less violent, more wholesome diet.*
>
> *Do we really have to damage our health, deny food to the hungry, abuse and kill animals, and destroy our environment, just to put a piece of meat on our dinner plate? On March 20th, the first day of spring, join Doris Day, Casey Kasem, Ally Sheedy, River Phoenix, and thousands of other concerned folks in the Great American Meatout. "Kick the meat habit," at least for the day, and explore a less violent, more wholesome diet.*

These messages make use of previous research that has shown that mindful message processing may be promoted by introducing a counterattitudinal message with a question, leading to more intensive processing of content than an opening statement, even in situations of low involvement (Burnkrant and Howard, 1984).

STATE OF TENNESSEE
PROCLAMATION
BY THE GOVERNOR

WHEREAS, Tennesseans benefit from an agriculturally diverse and productive economy which includes the production of an abundant supply of high quality and fresh vegetables, fruits and other horticultural crops; and

WHEREAS, vegetable production provides a source of enjoyment and is a practical food income supplement for home gardeners; and

WHEREAS, the value of vegetable production in Tennessee, combined with fruits and other horticultural crops, is estimated at about $83 million; and

WHEREAS, vegetables are a valuable source of essential vitamins and nutrients for a wholesome, and delicious diet for today's health conscious consumers; and

WHEREAS, the Tennessee Department of Agriculture has worked in earnest to promote the sale and consumption of Tennessee produced vegetables through the "Pick Tennessee Products" promotional campaign;

NOW, THEREFORE, I, Ned McWherter, as Governor of the State of Tennessee, do hereby proclaim March 20, 1989, as

VEGETABLE ENJOYMENT DAY

in Tennessee, and do urge all our citizens to join me in this worthy observance.

IN WITNESS WHEREOF, I HAVE HEREUNTO SET MY HAND AND CAUSED THE GREAT SEAL OF THE STATE OF TENNESSEE TO BE AFFIXED AT NASHVILLE ON THIS 14TH DAY OF MARCH, 1989.

GOVERNOR

ATTEST:

SECRETARY OF STATE

FIGURE 14–10 Sample of State Proclamations Sent to Local Campaigners

Source: Courtesy of Farm Animal Reform Movement (FARM).

From the desk of
Dr. Alex Hershaft

Dear Fellow Meatout Coordinator:

A key objective of the Great American Meatout campaign is to maximize the media coverage that will carry the Meatout message to millions of Americans who we can not reach in person. You can promote this objective by following up on our media contacts and by initiating your own. The purpose of this mailing is to assist you with this task.

To this end, we are enclosing a guide to "Effective Use of Mass Media" and a listing of the media that we have contacted in your state. We are also enclosing a news release sent to news editors of newspapers, magazines, radio and television networks, and wire services, a mailer sent to radio and television talk show producers, and another sent to radio and television public service directors.

Currently, we are sending packets of Meatout materials with special cover letters to life style, food, health, science, and environment editors of major newspapers, magazines, radio and television networks, and wire services, as well as syndicated columnists and cartoonists. In the near future, we will be sending news releases listing major Meatout events around the country to key news editors.

We hope that this will help you with your own media effort which is absolutely crucial to a successful Meatout campaign. Please feel free to call if we can provide any additional assistance.

Sincerely yours,

Alex Hershaft

 FARM ANIMAL REFORM MOVEMENT, INC.
Box 70123 Washington, DC 20088·301-530-1737

FIGURE 14–11 Letter to Campaign Coordinators Stressing Effective Media Use

Source: Courtesy of Farm Animal Reform Movement (FARM).

Sources and Receivers The Meatout campaign continued to be endorsed by numerous celebrities and opinion leaders, including physicians. School children became an additional target group of specific and intensive focus as Pittsburgh, Pennsylvania public schools served meatless meals to children system wide for the day. This, in turn, generated new ideas for planning of future campaigns.

Evaluation

Following the fifth year's Meatout campaign, the letter sent to celebrities seeking their endorsement observed that some 250 groups in 43 states had taken part in the fifth year's campaign. Meatout's continued success represents effectiveness in attaining the primary objective of intensification, and some success in attaining significant formation and conversion of desired attitudes.

Year 6

The Meatout campaign marked its sixth year in 1990.

Planning

The emphasis on the media to promote awareness became a significant and formalized effort during the planning for the sixth Meatout, as exemplified in Figure 14–11.

Implementation

The network of supporters had grown during the previous five years, and so efforts to intensify support were even greater. In a letter to coordinators, Hershaft observes that to achieve the national goal of 100,000 signed pledges and the actual behavior will save destruction of over 6,000 cows, calves, pigs, and other animals. He observes that, "A key objective of the Great American Meatout campaign is to maximize the media coverage that will carry the Meatout message to millions of Americans who we can not reach in person" (cited in Powell, 1990).

Messages Examine Figures 14–12, 14–13, and 14–14. Key message components in the campaign include the pledge (Figure 14–12), memorable slogans (Figure 14–13), and informative posters (Figure 14–14). These slogans sometimes employ death metaphors, increasing the intensity of the language in the expressions, and an explicit subject to personalize the message, which increases the message's immediacy.

Channel The FARM Report for the spring of 1990 reported the extensive coverage by the nation's print and broadcast media. CNN Prime News, CBS News "Nightwatch" and "This Morning" carried stories. National stories appeared in the Associated Press, Copley, Gannett, PR Newswire, and other news services.

THE MEATOUT PLEDGE

- Consumption of animal fat and meat has been linked conclusively with an elevated incidence of heart failure, stroke, cancer, and other chronic diseases that cripple and kill 1.5 million Americans each year.
- Raising of animals for food wastes foodstuffs that should be used to feed the world's hungry people and depletes drastically our irreplaceable food production resources such as topsoil and groundwater.
- Raising of animals for food devastates forests and other wildlife habitats and dumps more pollutants into our lakes and streams than all other human activities combined.
- Raising of animals for food on today's "factory farms" involves the confinement, crowding, deprivation, mutilation, and other gross abuse and slaughter of nearly six billion feeling, innocent animals.

Therefore, "I pledge to kick the meat habit on March 20th (first day of Spring) and to explore a less violent, more wholesome diet."

Name_____ Address_____ Zip_____

FIGURE 14–12 Great American Meatout Pledge

Source: Courtesy of Farm Animal Reform Movement (FARM).

FARM ANIMAL REFORM MOVEMENT (FARM)
PO Box 30654, Bethesda, MD 20824   301-530-1737

SLOGANS FOR A LESS VIOLENT LIFESTYLE

Feel free to use these slogans, with our compliments, to promote a less violent lifestyle. We welcome additional suggestions for future editions.

BE KIND TO ANIMALS — DON'T EAT THEM
SO, YOU LOVE ANIMALS — FOR BREAKFAST, LUNCH, OR DINNER?
ANIMALS LOVE VEGETARIANS
VEGETARIANISM IS NEVER HAVING TO SAY YOU'RE SORRY
FRIENDS, DON'T LET FRIENDS EAT MEAT
MOTHER WAS RIGHT — EAT YOUR VEGETABLES

A NON-VIOLENT LIFESTYLE BEGINS AT BREAKFAST
VEGETARIANS SAVE LIVES EVERY DAY
VEGETARIANS DO IT FOR LIFE
VEGETARIANS ARE FULL OF LIFE
VEGETARIANS NEVER SAY DIE
VEGETARIANS DON'T HAVE TO MAKE A KILLING
PERFORM A DEATH-DEFYING ACT — BECOME A VEGETARIAN
EACH DAY, TWENTY MILLION ANIMALS ARE DYING TO FEED YOU
CHOOSE LIFE — KICK THE MEAT HABIT
MEAT KILLS — ARE YOU REALLY THAT HUNGRY?
EATING MEAT EACH DAY KEEPS GOOD HEALTH AWAY
IF YOU LIKE CHOLESTEROL AND DRUGS, YOU'LL LOVE MEAT
STOP CHEWING THE FAT — BECOME A VEGETARIAN
HUNGER HURTS — BE A VEGETARIAN
THE HUNGRY CHILDREN'S LOSS IS THE MEAT INDUSTRY'S GRAIN
IF YOU HATE FORESTS, EAT A HAMBURGER

THE PRICE OF MEAT IS SHEER MURDER
EATING MEAT CAN COST AN ARM AND A LEG
MEAT EATERS ARE FULL OF BULL
MEAT IS A FOUR-LETTER WORD
GET THE MEAT OUT

FIGURE 14–13 Great American Meatout Slogans

Source: Courtesy of Farm Animal Reform Movement (FARM).

YOU'RE NOT THE ONLY ONE DYING FOR A HAMBURGER.

Hamburger, the All-American food. To most people, it's just a piece of meat. But the truth behind our meat consumption is more than a dying shame.

Each year nearly 1.5 million Americans die or are crippled from heart disease, cancer, and kidney failure, health problems directly associated with the over-consumption of meat.

More than 150 million animals and 3 billion birds are slaughtered every year. They are confined, chained, or imprisoned in permanent darkness until they are finally put to death.

All throughout the world children needlessly starve, while 90% of the grain grown in this country feeds factory animals destined for the slaughterhouse. To produce just one pound of meat, a steer must be fed 16 pounds of grains, food which could help to feed the world.

Over 260 million acres of forest lands have already been leveled for use as pastures to feed cattle. To package 8 billion fast-food burgers, nearly 890 square miles of forest land will be razed, depleting the topsoil and creating vast wastelands.

For yourself and your world, please observe The Great American Meatout. Some things are just not worth dying for.

THE GREAT AMERICAN MEATOUT
MARCH 20th -- First Day of Spring

National coordinator: Farm Animal Reform Movement

FIGURE 14–14   Great American Meatout Poster

Source: Courtesy of Farm Animal Reform Movement (FARM).

Sources   Endorsements of Meatout continued to include an array of celebrities, like Doris Day, Casey Kasem, Ally Sheedy, River Phoenix, Caesar Chavez, Cleveland Amory, Berke Breathed, Harvey and Marilyn Diamond, David Goldbeck, Tony LaRussa, and Jeremy Rifkin. Proclamations were issued by governors of Maine and Ohio, and the mayors of Asheville, Chapel Hill, Charlotte, Raleigh, and Durham in North Carolina; Birmingham and Mobile in Alabama; and Indianapolis, Philadelphia, Portland, Cincinnati, and Des Moines.

Receivers   The growth of the campaign resulted in the appointment of 50 state coordinators for this sixth annual campaign. Portland Vegetarians organized the serving of a meatless meal in Portland, Oregon public school system. The Triangle Vegetarian Society promoted the serving of 115,000 students meatless lunches in North Carolina schools. The audience of young people has become an important audience.

Evaluation

More than 400 events in all 50 states as well as several Canadian provinces marked the observance of the sixth annual Great American Meatout. The FARM Report for the Spring of 1990 noted in its headline that the "Great American Meatout Exceeds All Expectations." In sum, this campaign has succeeded in involving a large societal audience in action that promotes their own and others' wellness. Campaigners have generated support throughout the nation, sustaining enthusiasm among early supporters, and incrementally achieving change in a large group of uninformed, unmotivated, and apathetic Americans. This social action campaign illustrates the increased formalization of the planning that occurs in a campaign that starts at the grass roots level. It also illustrates the tendency of underfunded campaigns to eschew formal evaluation. The criticisms associated with such failure apply in this case, as the campaign was unable to claim with certitude what causes led to their success.

Conclusion

Commercial campaigns are product-oriented, whereas political campaigns are person-oriented, intentionally addressing the aim of putting someone into a position in government. Social action campaigns are event- or action-oriented, intentionally addressing aims greater than any single individual, but likely to affect a group or groups within the society.

The evaluation phase of campaigning is where commercial, political, and social action campaigns differ most strikingly. For commercial campaigners, success is measured by sales and profits. For political campaigners, success is measured by the election to office of the individual the campaign promoted; failure means the opponent was elected. For social action campaigners, the success is measured by improvement or lack of further deterioration of a societal condition (e.g., the environment, jobs for the homeless, rate of skin cancer).

Achieving the desired outcome in social action campaigns often means working with some of those individuals who hold positions in government. It may also mean seeking financial support from businesses and corporations. Thus, in this society, social action, political, and commercial campaigns may be closely connected during the implementation phase of the social action campaign. The same spokespersons may be deemed appropriate to put into office a candidate as are appropriate to improve a societal condition or represent a product. The same messages may even be useful in the three types of campaigns. In fact, within the United States, social action campaigners may be most successful when working with commercial and political campaigners to achieve the desired objectives of all three.

Suggestions for Further Reading

Doyle, J. B., Wilcox, B. L., & Reppucci, N. D. (1983). Training for social and community change. In E. Seidman (Ed.), *Handbook of Social Intervention* (pp. 615–638). Beverly Hills, CA: Sage.

Galician, M. and Pasternack, S. (1987). Balancing good news and bad news: An ethical obligation? *Journal of Mass Media Ethics, 2,* 82–92.

Inglehart, R. (1979). Political action: The impact of values, cognitive level, and social background. In S. H. Barnes & M. Kaase (Eds.), *Political Action: Mass Participation in Five Western Democracies* (pp. 343–380). Beverly Hills, CA: Sage.

Kotler, P. and Roberto, E. L. (1989). *Social Marketing: Strategies for Changing Public Behavior.* New York: The Free Press.

Manoff, R. K. (1985). *Social Marketing: New Imperative for Public Health.* New York: Praeger.

References

A New Era (1990, April 23). A new era of attack politics: Sunbelt Democrats try to win by a mudslide. *Newsweek*, pp. 22–23.

Aaker, D. A. and Bruzzone, D. E. (1981, October). Viewer perceptions of prime-time television advertising. *Journal of Advertising Research, 21*, 15–23.

Aaker, D. A. and Stayman, D. M. (1989). What mediates the emotional response to advertising? The case of warmth. In P. Cafferta and A. M. Tybout (Eds.), *Cognitive and Affective Responses to Advertising* (pp. 287–303). Lexington, MA: D. C. Heath and Company.

Aaker, D. A., Stayman, D. M., and Hagerty, M. R. (1986). Warmth in advertising: Measurement, impact, and sequence effects. *Journal of Consumer Research, 12*, 365–381.

Abelson, R. P., Kinder, D. R., Peters, M. D., and Fiske, S. T. (1982). Affective and semantic components in political person perception. *Journal of Personality and Social Psychology, 42*, 619–630.

Abrams, B. (1982, February 25). The 1981 TV advertisements that people remember most. *The Wall Streeet Journal*, p. 25.

Adams, W. C. (1987). As New Hampshire goes . . . In G. R. Orren and N. W. Polsby (Eds.), *Media and Momentum: The New Hampshire Primary and Nomination Politics* (pp. 42–59). Chatham, NJ: Chatham House Publishers, Inc.

AIADA Congress draws dealers to nation's capitol (1984, July). *Washington Report* (Vol. IV, No. 2), p.1

Aiken, H. D. (1956). *The Age of Ideology: The Nineteenth Century Philosophers*. New York: New American Library.

Alba, J.W. and Chattopadhyay, A. (1985). The effects of context and part–category cues on the recall of competing brands. *Journal of Marketing Research, 22*, 349–359.

Alba, J. W. and Hutchinson, J. W. (1987). Dimensions of consumer expertise. *Journal of Consumer Research, 13*, 411–454.

Albright, L., Kenny, D. A., and Malloy, T. E. (1988). Consensus in personality judgments at zero acquaintance. *Personality and Social Psychology Bulletin, 12*, 381–389.

Alcalay, R. and Taplin, S. (1989). Community health campaigns: From theory to action. In R. E. Rice and C. K. Atkin (Eds.), *Public Communication Campaigns* (2nd ed., pp. 105–129). Newbury Park, CA: Sage Publications.

Alesandrini, K. L. (1982). Imagery–illiciting strategies and meaningful learning. *Journal of Mental Imagery, 6*, 125–140.

Alesandrini, K. L. (1983). Strategies that influence memory for advertising communication. In R. J. Harris (Ed.), *Information Processing Research in Advertising* (pp. 65–82). Hillsdale, NJ: Lawrence Erlbaum Associates.

Alfstad, S. (1991, September 9). Don't shrug off zapping: Advertising must overcome television grazing. *Advertising Age*, p. 20.

Alicke, M. D., Smith, R. H., and Klotz, M. L. (1987). Judgments of physical attractiveness: The role of faces and bodies. *Personality and Social Psychology Bulletin, 12,* 381–389.

Allen, R. L. and Taylor, B. F. (1985). Media public affairs exposure: Issues and alternative strategies. *Communication Monographs, 52,* 186–201.

Allport, G. W. (1954). The historical background of modern social psychology. In G. Lindzey and E. Aronson (Eds.), *The Handbook of Social Psychology* (Vol. 1, pp. 3–56). Reading, MA: Addison-Wesley Publishing Company.

Alperstein, N. M. (1991). Imaginary social relationships with celebrities appearing in television commercials. *Journal of Broadcasting and Electronic Media, 35,* 43–58.

Alsop, R. (1986, March 13). Lionel Richie has no. 1 hit, but it isn't on record charts. *The Wall Street Journal*, p. 27.

Altheide, D. L. and Snow, R. P. (1979). *Media Logic*. Beverly Hills: Sage Publications.

American International Automobile Dealers Association (1984, November). *Setting the Record Straight: Fact and Fiction About Automobile Trade*. Washington, D.C.: AIADA.

Anderson, L. R. and McGuire, W. J. (1965). Prior reassurance of group consensus as a factor in producing resistance to persuasion. *Sociometry, 28,* 44–56.

Argenta, D. M., Stoneman, Z., and Brody, G. H. (1986). The effects of three different television programs on young children's peer interactions and toy play. *Journal of Applied Developmental Psychology, 7,* 355–371.

Armstrong, R. (1988). *The Next Hurrah: The Communications Revolution in American Politics*. New York: Beech Tree Books.

Arndt, J. (1967). Word–of–mouth advertising and informal communication. In D. F. Cox (Ed.), *Risk Taking and Information Handling in Consumer Behavior* (pp. 188–239). Boston: Harvard University Graduate School of Business Administration.

Arnold, D. C. (1985, September 22). Defenseless disciples of sanctuary. *The Arizona Daily Star*, p. F–1.

As creatives rate them: Agency executives give their reaction to Ad Council campaigns (1991, November 11). [The Advertising Council: 50 years of public service]. *Advertising Age*, p. A–10.

Asher, H. (1980). *Presidential Elections and American Politics: Voters, Candidates, and Campaigns Since 1952* (rev. ed.). Homewood, IL: The Dorsey Press.

Atkin, C. K. (1973). Instrumental utilities and information seeking. In P. Clarke (Ed.), *New Models for Mass Communication Research* (pp. 205–242). Beverly Hills, CA: Sage Publications.

Atkin, C. K. (1984). Consumer and social effects of advertising. In B. Dervin and M. J. Voight (Eds.), *Progress in Communication Sciences* (Vol. 4, 205–248). Norwood, NJ: Ablex Publishing Corporation.

Atkin, C. K. and Arkin, E. B. (1990). Issues and initiatives in communicating health information. In C. Atkin and L. Wallack (Eds.), *Mass Communication and Public Health: Complexities and Conflicts*. Newbury Park, CA: Sage Publications.

Atkin, C. K., Bowen, L., Nayman, O. B., and Sheinkopf, K. G. (1973). Quality versus quantity in televised political ads. *Public Opinion Quarterly, 37,* 209–224.

Atkin, C. K. and Freimuth, V. (1989). Formative evaluation research in campaign design. In R. E. Rice and C. K. Atkin (Eds.), *Public Communication Campaigns* (2nd edition, pp. 131–150). Newbury Park, CA: Sage Publications.

Atkinson, M. (1984). *Our Masters' Voices: The Language and Body Language of Politics*. London: Methuen.

Atkinson, M. (1986). The 1983 election and the demise of live oratory. In I. Crewe and M. Harrop (Eds.), *Political Communications: The General Election Campaign of 1983* (pp. 38–55). Cambridge: Cambridge University Press.

Atlanta Journal and Constitution (1992, February 14). [classified ad], p. S–22.

Auerbach, S. (1983a, November 2). Domestic content bill set back. *Washington Post*, p. D–7.

Auerbach, S. (1983b, November 3). House abruptly stops "content" debate. *Washington Post,* p. D-1.

Auerbach, S. (1983c, November 4). House approves "content" bill. *Washington Post,* p. E1.

Augustin, M. S., Stevens, E., and Hicks, D. (1973). An evaluation of the effectiveness of a children and youth project. *Health Services Report, 88,* 942-946.

Axelrod, D. (1988, November 9). Broadcast views. *Advertising Age,* pp. 68, 91-92.

Axelrod, R. (1972). Where voters came from: An analysis of electoral coalitions, 1952-1968. *American Political Science Review, 66,* 11-20.

Baggaley, J. (1989, June). *Media AIDS Education: The Boomerang Effect.* Paper presented to Fifth International Conference on AIDS, Montreal, Quebec, Canada.

Bailey, C. J. N. (1981). Theory, description, and differences among linguists (Or, what keeps linguistics from becoming a science). *Language and Communication, 1,* 39-66.

Bailey, T. A. (1966). *The American Pageant: A History of the Republic* (3rd ed.). Lexington, MA: D. C. Heath and Company.

Baldwin, H. (1989). *How to Create Effective TV Commercials* (2nd ed.). Lincolnwood, IL: National Textbook Company.

Ball, P., Giles, H., Byrne, J. L., and Berechee, P. (1984). Situational constraints on the evaluative significance of speech accommodation: some Australian data. *International Journal of the Sociology of Language, 46,* 115-129.

Ball-Rokeach, S. and Rokeach, M. (1989). The great American values test. In R.E. Rice and C. K. Atkin (Eds.), *Public Communication Campaigns* (pp. 218-221). Newbury Park, CA: Sage Publications.

Bandura, A. (1977a). Self-efficacy: Toward a unifying theory of behavioral change. *Psychological Review, 84,* 191-215.

Bandura, A. (1977b). *Social Learning Theory.* Englewood Cliffs, NJ: Prentice Hall, Inc.

Bandura, A. (1982). The self and mechanisms of agency. In J. Suls (Ed.), *Psychological Perspectives on the Self.* Hillsdale, NJ: Lawrence Erlbaum.

Bandura, A. and Cervone, D. (1986). Differential engagement of self-reactive influences on cognitive motivation. *Organizational Behavior and Human Decision Processes, 38,* 92-113.

Barber, J. D. (1978). Characters in the campaign: The educational challenge. In J. D. Barber (Ed.), *Race for the Presidency: The Media and the Nominating Process* (pp. 173-198). Englewood Cliffs, NJ: Prentice Hall, Inc.

Barnes, S. H. and Kaase, M. (1979). *Political Action.* Beverly Hills, CA: Sage Publications.

Barry, T. E. and Tremblay, R. L (1975). Comparative advertising: Perspectives and issues. *Journal of Advertising, 4,* 15-20.

Barthes, R. (1982). *Empire of Signs.* New York: Hill and Wang.

Barwise, T. P., Ehrenberg, A. S. C., and Goodhardt, G. J. (1982). Glued to the box? Patterns of TV repeat-viewing. *Journal of Communication, 32,* 22-29.

Batra, R. and Ray, M. L. (1983). Advertising situations: The implications of differential involvement and accompanying affect responses. In R. J. Harris (Ed.), *Information Processing Research in Advertising* (pp. 127-151). Hillsdale, NJ: Lawrence Erlbaum Associates.

Batra, R. and Ray, M. L. (1985). How advertising works at contact. In L. F. Alwitt and A. A. Mitchell (Eds.), *Psychological Processes and Advertising Effects: Theory, Research, and Applications* (pp. 13-43). Hillsdale, NJ: Lawrence Erlbaum Associates, Publishers.

Bauer, B. (1986, June 4). 15-second television commercials 'ad up' fast. *USA Today,* p. 1.

Beck, M. (1990, April 23). Going for the gold: Selling to the over-50s presents big opportunities and big risks. *Newsweek,* pp. 74-76.

Becker, L. B. (1982). The mass media and citizen assessment of issue importance: A reflection on agenda-setting research. In D. C. Whitney and E. Wartella (Eds.), *Mass Communication Review Yearbook* (vol. 3, pp. 521-536). Beverly Hills, CA: Sage Publications.

Becker, S. W. and McCombs, M. E. (1978). The role of the press in determining voter reaction to presidential primaries. *Human Communication Research, 4,* 301-307.

Bee, H. (1985). *The Developing Child* (4th ed.). New York: Harper and Row.

Belch, G. E. (1981). An examination of comparative and noncomparative television commercials: The effects of claim variation and repetition on cognitive response and message acceptance. *Journal of Marketing Research, 18*, 333–349.

Belch, G. E. (1982). The effects of television commercial repetition on cognitive response and message acceptance. *Journal of Consumer Research, 9*, 56–65.

Beltramini, R. F. and Kelley, L. D. (1983). Lifestyle research applications in advertising intermedia comparisons. In D. W. Jugenheimer (Ed.), *Proceedings of the 1983 Convention of the American Academy of Advertising* (pp. 6–9). Lawrence, KS: Donald W. Jugenheimer, William Allen White School of Journalism and Mass Communication, University of Kansas.

Belville, H. J. (1988). *Audience Ratings: Radio, Television, Cable* (2nd ed). Hillsdale, NJ: Lawrence Erlbaum Associates.

Bem, D. J. (1965). An experimental analysis of self persuasion. *Journal of Experimental Social Psychology, 1*, 199–218.

Bem, D. J. (1967). Self–perception: An alternative interpretation of cognitive dissonance phenomena. *Psychological Review, 74*, 183–200.

Bem, D. J. (1972). Self–perception theory. In L. Berkowitz (Ed.), *Advances in Experimental Social Psychology*, (vol. 6, pp. 1–62). New York: Academic Press.

Beniger, J. R. (1987). Personalization of mass media and the growth of pseudo–community. *Communication Research, 14*, 352–370.

Bennett, P. D. and Kassarjian, H. H. (1972). *Consumer Behavior*. Englewood Cliffs, NJ: Prentice Hall, Inc.

Berelson, B. R., Lazarsfeld, P. F., and McPhee, W. N. (1954). *Voting: A Study of Opinion Formation in a Presidential Campaign*. Chicago: University of Chicago Press.

Berger, C. R. (1977). The covering law perspective as a theoretical basis for the study of human communication. *Communication Quarterly, 25*, p. 7–18.

Berger, C. R. and Calabrese, R. J. (1975). Some explorations in initial interaction and beyond: Toward a developmental theory of interpersonal communication. *Human Communication Research, 1*, 99–112.

Berger, C. R. and Chaffee, S. H. (1987). The study of communication as a science. In C. R. Berger and S. H. Chaffee (Eds.), *Handbook of Communication Science* (pp. 15–19). Beverly Hills, CA: Sage Publications.

Berk, R. A. and Rossi, P. H. (1990). *Thinking About Program Evaluation*. Newbury Park, CA: Sage Publications.

Berkman, R. and Kitch, L. W. (1986). *Politics in the Media Age*. New York: McGraw–Hill.

Berkowitz, T. L. (1985). Political television advertising objectives: The viewpoint of political media consultants (Doctoral dissertation, Wayne State University). *Dissertation Abstracts International, 46*, 1117A.

Berlo, D. K. (1960). *The Process of Communication*. New York: Holt, Rineheart, and Winston.

Berman, R. (1981). *Advertising and Social Change*. Beverly Hills, CA: Sage Publications.

Biehal, G. and Chakravarti, D. (1986). Consumers' use of memory and external information in choice: Macro and micro perspectives. *Journal of Consumer Research, 12*, 382–405.

Big new celebrity boom (1978, May 22). *Business Week*, pp. 79–80.

Bingham, S. G. (1991). Communication strategies for managing sexual harassment in organizations: Understanding message options and their effects. *Journal of Applied Communication Research, 19*, 88–115.

Bird, C. D. (1987). Influence of the spacing of trait information on impressions of likability. *Journal of Experimental Social Psychology, 23*, 481–497.

Birkel, R. C. and Reppucci, N. D. (1983). Social networks, information–seeking, and the utilization of services. *American Journal of Communication Psychology, 11*, 185–205.

Bither, S. W., Dolich, I. J., and Nell, E. B. (1971). The application of attitude immunization techniques in marketing. *Journal of Marketing Research, 18*, 56–61.

Bloom, D. E. (1989). Women and work. In R. Hovland and G. B. Wilcox (Eds.), *Advertising in Society: Classical and Contemporary Readings on Advertising's Role in Society* (pp. 143–152). Lincolnwood, IL: National Textbook Company.

Blum, J. M., Catton, B., Morgan, E. S., Schlesinger, A. M., Jr., Stampp, K. M., and Van Woodward, C. (1968). *The National Experience: A History of the United States* (2nd ed.). New York: Harcourt, Brace and World, Inc.

Blumenthal, S. (1982). *The Permanent Campaign* (rev. ed.). New York: Simon & Schuster.

Blumler, J. G. (1985). The social character of media gratifications. In K. E. Rosengren, L. A. Wenner, and P. Palmgreen (Eds.), *Media Gratifications Research: Current Perspectives* (pp. 41–60). Beverly Hills, CA: Sage Publications.

Boddewyn, J. J. and Marton, K. (1978). *Comparison Advertising: A Worldwide Study*. New York: Hastings House.

Bogart, L. (1967). *Strategy in Advertising*. New York: Harcourt, Brace and World, Inc.

Bogart, L. (1990). *Strategy in Advertising: Matching Media and Messages to Markets and Motivations* (2nd ed.). Lincolnwood, IL: National Textbook Company.

Bond, R., Welkowitz, J., Goldschmidt, H., and Wattenberg, S. (1987). Vocal frequency and person perception: Effects of perceptual salience and nonverbal sensitivity. *Journal of Psycholinguistic Research, 16,* 335–350.

Boorstin, D. J. (1975). *The Image: A Guide to Pseudo-events in America*. New York: Atheneum.

Borgida, E. and Howard–Pitney, B. (1983). Personal involvement and the robustness of perceptual salience effects. *Journal of Personality and Social Psychology, 45,* 560–570.

Boschwitz Botches It (1990, November 19). He loses to the professor who will "be in Helms' face." *Time,* p. 43.

Boster, F. J. and Mongeau, P. (1984). Fear–arousing persuasive messages. In R. N. Bostrom (Ed.), *Communication Yearbook* (Vol. 8, pp. 330–375). Beverly Hills, CA: Sage Publications.

Boulding, K. E. (1977). *The Image: Knowledge in Life and Society*. Ann Arbor, MI: University of Michigan Press.

Bowen, D. J. and Grunberg, N. E. (1987). The expectancy construct within the social learning theories of Rotter and Bandura. *Journal of Applied Social Psychology, 17,* 622–640.

Bowers, J. W., Courtright, J. A., and Bradac, J. J. (1979). Three language variables in communication research: Intensity, immediacy, and diversity. *Human Communication Research, 5,* 257–269.

Bradburn, N. M. and Sudman, S. S. (1988). *Polls and Surveys: Understanding What They Tell Us.* San Francisco: Jossey-Bass.

Brady, H. E. and Johnston, R. (1987). What's the primary message: Horse race or issue journalism. In G. R. Orren and N. W. Polsby (Eds.), *Media and Momentum: The New Hampshire Primary and Nomination Politics* (pp. 127–186). Chatham, NJ: Chatham House Publishers, Inc.

Brehm, J. W. and Cohen, A. R. (1962). *Explorations in Cognitive Dissonance*. New York: John Wiley and Sons.

Brewer, W. E. and Dupree, D. A. (1983). Use of plan schemata in the recall and recognition of goal–directed actions. *Journal of Experimental Psychology, 9,* 117–129.

Brinker, R. P. (1982). Contextual contours and the development of language. In M. Beveridge (Ed.), *Children Thinking Through Language,* pp. 7–23. London: Edward Arnold, Ltd.

Broadcast Advertising Reports (1985, December 30). Political advertising. *The Wall Street Journal,* p. 11.

Broder, D., Edsall, T. B., Ifill, G., Taylor, P., and Rhoney, C. T. (1988). The candidates nobody wants. *Washington Post National Weekly Edition, 5,* 9–10.

Brown, W. (1983, November 2). U.S.-Japan auto pact hurts GM; Firm can't meet import goal. *Washington Post,* p. D7.

Brudney, J. L. and Brown, M. M. (1990). Training in volunteer administration: Assessing the needs of the field. *The Journal of Volunteer Administration, 9,* 21–28.

Brummett, B. (1988). The homology hypothesis: Pornography on the VCR. *Critical Studies in Mass Communication, 5,* 202–216.

Bruner, J. (1981). The social context of language acquisition. *Language and Communication, 1,* 155–178.

Burgoon, J. K. (1980). Nonverbal communication research in the 1970s: An overview. In D. Nimmo (Ed.), *Communication Yearbook IV* (pp. 179–197). New Brunswick, NJ: Transaction Books.

Burgoon, J. K., Buller, D. B., and Woodall, W. G. (1989). *Nonverbal Communication: The Unspoken Dialogue*. New York: Harper and Row.

Burgoon, J. K., Burgoon, M., Miller, G. R., and Sunnafrank, M. (1981). Learning theory approaches to persuasion. *Human Communication Research, 7,* 161–179.

Burgoon, J. K. and Hale, J. L. (1987). Validation and measurement of the fundamental themes of relational communication. *Communication Monographs, 54,* 19–41.

Burgoon, M. (1990). Language and social influence. In H. Giles and P. Robinson (Eds.), *Handbook of Social Psychology and Language,* (pp. 51–72). London: John Wiley and Sons.

Burgoon, M., Jones, S. B., and Stewart, D. (1975). Toward a message-centered theory of persuasion: Three empirical investigations of language intensity. *Human Communication Research, 1,* 240–256.

Burgoon, M. and Miller, G. R. (1985). An expectancy interpretation of language and persuasion. In H. Giles and R. N. St. Clair (Eds.), *Recent Advances in Language, Communication, and Social Psychology* (pp. 199–229). London: Lawrence Erlbaum Associates.

Burgoon, M., and Miller, G. R. (1990). Paths. *Communication Monographs, 57,* 152–160.

Burgoon, M. and Miller, M. (1986). Persuasive communication. In C. Fernandez-Collado and G. L. Dahnke (Eds.), *Social Science of Communication* (pp. 223–249). Mexico City: McGraw Hill de Mexico.

Burgoon, M., Pfau, M., Birk, T., and Clark, J. E. (1985). [An application and extension of an inoculation theory explanation for the effects of corporate advertorial campaigns]. Unpublished raw data.

Burke, R. R. and Srull, T. K. (1988). Competitive interference and consumer memory for advertising. *Journal of Consumer Research, 15,* 55–67.

Burnham, W. D. (1965). The changing shape of the American political universe. *American Political Science Review, 59,* 7–28.

Burnkrant, R. E. and Howard, D. J. (1984). Effects of the use of introductory rhetorical questions versus statements on information processing. *Journal of Personality and Social Psychology, 47,* 1218–1230.

Burnstein, E. (1967). Sources of cognitive bias in the representation of simple social structures: Balance, minimal change, positivity, reciprocity, and the respondent's own attitude. *Journal of Personality and Social Psychology, 7,* 36–48.

Cacioppo, J. T. and Petty, R. E. (1979). Attitudes and cognitive response: An electrophysiological approach. *Journal of Personality and Social Psychology, 37,* 2181–2199.

Cacioppo, J. T. and Petty, R. E. (1985). Central and peripheral routes to persuasion: The role of message repetition. In A. Mitchell and L. Alwitt (Eds.), *Psychological Processes and Advertising Effects.* Hillsdale, NJ: Lawrence Erlbaum Associates.

Cacioppo, J. T. and Petty, R. E. (1987). Stalking rudimentary processes of social influence: A psychophysiological approach. In M. P. Zanna, J. M. Olson and C. P. Herman (Eds.), *Social Influence: The Ontario Symposium* (Vol. 5, pp. 41–74). Hillsdale, NJ: Lawrence Erlbaum Associates.

Cacioppo, J. T., Petty, R. E., and Sidera, J. (1982). The effects of a salient self-schema on the evaluation of proattitudinal editorials: Top-down versus bottom-up message processing. *Journal of Experimental Social Psychology, 18,* 324–338.

Caddell, P. (1985, December 30). Baby boomers come of political age. *Wall Street Journal,* p 12.

Cafferata, P. and Tybout, A. (1989). *Cognitive and Affective Responses to Advertising.* Lexington, MA: Lexington Books.

Cain, C. (1986, August 17). Advertisers flock to famous faces. *Sioux Falls Argus Leader,* pp. 1E and 2E.

Calder, B. J. (1979). When attitudes follow behavior–A self-perception/dissonance interpretation of low involvement. In J. C. Maloney and B. Silverman (Eds.), *Attitude Research Plays for High Stakes.* Chicago: American Marketing Association.

Calder, B. J., and Gruner, C. L. (1989). Emotional advertising appeals. In P. Cafferata and A. M. Tybout (Eds.), *Cognitive and Affective Responses to Advertising* (pp. 277–285). Lexington, MA: Lexington Books.

Calder, B. J. and Sternthal, B. (1980). Television commercial wearout: An information processing view. *Journal of Marketing Research, 17*, 173–186.

Campbell, A., Conserve, P. E., Miller, W. E., and Stokes, D. E. (1960). *The American Voter*. New York: John Wiley and Sons.

Campbell, A., Conserve, P. E., Miller, W. E., and Stokes, D. E. (1966). *Elections and the Political Order*. New York: John Wiley and Sons.

Campbell, A., Gurin, G., and Miller, W. E. (1954). *The Voter Decides*. Evanston, IL: Row, Peterson and Company.

Cannon, J. P. (1981, November). *Institutional Political Advertising in the 1980 Elections*. Paper presented at the annual meeting of the Speech Communication Association, Anaheim, CA.

Carlson, M. B. (1988, August 8). Shoot-out at gender gap: Why women don't take a liking to Bush? *Time*, pp. 13 and 15.

Carpenter, E. (1986). The new languages. In G. Gumpert and R. Cathcart (Eds.), *Inter/Media: Interpersonal Communication in a Media World* (3rd ed., pp. 353–367). New York: Oxford University Press.

Carroll, L. (1960). *Through the Looking-Glass*. New York: New American Library, Inc.

Carton, B. (1990, September 23). Ad agencies cope with baby boomers' midlife crisis. *Chicago Tribune*, p. 7–9D.

Caughey, J. (1984). *Imaginary Social Worlds: A Cultural Approach*. Lincoln, NE: University of Nebraska Press.

Cecil, M. (1990, October 4). Pressler refuses to answer charges about missed vote. *Sioux Falls Argus Leader*, p. 1C.

Center, A. H. and Walsh, F. E. (1985). Public relations practices: Managerial case studies and problems (3rd ed.), Englewood Cliffs, NJ: Prentice Hall.

Chaffee, S. H. (1972). The interpersonal context of mass communication. In F. H. Kline and P. J. Tichenor (Eds.), *Current Perspectives in Mass Communication* (pp. 95–120). Beverly Hills, CA: Sage Publications.

Chaffee, S. H. (1978). Presidential debates—Are they helpful to voters? *Communication Monographs, 45*, 330–346.

Chaffee, S. H. (1981). Mass media in political campaigns: An expanding role. In R. E. Rice and W. J. Paisley (Eds.), *Public Communication Campaigns* (pp. 181–198). Beverly Hills, CA: Sage Publications.

Chaffee, S. H. (1982). Mass media and interpersonal channels: Competitive, convergent, or complementary? In G. Gumpert and R. Cathcart (Eds.), *Inter/media: Interpersonal Communication in a Media World* (2nd ed., pp. 57–77). New York: Oxford University Press.

Chaffee, S. H. and Choe, S. Y. (1980). Time of decision and media use during the Ford–Carter campaign. *Public Opinion Quarterly, 44*, 53–69.

Chaffee, S. H. and Hochheimer, J. L. (1985). The beginnings of political communication research in the United States: Origins of the "limited effects" model. In E. M. Rogers and F. Balle (Eds.), *The Media Revolution in America and in Western Europe* (pp. 267–296). Norwood, NJ: Ablex Publishing Corporation.

Chaiken, S. (1980). Heuristic versus systematic information processing and the use of source versus message cues in persuasion. *Journal of Personality and Social Psychology, 39*, 752–766.

Chaiken, S. (1987). The heuristic model of persuasion. In M. P. Zanna, J. M. Olson, and C. P. Herman (Eds.), *Social Influence: The Ontario Symposium* (Vol. 5, pp. 3–39). Hillsdale, NJ: Lawrence Erlbaum Associates.

Chaiken, S. and Baldwin, M. W. (1981). Affective–cognitive consistency and the effect of salient behavioral information on the self-perception of attitudes. *Journal of Personality and Social Psychology, 41*, 1–12.

Chaiken, S. and Eagly, A. H. (1976). Communication modality as a determinant of message persuasiveness and message comprehensibility. *Journal of Personality and Social Psychology, 3*, 605–614.

Chapman, S. (1985, August 25). The hazards of protectionism. *Chicago Tribune.*

Chen, H. and Rossi, P. H. (1980). The multi-goal, theory driven approach to evaluation: A model linking basic and applied social science. *Social Forces, 59*, 106–122.

Cherry, C. (1973). On signs, languages, and communication. In, *On Human Communication: A Review, a Survey and a Criticism* (3rd ed., pp. 68–125). Cambridge, MA: The MIT Press.

Chesebro, J. W. (1984). The media reality: Epistemological functions of media in cultural systems. *Critical Studies in Mass Communication, 1*, 111–130.

Childer, T. L., and Houston, M. J. (1984). Conditions for a picture–superiority effect on consumer memory. *Journal of Consumer Research, 11*, 643–654.

Chira, S. (1985a, March 28). Japan car flow may rise 24.3%. *New York Times*, pp. IV–1.

Chira, S. (1985b, March 29). Rise in car exports confirmed by Japan. *New York Times*, p. IV–15.

Choudhury, P. K. (1974). Social responsibility: An alternate strategy of marketing. *Academy of Marketing Science Journal, 2*, 213–222.

Christ, W. G., Caywood, C., and Thorson, E. (1991, May). *Do Attitudes Toward Negative Political Advertising Affect Information Processing?* Paper presented at the annual meeting of the International Communication Association, Chicago, IL.

Christianson, J. B. (1984). Provider participation in competitive bidding for indigent patients. *Inquiry, 21*, 161–177.

Christianson, J. B., Hillman, D. G., and Smith, K. R. (1984). Competitive bidding for indigent patients. *Inquiry, 21*, 161–177.

Cialdini, R. B. (1984a). *Influence: The New Psychology of Modern Persuasion.* New York: Quill.

Cialdini, R. B. (1984b, February). The triggers of influence. *Psychology Today*, pp. 40–45.

Cicero. *De Inventione* (H. M. Hubbell, tr.; 1949). Cambridge, MA: Loeb Classical Library.

Clancy, K. (1992, January 20). CPMS must bow to 'involvement' measurement. *Advertising Age*, p. 26.

Clark, E. (1988). *The Want Makers: The World of Advertising: How They Make You Buy.* New York: Viking.

Clark, P. and Fredin, E. (1978). Newspapers, television, and political reasoning. *Public Opinion Quarterly, 42*, 143–160.

Cleaver, J. Y. (1988, March 7). Lifestyle ads boost banks, insurers. *Advertising Age*, pp. S8–S10.

Coady, E. (1991, July 6), Bush raises import level for peanuts: Georgia farmers could lose $50 million. *The Atlanta Journal and Constitution*, p. A–1.

Cobbey, R. (1980). Audience attitudes and readership. *ANPA News Research Reports, 29*, 8–9.

Coen, R. J. (1987, November 30). TV forms hot; print, outdoor waver. *Advertising Age*, pp. S–2, S–4, S–5.

Cohen, B. C. (1963). *The Press and Foreign Policy.* Princeton, NJ: Princeton University Press.

Colford, S. W. (1988a, March 14). Politicos resort to "ambush" ads on TV. *Advertising Age*, p. 3.

Colford, S. W. (1988b, June 27). Hail to the image: Reagan legacy: Marketing tactics change politics. *Advertising Age*, pp. 3 and 32.

Colley, R. H. (1961). *Defining Advertising Goals for Measuring Advertising Results.* New York: Association for National Advertisers.

Combs, J. E. (1980). *Dimensions of Political Drama.* Santa Monica, CA: Goodyear Publishing Company, Inc.

Conference of Mayors (1980, April). Targeting in on handgun control. *The US Conference of Mayors Handgun Control Staff Newsletter* (Vol. 6, No. 1), pp. 1–4.

Conway, M. M. (1985). *Political Participation in the United States.* Washington, DC: Congressional Quarterly Press.

Converse, J. and Cooper, J. (1979). The importance of decisions and free–choice attitude change: A curvilinear finding. *Journal of Experimental Social Psychology, 15*, 48–61.

Cook, P. S., Petersen, R. C., and Moore, D. T. (1990). Alcohol, tobacco, and other drugs may harm the unborn. DHHS publication No. (ADM) 90-1711. Rockville, MD.

Cook, R. (1989). The nominating process. In M. Nelson (Ed.), *The elections of 1988* (pp. 25–61). Washington, DC: Congressional Quarterly Press.

Cooper, J. and Fazio, J. (1984). A new look at dissonance theory. *Advances in Experimental Social Psychology, 17*, 229–266.

Correcting misperceptions about US–Japan auto trade (1984, July). *Washingtion Report* (Vol. IV, No. 2), pp. 5–6.

Cott, N. F. (1987). *The Grounding of Modern Feminism.* New Haven: Yale University Press.

Cotton, J. L. (1985). Cognitive dissonance in selective exposure. In D. Zillmann and J. Bryant (Eds.), *Selective Exposure to Communication* (pp. 11–33). Hillsdale, NJ: Lawrence Erlbaum.

Cox, J. (1990, March 15). At the Ford–Chevy battleground: Residents puzzled by ad flap. *USA Today*, p. 4B.

Cronkhite, G. (1969). *Persuasion: Speech and Behavioral Change.* New York: Bobbs–Merrill Company, Inc.

Curti, M. (1967). The changing concept of "human nature" in the literature of American advertising. *Business History Review, 41*, 335–357.

Cutbirth, C. W., Monroe, P. S., Kirch, M., Case, J., and Mikesell, B. (1989, April 12–14). *Negative Campaigning: 1988.* Paper presented at the annual meeting of the Central States Communication Association, Kansas City, MO.

Cutler, N. E. and Danowski, J. A. (1980). Process gratification in aging cohorts. *Journalism Quarterly, 57*, 269–277.

Daines, G. (1984). The first forty years. *Fire Management Notes, 45*, 13–14.

Danforth, J. C. (1985, February 23). Hill set to pressure Japanese on auto imports. *Congressional Quarterly*, pp. 355–390.

Daniels, A. K. (1988). *Invisible Careers: Women Civic Leaders from the Volunteer World.* Chicago: University of Chicago Press.

Dardenne, P. (1981, November). The cost of corporate advertising. *Public Relations Journal,* pp. 30–35 and 38–42.

Dealer muscle needed to combat protectionist trade legislation (1986, July). *Toyota Today* (Vol. 14), p. 3.

Dealers and consumers unite to oppose domestic content (1984, July). *Washington Report* (Vol. IV, No. 2), pp. 2–3.

DeCarlo, T. and Parrott, R. (1991, April). *Perceptions of the Effectiveness of Alcohol Warning Labels.* Paper presented at the annual conference of the Southern Communication Association, Florida.

De Fleur, M. L., and Ball–Rokeach, S. (1982). *Theories of Mass Communication.* New York: Longman.

De Fleur, M. L. and Dennis, E. E. (1985). *Understanding Mass Communication* (2nd ed.). Boston: Houghton Mifflin Company.

Delia, J. G. (1977). Alternative perspectives for the study of human communication: Critique and reponse. *Communication Quarterly, 25*, 46–62.

Delia, J. G. (1987). Communication research: A history. In C. R. Berger and S. H. Chaffee (Eds.), *Handbook of Communication Science* (pp. 20–98). Beverly Hills, CA: Sage Publications.

DeMeuse, K. P. (1987). A review of the effects of nonverbal cues in the performance appraisal process. *Journal of Occupational Psychology, 60*, 207–226.

Denton, R. E., Jr. (1983, April). *"Be All You Can Be": The Development of the United States Army's Advertising Campaign.* Paper presented at the annual meeting of the Central States Speech Association, Lincoln, NE.

Denton, R. E. Jr., and Woodward, G. C. (1985). *Political Communication in America.* New York: Praeger Publishers.

Department of Health and Human Services in conjunction with the Public Health Service and the Centers for Disease Control. *American Response to AIDS. What Is HIV Infection? And What Is AIDS?* Atlanta, GA: Centers for Disease Control.

Dervin, B. (1989). Audience as listener and learner, teacher and confidante: The sense-making approach. In R. E. Rice and C. K. Atkin (Eds.), *Public Communication Campaigns* (2nd ed., pp. 67–86). Newbury Park, CA: Sage Publications.

Dervin, B., Harlock, S., Atwood, R., and Garzona, C. (1980). The human side of information: An exploration in a health communication context. In D. Nimmo, (Ed.), *Communication Yearbook* (Vol. 4, pp. 591–608). New Brunswick, NJ: Transaction Books.

Devlin, L. P. (1986). An analysis of presidential television commercials, 1952–1984. In L. L. Kaid, D. Nimmo, and K. R. Sanders (Eds.), *New Perspectives on Political Advertising* (pp. 21–54). Carbondale, IL: Southern Illinois University Press.

Devlin, L. P. (1989). Contrasts in presidential campaign commercials of 1988. *American Behavioral Scientist, 32,* 389–414.

Diamond, E. and Friery, K. (1987). Media coverage of presidential debates. In J. L. Swerdlow (ed.), *Presidential Debates: 1988 and Beyond* (pp. 43–51). Washington, DC: Congressional Quarterly Press.

Dollar, S. and Yandel, G. (1991, July 19). Atlanta at the top when it comes to TV. *The Atlanta Journal and Constitution,* pp. A-1 and A-9.

Donius, J. F. (1983). Campaign simulation via multiple exposures on-air copytesting: An experiment. *Journal of Advertising Research, 23,* 35–39.

Doyle, J. B., Wilcox, B. L., and Reppucci, N. D. (1983). Training for social and community change. In E. Seidman (Ed.), *Handbook of Social Intervention* (pp. 615–638). Beverly Hills, CA: Sage Publications.

Dougherty, P. H. (1973, November 14). Advertising: Comparison issue. *The New York Times,* p. 61.

Easterbrook, G. (1987, January 26). The revolution in medicine. *Newsweek,* pp. 40–74.

Edel, R. (1988, February 22). Unwired nets snare marketers' dollars. *Advertising Age,* p. S-12.

Edell, J. A. and Burke, M. C. (1987). The power of feelings in understanding advertising effects. *Journal of Consumer Research, 14,* 421–433.

Edelman, M. (1964). *Politics as Symbolic Action: Mass Arousal and Quiescence.* New York: Academic Press.

Edelman, M. (1967). *The Symbolic Uses of Politics.* Urbana, IL: University of Illinois Press.

Ehrenhalt, A. (1985). Technology, strategy bring new campaign era. *Congressional Quarterly Weekly Report, 43,* 2559–2565.

Ellis, D. G. (1982). Language and speech communication. In M. Burgoon (Ed.), *Communication Yearbook* (Vol. 6, pp. 34–62). Beverly Hills, CA: Sage Publications.

Elmore, R. F. (1983). Social policymaking as strategic intervention. In E. Seidman (Ed.), *Handbook of Social Intervention* (pp. 212–236). Beverly Hills, CA: Sage Publications.

Erickson, J. K. (1988, March 7). Marketing to women: It's tough to keep up with changes. *Advertising Age,* p. S1.

Etgar, M. and Goodwin, S. A. (1978). Comparative advertising: Issues and problems. In H. K. Hunt (Ed.), *Advances in Consumer Research* (Vol. 5, pp. 63–71). Chicago: Association for Consumer Research.

Ettema, J. S., Brown, J. W., and Luepker, R. V. (1983). Knowledge gap effects in a health information campaign. *Public Opinion Quarterly, 47,* 516–527.

Expert ratings (1991, November 11). [The Advertising Council: 50 years of public service]. *Advertising Age,* p. A-12.

Farah, B. G. and Klein, E. (1988, June 20). The return of the gender gap. *The Polling Report, 4,* 1 and 6–7.

Farah, B. G. and Klein, E. (1989). Public opinion trends. In G. M. Pomper et. al. (Eds.), *The Election of 1988: Reports and Interpretations* (pp. 103–128). Chatham, NJ: Chatham House Publishers.

Farnsworth, C. H. (1985, March 27). Anti-Japan trade bill in Senate; Nation called "unfair" in plea for retaliation. *New York Times,* p. IV-15.

Feds put squeeze (1991, April 25). Feds put squeeze on OJ labels: FDA: Juice made from concentrate isn't fresh. *Atlanta Journal and Constitution,* p. A1.

Feick, L. F. and Price, L. L. (1987). The market maven: A diffuser of marketplace information. *Journal of Marketing, 51,* 83–97.

Feldstein, M. and Feldstein, K. (1985, August 30). Protection: A good first step. *Washington Post.*

Festervand, T. A. and Lumpkin, J. R. (1989). Response of elderly consumers to their portrayal by advertisers. In R. Hovland and G. B. Wilcox (Eds.), *Advertising in Society: Classic and Contemporary Readings on Advertising's Role in Society* (pp. 165–190). Lincolnwood, IL: National Textbook Company.

Festinger, L. (1957). *A Theory of Cognitive Dissonance.* Stanford, CA: Stanford University Press.

Festinger, L. (1964). *Conflict, Decision, and Dissonance.* Stanford, CA: Stanford University Press.

Fimbres, G. (1985, September 14). MASH star declares war on "Rambo" thinking. *Tucson Citizen,* p. A–4.

Finding out what makes us tick (1987, January 27). *The Christian Science Monitor,* pp. 1, 16–17.

Fink, E. J., Monahan, J. L., and Kaplowitz, S. A. (1989). A spatial model of the mere exposure effect. *Communication Research, 16,* 746–769.

Finnegan, J. R., Jr., Bracht, N., and Viswanath, K. (1989). Community power and leadership analysis in lifestyle campaigns. In C. T. Salmon (Ed.), *Information Campaigns: Balancing Social Values and Social Change* (pp. 54–84). Newbury Park, CA: Sage Publications.

Fiske, S. T., Kinder, D. R., and Larter, W. M. (1983). The novice and the expert: Knowledge-based strategies in political cognition. *Journal of Experimental Social Psychology, 19,* 381–400.

Fiske, S. T. and Taylor, S. E. (1984). *Social Cognition.* Reading, MA: Addison-Wesley.

Fitzgerald, K. (1989a, May 8). Long–distance ad wars: Phone companies set big push. *Advertising Age,* p. 3.

Fitzgerald, K. (1989b, July 17). Sprint hangs up on humorous ads. *Advertising Age,* p. 4.

Fitzgerald, K. (1989c, August 21). Rivals reach out, lash AT&T. *Advertising Age,* p. 64.

Fitzgerald, K. (1989d, September 18). Sprint TV ads reduce the static about prices. *Advertising Age,* p. 70.

Fitzgerald, K. (1990a, June 4). Ringing up recall. *Advertising Age,* p. 47.

Fitzgerald, K. (1990b, October 22). Hello? Is anybody listening? *Advertising Age,* p. 34.

Flexner, E. (1975). *Century of Struggle: The Woman's Rights Movement in the United States* (rev. ed.). Cambridge, MA: Harvard University Press.

Flora, J. A., Maccoby, N., and Farquhar, J. W. (1989). Communication campaigns to prevent cardiovascular disease: The Stanford community studies. In R. E. Rice and C. K. Atkin (Eds.), *Public Communication Campaigns* (2nd ed., pp. 233–252). Newbury Park, CA: Sage Publications.

Foell, E. W. (1985, August 8). Hiroshima, Mazda cars, and the perils of protectionism. *The Christian Science Monitor,* pp. A1–2.

Foltz, K. (1990, August 6). Rebuttal spot by US Sprint to AT&T. *New York Times,* p. D13.

Forciea, P. (1991, April 15). [Interview with Patrick Forceia, Director and chief strategist of the Wellstone campaign]. Minneapolis, MN.

Fowler, F. J., JR. (1984). *Survey Research Methods.* Newbury Park, CA: Sage Publications.

Fox, S. (1984). *The Mirror Makers: A History of American Advertising and its Creators.* New York: William Morrow and Company.

Francese, P. (1988, November 9). A symphony of demographic change. *Advertising Age,* pp. 130–132.

Franklin, J. H. (1967). *From Slavery to Freedom: A History of Negro Americans* (3rd ed.). New York: Alfred A. Knopf.

Frankovic, K. A. (1982, Summer). Sex and politics–New alignments, old issues. *PS,* 439.

Frantzich, S. E. (1989). *Political Parties in the Technological Age.* New York: Longman.

Freeman, H. E., Blendon, R. J., Aiken, L. H., Sudman, S., Mullinix, C. S. and Corey, C. R. (1987, Spring). American's report on their access to health care. *Health Affairs,* 6–17.

Freimuth, V. S., Hammond, S. L., Edgar, T., and Monahan, J. L. (1990). Reaching those at risk: A content–analytic study of AIDS PSAs. *Communication Research, 17,* 775–791.

Freimuth, V. S. and Van Nevel, J. P. (1981, Spring). Reaching the public: The asbestos awareness campaign. *Journal of Communication,* 155–167.

Frey, D. (1986). Recent research on selective exposure to information. *Advances in Experimental Social Psychology, 19,* 41–80.

Galician, M. and Pasternack, S. (1987). Balancing good news and bad news: An ethical obligation? *Journal of Mass Media Ethics, 2,* 82–92.

Garramone, G. M. (1984). Voter responses to negative political ads. *Journalism Quarterly, 61,* 250–259.

Garramone, G. M. (1985). Effects of negative political advertising: The roles of sponsor and rebuttal. *Journal of Broadcasting and Electronic Media, 29,* 147–159.

Geer, J. G. (1987, April). *The Effects of Presidential Debates on the Electorate's Preferences for Candidates.* Paper presented at the annual meeting of the Midwest Political Science Association, Chicago, IL.

Geller, E. S. (1989). Using television to promote safety belt use. In R. E. Rice and C. K. Atkin (Eds.), *Public Communication Campaigns* (2nd ed., pp. 201–203). Newbury Park, CA: Sage Publications.

Gerbner, G., Gross, L., Signorelli, N., Morgan, M., and Jackson-Beeck, M. (1979). The demonstration of power: Violence profile No. 10. *Journal of Communication, 29,* 177–196.

Gergen, D. R. and Gest, T. (1989, March 8). Secrets behind the gun lobby's staying power: The NRA is doing quite well despite public opposition. *US News and World Report,* p. 26.

Gibney, F. B. (1985, August 25). Japan and the US: Partners in problems. *Los Angeles Times.*

Gibson, J. T. and Haritos-Fatouros, M. (1986, November). The education of a torturer. *Psychology Today,* pp. 50–58.

Giges, N. (1977, January 3). Coca-Cola–Reluctant entrant into comparative ad warfare. *Advertising Age,* pp. 2 and 35.

Giges, N. (1987, March 2). Renewed: Coke's NBC buy launches brand's "new feeling" ads. *Advertising Age,* pp. 2 and 70.

Giles, H. and Smith, P. (1979). Accommodation theory: Optimal levels of convergence. In H. Giles and R. N. St. Clair (Eds.), *Language and Social Psychology,* (pp. 45–65). Oxford: Blackwell.

Gillespie, D. F., and King, A. E. (1985). Demographic understanding of volunteerism. *Journal of Sociology and Social Welfare, 12,* 798–816.

Gilligan, C. (1982). *In a Different Voice: Psychological Theory and Women's Development.* Cambridge, MA: Harvard University Press.

Ginger, R. (1965). *Age of Excess: The United States from 1877 to 1914.* London: The Macmillan Company.

GM chief: US, Japan should end name-calling. (1992, February 8). *Atlanta Journal and Constitution,* p. C-3.

GM chief: US, Japan should end name-calling. (1992, February 14). *Atlanta Journal and Constitution,* p. S-6.

Godfrey, D., Jones, E., and Lord, C. (1986). Self-promotion is not ingratiating. *Journal of Personality and Social Psychology, 50,* 106–115.

Godin, V. and Sheppard, R. J. (1990). Use of attitude–behaviour models and exercise promotion. *Sports Medicine, 10,* pp. 103–121.

Godwin, R. K. (1988). *One Billion Dollars of Influence: The Direct Marketing of Politics.* Chatham, NJ: Chatham House Publishers.

Gold, E. R. (1988). Ronald Reagan and the oral tradition. *Central States Speech Journal, 39,* 159–176.

Golden, L. L. (1979). Consumer reactions to explicit brand comparisons in advertisements. *Journal of Marketing Research, 16,* 517–532.

Golden, J. L. (1987). Contemporary trends and historical roots in communication: A personal view. *Central States Speech Journal, 38,* 262–270.

Golden, L. L. (1974). Consumer reactions to comparative advertising. In B. B. Anderson (Ed.), *Advances in Consumer Research* (Vol. 3, pp. 63–67). Urbana, IL: Association for Consumer Research.

Goldman, P. and Fuller, T. (1985). *The Quest for the Presidency 1984.* New York: Bantam Books.

Goodman, E. (1986, September 27). Study: Self-interest doesn't appeal to women voters. *Sioux Falls Argus Leader*, p. 8A.

Goodwin, S. and Etgar, M. (1980). An experimental investigation of comparative advertising: Impact of message appeal, information load, and utility of product class. *Journal of Marketing Research, 17*, 187–202.

Gopoian, J. D. (1982). Issue preferences and candidate choice in presidential primaries. *American Journal of Political Science, 26*, 524–546.

Gorn, G. J. (1982). The effects of music in advertising on choice behavior: A classical conditioning approach. *Journal of Marketing, 46*, 94–101.

Gorn, G. J. and Goldberg, M. E. (1980). Children's responses to repetitive television commercials. *Journal of Consumer Research, 6*, 421–424.

Graber, D. A. (1976). Press and TV as opinion resources in presidential campaigns. *Public Opinion Quarterly, 40*, 285–303.

Graber, D. A. (1980). *Mass Media and American Politics*. Washington, DC: Congressional Quarterly Press.

Graber, D. A. (1981). Political languages. In D. D. Nimmo and K. R. Sanders (Eds.), *Handbook of Political Communication* (pp. 195–223). Beverly Hills, CA: Sage Publications.

Graber, D. A. (1987). Television news without pictures? *Critical Studies in Mass Communication, 4*, 74–78.

Graber, D. A. (1990). Seeing is remembering: How visuals contribute to learning from television news. *Journal of Communication, 40*, 134–155.

Grass, R. C. and Wallace, W. H. (1974). Advertising communication: Print vs. TV. *Journal of Advertising Research, 14*, 19–23.

Greenberg, B. and Gantz, W. (1989). Singing the (VD) blues. In R. E. Rice and C. K. Atkin (Eds.), *Public Communication Campaigns* (2nd ed., pp. 203–206). Newbury Park, CA: Sage Publications.

Greenberg, S. R. (1975). Conversations as units of analysis in the study of personal influence. *Journalism Quarterly, 52*, 128–131.

Greenwald, A. G. (1980). The totalitarian ego: Fabrication and revision of personal history. *American Psychologist, 35*, 603–618.

Greenwald, A. G. and Pratkanis, A. R. (1984). The self. In R. S. Wyer and T. K. Srull (Eds.), *Handbook of Social Cognition* (Vol. 3, pp. 129–178). Hillsdale, NJ: Lawrence Erlbaum Associates.

Gregg, R. B. (1977). The rhetoric of political newscasting. *Central States Speech Journal, 28*, 221–237.

Gronhaug, K. (1974). Education and buyer behavior. *Acta Sociologica, 17*, 179–189.

Gross, T. F. (1985). *Cognitive Development*. Belmont, CA: Brooks/Cole.

Gruner, C. R. (1970). The effect of humor in dull and interesting and informative speeches. *Central States Speech Journal, 21*, 160–166.

Grunig, J. E. (1989). Publics, audiences, and market segments: Segmentation principles for campaigns. In C. T. Salmon (Ed.), *Information Campaigns: Balancing Social Values and Social Change* (pp. 199–228). Newbury Park, CA: Sage Publications.

Gunter, B. (1980). Remembering television news: Effects of picture content. *The Journal of General Psychology, 102*, 127–133.

Gunter, B. (1987). *Poor Reception: Misunderstanding and Forgetting Broadcast News*. Hillsdale, NJ: Lawrence Erlbaum Associates.

Gunter, B., Furnham, A., and Jarrett, J. (1984). Personality, time of day and delayed memory for television news. *Human Learning, 2*, 261–267.

Gusfield, J. R. (1976). *Symbolic Crusade: Status Politics and the American Temperance Movement*. Urbana: University of Illinois Press.

Guskind, R. and Hagstrom, J. (1988). In the gutter. *National Journal, 20*, 2782–2790.

Guttman, L. (1944). A basis for scaling qualitative data. *American Sociological Review, 9*, 139–150.

Hagstrom, J. and Guskind, R. (1986, November 1). Selling the candidates. *National Journal*, pp. 2619–2629.

Halberstam, D. (1981, January 11). How television failed the American voter. *Parade*, pp. 4–8.

Hale, P. L., Immel, T., and Moher, S. (1984). Is AHCCCS working in the rural areas? *Arizona Medicine, 41*, 455–458.

Hall, G. (1990, October 14). 40s groups of boomers will change marketing. *Argus Leader*, p. 1–D.

Hamilton, D. L. and Zanna, M. P. (1972). Differential weighting of favorable and unfavorable attributes in impressions of personality. *Journal of Experimental Research in Personality, 6*, 204–212.

Hamilton, S. F. and Fenzel, L. M. (1988). The impact of volunteer experience on adolescent social development: Evidence of program effects. *Journal of Adolescent Research, 3*, 65–80.

Hammond, K. R. (1975). Social judgment theory: Its use in the study of psychoactive drugs. In K. R. Hammond and C. R. B. Joyce (Eds.), *Psychoactive Drugs and Social Judgment: Theory and Research*. New York: John Wiley and Sons.

Hample, D. (1977). Testing a model of value argument and evidence. *Communication Monographs, 44*, 106–120.

Hanily, M. L. (1991). *There's Nothing Mightier Than the Sword: The American Cancer Society's New Image Campaign, a Formative Evaluation*. Unpublished manuscript. School of Journalism, University of Georgia.

Hanneman, G., McEwen, W., and Coyne, S. (1973). Public service advertising on television. *Journal of Broadcasting, 17*, 387–404.

Harkins, S. G. and Petty, R. E. (1981). Effects of source magnification of cognitive effort on attitudes: An information–processing view. *Journal of Personality and Social Psychology, 40*, 401–413.

Harris, J. (1990, November 11). AM owners not singing a happy tune. *Sioux Falls Argus Leader*, p. 1–D.

Harris, T. (1992a, April). *A Campaign for Cultural Diversity Within Law School, Faculty, and Law Firms Across the Nation: Affirmative Action Revisited*. Paper presented to the annual conference of the Southern States Communication Association, San Antonio, TX.

Harris, T. (1992b, May). *A Campaign for Cultural Diversity Within Law Schools, Faculty, and Law Firms Across the Nation: Can the Dream Become Reality?* Paper presented to the annual conference of the International Communication Association, Miami, FL.

Harvey, J. H., Ickes, W. J., and Kidd, R. F. (1976). *New Directions in Attribution Research*. New York: John Wiley and Sons.

Harvey, P. (1984). Advertising family planning in the press: Direct response results from Bangladesh. *Studies in Family Planning, 15*, 40–42.

Hass, R. G. and Linder, D. E. (1972). Counterargument availability and the effects of message structure on persuasion. *Journal of Personality and Social Psychology, 23*, 219–233.

Haug, M. and Lavin, B. (1983). *Consumerism in Medicine: Challenging Physician Authority*. Beverly Hills: Sage.

Hearings Before the Committee on Commerce, Science, and Transportation, United States Senate, S. 707, Fair Practices in Automotive Products Act (Serial No. 98-95) (1984). Washington, DC: US Government Printing Office.

Hearings Before the Subcommittee on Commerce, Transportation, and Tourism of the Committee on Energy and Commerce, House of Representatives, H.R. 1234, US Auto Trade Problems (Serial No. 98-47) (1983). Washington, DC: US Government Printing Office.

Hearings Before the Subcommittee on Trade of the Committee on Ways and Means, House of Representatives, H.R. 5133, Fair Practices in Automative Products Act (Serial No. 97-80) (1982). Washington, DC: US Government Printing Office.

Hearold, S. (1986). A synthesis of 1043 effects of television on social behavior. In G. Comstock (Ed.), *Public Communication and Behavior* (Vol. 1, pp. 65–133). Orlando, FL: Academic Press, Inc.

Heesacker, M., Petty, R. E., and Cacioppo, J. T. (1983). Field dependence and attitude change: Source credibility can alter persuasion by affecting message relevant thinking. *Journal of Personality, 51*, 653–666.

Heeter, C., D'Allessio, D., Greenburg, B. S., and McVoy, D. S. (1983, May). Cable-viewing. paper presented at the annual meeting of the International Communication Association in Dallas, TX.

Heider, F. (1946). Attitudes and cognitive organization. *Journal of Psychology, 21,* 107–112.

Hellweg, S. A., Pfau, M., and Brydon, S. R. (1992). *Televised Presidential Debates: Advocacy in Contemporary America.* New York: Praeger Publishers.

Heritage, J. and Greatbatch, D. (1986). Generating applause: A study of rhetoric and response at party political conferences. *American Journal of Sociology, 92,* 110–157.

Hershey, M. R. (1989). The campaign and the media. In G. M. Pomper (Ed.), *The Elections of 1988: Reports and Interpretations* (pp. 73–102). Chatham, NJ: Chatham House Publishers.

Hess, A. K. and Gossett, D. (1974). Nixon and the media: A study of non–immediacy in newspaper editorials as reflective of geographical attitude differences. *Psychological Reports, 34,* 1055–1058.

Hicks, J. D. (1961). *The Populist Revolt: A History of the Farmers' Alliance and the People's Party.* Lincoln, NE: University of Nebraska Press.

Hillsman, B. (1991, April 14). [Interview with Bill Hillsman, North Woods Advertising, in charge of creating Wellstone's ads for all media, Minneapolis, MN].

Hirsch, P. M. (1980). An organizational perspective on television (Aided and abetted by models from economics, marketing, and the humanities). In S. B. Withey and R. P. Abeles (Eds.), *Television and Social Behavior: Beyond Violence and Children* (pp. 83–102). Hillsdale, NJ: Lawrence Erlbaum Associates.

Hirshfield, D. S. (1970). *The Lost Reform.* Cambridge, MA: Harvard University Press.

Hodges, B. H. (1974). Effect of valence on relative weighting in impression formation. *Journal of Personality and Social Psychology, 30,* 378–381.

Hofstetter, C. R. and Buss, T. F. (1980). Politics and last–minute political television. *Western Political Quarterly, 33,* 24–37.

Hofstetter, C. R. and Zukin, C. (1979). TV network news and advertising in the Nixon and McGovern campaigns. *Journalism Quarterly, 56,* 106–115, 152.

Hogan, R., Jones, W., and Cheek, J. (1985). Socioanalytic theory: An alternative to armadillo psychology. In B. R. Schlenker (Ed.), *The Self and Social Life,* (pp. 175–198). New York: McGraw–Hill.

Holbrook, M. B. and Batra, R. (1987). Assessing the role of emotions as mediators of consumer responses to advertising. *Journal of Consumer Research, 14,* 404–420.

Hole, J. and Levine, E. (1971). *Rebirth of Feminism.* New York: Quadrangle Books.

Holland, N. N. (1982). *Laughing: A Psychology of Humor.* Ithaca, NY: Cornell University Press.

Hollander, S. W. and Jacoby, J. (1973). Recall of crazy, mixed–up TV commercials. *Journal of Advertising Research, 13,* 39–42. 757

Holloway, H. and George, J. (1979). *Public Opinion: Coalitions, Elites, and Masses.* New York: St. Martin's Press.

Holsendolph, E. (1992, February 5). Japanese remarks might alienate US consumers. *The Atlanta Journal and Constitution,* p. B-1.

Holuska, J. (1985, April 13). Big bonuses at the big three again. *New York Times,* p. I-31.

Honomichl, J. J. (1988, November 9). Winning the bottom line. *Advertising Age,* pp. 12–13, 136, 138.

Hornig, S. (1990). Television's NOVA and the construction of scientific truth. *Critical Studies in Mass Communication, 7,* 11–23.

Hornik, J. and Schlinger, M. J. (1981). Allocation of time to the mass media. *Journal of Consumer Research, 7,* 343–354.

Hornik, R. C. (1989). Channel effectiveness in development communication programs. In R. E. Rice and C. K. Atkin (Eds.), *Public Communication Campaigns* (pp. 218–22). Newbury Park, CA: Sage Publications.

Horton, D. L. and Mills, C. B. (1984). Human learning and memory. *Annual Review of Psychology, 35,* 361–394.

Horton, D., and Wohl, R. R. (1956). Mass communication and parasocial interaction: Observations on intimacy at a distance. *Psychiatry, 19,* 215–229.

Hotakainen, R. and Schmickle, S. (1990, November 7). Boschwitz stunned while euphoria grips Wellstone backers. *Minneapolis Star Tribune,* p. 11A.

Houghton, J. C. (1987, March 16). Semiotics on the assembly line. *Advertising Age,* p. 18.

Hovland, C. I., Janis, I. L., and Kelley, H. H. (1953). *Communications and Persuasion: Psychological Studies of Opinion Change.* New Haven, CT: Yale University Press.

Hovland, C. I., Lumsdaine, A. A., and Sheffield, F. D. (1949). *Experiments on Mass Communication.* Princeton, NJ: Princeton University Press.

Howard, J. A. and Sheth, J. N. (1969). *The Theory of Buying Behavior.* New York: John Wiley and Sons.

Hubbell, H. M. (1949). Translation of *Cicero's: De Inventione.* Cambridge, MA: Loeb Classical Library.

Hubley, J. H. (1986). Barriers to health education in developing countries. *Health Education Research: Theory and Practice, 1,* 233–245.

Hulin-Salkin, B. (1987, July 20). Stretching to deliver readers' needs. *Advertising Age,* pp. S-1, S-2, S-4, S-6.

Hull, C. L. (1943). *Principles of Behavior: An Introduction to Behavior Theory.* New York: Appleton-Century.

Hume, S. (1988a, February 29). "Mac attack" wins battle for ad recall. *Advertising Age,* p. 6.

Hume, S. (1988b, November 9). Joe's beef: The hard sell. *Advertising Age,* pp. 44–46 and 147.

Hunter, J. E., Hamilton, M. A., and Allen, M. (1989). The design and analysis of language experiments in communication. *Communication Monographs, 56,* 341–363.

Hyman, R. H. (1959). *Political Socialization.* Glencoe, IL: The Free Press.

Inglehart, R. (1979). Political action: The impact of values, cognitive level, and social background. In S. H. Barnes and M. Kaase (Eds.), *Political Action: Mass Participation in Five Western Democracies* (pp. 343–380). Beverly Hills, CA: Sage Publications.

Insko, C. A., Lind, E. A., and LaTour, S. (1976). Persuasion, recall, and thoughts. *Representative Research in Social Psychology, 7,* 66–78.

Ittelson, W. H. (1973). *Environment and Cognition.* New York: Seminar Press.

Iyengar, S. (1991). *Is Anyone Responsible: How Television Frames Political Issues.* Chicago: University of Chicago Press.

Iyengar, S., Peters, M. D., and Kinder, D. R. (1982). Experimental demonstrations of the "not-so-minimal" consequences of television news programs. *American Political Science Review, 76,* 848–857.

Jackson, S. and Jacobs, S. (1983). Generalizing about messages: Suggestions for design and analysis of experiments. *Human Communication Research, 9,* 169–191.

Jacobson, B. (1982). *The Lady Killers: Why Smoking is a Feminist Issue.* New York: Continuum Publishing Company.

Jacobson, G. C. (1989). Congress: A singular continuity. In M. Nelson (Ed.), *The Elections of 1988* (pp. 127–152). Washington, DC: Congressional Quarterly Press.

Jacoby, J. and Kyner, D. B. (1973). Brand loyalty vs. repeat purchasing behavior. *Journal of Marketing Research, 10,* 1–9.

Jain, S. C. and Hackleman, E. C. (1978). How effective is comparison advertising for stimulating brand recall? *Journal of Advertising, 7,* 20–25.

Jamieson, K. H. (1984). *Packaging the presidency: A History and Criticism of Presidential Campaign Advertising.* New York: Oxford University Press.

Jamieson, K. H. (1988). *Eloquence in an Electronic Age: The Transformation of Political Speechmaking.* New York: Oxford University Press.

Jamieson, K. H. (1988, October 30). For televised mandacity: This year is the worst ever. *Washington Post,* Outlook, pp. C1–C2.

Jamieson, K. H. (1989). Context and the creation of meaning in the advertising of the 1988 Presidential campaign. *American Behavioral Scientist, 32,* 415–424.

Jamieson, K. H. and Birdsell, D. S. (1988). *Presidential Debates: The Challenge of Creating an Informed Electorate*. New York: Oxford University Press.

Janis, I. L. and Feshbach, S. (1953). Effects of fear-arousing communications. *Journal of Abnormal Social Psychology, 48*, 78–92.

Jaworski, L. (1976). *The Right and the Power: The Prosecution of Watergate*. Houston: Gulf Publishing Company.

Jeffres, L. W. (1975). Functions of media behaviors. *Communication Research, 2*, 137–161.

Jeffres, L. W. (1986). *Mass Media Processes and Effects.* Prospect Heights, IL: Waveland Press, Inc.

Jenkens, J. J. (1974). Remember that old theory of memory? Well, forget it! *American Psychologist, 29*, 785–795.

Jensen, J. V. (1981). *Argumentation: Reasoning in Communication*. New York: D. Van Nostrand Co.

John, D. R., Scott, C. A., and Bettman, J. R. (1986). Sampling data for covariation assessment: The effect of prior beliefs on search patterns. *Journal of Consumer Research, 13*, 38–47.

Johnson, D. (1990, November 11). Minnesota professor's "everyman" appeal wins a Senate seat. *New York Times*, p. 26.

Johnson, R. D. (1985). The bias against incomplete information: Inferences and framing interpretations (Doctoral dissertation, University of Iowa). *Dissertation Abstracts International, 46*, 2098B.

Johnson-Cartee, K. and Copeland, G. (1991). *Negative Political Advertising: Coming of Age.* Hillsdale, NJ: Lawrence Erlbaum Associates.

Johnstone, C. L. (1985, November). *Rhetoric, Politics, and the "Ideological Election": Some Ethical Dimensions of the 1984 Campaign.* Paper presented at the annual meeting of the Speech Communication Association, Denver, CO.

Joslyn, R. A. (1980). The content of political spot ads. *Journalism Quarterly, 57*, 92–98.

Joslyn, R. A. (1981). The impact of campaign spot advertising on voting defections. *Human Communication Research, 7*, 347–360.

Jowett, G. S. and O'Donnell, V. (1986). *Propaganda and Persuasion.* Newbury Park, CA: Sage Publications.

Jugenheimer, D. W. and Chowins, C. W. (1981). Consumer perspectives of advertising informational content. In H. K. Hunt (Ed.), *Proceedings of the Annual Conference of the American Academy of Advertising, 1981: Advertising in a New Age* (pp. 35–39). Provo, UT: Institute of Business Management, Graduate School of Management, Brigham Young University.

Just, M., Crigler, A., and Wallach, L. (1990). Thirty seconds or thirty minutes: What viewers learn from spot advertisements and candidate debates. *Journal of Communication, 40*, 120–133.

Kahle, L. R. and Homer, P. M. (1985). Physical attractiveness of the celebrity endorser: A social adaptation perspective. *Journal of Consumer Research, 11*, 954–961.

Kaid, L. L. (1977). The neglected candidate: Interpersonal communication in political campaigns. *Western Journal of Speech Communication, 41*, 245–252.

Kaid, L. L. and Davidson, D. K. (1986). Elements of videostyle: Candidate presentation through television advertising. In L. L. Kaid, D. Nimmo, and K. R. Sanders (Eds.), *New Perspectives on Political Advertising* (pp. 184–209). Carbondale, IL: Southern Illinois University Press.

Kaid, L. L., Nimmo, D., and Sanders, K. R. (Eds.) (1986). *New Perspectives on Political Advertising.* Carbondale, IL: Southern Illinois University Press.

Kaid, L. L. and Sanders, K. R. (1985). Survey of political communication theory and research. In K. R. Sanders, L. L. Kaid and D. Nimmo (Eds.), *Political Communication Yearbook: 1984* (pp. 283–308). Carbondale, IL: Southern Illinois University Press.

Kamhi, A. G., Nelson, L. K., Lee, R. F., and Gholson, B. (1985). The ability of language-disordered children to use and modify hypotheses in discrimination learning. *Applied Psycholinguistics, 6*, 435–451.

Kamins, M. A. and Asseal, H. (1987). Two-sided versus one-sided appeals: A cognitive perspective on argumentation, source derogation, and the effect of disconfirming trial on belief change. *Journal of Marketing Research, 24*, 29–39.

Kanouse, D. E. and Hanson, L. R. Jr. (1972). Negativity in evaluations. In E. L. Jones et al. (Eds.), *Attribution: Perceiving the Causes of Behavior*. Morristown, NJ: General Learning Press.

Kassarjian, H. H. and Robertson, T. S. (1973). *Perspectives in Consumer Behavior* (rev. ed.). Glenview, IL: Scott, Foresman and Company.

Katz, E. and Lazarsfeld, P. F. (1955). *Personal Influence: The Part Played by People in the Flow of Mass Communications*. New York: The Free Press.

Keating, J. P. and Latane, B. (1976). Politicians on TV: The image is the message. *Journal of Social Issues, 32*, 116–132.

Keim, G. and Zeithaml, V. (1981, November). Improving the return on advocacy advertising. *Financial Executive*, pp. 40–44.

Keller, K. L. (1987). Memory factors in advertising: The effect of advertising retrieval cues on brand evaluations. *Journal of Consumer Research, 14*, 316–333.

Kellermann, K. and Reynolds, R. (1990). When ignorance is bliss: The role of motivation to reduce uncertainty in uncertainty reduction theory. *Human Communication Research, 17*, 5–75.

Kelley, H. H. (1972). *Causal Schemata and the Attribution Process*. New York: General Learning Press.

Kelley, H. H. (1973). The process of causal attribution. *American Psychologist, 28*, 107–128.

Kendall, W. (Ed.) (1954). *Jean Jacques Rousseau: The Social Contract*. Chicago: The Henry Regnery Company.

Kennamer, J. D. and Chaffee, S. H. (1982). Communication of political information during early presidential primaries: Cognition, affect, and uncertainty. In M. Burgoon (Ed.), *Communication Yearbook 5*, (pp. 627–650). New Brunswick, NJ: Transaction Books.

Kern, M. (1989). *30-second Politics: Political Advertising in the Eighties*. New York: Praeger Publishers.

Kern, M. (1991, June). *The Mass Media Election on the Congressional and Statewide Level: Will Eighties Patterns Persist into the Nineties?* Paper presented at the annual meeting of the International Communication Association, Chicago, IL.

Kernall, S. (1977). Presidential popularity and negative voting: An alternative explanation of the midterm congressional decline of the President's party. *American Political Science Review, 71*, 44–66.

Kessler, F. (1986, July 7). High-tech shocks in ad research. *Fortune*, pp. 58–59, 62.

Key, Jr., V. O. (1953). *Politics, Parties, and Pressure Groups* (3rd ed.). New York: Thomas Y. Crowell Company.

Kiesler, C. A., Collins, B. E., and Miller, N. (1969). *Attitude Change: A Critical Analysis of Theoretical Approaches*. New York: John Wiley and Sons.

Kim, S., McLeod, J., and Palmgren, C. L. (1989). The impact of the "I'm special" program on student substance abuse and other related student problem behavior. *Journal of Drug Education, 19*, 83–95.

Kim, S., McLeod, J. H., and Shantzis, C. (1989). An outcome evaluation of refusal skills program as a drug abuse prevention strategy. *Journal of Drug Education, 19*, 363–371.

King, J. A., Morris, L. L., and Fitz-Gibbon, C. T. (1987). *How to Assess Program Implementation*. Beverly Hills, CA: Sage Publications.

Kish, L. (1987). *Statistical Design for Research*. New York: John Wiley and Sons.

Klapper, J. T. (1960). *The Effects of Mass Communication*. New York: The Free Press.

Kline, F. G. (1976). Media vital to current political campaigns. *Racham Reports, 3*, 2.

Koerner, K. (1983). The Chomskyan "revolution" and its historiography: A few critical remarks. *Language and Communication, 3*, 147–169.

Kohn, P. M., Goodstadt, M. S., Cook, G. M., Sheppard, M., and Chan, G. (1982). Ineffectiveness of threat appeals about drinking and driving. *Accident Analysis and Prevention, 14*, 457–464.

Koop, C. E. (1988). *Understanding AIDS: A Message from the Surgeon General* (DHHS Publication No. 88-8404). Washington, DC: Department of Health and Human Services.

Kornhauser, W. (1959). *The Politics of Mass Society*. New York: The Free Press.

Kosobud, R. F. and Morgan, J. N. (Eds.) (1964). *Consumer Behavior of Individual Families Over Two and Three Years.* Ann Arbor, MI: University of Michigan Press.

Koten, J. (1984, February 23). After serious '70s, advertisers are going for laughs again. *The Wall Street Journal*, p. 29.

Kotler, P. and Roberto, E. L. (1989). *Social Marketing: Strategies for Changing Public Behavior.* New York: The Free Press.

Kotler, P. and Zaltman, G. (1971). Social marketing: An approach to planned social change. *Journal of Marketing, 35,* 3–12.

Kramer, T. H., Cancellieri, F. R., Ottomanelli, G., Mosely, J. A., Fine, J., and Bihari, B. (1989). A behavioral measure of AIDS information seeking by drug and alcohol inpatients. *Journal of Substance Abuse Treatment, 6,* 83–85.

Kraus, S. and Davis, D. (1976). *The Effects of Mass Communication on Political Behavior.* University Park: The Pennsylvania State University Press.

Kretch, D. and Crutchfield, R. (1948). *Theory and Problems in Social Psychology.* New York: McGraw-Hill.

Kroger, F. (1992, February 14). *The Current Status of the AIDS Information and Education Program.* Seminar presented at the Emory School of Public Health, Atlanta, GA.

Krugman, H. E. (1965). The impact of television advertising: Learning without involvement. *Public Opinion Quarterly, 29,* 349–356.

Krugman, H. E. (1971). Brain wave measures of media involvement. *Journal of Advertising Research, 11,* 3–9.

Krugman, H. E. (1977, August). Memory without recall, exposure without perception, *Journal of Advertising Research, 17,* 7–12.

Krugman, H. E. (1986). Low recall and high recognition of advertising. *Journal of Advertising Research, 26,* 79–86.

Krugman, H. E. (1972). Why three exposures may be enough. *Journal of Advertising Research, 12,* 11–14.

Kuhlthau, C. C. (1991). Inside the search process: Information seeking from the user's perspective. *Journal of the American Society for Information Science, 42,* 361–371.

Kulman, I. R. and Akamatsu, T. J. (1988). The effects of television on large-scale attitude change. *Journal of Applied Psychology, 18,* 1121–1132.

Kumar, V. and Rust, R. T. (1989, August/September). Market segmentation by visual inspection. *Journal of Advertising Research*, pp. 23–29.

Kymlicka, B. B. and Matthews, J. (1988). *The Reagan Revolution?* Chicago: Dorsey Press.

Lafer, B. (1989). Predicting performance and persistence in hospice volunteers. *Psychological Reports, 65,* 467–472.

Lamb, C. W., Jr., Pletcher, B. A., and Pride, W. M. (1979). Print readers' perceptions of various advertising formats. *Journalism Quarterly, 56,* 328–335.

Lamb, C. W., Jr., Pride, W. M., and Pletcher, B. A. (1978). A taxonomy for comparative advertising research. *Journal of Advertising, 7,* 43–47.

Langer, E. J. (1978). Rethinking the role of thought in social interaction. In J.H. Harvey, W.J. Ickes, and R.F. Kidd (Eds.), *New Directions in Attribution Research* (Vol. 2, pp. 35–58). Hillsdale, NJ: Lawrence Erlbaum.

Lanigan, R. L. (1979). Communication models in philosophy: Review and commentary. In D. Nimmo (Ed.), *Communication Yearbook 3,* (pp. 29–49). New Brunswick, NJ: Transaction Books.

Lansing, J. B. and Kish, L. (1957). Family life cycle as an independent variable. *American Sociological Review, 22,* 512–519.

Larson, C. U. (1982). Media metaphors: Two perspectives for the rhetorical criticism of TV commercials. *Central States Speech Journal, 33,* 533–546.

Larson, C. U. (1984, November). *Media Metaphors and Candidates: Television Spot Commercials.* Paper presented at the annual meeting of the Speech Communication Association, Chicago, IL.

Larson, C. U. (1989). *Persuasion: Reception and Responsibility* (5th ed.). Belmont, CA: Wadsworth Publishing Company.

Larson, M. S. (1991). Health-related messages embedded in prime-time television entertainment. *Health Communication, 3,* 175–184.

.asswell, H. (1927). *Propaganda Techniques in the World War.* New York: Knopf.

Lasswell, H. (1935). *Propaganda and Promotional Activities.* Minneapolis: University of Minnesota Press.

Lau, R. R. (1982). Negativity in political perception. *Political Behavior, 4,* 353–377.

Lau, R. R. (1985). Two explanations for negativity effects in political behavior. *American Journal of Political Science, 29,* 119–138.

Lazarsfeld, P. F., Berelson, B., and Gaudet, H. (1968). *The People's Choice: How the Voter Makes up his Mind in a Presidential Campaign* (3rd ed.). New York: Columbia University Press.

Lazer, W. and Shaw, E. H. (1987, September). How older Americans spend their money. *American Demographics,* pp. 36–41.

Leavitt, C. (1966). The communication response. In L. Bogart (Ed.), *Psychology in Media Strategy.* Chicago: American Marketing Association.

Lemann, N. (1985). Implications: What Americans wanted. In M. Nelson (Ed.), *The Elections of 1984* (pp. 259–275). Washington, DC: Congressional Quarterly Press.

Lemon, N. (1973). *Attitudes and their Measurement.* New York: John Wiley.

Le Poire, B. (1991). Orientation and defensive reactions as alternatives to arousal in theories of nonverbal reactions to changes in immediacy. *Southern Communication Journal, 56,* 138–146.

Levin, G. (1987, March 2). "TV Guide" tops "Digest" in circulation. *Advertising Age,* p. 66.

Levin, G. (1988, November 9). The ad factor. *Advertising Age,* pp. 8 and 10.

Levine, P. (1976). Commercials that name competing brands. *Journal of Advertising Research, 16,* 1–14.

Levy, M. R. and Windahl, S. (1985). The concept of audience activity. In K. E. Rosengren, L. A. Wenner, and P. Palmgreen (Eds.), *Media Gratifications Research: Current Perspectives* (pp. 109–11). Beverly Hills, CA: Sage Publications.

Levy, R. (1987, February). Big resurgence in comparative ads. *Dun's Business Month, 129,* pp. 56–58.

Lewis, J. D. (1967). *Anti-Federalists versus Federalists: Selected Documents.* Scranton, PA: Chandler Publishing Company.

Leymore, V. (1982). The structural factor in systems of coummunication. *British Journal of Sociology, 33,* 421–434.

Li, D., Zhang, F. and Jin, Y. (1985). Characteristics of children's deductive reasoning for hypothetical judgment. *Information on Psychological Sciences, 1,* 4–10.

Liesse, J. (1991, December 2). Brands in trouble: As brand loyalty crumbles, marketers look for new answers. *Advertising Age,* pp. 16, 18, 50.

Lillehaug, D. (1991, April 15). [Interview with David Lillehaug, attorney, who coached Wellstone for his television debate, Minneapolis, MN].

Lincoln, D. J. and Samli, A. C. (1979). Empirical evidence of comparative advertising's effects: A review and synthesis. In N. Beckwith, M., et al. (Eds.), *1979 Educators' Conference Proceedings* (pp. 367–372). Chicago: American Marketing Association.

Linsky, M. (Ed.) (1983). *Television and the Presidential Elections: Self-interest and the Public Interest.* Lexington, MA: D. C. Heath and Company.

Lippmann, W. (1922). *Public Opinion.* New York: Macmillan.

Lopez, L. (1985, March 15). Senate health panel passes bill to extend AHCCCS for two years. *Arizona Daily Star,* p. B-1.

Low, S. M. (1981). The urban patient: Health-seeking behavior in the health care system of San Jose, Costa Rica. *Urban Anthropoloy, 10,* 27–52.

Luks, A. (1988). Helpers high: Volunteering makes people feel good, physically and emotionally. *Psychology Today, 22,* 39–40.

Lunn, T. (1986). Segmenting and constructing markets. In R. M. Worcester and J. Downham (Eds.), *Consumer Market Research Handbook* (3rd ed., pp. 387–423). Amsterdam: North Holland.

Lutz, K. A. and Lutz, R. J. (1978). Imagery-eliciting strategies: Review and implications of research. In H. K. Hunt (ed.), *Advances in Consumer Research* (Vol. 5, pp. 611–620). Ann Arbor, MI: Assoiciation for Consumer Research.

Lutz, R. J. (1985). Affective and cognitive antecedents of attitude toward the ad: A conceptual framework. In L. F. Alwitt and A. A. Mitchell (Eds.), *Psychological Processes and Advertising Effects: Theory, Research, and Applications* (pp. 45–63). Hillsdale, NJ: Lawrence Erlbaum Associates.

Lynch–Schneider, D. (1991, November). *Volunteerism 1990: A Communication Perspective.* A paper presented at the annual conference of the Speech Communication Association in Atlanta, Georgia.

Lynn, J. R. (1974, Winter). Effects of persuasive appeals in public service advertising. *Journalism Quarterly*, pp. 622–630.

MacWilliams, M. C., Burns, A., and Greer and Associates (1988a). *Volunteer Organization.* Washington, DC: Democratic National Training Institute.

MacWilliams, M. C., Burns, A., and Greer and Associates (1988b). *Voter Contact.* Washington, DC: Democratic National Training Institute.

Maddala, G. S. (1983). *Limited Dependent and Qualitative Variables in Econometrics.* London: Cambridge University Press.

Magnuson, E. (1986, February 10). They slipped the surly bonds of Earth to touch the face of God. *Time*, pp. 24–31.

Mandel, R. B. (1982). How women vote: The new gender gap. *Working Woman, 7,* 128–131.

Mandese, J. (1991, November 18). Rival sports cluttering television. *Advertising Age*, p. 6.

Mann, T. E. (1984). Public awareness of congressional candidates. In R. G. Niemi and H. F. Weisberg (Eds.), *Controversies in Voting Behavior* (2nd ed., pp. 251–268). Washington, DC: Congressional Quarterly Press.

Mann, T. E. and Wolfinger, R. E. (1984). Candidates and parties in congressional elections. In R. G. Niemi and H. F. Weisberg (Eds.), *Controversies in Voting Behavior* (2nd ed., pp. 269–291). Washington, DC: Congressional Quarterly Press.

Manoff, R. K. (1985). *Social Marketing: New Imperative for Public Health.* New York: Praeger.

Martineau, P. (1957). *Motivation in Advertising.* New York: McGraw–Hill.

Martineau, P. (1971). *Motivation in Advertising: Motives That Make People Buy.* New York: McGraw–Hill.

Martinez, M. D. and DeLegal, T. (1988, April). *Negative Ads and Negative Attitudes: Effects and Non-effects on Trust and Efficacy.* Paper presented at the annual meeting of the Midwest Political Science Association, Chicago.

Martz, L. (1990, April 23). A new era of attack politics: Sun–belt Democrats try to win by a mudslide. *Newsweek*, pp. 22–23.

Maslow, A. H. (1943). A theory of human motivation. *Psychological Review, 50,* 370–396.

Maslow, A. H. (1970). *Motivation and Personality* (2nd ed.). New York: Harper and Row.

Matthews, R. (1992, January 2). Why must the protectionists lie about Japan? *The Atlanta Journal and Constitution*, p. A-12.

Mauser, G. A. (1983). *Political Marketing: An Approach to Campaign Strategy.* New York: Praeger Publishers.

Mayer, C. S. (1970). CATV test laboratory panels. *Journal of Advertising Research, 10,* 37–43.

Mayer, J. P. (Ed.) (1969). *Alexis de Tocqueville: Democracy in America.* New York: Doubleday.

Mayer, W. G. (1987). The New Hampshire primary: A historical overview. In G. R. Orren and N. W. Polsby (Eds.), *Media and Momentum: The New Hampshire Primary and Nomination Politics* (pp. 9–41). Chatham, NJ: Chatham House Publishers, Inc.

Mazis, M. B. (1976). *A Theoretical and Empirical Examination of Comparative Advertising.* College of Business Administration Working Paper, University of Florida.

McAlister, A., Perry, C., Killen, J., Slinkard, L. A., and Maccoby, N. (1980). Pilot study of smoking, alcohol, and drug abuse prevention. *American Journal of Public Health, 70,* 719–721.

McAlister, A., Ramirez, A. G., Galavotti, C., and Gallion, K. J. (1989). Antismoking campaigns: Progress in the application of social learning theory. In R. E. Rice and C. K. Atkin (Eds.), *Public Communication Campaigns* (2nd ed., 291–308). Newbury Park, CA: Sage Publications.

McCombs, M. E. and Shaw, D. L. (1972). The agenda-setting function of the mass media. *Public Opinion Quarterly, 36,* 176–187.

McCombs, M. E. and Washington, L. (1983, February). Opinion surveys offer conflicting clues as to how public views press. *Presstime,* pp. 4–9.

McCracken, G. (1986). Culture and consumption: A theoretical account of the structure and movement of the cultural meaning of consumer goods. *Journal of Consumer Research, 13,* 71–84.

McCroskey, J. C. (1968). *An Introduction to Rhetorical Communication.* Englewood Cliffs, NJ: Prentice Hall.

McCullough, J. L. and Ostrom, T. M. (1974). Repetition of highly similar messages and attitude change. *Journal of Applied Psychology, 59,* 395–397.

McCurry, B. (1985, October). Don't take the choice away from the consumer. *Toyota Today, 13,* 15.

McDougall, G. H. G. (1977). Comparative advertising: Consumer issues and attitudes. In B. A. Greenberg and D. N. Bellenger (Eds.), *Contemporary Marketing Thought: 1977 Educators' Proceedings* (pp. 286–291). Chicago: American Marketing Association.

McGrath, D. J. (1990, November 11). With more humor than cash, he won it his way. *Minneapolis Star Tribune,* pp. 1, 16A–21A.

McGrath, D. J. (1991, April 15). [Interview with Dennis McGrath, *Minneapolis Star Tribune* reporter, who covered the Wellstone campaign throughout, Minneapolis, MN].

McGregor, G. (1984). Conversation and communication. *Language and Communication, 4,* 71–83.

McGuire, W. J. (1961). The effectiveness of supportive and refutational defenses in immunizing and restoring beliefs against persuasion. *Sociometry, 24,* 184–197.

McGuire, W. J. (1962). Persistance of the resistance to persuasion induced by various types of prior belief defenses. *Journal of Abnormal and Social Psychology, 64,* 241–248.

McGuire, W. J. (1966). The nature of attitudes and attitude change. In G. L. Lindzey and E. Aronson (Eds.), *The Handbook of Social Psychology* (Vol. 3: The individual in a social context, pp. 136–314). Reading, MA: Addison-Wesley Publishing Company.

McGuire, W. J. (1986). The myth of massive media impact: Savagings and salvagings. In G. Comstock (Ed.), *Public Communication and Behavior* (Vol. 1, pp. 173–257). Orlando, FL: Academic Press.

McGuire, W. J. (1989). Theoretical foundations of campaigns. In R. E. Rice and C. K. Atkin (Eds.), *Public Communication Campaigns* (2nd ed., pp. 43–65). Newbury Park, CA: Sage Publications.

McGuire, W. J. and Papageorgis, D. (1961). The relative efficacy of various types of prior belief-defense in producing immunity against persuasion. *Journal of Abnormal and Social Psychology, 62,* 327–337.

McKelvie, S. J. and Demers, E. G. (1979). Individual differences in reported visual imagery and memory performance. *British Journal of Psychology, 70,* 51–57.

McKeon, R. (1947). *Introduction to Aristotle.* New York: The Modern Library

McLeod, J. M. (1965). *Political Conflict and Information-Seeking.* Paper presented at the annual conference of the American Psychological Association, Chicago, IL.

McLeod, J. M. and Becker, L. B. (1981). The uses and gratifications approach. In D. D. Nimmo and K. R. Sanders (Eds.), *Handbook of Political Communication* (pp. 67–99). Beverly Hills, CA: Sage Publications.

McNamara, E. F., Kurth, T. and Hansen, D. (1989). Smokey Bear (summary and adaptation of chapter from first edition). In R. E. Rice and C. K. Atkin (Eds.), *Public Communication Campaigns* (2nd ed., pp. 215–218). Newberry Park, CA: Sage Publications.

Meadow, R. G. (1989). Political campaigns. In R. E. Rice and C. K. Atkin (Eds.), *Public Communication Campaigns* (2nd ed., pp. 253–272). Newbury Park, CA: Sage Publications.

Medlyn, B. (1985, July 21). Retarded in Arizona have "license to kill." *Tucson Citizen*, p. A-1.

Melder, K. (1989). Creating candidate imagery: The man on horseback. In L. J. Sabato (Ed.), *Campaigns and Elections: A Reader in Modern American Politics* (pp. 5–11). Glenview, IL: Scott, Foresman and Company.

Mendelsohn, H. and O'Keefe, G. J. (1976). *The People Choose a President*. New York: Praeger Publishers.

Merritt, S. (1984). Negative political advertising: Some empirical findings. *Journal of Advertising, 13*, 27–38.

Meyers, J. (1988a, October 31). Dilemma over paid AIDS ads: Will they hurt public service work? *Advertising Age*, p. 41.

Meyers, J. (1988b, November 9). Learning to deploy a strategic weapon. *Advertising Age*, p. 94.

Meyers-Levy, J. (1989). Gender differences in information processing: A selectivity interpretation. In P. Cafferata and A. M. Tybout (Eds.), *Cognitive and Affective Responses to Advertising* (pp. 219–260). Lexington, MA: D. C. Heath and Company.

Meyrowitz, J. (1985). *No Sense of Place: The Impact of the Electronic Media on Social Behavior*. New York: Oxford University Press.

Mick, D. G. (1986). Consumer research and semiotics: Exploring the morphology of signs, symbols, and significance. *Journal of Consumer Research, 13*, 196–213.

Miles, M. and Huberman, A. M. (1984). *Qualitative Data Analysis*. Beverly Hills, CA: Sage Publications.

Millar, M. G. and Tesser, A. (1986). Thought–induced attitude change: The effects of schema structure and commitment. *Journal of Personality and Social Psychology, 51*, 259–269.

Miller, A. H. (1988). Gender and the vote: 1984. In C. M. Meuller (Ed.), *The Politics of the Gender Gap: The Social Construction of Political Influence* (Vol. 12 of Sage Yearbooks in Women's Policy Studies, pp. 258–282). Beverly Hills: Sage Publications.

Miller, A. H. (1990). Public judgments of Senate and House candidates. *Legislative Studies Quarterly, 15*, 525–542.

Miller, A. H., Wattenburg, M. P., and Malanchuk, O. (1986). Schematic assessment of Presidential candidates. *American Political Science Review, 80*, 521–540.

Miller, G. A. (1973). Psychology and meaning. In G. A. Miller (Ed.), *Communication, Language, and Meaning* (pp. 3–22). New York: Basic Books, Inc.

Miller, G. R. (1980). On being persuaded: Some basic distinctions. In M. Roloff and G. Miller (Eds.), *Persuasion: New Directions in Theory and Research* (pp. 11.28). Beverly Hills, CA: Sage Publications.

Miller, G. R. (1987). Persuasion. In C. R. Berger and C. H. Chaffee Eds.), *Handbook of Communication Science* (pp. 446–483). Newbury Park, CA: Sage Publications.

Miller, G. R. and Burgoon, M. (1973). *New Techniques of Persuasion*. New York: Harper & Row.

Miller, G. R. and Burgoon, M. (1990). Paths. *Communication Monographs, 57*, 152–160.

Miller, G. R., Burgoon, M., and Burgoon, J. K. (1984). The functions of human communication in changing attitudes and gaining compliance. In C. C. Arnold and J. W. Bowers (Eds.), *Handbook of Rhetorical and Communication Theory* (pp. 400–474). Boston: Allyn and Bacon, Inc.

Miller, R. L. (1976). Mere exposure, psychological reactance, and attitude change. *Political Opinion Quarterly, 40*, 229–233.

Misperceptions about US-Japan auto trade (1984, July). *Washington Post* (Vol. IV, No. 2), pp. 5–6.

Mitchell, A. A. (1978). Involvement: A potentially important mediator of consumer behavior. In W. L. Wilkie (Ed.), *Advances in Consumer Research: Proceedings for the Association for Consumer Research Ninth Annual Conference Miami Beach, Florida, October 1978* (Vol. 6, pp. 191–196). Urbana, IL: Association for Consumer Research.

Mitchell, R. (1990, November 26). Have you heard the one about the funny campaign ad? They worked for Wellstone in Minnesota—and may start a trend. *Business Weekly*, p. 62.

Montgomery, B. M. (1981). Verbal immediacy as a behavioral indicatior of open communication content. *Communication Quarterly, 30,* 28–34.

Montgomery, J. (1984, March 7). Coca-Cola is seen claiming Diet Coke has passed 7-Up as the No. 3 soft drink. *The Wall Street Journal,* p. 14.

Moore, D. L. and Hutchinson, J. W. (1985). The influence of affective reactions to advertising: Direct and indirect mechanisms of attitude change. In L. F. Alwitt and A. A. Mitchell (Eds.), *Psychological Processes and Advertising Effects: Theory, Research, and Applications* (pp. 65–87). Hillsdale, NJ: Lawrence Erlbaum Associates.

Moore, D. W. (1987). Political campaigns and the knowledge-gap hypothesis. *Public Opinion Quarterly, 51,* 186–200.

Moreland, R. L. and Zajonc, R. B. (1977). Is stimulus recognition a necessary condition for the occurrence of exposure effects? *Journal of Personality and Social Psychology, 35,* 191–199.

Morley, D. D. (1988). Meta-analytic techniques: When generalizing to message populations is not possible. *Human Communication Research, 15,* 112–126.

Morner, A. L. (1978, February 13). It pays to knock your competitor. *Fortune,* pp. 104–106, 110–111.

Mortensen, C. D. (1968). The influence of television on policy discussion. *Quarterly Journal of Speech, 54,* 277–281.

Moshman, D. and Franks, B. A. (1986). Development of the concept of inferential validity. *Child Development, 57,* 153–165.

Moyer, R. S. (1985, January). The enemy within: Our minds pose as great a threat to world security as the bombs and missiles they've conceived. *Psychology Today,* pp. 30–37.

Moyers, B. (1984). *The Thirty-second President* [Video]. New York: PBS.

Murphy, J. and Kauffman, J. (1984). AHCCCS—the Pima county experience. *Arizona Medicine, 41,* 422–447.

National Organization for Women (1972). *Women in the Wasteland Fight Back.* Washington, DC: NOW.

NBC TV News Network Report (1990). *Sex Buys and Advertising* [Video]. New York: National Broadcasting Company.

Neisser, U. (1976). *Cognition and Reality.* San Francisco: Freeman.

Nesbit, D. D. (1988). *Videostyle in Senate Campaigns.* Knoxville, TN: The University of Tennessee Press.

Newcomb, T. M. (1953). An approach to the study of communicative acts. *Psychological Review, 50,* 393–404.

Nichols, A. (1984). AHCCCS—a mid-life crisis: Changes made and lessons learned. *Arizona Medicine, 41,* 422–447.

Nie, N. H. and Anderson, K. (1976). Mass belief systems revisited: Political change and attitude structure. In E. C. Dryer and W. A. Rosenbaum (Eds.), *Political Opinion and Behavior: Essays and Studies* (3rd ed., pp. 289–324). North Scituate, MA: Duxbury Press.

Nie, N. H., Verba, S., and Petrocik, J. R. (1976). *The Changing American Voter.* Cambridge, MA: Harvard University Press.

Nimmo, D. D. (1970). *The Political Persuaders: The Techniques of Modern Election Campaigns.* Englewood Cliffs, NJ: Prentice Hall.

Nix, H. L., Dressel, P. L., and Bates, F. L. (1977). Changing leaders and leadership structure: A longitudinal study. *Rural Sociology, 42.*

Norris, J. S. (1990). *Advertising* (4th ed.). Englewood Cliffs, NJ: Prentice Hall.

Norris, V. P. (1989). Advertising history—According to the textbooks. In R. Hovland and G. B. Wilcox (Eds.), *Advertising in Society: Classic and Contemporary Readings on Advertising's Role in Society* (pp. 99–118). Lincolnwood, IL: National Textbook Company.

Norton, R. W. (1978). *Communicator Style: Theory, Applications, and Measures.* Beverly Hills, CA: Sage Publications.

Nugent, J. F. (1987, March/April). Positively negative. *Campaigns and Elections,* pp. 47–49.

Nyhan, D. (1988). *The Duke: The Inside Story of a Political Phenomenon.* New York: Warner Books.

O'Connor, B. P. and Gifford, R. (1988). A test among models of nonverbal immmediacy reactions: Arousal–labeling, discrepancy–arousal, and social cognition. *Journal of Nonverbal Behavior, 12,* 6–33.

Ogilvy D. (1963). *Confessions of an Advertising Man.* New York: Ballantine Books.

Ogilvy and Mather Research (1976). *The Effects of Comparative Television Advertising That Names Competing Brands.* New York: Ogilvy and Mather.

Ogilvy and Mather Research (1977). *A Further Investigation into the Effects of Comparative Television Advertising that Names Competing Brands.* New York: Olilvy and Mather.

O'Keefe, D. J. (1990). *Persuasion: Theory and Research.* Newbury Park, CA: Sage Publications.

O'Keefe, G. J. (1989). Strategies and tactics in political campaigns. In C. T. Salmon (Ed.), *Information Campaigns: Balancing Social Values and Social Change* (pp. 259–284). Newbury Park, CA: Sage Publications.

O'Keefe, G. J. and Liu, J. (1980). First–time voters: Do media matter? *Journal of Communication, 30,* 122–129.

O'Keefe, G. J. and Atwood, L. E. (1981). Communication and election campaigns. In D. D. Nimmo and K. R. Sanders (Eds.), *Handbook of Political Communication* (pp. 329–358). Beverly Hills, CA: Sage Publications.

O'Keefe, G. J. and Mendelsohn, H. (1979). Media influences and their anticipation. In S. Kraus (Ed.), *The Great Debates: Carter vs. Ford, 1976* (pp. 405–417). Bloomington, IN: Indiana University Press.

O'Keefe, G. J. and Reid, K. (1989). The McGruff crime prevention campaign. In R. E. Rice and C. K. Atkin (Eds.), *Public Communication Campaigns* (2nd ed., pp.210–212). Newbury Park, CA: Sage Publications.

Oldroyd, D. (1986). *The Arch of Knowledge: An Introductory Study of the History of the Philosophy and Methodology of Science.* New York: Methuen and Co., Inc.

Osgood, C. E. (1965). Cross cultural comparability in attitude research via multilingual semantic differentials. In I. Steiner and M. Fishbeing (Eds.), *Current Studies in Social Psychology.* New York: Holt, Rinehart and Winston.

Osgood, C. E., Suci, G. J., and Tannenbaum, P. H. (1957). *The Measurement of Meaning.* Urbana, IL: University of Illinois Press.

Osgood, C. E. and Tannenbaum, P. H. (1955). The principle of congruity in the prediction of attitude change. *Psychological Review, 62,* 42–55.

O'Toole, P. (1981, September). Chrysler: Now the good news. *Savvy,* pp. 66–71.

Overton, W. F., Ward, S. L., Noveck, I. A., and Black, J. (1987). Form and content in the development of deductive reasoning. *Developmental Psychology, 23,* 22–30.

Owen, D. (1991). *Media Messages in American Presidential Elections.* New York: Greenwood Press.

Packard, V. (1957). *The Hidden Persuaders.* New York: Simon and Schuster.

Packwood: Hearings in May on content bill (1984, February 25). *Washington Post,* p. D9.

Paisley, W. (1989). Public communication campaigns: The American experience. In R. E. Rice and C. L. Atkin (Eds.), *Public Communication Campaigns* (2nd ed., pp. 15–38). Newbury Park, CA: Sage Publications.

Paletz, D. L. and Guthrie, K. K. (1987). Three faces of Ronald Reagan. *Journal of Communication, 37,* 7–23.

Palmer, E. (1981). Shaping persuasive messages with formative research. In R. E. Rice and W. J. Paisley, (Eds.), *Public Communication Campaigns* (pp. 227–238). Beverly Hills, CA: Sage Publications.

Palmgreen, P., Wenner, L. A., and Rosengren, K. E. (1985). Uses and gratifications research: The past ten years. In K. E. Rosengren, L. A. Wenner, and P. Palmgreen (Eds.), *Media Gratifications Research: Current Perspectives* (pp. 11–40). Beverly Hills, CA: Sage Publications.

Papageorgis, D. and McGuire, W. J. (1961). The generality of immunity to persuasion produced by pre–exposure to weakened counterarguments. *Journal of Abnormal and Social Psychology, 62,* 475–481.

Park, C. W., Easwar, S. I., and Smith, D. C. (1989). The effects of situational factors on in-store grocery shopping behavior: The role of store environment and time available for shopping. *Journal of Consumer Research, 15,* 422–433.

Park, R. E. (1975). The natural history of the newspaper. In W. Schramm (Ed.), *Mass Communications* (2nd ed., pp. 8–23). Urbana, IL: University of Illinois Press.

Parrott, R. (1992). Adult Arizonans' understanding of skin cancer's causes and recommendations for future messages. *Journal of Applied Communication Research.* In review.

Parrott, R., Glassman, M., and Burgoon, M. (1989, November). Arizona's Campaign to Stop Overexposure to the Sun: An Analysis of Print Media. Paper presented at the annual meeting of the Speech Communication Association in San Francisco, CA.

Parrott, R. and Ross, C. (1990, November). *A Proposed Model of Influence-seeking.* Paper presented at the annual meeting of the Speech Communication Association, Chicago, IL.

Parrott, R. and Ross, C. (1991, November). *Personal Relevance and Purposive Influence-seeking Events.* Paper presented at the annual meeting of the Speech Communication Association in Atlanta, Georgia.

Parton, J. (1964). *Life and Times of Benjamin Franklin.* New York: Mason Brothers.

Patterson, T. E. (1980). *The Mass Media Election: How Americans Choose Their President.* New York: Praeger Publishers.

Patterson, T. E., and Davis, R. (1985). The media campaign: Struggle for the agenda. In M. Nelson (Ed.), *The Elections of 1984* (pp. 111–127). Washington, DC: Congressional Quarterly Press.

Patterson, T. E. and McClure, R. D. (1976). *The Uunseeing Eye: The Myth of Television Power in National Elections.* New York: G. P. Putnam's Sons.

Patti, C. H. and Frazer, C. F. (1988). *Advertising: A Decision-making Approach.* New York: The Dryden Press.

Patton, M. Q. (1978). *Utilization-focused Evaluation.* Beverly Hills, CA: Sage Publications.

Patton, M. Q. (1982). *Practical Evaluation.* Beverly Hills, CA: Sage Publications.

Paulos, J. (1977). The logic of humour and the humour of logic. In A. J. Chapman and H. C. Foot (Eds.), *It's a Funny Thing, Humour* (pp. 113–114). Oxford: Pergamon.

Pavio, A. (1971). *Imagery and Verbal Processes.* New York: Holt, Rinehart and Winston.

Pechmann, C. and Stewart, D. W. (1989). The multidimensionality of persuasive communications: Theoretical and empirical foundations. In P. Cafferata and A. M. Tybout (Eds.), *Cognitive and Affective Responses to Advertising* (pp. 31–56). Lexington, MA: Lexington Books.

Pendleton, J. (1988, November 9). A higher personal vision. *Advertising Age,* pp. 52–53.

People for the Ethical Treatment of Animals (1990). *Animal Rights—A Question of Conscience.* Mass mailing.

Perkins, J. (1985, September 18). *There's Alligators in Those Free Trade Waters.* [Speech made to the American Association of Port Authorities.]

Perry, J. M. and Langley, M. (1988, October 27). Bush thrives on one-a-day T.V. message capsules prescribed by his skilled poli-tech image makers. *The Wall Street Journal,* p. A24.

Perse, E. M. and Rubin, R. B. (1989). Attribution in social and parasocial relationships. *Communication Research, 16,* 59–77.

Petty, R. E. and Cacioppo, J. T. (1979). Issue involvement can increase or decrease persuasion by enhancing message-relevant cognitive responses. *Journal of Personality and Social Psychology, 37,* 1915–1926.

Petty, R. E. and Cacioppo, J. T. (1984). The effects of involvement in responses to argument quantity and quality: Central and peripheral routes to persuasion. *Journal of Personality and Social Psychology, 46,* 69–81.

Petty, R. E. and Cacioppo, J. T. (1986). The elaboration likelihood model of persuasion. *Advances in Experimental Social Psychology, 19,* 123–205.

Petty, R.E., Cacioppo, J.T., and Goldman, R. (1981). Personal involvement as a determinant of argument-based persuasion. *Journal of Personality and Social Psychology, 41,* 847–855.

Petty, R.E., Cacioppo, J.T., and Heesacker, M. (1981). The use of rhetorical questions in persuasion: A cognitive response analysis. *Journal of Personality and Social Psychology, 40*, 432–440.

Pfau, M. (1987). The influence of intra-party political debates on candidate preference. *Communication Research, 14*, 687–697.

Pfau, M. (1988). Intra-party political debates and issue learning. *Journal of Applied Communication Research, 16*, 99–112.

Pfau, M. (1990). A channel approach to television influence. *Journal of Broadcasting and Electronic Media, 34*, 195–214.

Pfau, M. (1991a). The potential of inoculation in promoting resistance to the effectiveness of comparative advertising messages. *Communication Quarterly, 40*, pp. 26–44.

Pfau, M. (1991b). *Impact of Product Involvement, Message Format, and Receiver Gender of the Efficacy of Comparative Advertising Messages.* Paper presented at the annual meeting of the Speech Communication Association, Atlanta, GA.

Pfau, M. and Burgoon, M. (1988). Inoculation in political campaign communication. *Human Communication Research, 15*, 91–111.

Pfau, M. and Burgoon, M. (1989). The efficacy of issue and character attack message strategies in political campaign communication. *Communication Reports, 2*, 53–61.

Pfau, M. and Kenski, H. C. (1990). *Attack Politics: Strategy and Defense.* New York: Praeger Publishers.

Pfau, M., Kenski, H. C., Nitz, M., and Sorenson, J. (1990). Efficacy of inoculation strategies in promoting resistance to political attack messages: Application to direct mail. *Communication Monographs, 57*, 25–43.

Pfau, M., Kenski, H. C., Nitz, M., and Sorenson, J. (1989, November). *Use of the Attack Message Strategy in Political Campaign Communication.* Paper presented at the annual meeting of the Speech Communication Association, San Francisco, CA.

Phillips, J. S. and Lord, R. G. (1980). Determinants of intrinsic motivation: Locus of control and competence information as components of Deci's cognitive evaluation theory. *Journal of Applied Psychology, 65*, 211–218.

Piaget, J. (1962). *Comments.* Cambridge, MA: The MIT Press.

Pierce, J. C. and Sullivan, J. L. (1980). An overview of the American electorate. In J. C. Pierce and J. L. Sullivan (Eds.), *The Electorate Reconsidered* (pp. 11–29). Beverly Hills, CA: Sage Publications.

Pillsbury sues Hydrox. (1991, July 4). *Atlanta Journal and Constitution*, p. B–3.

Pines, M. (1981, May). Unlearning blind obedience in German schools. *Psychology Today*, pp. 59–65.

Planalp, S. and Hewes, D. E. (1982). A cognitive approach to communication theory: Cogito ergo dico? In M. Burgoon (Ed.), *Communication Yearbook 5*, (pp. 49–77). Beverly Hills, CA: Sage Publications.

Pollay, R. W. (1989). Campaigns, change and culture: On the polluting potential of persuasion. In C. T. Salmon (Ed.), *Information Campaigns: Balancing Social Values and Social Change* (pp. 185–198). Newbury Park, CA: Sage Publications.

Polsby, N. W. and Wildavsky, A. (1984). *Presidential Elections: Strategies of American Electoral Politics* (6th ed.). New York: Charles Scribner's Sons

Pomice, E. (1990, June 11). Misery loves Madison Ave.: Public–service ads pack a powerful new punch. Do they work? *U. S. News and World Report*, p. 53.

Pomper, G. M. (1975). *Voter's Choice: Varieties of American Electoral Behavior.* New York: Harper and Row.

Pomper, G. M. and Lederman, S. S. (1980). *Elections in America: Control and Influence in Democratic Politics* (2nd ed.). New York: Longman.

Pope, D. (1983). *The Making of Modern Advertising.* New York: Basic Books, Inc.

Postal, P. M. (1973). The realm of syntax. In G. A. Miller (Ed.), *Communication, Language, and Meaning* (pp. 23–35). New York: Basic Books, Inc.

Postman, N. (1988). Critical thinking in the electronic era. In T. Govier (Ed.), *Selected Issues in Logic and Communication* (pp. 11–19). Belmont, CA: Wadsworth.

Powell, K. (1990, July). Interview with Alex Hershaft. Washington, DC.

Pratkanis, A. R. and Greenwald, A. G. (1985). A reliable sleeper effect in persuasion: Implications for opinion change theory and research. In L. F. Alwitt and A. A. Mitchell (Eds.), *Psychological Processes and Advertising Effects: Theory, Research, and Applications* (pp. 157–173). Hillsdale, NJ: Lawrence Erlbaum Associates.

Pribram, K. H. (1976). Language in a sociobiological frame. In S. R. Harnad, H. D. Steklis, and J. Lancaster (Eds.), *Annals of the New York Academy of Sciences* (Vol. 280, pp. 798–809).

Pride, W. M., Lamb, C. W., Jr., and Pletcher, B. A. (1977). Are comparative advertisements more informative for owners of the mentioned competing brand than for nonowners. In B. A. Greenberg and D. N. Bellenger (Eds.), *Contemporary Marketing Thought: 1977 Educators' Proceedings* (pp. 298–301). Chicago: American Marketing Association.

Pride, W. M., Lamb, C. W., Jr., and Pletcher, B. A. (1979). The informativeness of comparative advertisements: An empirical investigation. *Journal of Advertising, 8,* 29–48.

Prideaux, G. D. (1985). *Psycholinguistics: The Experimental Study of Language.* New York: Guilford Press.

Profiles of the Senate Freshmen (1990, November 10). *Congressional Quarterly Weekly Report,* p. 3831.

Quera, L. (1977). *Advertising Campaigns: Formulation and Tactics* (2nd ed.). Columbus, OH: Grid, Inc.

Quirk, P. J. (1989). The election. In M. Nelson (Ed.), *The Elections of 1988* (pp. 63–92). Washington, DC: Congressional Quarterly Press.

Raasch, C. (1990, September 2). Negative ads out; "warm, fuzzy" ads in, experts say. *Sioux Falls Argus Leader,* p. 16A.

Ranney, A. (1983). *Channels of Power: The Impact of Television on American Politics.* New York: Basic Books, Inc.

Ratcliffe, W. D. and Wittman, W. P. (1983). Parenting education: Test-market evaluation of media campaign. *Prevention in Human Services, 2,* 97. 109.

Ray, M. L. (1982). *Advertising and Communication management.* Englewood Cliffs, NJ: Prentice Hall.

Ray, M. L. and Webb, P. (1976). *Experimental Research on the Effects of TV Clutter: Dealing With a Difficult Media Environment.* Cambridge: Marketing Science Institute, Report No. 76–102.

Raymond, C. (1976). *Advertising Research: The State of the Art.* New York: Association of National Advertisers, Inc.

Raynolds, J. F. and Raynolds, E. R. (1988). *Beyond Success: How Volunteer Service Can Help You Begin Making a Life Instead of Just a Living.* New York: Master Media.

Reardon, K. K. (1989). The potential role of persuasion in adolescent AIDS prevention. In R. E. Rice and C. K. Atkin (Eds.), *Public Communication Campaigns* (2nd ed., pp. 273–290). Newbury Park, CA: Sage Publications.

Reike, R. E. and Sillars, M. O. (1975). *Argumentation and the Decision Making Process.* New York: John Wiley and Sons, pp. 6–7.

Reinard, J. C. (1988). The empirical study of the persuasive effects of evidence: The status after fifty years of research. *Human Communication Research, 15,* 3–59.

Remley, A. (1988, October). The great parental value shift: From obedience to independence. *Psychology today,* pp. 56–59.

Republican's Net Loss (1990, November 10). Republican's net loss: One seat and many expectations. *Congressional Quarterly Weekly Report,* pp. 3824–3829.

Resnik, A. and Stern, B. L. (1977). An analysis of the information content in television advertising. *Journal of Marketing, 41,* 50–53.

Resnick, C. (1984, July 19). *AHCCCS: Past, Present, and Future.* Chair of Health Committee. Unpublished personal interview.

Reynolds, F. D. and Wells, W. D. (1977). *Consumer Behavior.* New York: McGraw Hill.

Rhodes, P. and Wolitski, R. J. (1990). Perceived effectiveness of fear appeals in AIDS education: Relationship to ethnicity, gender, age, and group membership. *AIDS Education and Prevention, 2*, 1–11.

Rice, B. (1988, March). The selling of lifestyles. *Psychology Today*, pp. 46–50.

Rice, R. E. and Atkin, C. K. (1989). *Public Communication Campaigns* (2nd ed.). Newbury Park, CA: Sage Publications.

Rice, R. E. and Paisley, W. J. (1981). *Public Communication Campaigns*. Beverly Hills, CA: Sage Publications.

Robberson, M. R. and Rogers, R. W. (1988). Beyond fear appeals: Negative and positive persuasive appeals to health and self-esteem. *Journal of Applied Social Psychology, 18*, 277–287.

Robinson, J. P. and Converse, P. E. (1972). The impact of television on mass media usages: A cross–national comparison. In A. Szalai (Ed.), *The Use of Time: Daily Activities of Urban and Suburban Populations in Twelve Countries* (pp. 197–212). The Hague: Mouton and Company.

Robinson, J. P and Davis, D. K. (1990). Television news and the informed public: An information–processing approach. *Journal of Communication, 40*, 106–119.

Robinson, J. and Holm, J. (1980, April/May). Ideological voting is alive and well. *Public Opinion*, pp. 52–58.

Robinson, M. J. (1981). The media in 1980: Was the message the message? In A. Ranney (Ed.), *The American Elections of 1980*. Washington, DC: American Enterprise Institute.

Rockefeller, J. D. (1972, March 27). *Report of the Commission on Population Growth and the American Future*. Washington, DC: Government Printing Office.

Rogers, E. M. (1962). *Diffusion of Innovations*. Glencoe, IL: The Free Press.

Rogers, E. M. and Chaffee, S. H. (1983). Communication as an academic discipline: A dialogue. [Ferment in the field]. *Journal of Communication, 33*, 18–30.

Rogers, E. M. and Storey, J. D. (1987). Communication campaigns. In C. R. Berger and S. H. Chaffee (Eds.), *Handbook of Communication Science* (pp. 817–846). Newbury Park, CA: Sage Publications.

Rook, D. W. (1987). The buying impulse. *Journal of Consumer Research, 14*, 189–199.

Ross, R. S. (1990). *Understanding Persuasion* (3rd ed.). Englewood Cliffs, NJ: Prentice Hall.

Rossel, R. D. (1981). Word play: Metaphor and humor in the small group. *Small Group Behavior, 12*, 116–136.

Rossi, P. H. and Freeman, H. E. (1989). *Evaluation: A Systematic Approach*. Newbury Park, CA: Sage Publications.

Rossiter, C. (Ed.) (1961). *The Federalist Papers. Alexander Hamilton, James Madison, John Jay*. New York: The New American Library.

Rossiter, J. R. and Percy, L. (1983). Visual communication in advertising. In R. J. Harris (Ed.), *Information Processing Research in Advertising* (pp. 83–125). Hillsdale, NJ: Lawrence Erlbaum Associates.

Rothschild, M. L. and Ray, M. L. (1974). Involvement and political advertising effect: An exploratory experiment. *Communication Research, 1*, 291–308.

Rothwell, J. D. (1982). *Telling It Like It Isn't*. Englewood Cliffs, NJ: Prentice Hall.

Rubin A. M. (1984). Ritualized and instrumental television viewing. *Journal of Communication*, Summer, 67–77.

Rubin, A. M. (1985). Media gratifications through the life cycle. In K. E. Rosengren, L. A. Wenner, and P. Palmgreen (Eds.), *Media Gratifications Research: Current Perspectives* (pp. 195–208). Beverly Hills, CA: Sage Publications.

Rubin, B. (1977). *Big Business and the Mass Media*. Lexington, MA: Lexington Books.

Rubin, R. B., Perse, E. M., and Barbato, C. A. (1988). Conceptualization and measurement of interpersonal communication motives. *Human Communication Research, 14*, 602–628.

Rusk, J. G. (1970). The effect of the Australian ballot reform on split ticket voting: 1976–1908. *American Political Science Review, 64*, 1220–1238.

Russell, J. T. and Lane, R. (1990). *Kleppner's Advertising Procedure* (11th ed.). Englewood Cliffs, NJ: Prentice Hall.

Sabato, L. J. (1981). *The Rise of Political Consultants: New Ways of Winning Elections*. New York: Basic Books, Inc.

Saisslin, R. and Parrott, R. (1992). Personalizing AIDS messages: The superiority of immediate language in changing risky sexual behaviors. *Communication Monographs*. In review.

Salmon, C. T. (1986). Perspectives on involvement in consumer and communication research. In B. Dervin and M. J. Voigt (Eds.), *Progress in Communication Sciences* (Vol. 7, pp. 243–268). Norwood, NJ: Ablex Publishing Corporation.

Salmon, C. T. (1989). *Information Campaigns: Balancing Social Values and Social Change*. Newbury Park, CA: Sage Publications.

Salmore, S. A. and Salmore, B. G. (1985). *Candidates, Parties, and Campaigns: Electoral Politics in America*. Washington, DC: Congressional Quarterly Press.

Salomon, G. (1979). *Interaction of Media, Cognition, and Learning*. San Francisco: Jossey–Bass.

Salomon, G. (1981). *Communication and Education: Social and Psychological Interactions*. Beverly Hills: Sage Publications.

Salomon, G. (1987). *Interaction of Media, Cognition, and Learning: An Exploration of How Symbolic Forms Cultivate Mental Skills and Affect Knowledge Acquisition*. San Francisco, CA: Jossey–Bass.

Salomon, G. and Leigh, T. (1984). Predispositions about learning from print and television. *Journal of Communication, 34*, 119–135.

Sandage, C. G., Fryburger, V., and Rotzoll, K. (1989). *Advertising: Theory and Practice*. New York: Longman.

Sandefur, G. D., Freeman, H. E., and Rossi, P. H. (1986). *Workbook for Evaluation: A Systematic Approach* (3rd ed.). Beverly Hills, CA: Sage Publications.

Sawyer, A. G. (1977). Repetition and affect: Recent empirical and theoretical developments. In A. G. Woodside, J. N. Sheth and P. D. Bennett (Eds.), *Consumer and Industrial Buying Behavior*. New York: North–Holland.

Sawyer, A. G. and Ward, S. (1979). Carry–over effects in advertising. *Research in Marketing, 2*, 259–314.

Schickel, R. (1985). *Intimate Strangers: The Culture of Celebrity*. New York: Doubleday.

Schram, M. (1987). *The Great American Video Game: Presidential Politics in the Television Age*. New York: William Morrow and Company.

Schramm, W. (1983). The unique perspective of communication: A retrospective view. *Journal of Communication, 33*, 6–17.

Schudson, M. (1984). *Advertising, the Uneasy Persuasion: Its Dubious Impact on American Society*. New York: Basic Books, Inc.

Schudson, M. (1989). Advertising as capitalist realism. In R. Hovland and G. B. Wilcox (Eds.), *Advertising in Society* (pp. 73–98). Lincolnwood, IL: National Textbook Company.

Schul, T. and Burnstein, E. (1990). Judging the typicality of an instance: Should the category be assessed first? *Journal of Personality and Social Psychology, 58*, 964–975.

Schultz, D. E. (1990). *Strategic Advertising Campaigns* (3rd ed.). Lincolnwood IL: National Textbook Company.

Schultz, D. E., Martin, D., and Brown, W. P. (1984). *Strategic Advertising Campaigns* (2nd ed.). Lincolnwood, IL: National Textbook Company.

Schultz, D. E. and Tannenbaum, S. I. (1989). *Essentials of Advertising Strategy* (2nd ed.). Lincolnwood, IL: National Textbook Company.

Scott, J. (1989, October 29). The old thrill is gone from some ads: Advertisers split on using sexy images to attract consumers. *Atlanta Journal and Constitution*, p. G–1.

Scott, J. (1992, January 21). Business report: On media and advertising. *Atlanta Journal and Constitution*, p. D–2.

Searle, J. R. (1969). *Speech Acts: An Essay in the Philosophy of Language*. London: Cambridge University Press.

Sears, D. O.,and Chaffee, S. H. (1979). The uses and effects of the 1976 debates: An overview of empirical studies. In S. Kraus (Ed.), *The Great Debates: Carter vs. Ford, 1976* (pp. 223–261). Bloomington, IN: Indiana University Press.

Senate eludes protectionists, oks trade bill (1984, September 27). *Congressional Quarterly Weekly Report* (Vol. 42, No. 38).

Serafin, R. and Horton, C. (1988, October 3). Car ad themes: Meant to last. *Advertising Age*, pp. 4 and 66.

Severin, W. J. and Tankard, J. W., Jr. (1979). *Communication Theories: Origins, Methods, Uses*. New York: Hastings House, Publishers.

Shaffer, D. R. (1988). *Social and Personality Development* (2nd ed.). Pacific Grove, CA: Brooks/Cole.

Shannon, W. W. (1991, January/February). Divided we stand. *The Public Perspective*, pp. 12–14.

Shaw, D. L. and McCombs, M. E. (1977). *The Emergence of American Political Issues: The Agenda-Setting Function of the Press*. St. Paul, MN: West Publishing Co.

Sheingold, C. A. (1973). Social networks and voting: The resurrection of a research agenda. *American Sociological Review, 38*, 712–720.

Sheluga, D. A. and Jacoby, J. (1978). Do comparative claims encourage comparative shopping? The impact of comparative claims on consumers' acquisition of product information. In J. Leigh and C. R. Martin (Eds.), *Current Issues and Research in Advertising* (pp. 23–37). Ann Arbor, MI: Division of Research, Graduate School of Business Administration, the University of Michigan.

Sherif, C. W., Sherif, M., and Nebergall, R. E. (1965). *Attitude and Attitude Change: The Social Judgment-Involvement Approach*. Philadelphia: Saunders.

Sherman, S. P. (1985, August 19). When you wish upon a star. *Fortune*, pp. 66–71.

Sherry, J. F. and Camargo, E. G. (1987). "May your life be marvelous": English language labelling and the semiotics of Japanese promotion. *Journal of Consumer Research, 14*, 174–188.

Sheth, J. N. (1971, June). Word-of-mouth in low risk innovations. *Journal of Advertising Research, 11*, 15–18.

Shimanoff, S. B. (1980). *Communication Rules: Theory and Research*. Beverly Hills, CA: Sage Publications.

Shimp, T. A. and Dyer, D. C. (1978). The effects of comparative advertising mediated by market position of sponsoring brand. *Journal of Advertising, 7*, 13–19.

Should an Ad (1979, September 24). Should an ad identify brand X? *Business Week*, pp. 156 and 161.

Shyles, L. (1986). The televised political spot advertisement. In L. L. Kaid, D. Nimmo, and K. R. Sanders (Eds.), *New Perspectives on Political Advertising* (pp. 107–138). Carbondale, IL: Southern Illinois University Press.

Siegel, K. (1988). Public education to prevent the spread of HIV infection. *New York State Journal of Medicine, 88*, 642–646.

Silk, A. J. and Varva, T. G. (1974). The influence of advertising's affective qualities on consumer response. In D. Hughes and M. L. Ray (Eds.), *Buyer/Consumer Information Processing* (pp. 157–186). Chapel Hill, NC: University of North Carolina Press.

Simmons, R. E. (1990). *Communication Campaign Management: A Systems Approach*. New York: Longman.

Simons, H. W. (1986). *Persuasion: Understanding, Practice, and Analysis*. New York: Random House.

Simonson, I., Huber, J., and Payne, J. (1988). The relationship between prior brand knowledge and information acquisition order. *Journal of Consumer Research, 14*, 566–578.

Sing, B. (1985, October 24). U. S., Japanese public split on trade issues. *Los Angeles Times*.

Sissors, J. Z. and Surmanek, J. (1982). *Advertising Media Planning* (2nd ed.). Chicago: Crain Books.

Smith, C. A. (1990). *Political Communication*. San Diego, CA: Harcourt Brace Janonovich, Publishers.

Smith, D. (1990a, November 1). Boschwitz accentuates the negative. *Minneapolis Star Tribune*, pp. 1A and 12A.

Smith, D. (1990b, November 5). Walter Mondale criticizes Boschwitz's ads. *Minneapolis Star Tribune*, pp. 1B and 4B.

Smith, D. (1990c, November 6). Boschwitz attack brings tough Wellstone replies. *Minneapolis Star Tribune*, p. 10A.

Smith, D. (1990d, November 7). Negative tactics hurt Perpich and Boschwitz. *Minneapolis Star Tribune*, p. 11A.

Smith, J. J. (1982). Cognitive schemata and persuasive communication: Toward a contingency rules theory. In M. Burgoon (Ed.), *Communication Yearbook* 6 (pp. 330–363). Beverly Hills: Sage Publications.

Smith, N., and Wilson, D. (1979). *Modern Linguistics: The Results of Chomsky's Revolution*. Bloomington: Indiana University Press.

Solmsen, F. (Ed.) (1954). *The Rhetoric and Poetics of Aristotle*. New York: Random House.

Solomon, D. S. (1989). A social marketing perspective on communication campaigns. In R. E. Rice and C. K. Atkin (Eds.), *Public Communication Campaigns* (2nd ed., pp. 87–104). Newbury Park, CA: Sage Publications.

Sproule, J. M. (1987). Propaganda studies in American social science: The rise and fall of the critical paradigm. *Quarterly Journal of Speech, 73*, 60–78.

Staples, B. (1990, November 11). Dirty political ads, reconsidered. *New York Times*, p. 16.

Steadman, M. (1969). How sexy illustrations affect brand recall. *Journal of Advertising Research, 9*, 15–19.

Stechert, K. (1986, June). Can't you take a joke. *Savvy*, pp. 36–40.

Steinberg, A. (1979). *Political Campaign Management: A Systems Approach*. Lexington, MA: Lexington Books.

Steinberg, J. (1988, March 7). Signs point to great reach via outdoors. *Advertising Age*, pp. S2 and S10.

Sterelny, K. (1983). Linguistic theory and variable rules. *Language and Communication, 3*, 47–69.

Stewart, C. J. (1975). Voter perceptions of mudslinging in political communication. *Central States Speech Journal, 26*, 279–286.

Story, M. (1990). Study group report on the impact of television on adolescent nutritional status. *Journal of Adolescent Health Care, 11*, 82–85.

Stouffer, S. A. (1949, May). A study of attitude. *Scientific American*, pp. 3–7.

Street, R. L. and Giles, H. (1982). Speech accommodation theory: A social cognitive approach to language and speech behavior. In M. E. Rolloff and C. R. Berger (Eds.), *Social Cognition and Communication* (pp. 193.225). Beverly Hills: Sage Publications.

Sujan, M. and Dekleva, C. (1987). Product categorization and inference making: Some implications for comparative advertising. *Journal of Consumer Research, 14*, 372–378.

Surlin, S. H. and Gordon, T. F. (1977). How values affect attitudes toward direct reference political advertising. *Journalism Quarterly, 54*, 89–98.

Swanson, D. L. (1977). And that's the way it was? Television covers the 1976 presidential campaign. *Quarterly Journal of Speech, 63*, 239–248.

Swanson, D. L. (1987). Gratification seeking, media exposure, and audience interpretations: Some directions for research. *Journal of Broadcasting and Electronic Media, 31*, 237–254.

Swanson, D. L. (1976). Information utility: An alternative perspective in political communication. *Central States Speech Journal, 27*, 95–101.

Swinyard, W. R. (1981). The interaction between comparative advertising and copy claim variation. *Journal of Marketing Research, 28*, 175–186.

Szybillo, G. J. and Heslin, R. (1973). Resistance to persuasion: Inoculation theory in a marketing context. *Journal of Marketing Research, 20*, 396–403.

Taylor, P. (1986). Accentuating the negative: Forget issue; Campaign ads this year are heavy on "air pollution". *The Washington Post National Weekly Edition, 3*, 6–7.

Taylor, P. (1989, January 17). Consultants: Winning on the attack. *Washington Post*, pp. A1 and A14.

Taylor, P. (1990). *See How They Run: Electing the President in an Age of Mediaocracy*. New York: Alfred A. Knopf.

Taylor, P. and Broder, D. S. (1988). How the presidential campaign got stuck on the low road. *Washington Post National Weekly Edition, 6,* 14–15.

Taylor, S. E. and Crocker, J. (1981). Schematic bases of social information processing. In E. T. Higgins, C. P. Herman, and M. P. Zanna (Eds.), *Social Cognition: The Ontario Symposium* (Vol. 1, pp. 89–134). Hillsdale, NJ: Lawrence Erlbaum Associates.

Taylor, S. E. and Fiske, S. T. (1978). Salience, attention, and attribution: Top of the head phenomena. In L. Berkowitz (Ed.), *Advances in Experimental Social Psychology* (Vol. 11). New York: Academic Press.

Taylor, S. E. and Thompson, S. C. (1982). Stalking the illusive vividness effect. *Psychological Review, 89,* 155–181.

Taylor, T. J. (1981). A Wittgensteinian perspective in linguistics. *Language and Communication, 1,* 263–274.

Tedeschi, J. T., and Norman, W. (1985). Social power, self–presentation, and the self. In B. R. Schlenker (Ed.), *The Self and Social Life* (pp. 293–322). New York: McGraw-Hill.

Teinowitz, I. (1988, August 1). Miller looks for Lite touch to tap youth. *Advertising Age,* pp. 3 and 50.

Terris, M. (1968). A social policy for health. *American Journal of Public Health, 58,* 5–12.

Tetlock, P. E. and Manstead, A. S. R. (1985). Impression management versus intrapsychic explanations in social psychology: A useful dichotomy? *Psychological Review, 92,* 59–77.

Thomas, L. F. (1985). Nothing more theoretical than good practice: Teaching for self–organized learning. In D. Bannister (Ed.), *Issues and Approaches in Personal Construct Theory* (pp. 233–252). London: Academic Press.

Thornburg, H. D. (1984). *Introduction to Educational Psychology.* St. Paul, MN: West Publishing.

Thorson, E. and Snyder, R. (1984). Viewer recall of television commercials: Prediction from the propositional structure of commercial scripts. *Jounal of Marketing Research, 21,* 127–216.

Thum, G. and Thum, M. (1974). *The Persuaders: Propaganda in War and Peace.* New York: Atheneum.

Thurstone, L. L. (1928). Attitudes can be measured. *American Journal of Sociology, 33,* 529–554.

Time (1986, June 2). Betty Crocker goes yuppie.

Toulmin, S. (1959). *The Uses of Argument.* London: Cambridge University Press.

Toyota: The First 20 Years In The U.S.A. (1977). Torrance, CA: Toyota Motor Sales, Inc.

Toyota Today (1985a, July). Torrance, CA: Toyota Motor Sales, Inc.

Toyota Today (1985b, October). Torrance, CA: Toyota Motor Sales, Inc.

Toyota Today (1985c, September). Torrance, CA: Toyota Motor Sales, Inc.

Traugott, M. W. and Tucker, C. (1984). Strategies for predicting whether a citizen will vote and estimation of electoral outcomes. *Public Opinion Quarterly, 48,* 330–343.

Trenholm, S. (1989). *Persuasion and Social Influence.* Englewood Cliffs, NJ: Prentice Hall.

Trent, J. S and Friedenberg, R. V. (1991). *Political Campaign Communication: Principles and Practices* (2nd ed.). New York: Praeger Publishers.

Triandis, H. C. (1979). Values, attitudes, and interpersonal behavior. In *Nebraska Symposium on Motivation* (pp. 195–229). Lincoln, NE: University of Nebraska Press.

Trice, A. D. (1982). Ratings of humor following experience with unsolvable tasks. *Psychological Reports, 51,* 1148.

Trice, A. D. and Price-Greathouse, J. (1986). Joking under the drill: A validity study of the coping humor scale. *Journal of Social Behavior and Personality, 1,* 265–266.

Tse, D. K., Belk, R. W., and Zhou, N. (1989). Becoming a consumer society: A longitudinal and cross–cultural content analysis of print ads from Hong Kong, the People's Republic of China, and Taiwan. *Journal of Consumer Research, 15,* 457–472.

Tsiantar, D, and Miller, A. (1989, April 17). Tuning out television ads. *Newsweek,* pp. 42–43.

Tubbs, S. (1968). Explicit versus implicit audience conclusions and audience commitment. *Speech Monographs, 35,* 14–19.

Tunmer, W. E. and Nesdale, A. R. (1983). The development of young children's awareness of logical inconsistencies. *Journal of Experimental Child Psychology, 36,* 97–108.

Tybout, A. (1989). Introduction. In P. Cafferata and A. M. Tybout (Eds.), *Cognitive and Affective Responses to Advertising* (pp. 1–9). Lexington, MA: Lexington Books.

Tyebjee, T. T. (1979). Refinement of the involvement concept: An advertising planning point of view. In J. C. Maloney and B. Silverman (Eds.), *Attitude Research Plays for High Stakes* (pp. 94–111). Chicago: American Marketing Association.

Ulanoff, S. M. (1977). *Advertising in America: An Introduction to Persuasive Communication.* New York: Hastings House, Publishers.

U.S. Forest Service (1960). *History of the Smokey Bear Program.* Washington, D. C.

U.S. Forest Service (1973). *Second National Smokey Bear Workshop.* Washington, D. C.

Users Are Losers (1988, October). *Psychology Today,* p. 10.

Vadehra, D. (1982, April 26). Miller Lite spots draw heavy acclaim: Viewers pick the 25 top television campaigns of the year. *Advertising Age,* pp. M40–M44.

Valentine, C. (1985, October). Who could ask for anything more! *Toyota Today, 13,* 13.

Vinokur–Kaplan, D., and Bergman, S. (1986). Retired Israeli social workers: Work, volunteer activities, and satisfaction among retired professionals. *Journal of Gerontological Social Work, 9,* 73–86.

Wallach, V. (1988, November 9). Matters of survival. *Advertising Age,* pp. 119–120 and 148–150.

Wallack, L. (1989). Mass communication and health promotion: A critical perspective. In R. E. Rice and C. K. Atkin (eds.), *Public Communication Campaigns* (2nd ed., pp. 353–367). Newbury Park, CA: Sage Publications.

Walley, W. (1988, November 28). Point of attack: If in doubt, promote. *Advertising Age,* p. 5–7.

Walley, W. (1988, November 28). Victim of its own success. *Advertising Age,* pp. S–7 and S–22.

Wandersman, A., Florin, P., Friedmann, R. R., and Meier, R. B. (1987). Who participates, who does not, and why? An analysis of voluntary neighborhood organizations in the United Stages and Israel. *Sociological Forum, 2,* 534–555.

Warshaw, P. R. (1978). Application of selective attention theory to television advertising displays. *Journal of Applied Psychology, 63,* 366–372.

Watson, J. B. (1924). The place of kinaesthetic, visceral and laryngeal organization in thinking. *The Psychological Review, 31,* 339–347.

Wattenberg, M. P. (1986). *The Decline of American Political Parties, 1952–1984.* Cambridge, MA: Harvard University Press.

Wattenberg, M. P. (1991). *The Rise of Candidate-Centered Politics.* Cambridge, MA: Harvard University Press.

Weaver, D. H., Graber, D. A., McCombs, M. E., and Eyal, C. H. (1981). *Media Agenda-Setting in a Presidential Election: Issues, Images, and Interest.* New York: Praeger.

Weaver, P. H. (1976, August 29). Captives of melodrama. *New York Times Magazine,* pp. 6 and 48.

Weibull, L. (1985). Structural factors in gratifications research. In K. E. Rosengren, L. A. Wenner, and P. Palmgreen (Eds.), *Media Gratifications Research: Current Perspectives* (pp. 123–149). Beverly Hills, CA: Sage Publications.

Weilbacher, W. M. (1984). *Advertising* (2nd ed.). New York: Macmillan.

Weiss, W. (1966). Repetition in advertising. In L. Bogart (Ed.), *Psychology in Media Strategy.* Chicago: American Marketing Association.

Welch, W. M. (1988, October 13). Negative trend snowballs. *Sioux Falls Argus Leader,* p. 7A.

Wenner, L. A. (1985). Transaction and media gratifications research. In K. E. Rosengren, L. A. Wenner, and P. Palmgreen (Eds.), *Media Gratifications Research: Current Perspectives* (pp. 73–94). Beverly Hills, CA: Sage Publications.

White, G. L. and Gerard, H. B. (1981). Postdecision evaluation of choice alternatives as a function of valence of alternatives, choice, and expected delay of choice consequences. *Journal of Research in Personality, 15,* 371–382.

White, T. H. (1982). *America in Search of Itself: The Making of the President 1956–1980.* New York: Harper and Row.

Wicklund, R. A. and Duval, S. (1971). Opinion change and performance facilitation as a result of object self-awareness. *Journal of Experimental Social Psychology, 7,* 319–342.

Wiener, M. and Mehrabian, A. (1968). *Language Within Language: Immediacy, a Channel in Verbal Communication*. New York: Appleton-Century Crofts.

Wilcox, D. L., Ault, P. H., and Agee, W. K. (1989). *Public Relations: Strategies and Tactics* (2nd ed.). New York: Harper and Row.

Williams, M. J. (1986, June 9). How to cash in on do-good pitches. *Fortune*, p. 71.

Williams, R., Hall, J., Lapointe, M., Parrott, R., Siegert, K., and Shapiro, P. (1990). *Your Baby's First Six Months* [Three-part program 1/2 inch VHS videocassette]. Biomedical Communications, The University of Arizona Health Sciences Center.

Wilson, C. (1988, November 9). The last titan of advertising. *Advertising Age*, p. 32.

Wilson, R. D. (1976). An empirical evaluation of comparative advertising messages: Subjects' responses on perceptual dimensions. In B. B. Anderson (Ed.), *Advances for Consumer Research* (Vol. 3, pp. 53–57). Association for Consumer Research.

Wilson, R. D. and Mudderisoglu, A. (1979, August). An analysis of cognitive responses to comparative advertising. *Working Series in Marketing Number 84*. Pennsylvania State University.

Wing, K. R. (1984). Recent amendments to the Medicaid program: Political implications. *American Journal of Public Health, 74*, 83–84.

Winter, D. G. (1988, July 8). What makes Jesse run? *Psychology Today*, p. 20–24.

Witty, S. (1983, August). The laugh-makers: New Studies spotlight the growth of the human funny bone. *Psychology Today*, pp. 22–29.

Wodarski, J. S. and Lenhart, S. D. (1982). *Alcohol Education by the Teams-Games-Tournaments Method*. Minneapolis, MN: Burgess Publishing Co.

Wright, P. L. (1974). Analyzing media effects on advertising responses. *Public Opinion Quarterly, 38*, 192–205.

Wyer, R. S. (1974). *Cognitive Organization and Change: An Information Processing Approach*. Potomac, MD: Lawrence Erlbaum Associates.

Yoos, G. E. (1979). A revision of the concept of ethical appeal. *Philosophy and Rhetoric, 12*, 41–58.

Young, M. (1987). *American Dictionary of Campaigns and Elections*. Lanham, MD: Hamilton Press.

Zaichkowsky, J. L. (1985). Measuring the involvement construct. *Journal of Consumer Research, 12*, 341–352.

Zajonc, R. B. (1980). Feeling and thinking: Preferences need no inferences. *American Psychologist, 35*, 151–175.

Zajonc, R. B. and Markus, H. (1982). Affective and cognitive factors in preferences. *Journal of Consumer Research, 9*, 123–131.

Zeifman, L. H. (1988, November 9). The sound of music. *Advertising Age*, p. 162.

Zimbardo, P. and Ebbesen, E. B. (1969). *Influencing Attitudes and Changing Behavior*. Reading, MA: Addison-Wesley.

Zoglin, R. (1990, July 9). The tuned-out generation: A new survey reveals that young people are ignoring the news. *Time*, p. 64.

100 Leading National Advertisers. (1990, September 26). *Advertising Age*, p. 17.

100 Leading National Advertisers. (1992, January 6). *Advertising Age*, p. S-2.

Author Index

Subject Index